Annihilating Difference

CALIFORNIA SERIES IN PUBLIC ANTHROPOLOGY

The California Series in Public Anthropology emphasizes the anthropologist's role as an engaged intellectual. It continues anthropology's commitment to being an ethnographic witness, to describing, in human terms, how life is lived beyond the borders of many readers' experiences. But it also adds a commitment, through ethnography, to reframing the terms of public debate—transforming received, accepted understandings of social issues with new insights, new framings.

Series Editor: Robert Borofsky (Hawaii Pacific University)
Contributing Editors: Philippe Bourgois (UC San Francisco), Paul Farmer
(Partners in Health), Rayna Rapp (New York University), and
Nancy Scheper-Hughes (UC Berkeley)
University of California Press Editor: Naomi Schneider

Annihilating Difference

The Anthropology of Genocide

EDITED BY

Alexander Laban Hinton

With a foreword by
Kenneth Roth
Human Rights Watch

UNIVERSITY OF CALIFORNIA PRESS

Berkeley   Los Angeles   London

University of California Press
Berkeley and Los Angeles, California

University of California Press, Ltd.
London, England

© 2002 by The Regents of the University of California

Library of Congress Cataloging-in-Publication Data

Annihilating difference : the anthropology of genocide / edited by
Alexander Laban Hinton ; with a foreword by Kenneth Roth.
    p.   cm.—(California Series in Public Anthropology; 3)
Includes bibliographical references and index.
  ISBN 978-0-520-23029-3 (Paper : alk. paper)

  1. Genocide.   2. Ethnic conflict.   I. Hinton, Alexander Laban.
II. Series.
HV6322.7 .A64 2002
304.6'63—dc21   2001007073

Manufactured in the United States of America
10 09 08 07
10 9 8 7 6 5 4

CONTENTS

FIGURES AND TABLES

FIGURES

FOREWORD

Anthropologists and human rights activists have not been natural partners. An anthropologist tends to accept a culture as it is. A human rights activist tends to identify injustices in a culture and work to change them. An anthropologist illuminates the differences among cultures. A human rights activist highlights cross-cultural commonality. An anthropologist respects a broad range of value systems that are seen as culturally variable. A human rights activist promotes a particular value system that is seen as universal.

Yet behind this tension there has always been a potential for partnership. Classic human rights advocacy depends at the outset on careful observation—on the detailed recording of the plight of particular individuals who have suffered abuse. Long gone are the days when a human rights "investigation" consisted of several prominent foreigners parachuting into a country (usually only its capital) for a quick few days of conversation with diplomats, journalists, and other elite observers. Today, as human rights organizations have grown in sophistication and rigor, an effective human rights researcher must become immersed in the country under study, speaking the language, interviewing the victims and witnesses, and becoming intimately familiar with local customs, politics, and governance.

In short, the investigative work of a human rights researcher increasingly resembles the careful fieldwork of an anthropologist. And so it should, since the tools of anthropology offer valuable assistance not only to those who seek to understand a society but also to those who hope to change it. Understanding the architecture of a society is valuable not only in its own right—as a work of anthropology—but also as a blueprint for change. It helps us identify the social pathologies that might lead to human rights abuse and the steps that can be taken to end or prevent them.

Of the many abuses that might be studied, there is none so grave as genocide. The crime that gave rise to the vow "never again" has, to humanity's great shame, reared its head again and again. What prompts a society to seek to eradicate a category of people? What combination of hatred and fear leads people to see their neighbors not as fellow human beings entitled to lead their own lives but as an intolerable presence that must be isolated and eliminated?

Human rights activists seek to monitor, curb, and punish such atrocities. They identify proximate causes or individuals who bear special responsibility. But in a fundamental sense they do not really explain these abuses. For a deeper explanation, they must turn to other disciplines. In this quest, anthropology has much to offer.

This volume—a collection of writings on genocide from the perspective of anthropology—seeks this deeper understanding of our era's most heinous crime. It asks not only what happened but also why it happened. It seeks not simply to describe but to explain. And in offering an explanation of this horrendous social malady, it points in the direction of a possible cure.

At one level, that cure is preventive. Anthropology helps us understand the social and political tensions that are most likely to explode in genocide. It helps explain the loyalties and hatreds, the aspirations and fears, that might motivate one group to try to eliminate another from its midst. As such, anthropologists can serve as an important source of early warning, a culturally sensitive Dew Line to alert us to imminent genocidal attack.

But as human rights activists are painfully aware, early warning is not enough. There are too many cases when the world knew all too well of an impending or even active genocide—but did nothing. As genocide unfolded in Rwanda, the Clinton administration refused even to utter the "G" word for fear of the ensuing legal obligation to try to stop it. As genocide raged in Bosnia, the West offered humanitarian aid in lieu of military defense. As Saddam Hussein depopulated the Kurdish highlands and executed those who refused to leave, the international community chose not to look too closely at the unfolding genocide for fear of jeopardizing commercial interests with an oil-rich government. As genocide spread through Guatemala's indigenous community, the West conveniently overlooked the slaughter—indeed, actively denied its existence—in the name of Cold War exigencies.

Anthropology alone cannot overcome this political cowardice, this deadly calculus of passivity. But it can help make inaction more costly by highlighting the feasibility of action. Those who would turn their backs on genocide tend to invoke the same litany of excuses. Ancient hatreds, age-old animosities, entrenched enmities—these are the myths propagated to suggest that action is beside the point, that efforts to stop genocide are impractical, that attempts to change the course of history are futile.

By giving the lie to these myths, anthropology can be a spur to action. By demonstrating the human agency behind the allegedly immutable forces of history, anthropology can help to reveal the individual volition behind any outbreak of genocide, to identify the particular people who choose this deadly path. Understanding this personal dimension of genocide is the first step toward combating it, since although the relentless march of history is indeed unstoppable, individual actors are not. Condemnations, sanctions, prosecutions, interventions—these may well be pointless against an inevitability of the ages, but they can be extraordinarily powerful against the particular individuals who, anthropology helps us understand, are the agents of genocide.

After a genocide has occurred, anthropology can also help a society determine how to move on. For some two decades, human rights activists have debated how to rebuild such societies. Are they better served by closing the book on a horrendous past and attempting to move forward or by insisting that those behind atrocities be held accountable? Is accountability best established through truth telling, criminal trials, or a combination? Is amnesty an appropriate act of forgiveness or an act of impunity that risks promoting further slaughter?

Debates of this sort have too often been dominated by cheap metaphors and facile assumptions. Proponents of forgiveness speak of the importance of closing the book on the past, of allowing society's wounds to heal, of permitting reconciliation. Advocates of accountability talk of the need to establish the rule of law, to deter future crimes, and to pay respect to the victims and their families. The debate cries out for the empirical contributions of anthropology. How do actual societies deal with traumas such as genocide? How do they move forward without inviting revenge from the past? How do they balance the imperative of justice and the need for stability? There are no easy answers to these problems of transitional justice, but anthropology's firm grounding in how societies address traumas would greatly enrich the debate.

In sum, this volume signals the launching of what I hope is a new and vigorous partnership. The human rights movement was built foremost on the power of exposing the truth. By adding anthropology's depth of insight and patient perspective, our understanding of the truth is deepened, and the cause of stopping future genocides is strengthened.

Kenneth Roth
Executive Director
Human Rights Watch

ACKNOWLEDGMENTS

Throughout history, entire populations have fallen victim to systematic genocide. During the twentieth century alone, we have witnessed the intentional destruction, in whole or in part, of such groups as Armenians, Jews, Cambodians, Hutus and Tutsis, Bosnians, and indigenous peoples. Despite the urgent need to understand the origins and effects of such devastation, anthropologists have not yet fully engaged this topic of study. The present book arose from "The Anthropology of Genocide," an invited session (by the General Anthropology Division and the Committee on Human Rights) at the 1998 meeting of the American Anthropological Association. Like the panel, the book is devoted to stimulating anthropological debate on genocide and pointing the way toward an anthropology of genocide.

A number of people have helped the book come to fruition. First, I'd like to sincerely thank the contributors to the volume, all of whom are dedicated scholars who have many commitments. From the onset, Naomi Schneider, our editor at the University of California Press, expressed strong interest in and support for the volume. We are all grateful for her efficiency, incisive comments, and commitment. Ellie Hickerson, her editorial assistant, was also of great help, as were Annie Decker, Martin Hanft, and Suzanne Knott. The anonymous reviewers of the manuscript provided important feedback that strengthened the volume in several respects. I am grateful to Michael Mattis for giving us permission to use the photograph *Grief* on the cover. And thanks are due to Katie Joice of Berg Publishers and Eric Fichtl of the North American Congress on Latin America for agreeing to allow us to include modified versions of previously published works by Christopher Taylor and Carole Nagengast:

Chapter 4 of Christopher Taylor's *Sacrifice As Terror* (Oxford: Berg Publishers, 150 Cowley Road, Oxford OX4 1JJ UK).
Carole Nagengast's article "Militarizing the Border Patrol," *NACLA Report on the Americas* 32, no. 3 (1998): 37–41.

My deepest gratitude goes to Kenneth Roth for writing the foreword to this volume and to Robert Borofsky, series editor, for his enthusiastic support and help in envisioning the book as part of the California Series in Public Anthropology.

Finally, I want to thank Nicole Cooley for her encouragement, comments, and thoughts on the structure of the volume. Without her help, the book would not have achieved its current form.

The Dark Side of Modernity

Toward an Anthropology of Genocide

Alexander Laban Hinton

As we stand on the edge of the millennium, looking back at modernity's wake, genocide looms as the Janus face of Western metanarratives of "civilization" and "progress."[1] With the rise of the nation-state and its imperialist and modernizing ambitions, tens of millions of "backward" or "savage" indigenous peoples perished from disease, starvation, slave labor, and outright murder. Sixty million others were also annihilated in the twentieth century, often after nation-states embarked upon lethal projects of social engineering intent upon eliminating certain undesirable and "contaminating" elements of the population. The list of victim groups during this "Century of Genocide"[2] is long. Some are well known to the public—Jews, Cambodians, Bosnians, and Rwandan Tutsis. Others have been annihilated in greater obscurity—Hereros, Armenians, Ukrainian peasants, Gypsies, Bengalis, Burundi Hutus, the Aché of Paraguay, Guatemalan Mayans, and the Ogoni of Nigeria.

Clearly, this devastation poses a critical challenge to scholars: Why does one group of human beings set out to eradicate another group from the face of the earth? What are the origins and processes involved in such mass murder? How do we respond to the bodily, material, and psychological devastation it causes? How might we go about predicting or preventing it in the twenty-first century? Because of their experience-near understandings of the communities in which such violence takes place, anthropologists are uniquely positioned to address these questions. Unfortunately, with few exceptions anthropologists have remained remarkably silent on the topic of genocide, as illustrated by the fact that they have written so little on what is often considered the twentieth-century's paradigmatic genocide, the Holocaust.[3] Although anthropologists have long been at the forefront of advocating for the rights of indigenous peoples and have conducted rich analyses of violence, conflict, and warfare in substate and prestate societies, they have only recently (since the 1980s) begun to focus their attention intensively on political violence in complex state societies.

Some of the factors fueling this shift in focus include: the broadening and de-essentializing of the concept of culture; the growing awareness that anthropology must deal conceptually with globalization, history, and the nation-state; a theoretical and ethnographic move away from studying small, relatively stable communities toward looking at those under siege, in flux, and victimized by state violence or insurgency movements; and the dramatic rise in ethnonationalist conflict and state terror in the wake of colonialism and the fall of the Berlin Wall. In addition, anthropologists may have felt uncomfortable engaging with this topic insofar as anthropologists themselves and anthropological conceptions (such as race, ethnicity, and "culture") have contributed to the genocidal process (see Arnold, Bowen, Schafft, and Scheper-Hughes, this volume). Moreover, anthropologists who did engage in such large-scale sociopolitical analyses during World War II and the Vietnam War often found themselves mired in moral quandaries and controversies. Still other anthropologists may have felt their analytical frameworks and insights were somehow insufficient to deal with the horrors of genocide.[4]

Finally, cultural relativism has likely played a key role in inhibiting anthropologists from studying genocide. As introductory textbooks in anthropology highlight, one of the fundamental features of anthropology is the view that cultural values are historical products and, therefore, that one should not ethnocentrically assume that the values of one's own society are more legitimate, superior, or universal than those of other peoples. This perspective informed the American Anthropological Association's official response to the 1948 Universal Declaration of Human Rights, which the organization critiqued for being a "statement of rights conceived only in terms of the values prevalent in the countries of Western Europe and America" (1947:539). Although legitimately fighting against cultural imperialism, this type of relativistic perspective has great difficulty responding to, let alone condemning, the atrocities committed during genocides and other forms of political violence. For, if one assumes that the values of other societies are as legitimate as one's own, how can one condemn horrendous acts that are perpetrated in terms of those alternative sets of morals, since the judgment that something is "horrendous" may be ethnocentric and culturally relative? (Not surprisingly, many ruthless governments have invoked cultural relativism to defend atrocities committed under their rule.) I suspect that the difficulty of dealing with such questions has contributed greatly to the anthropological reticence on genocide (see also Scheper-Hughes, this volume).[5]

This book represents an attempt to focus anthropological attention directly on the issue of genocide and to envision what an "anthropology of genocide" might look like. To broaden the scope of the volume, the essays examine a variety of cases (ranging from indigenous peoples to the Holocaust) and have been written from a variety of subdisciplinary backgrounds (ranging from archaeology to law). Moreover, the final chapters reflect on the book as a whole and suggest ways in which anthropologists might make a greater contribution to the study of genocide. In the introductory discussion that follows, I frame the essays along two axes. On the one hand, I suggest that genocide is intimately linked to modernity, a concept I define in more detail below. On the other hand, genocide is always a local process and therefore may be analyzed and understood in important ways through the ethnohistorical lens of anthropology. The introduction concludes by suggesting some key issues with which an anthropology of genocide might be concerned.

GENOCIDE: WHAT IS IT?

In the present Convention, genocide means any of the following acts committed with intent to destroy, in whole or in part, a national, ethnical, racial or religious group, as such:
(a) Killing members of the group;
(b) Causing serious bodily or mental harm to members of the group;
(c) Deliberately inflicting on the group conditions of life calculated to bring about its physical destruction in whole or in part;
(d) Imposing measures intended to prevent births within the group;
(e) Forcibly transferring children of the group to another group.
  —Article II, 1948 United Nations Genocide Convention

Prior to the twentieth century, the concept of genocide did not exist. The term was coined by the Polish jurist Raphäel Lemkin, who combined the Greek word *genos* (race, tribe) with the Latin root *cide* (killing of).[6] Lemkin lobbied incessantly to get genocide recognized as a crime, attending numerous meetings and writing hundreds of letters in a variety of languages. His efforts ultimately helped lead the United Nations to pass a preliminary resolution (96-I) in 1946, stating that genocide occurs "when racial, religious, political and other groups have been destroyed, entirely or in part." It is crucial to note that this preliminary resolution included the destruction of "political and other groups" in its definition. Much of the subsequent U.N. debate over the legislation on genocide revolved around the question of whether political and social groups should be covered by the convention (Kuper 1981).[7] A number of countries—particularly the Soviet Union, which, because of the atrocities it perpetrated against the kulaks and other "enemies of the people," feared accusations of genocide—argued that political groups should be excluded from the convention since they did not fit the etymology of genocide, were mutable categories, and lacked the distinguishing characteristics necessary for definition. In the end, the clause on "political and other groups" was dropped from the final version of the 1948 Genocide Convention on the Prevention and Punishment of Genocide, which dealt only with "national, ethnical, racial or religious groups."[8]

This omission has generated a great deal of debate. As currently defined, the U.N. Convention definition has difficulty accounting for such events as the Soviet liquidation of its "enemies" or the Nazi annihilation of tens of thousands of "lives not worth living" (that is, mentally challenged or mentally ill individuals), homosexuals, social "deviants," and communists. Regardless, some genocide scholars prefer to adhere to the strict, legal definition of the Genocide Convention while attempting to account for violence against political and social groups under such alternative rubrics as "related atrocities" (Kuper 1981) or "politicides" (Harff and Gurr 1988). Many other scholars have proposed more moderate definitions of genocide that cover political and social groups but exclude most deaths resulting from military warfare (e.g., Chalk and Jonassohn 1990; Fein 1990). Thus Helen Fein states: "Genocide is sustained purposeful action by a perpetrator to physically destroy a collectivity directly or indirectly, through interdiction of the biological and social reproduction of group members, sustained regardless of the surrender or lack of threat offered by the victim" (Fein 1990:24). Finally, a few scholars use a very broad definition of genocide that covers more types of military warfare (e.g., Charny 1994; Kuper 1994).

From an anthropological perspective, the U.N. definition is problematic in several respects. In particular, it gives primacy to an overly restricted set of social categories. While the marking of difference occurs in every society, the social groupings that are constructed vary dramatically. Race, ethnicity, nation, and religion are favored categories in modern discourse. However, as anthropologists and other scholars have demonstrated, many other social classifications exist, including totemistic groups, clans, phratries, lineages, castes, classes, tribes, and categories based on sexual orientation, mental or physical disability, urban or rural origin, and, of course, economic and political groups. Surely, if a government launched a campaign to obliterate the "Untouchables," everyone would characterize its actions as genocide. Likewise, there is no a priori reason why the intentional destruction of a political group or the handicapped should not be characterized as genocidal. The criterion that distinguishes genocide as a conceptual category is the *intentional* attempt to annihilate a social group that has been marked as different.

Some scholars might challenge this assertion by arguing that many of the social categories I have mentioned are too malleable. Such an argument could be refuted in its own terms—it is often extremely difficult to stop being an Untouchable or to stop having a disability. One may much more easily convert to a different religion. Accordingly, I believe it is crucial to note that even categories such as race, ethnicity, and nationality, which are frequently given a primordial tinge, are historically constructed groupings that have shifting edges and fuzzy boundaries.

This point is illustrated in Paul Magnarella's essay "Recent Developments in the International Law of Genocide: An Anthropological Perspective on the International Criminal Tribunal for Rwanda." Magnarella provides a detailed overview of the original provisions of the 1948 U.N. Genocide Convention and recent steps toward implementation. Since its inception, the convention has been plagued by the problem of enforcement. Although the convention provides for recourse on the state and international level, crimes of genocide have occurred without intervention or prosecution, since the state itself is usually the perpetrator of genocide and will not acknowledge the atrocities taking place within its borders. During the 1990s, the U.N. Security Council used its authority to establish tribunals in the former Yugoslavia and Rwanda. (An anthropologist and a lawyer, Magnarella served as a consultant and researcher for these tribunals.) Moreover, in July 1998, delegates at a

U.N. conference in Rome approved a statute calling for the creation of a permanent International Criminal Court, despite the protests of the United States and a handful of other countries, including Iran, Iraq, China, Lybia, Algeria, and Sudan. President Clinton finally signed the treaty in January 2001, days before leaving office. Senate confirmation remains in doubt.

After tracing these developments, Magnarella describes the process by which the International Criminal Tribunal for Rwanda (ICTR) conducted the first trial for the crime of genocide ever held before an international court. In September 1998, fifty years after the adoption of the U.N. Convention, former Rwandan mayor and educator Jean-Paul Akayesu was convicted of various acts of genocide, as well as crimes against humanity. Magnarella recounts the testimony of one woman who, despite seeking Akayesu's protection, was repeatedly raped in public; Akayesu reportedly encouraged one of the rapists, saying: "Don't tell me that you won't have tasted a Tutsi woman. Take advantage of it, because they'll be killed tomorrow." Akayesu, in turn, claimed that he was a minor official who was unable to control the atrocities that took place in his municipality.

Because of its unprecedented work, the ICTR faced many difficulties in achieving the conviction of Akayesu. One of the foremost problems was the U.N. Convention's lack of a definition of a "national, ethnical, racial or religious group." Background research revealed that the drafters of the convention restricted the definition of the term *genocide* to "stable, permanent groups, whose membership is determined by birth." Based on that conceptual distinction, the ICTR came up with provisional definitions of the aforementioned groups. However, the more fluid Hutu/Tutsi/Twa distinction did not clearly fit any of the proposed definitions. Noting that Rwandans readily identified themselves in these terms and that the labels were used in official Rwandan documents, the ICTR nevertheless concluded that such emic distinctions could serve as a basis for prosecution.

Magnarella points out that the ICTR effectively expanded the coverage of the convention by adding any "stable and permanent group, whose membership is largely determined by birth" to the pre-existing national, ethnic, racial, and religious categories. Thus, atrocities committed against those of different castes, sexual orientations, or disabilities might qualify as genocidal. In addition, the ICTR set a precedent for examining local understandings of social difference, since etic ones are too often indeterminate and vague. In fact, as I will later point out, this very uncertainty about identity often leads perpetrators to inscribe difference upon the bodies of their victims (Appadurai 1998; Feldman 1991; Taylor 1999). Although the ICTR ultimately maintained a criterion of enduring difference, its difficulty in using "national, ethnical, racial or religious" designations illustrates that even these seemingly stable categories refer to sets of social relations that have fuzzy boundaries and vary across time and place (see also Bowen, this volume).

Accordingly, I would advocate the use of a more moderate definition of *genocide*, such as the one Fein proposes, because it can, without losing analytic specificity, more easily account for the fact that group boundaries are socially constructed across contexts and through time. From an anthropological perspective, the reification of concepts such as race and ethnicity (while not surprising, given the historical privileging of perceived biological difference in much Western discourse) is problematic because—like class, caste, political or sexual orientation, and physical and mental disability—the terms reference "imagined communities," to borrow Benedict Anderson's (1991) term. Genocides are distinguished by a process of "othering" in which the boundaries of an imagined community are reshaped in such a manner that a previously "included" group (albeit often included only tangentially) is ideologically recast (almost always in dehumanizing rhetoric) as being outside the community, as a threatening and dangerous "other"—whether racial, political, ethnic, religious, economic, and so on—that must be annihilated.

Before turning to describe some of the other themes and essays in this volume, I would like to briefly discuss how genocide might be distinguished from other forms of violence. The English word *violence* is derived from the Latin *violentia*, which refers to "vehemence, impetuosity, ferocity" and is associated with "force."[9] In its current usage, *violence* may refer specifically to the "exercise of physical force so as to inflict injury on, or cause damage to, persons or property" (*Oxford English Dictionary* 1989:654) or quite generally to any type of physical, symbolic, psychological, or structural force exerted against someone, some group, or some thing.[10] Political violence is a subset of violence broadly encompassing forms of covert or, as Carole Nagengast has stated, "overt state-sponsored or tolerated violence" that may include "actions taken or not taken by the state or its agents with the express intent of realizing certain social, ethnic, economic, and political goals in the realm of public affairs, especially affairs of the state or even of social life in general" (1994:114).

Political violence, in turn, subsumes a number of potentially overlapping phenomena including terrorism, ethnic conflict, torture, oppression, war, and genocide. What distinguishes genocide from these other forms of political violence is the perpetrators' sustained and purposeful attempt to destroy a collectivity (Fein 1990:24). Thus, while genocide *may* involve terrorism (or acts intended to intimidate or subjugate others by the fear they inspire), ethnic conflict (or violence perpetrated against another ethnic group), torture (or the infliction of severe physical pain and psychological anguish to punish or coerce others), oppression (or the use of authority to forcibly subjugate others), and war (or a state of armed conflict between two or more nations, states, or factions), it differs from them conceptually insofar as genocide is characterized by the intention to annihilate "the other."[11] Clearly, the boundaries between these different forms of political violence blend into one another. Moreover, as with all conceptual categories, genocide is based on certain presuppositions that are subject to debate and challenge. Nevertheless, I believe that we may legitimately delineate the domain of "an anthropology of genocide" as encompassing those cases in which a perpetrator group attempts, intentionally and over a sustained period of time, to annihilate another social or political community from the face of the earth.

MODERNITY'S EDGES: GENOCIDE AND INDIGENOUS PEOPLES

[As] you are aware, in undertakings like ours the capital is applied to and spent in conquering or more properly attracting to work and civilization the savage tribes, which, once this is attained . . . brings to us the property of the very soil they dominated, paying afterwards with the produce they supply, the value of any such advance. In undertakings like ours any amounts so applied are considered capital.
—*Report and Special Report from the Select Committee on Putumayo*[12]

But humbled be, and thou shalt see these Indians soon will dy.
A Swarm of Flies, they may arise, a Nation to Annoy,
Yea Rats and Mice, or Swarms of Lice a Nation may destroy.
—CAPTAIN WAIT WINTHROP, 1675, *Some Meditations*[13]

If the concept of genocide is a twentieth-century invention, the types of destructive behaviors it references go far back in history. Many of the earliest recorded episodes were linked to warfare and the desire of the perpetrators to either eliminate an enemy or terrify potential foes into submission, what Helen Fein (1984) has called "despotic genocides."[14] The ancient Assyrians, for example, attempted to rule by fear, repeatedly massacring or enslaving those peoples who failed to submit to their authority. Seenacherib's destruction of Babylon in 689 B.C. provides one illustration: "[He] made up his mind to erase rebellious Babylon from the face of the earth. Having forced his way into the city, he slaughtered the inhabitants one by one, until the dead clogged the streets. . . . He would have the city vanish . . . from the very sight of mankind" (Ceram 1951:269). Ironically, the Assyrians themselves were later annihilated at the end of a war. Similarly, the Athenian empire made a terrifying example of upstart Melos by killing all Melinian men of military age and selling their women and children into slavery. The Mongols of Genghis Khan, in turn, developed a ferocious reputation for the massacres they carried out. Mongol soldiers were sometimes ordered to prove they had killed a requisite number of people by cutting off their victims' ears, which were later counted.

With the advent of modernity, however, genocidal violence began to be motivated by a new constellation of factors. The term *modernity* is notoriously difficult to define and can perhaps best be described as a set of interrelated processes, some of which began to develop as early as the fifteenth century, characterizing the emergence of "modern society."[15] Politically, modernity involves the rise of secular forms of government, symbolized by the French Revolution and culminating in the modern nation-state. Economically, modernity refers to capitalist expansion and its derivatives—monetarized exchange, the accumulation of capital, extensive private property, the search for new markets, commodification, and industrialization. Socially, modernity entails the replacement of "traditional" loyalties (to lord, master, priest, king, patriarch, kin, and local community) with "modern" ones (to secular authority, leader, "humanity," class, gender, race, and ethnicity). Culturally, modernity encompasses the movement from a predominantly religious to an emphatically secular and materialist worldview characterized by new ways of thinking about and understanding human behavior.

In many ways, this modern worldview was epitomized by Enlightenment thought, with its emphasis on the individual, empiricism, secularism, rationality, progress, and the enormous potential of science. For Enlightenment thinkers and their heirs, the social world, like nature, was something to be analyzed and explained in a rational, scientific manner. Ultimately, such empirical research would yield universal laws of human behavior and provide knowledge that could be used to advance the human condition. This optimistic bundle of ideas contributed greatly to the emergence of a key metanarrative of modernity—the teleological myth of "progress" and "civilization."[16] On the one hand, the human condition was portrayed as involving the inexorable march of progress from a state of savagery to one of civilization. On the other hand, reason and science provided the means to facilitate this march through social engineering; human societies, like nature, could be mastered, reconstructed, and improved.

Despite the optimistic promises of this metanarrative, modernity quickly demonstrated that it has a dark side—mass destruction, extreme cruelty, and genocide. Indigenous peoples, who lived on the edges of modernity, were often devastated by its advance (Bodley 1999; Maybury-Lewis 1997). Beginning with the fifteenth-century explorations of the Portuguese and Spanish, European imperialists began a process whereby newly "discovered" lands were conquered and colonized and the indigenous people living within them enslaved, exploited, and murdered. Tens of millions of indigenous peoples perished in the years that followed. Because the European expansion was largely driven by a desire for new lands, converts, wealth, slaves, and markets, some scholars refer to the resulting annihilation of indigenous peoples as "development" or "utilitarian" genocides (Fein 1984; Smith 1987). This devastation was legitimated by contradictory discourses that simultaneously asserted that the colonizers had the "burden" of "civilizing" the "savages" living on their newly conquered territories and that their deaths mattered little since they were not fully human. Metanarratives of modernity supplied the terms by which indigenous peoples were constructed as the inverted image of "civilized" peoples. Discourse about these "others" was frequently structured by a series of value-laden binary oppositions (see also Bauman 1991; Taussig 1987):

modernity/tradition
civilization/savagery
us/them
center/margin
civilized/wild
humanity/barbarity
progress/degeneration
advanced/backward

developed/underdeveloped
adult/childlike
nurturing/dependent
normal/abnormal
subject/object
human/subhuman
reason/passion
culture/nature
male/female
mind/body
objective/subjective
knowledge/ignorance
science/magic
truth/superstition
master/slave
good/evil
moral/sinful
believers/pagans
pure/impure
order/disorder
law/uncontrolled
justice/arbitrariness
active/passive
wealthy/poor
nation-state/nonstate spaces
strong/weak
dominant/subordinate
conqueror/conquered

In this volume, the chapters by Maybury-Lewis and Totten, Parsons, and Hitch-cock (see also Arnold, this volume) illustrate how such binary oppositions of moder-nity have been and continue to be invoked to legitimate abuses perpetrated against indigenous peoples.[17]

Maybury-Lewis's essay, "Genocide against Indigenous Peoples," notes that, while we will never know the exact numbers, somewhere between thirty and fifty million (or more) indigenous people—roughly 80 percent—perished from the time of first contact to their population low points in the late nineteenth and early twen-tieth centuries (see also Bodley 1999). Because of the technological and military superiority of European imperialists, various indigenous peoples stood little chance of resisting their advance and exploitative policies, particularly when coupled with the devastating effects of disease. As Maybury-Lewis points out, not all of the devastation was caused by genocide. Indigenous peoples perished from European diseases to which they had no resistance, from forced labor, from starvation caused by their loss of land and the disruption of their traditional ways of life, and from outright murder. Some of the deaths were intentionally perpetrated; others were caused indirectly.

Maybury-Lewis describes how the inhumane and genocidal treatment of indigenous peoples was often framed in metanarratives of modernity, particularly the notion of "progress." Thus, the annihilation of Tasmanians was legitimated as an attempt to "bring them to civilization," and Theodore Roosevelt justified the westward expansion of the United States by arguing that the land should not remain "a game preserve for squalid savages." Likewise, General Roca, who led the infamous "Conquest of the Desert" against indigenous Indians, told his fellow Argentineans that "our self-respect as a virile people obliges us to put down as soon as possible, by reason or by force, this handful of savages who destroy our wealth and prevent us from definitively occupying, in the name of law, progress and our own security, the richest and most fertile lands of the Republic" (Maybury-Lewis, this volume). Similar arguments were made to legitimate the massacre of thousands of Herero.

As Maybury-Lewis highlights, the perpetrators' greed and cruelty is astounding and, often, sickening. In the above examples, indigenous peoples were displaced and killed for their land. In other instances, they were terrorized into performing slave labor. Rubber-plantation owners in South America and the Congo were particularly brutal; they held relatives of the workers as hostages, raped women, tortured and maimed the recalcitrant, and sometimes abused and killed simply for amusement (see also Taussig 1987). In more recent times, indigenous peoples have been devastated by another metanarrative of modernity—discourses asserting the need for "development." The "development" of Nigeria's oil resources (through the collaboration of the government and multinational companies such as Shell), for example, has led to massive environmental damage and the enormous suffering of the Ogoni who reside in oil-rich areas (see also Totten, Parsons, and Hitchcock, this volume). In his own work at *Cultural Survival,* Maybury-Lewis continues to inform the public about the suffering of indigenous peoples around the globe, including contemporary cases in which states have waged war against indigenous peoples within their borders who have resisted—or been perceived as resisting—the state's authority (for example, the Naga of India, various non-Burmese peoples, Guatemalan Mayans, and Sudanese Christians). Maybury-Lewis's chapter concludes by summarizing some of the factors that have contributed to the genocide of indigenous peoples— the resources of the land upon which they live, extreme dehumanization, marginality and political weakness, and metanarratives of modernity. Perhaps, he suggests, the plight of indigenous peoples will improve in an era of globalization as nation-states are increasingly reorganized along more pluralist lines.

If Maybury-Lewis's essay outlines the long history of genocidal atrocities committed against indigenous peoples throughout the world, Samuel Totten, William Parsons, and Robert Hitchcock's chapter, "Confronting Genocide and Ethnocide of Indigenous Peoples: An Interdisciplinary Approach to Definition, Intervention, Prevention, and Advocacy," constitutes an interdisciplinary effort to clarify key issues related to the prevention of such atrocities. As cultural, applied, forensic, and other anthropologists have taken an increasingly proactive role in defending indigenous peoples, they have found themselves working with scholars from other fields, policy-makers, and indigenous peoples themselves. Unfortunately, the participants in such collaborative efforts often use terms like *genocide* in very different ways. Prevention, intervention, and advocacy, the authors argue, require precise conceptual distinctions that may lead to disparate preventative strategies.

The very definition of the term *indigenous people* is problematic, since in many places groups may migrate and identify themselves in different ways. Totten, Parsons, and Hitchcock note that the Independent Commission on International Humanitarian Issues identifies four key characteristics of indigenous peoples—pre-existence, non-dominance, cultural difference, and self-identification as indigenous—that parallel Maybury-Lewis's definition of indigenous peoples as those who "have been conquered by invaders who are racially, ethnically, or culturally different from themselves." Crucial issues revolve around the question of how one defines indigenous peoples. Several African and Asian governments, for example, have tried to deny that indigenous peoples live within their borders or argue that all the groups in the country are indigenous. By doing so, they attempt to avoid international inquiries on the behalf of indigenous peoples and undercut their claims for compensation or land rights.

Totten, Parsons, and Hitchcock also make useful distinctions between physical genocide (that is, the intentional killing of the members of a group), cultural genocide or "ethnocide" (the deliberate destruction of a group's way of life), "ecocide" (the destruction of a group's ecosystem by state or corporate entities), and various typologies of genocide (such as retributive, despotic, developmental, and ideological).[18] With such conceptual distinctions in mind, anthropologists and other advocates may more effectively promote the rights of indigenous peoples by developing explicit standards to monitor and defend groups at risk. In addition, scholars and policy makers may work to develop early-warning systems that trigger an alarm when the possibility of genocide is high in a locale. By using their "on the ground experience" to help warn about impending genocides and by helping to develop educational initiatives, anthropologists may play a crucial role in such efforts at prevention, intervention, and advocacy.

Such efforts, Totten, Parsons, and Hitchcock argue, are of crucial importance since indigenous peoples continue to endure a wide range of abuses, ranging from involuntary relocation and the forcible removal of children to arbitrary executions and genocide. Like Maybury-Lewis's essay, their chapter illustrates how such devastation is often implicitly or explicitly legitimated by metanarratives of modernity. Governments, agencies, companies, and multinational corporations frequently portray the suffering and death of indigenous peoples as a "necessary by-product" of "development" and "progress," which come in the form of logging, mineral extraction, hydroelectric projects, oil fields, and land grabs in resource-rich areas. Totten, Parsons, and Hitchcock carefully document how such projects result in enormous environmental damage, displacement, and, all too often, the deaths of indigenous peoples such as the Ogoni.

Ultimately, the very need for such harmful "development" projects is linked to other dimensions of modernity, the colonial endeavor and the creation of nation-states. As European imperialists set out to conquer new territories, they laid claim to large swaths of land throughout the world. Colonial boundaries were "rationally" demarcated in terms of major landmarks and the claims of competing powers. This pattern of "rational planning," establishing territorial borders, and ordering from above is one of the hallmarks of modernity. In order to create a map or grid that can be centrally controlled and manipulated, the modern state reduces and simplifies complex phenomena into a more manageable, schematized form; unfortunately, the results are often disastrous, particularly when local knowledge is ignored (Scott 1998). Colonial powers usually paid little attention to local understandings of sociopolitical difference when mapping out new political boundaries. After the colonial powers withdrew, newly independent nations found themselves in control of minority (and sometimes even majority) populations—including indigenous peoples—that wanted greater autonomy, more power, or the right to secede outright. Moreover, because of the exploitative economic practices of the colonial powers, many nations lacked basic infrastructure and trained personnel and were plagued by poverty and high rates of population growth. Colonialism therefore laid the foundation for much of the violent conflict and suffering that has plagued the twentieth-century world, as recently exemplified by the genocidal events in Rwanda.

ESSENTIALIZING DIFFERENCE: ANTHROPOLOGISTS IN THE HOLOCAUST

> Modern genocide is genocide with a purpose.... *It is a means to an end....* The end itself is a grand vision of a better, and radically different, society.... *This is the gardener's vision, projected upon a world-size screen.... Some gardeners hate the weeds that spoil their design—that ugliness in the midst of beauty, litter in the midst of serene order. Some others are quite unemotional about them: just a problem to be solved, an extra job to be done. Not that it makes a difference to the weeds; both gardeners exterminate them.*
> —ZYGMUNT BAUMAN, *Modernity and the Holocaust*[19]

If all human beings are born with a propensity to distinguish difference, modern societies are distinguished by the degree to which such differences are reified. In other words, modernity thrives on the essentialization of difference. Several factors have contributed to this tendency. First, during the Age of Expansion, European explorers found themselves confronted with groups of people whose appearance and ways of life differed dramatically from their own. To comprehend such difference and to justify their imperialist, exploitative enterprises, Europeans frequently constructed the wide array of peoples they encountered in a similar fashion—as "primitive" others who lived in a degenerate and lawless state. As noted in the last section, these "others" served as an inverted mirror of modernity, giving rise to the type of "Orientalist" constructions that Edward Said (1985) has so vividly described. The west (us) was frequently opposed to "the rest" (them) in a unidimensional, stereotypic, and essentialized manner.

Second, the nation-state covets homogeneity. In contrast to earlier state formations, the modern nation-state is characterized by fixed territorial borders, centralized control of power, impersonal forms of governance, and a representational claim to legitimacy (see Held 1995). The very existence of the nation-state is predicated upon the assumption that there is a political "imagined community" of theoretically uniform "citizens" who, despite living in distant locales and disparate social positions, read the same newspapers and share a similar set of interests, legal rights, and obligations (Anderson 1991). It is in the nation-state's interest to use whatever means are at its disposal—national holidays, the media, institutional policy, flags, and anthems—to promote this vision of homogeneity. This tendency frequently culminates in a naturalized identification between person and place, often expressed in origin myths and arborescent metaphors that physically "root" nationals to their homeland and assert the identification of blood, soil, and nation (see Malkki 1997; Linke, this volume).

Third, science searches for regularity. This quest is exemplified by its theoretical laws, quantitative measures, methodologies, empiricism, and classificatory systems. Enlightenment thinkers extended the emerging scientific mentality to human beings, who, the colonial encounter revealed, seemed to come in a variety of shapes, colors, and sizes. People, like other species and the physical world itself, had a "nature" that could be apprehended, classified, and theorized. Ultimately, this analogy had a lethal potentiality, which was actualized when hierarchical typologies of human difference were reified in terms of biological origins. "Otherness" became an immutable fact. Science thereby provided a legitimizing rationale for slavery, exploitation, and, ultimately, genocide in the modern era.

And, finally, to have "progress," one must have places and peoples to which it may be brought (savage "others" living in a "backward" state) and a standard (the end-point or goal) against which it may be judged (the "advanced" state of "civilization"). The means of "progress" are exemplified by modernity's projects of social engineering (Bauman 1991; Scott 1998). "Development" requires rational design (and, of course, the centralized control of the modern nation-state); rational design, in turn, requires legible, precise units that can be manipulated from above. From the perspective of the social engineer, groups of people are conceptualized as homogenous units having specifiable characteristics, which, like scientific variables, can be manipulated to achieve the desired end.

As Zygmunt Bauman (1991) has so effectively demonstrated, these essentializing impulses of modernity contributed to the paradigmatic genocide of the twentieth century, the Holocaust. In their attempt to create a homogenous German "folk community," the Nazis embarked on a lethal project of social engineering that was to eliminate "impure" groups that threatened the Aryan race. Difference was biologized into an immutable physiological essence that could not be changed. More than 200,000 severely disabled or mentally ill people, classified by German physicians as "lives not worth living," were murdered in the name of eugenics and euthanasia. Similarly, the Nazis executed up to six million Jews who were ideologically portrayed as a "disease," as "bacilli," and as "parasites" that threatened to poison the German national body and contaminate the purity of German blood (Koenigsberg 1975; Linke 1999). Gypsies and other undesirable groups were also targeted for elimination.

Once difference was essentialized and sorted into categories, the Nazis employed modern instruments to carry out their genocidal acts—state authority (the Nazis' centralized powers and control over the means of force), bureaucratic efficiency (managerial expertise regulating the flow of victims and the means of their annihilation), a technology of death (concentration camps, cyanide, railroad transport, crematoriums, brutal scientific experiments), and, of course, rational design (the Nazis' abstract plan for a "better" world). The Nazi genocide represented the culmination of modernity's lethal potentiality, as the German state, like Bauman's gardener, set out to reshape the social landscape by systematically and efficiently destroying the human weeds (Jews, Gypsies, "lives not worth living") that threatened to ruin this rational garden of Aryan purity.

As Bettina Arnold's and Gretchen Schafft's chapters suggest, anthropology, like other academic disciplines, was deeply implicated in this genocidal project of modernity and its essentializing tendencies. In fact, the rise of anthropology as a discipline was linked to the colonial encounter as Euroamerican missionaries, officials, travelers, and scholars attempted to comprehend the strange "others" they encountered. In other words, anthropology arose as one of modernity's disciplines of difference. Working from the Enlightenment belief in "progress" and the possibility of discovering scientific laws about human societies, anthropology's early progenitors, such as Spencer and Morgan, proposed that human societies advance through increasingly complex stages of development—from "savagery" to "barbarism" to modernity's apex of human existence, "civilization." Diverse ways of life were compressed into relatively stable categories, a homogenizing tendency that was paralleled by the anthropological typologies of race. If later anthropologists moved toward a more pluralistic conception of cultural diversity (via Herder and Boas), the discipline nevertheless continued to employ a concept of culture that was frequently reified and linked to the fixed territorial boundaries upon which the modern nation-state was predicated. In Germany, all of these essentializing tendencies coalesced under the Nazis, who asserted an equation between German blood and soil and the superiority of the German folk community. As experts on human diversity, German anthropologists were quickly enlisted to help construct this genocidal ideology of historical and physical difference, a process I have elsewhere called "manufacturing difference" (Hinton 1998, 2000).

Bettina Arnold's essay, "Justifying Genocide: Archaeology and the Construction of Difference," illustrates how historical difference is manufactured with archaeological "evidence" that provides an imagined identification between people and place. Such national identifications are notoriously susceptible to ideological manipulation because the categories upon which they are predicated—race, nation, ethnicity, religion, language, culture—are fuzzy and may shift across time, place, and person. Almost anyone can find an imagined origin for "their" group if they look hard enough, as recently illustrated by the violent conflict in the former Yugoslavia.

German National Socialism proved adept at such historical imaginings, which attempted to construct a mythic linkage between the Germanic people and their homeland. Arnold illustrates how German archaeologists, such as Gustaf Kossinna, reconstructed the past to provide a "pure," continuous line of Germanic cultural development from their ethnoparthenogenetic origin in the Paleolithic period up to the "post-Germanic" phase. Since the German people were supposed to be the most advanced race ever to have inhabited the earth, the Nazis sought to construct an archaeological record that demonstrated that the major advances in European history were of Nordic origin and denied that the Germanic people had been influenced by those of a "lesser" racial stock. Thus, through the creation of a mythic north-south migration route, the great achievements of ancient Greece and Rome were given a Germanic origin. Migration theory could also provide a basis for Nazi expansionist claims that the regime was merely retaking lands that had historically been Germanic territories. Ultimately, by constructing origin myths for the German nation-state and the superiority of the Aryan race, German archaeologists helped create essentialized categories of difference that served as an underpinning and justification for genocide.

Arnold notes that archaeology has also been used to legitimate genocide in other contexts. In the United States, for example, European settlers were sometimes dramatically confronted with the complex cultural achievements of Native Americans, such as the earthen mounds discovered in Ohio and the Mississippi River Valley. According to models of evolutionary progress, the "savage" natives could not possibly have built such sophisticated structures. To deal with this paradox, nineteenth-century archaeologists proposed the "Moundbuilder Myth," which held that the mounds had been built by a vanished race. By reconstructing the past to agree with their metanarratives of modernity, the European colonizers were able to legitimate their continued destruction of Native American societies, whose very "savagery" was confirmed by their suspected annihilation of the "civilized" Moundbuilders. The archaeological record was used in similar ways in Africa and other colonial territories. Arnold concludes by pointing out that archaeological evidence continues to be manipulated by various peoples around the globe—Chinese, Japanese, Celts, Estonians, Russians, Israelis—to legitimate their nationalist claims. By carefully examining and monitoring the ways in which archaeology continues to be used to manufacture difference, she suggests, anthropologists stand to make an important contribution to the prevention of genocide.

Although Arnold does not discuss Rwanda and the former Yugoslavia, her arguments about the lethal potentialities implicit in the association between people and place could certainly be applied to these genocides. In both cases, origin myths served as a basis for essentializing difference and legitimating the annihilation of victims. In colonial Rwanda, German and later Belgian officials reimagined social differences in terms of the "Hamitic Hypothesis," which held that Tutsis were more "civilized" Hamites who had migrated south from Egypt and the Nile Valley and introduced more "advanced" forms of "development" into the region (see Taylor 1999, and this volume; see also Malkki 1995). Tutsis therefore shared racial characteristics that enabled them to be more effective leaders than the allegedly racially inferior Hutus, who were supposedly of Bantu stock. In the postcolonial period, this origin myth was reinvented by Hutus to argue that the Tutsis were "tricky," impure foreign invaders who had to be expunged from what was Hutu soil—an image reminiscent of Nazi discourse about Jews.

Similarly, in Bosnia-Herzegovina in the 1990s, Serb and Croat historiographers vied to construct historical linkages connecting themselves to Muslims ("converts" and "heretics") and the territories in which they lived; Muslim scholars, in turn, argued that they were a national group (*narod*) that shared a way of life, religious beliefs, and legacy of residence on their lands (Bringa 1995, and this volume). Political ideologues played upon these different vantage points, arguing that their group had the right to lands that "others" now occupied. Genocide and ethnic cleansing were used to reconstruct an equivalence between national group and soil. As in Nazi Germany, in Rwanda and Bosnia an origin myth was ideologically deployed to essentialize identity, creating an "us" that belonged and a "them" that needed to be expunged—by forced removal or by death.

Gretchen Schafft's essay, "Scientific Racism in Service of the Reich: German Anthropologists in the Nazi Era," illustrates how Nazi anthropologists were deeply implicated in another form of manufacturing difference—constructing the alleged "characteristics" of various social groups. Many of these anthropologists worked in the anthropology division of the Kaiser Wilhelm Institute (KWI), which received large grants from the Rockefeller Foundation to conduct its studies on race and genetics. (This funding continued long after Hitler had begun to impose his anti-Semitic policies.) Schafft notes that, during the course of the 1930s, the anthropologists at the KWI's Institute for Anthropology, Human Heredity, and Genetics became increasingly involved in the racial politics of the Third Reich. On a practical level, these anthropologists acted as judges of identity and, therefore, had a considerable impact on an individual's chances for survival in Nazi Germany. Some certified racial backgrounds by examining an individual's blood type and physical features; others served as members of Nazi Racial Courts that enforced racial policy and heard appeals, though these were rarely granted. On a theoretical level, German and Austrian anthropologists helped buttress Nazi ideology by publishing articles on race and by training hundreds of SS doctors in the theory and practice of racial hygiene. In fact, one anthropologist, Otmar von Verscheur, founded *Der*

Erbartz, a leading medical journal that frequently published articles supporting Nazi policy on eugenics and race.

Schafft illustrates how, after World War II broke out, many Nazi anthropologists became even more intimately involved in the atrocities perpetrated during the Holocaust. Verschuer, who replaced the retiring Eugon Fischer as head of the KWI's Anthropology Institute in 1942, acted as a mentor to Josef Mengele, who himself had degrees in anthropology and medicine. Their collaboration continued while Mengele performed his notorious experiments at Auschwitz; in fact, Mengele sent blood samples and body parts to the Anthropology Institute for further analysis. After Germany invaded Poland, a number of anthropologists began working at the Institute für Deutsche Ostarbeit (Institute for Work in the East, or IDO) in the Race and Ethnic Research section. Some of these Nazi anthropologists were given responsibility for examining ethnic and racial differences in the newly conquered Eastern European territories. They conducted ethnographic research in a variety of locales, ranging from Polish villages to delousing centers and concentration camps. In many situations, SS guards provided these anthropologists with protection and forced their subjects, sometimes at gunpoint, to be examined, measured, and interviewed. Other anthropologists at the IDO examined the effects of "racial mixing" and identified various "racial strains." Like their colleagues at the KWI, Nazi anthropologists at the IDO were ultimately in the business of manufacturing difference—sorting diverse peoples into a fabricated hierarchy of essentialized biosocial types. The work of all of these Nazi anthropologists contributed directly to genocide, since they identified and judged the racial background of various individuals, forcibly used helpless victims (or their body parts) in their research projects, and, ultimately, provided a theoretical foundation for euthanasia, "racial hygiene," and the annihilation of Jews and other "impure" racial groups.

Schafft further considers why Nazi anthropologists participated in genocide. She suggests that anthropologists like Eugon Fischer, who altered his views about the benefits of "racial mixing" after Hitler took power, were driven, in part, by the desire for advancement and to continue conducting scientific research. (Those who protested in the Third Reich quickly lost their positions or were arrested.) Other Nazi anthropologists might have wanted to avoid military service. Many of these individuals may have believed that the lethal racist policies of the Third Reich were backed by scientific research. Still, the fact that these Nazi anthropologists often used vague and euphemistic language suggests that, on some level, they may have experienced qualms about what they were doing.[20] This vagueness subsequently enabled many Nazi anthropologists to escape punishment and continue their careers after the war, sometimes in positions of prominence. Finally, Schafft asks why anthropologists have been so hesitant to explore this dark chapter of their disciplinary history. Perhaps anthropologists don't want to draw further attention to the fact that their participation in public projects has sometimes been ethically suspect and had disastrous results. Others might reply that the Nazi anthropologists were a small fringe group whose work fell outside the mainstream of anthropological thought. Schafft responds by noting that anthropologists throughout the world were using many of the same conceptual categories as Nazi anthropologists, including notions of race, eugenics, and social engineering.

Ultimately, I suspect that the Holocaust is difficult for us to look at because it illustrates how our most fundamental enterprise—examining and characterizing human similarity and difference—may serve as the basis for horrendous deeds, including genocide. Genocidal regimes thrive on the very types of social categories that anthropologists analyze and deploy—peoples, cultures, ethnic groups, nations, religious groups. Anthropology is, in large part, a product of modernity and its essentializing tendencies. However, our discipline has another side, tolerance, which also has its roots in Enlightenment thought and was forcefully expressed by some of the founding figures of anthropology, such as Johann Herder and Franz Boas. Following this other disciplinary tradition, anthropologists have fought against racism and hate, defending the rights of indigenous peoples, demonstrating that categories like race are social constructs situated in particular historical and social contexts, and advocating a general respect for difference. These insights can certainly be extended to combat discourses of genocide. Nevertheless, an understanding of Nazi anthropology may help us to acknowledge and remain aware of our discipline's reductive propensities and the ways in which the forms of knowledge we produce can have powerful effects when put into practice.

ANNIHILATING DIFFERENCE:
LOCAL DIMENSIONS OF GENOCIDE

Although I have frequently referred to modernity in the singular, I want to emphasize that modernity is not a "thing." The term refers to a number of interrelated processes that give rise to distinct local formations, or "modernities." If genocide has frequently been motivated by and legitimated in terms of metanarratives of modernity, genocide, like modernity itself, is always a local process and cannot be fully comprehended without an experience-near understanding. Thus, modernity and genocide both involve the essentialization of difference, but the ways in which such differences are constructed, manufactured, and viewed may vary considerably across time and place. Moreover, the form and experience of genocidal violence is variably mediated by local knowledge.

These two key dimensions of genocide, modernity and the local, are exemplified by the many "ideological genocides" that have plagued the twentieth century (Smith 1987). In Nazi Germany and Cambodia, for example, genocide was structured by metanarratives of modernity—social engineering, progress, rationality, the elimination of the impure—and related sets of binary oppositions, including:

us/them
good/evil
progress/degeneration

order/chaos
belonging/alien
purity/contamination

Nevertheless, the meaning of such conceptual categories took on distinct local forms. Both the Nazis and the Khmer Rouge sought to expunge the impure, but they constructed the impure in different ways. Thus, even as the Nazis justified their destruction of the Jews and other sources of "contamination" in terms of "scientific" knowledge about race and genes, their ideology of hate also drew heavily on German notions of blood, soil, bodily aesthetics, contagion, genealogy, community, and anti-Semitism (Linke 1999, and this volume).

The Khmer Rouge, in turn, legitimated their utopian project of social engineering in terms of Marxist-Leninist "science," which supposedly enabled the "correct and clear-sighted leadership" to construct a new society free of "contaminating" elements (Hinton, forthcoming). In Khmer Rouge ideology, however, the "impure" was often conceptualized in terms of agrarian metaphors and Buddhist notions of (pure) order and (impure) fragmentation. Further, to increase the attractiveness of their message and to motivate their minions to annihilate their "enemies," the Khmer Rouge frequently incorporated pre-existing, emotionally salient forms of Cambodian cultural knowledge into their ideology (Hinton 1998, forthcoming). The essays described in this section of the introduction illustrate the importance of taking into account such local dimensions of genocide.

As suggested by its title, "The Cultural Face of Terror in the Rwandan Genocide of 1994," Christopher Taylor's chapter argues that, while historical, political, and socioeconomic factors played a crucial role in the Rwandan genocide, they remain unable to explain why the violence was perpetrated in certain ways—for example, the severing of Achilles tendons, genital mutilation, breast oblation, the construction of roadblocks that served as execution sites, bodies being stuffed into latrines. This violence, he contends, was deeply symbolic and embodied a cultural patterning. Accordingly, it is imperative for scholars to take cultural factors into account when explaining the genocidal process. Contrasting his position to the cultural determinism of Daniel Goldhagen's (1996) controversial analysis of German political culture, Taylor emphasizes that Rwandan cultural knowledge did not "cause" the genocide and that it is variably internalized by Rwandans. These pre-existing "generative schemes" only came to structure mass violence within a particular ethnohistorical context, one in which other tendencies and metanarratives of modernity—race, essentializing difference, biological determinism, national belonging—were also present.

Drawing on his ethnographic fieldwork in Rwanda, Taylor points out that Rwandan conceptions of the body are frequently structured in terms of a root metaphor of (orderly) flow and (disorderly) blockage. Health and well-being depend upon proper bodily flow. Thus, the bodies of newborn infants are carefully examined to ensure that they are free of "obstructions," such as anal malformations, that would indicate an inability to participate in (flows) of social exchange. Similarly, traditional Rwandan healing practices often center on the attempt to remove obstructing blockages and restore the stricken person's "flow." This root metaphor is analogically linked to a variety of other conceptual domains, ranging from topography to myth. Social exchange constitutes another flow that can be blocked by the deaths of daughters linking families or the failure to fulfill interpersonal obligations. Rwandan kings were sometimes ritually depicted as symbolic conduits through which substances of fertility and nourishment flowed to their subjects. Kings also had the responsibility of removing obstructing beings, such as women who lacked breasts or enemies who threatened the realm. Their power thus contained two contradictory elements: the ability to block obstructing beings and the capacity to guarantee proper social flows. In a variety of domains, then, blockage signified the antithesis of order, an obstruction that had to be removed to ensure personal and communal well-being.

Taylor contends that a great deal of the violence perpetrated during the Rwandan genocide embodied this root metaphor of flow and blockage. In Hutu nationalist discourse, Tutsis were frequently portrayed as the ultimate blocking beings— contaminating foreign "invaders from Ethiopia" who were inherently malevolent and obstructed the social flows of the Hutu nation. Motivated by this ideology of hate and their own self-implicating understandings of blockage and flow, Hutu perpetrators displayed a tendency to carry out their brutal deeds in terms of this cultural idiom. Thus, thousands of "obstructing" Tutsis were dumped in rivers—a signifier of flow in Rwandan cosmology—and thereby expunged from the body politic's symbolic organs of elimination. This analogy between Tutsis and excrement was expressed in another manifestation of violence, the stuffing of Tutsi bodies into latrines.

Throughout the country, Hutu militias also established roadblocks and barriers at which Tutsis were identified, robbed, raped, mutilated, and killed. These sites served as liminal domains in which the Tutsi "obstructors" were blocked and eliminated. Such violence was often perpetrated in ways that inscribed the obstructing status of the victims upon their bodies. To mark Tutsis as blocked beings, Hutus deprived these victims of their ability to move and live (stopping Tutsis at barriers, where their Achilles tendons were often severed before they were killed in cruel ways); removed their symbolic organs of reproductive social flow (genital mutilation and breast oblation); clogged their bodily conduits (impalement from anus or vagina to mouth); compelled them to engage in asocial acts signifying misdirected flow (rape and forced incest). Taylor concludes by arguing that, while the atrocities committed during the Rwandan genocide were motivated by other factors as well, the pattern of many of the horrible acts must be at least partially explained in terms of local understandings of blockage and flow.

Toni Shapiro-Phim's essay, "Dance, Music, and the Nature of Terror in Democratic Kampuchea," explores another experience-near dimension of genocide, the relation between state-sanctioned ideology and daily life. In particular, she analyzes the conjunction between everyday terror and music, song, and dance in the Cambodian genocide. As signifiers of identity, passion, and embodied experience, these aesthetic practices constitute a powerful means of communication and influence. Recognizing this potential efficacy and appeal, sociopolitical organizations—ranging from national governments to religious revivalists—frequently deploy music, song, and dance to inspire their followers. Unfortunately, genocidal regimes also use music, song, and dance to disseminate their discourses of hate.

Democratic Kampuchea (DK) provides a clear illustration of this point. During this genocidal period, Shapiro-Phim notes, the Khmer Rouge banned older, "counterrevolutionary" aesthetic practices. To promote revolutionary change and encourage the destruction of the regime's enemies, the Khmer Rouge created hundreds of new songs and dances. At work sites and meetings, in crammed vehicles, and in mess halls, Cambodians, many of whom were exhausted, malnourished, and ill, found themselves inundated with the revolutionary arts. DK songs lauded the sacrifice of slain revolutionaries and urged the populace to seek out and destroy enemies who remained hidden within their midst. Many of these songs, such as "Children of the New Kampuchea," specifically targeted children, who were viewed as "blank slates" upon whom revolutionary attitudes and a selfless devotion to the Party could be more easily imprinted. On more important occasions, revolutionary art troupes performed dances and skits that conveyed a similar message of indoctrination, often modeling revolutionary attitudes and behavior through their dress, lyrics, and movements. To highlight the new ideal of gender equality, male and female performers often dressed and danced similarly. Brusque movements and military demeanor, in turn, suggested that the country was still at war, fighting nature and counterrevolutionaries.

In terms of everyday life, however, there was sometimes a great discrepancy between the ideological discourses embodied in music, song, and dance and the experiences of individuals. Drawing on three life histories, Shapiro-Phim points out that, despite the fact that up to 90 percent of Cambodia's professional artists perished during DK, many precisely because of their "reactionary" backgrounds, other artists survived for the same reasons. Thus, Dara, a former art student, was arrested one night after playing his flute. Even after learning that Dara had been an artist during the old regime, a Khmer Rouge cadre spared Dara's life in return for Dara's promise to play music for him each evening. Similarly, Bun, a former court dancer, survived imprisonment after his interrogator learned of his past vocation. After dancing for the prison that evening, Bun received better treatment and additional food and was one of a small number of the prisoners to survive incarceration. Shapiro-Phim argues that this evidence illustrates that there is no one-to-one correspondence between state ideology and individual practice. Khmer Rouge cadre and soldiers made choices about how to act within varying sets of situational constraints. Moreover, the very inconsistencies and uncertainties that emerge from the discrepancy between official policy and local realities help generate an atmosphere of fear and terror.

Tone Bringa's essay, "Averted Gaze: Genocide in Bosnia-Herzegovina 1992–1995," illustrates what happens when the international community fails to act in the face of an escalating cycle of dehumanization, exclusionary rhetoric, political violence, and, ultimately, genocide. Bringa carefully examines how the Bosnian genocide emerged in the wake of the breakup of the former Yugoslavia. Although all of the Yugoslav republics, except for Bosnia-Herzegovina, were designated as the "national home" of a particular people (narod), Tito's Yugoslavia encouraged a superordinate loyalty to the state. On a structural level, transethnic identification was facilitated by the Yugoslav Communist Party and the Yugoslav People's Army. Ideologically, Tito encouraged interethnic ties through a cult of personality and the rubric of "Brotherhood and Unity," a key state tenet (along with "self-management") that played upon a traditional model of cooperation and interaction between various ethnoreligious communities. Drawing on her ethnographic fieldwork in Bosnia in the late 1980s, Bringa emphasizes that, in contrast to common portrayals of Bosnia-Herzegovina as either a seething cauldron of ethnic hatreds or an idyllic, harmonious, multiethnic society, a number of cultural models for interethnic relations existed, some promoting interaction, others exclusion. Moreover, the salience of these models varied across time, person, and place.

Bringa notes that all societies contain the potential for war and peace; these potentialities are actualized within shifting historical contexts. In the former Yugoslavia, Tito's death in 1980 marked the beginning of a gradual process whereby power increasingly devolved to the republics. This process was accelerated toward the end of the 1980s by the fall of the Berlin wall, economic crisis, and the emergence of strident ethnonationalist politicians who played upon popular fears and uncertainty. Whereas Tito had glossed over past conflicts between Yugoslavia's ethnoreligious groups, these new power elites invoked them with a vengeance. In a great irony of history, Slobodan Milosevic and other Serbian leaders frequently referred to the "genocide" that supposedly had been or was being perpetrated against the Serbs, thereby heightening fears of the ethnoreligious "other." Bringa points out that such tactics were part of a larger attempt to radically redefine categories of belonging as the former Yugoslavia broke apart. Modernity's essentializing tendencies once again took a lethal form, as ethnic difference was essentialized and the equation between people and place was redrawn. In an eerie parallel with Nazi anthropology, scholars frequently provided historical, cultural, and linguistic "evidence" to support the exclusionary claims of their leaders. Former friends and neighbors were suddenly redefined as dangerous "foreign enemies" who threatened the survival of the new ethnoreligious state-in-the-making.

Through the manipulation of fear and the "rhetoric of exclusion," ethnonationalist leaders legitimated forced relocations, rape, death camps, and mass violence, which culminated in the genocidal massacres carried out in places like Srebrenica. By the summer of 1992, Serb forces had "ethnically cleansed" more than 70 percent of Bosnia-Herzegovina. Meanwhile, the international community stood by watching, despite numerous reports of what was happening. Why, Bringa asks, did the international community fail to act? In some ways, their inaction was indirectly legiti-mated through the use of the vague term *ethnic cleansing*, which both exoticized the violence and, unlike the term *genocide*, did not carry the legal imperative of interven-tion. The conflict was also often portrayed as being the result of centuries-old hatreds that, because of their supposedly primordial nature, could not be (easily) stopped and, ultimately, seemed to support the power elite's claims that "we cannot live together." Bringa concludes with a plea for scholars and policy-makers to use both macro- and local-level analyses to develop better strategies for predicting and preventing such atrocities from recurring in the future.

GENOCIDE'S WAKE: TRAUMA, MEMORY, COPING, AND RENEWAL

With the fury of a tidal wave, genocide unleashes tragedy upon near and distant shores, creating terror upon its arrival, leaving devastation in its wake. Its death toll in the modern era is astounding: well over a hundred million dead. Although ulti-mately incalculable, the destructive force of genocide is even more widespread, as hundreds of millions of other people—generations of survivors, perpetrators, by-standers, and observers—have been struck, directly and indirectly, by the rippling currents of calamity.[21] On the domestic front, genocide leads to massive infrastruc-ture damage and prolonged social suffering, which may include poverty, hunger, men-tal illness, trauma, somatic symptoms, painful memories, the loss of loved ones, an increased incidence of disease and infant mortality, disrupted communal ties, desta-bilized social networks, a landscape of mines, economic dependency, desensitization, continued conflict and violence, and massive dislocations of the population. The in-ternational community, in turn, touches and is touched by genocide in the form of international aid, media coverage, its acceptance of refugees, the work of U.N. agen-cies and NGOs, the creation of international tribunals and laws, peace-keeping and military operations, academic scholarship, arms manufacturing (including mines), and the burdensome legacy of its own inaction, as foreign governments have too of-ten stood by, passively watching genocide unfold (see Bringa; Magnarella; Maybury-Lewis; Totten, Parsons, and Hitchcock; and other chapters in this volume).

May Ebihara's and Judy Ledgerwood's chapter, "Aftermaths of Genocide: Cam-bodian Villagers," illustrates how anthropologists can provide an experience-near analysis of the devastation that follows in genocide's wake and how survivors at-tempt to rebuild their ravaged lives. Ebihara's and Ledgerwood's analysis loosely focuses on a hamlet in central Cambodia where approximately half of the popu-lation studied by Ebihara in 1959–60 died of starvation, disease, overwork, or out-right execution during Democratic Kampuchea (DK), the period of Khmer Rouge rule. These figures exceed the national averages, which are nevertheless appalling: scholars have estimated that 1.7 million of Cambodia's 7.9 million inhabitants, more than 20 percent of the population, perished during this genocidal period (Kiernan 1996; see also Chandler 1991).

When the Khmer Rouge took power, they immediately set out to transform Cambodian society into a socialist utopia. Many of the socioeconomic changes the Khmer Rouge imposed attacked, directly or indirectly, the solidarity of the family/household unit, which previously had been a foundation of social life, economic production, moral obligation, and emotional attachment. In an attempt to subvert this threatening source of loyalty, the Khmer Rouge undercut the familial bond by separating (or killing) family members, inverting age hierarchies, and co-opting familial functions and sentiments. Immediately after DK, Cambodians crisscrossed the country, looking for lost loved ones. Ebihara and Ledgerwood point out how, in Svay and other parts of Cambodia, families slowly began to reconstitute themselves and re-establish social and kinship networks. Earlier patterns of interaction—such as reciprocal aid, economic cooperation, mutual concern, social interchange—gradually re-emerged, though many families have had to grapple with a shortage of male labor, poverty, emotional wounds, and the loss of loved ones.

The Khmer Rouge also attacked another key social institution that commanded popular loyalty, Buddhism. During DK, the Khmer Rouge banned the religion, forced monks to disrobe, and destroyed and desecrated temples, which were sometimes used as prisons, torture and interrogation centers, and execution sites. Like the family and the household, Buddhism has re-emerged as a dominant focus of Cambodian life. Throughout Cambodia, communities have reconstructed temples and re-established the monastic order. Thus, by 1997, the Svay villagers had largely rebuilt the devastated temple compound and supported monks who, as before DK, again play a crucial role in Cambodian life ceremonies. Buddhist beliefs, communal functions, healing rituals, and ceremonies for the dead have also provided Cambodians with an important means of coping with their enormous suffering and loss.

Sadly, despite their admirable accomplishments in rebuilding their lives and overcoming the trauma of genocide, Cambodians have been forced to continue living in an atmosphere of uncertainty and terror. For more than a decade after DK, people feared the return of the Khmer Rouge, who, supported by the United States and other foreign powers, battled government forces in many areas. In addition, armed men and bandits have terrorized people in many parts of the country. Innocent Cambodians have been robbed and killed in random acts of violence, sometimes perpetrated by rogue military or police units that feel they can act with impunity. Elsewhere, military units have appropriated land from defenseless peasants or participated in intensive logging, which represents a serious threat to Cambodia's agricultural and ecological systems. After twenty-five years of conflict, much of it linked to self-serving U.S. policies dating back to the Vietnam War, Cambodia is rife with landmines and guns, and the people still suffer from political instability and violence. Still, despite this uncertain atmosphere, Cambodians continue to rebuild their lives and look forward to a better future.

If Ebihara's and Ledgerwood's chapter focuses on the process by which communities rebuild social institutions in the aftermath of genocide, Beatriz Manz's chapter, "Terror, Grief, and Recovery: Genocidal Trauma in a Mayan Village in Guatemala," explores how the victims of genocide cope with trauma. On February 25, 1999, the Commission for Historical Clarification reported that, from 1981 to 1983 alone, Guatemala's Mayan population was the target of a genocidal campaign that included more than six hundred massacres carried out primarily by Guatemalan troops. Over the course of three decades of conflict, over 200,000 Guatemalans were killed or disappeared and another 1.5 million people were displaced.

Manz's essay focuses on Santa Maria Tzejá, a Mayan village where she has conducted research since the early 1970s and that is located in El Quiché province, where 344 massacres took place. Like so many of its surrounding communities, Santa Maria Tzejá was the site of a brutal massacre in which more than a dozen people were slaughtered and the village razed. How, Manz asks, do people cope with such ordeals and a life spent in a climate of fear and terror? The psychological toll of such conflicts runs deep in places like Santa Maria Tzejá, where survivors are haunted by painful memories, emotional swings, somatic pains, and chronic anxiety. Some withdraw into silence, resignation, emotional numbing, or a passivity that impairs their recovery. In addition, familial and communal bonds are often fractured by emotional strain, mistrust, political impunity, and the undermining of social institutions.

What is remarkable about Santa Maria Tzejá, however, is the way in which, despite such trauma and social upheaval, the community has recently been facing this genocidal past. Through public initiatives, such as human rights workshops and communal gatherings, the villagers have broken the veil of silence and fear and initiated a more public form of grieving. Perhaps most strikingly, a group of teenagers helped write and produce a play, *There Is Nothing Concealed That Will Not Be Discovered (Mathew 10:26)*, that directly discusses how the military abused the population and violated various articles in the Guatemalan constitution. Not only did the play have a cathartic effect in Santa Maria Tzejá but it also gained wider national and even international attention for its attempt to come to grips with and provide a healing form of remembering for the traumas of the past. Unfortunately, the village has paid a price for their communal grieving. On May 14, 2000, just ten days after some Santa Maria Tzejá villagers filed a suit against three military generals on charges of genocide, the village's cooperative store was burned to the ground.

Implicated in the origins of genocide, modernity has shaped its aftermath as well. On the conceptual level, terms like *trauma, suffering*, and *cruelty* are linked to discourses of modernity. All of them presume a certain type of human subject— citizens with rights over their bodies, which are the loci of social suffering.[22] Paradoxically, however, modernity is also associated with the centralization of political control and the predominance of state sovereignty, creating a situation in which modern subjects are regulated by state disciplines that may necessitate the very type of bodily suffering their "rights" are supposed to protect against (for example, the cruelties perpetrated against prisoners, protesters, adversaries in war, "traitors," threatening minorities). Moreover, since modern states, like modern subjects, are supposed to have "rights" over their body politic, other states cannot violate their sovereignty, leading to another paradox in which international inaction about genocide is legitimated by metanarratives of modernity.

Suffering itself has been harnessed by the economic engine of modernity—capitalism. In the mass media, the victims of genocide are frequently condensed into an essentialized portrait of the universal sufferer, an image that can be commodified, sold, and (re)broadcast to global audiences who see their own potential trauma reflected in this simulation of the modern subject.[23] Refugees frequently epitomize this modern trope of human suffering; silent and anonymous, they signify both a universal humanity and the threat of the premodern and uncivilized, which they have supposedly barely survived. However, refugees also threaten modernity in another way. As "citizens" uprooted from their homeland, refugees occupy a liminal space that calls into question modernity's naturalizing premise of sociopolitical homogeneity and nationalist belonging.[24] Likewise, when refugee populations are resettled abroad, they raise the same question that unsettles the nation-state—where do *they* belong? Particularly in the global present, as such diverse populations and images flow rapidly across national borders, the primacy of the nation-state has come under siege. If modernity inflects genocide, then genocide, in turn, inverts modernity, as it creates diasporic communities that threaten to undermine its culminating political incarnation, the nation-state.

Uli Linke's essay, "Archives of Violence: The Holocaust and the German Politics of Memory," examines such linkages between modernity and genocide through the idea of social memory. Drawing on her earlier work (Linke 1999), Linke argues that Nazi racial aesthetics—exemplified by tropes of blood, purity and contamination, the body, and excrement—have persisted in German cultural memory and are manifest in a variety of sociopolitical forms. In exploring this issue, Linke's essay addresses an issue too often ignored in genocide studies: the effect of genocide on perpetrators and bystanders and their descendants. Linke notes that, immediately after the Holocaust, Germans reacted to their painful and embarrassing legacy with silence, denial, and concealment.

In the 1960s, however, German youths began to confront their Nazi past in at least two salient ways. First, many youths began to act as if the atrocities were carried out by another generation that had led them, like Jews, to suffer greatly under a historical burden.[25] And, second, the West German New Left student movement attempted to negate the values of the past. White nakedness, in particular, emerged as an emblem of coping and restoration. If uniformed German male bodies were the instruments of genocide, their brutal deeds could be symbolically overcome through public nudity, which both expressed the legacy of shame (by uncovering the body like the hidden past) and freed German youths from this burden (by signifying the possibility of return to a pure and "natural" way of life, untainted by Auschwitz). However, the glorification of nature and the German body resonated eerily with Nazi *volk* ideology and Aryan ideals.

Even more disturbing was the direct manifestation of such Nazi racial aesthetics in German political discourse. On the far right, German politicians have portrayed immigrants as impure foreign bodies that, like Jews during the Holocaust, must be removed from the German body politic. Some German leftists, in turn, have used similar images of disease and pollution to characterize the far right, who are portrayed as Nazi "filth" that must be expunged. In both cases, modernity's essentializing impulses re-emerge in the quest for national homogeneity, racial purity, and the expulsion of impure and dehumanized "others," who are likened to polluting excrement.

Linke notes that, when making this argument in Germany, she has encountered great resistance and opposition. She argues that these attitudes are another manifestation of modernity's teleological myth of "progress" and "civilization," which portrays such violent imagery as a regressive aberration. Following Bauman (1991), Linke maintains that modernity, with its impulses toward centralized state control, exterminatory racism, and social engineering, is directly implicated in genocide. Genocide, in other words, is a product of, not an aberration from, modern social life. Obviously, modernity does not lead to genocide in any direct causal sense. It emerges only within certain historical contexts, usually involving socioeconomic upheaval, polarized social divisions, extreme dehumanization, and a centralized initiative to engage in mass killing (see Kuper 1981). Thus, despite the fact that some Nazi racial aesthetics seem to have endured in German social memory, there is little likelihood of a genocide taking place in contemporary Germany. Nevertheless, it is important for scholars to monitor and examine how such discourses persist over time, shaping genocide's wake.

CRITICAL REFLECTIONS:
ANTHROPOLOGY AND THE STUDY OF GENOCIDE

Although the behaviors it references have an ancient pedigree, the concept of genocide, like the idea of anthropology, is thoroughly modern. It is predicated upon a particular conception of the human subject, who is "naturally" endowed with certain rights—the foremost of which is, of course, the right to life. This modern subject, however, lives in a paradoxical world. While supposedly equal, people are also different. Modern subjects are imagined as containers of natural identities—race, ethnicity, nationality, religion—that are resistant to change. The nation-state is metaphorically likened to the individual; it, too, has an essential identity and certain rights, such as "sovereignty," that should not be violated. "Law" and "justice" serve as mechanisms to protect these rights. The United Nations Convention on Genocide manifests all of these discourses of modernity: a law against genocide is enacted to protect the natural rights of individuals who, because of their natural identities, have been targeted for annihilation. The paradox of genocide lies in the fact that the very state that is supposed to prevent genocide is usually the perpetrator. International legal mechanisms, in turn, falter because the international community fears "violating" the sovereignty of one of its members. After all, it might set a dangerous precedent. The usual result, recently illustrated in Rwanda, is prolonged debate, delay, and inaction.

Like genocide, anthropology is premised upon discourses of modernity. As noted earlier, anthropology emerged from the colonial encounter as modernity's discipline of difference. Using "scientific" methods, early anthropologists set out to characterize and discover laws about human similarity and variation. Sadly, their early pronouncements too often contributed to genocidal ideologies about "progress" and essentialized difference. This linkage between genocide and modernity constitutes one of the main undercurrents of John Bowen's critical reflections on the volume, entitled "Culture, Genocide, and a Public Anthropology." Bowen warns that anthropologists, who are in the business of explaining human variation, must be extremely cautious about the way they characterize difference, since the resulting categories have been incorporated into public projects of hate—ranging from Nazi notions of racial hierarchy (Schafft and Arnold) to ethnic stereotypes of Latinos in the United States (Nagengast). The very act of categorizing entails essentialization, as certain naturalized traits are attributed to given groups. Nationalist ideologies thrive on such characterizations, since they construct unmarked categories of normalcy that privilege, and often legitimate, domination by one type of person over another (marked, subordinated, binary opposite, dehumanized) one. In extreme cases, such discourses of hierarchical difference may serve to underwrite genocide. Accordingly, anthropologists must carefully consider how to best transmit their ideas to the general public and monitor the ways in which notions of difference are later invoked in the public domain.

At the same time, Bowen notes that the anthropological expertise in unpacking local categories might also help us to better understand mass violence. On the domestic and international fronts, anthropologists can point out how public discourses about violence inform political policy and response. The term *ethnic conflict*, for example, invokes a set of explanatory narratives implying that violence is the inevitable result of a "seething cauldron" of endogenous, ancient hatreds that erupt when not suppressed by the state. Popular narratives of "genocide," in turn, suggest that mass murder has an exogenous origin, as leaders like Hitler, Stalin, and Pol Pot manipulate their followers to annihilate victims. Both of these overly reductive narratives have influenced media portrayals of, and political responses to, genocidal violence.

Both narratives also oversimplify perpetrator motivation. Thus, in Indonesia, where Bowen has conducted ethnographic research, the media commonly portrays violence in places like Ambon, Kalimantan, and Aceh as primordial religious or ethnic conflict. Bowen points out that the actors in these locales have complex motivations that are more about local fears and struggles over local resources, autonomy, and power than about "ancient hatreds" (see also Bringa). Several essays in this volume directly or indirectly unpack the narratives associated with terms such as *ethnic conflict* (Bringa, Taylor) and *indigenous peoples* (Maybury-Lewis; Totten, Parsons, and Hitchcock), and the "stable and permanent groups" invoked in the U.N. Genocide Convention (Bringa, Magnarella), which have often contributed to political inaction and legal paradoxes. Other essays illustrate the ways in which cultural analysis may be used to explicate how the forms of violence are shaped by local idioms in a nonreductive manner (Linke, Nagengast, Shapiro-Phim, Taylor). For Bowen, then, an anthropology of genocide needs to move carefully between an understanding of the local knowledge that structures the forms of violence and the "second-order representations"—including those of anthropologists—that shape popular discourses and public policy. As opposed to deploying reductive, essentialized categories, we need to focus on process.

Elsewhere, I have suggested that we might use the term *genocidal priming* to reference the set of interwoven processes that generate such mass violence (Hinton 2002). To "prime" something is to make it ready or prepared, as in preparing "(a gun or mine) for firing by inserting a charge of gunpowder or a primer." The intransitive form of the verb means "to prepare someone or something for future action or operation" (*American Heritage Dictionary* 1976:1040), and, like the transitive verb, implies that which comes first. By genocidal priming, then, I refer to a set of processes that establish the preconditions for genocide to take place within a given sociopolitical context. Considering the "charged" connotations of the term, we might further conceptualize genocidal priming using a metaphor of heat: specific situations will become more or less "hot" and volatile—or more likely to be "set off"—as certain processes unfold.[26] What are these processes?

Although genocide is a complex phenomenon that cannot be reduced to a uniform pattern, many genocides are characterized by common processes that make the social context in question increasingly "hot," including socioeconomic upheaval, polarized social divisions, structural change, and effective ideological manipulation (Fein 1990; Harff and Gurr 1998; Kuper 1981). All of the cases discussed in this volume are suggestive in this regard. First, genocides are almost always preceded by some sort of socioeconomic upheaval—ranging from the epidemic diseases that devastated indigenous peoples in the Americas to the Vietnam War that wreaked havoc in Cambodia—which may generate anxiety, hunger, a loss of meaning, the breakdown of pre-existing social mechanisms, and struggles for power. Second, as Leo Kuper (1981; see also Furnivall 1956) has so vividly illustrated, the likelihood of genocide increases as social divisions are deepened because of segregation and differential legal, sociocultural, political, educational, and economic opportunities afforded to social groups. Thus, in postcolonial Rwanda, Tutsis were systematically excluded from political power and faced discrimination across a range of social contexts; Armenians, Jews, and many indigenous peoples have faced similarly difficult circumstances. Third, perpetrator regimes frequently introduce legislation or impose policies that further polarize social divisions. The Nuremberg Laws, the disarming of Armenians, the "privatization" of indigenous lands, and the Khmer Rouge's radical transformation of Cambodian society constitute some of the more infamous examples of such structural changes. And, fourth, the likelihood of genocide increases greatly when perpetrator regimes effectively disseminate messages of hate. Such ideological manipulation, which frequently draws upon local idioms that are highly salient to at least some social groups, serve to essentialize difference and legitimate acts of genocidal violence against victim groups, who are usually portrayed as subhuman outsiders standing in the way of the purity, well-being, or progress of the perpetrator group. In this manner Hutus are set against Tutsis, Germans against Jews, and the "civilized" against the "savage."

As these and other facilitating processes unfold, genocide becomes increasingly possible. Not all of these "hot" situations, however, result in mass violence. International pressures, local moral restraints, political and religious mechanisms, or a lack of ideological "take" may hold potential perpetrator regimes in check and, in the long run, facilitate a cooling of tensions (see Kuper 1981). In other situations, such as the plight of Latinos in the United States (Nagengast, this volume), the process of genocidal priming may never be more than "lukewarm." However, when the priming is "hot" and genocide does take place, there is almost always some sort of "genocidal activation" that ignites the "charge" that has been primed. Bowen notes that this "push" often comes from leaders who use panic, fear, and material gain to incite their followers to kill. For example, in Rwanda, which became primed for genocide over the course of several years, the mysterious shooting down of President Habyarimana's plane served as the pretext for Hutu extremists to instigate mass killing.

Anthropologists have a great deal to contribute to our understanding of genocidal priming and activation. Scholars working in the Boasian tradition have an expertise in analyzing cultural knowledge that can help us better understand how genocidal violence is patterned and why given ideological messages have greater or lesser "take" among different segments of a population. An examination of the cultural construction of emotion and other embodied discourses could be extremely revealing about perpetrator motivation and the efficacy of ideology. Symbolic anthropologists, in turn, have developed analytical tools that would yield rich insights about structure and meaning of perpetrator rituals, key symbols and iconography, use of time and space, and political rites. Further, we could use our expertise at unpacking local idioms to describe how categories of difference are invoked in "hot" situations and suggest ways they might be "cooled down" by alternative discourses that, in a culturally sensitive manner, stress intergroup ties, promote local mechanisms of conflict resolution, and rehumanize potential victim groups. Moreover, since anthropologists often have ethnographic experience in the locales in which genocidal priming becomes "hot," they are ideally situated to issue public warnings about what might occur. Since the early days of British structural-functionalism, anthropologists have also examined structural dynamics, a concern that has most recently been inflected by Marxist and poststructuralist theorists. Surely anthropological insights gleaned from such research—about structural inequality, political legitimacy, structural order, symbolic violence, rites of passage, schizmogenesis, group solidarity, and so forth—could be applied to the study of genocide.

Nancy Scheper-Hughes's essay, "Coming to Our Senses: Anthropology and Genocide," touches on several of these issues. Because of their disciplinary training methods, relativist ethos, and (in)direct involvement in questionable projects,

Scheper-Hughes notes, anthropologists have been predisposed to overlook the forms of political terror and "everyday violence" that often afflict the peoples whom they study. Even more troubling are the instances in which anthropologists—including some of the discipline's founding figures—have passively stood by while genocide took place, sometimes accepting the dehumanizing metanarratives that legitimate the destruction of victim groups. The very idea of "salvage ethnography" reflects anthropology's ambivalent relation to genocide. On the one hand, early anthropologists often accepted the destruction of indigenous peoples as the inevitable consequence of social evolution and "progress." On the other, many of these same scholars took an active role in preserving and documenting the cultural life of these disappearing groups.

Scheper-Hughes illustrates this point with a detailed analysis of Alfred Kroeber's relationship with Ishi, whom he called the "last California aborigine," in the early twentieth century. At the same time that he befriended and helped Ishi, Kroeber failed to speak out about the genocide that had devastated Ishi's Yahis and other Native American groups. Moreover, Kroeber also allowed his key informant to be exhibited at the Museum of Anthropology at the University of California on Sundays and, most strikingly, he permitted Ishi's brain to be shipped to the Smithsonian Institution for examination and curation—despite Kroeber's knowledge of Yahi beliefs about the dead and Ishi's dislike of the study of skulls and other body parts. Rather than simply excusing Kroeber because he lived in a time period during which a different set of beliefs was ascendant, Scheper-Hughes argues that we must consider how things might have been done differently. The importance of such reflection was highlighted in 1999 when Ishi's brain was found in a Smithsonian warehouse, and the Berkeley Department of Anthropology deliberated issuing a statement about the department's role in what had happened to Ishi.

More broadly, Scheper-Hughes argues that anthropologists should directly confront a question at the heart of this volume: What makes genocide possible? She maintains that, to comprehend genocide fully, we must go beyond typical cases and examine "small wars and invisible genocides" in which the structural dynamics taken to an extreme in genocide are manifest in everyday life. "Rubbish people" suffer in both times of war and peace. Thus, street children in Brazil attempt to survive in a liminal, degraded space that is viewed as dangerous and threatening. Few people notice or care when these "dirty vermin" disappear or die, frequently at the hands of police and death squads who describe their murder as "trash removal," "street cleaning," or "urban hygiene." Similarly, the elderly are turned into rubbish people in nursing homes where underpaid workers often drop their personal names, ignore their wishes, associate them with the impure, and treat them like objects. Such institutionalized forms of everyday violence reconstruct the subjectivity of the elderly, who, lacking the means to resist, are ultimately forced to accept their new, dehumanized status. For Scheper-Hughes, it is precisely by examining this "genocidal continuum" in the practices of everyday life that anthropologists can contribute to the understanding of genocide.

In her essay, "Inoculations of Evil in the U.S.-Mexican Border Region: Reflections on the Genocidal Potential of Symbolic Violence," Carole Nagengast makes a similar argument about the genocidal potential of everyday symbolic violence. Following a tradition established by Leo Kuper (1981), Nagengast examines a situation in which difference has been essentialized—the plight of Latino "aliens" in the United States—yet hasn't led to genocide. She argues that, although Latinos are victimized by forms of symbolic and physical violence analogous to those that take place in genocide, certain constraints exist that have prevented such violence from escalating into genocide. It is precisely by making comparisons between cases and noncases of genocide that scholars may begin to develop predictive models and preventative solutions.

Beginning with examples of how U.S. Border Patrol agents have shot and killed innocent Latinos near the U.S.-Mexican border, Nagengast argues that the frequent abuse of Latinos has been legitimated and normalized by various forms of symbolic violence. Given that the nation-state seeks homogeneity, it is not surprising that nationalist discourse in the United States often deploys a set of images about "belonging" that mark difference from the norm—in this case, the unmarked category of white, middle-class, employed, "straight," English-speaking, married males. Although many people in the United States are excluded from this category, Latinos have been increasingly marked as "different" since the end of the Cold War and the subsequent search for new "enemies." In the media, political speeches, and community discourses, Latino "otherness" is constructed around myths of the violent Mexican drug runner, the welfare cheat, and the "illegal alien" who takes jobs away from U.S. citizens. Bit by bit, Nagengast contends, the American public has become "immunized" by these symbolic "inoculations of evil," which naturalize violence against the threatening "other" and seemingly justify drastic measures—racial profiling, "raids" on Latino neighborhoods, discrimination and mistreatment, and even such "unfortunate but necessary" excesses as rape, beatings, and murder. In fact, the "threat" posed by these "aliens" has been portrayed as so extreme as to legitimate the militarization of the border zone.

Ultimately, Nagengast maintains, these forms of symbolic and physical violence are analogous to those that take place in genocide: a despised group is demonized in dehumanizing discourses and, already in a weakened social position, is increasingly victimized by discriminatory state policy. Nevertheless, the plight of Latinos in the United States, while an issue of great concern, has not escalated into genocide. By examining the reasons why genocide does not occur in such situations, scholars may better understand the processes that lead to mass violence and the ways in which genocidal violence might be predicted or prevented. In this case, Latinos have been helped by immigrant rights organizations that use the legal system to defend the rights of Latinos and describe their plight to the media. (The media therefore plays a dual role in this situation, simultaneously highlighting the plight of Latinos and portraying Latinos as dehumanized and threatening "others.") Nevertheless, such organizations have had trouble generating a public outcry against the abuse of Latinos because of prejudice, and they face difficulties in a legal system that has increasingly restricted the rights of immigrants. Even in a liberal democracy like the United States, which supposedly guarantees the rights of minorities, then, genocide may take place—a point clearly demonstrated by the atrocities perpetrated against indigenous peoples. Accordingly, Nagengast's chapter argues that we must carefully monitor and publicly decry the plight of disempowered groups that are in the process of being victimized by forms of symbolic and physical violence that often precede genocide.

As Nagengast, Scheper-Hughes, Totten, Parsons, and Hitchcock; and other contributors to this volume suggest, the anthropology of genocide will greatly contribute to and benefit from research in other fields. Genocide is always a local process, so the experience-near, ethnographic understandings of anthropology will be of enormous importance to other scholars. Anthropologists, in turn, will benefit greatly from the (often) more macro-level insights about genocide and political violence from other fields. Concepts such as Foucault's "microphysics of power" provide an important link between such emic and etic levels of analysis. On a more practical level, the possibility exists for productive interdisciplinary collaboration and activism. Several contributors to this volume, including Tone Bringa and Paul Magnarella, have effectively worked with lawyers and other scholars on United Nations missions to and international tribunals in the former Yugoslavia and Rwanda. Likewise, Robert Hitchcock and David Mabury-Lewis have been at the forefront of a diverse movement to defend indigenous peoples. Forensic anthropologists have worked with health professionals, lawyers, photographers, and nongovernmental organizations to analyze physical remains and gather evidence with which to prosecute perpetrators. Certainly, many other examples could be provided.[27]

In conclusion, then, the essays in this volume suggest that, drawing on research and theory from a variety of disciplines, anthropologists stand poised to make an enormous contribution to the study of genocide. On the one hand, we can provide insight into the ethnohistorical causes of genocide by answering such questions as: How is genocide linked to modernity? How are notions of race, ethnicity, and other social identities essentialized and manipulated by genocidal regimes? What are the processes by which "imagined communities" are constructed to exclude dehumanized victim groups? What political, historical, and socioeconomic circumstances are conducive to genocide? How do genocidal regimes appropriate cultural knowledge to motivate their minions to kill? How might genocides be predicted or prevented? Can genocidal regimes sometimes be characterized as revitalization movements? How are ritual processes involved in genocide?

On the other hand, anthropologists have the ability to point out how genocide affects victim groups and how they respond to their plight. What are the mental, physical, and somatic consequences of genocide? How do victims deal with such trauma? How are social networks torn asunder through death, dislocation, and diaspora? How do victims go about reconstructing their social networks and using them as a means of coping with their suffering? How are images of victims manufactured in the media and how do such images influence the international response? As the essays in this volume demonstrate, by answering such questions, anthropologists can make great progress toward developing an anthropology of genocide.

NOTES

In addition to the two anonymous reviewers of the manuscript, I would like to thank Ladson and Darlene Hinton, Carole Nagengast, May Ebihara, Brian Ferguson, Gretchen Schafft, David Chandler, and, especially, Nicole Cooley for their helpful comments and suggestions.

1. See Bauman (1991) on the link between modernity and the Holocaust and on the "two faces" of modernity. See also Bodley (1999) and Maybury-Lewis (1997) on the devastating effects of modernity on indigenous peoples. Of course, the cluster of processes characterized as "modernity" cannot be viewed as a monocausal explanation of genocide, but they have been directly or indirectly involved in almost every case of genocide in recent history.

2. Smith (1987, 1999). See also Totten, Parsons, and Charny (1997).

3. Perhaps, as Zygmunt Bauman (1991) has argued about sociology, anthropological engagement with the Holocaust was partially diminished because of a perception that the Holocaust was a part of Jewish history and therefore could be relegated to the fields of Jewish studies and history. On the lack of anthropological research on the Holocaust and genocide studies, see De Waal (1994); Fein (1990); Hinton (1998, 2002); Kuper (1981); McC. Lewin (1992); Messing (1976); Shiloh (1975).

4. See Daniel (1996) and Taussig (1987) for anthropological responses to political violence that question the limits of scholarly analysis. On the difficulty of representing genocide, see Friedlander (1992).

5. Of course, as some scholars have pointed out, there are ways to escape such dilemmas of relativism. Elvin Hatch (1997), for example, has argued for a limited form of relativism in which scholars vigilantly maintain a skeptical attitude toward moral judgments made about other societies, yet acknowledge that, after intense reflection, their condemnation may be justified and not merely a matter of ethnocentric projection. Such an attitude would preserve the tolerant and self-critical spirit of relativism while allowing for action when we are faced with intolerable situations such as genocide. Moreover, in this age of global flows of ideas and technologies, the very concept of "human rights" has spread to most societies and become part of their understandings, albeit in localized forms.

6. Lemkin (1944:79). On Lemkin's efforts to make genocide a crime, see Andreopoulos (1994); Fein (1990); Jacobs (1999); Kuper (1981).

7. The question of intent was also hotly contested. Because intent is so difficult to prove, many countries feared that genocidal regimes would deny their culpability by stating that the atrocities they had committed were unintentional. Unfortunately, these concerns have proven to be prescient, as countries such as Brazil and Paraguay have denied that they intentionally tried to destroy indigenous peoples (see Kuper 1981).

8. Sadly, the United States did not ratify the Genocide Convention until 1986, and even then it did so conditionally. The delay was due, in part, to the fears of some conservative politicians and interest groups that the convention's vague language might be used against the United States by civil rights leaders, Native Americans, and even foreign governments such as Vietnam. See LeBlanc (1991) for a detailed analysis of the U.S. ratification process. More recently, the conservative U.S. attitude has been evident in the country's attempt to se-

verely weaken the jurisdiction of a proposed permanent international tribunal that would try cases of genocide, war crimes, and crimes against humanity.

9. *Violentia* is derived from the Latin word *vis* ("force"), which, in turn, is derived from the Indo-European word *wei-*, or "vital force." See the *Oxford English Dictionary* (1989:654); *American Heritage Dictionary* (1976:1548); White (1915:643).

10. For in-depth analyses of the various connotations of the term *violence*, see Bourdieu (1977); Nagengast (1994); Riches (1986); Williams (1985). See also Ferguson (1989) on the term *war*.

11. Wars are usually waged to vanquish a foe, not to wipe that foe off the face of the earth. Similarly, terrorism and torture are typically used to subjugate and intimidate, not obliterate, certain groups of people. Even ethnic conflicts, which may lead to and be a crucial part of genocide, often erupt over forms of domination and subordination and do not by definition involve a sustained and purposeful attempt to annihilate another ethnic group. For a discussion of various conceptual issues surrounding the concept of genocide, see Andreopoulos (1994); Fein (1990); Kuper (1981). The above parenthetical definitions of different forms of political violence are partially adapted from the *American Heritage Dictionary* (1976).

12. Cited in Taussig (1987:23).

13. Cited in Chalk and Jonassohn (1990:194).

14. The historical information that follows is primarily based on ibid.; Kuper (1981); and Maybury-Lewis (1997). I should also note that such typologies are not rigid categories, often overlap, and have analytic limitations. There are many cases that could be listed under more than one rubric. I use the typology to present the historical material because it provides one way to group complex cases and may serve as a starting point for critical analysis. Other alternatives certainly exist. My typological categories are drawn from Chalk and Jonassohn (1990); Fein (1984); Kuper (1981); and Smith (1987, 1999).

15. See Hall (1995:8). On modernity in general, see Hall, Held, Hubert, and Thompson (1995). Other important works on modernity include: Bauman (1991); Habermas (1983); Harvey (1989); Lyotard (1984); Toulmin (1990). For an anthropological perspective on the dark side of modernity, see Scott (1998).

16. See Bauman (1991) on the "etiological myth of Western Civilization." Many important social theorists have been influenced by this myth, including Marx, Durkheim, Freud, Elias, and Weber. "Modernization theory" constitutes one of its more recent formulations.

17. See also Arens (1976); Bischoping and Fingerhut (1996); Bodley (1999); Hitchcock and Twedt (1997); Kroeber (1961); Maybury-Lewis (1997); Taussig (1987); and many issues of *Cultural Survival*. For an interesting analysis of how some of these oppositions are encoded in the U.S. Thanksgiving celebration—in which the turkey symbolically indexes the conquered and "civilized" Native "other"—see Siskind (1992).

18. On the distinctions (and conceptual overlap) between the legal definitions of genocide, crimes against humanity, war crimes, and crimes against peace, see Andreopoulos (1994); Charny (1999); and Kuper (1981:21). For other analyses of genocide and related terms, see Scherrer (1999).

19. Bauman (1991:91–92).

20. See Hinton (1996) for a detailed discussion of such "psychosocial dissonance."

21. See Kleinman, Das, and Lock (1997).

22. See Asad (1997); Young (1995).

23. See Baudrillard (1988); Feldman (1994); Malkki (1996). For various ways in which the image of the universal sufferer is linked to capitalism and modernity, see Kleinman and Kleinman (1997).

24. Malkki (1996, 1997); Appadurai (1996). On post–Cold War challenges to the nation-state, see Ferguson (forthcoming).

25. As Linke, drawing on Omer Bartov's (1998) work, points out, the popularity of Daniel Goldhagen's (1996) book in Germany may have been, at least in part, due to the fact that it reinforced the notion that Nazi Germany was like another society and therefore didn't implicate the current generation.

26. Let me stress that, through the use of metaphors of priming and heat, I do not want to convey the image of genocide as a primordial conflict waiting to explode. In fact, I want to do exactly the opposite and emphasize that genocide is a *process* that emerges from a variety of factors, or "primes," and that always involves impetus and organization from above, what I call "genocidal activation." For another use of metaphors of "heat" and "cold" to describe ethnonationalist violence in a manner that argues against primordialist explanations, see Appadurai (1996: 164f).

27. The interdisciplinary possibilities for the study of genocide are evident from several recent educational initiatives, including a comprehensive encyclopedia, books, and teaching guides related to genocide (e.g., Andreopoulos and Claude 1997; Charny 1999; Fein 1990; Freedman-Apsel and Fein 1992). Similarly, several interdisciplinary edited volumes have also been published in recent years (e.g., Andreopoulos 1994; Chorbajian and Shirinian 1999; Fein 1990; Totten, Parsons, and Charny 1997; Wallimann 2000). For a more complete review, see Hinton (2002). Unfortunately, in part because of their lack of engagement with genocide, anthropologists have been underrepresented in such interdisciplinary projects.

REFERENCES CITED

American Anthropological Association Executive Board. 1947. "Statement on Human Rights." *American Anthropologist* 49(4):539–43.

American Heritage Dictionary of the English Language. 1976. William Morris, ed. Boston: Houghton Mifflin.

Anderson, Benedict. 1991. *Imagined Communities: Reflections on the Origin and Spread of Nationalism*. London: Verso.

Andreopoulos, George J., ed. 1994. *Genocide: Conceptual and Historical Issues*. Philadelphia: University of Pennsylvania Press.

Andreopoulos, George J., and Richard Pierre Claude, eds. 1997. *Human Rights Education for the Twenty-First Century*. Philadelphia: University of Pennsylvania Press.

Appadurai, Arjun. 1996. *Modernity at Large: Cultural Dimensions of Globalization*. Minneapolis: University of Minnesota Press.

———. 1998. "Dead Certainty: Ethnic Violence in an Era of Globalization." *Public Culture* 10(2):225–47.

Arens, Richard, ed. 1976. *Genocide in Paraguay*. Philadelphia: Temple University Press.

Asad, Talal. 1997. "On Torture, or Cruel, Inhuman, and Degrading Treatment." In *Social Suffering*. Arthur Kleinman, Veena Das, and Margaret Lock, eds. Pp. 285–308. Berkeley: University of California Press.

Bartov, Omer. 1998. "Defining Enemies, Making Victims: Germans, Jews, and the Holocaust." *American Historical Review* 103(3):771–816.

Baudrillard, Jean. 1988. *Selected Writings*. Mark Poster, ed. Stanford: Stanford University Press.

Bauman, Zygmunt. 1991. *Modernity and the Holocaust*. Ithaca, N.Y.: Cornell University Press.

Bischoping, Katherine, and Natalie Fingerhut. 1996. "Border Lines: Indigenous Peoples in Genocide Studies." *Canadian Review of Sociology and Anthropology* 33(4):481–506.

Bodley, John H. 1999. *Victims of Progress.* Mountain View, Calif.: Mayfield.

Bourdieu, Pierre. 1977. *Outline of a Theory of Practice.* New York: Cambridge University Press.

Bringa, Tone. 1993. "National Categories, National Identification and Identity Formation in 'Multinational' Bosnia." *Anthropology of East Europe Review* 11(1–2):27–34.

———. 1995. *Being Muslim the Bosnian Way.* Princeton: Princeton University Press.

Ceram, C. W. 1951. *Gods, Graves, and Scholars: The Story of Archaeology.* E. B. Garside, trans. New York: Alfred A. Knopf.

Chalk, Frank, and Kurt Jonassohn, eds. 1990. *The History and Sociology of Genocide: Analyses and Case Studies.* New Haven: Yale University Press.

Chandler, David P. 1991. *The Tragedy of Cambodian History: Politics, War and Revolution since 1945.* New Haven: Yale University Press.

Charny, Israel W. 1994. "Toward a Generic Definition of Genocide." In *Genocide: Conceptual and Historical Dimensions.* George J. Andreopoulos, ed. Pp. 64–94. Philadelphia: University of Pennsylvania Press.

Charny, Israel W., ed. 1999. *The Encyclopedia of Genocide.* Santa Barbara, Calif.: ABC-CLIO.

Chorbajian, Levon, and George Shirinian, eds. 1999. *Studies in Comparative Genocide.* New York: St. Martin's.

Daniel, E. Valentine. 1996. *Charred Lullabies: Chapters in an Anthropography of Violence.* Princeton: Princeton University Press.

De Waal, Alex. 1994. "Genocide in Rwanda." *Anthropology Today* 10(3):1–2.

Fein, Helen. 1984. "Scenarios of Genocide: Models of Genocide and Critical Responses." In *Toward the Understanding and Prevention of Genocide: Proceedings of the International Conference on the Holocaust and Genocide.* Israel Charny, ed. Pp. 3–31. Boulder, Colo.: Westview.

———. 1990. "Genocide: A Sociological Perspective." *Current Sociology* 38(1):v–126.

Feldman, Allen. 1991. *Formations of Violence: The Narrative of the Body and Political Terror in Northern Ireland.* Chicago: University of Chicago Press.

———. 1994. "From Desert Storm to Rodney King via ex-Yugoslavia: On Cultural Anaesthesia." *American Ethnologist* 21(2):404–18.

Ferguson, R. Brian. 1989. "Anthropology and War: Theory, Politics, Ethics." In *The Anthropology of War and Peace.* D. Pitt and P. Turner, eds. Pp. 141–59. South Hadley, Mass.: Bergin & Garvey.

Ferguson, R. Brian, ed. Forthcoming. *The State under Siege: Global Process, Identity, and Violence.* New York: Routledge.

Freedman-Apsel, Joyce, and Helen Fein, eds. 1992. *Teaching about Genocide: A Guidebook for College and University Teachers: Critical Essays, Syllabi and Assignments.* New York: Institute for the Study of Genocide.

Friedlander, Saul, ed. 1992. *Probing the Limits of Representation: Nazism and the "Final Solution."* Cambridge: Harvard University Press.

Furnivall, John Sydenham. 1956. *Colonial Policy and Practice.* New York: New York University Press.

Goldhagen, Daniel Jonah. 1996. *Hitler's Willing Executioners: Ordinary Germans and the Holocaust.* New York: Alfred A. Knopf.

Habermas, Jürgen. 1983. "Modernity—An Incomplete Project." In *The Anti-Aesthetic: Essays on Postmodern Culture.* Hal Foster, ed. Pp. 3–15. Port Townsend, Wash.: Bay Press.

Hall, Stuart. 1995. "Introduction." In *Modernity: An Introduction to Modern Societies.* Stuart Hall, David Held, Don Hubert, and Kenneth Thompson, eds. Pp. 1–18. Cambridge, Eng.: Polity.

Hall, Stuart, David Held, Don Hubert, and Kenneth Thompson, eds. 1995. *Modernity: An Introduction to Modern Societies.* Cambridge, Eng.: Polity.

Harff, Barbara, and Ted Gurr. 1988. "Toward Empirical Theory of Genocides and Politicides: Identification and Measurement of Cases since 1945." *International Studies Quarterly* 22:359–71.

———. 1998. "Systematic Early Warning of Humanitarian Emergencies." *Journal of Peace Research* 35(5):551–79.

Harvey, David. 1989. *The Condition of Postmodernity.* Oxford: Basil Blackwell.

Hatch, Elvin. 1997. "The Good Side of Relativism." *Journal of Anthropological Research* 53(3):371–81.

Held, David. 1995. "The Development of the Modern State." In *Modernity: An Introduction to Modern Societies.* Stuart Hall, David Held, Don Hubert, and Kenneth Thompson, eds. Pp. 55–89. Cambridge, Eng.: Polity.

Hinton, Alexander Laban. 1996. "Agents of Death: Explaining the Cambodian Genocide in Terms of Psychosocial Dissonance." *American Anthropologist* 98(4):818–31.

———. 1998. "Why Did the Nazis Kill? Anthropology, Genocide, and the Goldhagen Controversy." *Anthropology Today* 14(3):9–15.

———. 2000. "Under the Shade of Pol Pot's Umbrella: Mandala, Myth, and Politics in the Cambodian Genocide." In *The Vision Thing: Myth, Politics and Psyche in the World.* Thomas Singer, ed. Pp. 170–204. New York: Routledge.

———. Forthcoming in 2003. *Cambodia's Shadow: Cultural Dimensions of Genocide.*

Hinton, Alexander Laban, ed. 2002. *Genocide: An Anthropological Reader.* Malden, Mass.: Blackwell.

Hitchcock, Robert K., and Tara M. Twedt. 1997. "Physical and Cultural Genocide of Various Indigenous Peoples." In *Century of Genocide: Eyewitness Accounts and Critical Views.* Samuel Totten, William S. Parsons, and Israel W. Charny, eds. Pp. 372–408. New York: Garland.

Jacobs, Steven L. 1999. "The Papers of Raphael Lemkin: A First Look." *Journal of Genocide Research* 1(1):105–14.

Kiernan, Ben. 1996. *The Pol Pot Regime: Race, Power, and Genocide in Cambodia under the Khmer Rouge, 1975–79.* New Haven: Yale University Press.

Kleinman, Arthur, and Joan Kleinman. 1997. "The Appeal of Experience; The Dismay of Images: Cultural Appropriations of Suffering in Our Times." In *Social Suffering.* Arthur Kleinman, Veena Das, and Margaret Lock, eds. Pp. 1–23. Berkeley: University of California Press.

Kleinman, Arthur, Veena Das, and Margaret Lock, eds. 1997. *Social Suffering.* Berkeley: University of California Press.

Koenigsberg, Richard A. 1975. *Hitler's Ideology: A Study in Psychoanalytic Sociology.* New York: Library of Social Science.

Kroeber, Theodora. 1961. *Ishi in Two Worlds.* Berkeley: University of California Press.

Kuper, Leo. 1981. *Genocide: Its Political Use in the Twentieth Century.* New Haven: Yale University Press.

———. 1994. "Theoretical Issues Relating to Genocide: Uses and Abuses." In *Genocide: Conceptual and Historical Dimensions.* George J. Andreopoulos, ed. Pp. 31–46. Philadelphia: University of Pennsylvania Press.

LeBlanc, Lawrence J. 1991. *The United States and the Genocide Convention.* Durham: Duke University Press.

Lemkin, Raphael. 1944. *Axis Rule in Occupied Europe.* Washington, D.C.: Carnegie Endowment for International Peace.

Linke, Uli. 1999. *Blood and Nation: The European Aesthetics of Race.* Philadelphia: University of Pennsylvania Press.

Lyotard, Jean-François. 1984. *The Postmodern Condition: A Report on Knowledge.* Geoff Bennington and Brian Massumi, trans. Minneapolis: University of Minnesota Press.

Malkki, Liisa. 1995. *Purity and Exile: Violence, Memory, and National Cosmology among Hutu Refugees in Tanzania.* Princeton: Princeton University Press.

———. 1996. "Speechless Emissaries: Refugees, Humanitarianism, and Dehistoricization." *Cultural Anthropology* 11(3):377–404.

———. 1997. "The Rooting of Peoples and the Territorialization of National Identity among Scholars and Refugees." In *Culture, Power, Place: Explorations in Critical Anthropology.* Akhil Gupta and James Ferguson, eds. Pp. 52–74. Durham: Duke University Press.

Maybury-Lewis, David. 1997. *Indigenous People, Ethnic Groups, and the State.* Boston: Allyn and Bacon.

McC. Lewin, Carroll. 1992. "The Holocaust: Anthropological Possibilities and the Dilemma of Representation." *American Anthropologist* 94(1):161–66.

Messing, Simon D. 1976. "On Anthropology and Nazi Genocide." *Current Anthropology* 17(2):326–27.

Nagengast, Carole. 1994. "Violence, Terror, and the Crisis of the State." *Annual Review of Anthropology* 23:109–36.

Oxford English Dictionary. 1989. 2d ed. Prepared by J. A. Simpson and E. S. C. Weiner. Oxford: Clarendon Press.

Riches, David, ed. 1986. *The Anthropology of Violence.* New York: Oxford University Press.

Said, Edward. 1985. *Orientalism.* New York: Pantheon.

Scherrer, Christian P. 1999. "Towards a Theory of Modern Genocide. Comparative Genocide Research: Definitions, Criteria, Typologies, Cases, Key Elements, Patterns and Voids." *Journal of Anthropological Research* 1(1):13–23.

Scott, James C. 1998. *Seeing Like a State: How Certain Schemes to Improve the Human Condition Have Failed.* New Haven: Yale University Press.

Shiloh, Ailon. 1975. "Psychological Anthropology: A Case Study in Cultural Blindness." *Current Anthropology* 16(4):618–20.

Siskind, Janet. 1992. "The Invention of Thanksgiving: A Ritual of American Nationality." *Critique of Anthropology* 12(2):167–91.

Smedley, Audrey. 1999. 2d ed. *Race in North America: Origins and Evolution of a Worldview.* Boulder, Colo.: Westview.

Smith, Roger W. 1987. "Human Destructiveness and Politics: The Twentieth Century as an Age of Genocide." In *Genocide and the Modern Age: Etiology and Case Studies of Mass Death.* Isidor Wallimann and Michael N. Dobkowski, eds. Pp. 21–39. New York: Greenwood Press.

———. 1999. "State Power and Genocide Intent: On the Uses of Genocide in the Twentieth Century." In *Studies in Comparative Genocide.* Levon Chorbajian and George Shirinian, eds. Pp. 3–14. New York: St. Martin's Press.

Taussig, Michael. 1987. *Shamanism, Colonialism, and the Wild Man: A Study in Terror and Healing.* Chicago: University of Chicago Press.

Taylor, Christopher C. 1999. *Sacrifice as Terror: The Rwandan Genocide of 1994.* Oxford: Berg.
Totten, Samuel, William S. Parsons, and Israel Charny, eds. 1997. *Century of Genocide: Eyewitness Accounts and Critical Views.* New York: Garland Publishing.
Toulmin, Stephen. 1990. *Cosmopolis: The Hidden Agenda of Modernity.* Chicago: University of Chicago Press.
Wallimann, Isidor, and Michael N. Dobkowski, eds. 2000. *Genocide and the Modern Age: Etiology and Case Studies of Mass Death.* Syracuse: Syracuse University Press.
White, John T. 1915. *A Latin-English Dictionary for the Use of Junior Students.* Boston: Ginn.
Williams, Raymond. 1985. *Marxism and Literature.* New York: Oxford University Press.
Young, Allan. 1995. *The Harmony of Illusions: Inventing Post-Traumatic Stress Disorder.* Princeton: Princeton University Press.

PART ONE

Modernity's Edges

Genocide and Indigenous Peoples

2

Genocide against Indigenous Peoples

David Maybury-Lewis

It is sad that few of us are surprised when we hear of genocides committed against indigenous peoples. We may be outraged or sickened, but, if we have any knowledge of the grim history of contacts between indigenous peoples and other societies, we are unlikely to be surprised. The reason is that the defining characteristic of indigenous peoples is not simply, as is often supposed, that they were "there" (wherever they are) first. Such a definition works well enough in the Americas or Australia, but is unsatisfactory in Africa and Eurasia. There, populations have eddied backward and forward over given territories for centuries, so that their "original inhabitants" are not clearly defined and often are in polemical dispute. The defining characteristic of indigenous peoples is not therefore priority on the land but rather that they have been conquered by invaders who are racially, ethnically, or culturally different from themselves. Accordingly, indigenous peoples are those who are subordinated and marginalized by alien powers that rule over them. It follows that they are relatively powerless, and so they become prime targets for genocide (see Maybury-Lewis 1997:8).

Genocide committed against indigenous populations was a particularly nasty aspect of the European seizure of empires from the fifteenth to the nineteenth centuries, but it was neither invented nor practiced solely by European imperialists. Genocide is in fact a new name, invented in 1944 by Raphael Lemkin (Richard 1992:6), for a very old outrage, namely the massacre or attempted massacre of an entire people. Such annihilations took place in antiquity, such as when the Romans destroyed Carthage and sowed its fields with salt. They were later carried on by conquering peoples such as the Huns and the Mongols and countless others. European imperialism and the massacres of indigenous peoples to which it gave rise added a bloody chapter to the history of genocide, which began much earlier and is unfortunately not yet finished.

European imperialism, like other imperialisms, lent itself to genocide because both depended on a wide disparity of power, between imperialists and those they conquered, as between genocidal murderers and those they massacre. European military superiority was evident from the very beginning of the European expansion. Even at the end of the Middle Ages, when the Spanish invaded the Americas, it soon became clear that their firearms, their fine steel weapons, their armor— particularly when worn by mounted knights, who were the tanks of medieval warfare—enabled them to defeat much larger numbers of Indians, even when the latter fought, as they often did, with great courage. The Spanish could therefore establish themselves as the absolute overlords of the defeated populations and, if they were so inclined, could institute local reigns of terror involving torture, killings, and mass murder. It was the Spanish reign of terror in the Caribbean, the barbarities inflicted on the Indians, and the systematic annihilation of the indigenous populations of many of the larger islands that led Bartolomé de las Casas to publish his searing denunciation entitled *Brevísima Relación de la Destrucción de las Indias (The Devastation of the Indies: A Brief Account)* in 1552.

It was Las Casas' writings that gave birth to the *leyenda negra,* or black legend, of Spanish cruelty in the Indies. However, my point here is to stress the futility of a debate over whether the Spanish conquistadors were or were not more cruel than other imperialists, but rather to emphasize that barbarous cruelties, sometimes involving genocide, were committed at one time or another by all the imperial powers against their subject populations. The conquered peoples suffered such dramatic declines in population during the centuries of European rule that Herman Merivale, in his well-known book *Lectures on Colonisation and Colonies,* quoted Darwin as saying, "Wherever the European has trod, death seems to pursue the aboriginal" (Merivale 1861:541). It is difficult to calculate the extent of this depopulation. The best estimates indicate that there was death on a colossal scale among the indigenous populations conquered by Europeans. Bodley (1982:39–42) estimates that, from the time of their first contacts with Europeans to the nadir of their population in the late nineteenth and early twentieth centuries, indigenous populations at the margins worldwide were reduced by some thirty million (a conservative figure) or, more likely, by about fifty million. In other words, indigenous populations were reduced to about one-fifth of their precontact numbers.

Of course this mortality was not caused solely by genocide, but rather by a combination of causes, of which genocide was only one. Diseases introduced by Europeans were the major killers. Colonists may not always have intended to spread diseases among the natives of the lands they invaded, but they were certainly aware of their efficacy in eliminating inconvenient populations, so they factored them into their plans for the future and occasionally spread infections deliberately. Meanwhile they introduced regimes of forced labor that resulted in debilitation and death among their workers. Furthermore, the disruption of native communities, through seizure of their lands and coercion of their inhabitants, when combined with the effects of European diseases, frequently produced social disorganization and famine.

A discussion of genocide as practiced against indigenous peoples should not therefore focus solely or even principally on deliberate attempts to massacre entire societies. Often the widespread dying resulted not so much from deliberate killing but from the fatal circumstances imposed by the imperialists on the conquered. Where deliberate extermination was the cause, it is useful to refer to Charny's distinction between *genocide* and *genocidal massacre* (1994:76). Indigenous peoples have often been the victims of genocidal massacres, where the slaughter is on a smaller scale and results from a general attitude toward indigenous peoples rather than necessarily being part of a campaign for total elimination of the victim population. On the other hand, campaigns of extermination are characteristic of those phases of colonization in which the invaders have decided on a course of ethnic cleansing to rid a territory of its indigenous inhabitants and appropriate it for themselves. In the heyday of colonialism such exterminations were often justified in the name of progress. The indigenous populations were stigmatized as savages who ought to make way for civilization. In his book *The Winning of the West*, for example, Theodore Roosevelt justified the treatment meted out to the Indians of the United States in the following terms: "The settler and pioneer have at bottom had justice on their side; this great continent could not have been kept as nothing but a game preserve for squalid savages" (Roosevelt 1889:90). General Roca, the minister for war in Argentina at the end of the nineteenth century, put it even more bluntly when he stated the case for clearing the pampas of their Indian inhabitants. Speaking to his fellow countrymen he argued that "our self-respect as a virile people obliges us to put down as soon as possible, by reason or by force, this handful of savages who destroy our wealth and prevent us from definitively occupying, in the name of law, progress and our own security, the richest and most fertile lands of the Republic" (Serres Güiraldes 1979:377–78).[1] Roca then proceeded to lead a campaign, known in Argentine history as the Conquest of the Desert, whose express purpose was to clear the pampas of Indians. The Indians were not entirely exterminated physically, but they were eradicated socially, ceasing to exist as separate and identifiable peoples.

A similar campaign to exterminate an indigenous population was carried out in Tasmania during the nineteenth century. The settlers tired of acts of resistance committed by the native Tasmanians and therefore organized a drive in which a line of armed men "beat" across the island, as they would do if they were flushing game, only this time the quarry was the remaining Tasmanians. The official objective of this drive was to capture the Tasmanians and "bring them to civilization," but, as Davies reported in *The Last of the Tasmanians*, "the real motive in the hearts of most of the participants was nothing more than the destruction of vermin, backed by the fear not only of what the native might do to their persons, but also the menace he presented to their crops and their flocks. . . . The aborigines were killed and maimed and left to die in the bush" (1974:123). The line did not, in fact, exterminate the Tasmanians, but it harried and decimated them so severely that it hastened their eventual extinction.[2]

A similar line operation had been put into effect earlier in Australia, when General Macquarie organized colonists, soldiers, and constables to drive the aborigines of New South Wales beyond the Blue Mountains (ibid.:111), but such organized campaigns increasingly became exceptions in a land where aborigines could be hunted and shot at will (see Elder 1998). In fact the killing by imperialists of the subject peoples over whom they ruled was generally inspired by a mixture of motives. It was sometimes done to displace the natives and seize their lands, but it was often perpetrated against landless natives who posed little threat. It was simply the direct outcome of a culture of prejudice among rulers who considered their native subjects less than human and who possessed the power to casually brutalize and kill them.

Alternatively, such killings were carried out as a means of terrorizing people into performing forced labor. The most notorious examples of this were the horrors inflicted on the unfortunate people forced to gather rubber by sadistic overseers in Peru and the Congo. The rubber boom in South America at the end of the nineteenth century led unscrupulous entrepreneurs to seize whole communities of indigenous peoples and force some of them to gather rubber while holding the rest hostage to ensure that the tappers did not run away. The ghastly tortures that the overseers inflicted on the Indians, sparing neither men, women, nor little children, make sickening reading (see Hardenburg 1912; Taussig 1986) and lead one to wonder why those with the power so mistreated (and therefore reduced the productivity of) the people they had enslaved. Similar questions were asked by those who reported from what Joseph Conrad called "the heart of darkness" in the Congo. Here again it was rubber and, to a lesser extent, ivory that was to be gathered in a vast territory run at the beginning of the twentieth century as a private fief by King Leopold II of Belgium. Here the tortures and massacres were as revolting as those in Peru and inflicted on a larger scale. To cite a single example from the hundreds documented by those who were disgusted by these goings on, soldiers employed in the Congo stated in sworn affidavits that it was decided to make an example of several villages that had fallen short of their assigned rubber quotas. The villages were therefore surrounded, "every man, woman and child butchered without mercy, their remains mutilated in the most fiendish manner, and the villages then burnt" (Morel 1970:129).

The unbelievable barbarities visited on the rubber gatherers of two continents by overseers of different nationalities and backgrounds calls for some kind of explanation. What did these places have in common that produced such terrible results? They were both run as commercial enterprises located at the edges of the so-called civilized world, and in them greed appears to have been the overriding consideration. The Arana brothers in Peru and King Leopold's overseers in the Congo wanted to extract every last ounce of profit from their operations, even if that meant killing their workforce. They seem to have thought there was a limitless supply of native labor to be captured and exploited. Meanwhile the rhetoric of the rulers laid great stress on the fact that they were dealing with savages—

either savages to be tamed or savages to be civilized.[3] Either way they felt the necessity to be ruthless, and they were too far from the societies from which they came to feel any constraints. At the same time, precisely because they were operating at the margins of their world, exploiting indigenous peoples for the profit of alien rulers, the overseers were determined to demonstrate their overwhelming power, so that there could be no thought of resistance on the part of those whom they treated so cruelly. The most revolting aspect of these terrible regimes was the absolute corruption that accompanied the establishment of absolute power, to the extent that, when the overseers tired of "routine" floggings, burnings, and maimings, they amused themselves by inventing new ways in which to torture and kill the people they controlled.

It is difficult to tell whether the peoples of the Putumayo region or the considerably larger populations in the Congo would have been exterminated if these systems of exploitation had been allowed to run their course. Fortunately the horrors taking place were publicized and eventually moderated. Nevertheless the depopulation in both regions was devastatingly genocidal. Estimates of the death toll are more reliable for the Congo, where Roger Casement calculated that the population had been reduced by 60 percent (ibid.:235).

In terms of sheer numbers, the Congo genocide takes second place only to the loss of African life occasioned by the slave trade. Historians have calculated that fifteen to twenty million Africans were herded overseas as slaves and an equal number were killed in the whole process of slaving, giving a total of up to forty million who were either killed or removed forever from their homes (Hatch 1999:71). Yet the intensity of the killing in the Congo was greater. The slave trade, after all, lasted for centuries, as compared with a few decades for the Congo genocide. During the slave trade, in King Leopold's Congo and in the Peruvian rubber-gathering regime, genocide was quite simply a business expense, the human cost of capturing and coercing unwilling laborers to produce for the international export trade. In fact the connection between the brutalizing of Indians in the remote forests of the Americas and the export trade had been clearly demonstrated earlier by the Portuguese in sixteenth-century Brazil. The Portuguese were expert slavers who not only depopulated the banks of the Amazon and its major tributaries but also soon became masters of the art of penetrating deep into the rain forests and attacking Indian villages that had thought themselves protected by their remoteness. This prowess did not, however, enable them to bring in sufficient slave labor for the Brazilian colony, with the result that Brazil early became a major importer of African slaves to work the plantations upon which the economy of the colony depended.

Imperialist genocide against indigenous peoples was thus of two kinds. It was practiced in order to clear lands that invading settlers wished to occupy. It was also practiced as part of a strategy to seize and coerce labor that the settlers could not or would not obtain by less drastic means. It was often inspired furthermore by the rulers' determination to show who was master and who was, if not slave, then at least obedient subject; and it was often put into effect as deliberate policy where the masters felt that their subjects had to be taught a lesson. Acts of resistance or rebellion were often punished by genocidal killings.

A classic example of this, out of the scores that might be cited, was the German extermination of the Herero in Southwest Africa (see Drechsler 1980; Bridgman 1981). The German administration of their Southwest African colony decided that German settlers should pasture their cattle on the best grazing lands in what was by and large an arid region. This meant that they would take over the lands where the Herero had traditionally grazed their cattle. Since there were no alternative grazing lands, the Herero would thus be deprived of their cattle and left without other means of subsistence than to work for the German settlers. The German administration argued that it was in the interests of higher development and virtually a part of natural law that indigenous peoples become a class of workers in the service of the whites. The Herero did not see it that way, however, and when they were evicted from their grazing lands they fought back. The Germans therefore mounted a punitive expedition in 1904 that massacred thousands of Herero and drove the rest into the waterless desert. General von Trotha then established a line to ensure that no Herero could re-emerge from the desert, where they were starving to death. He insisted that they should all leave German territory on pain of being shot. The result was the virtual extermination of the Herero, who were reduced to a few thousand landless fugitives.

Genocides against indigenous peoples were not, however, solely a function of colonial policies. Genocidal massacres continued to be committed in the years of decolonization and beyond, only their rationale was different. Such massacres are now less frequently committed in the search for profit, though they still occur. The notorious treatment of the Ogoni in Nigeria is a case in point.[4] Oil has been extracted in large quantities from Ogoni lands since 1958, but few of the proceeds have found their way to the Ogoni themselves. Instead the Ogoni have seen their land turned into one vast environmental disaster by oil spillage, oil flaring, and other side effects of oil drilling. The health of the Ogoni has suffered and continues to do so, while their subsistence activities have been spoiled, their society disrupted, and their population reduced by illness and destitution. This is a classic case of an indigenous society being forced to suffer in the name of development.

The development rationale is in fact the modern version of the older justifications for mistreating indigenous peoples. In previous centuries, imperialists insisted that they were doing the peoples they conquered a favor by bringing them into the civilized world. That was, for example, the thinking of the German administration in Southwest Africa when they drove the Herero into revolt and then exterminated them. Nowadays indigenous peoples frequently find themselves threatened by a particular aspect of modern "civilization," namely "development." It is all too often argued by governments and developmental planners that indigenous peoples "must not be allowed to stand in the way of development." In fact, being accused of "standing in the way of development" these days is to stand accused of something between a sin and a crime. So, all too often, projects or programs are put into effect, even though they have serious negative consequences for indigenous peoples, because indigenous peoples must not be allowed to "stand in the way of development." These are flimsy justifications. It is possible to design development programs that benefit indigenous peoples as well as their nonindigenous neighbors. Such programs are rarely implemented, however, because they are more expensive and produce less profit for nonindigenous entrepreneurs or sectors of the population. Instead, noxious oil-drilling is carried out, as among the Ogoni, when there are other oil companies ready and willing to drill more carefully and with benefit to the local people. Dams are built that flood indigenous lands. Timber companies are permitted or actually invited to cut down the forests in which indigenous people live. Such development activities destroy the livelihoods of indigenous peoples, disrupt their societies, undermine their health, and leave whole populations in suicidal despair.

Loss of life promoted by callous developmentalism is a slow and insidious form of genocide against indigenous peoples. A more direct form in our present era is the massacre of indigenous peoples for reasons of state. Such genocides were common in the USSR, where they were inflicted both on nonindigenous and indigenous peoples. In the days when the country was ruled despotically by Stalin, all its constituent peoples could, in whole or in part, be uprooted, relocated, or scattered in remote regions, often with the utmost brutality. Such measures were all too often put into effect, especially in and around the period of World War II, so that few peoples of the Soviet Union escaped the deportations and massacres that were part of the political culture of the nation (see Deker and Lebed 1958). Such genocides were part of a schizophrenic policy that pretended to guarantee and encourage peoples to cultivate their distinctive ethnicities while simultaneously striving to make sure that local ethnic sentiments were weakened if not destroyed. Soviet genocides were thus a paradoxical result of the Soviet nationalities policy.

In other parts of the world, genocidal massacres have resulted from a state's making war on the peoples at its margins. For example, where northeastern India now meets Burma, the Nagas asked to form their own independent state when the British withdrew and India became an independent nation in 1947. They signed an agreement with India, under the terms of which the Nagas would have local autonomy under Indian trusteeship for ten years and then be allowed to vote on whether they would remain in India or not. The Nagas voted overwhelmingly for independence in 1951, but India did not accede to their wish. Instead India invaded Nagaland in 1954 and has been fighting against secessionist Naga guerrillas ever since. By some estimates India has 200,000 troops in the Naga area, in order to prevent some two-and-a-half million Nagas from joining with another half-million over the border in Burma to form their own state. Meanwhile the bulk of the Naga population becomes increasingly embittered by Indian repression and human rights abuses. It would have been relatively easy for India to grant Naga independence in the 1950s, but in the 1990s there are separatist movements in other parts of India, such as Kashmir or the Punjab, where militant Sikhs are demanding their own state. Granting Naga independence now is therefore opposed by those Indians who think it would establish a dangerous precedent, leading to further secessions from the Indian state (see Fürer-Haimendorf 1982; Singh 1981).

Similar considerations lie behind the warfare waged by the government of Burma against the non-Burmese peoples at its borders. Like the Nagas of India, these border peoples—the Shan, the Karen, the Kachin, the Mon, the Karenni, the Arakanese, and others—agreed to join the Burmese federation after the end of British rule in 1948. They did so on condition that their local autonomy would be respected and that they would have the right to withdraw from the federation after ten years if they so wished. The Burmese refused, however, to permit any of the border peoples to exercise that option and have waged war on those that showed any inclination to do so. The Burmese army has treated the border peoples in rebel areas with great brutality, imposing regimes of forced labor, beatings, torture, and sexual abuse as they seek to break the will to resist of those whom they consider "uncivilized" tribal peoples (see Mirante 1987).

This phenomenon of a state's making war on those of its own peoples it considers marginal is by no means restricted to southern or southeastern Asia. Recent examples could be cited from the Sudan in Africa and from Guatemala in the Americas. The Anglo-Egyptian condominium that ruled the Sudan from 1899 to 1955 administered the north as an Arab Islamic region quite distinct from the south, which was African and much influenced by Christian missionaries. There was some talk of these regions' being granted independence as separate states, but eventually the Sudan received its independence as a single country, governed from the northern capital of Khartoum. The south urged that the country be organized as a federation, granting considerable autonomy to its regions in order to allow their different cultural traditions to flourish. The Islamic government of the state refused, and the result was a protracted civil war that was brought to a temporary close by the Addis Ababa agreement of 1972, which granted the south the autonomy it had always sought. The agreement was greeted with great hope that it would usher in an era of Arab-African cooperation that could serve as a model for all of Africa, but it was soon undermined by the national government in the north, which imposed Islamic law as the law of the land and provoked non-Muslim regions into armed resistance once again (see Deng 1995). The devastation and famine caused by the war has taken a particularly heavy toll on the south, where it is estimated that more than a quarter of a million people died of starvation in 1988 alone (ibid.:341).

In Guatemala an equally long-running civil war was fought from the 1960s until it was brought to a hesitant close by the peace accords of 1996. Schirmer (1998) describes the militarization of the Guatemalan state during this process. She cites army officers who admitted that the military's brutally repressive counterinsurgency tactics in the 1970s served to swell the ranks of the guerrillas. The army therefore changed its strategy. It used the utmost brutality in certain areas whose Indian inhabitants were marked for total extermination. In other areas it used torture and selective killings to force the Indians to fight on the government side, or at least to fight against those whom the government had targeted as its enemies. In yet other areas it offered paternalistic protection and assistance to communities it sought to win over, so that the overall strategy was called one of beans and bullets. This strategy succeeded in turning the civil war into a stalemate, with the indigenous masses in the countryside being forced to absorb terrible punishment. Meanwhile the army succeeded in institutionalizing itself and its methods as central to the supposedly democratic state that had succeeded the openly authoritarian military regimes of previous decades.

In Nagaland, Burma, and the Sudan, national governments have waged war against marginalized indigenous peoples because they refused to grant them autonomy and would not allow them to secede. In Guatemala the national government and its army represent the elites who have presided for a long time over an unjust and repressive social system that discriminated against the country's indigenous masses. These forces were quite willing to torture and massacre the Indians in order to protect the status quo and to ward off such changes as would undermine their traditional dominance.

It should by now be clear how such conflicts degenerate all too easily into genocide. It is because genocide everywhere depends on the perpetrators' dehumanizing their intended victims, establishing them as radically alien creatures who deserve to be eliminated, and having the power to kill them. These conditions normally apply to indigenous peoples who are marginalized and treated as aliens, even in their own countries, and are invariably in a position of political weakness. Moreover, indigenous peoples have in the recent past, and in some places right up to the present day, been considered "savages" who had to be annihilated physically or socially. In recent years indigenous peoples have been threatened in the name of development or for reasons of state.

It is particularly dangerous for them when these two threats come together, as happens when there are valuable resources in indigenous territory that the state wishes to seize in the name of development, and when indigenous wishes to secede from the state (often precisely because the state is trying to take over indigenous resources) are held to constitute a threat to the state.

It is the idea of the threatened state that is particularly insidious and especially likely to lead to genocide.[5] The Enlightenment idea of the state that has dominated Western thinking until recently stressed the rationality of the modern state, which would treat its citizens equally and guarantee their liberty by protecting their rights. It was thus concerned with the rights of individuals rather than with the rights of groups such as ethnic minorities or indigenous peoples. It was supposed instead that ethnicity would evaporate in the modern state as a result of modernization itself. The grim history of the twentieth century and the ethnic conflicts and persecutions that have played such a prominent part in it have shown, however, that ethnicity and ethnic nationalism have not disappeared, nor are they about to. It follows that actual modern states have not turned out the way they were supposed to; meanwhile, in an era of unprecedented globalization, the nature and function of the "nation-state" is being rethought, and a major aspect of this rethinking has to do with the continuing place of ethnicity and ethnic minorities in the states of the future.

It is no longer considered necessary or even possible that each state should correspond to a single nation, possessing a mainstream culture in which all its citizens (including those who are considered minorities) must participate. On the contrary, states are increasingly expected to be pluralistic, permitting localized minorities and indigenous peoples to retain their cultures and to enjoy a certain autonomy within the system. Those states that make war on marginalized minorities are thus states in which pluralism has either failed or has not been given a chance. Successful multiethnic states are, on the other hand, the best guarantee of peace and the best defense against genocide.

NOTES

1. My translation from the Spanish.

2. It has been generally accepted for some time that Truganini, who died in 1876, was the last Tasmanian, but there are still a few people alive today who claim to be descendants of the original Tasmanians.

3. It is astonishing to read the justifications offered by the overseers in the Congo, starting with King Leopold himself, who stressed their philanthropic concern for the savages whom they were in the process of civilizing.

4. I rely here on the book by Ken Saro-Wiwa, the distinguished Ogoni writer who was hanged by the Nigerian government because of his ardent defense of Ogoni rights.

5. This discussion of the state is set out more fully in Maybury-Lewis 1997, ch. 4.

REFERENCES

Bodley, John H. 1982. *Victims of Progress*. Menlo Park, Calif.: Benjamin Cummings.

Bridgman, John. 1981. *The Revolt of the Hereros*. Berkeley: University of California Press.

Charny, Israel. 1994. "Toward a General Definition of Genocide." In *Genocide: Conceptual and Historical Dimensions*. George Andreopoulos, ed. Pp. 64–94. Philadelphia: University of Pennsylvania Press.

Davies, David. 1974. *The Last of the Tasmanians*. New York: Harper and Row.

Deker, Nikolai, and Andrei Lebed, eds. 1958. *Genocide in the USSR: Studies in Group Destruction*. New York: Scarecrow Press.

Deng, Francis M. 1995. *War of Visions: Conflict of Identities in the Sudan*. Washington, D.C.: Brookings Institution.

Drechsler, Horst. 1980. *Let Us Die Fighting: The Struggle of the Herero and the Nama against German Imperialism (1884–1915)*. London: Zed Press.

Elder, Bruce. 1998. *Blood on the Wattle: Massacres and Maltreatment of Aboriginal Australians since 1788*. Frenchs Forest, N.S.W: New Holland Press.

Fürer-Haimendorf, Christoph von. 1982. *Tribes of India: The Struggle for Survival*. Berkeley: University of California Press.

Hardenburg, W. E. 1912. *The Putumayo: The Devil's Paradise*. London: T. Fisher Unwin.

Hatch, John. [1969] 1999. *The History of Britain in Africa: From the Fifteenth Century to the Present.* London: Andre Deutsch.

Las Casas, Bartolomé de. [1552] 1974. *Brevísima Relación de la Destrucción de las Indias.* New York: Seabury Press.

Maybury-Lewis, David. 1997. *Indigenous Peoples, Ethnic Groups and the State.* Boston: Allyn and Bacon.

Merivale, Herman. 1861. *Lectures on Colonisation and Colonies.* London: Green, Longman and Roberts.

Mirante, Edith T. 1987. "Ethnic Minorities of the Burma Frontiers and Their Resistance Groups." In *Cultural Survival: Southeast Asian Tribal Groups and Ethnic Minorities: Prospects for the Eighties and Beyond.* Cambridge, Mass.: Cultural Survival.

Morel, Edmund D. [1904] 1970. *King Leopold's Rule in Africa.* Westport, Conn.: Negro Universities Press.

Richard, Guy. 1992. *L'histoire Inhumaine: Massacres et Génocides des Origines à Nos Jours.* Paris: Armand Colin.

Roosevelt, Theodore. 1889. *The Winning of the West: From the Alleghenies to the Mississippi, 1769–1776.* Vol. 1. New York: G. P. Putnam's Sons.

Saro-Wiwa, Ken. 1992. *Genocide in Nigeria: The Ogoni Tragedy.* Lagos: Saros International Publishers.

Schirmer, Jennifer. 1998. *The Guatemalan Military Project: A Violence Called Democracy.* Philadelphia: University of Pennsylvania Press.

Serres Güiraldes, Alfredo M. 1979. *La Estrategia de General Roca.* Buenos Aires: Pleamar.

Singh, Chandrika. 1981. *Political Evolution of Nagaland.* New Delhi: Lancers.

Taussig, Michael. 1986. *Shamanism, Colonialism and the Wild Man: A Study in Terror and Healing.* Chicago: University of Chicago Press.

3

Confronting Genocide and Ethnocide of Indigenous Peoples

An Interdisciplinary Approach to Definition, Intervention, Prevention, and Advocacy

Samuel Totten, William S. Parsons, and Robert K. Hitchcock

INTRODUCTION

The plight of indigenous peoples has been underscored by what one analyst has characterized as "the often genocidal process of colonization and the long history of land dispossession" (Burger 1987:5). Time and again, various indigenous groups have seen their lands, cultures, and their very lives encroached upon, if not outright destroyed (Chalk and Jonassohn 1990:194–222, 412–14; Churchill 1997; Hitchcock and Twedt 1997). Indigenous leaders and writers have spoken out strongly on what they believe are genocidal policies aimed at destroying them both physically and culturally (Moody 1988, I:83–122; Churchill 1997).

Indigenous peoples are often seen, as Fein (1990:36–37) points out, as outside the universe of obligation—the "other"—or as competitors for valued resources. Governments of countries in which indigenous peoples exist have assigned them to categories such as "wards of the state" and have denied them basic civil, political, and socioeconomic rights (Burger 1987, 1990; Bodley 1999). Not only are indigenous people some of the most impoverished and disadvantaged members of the societies of which they are a part but they are also exposed in a number of instances to harsh and unjust treatment (Hitchcock 1994; Maybury-Lewis 1997).

As Jason Clay of Rights and Resources has noted, there have "probably been more genocides, ethnocides, and extinctions of tribal and ethnic groups in this century than any in history" (Clay 1984:1). This is due in part to the fact that, according to Clay (1993:48), some states spend more money to fight their own citizens than they do for all social and economic programs combined. In 1988, the International Work Group for Indigenous Affairs (IWGIA:1) argued that a conservative estimate of the number of deaths of indigenous people by violent means was around thirty thousand annually, with many more dying through neglect and starvation. Since the time of colonization, several million indigenous people have lost their lives either directly or indirectly as a result of the actions of other groups, states, or agencies.

The focus of this chapter is on issues of intervention and prevention of genocide, including such concerns as genocidal massacres, genocidal killing, cultural genocide, or ethnocide, as they relate to indigenous peoples. This essay is written in the spirit that there is a dire need for those working in different disciplines (in this case, genocide studies, indigenous peoples studies, anthropology, and education) to communicate and share ideas in an attempt to prevent genocide from taking place. This effort can only help to strengthen what Burger (1987:265) has described as the worldwide movement of indigenous peoples and nongovernmental organizations to achieve very specific protection of human rights in international law and effective implementation and enforcement of those laws.

This chapter addresses the subject of genocide from an interdisciplinary perspective. It brings together work on the issue of genocide by anthropologists and archaeologists, development workers, sociologists, political scientists, educators, historians, psychologists, lawyers, and educators, among others. Anthropology, more than any other discipline, has focused attention on indigenous peoples, beginning with its work with Native American populations in North America in the mid-nineteenth century and continuing into the twentieth and now the twenty-first centuries in the Pacific, the Arctic, Australia, Asia, Africa, and Latin America. Anthropologists undertook detailed fieldwork with individual societies, and they often attempted to advocate on behalf of indigenous populations, one example being the work of James Mooney, who sought to convince the U.S. government that the Ghost Dance being performed by Native Americans was not a war dance but rather an expression of peaceful religious sentiment. His perspective went unheeded, culminating in the massacre of hundreds of Lakota and other Plains Indians, many of them elderly men, women, and children by the Seventh Cavalry of the U.S. Army at Wounded Knee, South Dakota, on December 29, 1890 (Mooney 1896; Jensen, Paul, and Carter 1991).

Anthropologists have had a mixed history when it comes to dealing with issues of genocide and human rights violations involving indigenous peoples. On the one hand, they have argued for taking a "cultural relativist" position, one in which each culture's practices and institutions are seen as having their own inherent values and thus arguably should be viewed objectively. On the other hand, some anthropologists have taken relativism so literally that they opposed the Universal Declaration of Human Rights in 1948. Anthropologists have also taken part in activities that had negative effects on indigenous and other societies, one example being the role that anthropologists played in carrying out investigations of Hill Tribes in southeast Asia that were used to assist the U.S. war effort in the region in the 1960s (Wakin 1992). Admittedly, a number of anthropologists have worked for various intelligence agencies, militaries, and governmental and international agencies that were involved in activities that resulted in human rights violations and the denial of fair treatment to some individuals and groups. There were also anthropologists who sought to warn indigenous peoples and governments of the potential risks of various policies and programs. Anthropologists have long sought to influence policies aimed at the development of pastoral peoples, for example, and they have warned against the harm of large-scale infrastructure projects such as large dams (Sanford 1983; World Commission on Dams 2000). Anthropologists and other social scientists told U.S. and U.N. agencies of the potential for violence in places such as Rwanda, Somalia, and Sierra Leone. Had these warnings been heeded, the number of people who died and the huge costs of postconflict intervention could have been reduced, or the tragedies even possibly prevented.

Increasingly, anthropologists are collaborating with people from other disciplines in looking at genocide-related issues. This can be seen in the work of archaeologists on forensic teams made up of doctors, lawyers, and criminologists who have investigated massacres and disappearances in places as far afield as Argentina, Guatemala, Rwanda, and the former Yugoslavia (Stover and Peress 1998; Neier 1998:8–11). It can also be seen in the efforts by anthropologists to develop curricula on human rights and genocide that can be used in courses at the secondary and postsecondary levels.

Anthropologists have worked extensively in complex field situations, often seeing firsthand the violence that can and sometimes does lead to genocide (Nordstrom and Robben 1995). Anthropologists along with psychologists, sociologists, historians, and political scientists have identified some of the preconditions of genocide, including the exclusion of people identified as being "different" from what Fein (1994) calls "the universe of obligation." By focusing on issues such as racism, sexism, ethnocentrism, nationalism, fundamentalism, and anti-Semitism, anthropologists and other social scientists and educators have contributed to efforts to discredit ideologies and perspectives that lead to differential treatment of groups and individuals.

The balance of this chapter addresses issues relating to indigenous peoples and genocide, the definitions of genocide and ethnocide, typologies of genocide, especially as they relate to indigenous peoples, strategies for coping with genocide, including prediction, intervention, and advocacy, and the varied roles of the discipline of anthropology as it relates to genocide and ethnocide issues. The conclusion of the paper deals with the importance of education as a means of dealing with genocide, ethnocide, and human rights violations.

INDIGENOUS PEOPLES AND GENOCIDE

Indigenous peoples are those people who are also referred to as aboriginal peoples, native peoples, tribal peoples, Fourth World peoples, or "first nations." No single agreed-upon definition of the term *indigenous peoples* exists. According to the Independent Commission on International Humanitarian Issues (1987:6), four elements are included in the definition of indigenous peoples: (a) pre-existence, (b) nondominance, (c) cultural difference, and (d) self-identification as indigenous. Today, there are approximately 450 million to 650 million indigenous people residing in some 75 of the world's 194 nation-states. In the majority of cases indigenous peoples are numerical minorities, and they do not control the governments of the states in which they live.

Indigenous peoples generally possess ethnic, religious, or linguistic characteristics different from those of the dominant groups in the societies where they exist. They tend to have a sense of cultural identity or social solidarity that many members attempt to maintain. Today there is a worldwide indigenous movement in which members of indigenous communities and groups are seeking to promote their social, cultural, economic, political, and religious rights.

The pace of destruction of indigenous peoples rose substantially in the twentieth century, in spite of the fact that international declarations were drawn up and statements of indigenous rights created to try to counteract physical and cultural destruction and discrimination. It is estimated that in Brazil alone, between 1900 and 1957, more than eighty Indian groups that were contacted ended up destroyed as a result of disease, deculturation, and physical destruction (Davis 1977:5). The situation was especially devastating for those groups situated near natural resources that could be extracted from the land (rubber and nut collection, for example, or mineral exploitation). Overall, the number of indigenous people in Brazil declined from more than a million to 200,000, a drop of 80 percent (ibid.:5).

Indigenous peoples are often blamed for their own destruction. They are sometimes said not to be utilizing land productively or are argued to be responsible for its degradation, as seen, for example, in the case of rain forest depletion resulting from shifting cultivation. All too often, those in power characterize them negatively: brigands, nomads, vagabonds, vermin, poachers, drunkards, aliens, thieves, dissidents, inferiors, and unproductive people. The use of these terms increases when the state, business companies, or individuals move into new areas where indigenous groups are living and using the resources, as occurred when Europeans entered Australia and North America.

It is apparent that there are numerous terms used by indigenous peoples and those who work with them to illustrate what these groups are dealing with. On the one hand, there is physical genocide, the destruction of indigenous peoples themselves; on the other there is cultural genocide, or ethnocide, the destruction of a group's culture (Kuper 1981:30–31; Palmer 1992:1–6).

The term *genocide* has been the focus of great debate over the past several decades (Kuper 1981, 1984, 1985; Charny 1984, 1985; Fein 1984, 1990; Chalk 1989; Chalk and Jonassohn 1990; Totten and Parsons 1991). If humanity is to develop sound conventions and genocide warning systems in order to stave off genocide, then we (indigenous peoples, scholars, activists, educators, members of nongovernment organizations, and government officials, among others) need to come to a general understanding of what does and does not constitute genocide. It is also necessary to understand the preconditions that lead up to and culminate in genocide (Charny 1984, 1991; Kuper 1985, 1992).

Too often an incidence of massacre or some other serious human rights infraction is incorrectly referred to or deemed to be genocide by survivors, victim groups, the media, activists, or scholars. As horrible as these infractions are, if they do not meet certain criteria they cannot legitimately be called genocide. This misuse of the term does not assist in either fully understanding or combating actual genocides. A key problem herein, and one that complicates the effort to be more exact, is the fact that scholars are still in the process of trying to develop a theoretically sound and, at the same time, practical definition of genocide.

In light of the significance of this issue, we will begin with a synopsis of definitions of *genocide, genocidal massacres, ethnocide,* and various typologies of *genocide* that have been developed. Next, we will highlight past and present cases that generally have been acknowledged by spokespersons of indigenous groups, scholars, and members of human rights organizations. We will conclude with an examination of efforts by scholars, activists, and others working to intervene in or prevent the genocide of indigenous peoples.

GENOCIDE: DEFINITIONAL ISSUES

Some have argued that if humanity truly hopes to develop an efficacious method for preventing genocidal crimes, what is needed, at the very least, is a consensus as to what genocide is. As we will show, that has been and continues to be a daunting task.

Ever since Raphael Lemkin coined the term *genocide* in 1944, scholars, activists, government officials, and representatives of intergovernmental organizations like the United Nations have been wrestling with the term in an effort to try to develop a definition that is not so inclusive that it is meaningless but not so exclusive that it denies protection to certain groups of people (Fein 1984, 1990; Walliman and Dobkowski 1987; Charny 1988; Chalk 1989; Chalk and Jonassohn 1990). Consensus has been extremely difficult to come by. Various scholars have recast the definition of *genocide* in an attempt to make it more workable, manageable, specific, or, as Chalk and Jonassohn (1990:15) put it, "analytically rigorous."

Various other terms have been coined in an effort to differentiate between the intent, scope, and type of crime against humanity that has been committed. Among these terms are *ethnocide* (Kuper 1981:31; Whitaker 1985:17; Palmer 1992:1–4), *cultural genocide* (Dadrian 1975:201–12; Kuper 1981:15, 30–31, 44; Whitaker 1985:17; Charny 1991:31–32), *selective genocide* (Kuper 1985:154–55), *genocidal process* (Kuper 1988:156), and *genocidal massacres* (Kuper 1981:10, 32, 60; Chalk and Jonassohn 1990:26; Charny 1991:20). The use of the various concepts is important because, as Kuper (1985:150) notes, different types of genocide imply different strategies for prevention and protective action.

Raphael Lemkin (1944), who waged a one-man crusade for establishment of an international convention against the perpetration of genocide, formed the term *genocide* by combining the Greek *genos* (race, tribe) and the Latin *cide* (killing). As he stated,

> Generally speaking, genocide does not necessarily mean the immediate destruction of a nation, except when accomplished by mass killings of all members of a nation. It is intended rather to signify a coordinated plan of different actions aiming at the destruction of essential foundations of the life of national groups with the aim of annihilating the groups themselves. The objectives of such a plan would be the disintegration of the political and social institutions of culture, language, national feelings, religion, economic existence of national groups and the destruction of the personal security, liberty, health, dignity, and even the lives of the individuals belonging to such groups. Genocide is directed against the national group as an entity, and the actions involved are directed at individuals, not in their individual capacity, but as members of the national groups.... Genocide has two phases: one, destruction of the national pattern of the oppressed group; the other, the imposition of the national pattern of the oppressor. (Lemkin 1944:79)

It is apparent from this definition that Lemkin considered both physical and cultural genocide—or ethnocide—to be part of the general concept of genocide. Basically, the term *ethnocide* refers to the destruction of a culture without the killing of its bearers. The genocide/ethnocide issue has engendered considerable discussion and heated debate (Chalk and Jonassohn 1990; Palmer 1992). Succinctly stated, those who have argued against the inclusion of ethnocide under the rubric of genocide suggest that there is a qualitative difference between those situations in which people are slain outright and those in which certain aspects of a peoples' culture are destroyed.

Following World War II and the annihilation by the Nazis and their collaborators of approximately six million Jews and five million other people, such as Gypsies, the physically and mentally handicapped, Poles and other Slavic peoples, the United Nations adopted a resolution on December 9, 1946, calling for international cooperation on the prevention of and punishment for genocide. It was this terrible slaughter and the methods of destruction used by the Nazi regime that provoked the United Nations formally to recognize genocide as a crime in international law.

From the outset, however, the development of the U.N. Genocide Convention was enmeshed in controversy. As Kuper (1985:10) has noted, nations with vastly different philosophies, cultures, and "historical experiences and sensitivities to human suffering" presented varying interpretations as to what constituted genocide, and as a consequence they argued in favor of a definition and wording in the convention that fit their own perspectives. The arguments and counterarguments resulted in what can best be described as a "compromise definition," one that significantly played down ethnocide as a component (Kuper 1981:23). At the same time, it broadened the definition by adding a new category of victim: "political and other groups" (Chalk and Jonassohn 1990:10).

However, the Soviet Union, Poland, and other nations argued against the inclusion of political groups, claiming that such a step would not conform "with the scientific definition of genocide and would, in practice, distort the perspective in which the crime should be viewed and impair the efficacy of the Convention" (Kuper 1981:25). The upshot was that political and social groups were excluded from the convention. The sagacity of excluding such groups has been questioned, if not outright criticized, by numerous scholars (Kuper 1981, 1985; Whitaker 1985; Charny 1984, 1991; Chalk and Jonassohn 1990; Totten 1991). Others believe that the exclusion of political groups from the convention was a sound move. LeBlanc (1988:292–94), for example, supports the exclusion of political groups because of what he sees as the difficulty inherent in selecting criteria for determining what constitutes a political group and their instability over time; other reasons he cites are the right of the state to protect itself and the potential misuse of the label "genocide" by antagonists in conflict situations.

On December 9, 1948, the Convention on Genocide was approved by the General Assembly of the United Nations. The convention defines genocide as follows:

> In the present Convention, genocide means any of the following acts committed with the intent to destroy, in whole or in part, a national, ethnical, racial or religious group, as such:
> a. Killing members of the group;
> b. Causing serious bodily or mental harm to members of the group;
> c. Deliberately inflicting on the group conditions of life calculated to bring about its physical destruction in whole or in part;
> d. Imposing measures intended to prevent births within the group;
> e. Forcibly transferring children of the group to another group.

It is important to note, as Kuper (1985:150) does, that the Genocide Convention draws no distinction between types of genocide, since it seeks to define the elements that they share in common. The convention differentiates only the means (ibid.:15). As Chalk and Jonassohn (1990:11) stress, the U.N. definition of genocide commingles physical destruction with causing mental harm to members of a group. Once again, this raises the issue of whether ethnocide should be subsumed under the larger definition of genocide.

Cultural genocide and ethnocide are basically synonymous and refer to the destruction of a group's culture. As Whitaker (1985:17) notes, cultural genocide constitutes "[a]ny deliberate act committed with intent to destroy the language, religion or culture of a national, racial or religious group on grounds of national or racial origin or religious belief such as: 1. Prohibiting the use of the language of the group in daily intercourse or in schools, or the printing and circulation of publications in the language of the group; 2. Destroying or preventing the use of libraries, museums, schools, historical monuments, places of worship." According to Whitaker (ibid.:17), at least one member of the Ad Hoc Committee preparing the United Nations Genocide Convention indicated that exclusion of the term *cultural genocide* from the final text left minorities unprotected.

Some members proposed at the 1985 meetings of the Sub-Commission on the Prevention of Discrimination and Protection of Minorities that the definition of genocide be broadened to include ethnocide, but it was opposed by some members who felt that this might result in political interference in the domestic affairs of states (ibid.: 16). It was also suggested that the protection of minorities' culture should be the responsibility of other international bodies besides the United Nations— meaning, presumably, organizations such as the United Nations Educational, Scientific, and Cultural Organization (UNESCO), the International Labour Organization (ILO), and the United Nations Industrial and Scientific Organization. Such a strategy, though, as was noted, might not be very effective, given the lack of enforcement capabilities and the staffing limitations of these institutions.

TYPOLOGIES OF GENOCIDE

A number of typologies of genocide have been presented, some of which include actions involving indigenous peoples specifically. Dadrian (1975), for example, identified five types of genocide: (a) cultural genocide, in which assimilation is the perpetrator's aim; (b) latent genocide, the result of activities with unintended consequences (for example, the spread of diseases during an invasion); (c) retributive genocide, that designed to punish a segment of a minority that challenges a dominant group; (d) utilitarian genocide, the using of mass killing to obtain control of economic resources; and (e) optimal genocide, which is characterized by the slaughter of a group to achieve its obliteration.

Chalk and Jonassohn (1990:12–15) identified four types of genocide: that designed (a) to eliminate a potential or future threat; (b) to acquire economic wealth; (c) to create terror; and (d) to implement a belief, theory, or ideology. As they point out, genocide associated with the expansion of economic wealth was closely associated with colonial expansion into Asia, Africa, and the Americas (Chalk and Jonassohn 1990:36). As will be discussed below, destruction of indigenous groups and their societies has continued and even increased during the twentieth century, due in part to rapidly expanding business activities and both large-scale and small-scale development projects (Burger 1987; Gedicks 1993; Wilmer 1993; Hitchcock 1994, 1997).

The process of contact between immigrant and indigenous groups all too often had tragic consequences. Some groups received especially harsh treatment in the context of colonial expansion, notably hunter-gatherers (Kuper 1985:151; Gordon 1992; Hitchcock and Twedt 1997). One of the cases cited most frequently is that of Tasmania (Turnbull 1948; Morris 1972; Jonassohn and Chalk 1987:130, 204–22; Barta 1987; Tatz 1991:97–98). The white residents of Tasmania planned and executed what they felt was a Final Solution to the "Aboriginal problem" (Morris 1972:61). As Synot (1993:15) notes, "The most graphic image in Tasmanian history remains that of a continuous line of armed invaders marching through the bush, driving tribes of Aboriginals before them into Foresters Peninsula where they were exterminated." In fact, however, the "Black Line," or cordon of military personnel and volunteers that was mounted in the late 1820s, resulted in the capture of only two aboriginals, one of whom was a small boy and the other of whom escaped shortly afterward (Morris 1972:66–67; Tatz 1991:97). As colonial forces discovered, it was not easy to eliminate hunter-gatherers, since they tended to stay in remote areas, were often widely dispersed across the landscape, and were eminently familiar with their surroundings.

The number of indigenous people in Tasmania did decline precipitously, from an estimated five thousand at the time of first contact with Europeans in 1642 to some three hundred in 1830 (Diamond 1993:57). Some of them died from disease, but substantial numbers died at the hands of colonists who shot them on sight, poisoned them, caught them in steel traps and then killed them with swords, and dashed out the brains of their children (Turnbull 1948:39–42). Aboriginal women were raped, men were emasculated, and children were captured and forced into slavery. Many of those who managed to survive the mistreatment, disease, and starvation were rounded up in the early 1830s and forcibly relocated to Flinders Island, where the majority of them died. With the death in 1876 of Truganini, an elderly full-blooded Aboriginal woman who lived her last days in Hobart, the last of Tasmania's aboriginals was gone. As the local newspaper, the *Mercury* noted, "For the first time in human history, dies out the last of a race, a race . . . which never knew the meaning of suffering, wretchedness, and contempt until the English, with their soldiers, bibles, and rum-puncheons, came and dispossessed them of their heritage" (*Mercury*, quoted in Morris 1972:70).

Truganini's mother had been stabbed to death by a European, her sister was raped by sealers, and her husband's hands were cut off; she herself lived her final days fearing that her body would be dissected by scientists (Turnbull 1948:235–36; Morris 1972:69–70). Her last words were, "Don't let them cut me up," and she begged the doctor who was attending her to ensure that she was buried "behind the mountains." After her death, her body was sent to the Tasmanian Museum, where it remained in a box in the basement (Turnbull 1948:236; Morris 1972:70). The descendants of Tasmanian Aboriginals and the people who colonized the island have pressed the government to treat the remains of Tasmania's indigenous peoples with greater respect, but the government continues to maintain that they do not deserve special treatment. Tasmanian Aboriginal spokespersons argue that they themselves were in fact subjected to "special treatment," treatment that was genocidal both in intent and practice.

There have been ongoing debates over the issue of genocide among indigenous peoples. The situation is perhaps best illustrated in the case of the Ache of eastern Paraguay, who were described in the 1970s as the victims of genocidal policies (Munzel 1973, 1974; Lewis 1974; Arens 1976, 1978; Smith and Melia 1979). In the 1870s the Ache were still hunter-gatherers who moved about the landscape in small groups. By the 1940s and 1950s some of the Ache groups were harassed and attacked by Paraguayan colonists (Hill and Hurtado 1995:49). The 1960s saw pacification efforts carried out, and some of the Ache were moved onto reservations.

Efforts were made in the early 1970s to bring additional Ache to the reservations. Munzel (1973, 1974), Lewis (1975), and Arens (1976, 1978) maintain that armed parties were sent out to bring people to the reservations and that violence was very much a part of what were described as "manhunts." According to these reports, men were murdered and women and children enslaved during the course of those operations, which reportedly were mounted from reservations that served essentially as staging grounds for hunts of "wild" Ache. Munzel (1973:24) noted that Ache slavery was not only widespread but that it was also tolerated officially, with prices for Ache Indians on the open market fluctuating between $1.15 and $5.00 apiece during the period up to 1972. Ache and other Indians were considered "inconvenient," especially after roads were built into the forests and land values increased (Arens 1976; Staub 1989:85).

There were disagreements over whether genocide had actually occurred among the Ache, not only on the part of the government of Paraguay and ranchers living in Ache areas but also between two advocacy organizations promoting the rights of indigenous peoples: Cultural Survival, based in Cambridge, Massachusetts; and Survival International, based in London (see Maybury-Lewis and Howe 1980; Survival International 1993). There is no question, however, that the Ache suffered at the hands of others; members of Ache groups were murdered, women were raped, Ache children were kidnapped and sometimes sold, and whole communities were moved onto reservations. The question is, to what extent were those actions carried out or condoned by the Paraguayan state, and was there the intent by the perpetrators to exterminate, in whole or part, the Ache?

Although there were reports that some of the killings and kidnappings of Ache were the work of the Paraguayan military (Munzel 1973, 1974; Arens 1976), others claimed that the state was not involved and that there was no evidence of genocide (Maybury-Lewis and Howe 1980). Hill and Hurtado (1995:168–69) pointed out that most of the killings of Ache occurred in the context of peasants attempting to take over Ache land or to carry out retaliatory actions for livestock or crop theft. They also argued that "*in no case* were armed parties sent out, nor was there any violence or physical coercion involved" in the efforts to get the Ache to move to reservations (Hill and Hurtado 1995:51, emphasis in original). The government of Paraguay rejected the charge of genocide that was leveled against it at the United Nations in March 1974, saying that there was no intention to destroy the Ache as a group (Lewis 1974:62–63). The Paraguayan minister of defense, for example, said, "Although there are victims and victimizer, there is not the third element necessary to establish the crime of genocide—that is 'intent' " (quoted in Kuper 1985:12). Hill and Hurtado (1995:168) concluded, "The Ache contact situation also resulted in extremely high mortality, but this was due to carelessness and incompetence rather than intention, and the contact history is not particularly different from any of hundreds that have taken place in the Amazon over the past two centuries." Clearly, the question of intent is a major issue when it comes to dealing with genocide.

The Ache case underscores the importance of careful documentation of cases and the judicious use of the charge of genocide. Although emotional appeals for better treatment of indigenous peoples are undoubtedly important, they should be backed up with carefully detailed field research, eyewitness testimonies, and analyses of a wide variety of data if they are to be credible and serve the interests of the people affected (Totten 1991; Hill and Hurtado 1995:476–80; Hitchcock and Twedt 1997).

With regard to "the decimation of native peoples in the new continents and states settled by Europeans," Fein (1990:79) argues that demographic studies seldom disentangle the relative importance and interaction of the causes of decline in the number of native peoples, a point also made by Hill and Hurtado (1995:168–69, 476–80). As Fein (1990:79) further notes, there are several causes of such decline, including (a) diseases imported by settlers to which the local population lack immunity; (b) land usurpation and destruction of the indigenous economy; (c) deculturation and demoralization of indigenous group, and alcoholism; (d) wars; and (e) slaughter by the colonists. Today, as Fein points out, we are apt to label the second and third causes as ethnocide and the fifth as genocide (ibid.:79). Fein herself uses what she describes as a "sociological" definition of genocide: "Genocide is sustained purposeful action by a perpetrator to physically destroy a collectivity directly or indirectly, through interdiction of the biological and social reproduction of group members, sustained regardless of the surrender or lack of threat offered by the victim" (ibid.:24). One of the advantages of this definition is that it includes the sustained destruction of non-violent political groups and social classes, something that few others do.

Fein developed a typology of genocide made up of the following four categories: (a) developmental genocide, in which the perpetrator intentionally or unintentionally harms the victims as a result of colonization or economic exploitation; (b) despotic genocide, in which the perpetrator's aim is to rid his domain of any opposition (actual, potential, or imagined) to his rule; (c) retributive genocide, in which the perpetrator responds to a challenge to the structure of domination when two peoples, nations, ethnic groups, tribes, or religious collectives are locked into an ethnically stratified order in a plural society; and (d) ideological genocide, whose causes "are the hegemonic myths identifying the victims as outside the sanctioned universe of obligation or myths based on religion [that] exclude the victim from the sanctified universe of salvation and obligation" (Fein 1984:11, 18). In the case of developmental genocides, Fein addresses both intentional and unintentional consequences. This differs from the United Nations Convention, which addresses only intentional consequences.

It is important to note that the forms of genocide seen among indigenous peoples are diverse and spring from different roots. Smith (1987) sees genocide as a product of war and development. He also notes (ibid. 23) that the Indians of Peru, Paraguay, and Brazil were "destroyed out of cold calculation of gain, and, in some cases, sadistic pleasure rather than as the result of a political or economic crisis." Indigenous peoples are often seen as different from the people in power in society or, in some cases, as competitors.

Kuper (1985:151) is emphatic that a major cause of the destruction of indigenous peoples has been colonization, especially in the "conquest" and "pacification" of indigenous groups. He does remind us, however, that "[s]ome of the annihilations of indigenous peoples arose not so much by deliberate act, but in the course of what may be described as a genocidal process: massacres, appropriation of land, introduction of diseases, and arduous conditions of labor" (Kuper 1988:156). He draws a distinction (1985:150) between what he calls "domestic genocides," those arising from internal divisions within a society, and those genocides that occur in the context of international warfare.

Domestic genocides can be subdivided on the basis of the nature of the victim group and the social contexts in which they are perpetrated (Kuper ibid.:150). Domestic genocides, he says (ibid.:150–55), include the following: (a) those against indigenous peoples; (b) those against what he terms "hostage groups," vulnerable minorities who serve as hostages to the fortunes of the dominant groups in the state; (c) those against groups in a two-tiered state structure following the end of colonialism; and (d) those committed against ethnic, racial, or religious groups seeking power, autonomy or greater equality. The latter type of genocide, according to Kuper (ibid.:155–56), would include the victimization of Guatemala's Indians, who constitute more than half of the country's population.

Cases of genocide in the context of international warfare include those that occurred when the Chinese invaded Tibet and the occupation by Indonesia of East Timor. Kuper (ibid.:157) also cites the atomic bombings of Hiroshima and Nagasaki in 1945 and the widespread destruction caused by the United States in Vietnam, Laos, and Cambodia during the Vietnam War as examples of genocide. Some scholars disagreed adamantly with Kuper that either the atomic bombings or the Vietnam War constituted genocide, since there was arguably no intent on the part of the United States to "destroy, in whole or in part, a national, ethnical, racial or religious group, as such." In light of the fact that political mass murder is not included in the United Nations Convention on Genocide, Kuper (ibid.:26) argued for the reinstatement of political mass murder, in part because that form of mass murder takes substantial numbers of lives and because in some cases political mass murders tend to be tied in with ethnic and religious massacres, the Holocaust being a classic example. Another example of a political mass murder that was brought about by policies that led to starvation is the Soviet treatment of the peoples of the Ukraine (Mace 1997).

Minority groups that are in areas where there is competition for resources frequently face the threat of intimidation, oppression, and destruction, especially if they actively oppose the efforts of outside agencies and individuals (Gurr 1993, 2000; Hitchcock 1997). Kuper (1985:151) sees contemporary small-scale indigenous societies as "the so-called victims of progress, victims, that is, of predatory economic development" (see also Bodley 1999). Smith (1987:24–25) distinguished three types of genocide, one of which, utilitarian genocide, was characterized by indigenous peoples being subjected to "genocidal attacks in the name of progress and development." Not only were the natural resources of indigenous groups exploited, but so, too, were their human resources, with their labor being utilized in the quest for economic profits (International Labour Office 1953). Mistreatment of minorities is a widespread part of genocidal actions (Kuper 1981, 1985; Chalk and Jonassohn 1990).

ETHNOCIDE, GENOCIDE OR VARIATIONS
THEREOF AGAINST INDIGENOUS PEOPLES

Literally scores of indigenous peoples have been and continue to be the victims of ethnocide, genocide, or some variation thereof. A detailed discussion of each of these cases is beyond the scope of this essay, but a table has been generated showing twentieth-century cases of genocide of indigenous peoples (Table 3.1). The table contains cases drawn from a variety of sources, including the *Urgent Action Bulletins* (UABs) of Survival International, reports and publications by the International Work Group for Indigenous Affairs, Cultural Survival, the Minority Rights Group, Human Rights Watch, Amnesty International, Anti-Slavery International, and African Rights, as well as from overviews of the situations of indigenous groups (Burger 1987, 1990; Miller 1993; Wilmer 1993; Maybury-Lewis 1997; Bodley 1999). Key citations have been provided below for readers who want to pursue the study of this issue in more depth.

The cases of twentieth-century genocide cited here represent a number of perspectives held by researchers regarding the fate of the various victim groups. As one will see upon reading the various essays and reports cited, while one scholar may view a particular situation as ethnocide, another may view it as part of a genocidal process, and yet another may perceive it as outright genocide. The latter situation makes it abundantly clear as to why certain scholars are working arduously on the development of new and more exact definitions and typologies of genocide. Until there is at least a general agreement as to what should and should not constitute genocide, there will continue to be a certain degree of murkiness in the field. In light of the ongoing debate and work vis-à-vis definitions, we have made the conscious choice not to categorize each tragedy specifically as either a case of ethnocide, genocide, or genocidal massacre because such decisions could be viewed as somewhat arbitrary. As these cases demonstrate, the genocide of indigenous peoples is a widespread phenomenon, occurring on every continent and in a variety of social, political, economic, and environmental contexts.

In virtually every case, genocide is a calculated and generally premeditated set of actions designed to achieve certain goals, such as the removal of competitors or the silencing of opponents. Indigenous peoples can also be harmed through the destruction of their resource base, as occurred, for example, on the Great Plains of North America with the near-extermination of the buffalo and in the equatorial zones of South America, Africa, and Asia with the purposeful destruction of tropical forests.

TABLE 3.1 Genocides of Indigenous Peoples in the Twentieth Century

Group Name	Country	Date(s)
Africa		
Bubi	Equatorial Guinea	1969–79
Dinka, Nuer	Sudan	1992–93
Herero	Namibia	1904–7
Hutu	Burundi	1972, 1988
Isaak	Somalia	1988–89
Karimojong	Uganda	1979–86
Nuba	Sudan	1991–92
San	Angola, Namibia	1980–90
Tuareg	Mali, Niger	1988–90
Tutsi	Rwanda	1994
Tyua	Zimbabwe	1982–83
Asia and the Pacific		
Armenians	Turkey	1915–18
Atta	Philippines	1987
Auyu	West Papua, Indonesia	1989
Cham	Kampuchea (Cambodia)	1975–79
Dani	Papua New Guinea	1988
H'mong	Laos	1979–86
Kurds	Iraq	1988, 1991
Nasioi	Bougainville, Papua N.G.	1990–91
Tamil	Sri Lanka	1983–86
Tribals	Chittagong Hills, Bangladesh	1979–present
Latin America and the Caribbean		
Ache	Paraguay	1966–76
Arara	Brazil	1992
Cuiva	Colombia	1967–71
Mapuche	Chile	1986
Maya Indians	Guatemala	1964–94
Miskito	Nicaragua	1981–86
Nambiquara	Brazil	1986–87
Nunak	Colombia	1991
Paez	Colombia	1991
Pai Tavytere	Paraguay	1990–91
Ticuna	Brazil	1988
Yanomami	Brazil	1988–89, 1993
North America		
Indians	United States, Canada	1500s–1900s

TYPES OF GENOCIDE INVOLVING INDIGENOUS PEOPLES

For purposes of this chapter, we will distinguish several types of genocide involving indigenous peoples. The first of these is genocide in the context of a struggle between a state and an indigenous group or collectivity of several collaborating groups that are resisting the actions of the state. Neitschmann (1994) has analyzed the conflicts that occur between states and what he terms "nations," those people who perceive themselves as a single entity and who share common ancestry, customs, ideology, language, and territory. Few, if any, nations have willingly given up their land and resources, and some have sought actively to assert their autonomy—sometimes violently, as seen in the cases of the Kurds of Iraq (Saeedpour 1992; Middle East Watch and Physicians for Human Rights 1993), the Maya of the western Highlands of Guatemala (Burger 1987: 76–85; Independent Commission on International Humanitarian Issues 1987:84–87; Montejo 1987; Carmack 1988; Manz 1988; Amnesty International 1992:11–13, 20–22, 43–44; Stoll 1993; Falla 1994), and the Chittagong Hill Tribes of Bangladesh (Chowdhury 1989; Jahan 1997). Gurr (1993:115) has noted that of all the minority group types that he identified, indigenous peoples experienced the greatest proportional increase in the magnitude of conflicts between the 1950s and the 1980s.

Often defined by governments as insurgents, separatists, or terrorists, resisting nations tend to consider themselves freedom fighters or people seeking self-determination. Many of these groups are outnumbered and outgunned by the state, so they resort to guerrilla tactics or civil disobedience. The peoples of West Papua and other areas claimed by Indonesia have been massacred and subjected to severe abuse at the hands of the Indonesian military (Hyndman 1994; Cribb 1997; Dunn 1997). The Isaaks of northern Somalia were treated brutally by Somali government forces, who not only bombed and shot them but also poisoned their wells and utilized a scorched-earth policy to destroy their resource base (Africa Watch 1990; Hitchcock and Twedt 1997). Similar kinds of tactics were used by the Germans against the Hereros in Namibia between 1904 and 1907 (Bridgman 1981; Bridgman and Worley 1997) and against the Nuba, Nuer, Dinka, and other ethnic groups in southern Sudan by the Sudanese government in recent years (African Rights 1995a; Deng 1995; Hutchinson 1996; Human Rights Watch/Africa 1995). The Chechens and members of other ethnic groups (such as the Karachai, Kalmyks, and Ingushi) were summarily rounded up and deported en masse by the Soviet state to exile camps in central Asia, where they faced inhumane conditions (Gurr 1993:190; Legters 1997). In the recent past, the Chechens have been subjected to artillery bombardments, bombings, and infantry operations by the Russian army. In all of these cases, the vast majority of people affected were noncombatants.

Over the past thirty years, tens of thousands of Quiche Maya and other Guatemalan Indians were killed, their villages destroyed, and their crops burned by the Guatemalan military, with the tacit and sometimes active support of the United States government (Carmack 1988; Stoll 1993; Falla 1994). The Guatemalan elite was not prepared to allow Indians to participate in the workings of the government or in local-level decision making. By the late 1970s some of the Indians had joined guerrilla groups that had as their aims the expansion of political participation and the improvement of the lives of peasants. The Guatemalan government responded to the organizational efforts of indigenous peoples and others with repressive tactics. Death squads kidnapped and murdered political leaders. Counterinsurgency operations were launched in the mid-1970s, and by the late 1970s and early 1980s the government was engaged in a full-scale frontal assault against indigenous peoples and peasants in Guatemala.

Indians joined the guerrilla movements not so much because they agreed with their ideology but because they saw such movements as being among the few means available for protecting themselves against the acts of terror perpetrated by the government forces (Carmack 1988). As Stoll (1993:xi) notes, most of the Maya "were rebels against their will, and they were coerced by the guerrillas as well as the army." In February 1996, anthropologists from the Guatemalan Forensic Anthropology Team, human rights workers, and local people excavated a mass grave at Agua Fria, a village in the state of Quiche. This grave is but one of literally dozens of clandestine cemeteries that contain the victims of brutal military operations against Indian peasants who were suspected of providing support for rebels opposed to the government of General Efrain Rios Montt, who ran Guatemala in 1982–83. The mass murders were part of a general campaign on the part of the government to terrorize the populace.

At the height of the Guatemalan civil war, there were as many as forty-five to fifty thousand Quiche Maya refugees living in camps in Mexico. Even there, people were not completely safe. There is evidence of assassins going into the refugee camps in Mexico and killing suspected guerrilla leaders (Victor Montejo, personal communication). Mayan peasants argued that they were "living between two fires" and that they wanted simply to be treated with respect by the government and those with whom they lived in rural Guatemala.

The second type of genocide that we will deal with here is retributive genocide, those actions taken by states or other entities in retribution for their behavior. A classic statement recommending retributive genocide came from a member of Chase Manhattan Bank's Emerging Markets Group, Riordan Roett, who, in January 1995, made the following comment about the Zapatista uprising in southern Mexico: "While Chiapas, in our opinion, does not pose a fundamental threat to Mexican political stability, it is perceived to be so by many in the investment community. The government will need to eliminate the Zapatistas to demonstrate their effective control of the national territory and of security policy" (quoted in the *Washington Post*, February 13, 1995). Amnesty International and other human rights organizations reported on human rights violations by the Mexican army in its efforts to quell the Zapatista uprising in 1994–95. Not only were members of the Zapatista Army of National Liberation (EZLN) killed, but so, too, were noncombatants (Collier and Quaratiello 1999). Although the Zapatistas were not wiped out, other indigenous associations and groups have not been so fortunate, as can be seen in the cases of the Chittagong Hill Tracts of Bangladesh, in Indonesia, and in Burma. It is important to note that of the 120-plus wars that were going on in 1993, 80 percent of them involved Fourth World nations resisting state military forces (Neitschmann 1994:233).

According to representatives of indigenous groups speaking at international forums on indigenous peoples and human rights, people defined as indigenous have experienced mass killings, arbitrary executions, torture, mental and physical mistreatment, arrests and detentions without trial, forced sterilization, involuntary relocation, destruction of their subsistence base, and the removal of children from their families (Ismaelillo and Wright 1982; Veber et al. 1993; Wilmer 1993; Churchill 1997). Some of these actions have been described as genocidal, others as pregenocidal or as situations that potentially could lead to genocide if allowed to continue without any attempts at intervention or alleviation.

Cases claiming genocide of indigenous peoples have been brought before the United Nations, but generally they have brought little result, in part because government representatives claimed that there had been no intent to destroy indigenous peoples as such, and that the groups were never eliminated "as an ethnic or cultural group" (Kuper 1985:12–13). Governments and other agencies usually state that the deaths of indigenous people were an "unintended consequence" of certain actions, such as colonizing remote areas, and that there were no planned efforts to destroy people on the basis of who they were. Indigenous groups in numerous countries, including Guatemala and Bangladesh, have stressed that violations of the right to life in many countries has had a distinctly ethnic or culturally targeted character, no matter what government officials claim.

Military repression of indigenous peoples that resist state-building efforts is not the only context in which conflict-related genocide occurs. Some states have conscripted members of indigenous groups into their armed forces, sometimes at gunpoint. The United States drew upon the services of the Montagnards of Vietnam, while the South African Defense Force drafted members of !Kung, Khwe, and Vasakela San groups in the war against the South West Africa People's Organization (SWAPO) in Angola and Namibia in the 1970s and 1980s. Indeed, the San of southern Africa have been described as "the most militarized ethnic group in the world" (Gordon 1992:2). Although the San have been treated poorly throughout their history (see ibid.; Hitchcock 1996), they did sometimes engage in violent actions against other people. The point here is that indigenous peoples have been and are on both sides of the genocide equation. Simply because one is indigenous does not mean that she or he is incapable of genocidal behavior.

An assumption is sometimes made that hunter-gatherers tended not to engage in genocide. Chalk and Jonassohn (1990:36), for example, state, "It seems unlikely that early man engaged in genocide during the hunting and gathering stage." One of the reasons for this position is that it is assumed that hunter-gatherers tend to be peace-loving peoples and that they preferred to have amicable relations with their neighbors rather than engaging in intergroup conflict. Indeed, there is mounting evidence that indicates that indigenous warfare increased significantly as a result of European expansionism (Ferguson and Whitehead 1992). Judging from the archaeological record, intergroup conflicts were much more common among state systems and settled agriculturalists than was the case among foragers. This should not be taken to mean, however, that genocide was primarily a product of sedentism, agriculture, and the rise of the state. Certainly early foragers had the skills, technology, and presumably the desire to eliminate other people in competitive situations.

Another context in which genocides and massive human rights violations against indigenous peoples occur is where efforts are made to promote social and economic development, often characterized as being "in the national interest." Sometimes called developmental genocides, these kinds of actions occur when states, agencies, companies, or transnational corporations oppress local peoples during the course of implementing various kinds of development projects.

All too frequently, local people have been killed or forced out of development project areas, often with little or no compensation either in the form of alternative land or cash for lost assets (see Table 3.2). The problem has become so widespread, in fact, that a new category of displaced persons has been proposed: "development refugees" (Horowitz 1989, 1991; Scudder 1990). River basin development projects, among other kinds of large-scale efforts, have sometimes employed violent means to ensure compliance on the part of local people. Dam projects such as those along the Narmada River in India, the Rio Negro in Guatemala, and the Manantali Dam on the Senegal River in west Africa witnessed repressive tactics by the companies or agencies involved, including the murder of political activists, disappearances, the shooting of demonstrators, arbitrary arrest, and the torture of detainees (Koening and Horowitz 1992; Human Rights Watch 1992:41–42; Scully 1996; Colajacomo 1999).

There are a number of cases where transnational corporations (TNCs) have allegedly been involved in serious human rights violations against indigenous peoples. These cases range from the actions of mining companies such as Freeport Indonesia, Inc., (FII) in Irian Jaya (West Papua) to oil companies such as Texaco and Maxus in Ecuador (see Table 3.2). Some companies, such as Royal Dutch/Shell in Nigeria, have been accused of being in complicity with governments that are oppressing their own citizens (Human Rights Watch/Africa 1995; Kretzman 1995). Companies have been cited as being guilty of a series of human rights crimes, including assassinations, disappearances, raids and the burning of villages, detentions without trial, torture, purposeful dumping of toxic substances, and intimidation of opponents (Human Rights Watch and Natural Resources Defense Council 1992; Gedicks 1993; Wilmer 1993; Hyndman 1994; Kane 1995; Sachs 1995; Hitchcock 1997). Justifications by company executives for their actions range from their right to protect their assets and the security of their employees to making profits, some of which go to the countries where they operate.

In spite of the fact that human rights concern has become widespread, indigenous peoples have continued to suffer severe abuse. Recent evidence suggests that

TABLE 3.2 Development Projects of Multinational
Corporations (MNCs) That Have Injured Indigenous Peoples'
Well-being and That Have Been Cited as Genocidal or Ethnocidal

Project and Company	Country	Effects
Ecuador Oil Developments (Texaco, Maxus Oil Co., and Conoco, etc.)	Ecuador	Waorani and other Indians forced off land, massive environmental problems with oil spills, poisoning of water, loss of biodiversity
Freeport-MacMoRan Copper and Gold Mining	West Papua (Irian Jaya)	Amungme and other West Papuans dispossessed, crackdowns on local people, ecological destruction, intimidation
Unocal	Burma	Alleged complicity in slavery, forced relocation, torture, murder, and disappearances in the area of a Unocal pipeline
Shell Oil	Nigeria	Development of oil production and refining facilities in the Ogoni region of Nigeria led to habitat destruction, pressure on the Ogoni people by the Nigerian state
Tanzania Wheat Project (CIDA)	Tanzania	Barabaig agropastoralists removed from their lands, harrassed and jailed, denied access to winter grazing
Logging Companies (e.g., Mitsubishi)	Malaysia	Deforestation, dispossession and oppression of resident Penan and other groups
Western Desert Uranium Mining (e.g., Rio Tito Zinc)	Australia	Aboriginals forced out of traditional areas, land and sacred sites affected, some problems with mining residues

NOTE: For additional case material, see Human Rights Watch and Natural Resources Defense Council (1992); Johnston (1994, 1997); Gedicks (1993); Sachs (1995); Hitchcock (1994, 1997); see also the *Multinational Monitor.*

the situations they face are actually getting worse in a number of areas, particularly as economic development reaches into the world's remoter regions (Durning 1992; Hitchcock 1994, 1997, 2000; Bodley 1999).

It is important to note that one of the defenses offered by both government and company officials to charges of genocide is that the killing of indigenous people cannot be defined as genocide if it is done for "economic" reasons (Kuper 1985:13). As one African indigenous leader put it at a March 1996 meeting of the United Nations Human Rights Commission, "We are killed out of greed." The poor treatment of indigenous peoples and the loss of their land has had a series of negative effects, including reduction of their subsistence base, nutritional deprivation, and heightened social tensions, some of which are manifested in higher rates of suicide, as was the case, for example, with the Guarani Kaiowa of Brazil in the late 1980s and 1990s.

Yet another context in which genocides occur is one that is not normally recognized in the human rights and environmental justice communities, conservation-related violations. In many parts of the world, national parks, game reserves, and other kinds of protection areas have been established, often at significant cost to local communities, many of which have been dispossessed as a result. Forced relocation out of conservation areas has all too often exacerbated problems of poverty, environmental degradation, and social conflict. In the course of state efforts to promote conservation, legal restrictions have been placed on hunting and fishing through national legislation. Such legislation not only reduces the access of indigenous peoples to natural resources, it also results in individuals and sometimes whole communities being arrested, jailed, and, in some cases, killed, as has been the case in Africa and Indonesia (Peluso 1993; Hitchcock 1994). Anthropologists have documented these situations and have attempted to pressure governments, international agencies, and environmental organizations to pay more attention to the rights of people exposed to what in effect is coercive conservation.

Genocidal actions also sometimes occur in situations in which there is purposeful environmental destruction. That can be seen, for instance, in cases where herbicides such as Agent Orange were used to clear forests so that counterinsurgency actions could proceed, as was the case in Vietnam. The so-called drug war, orchestrated in part by the U.S. Drug Enforcement Agency (DEA) in countries such as Bolivia, Colombia, and Peru, has had more than its share of human rights violations, some of them arising from raids on local communities and the use of chemicals to destroy coca and marijuana crops. Ecocide, the destruction of ecosystems by states, agencies, or corporate entities, is a problem facing substantial numbers of indigenous and other peoples in many parts of the world (Grinde and Johansen 1995).

Activists opposed to the degradation of the ecosystems have had to contend with efforts by transnational corporations and states to silence them, sometimes violently (Human Rights Watch 1992; Human Rights Watch and Natural Resources Defense Council 1992; Johnston 1994; Sachs 1995:19–23). The 1988 killing of Chico Mendez, the Brazilian rubber tapper who spoke out forcefully against the destruction of the tropical rain forests, and the execution by the Nigerian state of Ken Saro-Wiwa, the head of the Movement for the Survival of the Ogoni People (MOSOP), on November 10, 1995, underscored the dangers faced by environmental activists and the lengths to which their opponents are willing to go.

Anthropologists, too, have been killed for their efforts in behalf of social justice, as occurred in the case of antiapartheid activist David Webster in South Africa. There have also been cases in which anthropologists who served as whistle blowers about projects that were doing harm to indigenous peoples and others lost their jobs or were investigated by agencies ranging from the Federal Bureau of Investigation to the Internal Revenue Service. Advocacy in behalf of indigenous peoples by anthropologists has led to the establishment of human rights organizations aimed at promoting the well-being of indigenous groups, examples being the International Work Group for Indigenous Affairs, founded in Denmark in 1968 by Helge Kleivan and others, and Cultural Survival, Inc., founded by David and Pia Maybury-Lewis and their colleagues in Boston, Massachusetts, in 1972. Anthropologists have also collaborated with indigenous nongovernment organizations in their efforts to promote their rights, as can be seen in the cases of First People of the Kalahari (FPK), a San advocacy organization based in Ghanzi, Botswana, and the Working Group of Indigenous Minorities in Southern Africa (WIMSA), a regional San advocacy and networking organization.

COPING WITH GENOCIDES AGAINST INDIGENOUS PEOPLES

Efforts have been made at the international and the national levels to bring indigenous genocide cases to the attention of both the media and human rights and intergovernmental organizations, including the United Nations. In the 1970s, the United Nations was officially informed of the situations in Paraguay with the Ache and various indigenous groups in Brazil (Kuper 1985:151). Officials from both Paraguay and Brazil vehemently denied that their governments were responsible for genocide. Such was the case in 1969, when the Brazilian representative to the United Nations said that although Indians in Brazil had been "eliminated," it was done "for exclusively economic reasons, the perpetrators having acted solely to take possession of the lands of their victims" (United Nations Human Rights Communication no. 478, September 29, 1969, quoted in Kuper 1985:151). In other words, the killings of Brazilian Indians were not genocide because the purpose of the actions was economic. Economically motivated destruction of indigenous peoples has been and is a serious problem in Brazil (Davis 1977; Ramos and Taylor 1979; Bay 1984; American Anthropological Association 1991; Amnesty International 1992; Colby and Dennett 1995). Although wide-ranging efforts have been made to promote the rights of Brazilian Indians by indigenous communities, advocacy organizations, and human rights groups, their socioeconomic status continues to decline in many areas.

In August 1993 there was an international outcry over the killings of Yanomami (Yanomamo) Indians by gold miners on the Venezuela-Brazil border (Chagnon

1993a–c; Albert 1994; Ramos 1995). When it was learned that the number of people shot and dismembered was "only" sixteen, international interest in the case waned. Subsequently, when charges were traded about possible complicity on the part of social scientists and missionaries in the processes that led up to the massacre, public interest was piqued again, but it subsided after the governments of Brazil and Venezuela argued that the situation was not as bad as had been claimed.

The governments of countries in which indigenous peoples face severe human rights problems routinely deny that the situation is as bad as is portrayed in the media, by advocacy groups, or by the oral testimonies of individuals claiming violation of human rights. The same is true of those private companies in areas where indigenous peoples are being affected by development and environmental change. It should be emphasized that there are frequently serious conflicts of interest between states and private companies operating inside their borders. In the 1980s and early 1990s, the United Nations Economic and Social Council Commission on Transnational Corporations drew up a Code of Conduct for transnational corporations, but as of early 1999 the code had yet to be implemented.

There has been marked opposition to indigenous peoples' efforts to re-establish their land and resource rights, not only from states but also from private companies seeking access to minerals and other resources. Today, some of the greatest problems faced by indigenous groups in terms of land and resource rights derive from transnational corporations, private companies, and individuals who are pressuring governments to reduce their efforts in behalf of indigenous land rights, as can be seen, for example, in Australia, Brazil, and Mexico.

Efforts are being made by intergovernmental organizations, indigenous associations, development and human rights–oriented nongovernmental organizations, and interested individuals to draw up guidelines for development and conservation project implementation that protect both local people and their ecosystems. The problem with many of these guidelines, however, is that they rarely, if ever, are enforced. Although detailed international standards have been established for handling the resettlement of people affected by large-scale infrastructure projects (see, for example, World Bank 1991), there are few cases in which all or even most of the steps have been followed. The result has been that a majority of the people who have been forcibly relocated, numbering in the tens of millions, have ended up much worse off after relocation (Scully 1996; Scudder 1997a, 1997b; World Commission on Dams 2000).

There have been few cases where companies or development agencies have been required to change their tactics or to follow international standards. As yet there are no internationally accepted principles by which companies, development institutions, or conservation organizations must operate. The consequence is that indigenous groups face major problems.

In response, indigenous groups have begun to organize among themselves in an effort to oppose genocidal practices and promote human rights (Durning 1992; Wilmer 1993; Hitchcock and Biesele 2000). How successful these efforts will be very much depends on whether private companies, intergovernmental organizations, states, and nongovernment organizations are willing to (a) come up with strict internationally recognized human rights and environmental standards, (b) monitor development and conservation activities as they are implemented, and (c) enforce those standards.

Lawsuits have been filed by indigenous groups and their supporters against multinational corporations. In 1993, a group of lawyers in New York filed a $1 billion lawsuit against Texaco on behalf of the Huaorani Indians of Ecuador. In 1996 lawyers representing citizens of Burma filed a lawsuit in a U.S. federal court that alleged complicity on the part of the oil company Unocal in human rights abuses in an area of Burma where a natural gas pipeline was being built. The charges included complicity in enslavement of people, forced relocation, torture, murder, and intimidation of opponents of the pipeline (Strider 1995; Bray 1999). These lawsuits could set a legal precedent whereby environmental and human rights violations can be prosecuted under international law in the United States. What this would mean, in effect, is that private companies could be held to the same standards as governments. It may be necessary, in our opinion, to charge the chief executive officers (CEOs) of some of the world's major corporations with crimes against humanity and try them in a duly constituted and independent international court.

Publicizing the names of companies involved in human rights violations is helpful, and efforts are ongoing along those lines, with the assistance of a number of nongovernment organizations, some of which publicize the actions of multinationals on the worldwide web and in other forums. Nongovernment organizations and stockholder groups have called for the organization of boycotts and the imposition of sanctions on those companies involved in systematic human rights violations. It is only when company profits and stock values begin to decrease that efforts will be made to curb the kinds of systematic mistreatment of indigenous peoples that are so commonplace in many parts of the world today.

GENOCIDE EARLY WARNING SYSTEMS

Over the past decade or so, numerous scholars have begun working on what are commonly referred to as genocide early warning systems (GEWS) (Charny 1984, 1991, 1999:253–61; Kuper 1985:218–28, 1991; Whitaker 1985:41–45; Totten and Parsons 1991). These are systems that identify criteria for detecting conditions that increase the possibility of genocide. Their goal is to bring world attention to a potentially genocidal situation so that an objective outside agency can intervene. Such a system would be useful in many ways, but for indigenous groups it would be especially important, given that many of them are exposed to genocidal actions with little or no outside monitoring and limited channels of communication to the outside world.

Totten (1991) has suggested that a key component of any early warning system should be the collection and analysis of eyewitness accounts of events that might be leading up to a genocide, or of particular genocidal acts themselves. As Totten (ibid.: lvii) pointed out, "Time and again throughout this [the twentieth] century, some of the first warnings that a genocidal act was taking place were the appearance of first-person accounts by members of the victim group who either managed to escape or smuggle out reports, and/or accounts by other witnesses (e.g., journalists, consular officials, relief workers)." Besides eyewitness accounts, there are other indications of potential genocides, including increased rates of beatings, killings, kidnappings, and disappearances, and heightened refugee flows.

The threats facing indigenous peoples include the lack of efforts on the part of states and regional governments that contribute to the insecurity of indigenous peoples; these would include incomplete demarcation of reserve areas, failure to prosecute individuals or companies that enter reserves that have been legally gazetted, and allowing individuals or groups that have committed human rights violations against indigenous people to get away with their crimes. Preconditions for genocide include rising numbers of arrests, extrajudicial executions, disappearances, and heated rhetoric in the media, all of which were seen, for example, in the cases of Burundi and, more recently, Rwanda (African Rights 1995b; Neier 1998). Coming up with detailed assessments of the factors that result in genocides is crucial if these crimes are to be predicted.

We, along with Whitaker (1985:44), support the establishment of an international body to deal with genocide. Such a body could have a section that analyzes data on potential genocides and be empowered with the authority to bring any urgent situations to the attention of the secretary-general of the United Nations and other appropriate institutions.

In October 1992, the United Nations Security Council agreed, albeit somewhat reluctantly, to undertake a formal investigation into the allegations concerning death camps, ethnic cleansing, and mass rape in Bosnia. The panel, known as the Commission of Experts, was aimed in part at preparing the way for a war crimes tribunal. The War Crimes Tribunal was established in 1993, the first time such a tribunal had been set up since the trials held in Nuremberg and Japan following World War II. There has been a certain amount of reluctance on the part of the United Nations leadership to pursue high-level individuals as war criminals, but the tribunal is now issuing indictments. Indictments have also now been issued by the International Tribunal for Rwanda (ICTR). We hope that both of these tribunals will follow through on prosecution of those responsible for genocide and war crimes.

Anthropologists and archaeologists can play significant roles in predicting, documenting, and investigating pregenocidal and genocidal situations. Anthropologists sometimes find themselves in situations where they witness violence and poor treatment of people (Nordstrom and Robben 1995). Some of them have recorded their observations carefully and made them available to human rights organizations and to the media. Others have shared information on government plans that might affect local people, and some have assisted in organizing resistance efforts. Careful documentation of allegedly genocidal actions with the use of archaeological and forensic techniques has been done in Argentina, Chile, Guatemala, El Salvador, the Philippines, Ethiopia, Iraq, the former Yugoslavia, Haiti, Rwanda, and, recently, Zimbabwe (Geiger and Cook-Deegan 1993; Middle East Watch and Physicians for Human Rights 1993; Haglund and Sorg 1997; Stover and Peress 1998). The information obtained during the course of these activities can and will serve as part of the evidence for pursuit of human rights cases by courts and the International War Crimes Tribunals (for example, those for the former Yugoslavia and for Rwanda). The American Association for the Advancement of Science (AAAS), Physicians for Human Rights (PHR), Human Rights Watch, the Minnesota Lawyers International Human Rights Committee, and regional teams of forensic anthropologists, lawyers, and medical personnel collaborate in carrying out investigations, conducting workshops, and doing training exercises for people involved in the examination of instances of suspicious deaths.

GENOCIDE, ANTHROPOLOGY, AND EDUCATION

It is of the utmost necessity for university and secondary school curricula not to focus solely on genocidal acts themselves but also on the preconditions of genocide, as well as methods of intervention and prevention, including the role of individuals acting alone and in concert with others. A primary purpose of holding up clear examples of the abuse of human rights is to encourage people to look seriously at events and deeds in their own lives and the world about them that may increase the likelihood of bigotry and the possibility for violence.

The most effective pedagogy on genocide helps students think about issues such as the use and abuse of power, the implications of a society that violates civil and human rights, and the role and responsibilities of individuals, groups, and nations when confronting human rights violations and genocidal acts. Examining these issues can broaden students' understanding of key concepts and concerns, such as racism, prejudice, discrimination, blind obedience, loyalty, conflict, conflict resolution, decision making, justice, prevention, intervention, and survival, all of which can be useful when considering what constitutes responsible citizenship. If that is not done, the study is little more than an academic exercise.

If students at all levels of schooling across the globe are going to be reached effectively, then something more—much more—than traditional curricula and instructional efforts are needed. An all-out, well-coordinated educational and outreach effort is required, one that involves those groups working on the behalf of victims of genocide as well as those groups working on various genocidal and human rights issues, in conjunction with pedagogical experts. Working together, those three groups, we believe, could not only produce outstanding curricular materials but could also reach students in a way that has not been attempted thus far.

The protection of individuals and groups who are different is very much a contemporary issue, and students should be presented with opportunities (if they so desire) to move from studying and thinking to becoming actively involved in intervention and prevention work. The efforts of Amnesty International, the international human rights organization that was the recipient of the Nobel Prize for Peace in 1977, to involve students in human rights work is both admirable and something that could be emulated by other organizations working to protect indigenous peoples and other victims of discrimination and genocidal acts. The strength of such programs is that they provide students with an outstanding reason for studying human rights issues. It helps them appreciate the fact that human rights are not givens but something that must be protected. Likewise, it informs them about why and how human rights infractions are committed across the globe, and how individuals can work together to ameliorate these situations.

International Alert Against Genocide and Mass Killing (which has its headquarters in London) was established as a response to the realization that groups were not being protected against genocide and that there seemed to be an increasing incidence of the crime. It seeks "to promote awareness and a commitment to preventive action through teaching and research and by sounding international alerts on threatening crises in inter-group relations" (Leo Kuper, personal communication, August 10, 1990). Put another way, "it is the action component complementing the educational work" (Kuper, personal communication, May 29, 1991). This organization makes representations in the conventional channels (such as aid agencies, governments, and international organizations), but it also tries to explore new channels for effective action.

History demonstrates that encounters between indigenous peoples or ethnic minorities and other groups, states, and development agencies often culminate in indigenous peoples or minorities being stripped of their culture, physically decimated, or both. In light of that, the following comment by Irving Horowitz is worthy of considerable thought: "Genocide is always a conscious choice and policy. It is never just an accident of history or a necessity imposed by unseen economic growth requirements. Genocide is always and everywhere an essentially political decision" (Horowitz 1980:38). To some extent, the lack of awareness by the "average person" about the conditions of indigenous peoples is reminiscent of many of the conclusions reached by Michael Harrington (1963) in his book *The Other America*, which helped to bring the issue of poverty in the United States to the forefront of many peoples' minds. In his opening chapter, Harrington puts forth his main theme when he states: "The millions who are poor in the United States tend to become increasingly invisible. Here is a great mass of people, yet it takes an effort of the intellect and will even to see them" (ibid.:10). Like the poor that make up the "other America," the indigenous peoples of the world today are generally invisible, isolated, "off the beaten track," powerless, and "slipping out" of our "very experience and consciousness" (ibid.:11–13).

Anthropologists have worked extensively on marginalized groups and segments of society. They have examined poverty and underdevelopment; the causes and consequences of conflict, warfare, and genocide; and policies of separate development and differential treatment of groups on the basis of ethnicity, class, or background; they also have firsthand information on what happens to groups and individuals under stress. This material can be drawn upon in the development of university and secondary school curricula and case studies for workshops and training sessions relating to human rights, social justice, and equity. It can also be used in courses and programs on conflict resolution and conflict management. Having a better understanding of the roots of prejudice, discrimination, ethnic identity formation and manipulation, nationalism, and genocide will go a long way toward helping alleviate the conditions that bring about human rights violations and destruction of individuals, groups, and cultures.

CONCLUSIONS

When we read the lists of peoples that have been and are being destroyed, it is easy to forget that behind the names of these indigenous groups are unprotected mothers, fathers, children, grandparents—indeed, entire families. Awareness of this victimization and injustice forces us to make choices. Some of us choose to ignore and avoid the information, others strive to learn more, and still others search for ways to intervene or to prevent these events and deeds from happening. In this chapter we have attempted to analyze some of the major issues surrounding genocide and ethnocide as they affect indigenous peoples. We have stressed the need for genocide prediction and prevention efforts, as well as the need to intervene in situations where genocide might occur. We believe strongly that more work is needed on defining genocide. The fact that governments and other agencies have denied engaging in genocide while at the same time carrying out serious human rights violations underscores the need for modifications to the definition of genocide in the Genocide Convention.

Fein (1990:82) has addressed the crucial need for delineating clear policies for the protection and enhancement of the well-being of indigenous peoples:

> It seems wise . . . to me to have clear conceptual standards, discriminating specific policies and ways of monitoring the operation of state and settlers—laws, administration, equal justice, land settlement, health and educational services—so that we can assess both intentions and effects on indigenous peoples, rather than to label all population decline as a result of genocide and assume the inevitability of decimation of indigenous peoples. (Fein ibid.)

There is a clear need to document cases carefully and to come up with quantitative as well as qualitative analyses of the effects on indigenous peoples of actions by states, agencies, corporations, and other entities.

It would be useful, as Fein (ibid.) notes, to draw up a convention on ethnocide and lay out in very specific terms what the various obligations are of states in protecting the rights of indigenous peoples. Such a convention would be important because there are problems with the current Genocide Convention and with the United Nations' role in preventing genocides.

Many of these problems lie in the convention itself. First, the definition itself is lacking in clarity. Second, the convention concentrates primarily on punishment rather than prevention. Third, the lack of enforcement has meant that the Genocide Convention can be ignored by states and individuals without fear of retribution. Many states are reluctant to pursue genocide cases because they take the position that these situations are "internal matters"; taking strong action might be viewed as denying self-determination and states' rights. However, as Whitaker (1985:35) notes, genocide should be made a matter of universal jurisdiction. Only in that way will governments be held accountable for their actions.

Among the most important efforts to achieve the protection of the rights of indigenous peoples are those of various indigenous groups themselves. Indigenous groups today are "organizing to survive," as one San put it. Their actions are important for a number of key reasons. First of all, the efforts are a classic case of self-determination. The groups know what they need and desire, and they are working toward those goals, some on an individual basis and some collectively. Second, these actions, while not always successful, serve to provide important experience for indigenous groups, and they may serve to increase their knowledge and potential effectiveness. Third, they often serve to enhance the organizational capacity of the groups because they often require them to try various decision-making, participation, and leadership strategies. Fourth, the efforts, if successful even marginally, provide individuals and groups with much-needed self-confidence in the face of adversity.

Although most of these groups eventually come face to face with forces that are beyond their control, they are better equipped to cope with them for having attempted to mobilize themselves. The fact that they are forming coalitions and communicating more effectively through the electronic media and other means is indicative of their desire to establish broad-based networks and information dissemination mechanisms.

That said, one still needs to be circumspect in regard to what has been and still needs to be accomplished. For example, while it is certainly true that indigenous groups are making steady progress, it is also a fact that there are individual governments, big businesses, certain church organizations, and others that are doing everything in their power to circumvent the efforts and progress being made by indigenous groups within their realm of power or interest. What needs to be done by indigenous groups and nonindigenous organizations that support them is to form strong networks and coalitions that will work toward the same goals in the most efficacious manner. It can be hoped that such efforts will prevent factions from being formed and will lead to a more cohesive and stronger movement for the protection of all indigenous peoples.

Encouraging representatives of governments and indigenous peoples to reach agreement on international standards for protecting indigenous peoples is an ongoing task of the Working Group on Indigenous Populations of the United Nations, which is made up of representatives of indigenous peoples and groups that work with them (International Work Group for Indigenous Affairs 1999). Although broad agreement has been reached on many issues, there still exist many areas of dispute. Some of the most serious of these conflicts relate to protection of the land and resource rights of indigenous peoples, the recognition of collective rights, and the right to self-determination.

There are literally dozens of organizations and associations working on indigenous rights' issues. A major strength of these organizations is that they serve as advocates for those people who often find themselves voiceless or powerless against governments or business interests that encroach upon their land, threaten their way of life, or endanger their lives (Burger 1987; Durning 1992; Maybury-Lewis 1997; Hitchcock 1997). These organizations also assist those indigenous groups that are active on their own behalf in reaching a larger constituency or power base. In doing so they conduct research into the needs of and problems faced by indigenous peoples, serve as advocates for the groups in international and national meetings and governmental and nongovernmental forums, and educate the general public about the situation of indigenous peoples. In recent years, greater efforts have been made by these advocacy groups to get involved in human rights investigations and promotion of health, nutrition, and development activities that enhance the well-being of indigenous groups. All of these efforts will go a long way toward reducing the problems facing indigenous peoples.

Whitaker (1985:42) asserts that research on the causes and prevention of genocide "could help form one part of a wide educational program throughout the world against such aberrations [that is, genocide], starting at an early age in schools." To fail to educate students and the public at large about genocide, including the fate of indigenous peoples across the globe who have to face this crime, has, we believe, profound ramifications. To ignore genocide is to distort history. To talk about the conquest of the New World, colonialism in the Americas, or the confrontation between indigenous peoples and "technological advancement" today without discussing genocide is to present a false or sanitized picture of the way changes have occurred over time.

It is heartening to note that a growing number of communities are beginning to include the study of genocide in their curricula (Totten and Parsons 1991; Charny 1999). At present, twenty states in the United States recommend the teaching of the Holocaust and genocide. However, in spite of the surge in the study of genocide and the use of materials on genocide in schools, the level of understanding of the causes and consequences of genocide and human rights violations on the part of the public is limited at best.

The vast majority, if not all, of the curricula developed on genocide for use in schools do not address the plight of most indigenous peoples other than Native Americans and the Armenians in any systematic way. Even those students who do study some aspect of genocide still cannot intelligently discuss what it is that constitutes genocide, the preconditions and consequences of any genocide, or methods of intervention and prevention: those kinds of issues are not underscored in the curricula or the media. In addition, to a large extent, most of the current curricula available on genocide are not of a particularly high quality, although that situation is changing.

A particular area of concern among indigenous peoples as it relates to genocide and human rights violations is gender-related violence. Representatives of women's organizations, indigenous associations, and human rights groups have argued that rape and sexual assault should be considered crimes against humanity. Mass rape was used as a strategy to terrorize people in the former Yugoslavia (Stiglmayer 1994). Aboriginal women were raped and sexually abused by settlers in Tasmania and Australia (Turnbull 1948), as were Ache women in Paraguay (Munzel 1973, 1974; Arens 1976), American Indian women in the United States (Dunbar Ortiz 1984; Jaimes 1992; Churchill 1997), and Somali women, a number of whom were in refugee camps, in the Horn of Africa (Africa Watch 1989). The declaration of rape and sexual abuse as crimes against humanity will, in the opinion of indigenous leaders and others, result in greater efforts to deter gender-related violence both in wartime and peacetime.

If students and the public are to have greater knowledge of the plight of indigenous peoples, deprivation of human rights, and the causes and consequences of genocide, scholars in such fields as anthropology, history, sociology, political science, law, and genocide studies are going to have to work with teachers and school administrators to convince them of the necessity for addressing such concerns as well as to assist them in developing accurate content and pedagogically sound curricula. Scholars, indigenous groups and their supporters, and nongovernmental organizations need to assist educators in choosing cases that contribute significantly to an understanding of the survival problems facing indigenous peoples. An in-depth approach to well-documented cases encourages students and the public to develop more careful distinctions when making comparative generalizations, and it helps them to refrain from offering simple answers to complex human behavior.

For intervention and prevention of genocide and ethnocide against indigenous peoples to succeed, better progress needs to take place in increasing our level of awareness, in encouraging the citizens of the world to care, and in overcoming denial. For the most part, governments do not acknowledge or take responsibility for their genocidal acts, past or present, and most citizens would like to avoid dealing with ugly events and deeds perpetrated by their nation or others. Unfortunately, denial is reinforced because the historical record demonstrates that perpetrators of ethnocide or genocide are seldom brought to trial. A case in point is the fact that even the perpetrators of major twentieth-century genocides have escaped justice. Investigations of cases of alleged genocide and prosecution of the perpetrators would help to ensure that others will be less likely to engage in such actions in the future.

Resolving complex problems and injustices requires multiple approaches. Scholars need to continue grappling with the multitude of criteria and distinctions that help to define, understand, and prevent genocide and ethnocide. Educators need to learn about what has and is happening to indigenous peoples, and they need to develop strategies for bringing these lessons to their students in order to give intervention and prevention a real chance in the future. Activists need to keep involving others, expanding their efforts, and confronting those who violate the rights and freedoms of indigenous peoples.

The international business community needs to take further steps to develop a code of business ethics that protects the rights of people in areas where businesses are operating. Governments must live up to their obligation to protect indigenous peoples and not compromise their rights under the weight of so-called progress, economic growth, or nationalism. Finally, all institutions, whether states, corporations, nongovernment organizations, or indigenous support groups, need to work together to promote the rights not just of indigenous peoples but also of all human beings.

REFERENCES CITED

Adelman, Howard, and Astri Suhrke. 1996. "Early Warning and Response: Why the International Community Failed to Prevent the Rwanda Genocide." *Disasters* 20(3):295–304.
Africa Watch. 1989. *Zimbabwe, A Break with the Past? Human Rights and Political Unity.* New York and Washington, D.C.: Africa Watch Committee.
——. 1990. *Somalia: A Government at War with Its Own People: Testimonies about the Killings and the Conflict in the North.* New York: Human Rights Watch.
African Rights. 1995a. *Facing Genocide: The Nuba of Sudan.* London: African Rights.
——. 1995b. *Rwanda: Death, Despair, and Defiance.* London: African Rights.
——. 1996. *Rwanda: Killing the Evidence: Murders, Attacks, Arrests, and Intimidation of Survivors and Witnesses.* London: African Rights.
——. 1999. *Rwanda: The Insurgency in the Northwest.* London: African Rights.
Akhavan, Payyam. "Justice and Reconciliation in the Great Lakes Region of Africa: The Contribution of the International Criminal Tribunal for Rwanda." *Duke Journal of Comparative and International Law* 7:325–48.
Albert, Bruce. 1994. "Gold Miners and Yanomami Indians in the Brazilian Amazon: The Hashimu Massacre." In *Who Pays the Price? The Sociocultural Context of Environmental Crisis.* Barbara Rose Johnston, ed. Pp. 47–55. Washington D.C.: Island Press.
American Anthropological Association. 1991. *Report of the Special Commission to Investigate the Situation of the Brazilian Yanomami, June, 1991.* Washington, D.C.: American Anthropological Association.
Amnesty International. 1992. *Human Rights Violations against Indigenous Peoples of the Americas.* New York: Amnesty International.
Arens, Richard. 1978. *The Forest Indians in Stroessner's Paraguay: Survival or Extinction?* Survival International Document Series, No. 4. London: Survival International.
Arens, Richard, ed. 1976. *Genocide in Paraguay.* Philadelphia: Temple University Press.
Barta, Tony. 1987. "Relations of Genocide: Land and Lives in the Colonization of Australia." In *Genocide and the Modern Age: Etiology and Case Studies of Mass Death.* Isidor Walliman and Michael N. Dobkowski, eds. Pp. 237–51. Westport, Conn.: Greenwood Press.
Bay, Christian. 1984. "Human Rights on the Periphery: No Room in the Ark for the Yanomami?" *Development Dialogue* 1(2):23–41.

Biesele, Megan, and Robert K. Hitchcock. 2000. "The Ju/'hoansi San under Two States: Impacts of the South West African Administration and the Government of the Republic of South Africa." In *Hunters and Gatherers in the Modern World: Conflict, Resistance and Self-Determination.* Peter P. Schweitzer, Megan Biesele, and Robert K. Hitchcock, eds. Pp. 305–26. New York: Berghahn Books.

Bodley, John H. 1999. *Victims of Progress.* 4th ed. Mountain View, Calif.: Mayfield.

Bray, John. 1999. "Petroleum and Human Rights: The New Frontiers of Debate." *Oil and Gas Journal* (Nov. 1):65–69.

Bridgman, J. M. 1981. *The Revolt of the Hereros.* Berkeley: University of California Press.

Bridgman, Jon, and Leslie H. Worley. 1997. "Genocide of the Hereros." In *Century of Genocide: Eyewitness Accounts and Critical Views.* Samuel Totten, William S. Parsons, and Israel W. Charny, eds. Pp. 3–40. New York: Garland Publishing.

Burger, Julian. 1987. *Report from the Frontier: The State of the World's Indigenous Peoples.* London: Zed Press.

———. 1990. *The Gaia Atlas of First Peoples: A Future for the Indigenous World.* New York: Anchor Books.

Carmack, Robert M., ed. 1988. *Harvest of Violence: The Maya Indians and the Guatemalan Crisis.* Norman: University of Oklahoma Press.

Chagnon, Napoleon A. 1993a. "Anti-Science and Native Rights: Genocide of the Yanomami." *Human Behavior and Evolution Society Newsletter* 2(3):1–4.

———. 1993b. "Covering up the Yanomamo Massacre." *New York Times Op-Ed,* Saturday, October 23, 1993, p. 13.

———. 1993c. "Killed by Kindness? The Dubious Influence of the Salesian Missions in Amazonas." *Times Literary Supplement,* December 24, 1993, pp. 11–12.

Chalk, Frank. 1989. "Definitions of Genocide and Their Implications for Prediction and Prevention." *Holocaust and Genocide Studies* 4(2):149–60.

Chalk, Frank, and Kurt Jonassohn. 1990. *The History and Sociology of Genocide: Analyses and Case Studies.* New Haven: Yale University Press.

Charny, Israel W. 1985. "Genocide: The Ultimate Human Rights Problem." *Social Education* 49(6):448–52.

———. 1988. "The Study of Genocide." In *Genocide: A Critical Bibliographic Review.* Israel W. Charny, ed. Pp. 1–19. New York: Facts on File.

———. 1991. "Genocide: Intervention and Prevention." *Social Education* 55(2):124–27.

———. 1997. "Which Genocide Matters More? Learning to Care about Humanity." In *Century of Genocide: Eyewitness Accounts and Critical Views.* Samuel Totten, William S. Parsons, and Israel W. Charny, eds. Pp. xii–xix. New York: Garland Publishing.

Charny, Israel W., ed. 1984. *Toward the Understanding and Prevention of Genocide: Proceedings of the International Conference on the Holocaust and Genocide.* Boulder, Colo.: Westview Press.

———. 1999. *Encyclopedia of Genocide.* 2 vols. Santa Barbara, Calif.: ABC-CLIO.

Chowdhury, Akram H. 1989. "Self-Determination, the Chittagong, and Bangladesh." In *Human Rights and Development: International Views.* David P. Forsythe, ed. Pp. 292–301. New York: St. Martin's Press.

Churchill, Ward. 1997. *A Little Matter of Genocide: Holocaust and Denial in the Americas, 1492 to the Present.* San Francisco: City Lights Books.

Clay, Jason. 1984. "Genocide in the Age of Enlightenment." *Cultural Survival Quarterly* 12(3):1.

————. 1993a. "Hunger among Indigenous Peoples." In *Hunger 1993: Uprooted People, Third Annual Report on the State of World Hunger.* Marc J. Cohen, ed. Pp. 48–52. Washington, D.C.: Bread for the World Institute on Hunger and Development.

————. 1993b. "Looking Backward to Go Forward: Predicting and Preventing Human Rights Violations." In *State of the Peoples: A Global Human Rights Report on Societies in Danger.* Marc S. Miller, ed., with Cultural Survival. Pp. 64–71. Boston: Beacon Press.

————. 1994. "Resource Wars: Nation and State Conflicts of the Twentieth Century." In *Who Pays the Price? The Sociocultural Context of Environmental Crisis.* Barbara Rose Johnston, ed. Pp. 19–30. Covelo, Calif.: Island Press.

Colajamoco, Jaroshava. 1999. "The Chixoy Dam: The Aya Achi Genocide: The Story of Forced Resettlement." In *Dams, Indigenous Peoples, and Ethnic Minorities.* Marcus Colchester, ed. *Indigenous Affairs* 3–4/99. Pp. 64–78. Copenhagen: International Work Group for Indigenous Affairs.

Colby, Gerard, with Charlotte Dennett. 1995. *Thy Will Be Done: The Conquest of the Amazon— Nelson Rockefeller and Evangelism in the Age of Oil.* New York: HarperCollins.

Collier, George A., with Elizabeth Lowery Quaratiello. 1999. *Basta! Land and the Zapatista Rebellion in Chiapas.* 2d ed. Oakland, Calif.: Food First Books.

Cribb, Robert. 1997. "The Indonesian Massacres." In *Century of Genocide: Eyewitness Accounts and Critical Views.* Samuel Totten, William S. Parsons, and Israel W. Charny, eds. Pp. 236–63. New York: Garland Publishing.

Dadrian, Vahakn N. 1975. "A Typology of Genocide." *International Review of Modern Sociology* 5:201–12.

Davis, Shelton H. 1977. *Victims of the Miracle: Development and the Indians of Brazil.* Cambridge: Cambridge University Press.

Deng, Francis M. 1995. *War of Visions: Conflict of Identities in the Sudan.* Washington, D.C.: Brookings Institution.

Diamond, Jared. 1993. "Ten Thousand Years of Solitude." *Discover* (March):48–57.

Dunbar Ortiz, Roxanne. 1984. *Indians of the Americas: Human Rights and Self-Determination.* London: Zed Books.

Dunn, James. 1997. "Genocide in East Timor." In *Century of Genocide: Eyewitness Accounts and Critical Views.* Samuel Totten, William S. Parsons, and Israel W. Charny, eds. Pp. 264–90. New York: Garland Publishing.

Durning, Alan C. 1992. *Guardians of the Land: Indigenous Peoples and the Health of the Earth.* Washington, D.C.: WorldWatch Institute.

Falla, Ricardo. 1994. *Massacres in the Jungle: Ixcan, Guatemala, 1975–1982.* Boulder, Colo.: Westview Press.

Fein, Helen. 1984. "Scenarios of Genocide: Models of Genocide and Critical Responses." In *Toward the Understanding and Prevention of Genocide: Proceedings of the International Conference on the Holocaust and Genocide.* Israel W. Charny, ed. Pp. 3–31. Boulder, Colo.: Westview Press.

————. 1990. "Genocide: A Sociological Perspective." *Current Sociology* 38(1):1–126.

————. 1994. "Genocide, Terror, Life Integrity, and War Crimes: The Case for Discrimination." In *Genocide: Conceptual and Historical Dimensions.* George J. Andreopoulos, ed. Pp. 95–107. Philadelphia: University of Pennsylvania Press.

Fein, Helen, ed. 1994. *The Prevention of Genocide: Rwanda and Yugoslavia Reconsidered.* New York: Institute for the Study of Genocide.

Forsythe, David P. *Human Rights in International Relations.* Cambridge: Cambridge University Press, 2000.

Gedicks, Al. 1993. *The New Resource Wars: Native and Environmental Struggles against Multinational Corporations.* Boston: South End Press.

Geiger, Jack H., and Robin Cook-Deegan. 1993. "The Role of Physicians in Conflicts and Humanitarian Crises: Case Studies from the Field Missions of Physicians for Human Rights, 1988 to 1933." *Journal of the American Medical Association* 270:616–20.

Gordon, Robert J. 1992. *The Bushman Myth: The Making of a Namibian Underclass.* Boulder, Colo.: Westview Press.

Grinde, Donald A., and Bruce E. Johansen. 1995. *Ecocide of Native North America: Environmental Destruction of Indian Lands and Peoples.* Santa Fe, N.M.: Clear Light Publishers.

Gurr, Ted Robert. 1993. *Minorities at Risk: A Global View of Ethnopolitical Conflicts.* Washington, D.C.: U.S. Institute of Peace Press.

————. 2000. *Peoples versus States: Minorities at Risk in the New Century.* Washington, D.C.: United States Institute of Peace Press.

Haglund, William D., and Marcella H. Sorg. 1997. *Forensic Taphonomy: The Postmortem Fate of Human Remains.* Boca Raton, Fla.: CRC Press.

Harrington, Michael. 1963. *The Other America: Poverty in the United States.* New York: Macmillan Publishing Company.

Hill, Kim, and A. Magdalena Hurtado. 1995. *Ache Life History: The Ecology and Demography of a Foraging People.* New York: Aldine de Gruyter.

Hitchcock, Robert K. 1994. "International Human Rights, the Environment, and Indigenous Peoples." *Colorado Journal of International Environmental Law and Policy* 5(1):1–22.

————. 1996. *Kalahari Communities: Bushmen and the Politics of the Environment in Southern Africa.* Copenhagen: International Work Group for Indigenous Affairs.

————. 1997. "Indigenous Peoples, Multinational Corporations, and Human Rights." *Indigenous Affairs* 2:6–11.

————. 1999. "Indigenous Peoples, Genocide of." In *Encyclopedia of Genocide,* Volume II, I-Y. Israel W. Charny, ed. Pp. 349–54. Santa Barbara, Calif.: ABC-CLIO.

————. 2000. "The United States, Development, and Indigenous Peoples." In *The United States and Human Rights: Looking Outward and Inward.* David P. Forsythe, ed. Pp. 300–325. Lincoln: University of Nebraska Press.

Hitchcock, Robert K., and Megan Biesele. 2000. "Introduction." In *Hunters and Gatherers in the Modern World: Conflict, Resistance, and Self-Determination.* Peter P. Schweitzner, Megan Biesele, and Robert K. Hitchcock, eds. Pp. 1–27. New York: Berghahn Books.

Hitchcock, Robert K., and Tara M. Twedt. 1997. "Physical and Cultural Genocide of Various Indigenous Peoples." In *Century of Genocide: Eyewitness Accounts and Critical Views.* Samuel Totten, Israel W. Charny, and William S. Parsons, eds. Pp. 372–407. New York: Garland Publishing.

Horowitz, Irving Louis. 1980. *Taking Lives: Genocide and State Power.* Brunswick, N.J.: Transaction Books.

Horowitz, Michael M. 1989. "Victims of Development." *Development Anthropology Network* 7(2):1–8.

————. 1991. "Victims Upstream and Down." *Journal of Refugee Studies* 4(2):164–81.

Human Rights Watch/Africa. 1995. *Behind the Red Line: Political Repression in Sudan.* New York: Human Rights Watch/Africa.

Human Rights Watch and Natural Resources Defense Council. 1992. *Defending the Earth: Abuses of Human Rights and the Environment.* Washington, D.C.: Human Rights Watch and Natural Resources Defense Council.

Hutchinson, Sharon E. 1996. *Nuer Dilemmas: Coping with Money, War, and the State.* Berkeley: University of California Press.

Hyndman, David. 1994. *Ancestral Rain Forests and the Mountain of Gold: Indigenous Peoples and Mining in New Guinea.* Boulder, Colo.: Westview Press.

Independent Commission on International Humanitarian Issues. 1987. *Indigenous Peoples: A Global Quest for Justice.* London: Zed Books.

International Labour Office. 1953. *Indigenous Peoples: Living and Working Conditions of Aboriginal Populations in Independent Countries.* Geneva: ILO.

International Work Group for Indigenous Affairs. 1988. *IWGIA Yearbook 1987: Indigenous Peoples and Development.* Copenhagen: IWGIA.

———. 1999. *The Indigenous World 1998–99.* Copenhagen: IWGIA.

Ismaelillo and Robin Wright. 1982. *Native Peoples in Struggle: Cases from the Fourth Russell Tribunal and Other International Forums.* Bombay, New York: E.R.I.N. Publications.

Jahan, Rounaq. 1997. "Genocide in Bangladesh." *In Century of Genocide: Eyewitness Accounts and Critical Views.* Samuel Totten, William S. Parsons, and Israel W. Charny, eds. Pp. 291–316. New York: Garland Publishing.

Jaimes, M. Annette, ed. 1992. *The State of Native America: Genocide, Colonization, and Resistance.* Boston: South End Press.

Jensen, Richard E., R. Eli Paul, and John E. Carter. 1991. *Eyewitness at Wounded Knee.* Lincoln: University of Nebraska Press.

Johnston, Barbara Rose, ed. 1994. *Who Pays the Price? Examining the Sociocultural Context of Environmental Crisis.* Covelo, Calif.: Island Press.

———. 1997. *Life and Death Matters: Human Rights and the Environment at the End of the Millennium.* Thousand Oaks, Calif.: AltaMira Press.

Joyce, Christopher, and Eric Stover. 1991. *Witnesses from the Grave.* Boston: Little Brown.

Kane, Joe. 1995. *Savages.* New York: Alfred A. Knopf.

Koening, Dolores, and Michael Horowitz. 1992. "Involuntary Resettlement at Manantali, Mali." In *Social Change and Applied Anthropology: Essays in Honor of David W. Brokensha.* Miriam S. Chaiken and Anne K. Fleuret, eds. Pp. 69–83. Boulder, Colo.: Westview Press.

Kretzmann, Steve. 1995. "Nigeria's 'Drilling Fields': Shell Oil's Role in Repression." *Multinational Monitor* (January/February): 8–11, 25.

Kuper, Leo. 1981. *Genocide: Its Political Use in the Twentieth Century.* New Haven: Yale University Press.

———. 1984. "Types of Genocide and Mass Murder." In *Toward the Understanding and Prevention of Genocide: Proceedings of the International Conference on the Holocaust and Genocide.* Israel W. Charny, ed. Pp. 32–47. Boulder, Colo.: Westview Press.

———. 1985. *The Prevention of Genocide.* New Haven: Yale University Press.

———. 1988. "Other Selected Cases of Genocide." In *Genocide: A Bibliographical Review.* Israel W. Charny, ed. Pp. 155–71. New York: Facts on File.

———. 1991. "When Denial Becomes Routine." *Social Education* 55(2):121–23.

———. 1992. "Reflections on the Prevention of Genocide." In *Genocide Watch.* Helen Fein, ed. Pp. 135–61. New Haven: Yale University Press.

Le Blanc, Lawrence J. 1988. "The United Nations Genocide Convention and Political Groups: Should the United States Propose an Amendment?" *International Yale Journal of Law* 13(2):268–94.

Legters, Lyman H. 1997. "Soviet Deportation of Whole Nations: A Genocidal Process." In *Century of Genocide: Eyewitness Accounts and Critical Views*. Samuel Totten, William S. Parsons, and Israel W. Charny, eds. Pp. 113–35. New York: Garland Publishing.

Lemkin, Raphael. 1944. *Axis Rule in Occupied Europe.* Washington, D.C.: Carnegie Endowment for International Peace.

Lewis, Norman. 1974. *Genocide: A Documentary Report on the Conditions of Indian Peoples.* Berkeley: Indigena and the American Friends of Brazil.

Mace, James E. 1997. "Soviet Man-Made Famine in Ukraine." In *Century of Genocide: Eyewitness Accounts and Critical Views*. Sam Totten, William S. Parsons, and Israel W. Charny, eds. Pp. 78–112. New York: Garland Publishing.

Manz, Beatriz. 1988. *Refugees of a Hidden War: The Aftermath of Counterinsurgency in Guatemala.* Albany: State University of New York Press.

Maybury-Lewis, David. 1997. *Indigenous Peoples, Ethnic Groups, and the State.* Boston: Allyn and Bacon.

Maybury-Lewis, David, and James Howe. 1980. *The Indian Peoples of Paraguay: Their Plight and Their Prospects.* Cambridge: Cultural Survival.

McCully, Patrick. 1996. *Silenced Rivers: The Ecology and Politics of Large Dams.* London: Zed Books.

Middle East Watch and Physicians for Human Rights. 1993. *The Anfal Campaign in Iraqi Kurdistan: The Destruction of Koreme.* New York: Middle East Watch and Physicians for Human Rights.

Miller, Marc S., with Cultural Survival, ed. 1993. *State of the Peoples: A Global Human Rights Report on Societies in Danger.* Boston: Beacon Press.

Minority Rights Group International. 1997. *World Directory of Minorities.* London: Minority Rights Group International.

Montejo, Victor. 1987. *Testimony: Death of a Guatemalan Village.* Willamantic, Conn.: Curbstone Press.

Moody, Roger, ed. l988. *The Indigenous Voice: Visions and Realities.* 2 vols. London: Zed Press.

Mooney, James. 1896. *The Ghost-Dance Religion and the Sioux Outbreak of 1890.* Fourteenth Annual Report. Washington, D.C.: Bureau of American Ethnology.

Morris, James. 1972. "The Final Solution, Down Under." *Horizon* 14(1):60–71.

Morris, Virginia, and Michael Scharf. *An Insider's Guide to the International Criminal Tribunal for the Former Yugoslavia.* Irvington-on-Hudson, N.Y.: Transaction Publishers, 1995.

Munzel, Mark. 1973. *The Ache Indians: Genocide in Paraguay.* IWGIA Document No. ll. Copenhagen: International Work Group for Indigenous Affairs.

———. 1974. *The Ache: Genocide Continues in Paraguay.* Copenhagen: International Work Group for Indigenous Affairs.

———. 1985. "The Manhunts: Ache Indians in Paraguay." In *Case Studies on Human Rights and Fundamental Freedoms: A World Survey*, Vol. 4. Willem A. Veenhoven et al., eds. Pp. 351–403. The Hague: Nijhoff.

Neier, Aryeh. 1998. *War Crimes: Brutality, Genocide, Terror, and the Struggle for Justice.* New York: Times Books.

Neitschmann, Bernard. 1994. "The Fourth World: Nations versus States." In *Reordering the World: Geopolitical Perspectives on the 21st Century*. George J. Demoko and William B. Wood, eds. Pp. 225–42. Boulder, Colo.: Westview Press.

Nordstrom, Carolyn, and Antonius C. G. M. Robben, eds. 1995. *Fieldwork under Fire: Contemporary Studies of Violence and Survival.* Berkeley: University of California Press.

Palmer, Alison. 1992. "Ethnocide." In *Genocide in Our Time: An Annotated Bibliography.* Analytical Introductions by Michael N. Dobkowski and Isidor Wallimann. Pp. 1–6. Ann Arbor: Pierian Press.

Parsons, William S., and Samuel Totten. 1991. "Teaching and Learning about Genocide: Questions of Content, Rationale, and Methodology." *Social Education* 55(2):85–90.

Peluso, Nancy. 1993. "Coercing Conservation: The Politics of State Resource Control." In *The State and Social Power in Global Environmental Politics.* R. D. Lipschutz and K. Conca, eds. New York: Columbia University Press.

Ramos, Alcida Rita. 1995. *Sanuma Memories: Yanomami Ethnography in Times of Crisis.* Madison: University of Wisconsin Press.

Ramos, Alicida R., and Kenneth Taylor. 1979. *The Yanomami in Brazil.* IWGIA Document No. 37. Copenhagen: International Work Group for Indigenous Affairs.

Sachs, Aaron. 1995. *Eco-Justice: Linking Human Rights and the Environment.* WorldWatch Paper 127. Washington, D.C.: WorldWatch Institute.

Saeedpour, Vera Beaudin. 1992. "Establishing State Motives for Genocide: Iraq and the Kurds." In *Genocide Watch.* Helen Fein, ed. Pp. 59–69. New Haven: Yale University Press.

Sanford, Stephen. 1983. *Management of Pastoral Development in the Third World.* Chichester: John Wiley and Sons.

Scudder, Thayer. 1990. "Victims of Development Revisited: The Political Costs of River Basin Development." *IDA Development Anthropology Network* 8(1):1–5.

———. 1997a. "Social Impacts." In *Water Resources: Environmental Planning, Management, and Development.* Asit K. Biswas, ed. Pp. 623–65. New York: McGraw-Hill.

———. 1997b. "Resettlement." In *Water Resources: Environmental Planning, Management, and Development.* Asit K. Biswas, ed. Pp. 667–710. New York: McGraw-Hill.

Scully, Gerald W. 1997. *Murder by the State.* National Center for Policy Analysis, Report No. 211. Dallas, Tex.: National Center for Policy Analysis.

Smith, Robert Jerome, and Bartomev Melia. 1978. "Genocide of the Aché-Guyaki?" *Survival International Supplement* 3(1):8–13.

Smith, Roger W. 1987. "Human Destructiveness and Politics: The Twentieth Century as an Age of Genocide." In *Genocide and the Modern Age: Etiology and Case Studies of Mass Death.* Isidor Walliman and Michael N. Dobkowski, eds. Pp. 21–38. New York: Greenwood Press.

Staub, Ervin. 1989. *The Roots of Evil: The Origins of Genocide and Other Group Violence.* New York: Cambridge University Press.

Stiglmayer, Alexandra, ed. 1994. *Mass Rape: The War against Women in Bosnia-Herzegovina.* Lincoln: University of Nebraska Press.

Stoll, David. 1993. *Between Two Armies in the Ixil Towns of Guatemala.* New York: Columbia University Press.

Stover, J. Eric, and Gilles Peress. 1998. *The Graves: Srebenica and Vukovar.* Zurich: Scalo.

Strider, R. 1995. "Blood in the Pipeline." *Multinational Monitor* (Jan./Feb.) 1995:22–25.

Survival International. 1993. *The Denial of Genocide.* London: Survival International.

Synott, John P. 1993. "Genocide and Cover-up Practices of the British Colonial System against Australian Aborigines, 1788–1992." *Internet on the Holocaust and Genocide* 44–46:15–16.

Tatz, Colin. 1991. "Australia's Genocide: They Soon Forget Their Offspring." *Social Education* 55(2):97–98.

Totten, Samuel. 1991. *First-Person Accounts of Genocidal Acts Committed in the Twentieth Century.* New York: Greenwood Press.

Totten, Samuel, and William S. Parsons, eds. 1991. "Teaching about Genocide." Special Section of *Social Education* 55(2):85–133.

Totten, Samuel, William S. Parsons, and Israel Charny, eds. 1997. *Century of Genocide: Eyewitness Accounts and Critical Views*. New York: Garland Publishing.

Turnbull, Clive. 1948. *Black War: The Extermination of the Tasmanian Aborigines*. Melbourne: F. W. Cheshire.

Veber, Hanne, Jens Dahl, Fiona Wilson, and Espen Waehle, eds. 1993. *". . . Never Drink from the Same Cup": Proceedings of the Conference on Indigenous Peoples in Africa, Tune, Denmark, 1993*. IWGIA Document No. 74. Copenhagen: International Work Group for Indigenous Affairs and Center for Development Research.

Wakin, Eric. 1992. *Anthropology Goes to War: Professional Ethics and Counterinsurgency in Thailand*. Madison: Center for Southeast Asian Studies, University of Wisconsin.

Walliman, Isidor, and Michael Dobkowski, eds. 1987. *Genocide in the Modern Age: Etiology and Case Studies of Mass Death*. New York: Greenwood Press.

Whitaker, B. 1985. *Revised and Updated Report on the Question of the Prevention and Punishment of the Crime of Genocide*. New York: United Nations Economic and Social Council. E/CN.4/Sub.2/1985/6.

Wilmer, Franke. 1993. *The Indigenous Voice in World Politics: Since Time Immemorial*. Newbury Park, Calif.: Sage Publications.

World Bank. 1991. *Operational Directive on Indigenous Peoples*. Washington, D.C.: World Bank.

World Commission on Dams. 2000. *Dams and Development: A New Framework for Decision-Making: The Report of the World Commission on Dams*. London: Earthscan Publications.

PART TWO

Essentializing Difference

Anthropologists in the Holocaust

4

Justifying Genocide

Archaeology and the Construction of Difference

Bettina Arnold

It is one of the terrible ironies of the systematic extermination of one people by another that its justification is considered necessary. As Norman Cohn has argued, "[H]owever narrow, materialistic, or downright criminal their own motives may be, such men cannot operate without an ideology behind them. At least, when operating collectively, they need an ideology to legitimate their behavior, for without it they would have to see themselves and one another as what they really are—common thieves and murderers. And that apparently is something which even they cannot bear" (Leo Kuper [1981:84] quoting Norman Cohn [1967:263–64]). Obviously warrants for genocide can take many forms, and not all of them make explicit reference to the archaeological past. Those that do deserve closer examination. The starting point for this paper therefore is Leo Kuper's statement that "massive slaughter of members of one's own species is repugnant to man, and that ideological legitimation is a necessary precondition for genocide" (1981:84). I explore the symbiotic relationship between nationalism, race, and archaeology from a cross-cultural perspective in order to illustrate how archaeological research has been co-opted to ratify and reify genocide.

CULTURAL CAPITAL AND THE CONSTRUCTION OF DIFFERENCE

If the politics of memory and the psychology of politics are intimately related, as Hirsch suggests, and if memories, and the myths and hatreds constructed around them, may be manipulated by individuals or groups in positions of leadership to motivate populations to commit genocide or other atrocities (1995:3), then archaeology must be considered a potential contributing factor in such political systems. Archaeological research in contemporary contexts is in fact explicitly referred to as "cultural capital," a source to be mined for "useful" matter, much as natural resources are (Hamilakis and Yalouri 1996). The terms "heritage management" (Britain) and "cultural resource management" (United States), both used to describe archaeological research, especially government-funded research, illustrate this point (Arnold 1999:1). In the decades since 1945, the cultural capital represented by the "deep past quarry" of archaeological research has become heavily contested territory, without however being accompanied by the development of a clear set of ethical or programmatic policies within the discipline to cope with the potential for overt exploitation. Organizations such as ROPA (the Register of Professional Archaeologists) in the United States, or the Council of British Archaeology, have not as yet succeeded in raising the consciousness of practicing archaeologists in those countries to the level required if abuse of research results is to be avoided. As Hirsch points out, "[If] the connection between memory and politics is not clarified, the past may be ignored, reconstructed or manipulated, employed as a mythological justification for the present" (1995: 10).

On the other hand, the spate of recent publications on the archaeology of nationalism and ethnicity illustrates a dawning awareness of the significance of archaeological research to the ideological underpinnings of political systems (Olivier 1999; Legendre 1999; Halle and Schmidt 1999; Demoule 1999; Jones 1997; Atkinson, Banks and O'Sullivan 1996; Kohl and Fawcett 1995; Ligi 1993; Edwards 1991, 1999). To what extent do material culture remains "map" people, and what are the implications of this operating assumption for archaeology and for the discipline of anthropology more generally? The tendency to equate material culture assemblages with cultural subdivisions still dominates the field of archaeology (Wells 1998; among others), a theoretical dilemma that deserves closer attention. Archaeologists have traditionally claimed that ethnicity can be recognized in archaeological assemblages. Reduced to a simplistic formula, pots = people (Childe 1929:vi).[1] As a result of this assumption, archaeology acquires political significance. In other words, the way ethnicity is identified in the archaeological record and the way archaeology informs ethnicity in contemporary cultures must be seen as two sides of the same coin.

British archaeologist Stephen Shennan defines the term ethnicity very generally as "self-conscious identification with a particular social group" (1989:6). A more recent definition by South African archaeologist Martin Hall defines it as "an historically validated continuity of identity" (1994:176). As with most definitions, these raise more questions than they answer. What is meant by "self-conscious" or "historically validated"? How is a "social group" or an "identity" defined, and by whom? Siân Jones in her recent treatment of the topic of the archaeology of ethnicity (1997) argues that not enough attention is paid by archaeologists to distinguishing between the emic vs. etic classification of ethnic groups—self-identified ethnicity vs. that assigned by others. Her criticism is part of a growing recognition of the complexity and context-dependent fluidity of the term "ethnicity," which archaeologists have so long treated as normative and immutable (Graves-Brown, Jones, and Gamble 1996).

Part of the problem is the mutability of the term "ethnicity" itself, which is used expediently in modern discourse. It can be equated with religious belief, race, language, or cultural continuity within a specific location (Arnold 1998/99, 1999). Another term that needs to be defined is "nation." I am using the term in its most general sense: a group of people who feel themselves to be a community bound by ties of history, culture, and common ancestry. Is "nationalism" possible without notions of "ethnicity"? Is nationalism the inevitable result of the creation of ethnic identity in the postindustrial state? How do nationalist agendas affect archaeological interpretation, and how does archaeological evidence affect nationalist agendas, and in some cases, the genocidal expression of those agendas?

ARCHAEOLOGY AND GERMAN NATIONAL SOCIALISM

A particularly egregious, and therefore informative, example of the manipulation of the "deep" archaeological past for political, and ultimately genocidal, purposes is prehistoric German archaeology under the National Socialists. I have been doing research for some time now on the role played by archaeology in the creation of nationalist and ethnic identity in the German nation-state (Arnold 1990, 1992, 1998/99, 1999; Arnold and Hassmann 1995), and I will further develop some of those ideas in this chapter.

Michael Ignatieff (1994) has described nationalism as an emotional mix of "blood and belonging," and certainly it was blood, or race, that determined belonging in the German nation-state in the nineteenth century and particularly after 1933.[2] Language was a secondary, though important, defining characteristic (Kellas 1991:31), but the idea that race was what distinguished Germans from all other human groups had several ramifications. Unlike other defining ethnic characteristics, race was assumed by nationalists to be unaffected by cultural changes over time, which meant that "Germans" in 1933 could be considered part of an ethnic continuum in northern Europe going back as far as the Upper Paleolithic (that is, the first appearance of anatomically modern humans in the European archaeological record). Race as defined by German National Socialism was what qualified one to be a member of the Germanic community. It was more important than religion, language, or place of birth. It was, in fact, the basis for the "imagined community" that was the "German Reich." In the nineteenth and early twentieth centuries, Germany was wherever Germans were or could be shown to have been. Germans established territory by occupying it and leaving a distinctive material record of their presence. Once occupied, the territory could be reclaimed, which was why the identification of "Germanic" material culture in the archaeological record of eastern and northern Europe came to have such political significance for German territorial expansion under the National Socialists. Ernest Renan's prophetic 1882 essay decried this conflation of race and nation by German nationalists:

The Germanic family . . . has the right to reassemble the scattered limbs of the Germanic order, even when those limbs are not asking to be joined together again. The right of the Germanic order over such-and-such a province is stronger than the right of the inhabitants of that province over themselves. There is thus created a kind of primordial right analogous to the divine right of kings; an ethnographic principle is substituted for a national one. This is a very grave error, which, if it were to become dominant, would destroy European civilization. The primordial right of races is as narrow and as perilous for genuine progress as the national principle is just and legitimate. (1990:13)

The origin myth of the German people that developed between 1871 and 1918 laid the foundations for the abuse of archaeological research in the Third Reich, while also providing a justification for genocide. Hirsch has argued that origin myths frequently involve the identification of groups of people who are defined as being outside the "universe of obligation" that determines behavior toward members of the "in-group" (1995:99). Educational texts, films, and archaeological publications for popular audiences produced between 1933 and 1945 represent the origins of the German people as beginning with a form of ethnoparthenogenesis in northern Europe in the Paleolithic (Figure 4.1; Ströbel 1935). How these populations of anatomically modern humans got to Europe in the first place is shrouded in obscurity in most of these texts, since an eastern or African origin was inconsistent with the notion of a unique and superior Germanic gene pool. The redefining in 1935 of all post-Paleolithic cultural phases (Mesolithic, Neolithic, Bronze and Iron Ages) as permutations of an isolated and "pure" Germanic cultural development (Arnold 1990) was more than a semantic makeover. It exemplifies the way archaeology was expected to serve as handmaiden to the ideology of genocide in Nazi Germany. The Nazi cultural phases were renamed as follows:

Pre-Germanic	Paleolithic–3000 B.C.
Proto-Germanic	3000–2000 B.C.
Early Germanic	2000–700 B.C.
Old Germanic	700 B.C.–0 B.C.
High Germanic	0–A.D. 400
Late Germanic	400–A.D. 800
Post-Germanic	800–present (Dinstahl 1936)

Each of these time periods has a counterpart in the evolutionary diagram in Figure 4.1, which was published in a school textbook in 1935 with the stirring title "Unseres Volkes Ursprung: 5000 Jahre Nordisch-Germanische Kulturentwicklung" ("The Origins of Our People: 5000 Years of Nordic-Germanic Cultural Evolution") (Ströbel 1935). The diagram was intended to link German children in their 1935 classrooms to the unbroken chain of "Germanic" peoples, protagonists in the latest chapter of a cycle of repeated testing, represented by genetic and cultural crises and eventual triumph in the twentieth century (the "Reawakening/Self-awakening"

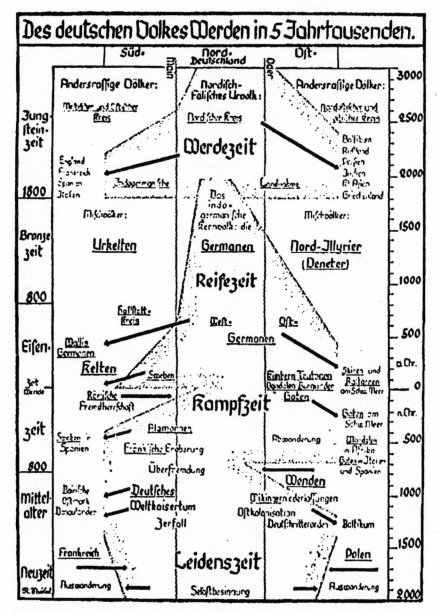

Figure 4.1. A Representative Blueprint of the National Socialist "Origin Myth."
Prehistoric and historic periods are used in this "ontogeny" of the Germanic people:
Time of Becoming, Time of Maturation, Time of Struggle, Time of Suffering/Testing,
Time of Self-Awakening (Ströbel 1935).

at the very bottom of the diagram). In effect, the diagram is a simplified blueprint for the construction of notions of cultural difference and genetic superiority, aimed at the impressionable minds of schoolchildren.

The "Proto-Germanic" period of National Socialist archaeologists is represented by the *Werdezeit* (Time of Becoming) phase in Ströbel's diagram. The geographically designated racial "core" of the German people at this time is represented by the middle column, entitled *Norddeutschland,* the home of the *Nordisch-Fälisches Urvolk* (Nordic-Phalian Ur-Peoples). According to Ströbel's blueprint, some of these "pure" Nordic people migrated out of their northern European homeland into regions to the south and east during what he calls the "Indo-Germanic Land-Taking." The rest remained in the northern core, where they presumably kept the home fires burning pure through the centuries that followed. Threats to racial homogeneity and "Nordic" cultural dominance are associated throughout the diagram with the south and east, whence are found *Andersrassige Völker* (literally "Other-racial, that is, non-Nordic Peoples"). So-called *Mischvölker* (literally "mixed peoples") include the Celts and the Northern Illyrians. Significantly, most of the arrows that Ströbel uses to illustrate migration radiate out of the Nordic-Germanic core rather than into it; the first incursion is represented by the Romans around the time of the birth of Christ. Not coincidentally, the Roman conquest also marks the appearance of the first historical records in northern Europe, less easily manipulated than the archaeological record of prehistoric times—hence the first indication in the diagram of outside influence within the "Germanic core." This unidirectional representation of cultural and genetic influences on the evolution of the "Germanic" people appears repeatedly in German archaeological publications of the 1930s and 1940s. A particularly good example, applied to the penultimate symbol of German National Socialism, is Jörg Lechler's 1934 diagram (Figure 4.2) purporting to show the origins and distribution of the swastika (Lechler 1934).

The period designated as "High Germanic" represents what archaeologists today would call the late Iron Age, when Germanic-speaking peoples are first documented historically as well as archaeologically within and outside the boundaries of the Roman empire in west-central Europe. This corresponds to the period designated as the *Kampfzeit* (Time of Struggle) in Figure 4.1. The four preceding "cultural phases" are neither linguistically nor culturally identifiable as "Germanic" but are defined as Celtic (early Bronze Age through the Roman period) or pre-Celtic, Indo-European-speaking peoples (Mesolithic through the late Neolithic) by both linguists and archaeologists today (Zvelebil 1996).

The year A.D. 800 was chosen by National Socialist archaeologists (and by Ströbel) as the division between the supposedly uncompromised cultural and biological development of the German people (apart from the Roman influence) and the "Post-Germanic" period because it marked a historical event that had symbolic as well as political significance for National Socialist ideologues: in that year Charles the Great, king of the Franks, was crowned in Aachen by Pope Leo III and became

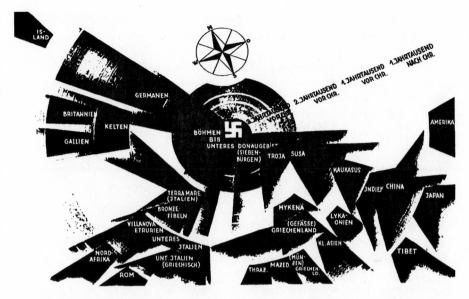

Figure 4.2. Diagram Showing the Origins and Diffusion of the Swastika as a Symbol (after Lechler 1934). The central position of the Germanic "core area" and the subsidiary role of the Mediterranean world are clearly indicated here. This relationship is repeated in other contexts as well; this is just one example.

the founder of the Holy Roman Empire. He was frequently vilified by the National Socialists for his campaigns against the tribes in northern Germany, which earned him the sobriquet "Carl the Saxon Slaughterer." As Charlemagne, he was a potent national symbol for the French, yet another reason for his disapprobation by the Nazi Party. In Figure 4.1, the period beginning with Charlemagne's crowning as Holy Roman Emperor is designated by the entries *Fränkische Eroberung* (Frankish Conquest) and *Überfremdung* (Foreign Infiltration). The link between "non-Nordic" political domination and genetic adulteration is made quite explicit here.

All of these cultural phases witnessed the movement of peoples into and out of west-central Europe; neither the linguistic nor the archaeological records show any evidence of "Germanic" peoples until the end of the last of these cultural phases, the late Iron Age. The "renaming" of these cultural phases by National Socialist prehistorians then was ideologically and politically significant. The denial of cultural or genetic change is an example of what has been called "pseudo-" or "social speciation" (Erikson 1996:53). This is one of the preconditions of genocide, as well as other forms of intraspecies violence. In the words of Kai Erikson: "At its worst . . . social speciation is a process by which one people manages to neutralize the humanity of another to such an extent that the inhibitions which normally prevent creatures of the same species from killing one another wantonly are relaxed" (1996:55). The German word *Volk,* which is so difficult to translate into English, is a linguistic example of the sense of separateness, both cultural and biological, that characterized belonging in the German nation-state. It could be argued that this sense of separateness resulting from social speciation is still a distinguishing characteristic of the German nation today, since the precondition for citizenship continues to be blood and not soil (race rather than geography).[3] Archaeology helped to draw the boundaries of the German nation-state in geographic as well as biological terms by claiming to be able to distinguish ethnic groups in the material record.

GUSTAF KOSSINNA AND THE ARCHAEOLOGICAL "MAPPING" OF ETHNICITY

Gustaf Kossinna, a linguist by training who came late to archaeology, is credited by most contemporary scholars with developing the concept of defining ethnic boundaries on the basis of material culture patterns in the archaeological record. His work had considerable influence on National Socialist archaeology, and provides insight into the question of how it in turn could have helped underwrite genocide (Arnold 1999; Hassmann and Jantzen 1994; Veit 1984, 1989; Hagen 1985/86; Smolla 1979/80; Klejn 1974; Daniel 1962:146; Eggers 1950; among others). Kossinna's methodology developed within a specific cultural context that emphasized the biological and cultural uniqueness of the German people. He was not the first prehistorian to incorporate notions of ethnicity and race into his research, but his characterization of archaeology as a "preeminently national discipline" was new.

Kossinna defined his methodology as follows:

> For all of these sorts of questions prehistoric archaeology seems to me to provide the most secure foundation, indeed the only dependable guide, because it alone can take us into times long past about which other disciplines can provide only vague impressions and uncertain conclusions. The key is to identify a geographic area which seems appropriate for the homeland of a particular tribe, people, or social group—for example, that of the original Indogermanic people. After that it is just a matter of getting the culture history of that group out of the ground or, if that has been done already, to reconstruct it from existing excavated material. (Kossinna 1920:1)

Kossinna explicitly equated ceramic traditions and ethnic groups, since he believed that at least until the invention of the potter's wheel pottery was most often the result of autochthonous development rather than trade or diffusion. The so-called Pommeranian face urns, for example, which Kossinna assigned to a Germanic ethnic tradition, were the basis of his argument for returning territory to Germany ceded to Poland in 1918. Indeed, since 1990 archaeologists on both sides of that border have taken up the old fight using the same weapons Kossinna forged in the years just after World War I, something that should perhaps be grounds for concern.

National Socialist manipulation of migration theory, one of the elements of Kossinna's work, in the study of cultural evolution is relevant here as well (Anthony

1995:90–96). This ties in with party attitudes toward the Mediterranean cultures of Greece and Rome, which were ambivalent to say the least. Alexander von Humboldt exemplifies the pre-1933 hellenophilic perspective: " 'Knowledge of the Greeks is not merely pleasant, useful, or necessary to us—no, *in the Greeks alone* we find the ideal of that which we should like to be and produce' " (quoted in Morris 1994:18). The National Socialists rejected the Mediterranean world as a major influence on Germanic culture. Instead, party ideologues proposed that Classical Greek civilization was really the product of southeastward migration of peoples from the northern Germanic heartland, where the Nordic stock remained pure (Figure 4.2). Everything that was laudable, admirable, and positive about Greek or Roman civilization was the result of Nordic influence; everything that was reprehensible, degenerate, and negative was the result of native, non-Nordic dilution of the original, superior racial stock. This preserved the old narrative structure but reversed the direction of cultural influence (see Marchand 1996 for a more in-depth discussion). Allied to the north-south migration concept was the total denial of outside influence on German cultural evolution and an emphasis on autochthonous development. This manifested itself institutionally in witch hunts against *Römlinge*, archaeologists primarily concerned with the study of Greek or Roman civilization (Arnold 1990; Bollmus 1970; Kater 1974).

THE MIRAGE OF THE "SUPERIOR NORTH"

Inevitably and ironically, in creating this myth of a northern origin for the civilizations of the Mediterranean (Hermand 1992:196), National Socialist researchers had to lean heavily on written sources from that region. A good example is the Roman writer Tacitus. His account of the German people has been called "the birth certificate of the German race" (Schama 1995:76), and National Socialist school textbooks referred to it as the Old Testament of the German people (Ocklitz 1934). What was it about Tacitus's text that made it so important for the National Socialist metanarrative? Among other things, it supported the idea of cultural and racial parthenogenesis, so attractive to National Socialist ideologues. Tacitus described Tuisto, the primal deity of the German people, as literally issuing from the soil, giving birth to Mannus, the first man, who in turn had three sons. (The total absence of women, even in their officially sanctioned role as "hero-makers," is notable here.) Each of these sons was the ancestral father of a German tribe. "Beyond all other people, Tacitus seemed to be saying, the Germans were true indigenes, sprung from the black earth of their native land" (Schama 1995:76).

Party archaeologists between 1933 and 1945 supported the idea that the Germans not only "gave birth to themselves" but also succeeded in developing independently all the major technological advances of civilization, which they shared with all other, less fortunate European peoples through migration from their northern homeland. Another trope that the National Socialist ideologues looted from Tacitus (derived from Charles Darwin and filtered through Ernst Haeckel) was his theory of social geography as the reason for the tempered hardiness of the Germanic people, adapted to an environment at once cruel and ennobling. The "Forest Primeval" as the testing ground for the archetypal German warrior-hero is also reflected in the fairy tales of the Brothers Grimm, where the supernaturally gifted (read: biologically superior) protagonist must pass through and be tested by the forest to achieve transformation and emerge victorious. The following quotation from Hitler's *Mein Kampf* makes it clear that it is the innate (that is, racial) qualities of the German people that allow them to emerge unscathed from this testing (an example of noumenal racism, where physical traits and customs are the expressions of some internal occult quality):

> The scanty fertility of a living space may instigate one race towards the highest achievements, while with another race this may only become the cause for the most dire poverty.... The inner disposition of the peoples is always decisive for the way in which outward influences work themselves out. What leads one people to starvation, trains the other for hard work. (1939:396)

The east and south were to be viewed as recipients, but not donors, of superior culture and technology. If the "hero," the German people, had an eastern origin, then this argument was not tenable. School texts and other propaganda literature published in the 1930s reduced the formula to three main points: (a) The Germans are not barbarians, but rather are the carriers of a superior, indigenous culture; (b) German history begins not with Charlemagne (Carl the "Saxon Slaughterer") but with the Neolithic megalithic tombs of northern Europe; (c) the political history of Europe (including Classical Greek civilization) is unthinkable without the north and without the German people (see Dinstuhl 1936; Vogel 1939; Rude 1937; among others).

Ströbel's school text is particularly instructive, because his headings, subheadings, and highlighted passages demonstrate the exploitative nature of the relationship between National Socialist propaganda and prehistoric German archaeology. What follows is a sample: "German Prehistory, a Source of Strength for Our People," followed by a reference to the fact that Mussolini consciously built the new Italy on the foundations of ancient Rome (1935:3). "The Cultural Hiatus of Charlemagne Ripped Our Most Ancient Past from Us," followed by a diatribe against the forcible replacement of indigenous Germanic values by those of "Rome" (read: Mediterranean/southern).

Ströbel also stresses the fact that the archaeological record represents an "unbribable/uncontaminatable" witness to what "truly" happened in the past, ironically enough (ibid.: 4), since that was the last thing to concern party ideologues. Such claims regarding the objectivity of archaeological evidence ("the dirt doesn't lie"), accompanied by suppression or exaggeration of the existing evidence, are often invoked by propaganda texts during this period. Again, the legitimacy that archaeological evidence lends to claims made in the present is illustrated by such manipulation.

At the "lunatic fringe" end of the spectrum (mainstream archaeologists referred to this group as *Germanomanen* [Germanomaniacs])(Arnold 1990:470) are fictional accounts like those of Edmund Kiß, whose novels about the rise, fall, and ultimate triumphant rebirth of the "lost" civilization of Atlantis (supposedly originating somewhere in the Arctic Circle) tie ideas of Germanic racial superiority to pseudo-scientific concepts like Hans Hörbiger's *Glazial-Kosmogony* (Glacial Cosmogony) (Hermand 1992:193–98). Such amalgams of fiction, mythology, and selectively chosen archaeological evidence (archaeologist Hans Reinerth, a high-ranking official in the Rosenberg Office, was sent to Greece in the 1940s to search for evidence of a Nordic-Germanic invasion of the Mediterranean in the Neolithic, partly in response to Kiß's notions of a post-Atlantis diaspora) set the tone for at least some of the research conducted within organizations like Himmler's SS-Ahnenerbe (Ancestor Heritage Society) (Arnold 1990).

The National Socialist archaeo-mythology about Atlantis and Nordic migrations south and east might be dismissed by some as harmless, if disturbing, lunacy. The subtext is anything but harmless, however, and it demonstrates how readily such notions of ethnoparthenogenesis can be used to underwrite genocide. According to Kiß and others who exploited or supported the Atlantis myth, the "sons of the Sun" (read "Asa/Aryans/supermen"), whose superior bloodlines guaranteed their supremacy over all inferior (read "non-Aryan") peoples, were repeatedly threatened by miscegenation in their postcatastrophic wanderings around the globe. Ströbel's references to Mischvölker in Figure 4.1, and his reference to a Kampfzeit, is an example of the pervasiveness of this idea. Kiß's novels were also avidly read and praised by top Nazi officials, including Hitler (Hermand 1992:193). The eventual return to the Nordic homeland (with the Arctic Atlantis no longer habitable, northern Europe became a stand-in) and periodic recourse to "racial hygiene" practices (read: the genocidal extermination of undesirable elements in the gene pool) were necessary elements in the survival and maintenance of Nordic-Germanic racial and cultural supremacy, according to Kiß and his supporters. There are frequent references to metallurgy in descriptions of this cultural and genetic "refining" process (the terms "tempering" and "steel" appear repeatedly [ibid.:194]), and the motifs of the warrior-hero and the northern Forest Primeval as the ultimate testing ground are interwoven with concepts of purification and elimination.

The folkloric foundations of National Socialism have been extensively discussed elsewhere (ibid.; Dow and Lixfeld 1994; Lixfeld 1994; among others). A few elements can be linked to archaeological research in instructive ways. The Forest Primeval theme is perhaps one of the most pervasive (Schama 1995:75–134). It appears in the short-lived National Socialist attempt to create a neo-pagan state religion, centered on open-air theaters known as Thing-Stätten (Arnold 1992; Lurz 1975). These were constructed in carefully controlled "wild" settings with archaeological links to the Germanic past, either real, fabricated, or "enhanced." Morality plays and educational dramas were enacted at these open-air theaters, which incorporated the National Socialist meta-narrative in their plot lines: the noble, courageous German warrior-hero, the long-suffering, patient German mother (she is always a mother, never "just" a woman), and the evil, cunning Jewish antihero, locked in an eternal, three-cornered struggle.

If National Socialist Germany's "origin myth" was consciously modeled after a hero tale metanarrative, as I am suggesting here, it also was logically unable to cope with defeat. As Gellner has argued, "[T]he Nazi salvation was selective, it was reserved for the strong and victorious, and when they lost, there was no logical bolthole" (1994:147). Protagonists of hero-tales don't need boltholes, because their narratives have happy endings by definition. This may be why defeat in 1945 seems to have been especially traumatic in the discipline of prehistoric archaeology, which has maintained a kind of collective amnesia for more than fifty years on the subject of its role in the construction of the National Socialist metanarrative (Arnold 1990; Arnold and Hassmann 1995; but see Halle and Schmidt 1999). Other compromised academic disciplines eventually went through a self-critical and self-reflexive phase, the timing of which varied depending on the extent of their involvement. The fact that German prehistoric archaeology is only now beginning to come to terms with its past is, I believe, testimony to its involvement in the construction of the hero-tale that went so horribly wrong, and the degree to which it owed its existence as a legitimate discipline to the National Socialist state.

ARCHAEOLOGY AS THE HANDMAIDEN OF NATIONALISM

The mutability of archaeological approaches to ethnicity and the construction of nationalist narrative can be seen in the shifting focus on different ethnic groups by European nations in the twentieth century. For example, the Germanic tribes were manipulated for the purposes of political propaganda at least as early as Julius Caesar, who clearly had ulterior motives for the ethnic distinctions he made between the "barbarian" populations on the left ("Celtic") and right ("Germanic") banks of the Rhine. Tacitus's depiction of the Germanic character as the polar opposite of his dissolute and debauched Roman contemporaries has already been mentioned. The creation by the National Socialists of the myth of Germanic racial superiority is a more recent application of the archaeology of ethnicity to a political agenda that included the systematic extinction of whole segments of the population. George Andreopoulos argues that the "fiction of the nation-state often contains a prescription for the cultural destruction of a people through state policies of more or less compulsory assimilation and, at the limit, for genocide" (1994:6). He cites the example of the Belgian state: "Much as the colonial Gold Coast invented a 1000-year old historical pedigree by renaming itself Ghana, Belgian historians seek their roots in Caesar's *De Bello Gallico*. Never mind that Caesar's Belgae had only the most tenuous connection with today's Belgians" (ibid.:7–8).

Nazi Germany is by no means the only example of the use and abuse of the past by genocidal regimes, though it may be one of the most extreme. Another much-studied example comes from the United States. In the late eighteenth and nineteenth centuries the European population of the United States was engaged in displacing, physically eliminating, or culturally assimilating indigenous populations (McManamon 1999). This systematic erasure of peoples and cultures was justified according to the following assumptions about contemporary native groups: (a) eighteenth- and nineteenth-century Indian populations were not seen building or using the mound complexes of Ohio or the Mississippi Valley, and supposedly had no knowledge of who had built them; (b) they were thought to be too primitive to have constructed anything on the scale of structures such as Monk's Mound at the Mississippian site of Cahokia in Illinois, which was over a hundred feet high with a footprint close to that of the Great Pyramid at Giza; (c) "tablets" with "writing" purportedly found in some of the mounds were interpreted as having an Old World origin (suggestions for these pre-Columbian travelers ranged from wandering Egyptians to disoriented Welshmen); and (d) the moundbuilders were obviously much older than any contemporary Indian group, based on what later turned out to be erroneous tree-ring dating techniques applied to some of the mounds.

There were some early challenges to the view that contemporary Indian cultures could not have been associated with the moundbuilding cultures. Thomas Jefferson is one of the best known of those early skeptics. He based his interpretation on mounds he excavated on his own property rather than on speculative and racist assumptions of the cultural sophistication of contemporary Indian groups. Significantly, however, it was not until the end of the century, when Indian resistance to colonial advances and appropriations was beginning to wane, that the Bureau of American Ethnology in Washington hired an entomologist from Illinois by the name of Cyrus Thomas to systematically investigate the origins of the mounds. In his multivolume report submitted to the bureau in 1894, Thomas concluded that the mounds were not as old as originally claimed; there was solid evidence suggesting continuity between contemporary Indian burial practices and those seen in the mounds; and the de Soto expedition in the seventeenth century had observed and reported the construction and use of such mounds by tribes in the southeast, many of which had been decimated by disease and warfare by the time the first colonists arrived in the area.

Robert Silverberg, in his study of the Moundbuilder Myth, concluded that the idea of a vanished race of Old World origin was politically motivated, in part because it was "comforting to the conquerors" (1989:48). Why "comforting"? Kenneth Feder argues more explicitly as follows:

> Perhaps if the Indians were not the builders of the mounds and the bearers of a culture that impressed even the rather ethnocentric European colonizers of America, it made wiping out the presumably savage and primitive natives less troublesome. And, if Europeans could further convince themselves that the Indians were very recent interlopers—in fact, the very invaders who had savagely destroyed the gentle and civilized Moundbuilders—so much the better. And if, finally, it could be shown that the Moundbuilders were, in actuality, ancient European travelers to the Western Hemisphere, the circle was complete. In destroying the Indian people, Europeans in the 18th and 19th centuries could rationalize that they were . . . merely reclaiming terri-

tory once held by ancient Europe. The Moundbuilder myth was not just the result of
a harmless prank or a confusing hoax. It was part of an attempt to justify the destruction of American Indian societies. (1996:135)

In this particular case archaeology initially underwrote but later challenged the ideology justifying the extermination of Native Americans on the basis of their supposed cultural inferiority and recent arrival in the Americas—but the acknowledgment of native achievement did not come until the living descendants of the
populations to which the moundbuilding cultures were attributed had effectively
been disenfranchised and no longer posed a legitimate threat to the colonial regime.

Significant parallels to the Moundbuilder myth can be found in the history of the
archaeological investigation of the ruins known as Great Zimbabwe in what was
formerly the British colony of Rhodesia (Garlake 1983; Hall 1984; Kuklick 1991).

> Seeking to legitimate their rule, British settlers and African nationalists subscribed to
> very different accounts of the building of the ruins, placing their construction alter-
> nately in ancient times and the relatively recent past, and identifying the builders—
> or, at least the architects—either as representatives of some non-African civilization
> or dismissed the possibility that the Shona in the area could have built Great Zim-
> babwe. (Kuklick 1991: 139–40)

The list of supposed non-African "builders or architects" proposed by white researchers, settlers, and politicians includes some of the same peripatetic types cited
by the Moundbuilder fantabulists (minus Vikings and Welshmen): Phoenicians,
Egyptians, the Lost Tribes of Israel, and so forth. As in the North American case,
the local population was categorized as intellectually too degenerate to have been
able to produce such sophisticated structures; later, when an African origin for the
site became the accepted interpretation, the construction techniques were described
as primitive, giving with one hand and taking away with the other, while maintaining the trope of the inherent inferiority of the local African peoples. A similar
reversal can be found in North American archaeology post-Cyrus Thomas, where
the emphasis for many years was on the cultural immutability, even stasis, of Native American peoples (Trigger 1980b). To some extent this notion is still with us
today in the form of New Age interpretations of Native culture as "closer to Nature" because less evolved. This may currently be intended to be complimentary
but is nevertheless part of the same legacy of denigration of the colonized by the
colonizers that we already see in Tacitus, whose *Germania* has been described by
Schama as a "backhanded compliment from Barbarism to Civilization" (1995:76).[4]
In this sense archaeology historically has been in the business of what Alex Hinton calls "manufacturing difference" (1998:14), which is the first step toward, and
necessary precondition of, "social speciation" and, under certain conditions, genocide. As Barry Sautman has pointed out, "[M]yths of descent deployed as an instrument in the service of a modernizing, authoritarian state to artificially reconstruct the idea of a people are politically perilous. . . . The experiences of the former

USSR and Yugoslavia show that making dubious historicizing central to a nation-building project leads to ethnic outbidding in which the most virulent ultra-nationalists prevail and violence ensues" (1997:89).

The Khmer Rouge regime in Cambodia is another example of genocide underwritten by the past. Excavations and reconstruction by the French of parts of the site of Angkor Wat (ninth to fourteenth centuries A.D.) revealed that Cambodia had once been a great and powerful empire, rich in agricultural resources and conquered territory. Angkor Wat itself became the symbol of this past greatness; its five towers have been featured in stylized form on each of Cambodia's national flags since 1970 (Chandler 1993; Staub 1989:199). Interestingly, much of the rhetoric associated with the Khmer Rouge regime sounds very much like that used by the German totalitarian state in the 1930s and 1940s; the two regimes even share a characterization of the French as a paramount enemy: "The counterpart to the xenophobia implicit in the targeting of foreigners and ethnic groups was an idealization of Khmer racial purity and a 'mission to revive the ancient glory and honor of Cambodia and to ensure the perenniality of the Khmer race'" (Andreopoulos 1994:26–27, quoting Becker 1986:239).

The significance of origin stories in shaping contemporary attitudes is often underestimated. As Judy Ledgerwood correctly notes in a recent paper, "Not only do we learn from origin stories how we are to behave morally in the present, but the proper telling of these stories, the proper recitation of texts, can recreate this perception of order, of things being as they should be—that is, as they were in the beginning" (n.d.:23–24). She refers specifically to Cambodia in her discussion, elaborating on David Chandler's work (1982), which "plays on contrasting notions of order and disorder, of forest and field, and postulates that for Khmer in the 19th century, just emerging from a time of hardship and destruction, an appeal to notions of previous times when hierarchical relationships in society were as they should be was used tactically to re-assert order in the present" (ibid.:24).

The Khmer Rouge regime consciously and expediently modeled itself on the peoples who built Angkor Wat. Just as the majority of the population in Angkor in the thirteenth century were slaves (based on the report of a Chinese observer) (Staub 1989:196), so Pol Pot's regime created its own slave class, the "new people," many of whom were former elites. Inasmuch as the king in Angkor between the ninth and fourteenth centuries was an absolute monarch, with the great temples testimony to his right to rule, Pol Pot established himself as a peasant leader on the basis of that earlier system: "The role of the king in Cambodian society provided a cultural blueprint for absolute authority and made it easier for people to accept the absolute authority of the Khmer Rouge" (ibid.:198). As in the case of Germany after 1918, the "Khmer Rouge had a sense of superiority combined with underlying feelings of inferiority and vulnerability. This arose from a combination of long past glory, recent history and present circumstances" (ibid.:199). In Cambodia the resident Chinese and Vietnamese (as well as an extensive ancillary list that included Muslim Chams, members of the Lon Nol regime, internal "traitors," and "counterrevolutionaries") were constituted as the "Other" and became targets for extermination under the Khmer Rouge regime, whereas in Germany the targets were Jews, Gypsies, and other groups singled out for "social speciation." The anti-intellectual nature of both the German and Cambodian systems is another common denominator that seems to characterize genocidal regimes in other contexts as well, including the example from the nineteenth-century United States discussed above.

CONCLUSION

Examples of the symbiosis between archaeological research and racial nationalism are much more common than genocidal regimes making use of the past to justify the extermination of certain groups within a population, but the correlation between the two is important and worth discussing. Regimes that make reference to the archaeological past in their nationalist rhetoric are frequently in the preliminary stages of social speciation, and whether that process eventually leads to genocide is dependent on the changing context within which such manipulation of the past occurs. As Barry Sautman has succinctly put it, "[N]ationalism is both political and ethnic because race and nationalism overlap. In particular, race and nation are rooted in common myths about the significance of common descent" (1997:83). Recently, Uli Linke produced an eloquent exegesis on the concepts of blood and nation and their symbiotic relationship throughout European history (1999). In a sense, the deep past in the form of the archaeological record represents the concretization of both concepts, evidence of blood and belonging in material form, and it is this that gives archaeological research its symbolic and hence its political potency.

I have attempted to show in this discussion in what ways archaeology plays a role in the creation and maintenance of origin myths and notions of cultural difference. I hope I have demonstrated that there are enough common denominators in the appropriation of archaeology by political regimes to warrant keeping a close eye on nations exploiting the past in these ways. This includes nations like France, in which Celtic heritage and sites associated with the Roman-Gallic conflicts are explicitly referenced by political leaders (Dietler 1994); nations like Israel, where archaeology has been described as a "national sport" in which participants "volunteer to participate in archaeological excavations, make pilgrimages to reconstructed archaeological sites, and visit museums that display archaeological findings, as if through these activities they ritually affirm their roots in the land" (Zerubavel 1995:57);[5] and nations like China, in which racial nationalism is constructed "through the official propagation of myths of origin and descent. The former confer dignity through antiquity to a group and locate its 'primal habitat.' The latter trace descent to illustrious forebears and suggest nobility and solidarity" (Sautman 1997:80). Japanese scholars recently have made a point of the frightening parallels between the racist rhetoric of Japan in the 1930s and that of China today (ibid.:91; but for a discussion of Japanese nationalism and archaeology, see Edwards 1991, 1999). If the manipulation of the past, including the archaeological past, in the construction of difference along racial lines is a sort of canary in a coal mine, a harbinger of genocidal policies, then it seems imperative that anthropologists turn their attention to the study of political systems in which such manifestations appear.

What does the future hold? Is the appropriation of the past as a justification for authoritarian and occasionally genocidal regimes inevitable? That seems to depend on a number of variables, but there are some new configurations developing to counter the continuing parade of regimes intent on cannibalizing themselves in the name of cultural difference. For example, the Celts are currently the "ethnic" group that it is most expedient to claim as national patrimony in Germany, as well as a number of other western European nations. One can apply Gellner's observations regarding the connection between emerging states and a resurgent interest in ethnicity to this "Celtic renaissance." Whereas in the late nineteenth and early twentieth centuries the emphasis was on national differences, now, with the newly emergent European Community, it is on "pan-European-ness." The Celts are presented as the ultimate pan-European "ethnic" group (James 1999), stretching from Spain to Galicia during the late Iron Age. In fact, this archaeologically "documented" Celtic cultural uniformity is as much an "imagined community" as Tacitus's or Kossinna's constructions, since it is based mainly on similarities in material culture. As examples from ethnographic contexts such as New Guinea have shown (Terrell 1986), ethnicity need not map onto material culture, nor necessarily map onto language, or religion, or race, or any combination of the above. The question of how to define "cultures" in the material record of the past is in need of serious re-examination, not least because of the potential for abuse by political systems. Archaeologists can no longer afford to produce interpretations of the past on the sidelines of history. Whether they are actively involved in the construction of cultural difference or not, indirectly their research produces a potentially lethal weapon in the symbolic arsenal available to political regimes, including those bent on genocide. This places a tremendous responsibility on the producers of such knowledge, a burden that will only continue to grow as the demands placed on scholars increase in complexity in the coming decades. Archaeology as a discipline, which has tended to be focused inward, will need to adjust its modus operandi accordingly. The recent emergence of the concept of the archaeologist as "public intellectual" (Bonyhady and Griffiths 1997) suggests the direction that the discipline will need to take if it wants to adopt a proactive stance in the battle over the interpretation and exploitation of the archaeological past. At the same time, anthropology as a whole could benefit from acknowledging the actual and potential contributions of archaeological research to the increasingly pressing problem of how to recognize and take action against inter- and intragroup violence based on the cultural construction of difference. I therefore want to thank Alex Hinton for the opportunity to contribute an archaeological voice to the anthropological analysis of genocide—this is an endeavor that can only benefit from interdisciplinary cooperation.

NOTES

1. To quote V. Gordon Childe, one of the most influential archaeologists of the twentieth century (Trigger 1980a), who was himself influenced by Kossinna's "settlement archaeological method": "We find certain types of remains . . . constantly recurring together. Such a complex of regularly associated traits we shall term a 'cultural group' or just a 'culture.' We assume that such a complex is the material expression of what would today be called a 'people'" (1929:vi).

2. The metaphor of blood is discussed by Uli Linke in some detail in her study of race and nation in modern Germany (Linke 1997:559–61).

3. The Christian Democratic Party in Germany, for example, propagates the principle of *jus sanguinis* (right of the blood) and views Germans as a "community of destiny and ancestry" (Pfaff 1996:9, quoted in Sautman 1997:81). This is not a phenomenon unique to the German nation-state. The nationality laws of the People's Republic of China also rely on the concept of race through the "principle of blood lineage" (*xuetong zhuyi*); as with so-called ethnic Germans, individuals of Chinese descent not living in China may apply for PRC passports by virtue of their blood lineage (Sautman 1997:81).

4. Martin Hall makes this relationship between colonialism and archaeological manipulation of the past explicit: "In those countries where the archaeology of the colonized is mostly practised by descendants of the colonizers, the study of the past must have a political dimension. This has become overt in Australasia, where, as one Aboriginal representative has put it, the colonizers 'have tried to destroy our culture, you have built your fortunes upon the lands and bodies of our people and now, having said sorry, want a share in picking out the bones of what you regard as a dead past'" (Langford 1983:2, quoted in Hall 1984:455).

5. See Abu el-Haj (1998) for additional discussion of Israeli archaeology and nationalism.

REFERENCES CITED

Abu el-Haj, Nadia. 1998. "Translating Truths: Nationalism, the Practice of Archaeology, and the Remaking of Past and Present in Contemporary Jerusalem." *American Ethnologist* 25(2):166–88.

Anderson, Benedict. 1983. *Imagined Communities: Reflections on the Origins and Spread of Nationalism.* London: Verso.

Andreopoulos, George, ed. 1994. *Genocide: Conceptual and Historical Dimensions.* Philadelphia: University of Pennsylvania Press.

Anthony, David. 1995. "Nazi and Eco-Feminist Prehistories: Ideology and Empiricism in Indo-European Archaeology." In *Nationalism, Politics and the Practice of Archaeology.* Philip L. Kohl and Clare Fawcett, eds. Pp. 82–98. Cambridge: Cambridge University Press.

Arnold, Bettina. 1990. "The Past as Propaganda: Totalitarian Archaeology in Nazi Germany." *Antiquity* 64:464–78.

———. 1992. "The Past as Propaganda." *Archaeology* (July/August):30–37.

———. 1998/99. "The Power of the Past: Nationalism and Archaeology in 20th Century Germany." *Archaelogia Polona* (35/36):237–53.

———. 1999. "The Contested Past." *Anthropology Today* 15(4):1–4.

———. 2000. "A Transatlantic Perspective on German Archaeology." In *Archaeology, Ideology and Society: The German Experience.* Heinrich Härke, ed. Bern and Frankfurt: Fritz Lang Verlag.

Arnold, Bettina, and Henning Hassmann. 1995. "Archaeology in Nazi Germany: The Legacy of the Faustian Bargain." In *Nationalism, Politics and the Practice of Archaeology.* Philip Kohl and Clare Fawcett, eds. Pp. 70–81. Cambridge: Cambridge University Press.

Atkinson, John, Iain Banks, and Jerry O'Sullivan, eds. 1996. *Nationalism and Archaeology.* Glasgow: Cruithne Press.

Becker, Elizabeth. 1986. *When the War Was Over: The Voices of Cambodia's Revolution and Its People.* New York: Simon and Schuster.

Bollmus, Reinhard. 1970. *Das Amt Rosenberg and Seine Gegner. Studien zur Zeitgeschichte.* Stuttgart: Deutsche Verlagsanstalt.

Bonyhady, Tim, and Tom Griffiths. 1997. *Prehistory to Politics: John Mulvaney, the Humanities and the Public Intellectual.* Melbourne: Melbourne University Press.

Chandler, David P. 1982. "Songs at the Edge of the Forest: Perceptions of Order in Three Cambodian Texts." In *Moral Order and the Question of Change: Essays on Southeast Asian Thought.* D. K. Wyatt and A. Woodside, eds. Southeast Asian Monograph Series 24. Pp. 53–77. New Haven: Yale University Press.

———. 1993. 2d ed. *The Tragedy of Cambodian History: Politics, War and Revolution since 1945.* New Haven: Yale University Press.

Childe, V. Gordon. 1929. *The Danube in Prehistory.* Oxford: Oxford University Press.

Cohn, Norma. 1967. *Warrant for Genocide.* New York: Harper and Row.

Daniel, Glynn. 1962. *The Idea of Prehistory.* Cleveland: World.

Demoule, Jean-Paul. 1999. "Ethnicity, Culture and Identity: French Archaeologists and Historians." *Antiquity* 73(279):190–98.

Dietler, Michael. 1994. " 'Our Ancestors the Gauls': Archaeology, Ethnic Nationalism, and the Manipulation of Celtic Identity in Modern Europe." *American Anthropologist* 96(3):584–605.

Dinstuhl, Friedrich. 1936. *Deutsche Vorgeschichte im Unterricht.* Düsseldorf: NSLB-Düsseldorf.

Dow, James, and Hannjost Lixfeld. 1994. *The Nazification of an Academic Discipline: Folklore in the Third Reich.* Bloomington: University of Indiana Press.

Edwards, Walter. 1991. "Buried Discourse: The Toro Archaeological Site and Japanese National Identity in the Early Postwar Period." *Journal of Japanese Studies* 17(1):1–23.

———. 1999. " 'Monuments to an Unbroken Line': The Imperial Tombs and Japanese Nationalism." Paper presented at the Archaeological Institute of America annual meeting, Dallas. December.

Eggers, Hans-Jürgen. 1950. "Das Problem der Ethnischen Deutung in der Frühgeschichte." In *Ur- and Frühgeschichte als historische Wissenschaft.* Festschrift zum 60. Geburtstag von Ernst Wahle. H. Kirchner, ed. Heidelberg: Winter.

Erikson, Kai. 1996. "On Pseudospeciation and Social Speciation." In *Genocide, War and Human Survival.* Charles B. Strozier and Michael Flynn, eds. Pp. 51–57. Maryland: Rowman and Littlefield.

Feder, Kenneth. 1996. 2d ed. *Frauds, Myths, and Mysteries: Science and Pseudoscience in Archaeology.* Mountain View, Calif.: Mayfield.

Garlake, Peter. 1983. "Prehistory and Ideology in Zimbabwe." In *Past and Present in Zimbabwe.* J. D. Y. Peel and T. O. Tanger, eds. Pp. 3–19. Manchester: Manchester University Press.

Gellner, Ernest. 1994. *Nations and Nationalism.* Ithaca: Cornell University Press.

Graves-Brown, Paul, Siân Jones, and Clive Gamble, eds. 1996. *Cultural Identity and Archaeology: The Construction of European Communities.* London: Routledge.

Hagen, Anders. 1985/86. "Arkeologi og Politik." *Viking* 49:269–78.

Hall, Martin. 1984. "The Burden of Tribalism: The Social Context of Southern African Iron Age Studies." *American Antiquity* 49(3):455–67.

———. 1994. "Lifting the Veil of Popular History: Archaeology and Politics in Urban Capetown." In *Social Construction of the Past: Representation as Power.* G. C. Bond and A. Gilliam, eds. Pp. 167–82. London: Routledge.

Halle, Uta, and Martin Schmidt. 1999. "Es handelt sich nicht um Affinitäten von Archäologen zum Nationalsozialismus—das ist der Nationalsozialismus." Bericht über die Internationale Tagung "Die Mittel- und Osteuropäische Ur- und Frühgeschichtsforschung in den Jahren 1933–1945." *Archäologische Informationen* 22(1):41–52.

Hamilakis, Yannis, and Eleana Yalouri. 1996. "Antiquities as Symbolic Capital in Modern Greek Society." *Antiquity* 70(267):117–29.

Hassmann, Henning, and D. Jantzen. 1994. " 'Die Deutsche Vorgeschichte—Eine Nationale Wissenschaft.' Das Kieler Museum Vorgeschichtlicher Altertümer im Dritten Reich." *Offa* 51:6–35.

Hermand, Jost. 1992. *Old Dreams of a New Reich: Volkish Utopias and National Socialism.* Bloomington: Indiana University Press.

Hinton, Alex. 1998. "Why Did the Nazis Kill? Anthropology, Genocide and the Goldhagen Controversy." *Anthropology Today* 14(5):9–15.

Hirsch, Herbert. 1995. *Genocide and the Politics of Memory: Studying Death to Preserve Life.* Chapel Hill: North Carolina Press.

Hitler, Adolf. 1939. *Mein Kampf.* Boston: Houghton Mifflin Company.

Ignatieff, Michael. 1994. *Blood and Belonging: Journeys into the New Nationalism.* New York: Farrar, Strauss and Giroux.

James, Simon. 1999. *The Atlantic Celts: Ancient People or Modern Invention?* Madison: University of Wisconsin Press.

Jones, Siân. 1997. *The Archaeology of Ethnicity: Constructing Identities in the Past and Present.* London: Routledge.

Kater, Michael. 1974. *Das "Ahnenerbe" der SS 1935–1945. Studien zur Zeitgeschichte.* Herausgegeben vom Institut für Zeitgeschichte. Stuttgart: Deutsche Verlagsanstalt.

Kellas, J. G. 1991. *The Politics of Nationalism and Ethnicity.* New York: St. Martin's Press.

Klejn, Leo S. 1974. "Kossinna im Abstand von Vierzig Jahren." *Jahresschrift Halle* 58:7–55.

Kohl, Philip, and Clare Fawcett, eds. 1995. *Nationalism, Politics, and the Practise of Archaeology.* Cambridge: Cambridge University Press.

Kossinna, Gustaf. 1920. 2d ed. *Die Herkunft der Germanen: Zur Methode der Siedlungsarchäologie.* Leipzig: Kurt Zabitzsch.

Kuklick, Henrika. 1991. "Contested Monuments: The Politics of Archaeology in Southern Africa." In *Colonial Situations: Essays on the Contextualization of Ethnographic Knowledge.* George Stocking, Jr., ed. Pp. 135–69. History of Anthropology Vol. 7. Madison: University of Wisconsin Press.

Kuper, Leo. 1981. *Genocide: Its Political Use in the Twentieth Century.* New Haven: Yale University Press.

Langford, R. J. 1983. "Our Heritage, Your Playground." *Australian Archaeology* 16:1–6.

Lechler, Jörg. 1934. *Vom Hakenkreuz: Die Geschichte eines Symbols.* Leipzig: C. Kabitzsch.

Ledgerwood, Judy. n.d. "Ongoing Interdisciplinary Investigations at Angkor Borei, Cambodia." Manuscript.

Legendre, Jean-Pierre. 1999. "Archaeology and Ideological Propaganda in Annexed Alsace (1940–1944)." *Antiquity* 73(279):184–90.

Ligi, Priit. 1993. "National Romanticism in Archaeology: The Paradigm of Slavonic Colonization in Northwest Russia." *Fennoscandia Archaeologica* 10:31–9.

Linke, Uli. 1997. "Gendered Difference, Violent Imagination: Blood, Race, Nation." *American Anthropologist* 99(3):559–73.

————. 1999. *Blood and Nation: The European Aesthetic of Race.* Philadelphia: University of Pennsylvania Press.

Lixfeld, Hannjost. 1994. *Folklore and Fascism: The Reich Institute for German Volkskunde.* James R. Dow, trans. Bloomington: University of Indiana Press.

Lurz, Meinhold. 1975. *Die Heidelberger Thingstätte: Die Thingbewegung im Dritten Reich: Kunst als Mittel Politischer Propaganda.* Schriftenreihe zur Landschaft, Kultur und Geschichte Heidelbergs. Heidelberg: Schutzgemeinschaft Heiligenberg e.V.

Marchand, Susan. 1996. *Down from Olympus: Archaeology and Philhellenism in Germany 1750–1970.* Princeton: Princeton University Press.

McManamon, Francis P. 1999. "Nationalism and Ancient America." Paper presented at the Archaeological Institute of America annual meeting, Dallas. December.

Morris, Ian. 1994. *Classical Greece: Ancient Histories and Modern Archaeologies.* Cambridge: Cambridge University Press.

Ocklitz, Oskar. 1934. *Armin, der Führer der Ersten Nationalen Freiheitsbewegung.* Breslau: Handel.

Olivier, Laurent. 1999. "The Origins of French Archaeology." *Antiquity* 71(279):176–83.

Pfaff, William. 1996. "Immigration and the Racial Element." *International Herald Tribune,* March 22, p. 9.

Renan, Ernest. 1990. "What Is a Nation?" In *Nation and Narration.* Homi K. Bhabha, ed. Pp. 8–22. New York: Routledge.

Rude, Erwin. 1937. *Deutsche Vorgeschichte im Schulunterricht.* Berlin: A. W. Zickfeldt Verlag.

Sautman, Barry. 1997. "Racial Nationalism and China's External Behavior." *World Affairs* 160(2):78 ff.

Schama, Simon. 1995. *Landscape and Memory.* New York: Knopf.

Shennan, Stephen. 1989. "Introduction." In *Archaeological Approaches to Cultural Identity.* Stephen Shennan, ed. Pp. 1–32. One World Archaeology 10. New York: Unwin Hyman.

Silverberg, Robert. 1989. *The Moundbuilders.* Athens: Ohio University Press.

Smolla, Günter. 1979/80. "Das Kossinna Syndrom." *Fundberichte aus Hessen* 19(20):1–9.

————. 1984/85. "Gustaf Kossinna nach 50 Jahren. Kein Nachruf." *Acta Praehistoria et Archaeologia* 16(17):9–14.

Staub, Ervin. 1989. *The Roots of Evil: The Origins of Genocide and Other Group Violence.* Cambridge: Cambridge University Press.

Ströbel, Richard. 1935. *Unseres Volkes Ursprung: 5000 Jahre Nordisch-Germanische Kulturentwicklung.* Nationalpolitische Aufklärungsschriften Heft 2. Berlin: Propaganda Verlag Paul Hochmuth.

Terrell, John. 1986. *The Prehistory of the Pacific Islands: An Introduction to the Study of Variation in Language, Customs and Human Biology.* Cambridge: Cambridge University Press.

Trigger, Bruce. 1980a. *Gordon Childe: Revolutions in Archaeology.* London: Thames and Hudson.

————. 1980b. "Archaeology and the Image of the American Indian." *American Antiquity* 45:662–76.

Veit, Ulrich. 1984. "Gustaf Kossinna and V. Gordon Childe. Ansätze zu einer Theoretischen Grundlegung der Vorgeschichte." *Saeculum* 35:326–64.

————. 1989. "Ethnic Concepts in German Prehistory: A Case Study on the Relationship between Cultural Identity and Objectivity." In *Archaeological Approaches to Cultural Identity.* Stephen Shennan, ed. Pp. 35–56. London: Unwin Hyman.

Vogel, Paul. 1939. *Deutsche Vorgeschichte: Eine Erste Einführung.* Frankfurt: Verlag Moritz Diesterweg.

Wells, Peter. 1998. "Identity and Material Culture in the Later Prehistory of Central Europe." *Journal of Anthropological Research* 6(3):239–98.

Zerubavel, Yael. 1995. *Recovered Roots: Collective Memory and the Making of Israeli National Tradition.* Chicago: University of Chicago Press.

Zvelebil, Marek. 1996. "Farmers Our Ancestors and the Identity of Europe." In *Cultural Identity and Archaeology.* Paul Graves-Brown, Siân Jones, and Clive Gamble, eds. Pp. 145–66. London: Routledge.

5

Scientific Racism in Service of the Reich

German Anthropologists in the Nazi Era

Gretchen E. Schafft

BACKGROUND

Almost sixty years after the invasion of Poland by the Nazis in World War II, an old man stands shaking by his door, afraid to meet the anthropologists who have come to talk to him. He says he does not have anything to tell; he was sick, in the hospital at the time. Another villager is not hesitant and tells of the time of the Nazi occupation of Poland when anthropologists came into the town under SS guard, gave the townspeople a time to appear at the priest's house, and examined them from head to foot. (Few Jews remained in the villages by that time, having been moved to collection points and ghettoes.) Some were given German passports and told to appear for induction and transport to the Russian Front. Others were told to appear for delousing and assignment to labor battalions in Germany. Others escaped to the south and joined the resistance, or were shot attempting to do so. The few people who can remember this time complete a record that at last is being pieced together. They are the living memory of a period almost forgotten in anthropology's professional history.

The fact that German and, to a lesser extent, Austrian anthropologists were involved in the Holocaust as perpetrators, from its beginning to its conclusion, has never been fully acknowledged nor discussed by American anthropologists.[1] The role that American funding played in developing the Nazi ideology of race has also not been told. The information has been available, although not easy to access. Records of these anthropologists' theoretical and empirical studies, as well as their activities as trainers of SS doctors, members of racial courts, collectors of data from concentration camp medical experiments, and certifiers of racial identities have been "cleansed." Documents that should be available in archival files are missing. The biographies of many perpetrators include a cover story for the years 1933 through 1945.[2] The archives of the Rockefeller Foundation, which supported German anthropologists in their racial research, are also mysteriously missing important research plans and reports.

Perhaps the most interesting aspect of all this obscuration is that the perpetrators themselves were careful in how they described their activities, making the most obscene appear quite harmless.[3] They rarely stated explicitly what they were doing, and usually used euphemisms to describe what we now know were crimes against humanity. However, dedicated researchers have found enough corollary documentation to make an airtight case that anthropologists were deeply enmeshed in the crimes of the Third Reich. This documentation is found in archives in the United States and Europe and, increasingly, in books about and compilations of documents from the period (Lifton 1986; Proctor 1988; Klee et al. 1991; Drechsel 1993; Aly et al. 1994; Friedlander 1995; Klee 1997).

The arguments against bringing up this disastrous chapter of the discipline's history are strong. Anthropologists have asked: Why discredit our field so long after the deeds were done? Why discredit all anthropologists of the era when only a few were involved? Why should we give German anthropologists of that period so much attention when American anthropologists never took them seriously anyway?

The answer to these questions is simply that the issues that challenged the anthropologists of the Nazi era were not so different from the issues that have challenged anthropologists at other times as well. As a discipline we have had a strong desire to play a role in the governmental activities of our countries and to inform policy makers of our learned opinions regarding population groups. Anthropologists were involved in the administration of England's colonies; they have been involved in the conduct of war and have been advisers on racial and educational policy in the United States. This involvement has had both positive and negative effects on the people who were subject to the policies that evolved with anthropological input. Problems arise when the direction a government is taking is in opposition to the human rights of some of its people or those it has power to command. Does the anthropologist then abandon the desire to be a player, or does he or she adapt to the order of the day?

We must remind our critics that one does not discredit a discipline by looking closely at the mistakes, or crimes, its theoreticians and practitioners have committed, even when they are of the magnitude of a Holocaust. It is far more dangerous to ignore an infamous period and to learn nothing from it. Denial of unpleasant truths makes it easy to turn complicated events into myths by placing them in a simplistic format (Schafft 1998). When we do that, we fail to see the ways by which people come to follow the road to genocide. Particularly in our own time, following the turn of the century, we see no end to impulses to commit atrocities against ethnic groups. It is absolutely vital that we begin to look at the ways by which otherwise civilized people embrace the road to genocide, as Scheper-Hughes does in this book. What roles in society can fan the flames of ethnic violence or, more appropriately, stop the trend? What policies exacerbate or might be effective in restoring values that protect human life? Students in a class I teach on the Holocaust always ask, Why did it happen? Why didn't anyone stop it? Their questions are important. It is important to know why anthropologists became so involved in Nazi genocide and why no one inside or outside the discipline stopped them.

Unfortunately, it was not a single branch of European anthropology or only a few anthropologists who were engaged in creating and supporting events that were tied to the Holocaust's horrors. Physical anthropologists, eugenicists, ethnographers, and social anthropologists were equally busy during the first half of the 1900s in "racial" studies, in Mendelian genetics, in ethnographic studies of prisoners of war, and in sorting groups of people by psychological and physical characteristics. In these and in so many different ways they helped to determine the outcomes of the lives of their subjects.

German anthropology in this time period was often an interdisciplinary study and practice. It was common for medical doctors, biologists, or geneticists to take a second "practical" doctoral degree in anthropology. It was believed that anthropology could assist in making a better society by providing the theoretical basis for improving the biological structure of the population and the practical means of sorting those people into desirable and undesirable groups, using ethnographic as well as physical anthropological techniques.

Even before Hitler, many people around the world believed that it might be possible to gain control over many social problems by social and biological "engineering." In the 1920s, many were greatly concerned with the criminality that accompanied urbanization, industrialization, and population movements; mental illness, for which there were no effective treatments or cures; and mental retardation (Kühl 1994). Persons who were physically or mentally ill were left to individual or family care, with only the most dismal warehousing of patients the alternative to home care. The idea that a society in the next generation could be rid of the burden of this care—through the sterilization of a variety of persons who did not "fit," or were not self-sufficient or productive—was widely accepted. Sterilization of the mentally ill and handicapped, as well as criminals, was legal in many states in America before Hitler came to power in Germany (ibid.) These U.S. laws provided the justification and groundwork for some of his earliest decrees.

Anthropologists were able to introduce the concept of race to this bevy of concerns about building a healthy and masterful society. The concept of race came to mean to German anthropologists of the early 1900s distinct groups of people who, although they had mingled throughout the ages, remained identifiable. Ideas about kinship, therefore, were mixed with ideas of race. When anthropologists and other professionals combined these ideas with Mendelian ideas of heredity, they could develop a wide range of research aimed at ridding society of "life unworthy of life." Thus the first steps of genocide in the Nazi era were sterilization and eventual killing of the physically and mentally ill and those with handicaps, a practice referred to as euthanasia (Friedlander 1995; Lifton and Markusen 1990). When combined with racial beliefs, it was not difficult to extend this killing to supposed racial groups in order to cleanse the fatherland (Aly 1994).

At first interested in descriptive analyses of varieties of peoples around the world, anthropologists then turned to developing hierarchies of value and assigning them to their racial categories. It was a small step for anthropologists to chart the "races of the world," rank them in some way, and assign capabilities to each. Those imagined capabilities could then match the needs of the Reich, and population groups could be moved, placed, positioned, or eliminated to serve the needs of the "master race," those of German ancestry.

Ideas of "race" were almost immediately part of this kind of social engineering. If one could visualize a country in which the population became uniform in its excellent health, fitness, and mental capacity, then why not also uniform in its "racial" characteristics, which indeed were thought to be equated with such qualities? The idea of uniform "racial" identity became more important as the public embraced a hierarchical theory of valued "racial" groupings, as did the idea of a uniform physical and mental "type" that would represent the German "race."

Research regarding the concept of race was developed initially by German anthropologists at the Kaiser Wilhelm Institut für Anthropologie (KWIA), a part of the larger Kaiser Wilhelm Institut (KWI). This entity could be likened to a national academy of science with the broad goal of advancing knowledge and intellectual achievement. At first supported in part by the Rockefeller Foundation, the programs of the KWIA laid the groundwork for future disregard of human subjects and, ultimately, the genocide of unwanted (*unerwünscht*) groups in Germany and the occupied lands.

THE ROCKEFELLER FOUNDATION AND THE DEVELOPMENT OF THE KAISER WILHELM INSTITUT FÜR ANTHROPOLOGIE

The KWI was founded on October 10, 1910, on the day of Berlin University's centennial, under the premise that it would gain international recognition and cooperation in its research ventures. (In 1914 Albert Einstein became the director of the KWI Institute of Physics; he won the Nobel Prize in 1921, bringing honor to the Berlin complex.) The Institute of Anthropology, Human Heredity, and Genetics was founded in 1927, one of the later institutes in the KWI. Shortly before Hitler assumed power in 1933, the KWI had thirty-one institutes "divided into three classes: I. Institutes of chemistry, physics, technology; II. Institutes of biology, zoology and anthropology; III. Institutes of letters and art." [4] In a voice of optimism, the director of the Kaiser Wilhelm Gesellschaft, a major funding source for the institute, stated:[5]

> I have learned here that the Americans are just as eager as the European scientists to do all in their power towards cultivating and furthering the cause of international scientific development by the cooperation of the scholars of the world. They have realized the importance of such an institution dedicated to the interests of every nation and its tremendous value in promoting international peace and goodwill. We sincerely hope this house will serve as a span to bridge oceans and to bring the nations of the world more closely together. (op. cit.:6–7)

And indeed, "the Americans," namely the Rockefeller Foundation, provided money for many of the institutes, built facilities for them, bought land for them, and, in general, were enthusiastic supporters of the KWI until war broke out in 1939.[6]

The Section on Anthropology, Human Heredity, and Genetics had had an early interest in race. In particular, it wanted to map the "racial" characteristics of the German nation. In 1929 the Rockefeller Foundation gave the Notgesellschaft für Deutsche Wissenschaft, a kind of governmental funding agency for science, $125,000 dedicated to the Kaiser Wilhelm Institut für Anthropologie. It was to be used over a five-year period for the purpose of mapping the racial characteristics of the German nation.[7] Under the direction of Eugen Fischer, the institute's director, anthropologists went from community to community measuring their subjects and doing ethnographic inquiries, but they found great resistance among the population to this probing and prying (Loesch 1997). The resistance of the population was so great that even with Rockefeller funding progress was difficult.

By the time Hitler was elected chancellor of Germany in 1933, the Kaiser Wilhelm Institut für Anthropologie was a major research center in Germany. It had a reduced budget, because of the world financial crisis, of 71,200 Reich Marks (RMs), of which 12,345.51 RM came from the Rockefeller Foundation.[8] By 1935, the budget of the Institute for Anthropology, Human Heredity, and Genetics had risen to 140,000 RM, in large part because of the critical role it was playing in racial policy (Proctor 1998). Eugon Fischer had a powerful position as head of the institute and also rector of the University of Berlin.

Internal documents at the Rockefeller Foundation indicate that officials there watched the development of the Nazi regime but were not particularly concerned about supporting a research entity that had become closely aligned, because of funding and policy, with the new government. Correspondence that remains shows that officials were aware of the anti-Semitic policies that had come into force, but year by year the grants continued.[9]

Certainly many German anthropologists, although interested in race, were at first not in agreement with the "racial" doctrines that the Nazis espoused. The KWI, not a government agency but a recipient of government funding, was obliged to rid itself of Jewish workers and politically left-leaning personnel. The anthropologists at the KWI immediately set about cleansing their institute of these colleagues. Max Planck, director of the KWI throughout the Nazi era, went to see Hitler to tell him that the removal of Jewish scientists from the KWI would mean far fewer Nobel prizes in the future (Stern 1999). (Albert Einstein had left Germany in 1932.) This did not impress Hitler, who was determined that Germany would thrive without Jews. Nor did it deter Planck from continuing his work while complying with every government regulation.[10]

Eugen Fischer, who at first was not so sure about the Nazi idea of a pure German race,[11] soon was able to tell a learned audience:

We need—I repeat again—an *Erbpflege* [literally, a fostering of heredity], in large part conscious and goal directed. Erbpflege is a better word for genetics than racial hygiene; it promotes those who are healthy in mind and body, those with a Germanic heritage, those who carry our way of life. Only that is a population policy! If finally such is enacted, it is not too late to save our people, our German people . . . to [bring them to] the fortified National-Socialist State, a State that we all want, that is supported by our sense of duty, based on an ethical understanding of the future of our people.[12]

The monographs from the study of race in Germany were in the midst of being published when Hitler took power. The arrangement had been for the government's scientific funding agency, the Notgesellschaft für Deutsche Wissenschaft, to pay for the printing. Given the world economic depression in the late 1920s and the cuts in general funding, this cost was difficult to bear. The Rockefeller Foundation was asked to assume the costs. One can surmise what reasons the Rockefeller Foundation might have had to hesitate giving money to the Institute for Anthropology for racial studies, but the written record does not reveal the internal discussions on this matter. Instead, a note is made that 1934 money earmarked for the institute is given to the Notgesellschaft with the understanding that it will be used for this purpose.[13] The monographs were released under the title "Deutsche Rassenkunde," or "German Racial Studies." In its internal documents, the Rockefeller staff refers to the monographs as parts of the "Study of the German People."

The need for money within the Institute for Anthropology was partially alleviated by the source of funding that came from the Department of the Interior (Innenministerium). With the onset of Hitler's racial policies, the need for certification of "Germanness" was immediate, even within the KWI itself. Employees had to prove that they had no "Jewish blood" and were "pure Germans" in order to continue in their jobs. Kinship formed the basis of determining who was Jewish and who was not. Long before the Reich Citizenship Law was enacted in November 1935, spelling out the definition of a Jew became critical to the enforcement of the new German government policy. A Jew was defined under the law of November 1935 as a person:

- descended from three Jewish grandparents;
- descended from two Jewish grandparents and belonging to a Jewish religious community on September 15, 1935, or on a subsequent date; or
- married to a Jewish person on September 15, 1935, or on a subsequent date.

In addition, the offspring of a marriage contracted with a "three-quarters" or "full Jew" after September 15, 1935, or the offspring of an extramarital relationship with a "three-quarters" or "full Jew" born after July 31, 1936, were also considered Jewish (Hilberg 1985:31).

Although this law was not drafted by anthropologists, who better understood kinship and were in a position to certify it? Fischer made use of this expertise to further the fortunes of the institute. An examination was needed when church records did not establish the ethnicity of a person. The examination, when it was performed, consisted of a blood test, a look at the eye shape and physiology, the shape of the head, and a photograph, front and in profile. In the end the decision was based on personal opinion, for there were no criteria for determining who was Jewish, or of any other ethnicity.

Throughout the country people rushed to find *Gutachter*, or certifiers. Universities performed the service free of charge. Fischer rebelled against this volunteer service, however: "I would urgently advise against doing these certifications without cost. First, it is really not clear why some who have government funding should take the time, especially the scientific time, from public work to perform economic jobs that do not pay for the trouble."[14]

In 1938 Fischer declared that his institute prepared about seventy certificates yearly, bringing in an income of 1,652 RM in 1935–1936 and 1,117 RM from April to August of the next year.[15] According to the Interior Ministry, each certificate should cost about 90 RM. Most people seeking or requiring a certificate could pay for it themselves, leaving a shortfall of only 1,350 RM per year to the government as a whole.[16] Although eventually the government allowed the institute to keep the money it collected, it argued that the "research value" alone of doing the racial certifications should be a reward, particularly to the university departments of anthropology.[17]

Racial courts were established by the Nazis to handle violations of racial codes, to settle racial questions, and to enforce the racial standards. Anthropologists at the institute were asked to serve, and they did. In the "Report of Activities" of the institute from July 1933 to April 1935, Fischer reported:

> At the meeting of the Board of Directors in July 1933, Dr. Gütt, the Minister Director, stated that it was the wish and in the interest of the Reich government that exactly this Institute would be ready to advise on the enactment of laws regarding sterilization, research on the genetically ill, clinical handling and training of a genetic and racial-biological medical force. The Institute has tried to do this without restraint since that time. I have been aware that much of my scientific work has been somewhat reduced or given to others but that did not stop me. I am of the opinion that at the present time as we build the peoples' State, no other institution can serve this task as well as we, and it must be our priority. We have all done this—division leaders, assistants and volunteers—to the greatest degree possible.[18]

Fischer then went on to say that Professor Otmar von Verschuer, at that time second in command at the institute, had been a member of the Genetic Health Court "for a long time." Fischer himself had been a member of the Appellate Genetic Health Court in Berlin "from the beginning."

The Genetic Health Courts had a rapid influence and a chilling effect on the population. Those ordered to be sterilized because of what was thought to be a genetic flaw in their makeup could appeal their cases. In the first two months after they were established, the first court in Berlin heard 348 cases, of which 325 appeals were rejected and the sterilization was ordered (Proctor 1988:106).

Fischer also reported that Professor Fritz Lenz, an anthropologist who was the liaison between the universities and the institute before he became head of the Institute for Race Studies at the University of Berlin, took part in the Commission on Population and Racial Policy. This commission was a powerful source of planning for the occupation of lands to the east of Germany, the resettlement of various population groups, and the dispersion and eventual annihilation of Jews, Sinti, and Roma.

Certainly, the training of SS doctors was an important part of the service the institute was providing for the state. A textbook for doctors used at that time quotes Eugon Fischer as stating that the cultural life of mankind involves a domestication in which many weak and sick individuals come to be tolerated (Keiter 1941). This would not occur in free nature where variation and mutations would not survive. The textbook goes on to explain the implications of "contra-selection," the beginning arguments for euthanasia.

In the first year and a half of the regime, the institute trained eleven hundred doctors in the theory and practice of racial hygiene (Proctor 1988:42). These doctors were trained by the anthropologists to be ruthless in their approach to their patients. They proved their ability to be just that in their work in concentration camps, hospitals, and asylums.

By the late 1930s, most of the significant university positions in anthropology were being vetted by the Kaiser Wilhelm Insitut für Anthropologie in Berlin, which had a sterling record of loyalty to the government and its "racial" policies. It is safe to assume that few, if any, anthropologists had positions in German universities who were not ideologically committed to "racial" studies and actions to make Germany and the Reich uniform in its population. Racial certification was done by anthropology departments throughout Germany, research being parceled out to universities in Marburg, Munich, Jena, Gera, Leipzig, Frankfurt, Vienna, Graz, and other universities too numerous to mention.

Eugen Fischer remained the director of the Institute for Anthropology until he retired in 1942. His case illustrates how it could come about that one would move so easily from a study of differences to the conviction that differences could be gradated into a hierarchical value system. He began studies in South Africa of people of mixed "race" whom he called the "Rehobath Bastards." Despite the negative connotation of the word *bastard*, he was rather favorably impressed by "mixed race" people and decided that offspring from two different groups might prove beneficial to a society. This opinion was not looked upon with favor from those in the Hitler regime, and over a relatively short time his statements changed, until he had brought himself in line with government policy. He became so willing to go along with the order of the day that he instituted a series of measures that directly supported the move to make Germany a homogeneous nation. As already stated, he began courses for SS doctors in "Racial Hygiene" through the auspices of the institute and certified them in the theoretical basis of racism.[19] He supported sterilization in his writing, in his speeches, and as a member of the racial court.

Fischer had the chance to withdraw from the research arena in the Third Reich and go into "internal exile." Instead he chose to alter his beliefs based on his findings to come into congruence with the government's stance. The policy of *Gleichschaltung*, the homogeneous approach to all matters of organization and belief, was vigorously enforced by the Nazi government. The alternative for those who could not or would not stand with official policy was to be removed from any serious endeavor and to be regarded with suspicion by the police state. At some point, although Fischer was old enough to retire, he chose to play an active role even if it meant changing his position. In the end, this shift to endorsing Nazi ideology led him to support a line of research that developed into the most vivid horror of the Nazi era.[20]

The Rockefeller Foundation shifted its interest from racial studies to research on twins at the beginning of the Hitler era. Twins held the key to questions of heredity versus environment. The studies at the institute were the domain of Verschuer, who had been a professor at Frankfurt and maintained a post there as well as in Berlin. In a report from 1941, Fischer reported that Verschuer had "a material of 700 twin pairs on hand."[21]

Verschuer was interested in determining the influence of nature versus nurture in personality, especially criminal personality. For this purpose, he had identified 150 pairs of twins that he studied. "With clinician Diehl he is studying tuberculosis in twins and publishing on that subject. The investigation is supported by the Ministry of the Interior, the Prussian Welfare Ministry and the Rockefeller Foundation."[22] At first the study looked at these issues using 4,000 twin pairs he identified through public school records. Later he arranged for the twins to be admitted into a hospital facility at Berlin Buch, paid for by the Rockefeller Foundation.[23] There, research regarding resistance to infectious disease, including tuberculosis, was undertaken. In 1935 Fischer related to the Rockefeller Foundation that twin research under Verschuer comprised psychological studies, pathological studies, and "the reaction of twins to Atrophin, Pilocarpin, Adrenalin, Histamin. Dr. Werner can show that the pulse, blood pressure, saliva, etc. reacts more similarly among identical twins than the others, therefore the reactions are inherited."[24] What kind of experimentation was going on? It is not clear from the existing records, but introducing school-aged children to experimental doses of chemical substances predated twin experiments in Auschwitz by almost a decade. There is no indication that the Rockefeller Foundation staff raised ethical questions about the practices.

Early in the Hitler regime, Verschuer founded the professional journal *Der Erbartz* (*The Genetics' Doctor*), which became the most widely read journal by physicians in the Third Reich. It served as a publication venue for much of the work of the institute. Through this vehicle he was able to spread the eugenics and racial doctrine throughout the Reich, including the need for sterilization of handicapped individuals and the doctrine of creating a more perfect race for the state while abandoning the idea of the value of individual human beings.

CONTINUATION OF THE KAISER WILHELM INSTITUT
FÜR ANTHROPOLOGIE AFTER THE OUTBREAK OF WAR

The Rockefeller Foundation discontinued funding of the KWI after war was declared between the United States and Germany. That did not stop the Institute for Anthropology from continuing its activities, however. Many were intensified.

Fischer continued as director until 1942, when he retired. According to internal memos, he was past the retirement age and not in good health. Whatever other reasons he may have had are not known. He was replaced by Verschuer, who was often assisted in his work by Josef Mengele. Verschuer had been the "Doctor Father" (mentor) of Mengele, and they worked well together when Mengele could spare time from his SS duties. Mengele had gotten a doctorate in anthropology and then a second doctorate in medicine. Like Verschuer, he was both a medical doctor and an anthropologist. He was very interested in twin research and was able to provide some "materials" to the institute from Auschwitz.

> My assistant Dr. [Josef] Mengele (M.D., Ph.D.) has joined me in the branch of research. He is presently employed as *Hauptsturmführer* and camp physician in the concentration camp at Auschwitz. Anthropological investigations on the most diverse racial groups of this concentration camp are carried out with permission of the SS *Reichsführer* [Heinrich Himmler]; the blood samples are being sent to my laboratory for analysis.[25]

If only the investigations had been limited to blood samples. Unfortunately, there is ample evidence that eyes and other human body parts were sent to the institute for further study. Some of the twins survived to tell their stories:

> Mengele had two types of research programs. One set of experiments dealt with genetics and the other with germ warfare. In the germ experiments, Mengele would inject one twin with a germ. Then, if and when the twin died, he would kill the other twin to compare the organs at autopsy. (Annas and Grodin 1992)

The institute received a new assignment as Germany pushed into Poland and the Soviet Union. Could they advise the government on the nature of ethnic groups that would be found in the occupied lands? Another anthropological group was already working on this problem and had its own modus operandi.

THE INSTITUT FÜR DEUTSCHE OSTARBEIT
(THE INSTITUTE FOR WORK IN THE EAST)

Anthropologists in Germany and Austria were well-respected participants in the Nazi regime by the time Germany marched into Poland. They were counted on for advice, assistance, and active participation in many of the tasks of the expanding empire. They provided the justification, the theory, and the methodology for "Racial Science" and its applications, the backbone of the Third Reich.

On Hitler's birthday, April 20, 1940, The Institut für Deutsche Ostarbeit (IDO) was opened. Its purpose was to create policy and investigate modes of exploiting the newly conquered lands in the *Generalgouvernement* (GG), under Gouveneur Hans Frank. Five months earlier, just one month after the invasion of Poland, the Germans had tricked 183 professors of Cracow's Jagiellonian University into appearing for a meeting that was promptly dismissed, its participants packed into buses heading for German concentration camps where most were eventually killed (Burleigh 1988:253). This cleared the way for a new direction in the academy and space for the offices of the IDO.

The institute took over the beautiful buildings of the Jagiellonian University, which dated back to the age of Copernicus. Within the IDO were eleven sections, including prehistory, history, art history, law, language, economy, agriculture, landscape, forestry, earth science, and race and ethnic research. The structure was not unlike that of the Kaiser Wilhelm Institut in Berlin.

The section on Race and Ethnic Research had a relatively small number of permanent staff members augmented by Polish workers, most of whom were highly trained. Unlike the KWI, however, the anthropological part of the IDO was focused on ethnographic studies as well as anthropometric "racial" identifications. The section had three *Referat*, or divisions: Anthropology, Ethnology, and Jewish Research. The outcomes of research led to the same end as anthropological research elsewhere in the Third Reich: classifications of persons as outsiders, and a determination of their life chances within the Nazi world order.

> The *Referat* Ethnology is making efforts to carry the concept of ethnic research far beyond what has hitherto been understood by the term as it is used in academic circles. This ethnic research requires the total encompassing of the life history of peoples, what they carry with them from all sides, such as their racial history, their biology, their demographics, sociology, ethno-politics, and folk psychology. Ethnic investigation includes the health of a people, their limitations due to inherited illnesses and conditions, the (cultural) movements of the people, their customs and expressions of it in form and content, the feeling for nationhood and mythmaking, the problems and conflicts on the speech and ethnic boundaries, and much more—in short, all that contributes to a group's active or passive expression of race and identity.[26]

The anthropologists put forth the idea that Middle and Eastern Europe was composed of various "racial strains." Under the prevailing philosophy, each group should be assessed according to how the capabilities of its people could best assist in the development of the New Order of Nazi Germany (Gottong 1941:28–40). In practice this meant that the anthropologists of the IDO and their staffs intended to cast a "thick net" of investigations over the GG, as the former Polish districts of Warsaw, Cracow, Radom, and Lublin were known under Nazi occupation. The outcome of these ethnographic and anthropomorphic investigations was a sorting of people for slave labor, colonization of Ukrainian farmland, entry into the German Army, or death.

The German anthropologists were not satisfied with the descriptions of populations they could obtain from Polish scientists: "There is little worth in the materials presented to us by Polish anthropologists due to their peculiar point of view and the methods used. There is virtually no material on the races and their distribution; everything remains for the German scientists to do."[27]

Many of the anthropological positions were filled with university people from Vienna. Women anthropologists played a major role in the section, one becoming acting director when her predecessor was called to the front. Their duties were broad and strenuous, and the anthropologists, without a doubt, worked very hard.

In Cracow they took part in the confiscation of libraries and private collections of books useful to their cause. They oversaw the inventory of ethnographic museums throughout Poland and arranged for materials to be sent back to Germany for exhibits there; they also prepared exhibits for display in occupied Poland. A major thrust of these exhibits seemed to be the justification for the Nazi invasion. These justifications included the idea that Germanic tribes and peoples had populated the newly occupied lands in the twelfth and thirteenth centuries, and their "racial" heritage had provided every cultural advantage to the GG. This heritage needed to be redefined and protected in the future. They published unceasingly in journals, paid for by the IDO, devoted to examination of the discoveries of Eastern Europe, particularly the GG. They coordinated visits with anthropologists from the Reich and parceled out work to them.

Their most important task, however, was the ethnographic and anthropometric studies of the people of occupied Poland. During the four years of their IDO work, they investigated numerous villages, delousing centers, at least one ghetto, and concentration/prisoner-of-war camps. This ethnographic work was carried on in coordination with the SS, which provided protection to the scientists and ensured the compliance of the subjects. People were taken at gunpoint to collection places where they were measured, interviewed, and sometimes fingerprinted. Occasionally, hair samples were taken. Photographs were taken by SS photographers, and sketches of body hair were made of many of the subjects.[28]

In 1942 the section reported that it had made 13,258 separate notes in its research into Polish bibliographic sources! Many of these were historical descriptions of settlements in which the anthropologists had an interest. They had assembled these notes and placed them in a card catalog that was "completed up to the letter 'J.' "[29]

The Section on Jewish Research described its goal in a forthright way. The staff collected written material about Jews and hoped to publish materials showing the results of the "racial mixing" of societies in the occupied lands. "The final goal of all the individual research projects is the production of a history and course of study of the Jewish question in order to immunize the coming generations against renewed domination tendencies of Jews."[30]

By 1943 the section was more focused on practical matters.

Seldom has a region within Europe been so racially mixed and presented with the resulting ethnic problems as the *Generalgouvernement*. To investigate the full range of ethnic expression and to make the results useful to the State officials is the job of the Section.[31]

In this report it is clear that another concern bothered the Germans. Many Poles were being sent back to the Reich to work as slave laborers. Would they "mix" with the people there, infecting the "pure" German population with inferior genes? Only Poles with predominantly "Aryan" features should be risked. The anthropologists had to find these people and identify them.

The Jews of the Tarnower Ghetto were another group that had to be investigated quickly, for they were being eliminated. This investigation was carried out in conjunction with the Anthropological Institute in Vienna. The features identified in the Jews, many of whom had been forcibly removed from Vienna, would be available to trace traits that had been passed on to other groups through intermarriage and "racial" mixing in the future. The anthropologists were aware that the Jews would not be alive much longer.[32]

As far as the Jews' pictures are concerned, of course we will stand by the agreement we made as far as it just depends on us. I am in agreement with the times you have given, but I want to remind you that we don't know what measures regarding the expulsion of the Jews will be taken in the coming months, under which circumstances worthwhile material would be lost to us. It could happen that the natural family connections will be torn from their context, whereby not only the pictures themselves will be taken under difficult circumstances, but also the very possibility of taking pictures will be very much altered.[33]

There is little of a personal nature that has remained of the experiences of the anthropologists. Several female anthropologists from Vienna University, who were increasingly responsible members of the team as the male anthropologists were called to the Russian Front, carried on a limited correspondence. These are the only remaining indications that personal experiences entered into their lives as researchers.[34] In one such letter, Elfriede Fliethmann describes her trip to Hanozowa. "As I drove back from Hanozowa, I was almost hit by an avalanche. Workers there loaded a car with stones, and as I drove past they threw a whole forklift full at me. Luckily nothing happened to me, but you can imagine my fury."[35]

By the summer of 1944, the Russians had closed in on the GG, and Germany was in retreat. Concentration camp prisoners from Flossenburg and Ravensbrück were called in to pack up the materials and send them to two castles in Bavaria for safekeeping.[36] The staff of the IDO relocated with their materials, and some scientists tried to continue to work.

The U.S. Army discovered the staff and materials at the end of the war. They were convinced that these were harmless scientists who had been victims of the war. As such, they even arranged for them to be paid for a few more months! The materials from the IDO's Section on Race and Ethnic Research were sent to Washington and divided among several archives. Although much of the material had been deleted and destroyed—by whom cannot be ascertained—enough remained to give a picture of what had happened in Cracow.[37] Other archives stored various materials from the IDO, and their publications remain in several world libraries, including the Library of Congress.

NAZI ANTHROPOLOGISTS IN SUPPORT OF GENOCIDE

We return to the questions my students have raised about these anthropologists: why did they do it, and why did no one stop them? Perhaps the answers are not as difficult as they seemed at first. Hannah Arendt was right, there was a banality of evil (Arendt 1963).

It is now clear that the *process* by which the ultimate evil of the Holocaust came about was not begun under the Nazis, but many years earlier when the world looked for answers to hard questions raised by urbanization and modernity, described by Hinton in the first chapter of this book. The steps in the process were, first, international acceptance of initial research questions and the methods and context in which they were carried out. This context included the exclusion from the research teams of previously valued members because of political and "racial" identities. Second, career aggrandizement—rather than unemployment—offered a great motivation. Third, psychological protection reduced the psychosocial dissonance (Hinton 1996) and assisted anthropologists in handling the stress of conducting inhumane investigations. Fourth, values of the "normal" world were attached to their very abnormal activities.

How could the world be made healthier, more productive, and more efficient? The questions were asked not only in Germany but also in the United States and other Western countries. Despite its questionable methodologies, the German research of the 1920s that addressed these questions was supported in large part by the Rockefeller Foundation, an American institution.

The answers devised in the Third Reich were as follows: First, the state could arrange to sterilize those who reproduced or could reproduce offspring not valued by the state. Second, the state could allow and encourage experimentation on human subjects, referred to as "pieces" or "material," those who had no power to say "no." Next, the state could arrange to get rid of "life unworthy of life" and assign those considered least worthy to menial tasks under the control of those in charge of the New Order. Finally, the state could move masses of population groups from place to place, killing some and enslaving others for the benefit of the few who met the criteria of the "Master Race."

Why did the anthropological community in Germany offer no objection? First, individuals who stood against government policy were dealt with quickly in the first weeks, months, and years of the regime. Their ability to protest was brutally and quickly wiped out. We have no record of anthropologists who went to concentration camps for their adherence to a different moral order, but we can assume some did.

Others were motivated to continue their work by their own success. Never had their discipline been so well respected and received (Mosen 1991:9). Never had practitioners been so busy. Furthermore, their work, which was so closely tied to the SS, could provide exemptions from military service for the men. This was not a small consideration. All the motivation for cooperation with the Nazi regime was incorporated in career advancement, while the price for not cooperating was "internal exile," joblessness, or incarceration.

The academic discipline as a whole assisted the individual in handling the psychosocial dissonance by allowing anthropologists the opportunity to publish their research accounts with only vague references to their methods and selection of subjects. A cognitive dissociation between the treatment of human subjects and the descriptions of scientific research was actually encouraged. Despite the ruthlessness of the actions instigated by anthropologists and other scientists, the incipient shame and guilt they must have felt can be read into what they did *not* say and write. It takes a great deal of reading to find even hints of "smoking guns" among the remaining documents. For example, Mengele's files, once returned to the KWI, are not to be found. Only his victims indicate the enormity of his crime.

The practice of not specifying the actual activities undertaken in the name of science served the purpose of protecting the postwar careers of Nazi anthropologists and other perpetrators. Of the academics who worked in the IDO, virtually all went on to other esteemed positions following the war. Fischer retired in 1942 from the KWI, but Verschuer, after paying a small fine, was given other university positions until his connection with Mengele became known. Among the scientists of the IDO, most continued with government careers despite their participation in the genocide of Jews and Roma, as well as the rape of Poland.

Perhaps the anthropologists who witnessed genocide, and played a role in it, buffered their knowledge of their own involvement with a scientism that went beyond their convoluted verbiage. Perhaps they believed that the ethnographic studies they performed were valuable in their own right, even if they had to be conducted under SS guard and village people were shot at the edge of town during their research trips.

Some of their values matched those of the outside world. They spoke of better public health, better economic conditions, and a deeper intellectual understanding of diversity. By stressing those values and denying the enormity of the damage they were inflicting on people through their practice, the anthropologists could continue to feel they were making a contribution to a better world, one in which they would be ever more highly valued and their knowledge revered. This could happen only if the fate of those they defined as "Other" was justified by the search for a clean and purified "Folks' Society." Nazi anthropologists marched under their pseudo-science banner to the tune of health, cleanliness, and racial homogeneity, providing the state its justification for genocidal and criminal acts. The activities of the Nazi anthropologists linger with us through the suffering of survivors and often survivors' offspring, through their influence on a postwar generation of students, and through the garbled history they left behind them.

NOTES

The author would like to recognize the following archives and thank the staff members who were particularly helpful: The National Anthropological Archives (NAA), John Homiak, director, and Robert Leopold, archivist; The National Archives in Washington, D.C. (NAW); The Jagiellonian University Archive (JUA), Adam Cieślak, curator; The Bundesarchiv Koblenz (BAK), Gregor Pickro, archivist; the Archiv zur Geschichte der Max-Planck-Gesellschaft (AMPG); and the Rockefeller Archive Center (RAC). Gerhard Zeidler was a partner in most of the research reflected in this chapter, although the author alone is responsible for its content. Sonja Kämpgen assisted with the editing.

1. The exception to this silence is a chapter by Robert Proctor, "From Anthropologie to Rassenkunde in the German Anthropological Tradition," in *Bones, Bodies, Behavior: Essays on Biological Anthropology*, George Stocking, ed. (Madison: University of Wisconsin Press, 1988).

German anthropologists did not explore the history of their discipline's activities in the Third Reich until 1983, the fiftieth anniversary of the takeover by Hitler (Fischer 1990). Since that time, several universities have explored their own history, although there is often a great deal of resistance to such an enterprise (Mosen 1991:7). For further information on the view of German and Austrian anthropologists of this period, see among others Hauschild (1995), Linimayr (1994), Gerndt (1987), and Mosen (1991).

2. Personal conversation with Gregor Pickro, archivist at the Bundesarchive Koblenz, Germany, and experience in various archives.

3. Examples abound of scientists who "managed" their identities after the war. During the war they kept the descriptions of their activities innocuous, often by maintaining a university position while, in fact, "practicing" anthropology in a government-related office.

4. Speech by Dr. Adolf Morsbach, director of the Kaiser Wilhelm Society for the Promotion of Science, 1932, p. 3, RAC, RF, Record Group 1.1, Series A, Sub-Series 717, Box 10, Folder 64.

5. All translations in this chapter are the work of the author.

6. There was some discussion that the KWI would name its physics institute the Rockefeller Institut in return for a substantial investment of funds. RAC, Record Group 1.1, Series A, Box 4, Folder 46, pp. 6–7.

7. Memo from Professor Stark, president of the Notgesellschaft, to Eugen Fischer, director of Anthropological Studies of the German People. RAC, RF, Collection 1.1, Record Group A, Box 20, Folder 187.

8. RAC, RF, Record Group 1.1, Series 717, Sub-Series A, Box 10, Folder 63.

9. RAC, RF, Record Group 1.1, Subseries A, Box 4, Folder 46.

10. "Planck declared to Frick (Reichs Innenminister) his willingness 'to place the KWI at the systematic service of the Reich' " (Loesch 1987:312).

11. Loesch (pp. 234–253) states that there was a campaign against Fischer based on his pre-1933 research reports that claimed some benefit of mixed-race populations. After discussions with officials in the SS Office of Population and Genetic Health (SS-Amt für Bevölkerungspolitik und Erbgesundheitspflege), he realized that he would have a very restricted position and possibly be required to retire at sixty-five in 1939 if he did not agree to the line set out by the racial policy groups. This he did not want to do.

12. Eugen Fischer. "Die Fortschritte bei menschlichen Erblehre als Grundlage eugenischer Bevölkerungspolitik," p. 71 (source unidentified) RAC, RF, Record Group 1.1, Series A, Box 20, Folder 187.

13. RAC, RF, Record Group 1.1, Series A, Box 20, Folder 187.

14. AMPG, I Abt., Rep. 1A. Nr. 2399/3, Bl. 90.

15. Ibid.

16. Ibid., Bl. 80.

17. Ibid.

18. AMPG, I. Abt., 1A., Nr. 2404/3, Bl. 49.

19. RAC, RF, Record Group 1.1, Series A, Box 20, Folder 187.

20. Fischer is a good example of an anthropologist who was influenced, even formed, by the state and yet contributed to the viability and practice of the deadly ideology it embodied. Given his wish to conform, one can imagine that had he lived under a more humane or benign government, he might have been a different kind of professional.

21. AMPG, I. Abt., 1A, Nr. 2404/2, Bl. 14–17.

22. Ibid.

23. RAC, RF, Record Group 1.1, Series A, Box 4, Folder 46.

24. Ibid., Box 10, Folder 63.

25. Proctor 1988, 44, from Benno Müller-Hill, *Murderous Science* (Oxford: Oxford University Press, 1988); BAK, R 73/15342, fol.64.

26. NAA, Register to the Materials of the Institut für Deutsche Ostarbeit (IDO) collection (Schafft and Zeidler 1998).

27. Ernst R. Fugmann. "Das wirtschaftsgeographische Gefüge des Generalgouvernements." Unidentified article found in a collection at the Bundesarchiv Berlin-Lichterfelde.

28. NAA, IDO Collection.

29. Ibid.

30. Ibid.

31. Ibid.

32. Correspondence Fliethmann, IDO Collection, Folder 70.

33. JUA, IDO Collection, Folder 70.

34. These women anthropologists carried on research in their own assigned villages, usually traveling without their male colleagues but under heavy SS guard.

35. Ibid.

36. Ravensbrück is often thought of as solely a women's camp. It incorporated, however, both a youth camp and a men's camp.

37. One assumes from the nature of the collection that materials have been destroyed. Informants in Poland indicate that pictures of their naked bodies were taken, but only the portraits of faces and ethnographic shots of material goods and landscapes exist today. It is possible that some materials remain to be found.

REFERENCES CITED

Aly, Götz, P. Chroust, and C. Pross. 1994. *Cleansing the Fatherland*. Baltimore, Md.: Johns Hopkins University Press.

Annas, George, and M. A. Grodin. 1992. *The Nazi Doctors and the Nuremberg Code*. New York: Oxford University Press.

Arendt, Hannah. 1963. *Eichmann in Jerusalem: A Report on the Banality of Evil.* New York: Viking Press.

Burleigh, Michael. 1988. *Germany Turns Eastward: A Study of Ostforschung in the Third Reich.* New York: Cambridge.

Drechsel, Klaus-Peter. 1993. *Beurteilt, Vermessen, Ermordet: Die Praxis der Euthanasie bis zum Ende des deutschen Faschismus.* Duisburg: Duisburger Institut für Sprach- und Sozialforschung.

Fischer, Hans. 1990. *Völkerkunde im Nationalsozialismus.* Berlin: Dietrich Reimer Verlag.

Friedlander, Henry. 1995. *The Origins of Nazi Genocide: From Euthanasia to the Final Solution.* Chapel Hill: University of North Carolina Press.

Gerndt, Helge, ed. 1987. *Nationalsozialismus. Referate und Diskussionen einer Tagung der Deutschen Gesellschaft für Volkskunde, München, 23–25, Oktober 1986.* München: Münchener Vereinigung für Volkskunde, Band 7.

Gottong, Heinrich. 1941. "Bedeutung und Aufgaben der Sektion Rassen und Volkstumsforschung." *Deutsche Forschung im Osten* 1(6):28–40.

Hauschild, Thomas. 1995. *Lebenslust und Fremdenfurcht: Ethnologie im Dritten Reich.* Frankfurt/M: Suhrkamp.

Hilberg, Raul. 1985. *The Destruction of the European Jews.* New York: Holmes and Meier.

Hinton, Alexander Laban. 1996. "Agents of Death: Explaining the Cambodian Genocide in Terms of Psychosocial Dissonance." *American Anthropologist* 98(4):818–31.

Keiter, Friedrich. 1941. *Rassenbiologie und Rassenhygiene.* Stuttgart: Ferdinand Enke Verlag.

Klee, Ernst. 1997. *Auschwitz: Die NS-Medizin und ihre Opfer.* Frankfurt am Main: S. Fischer.

Klee, Ernst, W. Dressen, and V. Riess, eds. 1991. *The Good Old Days.* New York: Konecky and Konecky.

Kühl, Stefan. 1994. *The Nazi Connection: Eugenics, American Racism, and German National Socialism.* New York: Oxford University Press.

Lifton, Robert Jay. 1986. *The Nazi Doctors: Medical Killing and the Psychology of Genocide.* New York: Basic Books.

Lifton, Robert J., and Eric Markusen. 1990. *The Genocidal Mentality: Nazi Holocaust and Nuclear Threat.* New York: Basic Books.

Linimayr, Peter. 1994. *Wiener Völkerkunde im Nationalsozialismus. Ansätze zu einer NS-Wissenschaft.* Frankfurt/M: Europäische Hochschulschriften.

Loesch, Niels. 1997. *Rasse als Konstrukt: Leben und Werk Eugen Fischers.* Frankfurt/M: Peter Lang.

Mosen, Markus. 1991. *Der koloniale Traum.* Bonn: Holos.

Müller-Hill, Benno. 1984. *Tödliche Wissenschaft.* Reinbek bei Hamburg: Rowohlt Taschenbuch Verlag, GmbH.

Proctor, Robert. 1988. *Racial Hygiene: Medicine under the Nazis.* Cambridge: Harvard University Press.

Schafft, Gretchen. 1998. "Civic Denial and the Memory of War." *Journal of the American Academy of Psychoanalysis* 26(2):255–272.

Schafft, Gretchen, and Gerhard Zeidler. 1998. *Register to the Materials of the Institut für deutsche Ostarbeit.* Washington, D.C.: Smithsonian Institution, National Anthropological Archives.

Stern, Fritz. 1999. *Einstein's German World.* Princeton: Princeton University Press

PART THREE

Annihilating Difference

Local Dimensions of Genocide

6

The Cultural Face of Terror in the Rwandan Genocide of 1994

Christopher C. Taylor

INTRODUCTION

For the past fifteen years anthropology's central concept, the concept of culture, has come under withering attack. Some have criticized its use as overly reifying. Others claim that no human group has ever been characterized by a single coherent set of norms, beliefs, and attitudes. Still others view the notion of culture as excessively rule-oriented and deterministic—too much of a "cookie-cutter" and as such insufficiently sensitive to the expression of diverse human agencies. There are no such things as rules, say the latter, only contested meanings and negotiated realities arrived at, and only ephemerally, in the clash of conflicting interests and ideologies.

Yet those who claim that the anthropological notion of culture has been excessively totalizing sometimes ignore the fact that the analysts they criticize are often not guilty of the imputed charges (Sahlins 1999:404). Still the critique has not fallen on deaf ears. It cannot be denied that in its wake, much anthropological analysis has returned to a kind of methodological and ontological individualism. Eschewing homeostatic "social structures" and the decoding of "deep structures," many anthropologists have begun to prefer analytic approaches that emphasize diverse subjectivities, multivocality, and multiple interpretation (Clifford and Marcus 1986). These latter claim that anthropologists of intellectualist bent ignore or diminish the subject, that they depict social actors as mere bearers of their culture rather than its shapers. History as well, in the hands of the intellectualists, loses its dynamism as all becomes reduced to the recapitulation of the same or very similar structures of thought.

Yet among those who would fetishize difference, many appear bent upon abolishing the concept of culture altogether. In earlier versions of methodological individualism, as in transactionalism and rational choice theory, individuals everywhere seemed to think and to act alike. Like *Homo economicus*, social actors exercised their free will, maximizing utility, and choosing courses of action according to perceived cost/benefit ratios. Culture was additive, an aggregate generated by the sum total of individuals' choices (Barth 1959). Although more recent individualist approaches often criticize the presumed universality of a maximizing person, culture has nevertheless become fragmented into a cacophony of multiple and conflicting discourses in which the subject often disappears in a cloud of complexity and incoherence (Ortner 1995:183).

Yet it could also be argued that in the latter case the notion of the subject is a culture-bound one, grounded in individualist and egalitarian assumptions that "celebrate difference and interpretation" (Kapferer 1989:193). Culture, according to that strain of thought, has become epiphenomenal, a dependent variable, a mere instrument in the political or economic struggle rather than the ideational crucible in which these struggles find their significance. In earlier versions individualist assumptions were explicitly stated; more frequently today they are not. In either case cultural voluntarism and its more recent avatars continue to sound particularly Western in perspective.

Attempting to wend the way between an overly reified notion of culture and the concept's effective negation has presented anthropology with a formidable challenge; neither side appears to be completely right, nor completely wrong. Yet both sides are loath to consider the possibility that the analytic strength that one might derive from an axiomatically unified set of presuppositions may also be a weakness. Perhaps this is nowhere more apparent than in the domain of political anthropology, where scholars like John Gledhill are insisting that to understand the political behavior of elites in the non-Western world, one must understand not only the varied self-interests of social actors and the multiplicity of discourses they construct but also the cultural frameworks in which actions occur and that render those actions meaningful (Gledhill 1994). We cannot assume that the manifestations of power in the world are everywhere the same, for, as Gledhill shows, there are profound differences in political cultures. Economic and political behavior outside the Western context is unlikely to be understood without some sense of these differences.

Gledhill's work builds upon that of Michel Foucault, Pierre Bourdieu, and Bruce Kapferer. From Foucault, Gledhill pursues the insight that power involves not only the negative aspect of constraining the volition of others but also a positive aspect. Social actors in specific cultural and historical circumstances are constructed to think and to act in certain ways (ibid.:126). We need to understand the construction of the subject from the inside out in order to understand power in its fullest dimensions, and that, Gledhill argues, might best be accomplished by building upon conventional anthropological studies of symbolism (ibid.). To this end, Gledhill cites the work of Pierre Bourdieu and his use of the notion of *habitus*, and Bruce Kapferer and his use of the notion of ontology.

It is to these theorists that I turn in attempting to understand some of the cultural dimensions of what occurred during the 1994 genocide in Rwanda, where as many as one million people were killed—one-seventh of the country's population.[1] Although much of what I will concern myself with involves the politics of ethnicity in Rwanda, my major point is that we cannot make full sense of the Rwandan tragedy with an analytical approach that merely recapitulates the assumption of instrumental rationality that characterizes much neofunctionalist analysis. The violence that occurred in Rwanda cannot be reduced solely and simply to the competition for power, dominance, and hegemony among antagonistic factions. Much of the violence, I maintain, followed a cultural patterning, a structured and structuring logic, as individual Rwandans lashed out against a perceived internal other who threatened, in their imaginary, both their personal integrity and the cosmic order of the state. It was overwhelmingly Tutsi who were the sacrificial victims in what in many respects was a massive ritual of purification, a ritual intended to purge the nation of "obstructing beings," as the threat of obstruction was imagined through a Rwandan ontology that situates the body politic in analogical relation to the individual human body.

As I will attempt to show in this chapter, many of the representations concerning bodily integrity that I encountered in popular medicine during fieldwork in Rwanda in 1983 to 1985, 1987, and 1993 to 1994 emerged in the techniques of physical cruelty employed by Hutu extremists during the genocide. But there was no simple cultural determinism to the Rwandan genocide. I do not advance the argument that the political events of 1994 were in any way caused by these symbols, or by Rwandan "culture," conceived of in a cognitively determinist way in the manner of Goldhagen's controversial analysis of the Nazi genocide (1996). These representations operated as much during times of peace as during times of war. The "generative schemes"—the logical substrate of oppositions, analogies, and homologies—upon which the representations were based constituted for many Rwandans a practical, everyday sense of body, self, and others. Because these "generative schemes" were internalized during early socialization, they took on a nearly unconscious or "goes without saying" quality (Bourdieu 1990:67–79). Although many Rwandan social actors embodied this knowledge, they never explicitly verbalized it.

The symbolic system I describe here takes root in representations that go back at least to the nineteenth century: elements of it can be discerned in the rituals of Rwandan sacred kingship practiced during precolonial and early colonial times. In that sense, much of this symbolism is relatively old. It must be emphasized, however, that neither the symbolic nor the normative structures of early Rwanda were mechanically reproduced during the events of 1994. Moreover, the context in which the symbols appeared was quite contemporary, for the discourse of Hutu ethnic nationalism with its accompanying characteristics of primordialism, biological determinism, essentialism, and racism is nothing if not modern.

OTHER SCHOLARSHIP ON VIOLENCE
AND ITS RELATION TO RWANDA

The idea that violence may be culturally or symbolically conditioned is not new. In a work edited by C. Nordstrom and J. Martin (1992), the authors remark "that repression and resistance generated at the national level are often inserted into the local reality in culturally specific ways" (ibid.:5). Yet elsewhere in the volume the contributors seldom live up to this promise, showing instead that violence and terror split communities along fault lines that can be demarcated by social analysis, rather than that violence follows culturally specific modalities. Coming closer to this point, Michael Taussig describes the narrative forms that accompanied the emergence of a "culture of terror" in the rubber-collecting regions of early twentieth-century Colombia (1984). In Taussig's book *Shamanism, Colonialism and the Wild Man* (1987), he again takes up the subject of the Putumayo violence committed against Native Americans as reported by the English investigator Roger Casement:

> From the accounts of Casement and Timerman it is also obvious that torture and terror are ritualized art forms and that, far from being spontaneous, sui generis, and an abandonment of what are often called the values of civilization, such rites of terror have a deep history deriving power and meaning from those very values. (ibid.:133)

Taussig analyzes colonialist discourse and underscores the Manichean nature of its explicit opposition of savagery vs. civilization. He unmasks the bitterly ironic process of mimesis that was at work when rubber company overseers both imagined into existence and became the savage, in gratuitous acts of terrorism and torture. His point that the forms of violence practiced in Putumayo logically extended the ideological and normative patterns of colonizing culture, rather than being a departure from them, is well taken. Yet one is left to wonder, from the pithy statement cited above, whether there might be more to this claim than discourse analysis alone is capable of revealing—specific, art and ritual forms from colonizing cultures that Taussig might have analyzed and that tell us something about European preoccupation with the demonic, and the tendency to project fears of it onto convenient scapegoats, whether internal or external.

Rwanda as well, during the years leading up to the genocide of 1994, became a "culture of terror," and there were a number of narratives in circulation that Hutu extremists used to justify violence against the Tutsi. They included narratives of this sort, among others: "Tutsi are invaders from Ethiopia." "We carry the Tutsi on our backs." "Tutsi are lazy." "Tutsi are shrewd and conniving." "They use the beauty of their women to seduce us into working for them." Many of the narratives of Hutu extremism that I encountered in 1994 Rwanda, or in earlier fieldwork during the 1980s, closely resemble the "mythico-histories" discussed by Liisa Malkki, in her book *Purity and Exile* (1995), among Burundian Hutu refugees in a Tanzanian camp. Many of the narratives take root in the early colonial historiography that depicted Tutsi as intelligent "Hamite" invaders who conquered the slower-witted "Bantu" Hutu. The selective use of this historiography leads one to believe that the narratives, far from being recent creations, date from late colonial times and form something of a substrate for the ideology of Hutu ethnic extremism.

More germane to the purposes of this chapter, Malkki's book also describes the techniques of violence meted out against Hutu victims in Burundi during that country's genocidal events of 1972–73. Those techniques included impalement of men from anus to head or mouth, impalement of women from vagina to mouth, cutting fetuses from their mothers' wombs, forcing parents to eat the flesh of their children, and forcing a parent and child to commit incest by roping them together in a sexual position prior to killing them (ibid.:87–98). She raises interesting questions with regard to the forms that the violence took and the accounts about it:

> [It] is relevant to ask how the accounts of atrocity come to assume thematic form, how they become formulaic.... The first thing to be examined is the extent to which the techniques of cruelty actually used were already meaningful, already mythico-historical. (ibid.:94)
>
> One need only inspect reports from Amnesty International and other organizations whose main purpose is to document human-rights violations to begin to see that the conventionalization of torture, killing, and other forms of violence occurs not only routinely but in patterned forms in the contemporary world. Torture, in particular, is a highly symbolized form of violence. At this level, it can be said that historical actors mete out death and perpetrate violence mythically. (ibid.)

Nevertheless, despite the assertion that the violence in Burundi was already "mythico-historical" and that it was patterned—an assertion that would seem to cry out for ritual and symbolic analysis—Malkki's analysis does not pursue this avenue in other than general comments about the attempt on the part of Burundian Tutsi to humiliate and dehumanize their Hutu victims, to render them powerless, to destroy the life of their future generations, or to reverse natural processes (ibid.:98). Although all her statements are true, my contention is that Malkki's comments leave the ontological dimension of extremist violence in Burundi and Rwanda untouched. Many of the same forms of violence, the same techniques of cruelty, were encountered in Rwanda during the 1994 genocide: impalement, evisceration of pregnant women, forced incest, forced cannibalism of family members. There were also other forms of torture and terror in Rwanda that may or may not have occurred in Burundi: the widespread killing of victims at roadblocks erected on highways, roads, streets, or even on small footpaths; the severing of the Achilles tendons of human and cattle victims; emasculation of men; and breast oblation of women.

In order to make these forms of violence comprehensible in terms of the local symbolism, it is first necessary to understand, as Pierre Clastres (1974) instructs us, that social systems inscribe "law" onto the bodies of their subjects. Occasionally physical torture is an integral part of the ritual process intended to inculcate society's norms and values. As Foucault shows, measures of bodily discipline short of actual torture imposed on inmates in institutions such as schools, prisons, and the military also serve a similar purpose (Foucault 1977). Using *The Penal Colony* by way of illustration, Clastres states: "Here Kafka designates the body as a writing surface, a surface able to receive the law's readable text."[2] Clastres expands upon this by considering the cognitive role of the body in ritual, "The body mediates in the acquisition of knowledge; this knowledge inscribes itself upon the body."[3] And ritual, Clastres emphasizes, involves the mnemonics of ordeal and pain: "[S]ociety prints its mark on the body of its youth...."

The mark acts as an obstacle to forgetting; the body carries the traces of a memory printed upon it; *the body is a memory.*"[4]

Although the rituals of which Clastres speaks are rites of passage—specifically, male initiation rituals in so-called primitive societies—I believe that many of his insights could be fruitfully extended to the actions of modern nation-states, particularly actions of a violent and terroristic nature. It is here that Clastres presages Bruce Kapferer's work on nationalism, particularly with regard to the mythico-ritual dimensions of nationalism as these delineate an analogical space relating the body to the body politic. As Kapferer states: "I have shown that in the myths and rites of evil, as in the legends of history, the order of the body is identified with and produced within the order of the state" (1988:78). Kapferer shows that the passions, violence, and intolerance that characterize modern nationalism cannot be understood solely through analysis of the associated political pragmatics. Nor can these passions be interpreted in purely psychological terms, as simply the tension-dissipating response to psychological stress generated by disorder and rapid social change. In order to understand the passions of modern nationalism, as well as the violence and terror unleashed upon the bodies of its sacrificial victims, we need to understand its ontological dimensions.

Building upon Benedict Anderson, Kapferer says, "Nationalism makes the political religious and places the nation above politics" (ibid.:1). He then proceeds to analyze Sinhalese and Australian nationalisms, which, although quite different in their specific ontologies, are both constitutive of being and personhood. Condensed within these ontologies are the "myths, legends, and other traditions to which these nationalisms accord value" (ibid.:6). Further on in the book he describes the pre-reflective dimensions of ontology:

> [It] describes the fundamental principles of a being in the world and the orientation
> of such a being toward the horizons of its experience. It is an ontology confined within
> the structure of certain myths and, as I have shown, it is an ontology which governs
> the constitution and reconstitution of being in some rituals. (ibid.:79–80)

Borrowing from Louis Dumont's work, Kapferer describes Australian nationalism as "individualistic and egalitarian," that of Sri Lanka as "hierarchical and encompassing."[5] He also describes in both instances what these specific nationalisms posit as potentially destructive to the cosmic order of the state and malevolent to the person. In the Sri Lankan case, malevolence takes the form of resistance to the hierarchical, encompassing Buddhist state. Tamils may live peacefully in Sri Lanka but only as subordinated, encompassed, internal others. In the Australian case, malevolence takes the form of an arbitrary state contemptuous of, or indifferent to, issues of personal autonomy and integrity (ibid.:7).

DEMOCRACY AND HIERARCHY IN RWANDA

Rwandan nationalism more closely approaches the "hierarchical, encompassing" type that Kapferer describes, despite its frequent appeals to democratic values. In monarchical Rwanda, the state was a hierarchical and encompassing order much of whose potency was embodied in the person of the Tutsi king or *mwami*. After the Hutu Revolution of 1960, dictatorial power was vested in the person of the Hutu president. Nevertheless, the ideology of Rwanda's Hutu elite after 1960 emphasized democracy and egalitarianism. Of course what was implied by this ideology was tyranny of the majority, at least the tyranny of a small clique within the majority, and systematic monopolization of the state apparatus by this clique and its clients. During the political turmoil of the 1990s and before, Hutu extremist politicians made frequent use of the term *rubanda nyamwinshi*, meaning the "popular mass" or "rule by the popular mass"; and all Rwandans knew that Tutsi were excluded from that group. As long as Tutsis did not object to their "encompassed" status, which was more politically than economically prejudicial to them, they were left alone. Although they could not hold political office after 1960, they could gain wealth and status through other avenues. It was not until Rwanda's experiment with multiparty democracy beginning in 1989 that a few Rwandan Tutsi began to hold significant political positions.

In early Rwanda, rituals of the state were conducted under the aegis of the Rwandan sacred king (mwami) and his college of ritual specialists (*abiiru*). After the Hutu Revolution, nationalist rituals in the modern sense began to be celebrated. Although this was not my area of interest at the time, I occasionally witnessed such celebrations during my first fieldwork in Rwanda during 1983–85. The most common of these occurred every Wednesday afternoon and were called "animation." Virtually all Rwandans who were employed by the state, and including some who were employees in private enterprises, would be excused from work and would gather together in small groups to sing or chant. Organized into *cellules* and sometimes referring to themselves as *groupes de choc*, the groups would compose and rehearse litanies about the country's development, the accomplishments and qualities of President Habyarimana, or those of the political party that he had founded, the Mouvement Revolutionnaire pour le Developpement (MRND), the country's only political party between 1973 and 1989. On national holidays such as the July 5 celebration of Habyarimana's 1973 coup d'état, such groups would perform publicly, competing with one another in the expression of attachment to the nation and its leader. In these state rituals the values of democracy and equality would be extolled, and the overthrow of the Tutsi monarchy and rejection of *ubuhake* would be evoked by way of substantiating the Hutu government's commitment to those values.[6] Nevertheless, it was clear to most Rwandans that President Habyarimana held absolute power and that political and economic advancement were largely dependent upon one's proximity to the president and his coterie. Northern Hutu, especially those who were officers in the Rwandan Army, were the most favored under the regime, although some Tutsi and southern Hutu had become prosperous in other ways. At the time of my first fieldwork in 1983–85, Rwanda was more divided by class and region than by ethnicity, as the chasm between the military/merchant bourgeoisie (dominated by northerners) and the rural peasantry, 95 percent of the population, continued to grow.

Although it was ultimately along ethnic lines that the Rwandan social fabric tore asunder during the genocide of 1994, this was not a foregone conclusion. Rwanda's history has indeed been marked by other incidents of ethnic unrest, but in each case the passions that have fueled the violence have been far from primordial; they have had to have been rekindled and manipulated by unscrupulous politicians (cf. Taylor 1999b:35–53). After 1990 many events orchestrated by supporters of the president and the two political parties that were most avidly racialist in ideology— the MRND and the more extreme CDR (Coalition pour la Defense de la Republique)—subverted existing political alliances between Hutu and Tutsi opponents of the regime and precluded others from forming that might have prevented the genocide. Several key people who appealed to both southern Hutu and Tutsi were assassinated. One such assassination, that of Felicien Gatabazi, arguably Rwanda's most popular political leader and head of an ethnically mixed party, the Parti Social Democrate (PSD), occurred one evening (January 25, 1994) so close to my home in Kigali that I heard the three bursts of automatic rifle fire that killed him. My most informed Rwandan acquaintances at the time claimed that members of Habyarimana's elite presidential guard had carried out the assassination.

Gatabazi's party had been attempting to forge an alliance between peasants in southern Rwanda and liberal entrepreneurs and intellectuals of both ethnicities in the cities of Kigali and Butare. The party vehemently opposed the ethnic rift that the MRND and the CDR appeared bent upon deepening. Following Gatabazi's assassination, the depth of anger of PSD supporters was so profound that the next day, Hutu peasants in southern Rwanda pursued the leader of the extremist CDR, Martin Bucyana, in his car en route to Kigali from Butare. Furious over Gatabazi's murder, they eventually managed to stop the car. Then with hoes and machetes, they murdered all three occupants: Bucyana, his brother-in-law, and the car's driver. The incident underlined the fact that many Rwandans in the south were more incensed about regional favoritism and domination by the Habyarimana clique than they were about ethnicity. For two full days after the CDR leader's death, supporters of the regime fomented violence in Kigali in which Tutsi and PSD party members were specifically targeted; virtually everyone in the city stayed home from work (*ville morte*). A few people were killed; many more were intimidated into abandoning their houses in Kigali or coerced into paying "insurance" to *Interahamwe* militia members.[7] On the third day after Gatabazi's death, normalcy abruptly returned as if by command; the lesson to those who did not support the ethnicist line of the MRND and the CDR had been conveyed.

FIELDWORK IN RWANDA

I have lived for several extended periods in Rwanda. For eighteen months during 1983–1985, I studied Rwandan practices of popular medicine. Later I returned there during the summer months of 1987 to do follow-up work on popular medicine. In recent years some of my research in Rwanda has taken an applied direction. In May of 1993, for example, I journeyed to Rwanda and remained for one month serving as a consultant to Family Health International, a subcontractor for USAID. I participated in organizing an AIDS prevention project that was to be funded by USAID. It was again as an employee of FHI that I returned to Rwanda in late October 1993 to begin AIDS-related behavioral research. Although I had hoped to live in Rwanda for at least two years and to conduct research on sexual behavior and HIV transmission, that proved to be impossible because of the renewed outbreak of hostilities that followed the assassination of President Habyarimana on April 6, 1994. On April 9, most members of the American community in Rwanda were evacuated by land convoy to neighboring Burundi. From Burundi, I then flew to Nairobi, Kenya, where I spent the next four months.

During my last period of fieldwork in Rwanda, I witnessed the country's slow but inexorable slide into chaos. After several attempts to install the broad-based transitional government failed, I became keenly aware that the Habyarimana regime and the MRND had not been serious about the peace accords signed with the Rwandan Patriotic Front in Arusha during August of 1993. Encouraged by the unwavering support of French backers, Habyarimana and his supporters were treating the accords as "just a piece of paper." During the five months or so that I resided in Rwanda, the dogs of war were slowly unleashed. Acts of terrorist violence became more common, Interahamwe militia members grew bolder in their attacks upon civilians, and there were several assassinations.

It had not been my intention to study or to witness the degradation of the political situation in Rwanda. Originally I had hoped to further my explorations into the popular perceptions of sickness and, in particular, of sexually transmitted diseases. My job with FHI in Rwanda was to help adapt HIV prevention and intervention strategies to local social and cultural realities. I had been chosen for this task because FHI was aware of my previous research on popular medicine and, in particular, my research emphasizing the importance of bodily fluids in the local cognitive models of sickness. These were obviously important because HIV is transmitted by bodily fluids, and preventive strategies generally focus on "barrier methods" such as condoms. From previous research in Rwanda, I had advanced the hypothesis that impeding the passage of bodily fluids between partners was locally perceived as unhealthful, and that this resistance would have to be overcome in culturally appropriate ways in order to promote safer sexual practices (Taylor 1990).

RWANDAN SYMBOLISM AND THE BODY

Although the connection between local cognitive models of illness and ethnic nationalism may appear distant at first glance, their relatedness lies at the level of myth and symbol. The Rwandan body is, following Clastres, an imprinted body—imprinted with the condensed memories of history. Following Kapferer, it is only through myth and symbol that we can grasp the logic of these condensed memories and their significance to Rwandan Hutu nationalism, because the latter derived much of its passionate force from a mythic logic constitutive of being and personhood:

> Broadly, the legitimating and emotional force of myth is not in the events as such but in the logic that conditions their significance. This is so when the logic is also vital in the way human actors are culturally given to constituting a self in the everyday routine world and move out toward others in that world. Mythic reality is mediated by human beings into the worlds in which they live. Where human beings recognize the argument of mythic reality as corresponding to their own personal constitutions—their orientation within and movement through reality—so myth gathers force and can come to be seen as embodying ultimate truth. Myth so enlivened, I suggest, can become imbued with commanding power, binding human actors to the logical movement of its scheme. In this sense, myth is not subordinated to the interests of the individual or group but can itself have motive force. It comes to define significant experience in the world, experience which in its significance is also conceived of as intrinsic to the constitution of the person. By virtue of the fact that myth engages a reasoning which is also integral to everyday realities, part of the taken-for-granted or "habitus" [Bourdieu 1977] of the mundane world, myth can charge the emotions and fire the passions. (Kapferer 1988:46–47)

Nevertheless, in order to get at these mythic and prereflective dimensions of ontology, we need to move beyond Kapferer's and Dumont's categories of "egalitarian and individualistic" vs. "hierarchical and encompassing." We need to shift analysis to an almost "molecular" level and to consider the structures of thought that underlie the construction of the moral person in Rwanda and that constitute a specific practical logic of being in the world. These structures must be seen both in their formalist dimension and in specific instances of their use and enactment in everyday social life. Proceeding in this fashion we may then be able to appreciate that, lurking beneath the extraordinary events and violence of the genocide, one perceives the logic of ordinary sociality.

Much of this ordinary, practical logic can be discerned in Rwandan practices related to the body and aimed at maintaining it or restoring it to health and integrity. Based on Rwandan popular medical practices that I observed during the 1980s, I have elsewhere advanced the hypothesis that a root metaphor underlies conceptualizations of the body (Taylor 1992). Basically, these conceptualizations are characterized by an opposition between orderly states of humoral and other flows to disorderly ones.[8] Analogies are constructed that take this opposition as their base and then relate bodily processes to those of social and natural life. In the unfolding of human and natural events, flow/blockage symbolism mediates between physiological, sociological, and cosmological levels of causality. Popular healing aims at restoring bodily flows that have been perturbed by human negligence and malevolence. Bodily fluids such as blood, semen, breast milk, and menstrual blood are a recurrent concern, as is the passage of aliments through the digestive tract.[9]

Pathological states are characterized by obstructed or excessive flows, and perturbations of this sort may signify illness, diminished fertility, or death.

Fluid metaphors suffuse Rwandan popular medical practices, yet healers and their patients do not explicitly verbalize them in any local mode of exegesis. The model that I hypothesize for Rwandan popular medicine thus does not appear to be a fully conscious one. This is in sharp contrast to similar "image schemata" (Johnson 1987) found elsewhere in the world. For example, in some forms of Indian popular medicine, healers explicitly talk of illness in terms of interrupted flows of kundalini (Kakar 1982). Similarly, in many forms of Chinese popular medicine, concern is expressed about the flow of Qi through the body; therapeutic measures are taken to direct or unblock Qi flow (Farquhar 1994). Despite an apparently less than conscious quality in Rwanda, flow/blockage metaphors are imaged and enacted in a diverse array of domains. Although they may be most commonly encountered in popular healing, my research has revealed that similar representations are also present in myths, legends, and the rituals of sacred kingship, and that they involve potencies of various types (Taylor 1988).

Because of the implicit quality of this symbolism, it is not possible to ascertain the degree to which Rwandans from various regions and of differing ethnicity, gender, or class have internalized it. Although it may be possible in some instances to verify how many people have knowledge of a specific healing procedure or belief, it is impossible to affirm whether that specific knowledge, or lack of it, implies adherence to an associated mode of thought. This means that at a second level of understanding, attention needs to be shifted away from the study of the formal properties of the symbolism, to its various enactments in social life.

POPULAR MEDICINE

During my fieldwork in Rwanda in the 1980s, I found that illnesses were often characterized by perceived irregularities in fluid flows, and that these tended to have an alimentary or reproductive symptomatic focus. Concern with ordered flows and their proper embodiment was not just implicated in illness, however; it was also implicated in health. From the very moment that a human being enters this world, these metaphors figure prominently in the cultural construction of the person. Practices associated with childbirth, for example, focus upon certain portions of the child's anatomy. Rural Rwandans that I interviewed in both northern and southern Rwanda during the 1980s recounted versions of the following practices.

After giving birth a new mother is secluded for a period of eight days (today this period is often shorter). On the ninth day, the newborn child is presented to other members of the family and local community for the first time (*gusohora umwana*). This rite of passage can be performed only after the baby's body has been examined and found to be free of anal malformations. People at this occasion receive a meal, especially the children present, who are given favorite foods. These children in turn bestow a nickname on the newborn that will remain their name for the child. A few months later the parents give the child another name, but the children continue to call the infant by their name. The meal given to the children is termed *kurya ubunyano,* which means "to eat the baby's excrement," for Rwandans say that a tiny quantity of the baby's fecal matter is mixed with the food. This appellation celebrates the fact that the baby's body has been found to be an "open conduit," an adequate vessel for perpetuating the process of "flow." In a sense, the baby's feces are its first gift, and the members of his age class are its first recipients. The children at the ceremony incorporate the child into their group by symbolically ingesting one of his bodily products. Their bestowal of a name upon the infant manifests their acceptance of the child as a social being.

The confirmation of the baby's body as an "open conduit" is a socially and morally salient image. If the body were "closed" at the anal end, the baby would still be able to ingest, though not to excrete. The baby would be able to receive, but unable to give up or pass on that which it had received. In effect, its body would be a "blocked" conduit or pathway. In social terms, such a body would be unable to participate in reciprocity, for while it could receive, it could never give (see also Beidelman 1986). That gift-giving and reciprocity are important aspects where Rwandan concepts of the moral person are concerned can be discerned from the term for "man" in Kinyarwanda, *umugabo,* for it is derived from the verb *kugaba,* which means "to give." The construction of the moral person among rural Rwandans is contingent upon the social attestation that the person properly embodies the physiological attributes that analogically evoke the capacity to reciprocate. This entails the capacity to ingest and the capacity to excrete, or, in socio-moral terms, the capacity to receive and the capacity to give. Consequently, two portions of the anatomy and their unobstructed connection are at issue: the mouth and the anus. By analogical extension the concern with unobstructed connection and unimpeded movement characterizes earlier Rwandan symbolic thought about the topography of the land, its rivers, roads, and pathways in general.

Illnesses treated by Rwandan popular healers are often said to be caused by the malevolent actions of other human beings.[10] Sorcerers act upon others by arresting their flow of generative fluids; they make women sterile and men impotent. They are also vampirish, anthropophagic beings who parasitically and invisibly suck away the blood and other vital fluids of their victims. In other instances sorcerers may induce fluids to leave the body in a torrent, causing symptoms such as hemorrhagic menstruation, the vomiting of blood, projectile vomiting, and violent diarrhea. There are thus two basic expressions to symptoms in this model: "blocked flow" and "hemorrhagic flow."

One example of *uburozi* (spell, poisoning) that is quite commonly treated by both northern and southern Rwandan healers is that called *kumanikira amaraso* ("to suspend blood"). In this poisoning, a fluid is taken from the intended female victim: either her menstrual blood (*irungu*), her urine, or some of the fluid exuding from the vagina after parturition (*igisanza*). The sorcerer takes one of these fluids, adds medicines to it, puts it in a packet, and suspends the packet from the rafters of a house, or among rocks on the summit of a high hill where rain cannot touch it. If menstrual blood or urine has been taken from the woman, she will be unable to conceive. If igisanza has been taken from the woman, she will be able to conceive but unable to deliver the baby. The fetus will become turned transversally in the womb, or it will move upward toward the heart. In both variations of this poisoning, whether the woman is pregnant or not, the female victim's reproductive capacity is obstructed. Another variation of this spell, sometimes called *umuvu*, entails throwing the packet with the woman's menstrual blood or urine into a fast-moving stream. In this case the woman's menstrual flow becomes excessively abundant or prolonged.

In effect, by suspending a woman's blood or other fluids involved in sexuality or reproduction, the woman's reproductive functions are also suspended. Either she becomes unable to deliver the baby already in her womb, or her menstruation stops and she becomes sterile. By suspending the woman's bodily fluids in a position between sky and earth, or in a place where rain cannot touch them, the woman's body becomes "blocked." When her fluids are put into a body of fast-moving water, her menses become dangerously abundant, an example of "hemorrhagic flow."

Healers vary in their treatment of this poisoning; nevertheless, these variations possess features in common. One healer has the female victim of "suspended blood" lie naked on her back. The healer then climbs onto the roof of the victim's house, parts the thatch, and pours an aqueous mixture of medicines through the opening onto the woman's abdomen. Another person inside the house rubs the woman's stomach with the medicinal mixture. In this treatment the blockage within the woman's body is analogically posited as a blockage between sky and earth, for it is counteracted by someone's actually moving to the sky position (ascending to the roof of the house) and pouring fluids earthward. This time, however, the downward movement of fluids includes the woman's body in the circuit of flow from sky to earth. The cure is a virtually one-to-one homeopathic reversal of the symbolic operations accomplished in the poisoning, which removed the woman's body from the circuit of moving fluids by "suspending" her blood between earth and sky.

Another healer, Baudouin, treated kumanikira amaraso in a different yet symbolically comparable way. In one case that I observed, he gave the afflicted woman, who was unable to deliver despite being pregnant, water with a piece of hippopotamus skin in it. In addition, he administered a remedy concocted from the *umuhaanga* plant (*Kotschya aeschynomenoides; Kotschya strigosa* var. grandiflora; *Maesa lanceolata*) (Jacob 1984:449). The name of this plant comes from the verb *guhaanga*, which means: (a) to create, to restore, to invent; (b) to occupy a place first; (c) to germinate, to blossom; (d) to have one's first menstrual period. He also gave her a plant called *umumanurankuba*, a name that comes from the words *kumanura*—to make something descend, or to depend on; and *inkuba*—thunder. The full meaning of the name of this plant would be: "to make thunder descend, to depend on thunder," that is, to make rain fall.

Once again this is an image of restoring the sky-to-earth movement of rainfall, and by analogy, restoring orderly flows to the woman's body. In restoring the flow, the healer renders the woman capable of creating, capable of blossoming. The use of the hippopotamus follows the fact that it is an animal closely associated with terrestrial waters.

It is difficult to assess accurately the percentage of Rwandans whose thought during illness conforms to the model of flow/blockage. Rwandans among whom I studied popular medicine during my first two periods of fieldwork included Hutu, Tutsi, and Twa of both sexes, and urban as well as rural inhabitants. Many of these consulted only popular healers, while some, especially in cities, consulted only biomedical practitioners. In all probability, the majority of Rwandans with whom I interacted consulted both popular and biomedical specialists, and even at times acupuncturists and Chinese herbalists. Similar to medical systems elsewhere in the developing world, the one in Rwanda is highly pluralistic. Rwandan medicine in general, therefore, cannot be said to be characterized by theoretical, symbolic, or ideological unity. Be that as it may, I believe that I am on safe ground when I claim that the implicit model of flow/blockage characterizes the medical thinking of many, if not all, Rwandans. Attaining a higher level of precision than this, or conducting a survey to determine the percentage of a population who ascribe to an implicit model, strikes me as absurd. What can be affirmed is that the practice of kumanikira amaraso is encountered in northern and southern Rwanda, even in urban areas. A substantial number of respondents also claimed that "suspending blood" could be used intentionally as a means of contraception and was not always a malevolent spell intended to induce sterility. A few female respondents even admitted that their mothers had "suspended" their first menstrual blood in order to assure that they would not become pregnant out of wedlock.

Another female fertility disorder encountered in both northern and southern Rwanda and often treated by popular healers is that called *igihama*. A woman who lacks breast milk is called igihama, as are women who lack vaginal secretions during intercourse. The noun *igihama* is derived from the verb *guhama*, which means "to cultivate a field hardened by the sun; to have sexual relations with a woman who lacks vaginal secretions" (ibid.:437–38). Women who lack breast milk after childbirth and those who lack vaginal secretions during intercourse are similar, for in both cases their fertility is threatened.[11] Both women lack an essential bodily fluid, in one case the fluid that will nourish a child, and in the other case the fluid that is deemed necessary for the woman to have fruitful sexual relations and, by consequence, to conceive.

Close to the southern Rwandan town of Butare, I elicited the following illness narrative in 1984 from a woman named Verediana who had consulted a healer named Matthew. This narrative is remarkable in that it illustrates the imagery of perturbed menstruation, perturbed lactation, reduced fertility, and interruption during the course of a journey. At the time, however, I had little idea that the events related in this woman's story were connected in any other way than that which she persistently emphasized: these were persistent misfortunes whose seriality proved that they were due to the malevolent influence of sorcerers.

Verediana came to Matthew convinced that she had been poisoned. This time she had been sick since July 1983, approximately one year before I met her. Her primary symptom consisted of prolonged, abundant menstruation. Although she had visited a hospital and received injections that stopped her hemorrhagic periods, she still felt intensely afraid. She often had trouble eating. Recently she and her husband had separated. Immediately after their separation her symptoms improved, then they began to worsen anew.

According to Verediana, it was the older brother of her husband and his wife who were her poisoners. She believed that this man afflicted others through the use of malevolent spirits. In previous years she had been suspicious of another brother of her husband, a man who was suspected of sorcery and later killed by a group of his neighbors. She also felt that her husband was in league with his brothers, all of whom were eager to have her out of the way.

In recounting earlier misfortunes, Verediana explained that her third pregnancy had been interrupted by the baby's premature birth at eight and a half months. Somehow the child managed to survive despite her reduced lactation. Before this occurrence, she had lost a child. During the troubled events of 1973—revived tensions between Hutu and Tutsi and the government's inability to deal with the situation had led to a military coup—she was being transported to the hospital in labor. She recalls that there were numerous roadblocks and barriers erected on the roads. Despite these barriers, she finally arrived safely at the hospital. Her child was born alive but died the next day. When I suggested to her that her difficulty in reaching the hospital may have had more to do with national events in Rwanda than with actions of her persecutors, she replied, "Yes, but why did I go into labor at just such a time?"

Matthew's diagnosis was that Verediana was suffering from *amageza* affliction, a spirit illness that can cause excessive blood flow from the vagina.

Notice that in this narrative, Verediana speaks of disorderly bodily flows: hemorrhagic menstruation, premature birth, and diminished lactation. She also mentions physical obstructions encountered while en route to the hospital in 1973. The background to this incident, the political events of 1973, constitutes a moment when political relations between Rwanda's two most numerous ethnic groups, the Tutsi and the Hutu, had degenerated into violence.

Many of the details that Verediana employs in her narrative are images of incompletion, partial arrest, or obstruction: difficulty in eating, diminished lactation, barriers on the roads, a child who dies soon after birth, or a baby who was born prematurely—that is, it left her womb before it had been completely formed by the process of intensified mixing of husband's semen and wife's blood that is supposed to occur during the final stages of pregnancy (*gukurakuza*). Other details are images of excessive flow: menstrual periods that are prolonged and hemorrhagic.

She implicates several domains of problematic social relations that merge together in her story: difficulties with her husband in the context of a polygynous household, relations with her affines, political conflict between Tutsi and Hutu during 1973. This woman's story is remarkable in touching so many levels at once. Although the symptomatic focus is her body, an analogy is constantly being drawn between it and other domains of social life.

Verediana's complaint weaves a web of concentric circles composed of progressively more encompassing relational dyads. At the most personal level these consist of husband and wife, mother and child. At a more encompassing level: wife and cowives, consanguines and affines; and finally at the level of the nation, Tutsi and Hutu. Her narrative moves from her body, to the household, to the extended family, to the nation in a seamless series of symbolically logical leaps, for all are posed in terms of bodily and social processes whose movement or obstruction are causes for concern.

RWANDAN SACRED KINGSHIP

If flow/blockage symbolism can be discerned in the narratives of individual patients and in the therapeutic means employed by healers, it is logical to ask if similar symbolism can be found, as Verediana's narrative suggests it might, at the level of representations of the polity as a whole.

Although it is difficult to find clear evidence of this symbolism for the postcolonial Rwandan state and its rituals of nationalism (though it may exist), there is indeed strong historical evidence of it before independence at the time when Rwanda was a sacred kingdom. Here, the principal sources of symbolic material are texts of the royal rituals performed by the king and his college of ritualists, dynastic poetry, and popular narratives recounted about Rwandan kings.

As for the ritual texts, in the precolonial and early colonial period these were memorized by the king's ritual specialists. Later during the 1940s and 1950s, when it appeared that knowledge of the rituals might be lost forever as the last generation of royal ritualists begin to die off, the texts were transcribed by Rwandan and European scholars. In 1964, M. d'Hertfelt and A. Coupez published Kinyarwanda texts and French translations of seventeen of the royal rituals in a book entitled *La royaute sacree de l'ancien Rwanda.*

Although Coupez and d'Hertefelt do not attempt to date their versions of the ritual texts precisely, it is quite likely that they go back at least to the precolonial times of the nineteenth century. The last Rwandan king who presided over the enactment of the rituals, the last king who could be truly described as "sacred" in terms of local perceptions, was Yuhi V Musinga whose reign (1896–1931) straddles the end of the nineteenth century and the early period of Catholic evangelization. Musinga and his abiiru performed the rituals until the late 1920s, at which time they began to be neglected for fear that certain ritual practices might offend European and Catholic sensibilities. Despite Musinga's concession, Belgian colonial authorities deposed Musinga in 1931 and replaced him with his mission-educated son. In the texts published by d'Hertefelt and Coupez, there are procedures in the rituals that Europeans would have found difficult to accept: ritual copulation on the part of the king and his wives, human sacrifice, ritual war, and adornment of the royal drum with the genitals of slain enemies.

As for the ethnic origin of the rituals, although the central Rwandan monarchy was dominated by a Tutsi king and many of his closest associates were Tutsi, many scholars claim that similar rituals were being performed in Hutu polities prior to the central kingdom's existence (d'Hertefelt 1971:32). It is probable that the existence of the state in central Rwanda preceded its becoming a Tutsi-dominated institution. Therefore the rituals and their attendant symbolism cannot readily and simply be ascribed to later Tutsi dominance. In addition, although the Rwandan king was Tutsi, the rituals he enacted had to address the preoccupations of the Hutu majority, particularly the concern for orderly rainfall and an abundant sorghum harvest. Moreover, in material terms the king performed a redistributive function, concentrating wealth and then redisbursing it.

Careful reading of the ritual texts indicates recurrent preoccupation with maintaining orderly fluid flows and implicitly that of *imaana*. The term, *imaana*, although often translated as "God," only occasionally referred to a supreme being. More frequently, imaana was a generalized creative or transformative force, or, as d'Hertefelt and Coupez have translated the term, a "diffuse fecundating fluid" of celestial origin. Gaining access to the powers of imaana and keeping the fluids of production, consumption, and fertility in movement were arguably the most important ritual functions of the Rwandan king (mwami). The mwami was the ultimate human guarantor of the fertility of bees (for honey), cattle, women, and land. In times of drought, famine, epidemic, or epizootic, he could be deposed or called upon to offer himself (or a close relative) as a sacrificial victim (*umutabazi*), so that the shedding of his blood would conjure away collective peril. The king mediated between the sky and the earth. He was the most important rainmaker for the kingdom. He received the celestial gift of fertility and passed it downward to his subjects. In some instances this beneficence was conceptualized as milk, as is expressed in this dynastic poem:

> The King is not a man,
> O men that he has enriched with his cattle . . .
> He is a man before his designation to the throne . . .
> Ah yes! That is certain:
> But the one who becomes King ceases to be a man!
> The King, it is he Imaana
> And he dominates over humans . . .
> I believe that he is the Imaana who hears our pleas!
> The other Imaana, it's the King who knows him,
> As for us, we see only this Defender! . . .
> Here is the sovereign who drinks the milk milked by Imaana,
> And we drink that which he in turn milks for us!
>
> (from *La poésie dynastique au Rwanda*, pp. 53–55, cited by A. KAGAME [in French] in
> *La philosophie bantu-rwandaise de l'être*, 1956:15 [my translation])

The Rwandan king, mwami, could be compared to a hollow conduit through which celestial beneficence passed. He was the kingdom's most giving or "flowing being." The image of his body as conduit can be discerned in a legend that is sometimes recounted about Ruganzu Ndori, one of early Rwanda's most important kings. This particular version of the story was related to me by a certain Augustin, the gardener at the Institut National de Recherche Scientifique in Butare during my fieldwork there in 1987. Here fertility is restored to the earth by first passing through the mwami's digestive tract:

> Ruganzu Ndori was living in exile in the neighboring kingdom of Ndorwa, to the north of Rwanda. There he had taken refuge with his father's sister who was married to a man from the region. In the meantime, because the Rwandan throne was occupied by an illegitimate usurper, Rwanda was experiencing numerous calamities. Rain was not falling, crops were dying, cows were not giving milk, and the women were becoming sterile. Ruganzu's aunt encouraged him to return to Rwanda and re-take the throne and in this way, to save his people from catastrophe. Ruganzu agreed. But before setting forth on his voyage, his aunt gave him the seeds (*imbuto*) of several cultivated plants (sorghum, gourds, and others) to restart Rwandan cultures. While en route to Rwanda, Ruganzu Ndori came under attack. Fearing that the imbuto would be captured, he swallowed the seeds with a long draught of milk. Once he regained the Rwandan throne, he defecated the milk and seed mixture upon the ground and the land became productive once again. Since that time all Rwandan kings are said to be born clutching the seeds of the original imbuto in their hand.

The image of the king's body as exemplary of a flowing process is implied in the verb *kwamira*, from which the noun *mwami*, is derived. Kwamira has both a formal sense and a popular one. Its formal meaning is "to make, to create, or to render fertile," but another meaning is "to lactate" (Vansina, personal communication). In some parts of interlacustrine Bantu-speaking Africa, the sacred king was called mwami. In many other parts, such as Bunyoro, the sacred king was termed *mukama* from the verb *gukama*, which means "to milk." Sometimes even the Rwandan king was referred to as mukama. When the Bunyoro Mukama died, a man would ascend a ladder, pour milk onto the ground, and say: "The milk is spilt; the king has been taken away!" (Beattie 1960:28). The terms *mwami* and *mukama* thus encompass several semantic domains that are central to Rwandan symbolic thought: production, reproduction, the labor associated with extracting the aliment of highest esteem, milk, and their metaphorization in the popular imagination as a flowing process, lactation.

The assertion that the mwami was supposed to be the most "flowing being" of the kingdom, a hollow conduit through which fluids passed, is how I depict the concern on the part of traditional Rwandans that the mwami keep the rain falling regularly, the cows giving milk, the bees producing honey, and the crops growing. Of the seventeen royal rituals recorded and annotated by d'Hertefelt and Coupez, two concern rainfall, one concerns the production of honey, another conjures away cattle epizootics (assuring the production of milk), and one celebrates the sorghum harvest (most sorghum was brewed into beer). One of the most important rituals, "The Watering of the Royal Herds," which was accomplished only once every four reigns and which was intended to renew the dynastic cycle, deploys virtually the entire gamut of fluid symbols, including those concerning the two most important rivers of the kingdom, the Nyabugogo and the Nyabarongo, rivers that delineated sacred time and sacred space.[12]

The person of the mwami embodied flow/blockage imagery with regard to his physiological processes as well, for every morning the king imbibed a milky liquid called *isubyo*, which was a powerful laxative (Bourgeois 1956). Although the ostensible purpose of this matinal libation was to purge the mwami's body of any poison he might have absorbed, the reasoning behind the custom goes deeper than that, for the mwami's enemies were depicted as the antithesis of "flowing beings"; they were beings who interrupted production, exchange, and fertility. They were "obstructing beings." When seen from this perspective, the practice of kurya ubunyano (discussed above with regard to newborn children) makes eminent sense.

The Rwandan mythical archetype of the "blocking being" was a small old woman (*agakeecuru*). A legend recounts how Death, while being pursued by the mwami, Thunder, and God, sought refuge with this agakeecuru, while she was gathering gourds in a field. The tiny old woman sheltered Death in her uterus (Smith 1975:132), where he remained to subsist on her blood. Later in eating with her descendants, the agakeecuru communicated Death to them and they, in their turn, to the rest of the world. In this tale we see that Death is associated with beings whose fluids do not or no longer flow, for old women do not menstruate. The origin of Death is also the origin of sorcery, for the old woman passes the contagion of Death on to others by eating with them.[13]

One of the mwami's responsibilities was to eliminate beings who lacked the capacity "to flow." Two such beings included girls who had reached child-bearing age and who lacked breasts, called *impenebere*, and girls who had reached child-bearing age and who had not yet menstruated, called *impa* (d'Hertefelt and Coupez 1964:286). In both cases, the girls were put to death for want of the apparent capacity to produce an important fertility fluid, in one case, blood, in the other, milk. Obstructed in their perceived capacity to reproduce, the girls were thought to be potential sources of misfortune and aridity to the entire kingdom.

Although it might appear that the person of the mwami catalyzed flows and eliminated symbolic obstruction, in fact he embodied this metaphor in its entirety. While he was extolled as the being who "milked" for others, the being who acted as the conduit of imaana, the being who embodied the powers of both genders as a "lactating" male, the king was as much a "blocking being" as a "flowing" one. He was not simply a passive conduit through which beneficence passed; he was an active agent who possessed the power of life and death over his subjects. He could enrich his followers with gifts of cattle and land or he could impoverish them. Like a sorcerer who impedes fertility or inflicts death upon victims by invisibly sucking away their blood, the manifestation of the king's power was more likely to be felt in all those ways by which the king could obstruct human movement, economic processes, life, and human reproduction. This aspect of Rwandan sacred kingship was given less elaboration in ritual, poetry, or popular narratives, although there are aspects in the ritual texts in which the obstructive function of kingship can be discerned, albeit indirectly. This connectedness of the well-being of the polity with processes that can be promoted or inhibited can be discerned in the rituals associated with sacred kingship.

First let us take the Kinyarwanda ritual lexicon and examine the use of the term *flow.* In the "Path of the Watering," the royal ritual performed only once in every dynastic cycle of four kings and intended to revivify the entire magico-religious order of Rwandan kingship, there were several instances when a group of eight cows, representing all the deceased kings of the two previous dynastic cycles, along with one bull were presented to the living king. Occasionally this group of eight cows was referred to as *isibo* ("a flow") (ibid.:142). Examining the full meaning of the term *isibo,* we see that in other contexts it was used to designate: (a) a group of cattle rushing toward a watering trough; (b) (in war poetry) a flow of living beings, a swarming multitude; (c) force, élan, flight, impetuosity, as in *guca* isibo (especially when speaking of the *intoóre* [warrior] dances), which means, literally, "to cut the flow" in the context of dance—that is, to jump very high while dancing (Jacob 1985:169). But the verb from which *isibo* is derived, *gusiba,* means: (a) to plug, to fill up, to obstruct, to fill a hollow or empty space; (b) (neologism) to erase, to clear off; (c) to decimate, to eliminate, to make something disappear; (d) to hoe the earth without taking care to remove weeds; (e) to reduce an adversary to silence by an irrefutable argument; (f) (when speaking of mammary glands) to be obstructed; (g) (when speaking of a path) to become covered over with plants. Other usages include: gusiba *inkaru*—to do grave harm to someone; and gusiba *inzira*—(lit.: "to block the path") to lose one's daughter through death (ibid.:167).[14]

Notice, therefore, that the noun *isibo* and its root verb, *gusiba,* appear to encompass two apparently contradictory meanings. One field of meaning seems to center on the idea of living beings in movement. Another set of meanings seems to crystallize around the ideas of obstruction and loss. A single verbal concept in Kinyarwanda thus appears to encompass the idea of flow and its opposite, the idea of blockage. Furthermore, in this second instance, the notion of "blockage" is related to the idea of doing harm to someone, as in gusiba inkaru, as well as to the idea of losing one's daughter, as in gusiba inzira. With regard to gusiba inzira, an analogy is drawn between "blocking the path" and "losing one's daughter." In effect, when one loses a daughter, death blocks the "path" between one's own family and that of another family—that is, the alliance relation that could have resulted from the gift of one's daughter to a man from another family; it is preemptively extinguished. With regard to gusiba inkaru, an analogy is drawn between the action of "blocking" and the action of doing serious harm to someone, an idea that comes very close to Rwandan notions of sorcery.

This apparent antinomy between the fields of meaning denoted and connoted in the words *isibo* and *gusiba* might appear illogical to someone situated outside the context of Rwandan social action. Within this context, however, this contradiction was nothing less than an ineluctable corollary to the workings of social life itself. It was its internal dialectic. Just as imaana could "flow" or be "blocked," just as the sky could yield its fertilizing liquid in the right measure and at the right time, so could the body flow properly in health or improperly in illness. The words *isibo* and *gusiba* embody part of this recognition, the recognition that one cannot have "flow" without "blockage," just as one cannot "milk" (gukama) without incurring the risk of depleting the environment, and one cannot give to some without withholding one's gifts from others. Power in early Rwanda grew as much from the capacity to obstruct as from the capacity to give.

It was through obstruction, impoverishment, strangulation, murder, and sorcery that the Rwandan king manifested the coercive aspect of his power over subjects and adversaries. The precolonial Rwandan polity, through its king, unabashedly proclaimed its expansionist intent in the five royal rituals directly concerned with warfare. In one such ritual, *Inzira yo Kwambika Ingoma* ("The Path of Adorning the Drum"), the genitals of important slain enemies were ritually prepared in order to be placed within containers and then hung upon *Karinga* (the most important royal drum). Early Rwandan warriors carried a special curved knife that was used to remove the genitalia of slain enemies. During this ritual the king and his ritualists would shout:

Ngo twahotor Uburundi kuu ngoma
N'amahang adatuur umwami w'Irwanda
Twayahotora kuu ngoma
(D'HERTEFELT AND COUPEZ 1964:176)

May we strangle Burundi's drum
And all countries who do not pay tribute to Rwanda's king
May we strangle their drums.

Women were also victims of mutilation in earlier times. In disputes between rival lineages, for example, it was common for the victors to cut off the breasts of women belonging to the vanquished group, although these were not used in the above ritual.

The Rwandan monarchy manifested its control over flowing processes—rainfall, human fertility, bovine fertility, milk, and honey production—through its ritual capacity to catalyze or to interdict them. Kings thus encompassed the qualities of both "flow" and "blockage" and, in that sense, were ambiguous, "liminoid" beings, the embodiment of evil as well as good. At times of dire calamity to the polity as a whole, the king became the ultimate repository of ritual negativity, the ultimate "blocking being," and in those instances it was his blood that had to be sacrificially shed to reopen the conduits of imaana. According to Rwandan dynastic legends, many kings were said to have died as ritual sacrifices. Indeed, the events leading up to and including the 1994 genocide incorporate many elements of the "mythic logic" of king sacrifice.

RITUAL, POWER, AND GENOCIDE

Issues of personhood and the body, all of which are generally implicated in nationalistic expressions of violence, do not follow a universal logic. Likewise, this logic is not limited to the common exigency to eliminate as many of the regime's adversaries as possible. State-promoted violence persistently defies the state's attempts to rationalize and routinize it. The psychologically detached, dispassionate torturer does not exist; the acultural torturer who acts independently of the habitus that he or she embodies does not exist. Nor can the interposition of killing machines or technology efface what Kafka so perceptively recognized in *The Penal Colony*, that societies "write" their signatures onto the bodies of their sacrificial victims. As Foucault (1977) shows, power constructs human subjects, and a certain homology obtains between the quotidian disciplinary practices employed by social institutions like the army or the school to produce "docile bodies" and the more coercive measures employed against criminals and enemies of the state. Taking this observation further, one might justifiably ask: Why do the French guillotine, the Spanish garrote, the English hang, and the Americans electrocute, gas, or lethally inject those in their midst whom they wish to obliterate from the moral community? Among the numerous forms of state cruelty that Edward Peters examines in *Torture*, he notes that "there seem to be culturally-favoured forms of torture in different societies" (1996:171). Not all methods are used everywhere. In Greece, for example, there appears to be a preference for *falanga* (the beating of the soles of the feet), a torture that is not as common in Latin America and where electrical shock predominates. In Rwanda of 1994 torturers manifested a certain proclivity to employ violent methods with specific forms. These forms betrayed a preoccupation with the movement of persons and substances and with the canals, arteries, and conduits along which persons and substances flow: rivers, roadways, pathways, and even the conduits of the human body, such as the reproductive and digestive systems.

Controlling Flows

(1) Rivers.   In other work I have analyzed the ritual and symbolic importance of Rwanda's rivers in light of the generative scheme of flow vs. blockage. In the kingship ritual known as the "Path of the Watering," for example, the Nyabugogo and Nybarongo rivers served to revivify the magico-religious potency of the dynasty by recycling and reintegrating the ancestral benevolence of deceased kings (Taylor 1988). Although in the postcolonial Rwandan state these rivers appear to have lost their previous ritual significance, Rwanda's rivers were conscripted into the

genocide. This is apparent in statements made by one of the leading proponents of Hutu extremism, Leon Mugesera.

Well in advance of the genocide, Rwandan politicians made statements indicating that elements in the president's entourage were contemplating large-scale massacres of Tutsi. One of the baldest pronouncements in that regard came from the afore-mentioned Mugesera, an MRND party leader from the northern prefecture of Gisenyi. On November 22, 1992, Mugesera spoke to party faithful there. It was no ac-cident that a venue in Gisenyi Prefecture had been chosen for such an inflammatory speech, because this was the regime's home turf. Gisenyi solidly backed the Rwandan government and its president, for following Habyarimana's coup d'état in 1973, the re-gion had always received more than its allotted share of state jobs, secondary school placements, and so forth. Mugesera's words were not falling on deaf ears:

> The opposition parties have plotted with the enemy to make Byumba prefecture fall to the *Inyenzi*. . . . They have plotted to undermine our armed forces. . . . The law is quite clear on this point: "Any person who is guilty of acts aiming at sapping the morale of the armed forces will be condemned to death." What are we waiting for? . . . And what about those accomplices (*ibyitso*) here who are sending their children to the RPF? Why are we waiting to get rid of these families? . . . We have to take responsi-bility into our own hands and wipe out these hoodlums. . . . The fatal mistake we made in 1959 was to let them [the Tutsis] get out. . . . They belong in Ethiopia and we are going to find them a shortcut to get there by throwing them into the Nyabarongo River [which flows northward]. I must insist on this point. We have to act. Wipe them all out! (Text cited from Prunier 1995:171–72)

Shortly after this occurrence, Mugesera repeated the same speech in other Rwandan venues, and several violent incidents in which Tutsi were killed can be directly traced to its instigation. Although the minister of justice at the time, Stanis-las Mbonampeka, charged Mugesera with inciting racial hatred and gave orders to have him arrested, Mugesera took refuge at an army base where police dared not enter (ibid.).

In this speech there are several important elements, some of which are more ap-parent and others less so. That Mugesera is calling for the extermination of all en-emies of the regime and especially Tutsi seems clear. The old theme of Tutsi as originators from Ethiopia or "invaders from Ethiopia" has also resurfaced in this speech. The theme of Ethiopian origins, used during the late colonial era by apol-ogists of Tutsi domination (cf. A. Kagame 1959), has become, in the hands of Hutu extremists, a means of denying Tutsi any share in the patrimony of Rwanda. Yet also present in this speech is the first explicit postcolonial reference that I know of to the Nyabarongo River as a geographic entity with symbolic and political signi-ficance. In this speech the Nyabarongo has become the means by which Tutsi shall be removed from Rwanda and retransported to their presumed land of origin. Here, it should be emphasized, the river is again to serve an important ritualistic function—that of purifying the nation of its internal "foreign" minority.

It is no accident, then, that in the months of June, July, and August of 1994, when allegations of a massive genocide in Rwanda were just beginning to be taken seriously in the international media, thousands of bodies began washing up on the shores of Lake Victoria—bodies that had been carried there by the Nybarongo and then the Akagera rivers. So many Rwandan corpses accumulated in Lake Victoria that consumers in Kenya, Tanzania, and Uganda avoided buying fish taken from Victoria's waters, and the lake's important fishing industry was seriously jeopardized. In response, a publicity campaign was mounted to assure people that Lake Victoria fish species, such as tilapia and Nile River perch, do not feed on human corpses and that human remains only add more organic material to the water and do not diminish the edibility of the fish. Although these pleas aimed at minimizing the commercial impact of the large numbers of accumulated bodies, it was nonetheless clear that these latter were insalubrious to people living near the lake. Very quickly, local, national, and international efforts were mobilized to remove the decomposing corpses from the lake and its shores.

Rwanda's rivers became part of the genocide by acting as the body politic's organs of elimination, in a sense "excreting" its hated internal other. It is not much of a leap to infer that Tutsi were thought of as excrement by their persecutors. Other evidence of this is apparent in the fact that many Tutsi were stuffed into latrines after their deaths. Some were even thrown while still alive into latrines; a few of them actually managed to survive and to extricate themselves.

(2) Gusiba Inzira, "Blocking the Path." Among the accounts of Rwandan refugees that I interviewed in Kenya during the late spring and early summer of 1994, there was persistent mention of barriers and roadblocks. Like Nazi shower rooms in the concentration camps, these were the most frequent loci of execution for Rwanda's Tutsi and Hutu opponents of the regime. Barriers were erected almost ubiquitously and by many different groups. There were roadblocks manned by Rwandan government forces, roadblocks of the dreaded *Interhamwe* militia, Rwandan communal police checkpoints, barriers set up by neighborhood protection groups, opportunistic roadblocks erected by gangs of criminals, and even occasional checkpoints manned by the Rwandan Patriotic Front in areas under their control. For people attempting to flee Rwanda, evading these blockades was virtually impossible. Moreover, participation in a team of people manning a barrier was a duty frequently imposed upon citizens by Rwandan government or military officials.

Several Hutu informants who escaped Rwanda via an overland route explained to me that they had had to traverse hundreds of roadblocks. One informant estimated that he had encountered one barrier per hundred meters in a certain area. Another counted forty-three blockades in a ten-kilometer stretch on the paved road between Kigali and Gitarama. Leaving major highways was no solution, for one would encounter barriers erected across dirt roads and footpaths manned by local peasants. At every barrier fleeing people were forced to show their national identity card. Since the ID card bore mention of one's ethnicity, distinguishing Tutsi from Hutu was no problem, and almost always, fleeing Tutsi, said to be ibyitso, or "traitors," were robbed and killed. When a refugee claimed to have lost the ID card, his or her physical features were relied upon as ethnic identification. It was to one's advantage to look Hutu (to be of moderate height and to have a wide nose). One refugee that I interviewed, classified as Tutsi because his father was Tutsi and his mother was Hutu, escaped without showing his identity card because his features were typically Hutu. Another, classified as Hutu because his father was Hutu while his mother was Tutsi, narrowly missed being executed in Gitarama because of his Tutsilike physiognomy.

In order to traverse these barriers, even as a Hutu, it was often necessary to bribe those who were in control. One prosperous Hutu businessman whom I had known in Kigali, and who surely would have been killed because of his political affiliation (PSD) had he been recognized, told me that he had paid more than five thousand dollars in bribes.

Barriers were ritual and liminal spaces where "obstructing beings" were to be obstructed in their turn and cast out of the nation. The roadblocks were the space both of ritual and of transgression, following an ambivalent logic that Bourdieu underlines: "[T]he most fundamental ritual actions are in fact denied transgression" (1990:212). There were scenes of inordinate cruelty. Often the condemned had to pay for the quick death of a bullet, while the less fortunate were slashed with machetes or bludgeoned to death with nail-studded clubs. In many cases victims were intentionally maimed but not fully dispatched. Beside the line of motionless corpses awaiting pickup and disposal lay the mortally injured, exposed to the sun and still writhing, as their persecutors sat by calmly, drinking beer.

One refugee who had made it to Kenya by the circuitous route of fleeing south-ward to Burundi, told me that he and everyone else in his company had been forced to pay an unusual toll at one barrier. Each had been forced to bludgeon a cap-tured Tutsi with a hammer before being allowed to move on. Some in the party had even been made to repeat their blows a second or third time for lack of initial enthusiasm. The reasoning behind this can be clarified by considering the logic of sacrifice and the stigma that inevitably accrues to the sacrificer, the person who actually spills the victim's blood. As Bourdieu puts it:

> The magical protections that are set to work whenever the reproduction of the vital order requires transgression of the limits that are the foundation of that order, espe-cially whenever it is necessary to cut or kill, in short, to interrupt the normal course of life, include a number of ambivalent figures who are all equally despised and feared. (ibid.:213)

Requiring those who were being spared at the roadblocks to kill a hapless captive may seem unnecessary and purely sadistic, yet it served a useful psychological func-tion from the point of view of the genocide's perpetrators: that of removing the ambivalence of the sacrificial act and the stigma of the sacrificer/executioner by passing these on to everyone. The ritual obfuscated the boundary between *geno-*

cidiaires and those who were otherwise innocent Hutu. Not only were Tutsi and Hutu "traitors" being killed at the barriers; innocent Hutu were also being forced to become morally complicit in the genocide by becoming both "sacrificer" and "sacrifier" (Hubert and Mauss 1981) and shedding Tutsi blood.

Several Hutu refugees that I met in Kenya explained that they had used elaborate ruses to avoid, or to be excused from, "barrier duty." One of them, Jean-Damascene, told me that he had been obliged to spend two full days and nights at a barrier before being allowed to return to his nearby home. As he would have been resummoned for additional duty, Jean-Damascene and his wife concocted a persuasive alibi. Because she was already more than seven months pregnant and visibly so, his wife might be able to feign the onset of difficult labor. After less than twenty-fours of rest, Jean-Damascene returned to the barrier with his groaning, agitated wife and asked for permission to take her to Kigali hospital. The youthful Interahamwe in charge of the barrier seemed convinced by the charade and let them proceed, but only after Jean-Damascene left his wristwatch as a guarantee.

From there the couple walked a few kilometers to the center of Kigali, to a large, modern building where Jean-Damascene ordinarily worked. Gaining entrance into the building through doors that had been forced open by looters, the couple spent several nights sleeping on the floor of an upper-story corridor. During the day Jean-Damascene ventured outside to procure food and to ask people with vehicles if they were headed in the direction of Cyangugu (a city located on the southern edge of Lake Kivu and very close to the border with Zaire). Finally he found someone who was going to Cyangugu and who was willing to take him and his wife. Once in Cyangugu, the couple crossed the border into Zaire. In Bukavu (Zaire) they met a friend who gave Jean-Damascene enough money to buy a plane ticket to Nairobi. When I met Jean-Damascene in Nairobi, he was staying in the Shauri-Moyo Y.M.C.A., a place where many Rwandan refugees were being temporarily housed by the UNHCR. While in Nairobi, Jean-Damascene managed to raise enough money from family and friends to buy a plane ticket for his wife, who was still in Bukavu.

Hutu who were fleeing Rwandan government violence and that of the Interahamwe might traverse the barriers as long as they were not well-known opposition personalities who might be recognized. For Tutsi, escape was next to impossible. Most Tutsi refugees that I met in Nairobi had fled from Rwanda by other means. Several had made their way to Kigali airport during the week or so following President Habyarimana's assassination, a time when Belgian and French troops were evacuating their citizens via Kigali airport. Several had even been aided in their escape by a few Rwandan government army officers who had been willing to help them. Those who were saved this way were extremely lucky, for only some Belgian and some Senegalese troops made much of an attempt to save threatened Tutsi. French troops, allies of the genocidal regime, cynically abandoned Rwandan Tutsi to their fate, even those who had been former employees of the French embassy or the French Cultural Center.

One Tutsi man that I interviewed in Nairobi recounted that he, his wife, three of his children, and several other Tutsi employees of the French Cultural Center had been denied evacuation by French troops who remained at the center for several days before abruptly deciding to depart.[15] Belgian troops later occupied the Cultural Center and agreed to evacuate them; the Rwandans were placed among Westerners on Belgian Army trucks. Obliged to traverse several military roadblocks en route to the airport, the Tutsis hid beneath benches upon which Western evacuees were seated. Once at the airport, they were flown out of Rwanda on Belgian transport planes.

Although the barriers that fleeing Rwandans had to contend with were effective as a means of robbing and killing Tutsi civilians, roadblocks were next to useless as a means of halting the slow but inexorable RPF advance. In fact, the barriers defy military logic. Proliferated in all directions, they were counterproductive in any tactical sense, for they diverted manpower that could have been deployed in the field and they decentralized resistance to the RPF. Rwandan government forces and their associated Interahamwe militias were like a headless, tentacular beast expending its rage against Tutsi civilians and Hutu moderates while doing little to confront its real adversary. Even from the point of view of the military and militia who controlled the barriers, their utility defies ordinary logic. With roadblocks placed so close together, only one hundred meters apart in some instances, most were clearly redundant. Downstream barriers had little hope of catching people who had not already been stopped and fleeced of their money and belongings.

On April 9, 1994, as part of the U.S. embassy's overland evacuation from Rwanda, I had the opportunity to traverse many RGF barriers. At several roadblocks, soldiers could be seen openly drinking beer or whisky; there was a palpable sense of their frustration and disorientation. Yet they were very menacing. Soldiers paced suspiciously up and down the long line of stopped cars peering into them and asking questions whenever they saw a black face. Later that day and following it, subsequent evacuation convoys fared very badly at their hands. Suspected Tutsi or Hutu opposition party members were pulled from cars and summarily shot. Simply looking Tutsi was sufficient grounds for execution. A Mauritanian friend of mine had two of his children pulled from his car and threatened because of their facial features. Only tense negotiation and the showing of every possible identity paper convinced the soldiers that the children were not Tutsi but Mauritanian. Expending so much energy against the perceived internal enemy virtually ensured defeat for the Rwandan government forces and their allied militias, for while they wasted their time trying to stop fleeing civilians, the RPF methodically pressed its offensive, capturing one military base after another, one city after another.

If the movement of people could be obstructed with barriers, it could also be hindered by directly attacking the body. The parts of the body most frequently targeted to induce immobility were the legs, feet, and Achilles tendons. Thousands of corpses discovered after the violence showed evidence of one or both tendons having been sectioned by machete blows. Other victims later found alive in parts of Rwanda where humanitarian organizations were able to intervene had also sustained this injury. Medecins Sans Frontieres, when it entered eastern Rwanda in late June of 1994, declared in presentations to televised media that this injury was the one most frequently encountered in their area. Although MSF managed to save many lives among those so injured, the organization warned that in virtually every case, costly surgery would be needed to restore some mobility to the foot. This injury, known in medieval France as the *coup de Jarnac*, has sometimes been attributed to the influence of French troops and their alleged training of Interhamwe militia members (Braeckman 1994). While I have no evidence to refute that in this specific instance, Braeckman's assertion does not explain why the technique had been used in Rwanda during the violence of 1959–64 and in 1973. Moreover, in previous episodes of violence, as well as in 1994, assailants also mutilated cattle belonging to Tutsi by cutting the leg tendons. Although many cattle in 1994 were killed outright and eaten, and others were stolen, a large number were immobilized and left to die slowly in the field.

This technique of cruelty has a certain logic to it where human beings are concerned. In the presence of a large number of potential victims, too many to kill at once, Interahamwe might immobilize fleeing victims by a quick blow to one or both of the Achilles tendons. Then the killers could return at their leisure and complete their work. This makes sense, yet it does not explain why many who sustained this injury were children too young to walk, elderly people, people who were crippled or infirm, and people in hospital beds incapable of running away. It is here that the pragmatic logic of immobilizing one's enemies and the symbolic logic of "blocking the path," which are not contradictory in many cases, are in conflict. Why immobilize the immobile? As with barriers on paths and roadways, there is a deeper generative scheme that subtends both the killers' intentionality and the message inscribed on the bodies of their victims, even though these techniques of cruelty also involve a degree of improvisation. Power in this instance, in symbolic terms, derives from the capacity to obstruct. The persecutor "blocks the path" of human beings and impedes the movement of the material/symbolic capital necessary to the social reproduction of human beings—cattle. Even when it is apparently unnecessary to arrest the movement of the already immobile, the assertion of the capacity to obstruct is nonetheless the claim and assertion of power.

(3) The Body as Conduit.   In addition to the imagery of obstruction, numerous instances of the body as conduit can be discerned in the Rwandan violence of 1994. This imagery tends to center on two bodily foci: the digestive tract and the reproductive system. For example, after spending several days in Bujumbura, Burundi, following our land evacuation from Rwanda, my fiancée, a Rwandan Tutsi, and I took a plane to Nairobi, Kenya. When we arrived at the airport on April 15, 1994, we were surprised to see a group of about fifty or so Rwandans, mostly Tutsi, who had been stranded there for days. The Kenyan government, allied to the former Rwandan regime and already sheltering thousands of refugees

from other countries in UNHCR camps, had given instructions to immigration personnel to refuse entry visas to all Rwandans. Having been deposited in Nairobi by Belgian or U.N. evacuation planes, the Rwandans found themselves with nowhere to go and nowhere to return. As my fiancée and I were also denied entry visas for several hours until we received help from the U.S. embassy in Nairobi, we had ample time to talk to the stranded Rwandans. Virtually all of them had lost numerous family members, or spouses, lovers, and friends. All were suffering from their confinement at Nairobi airport. Unable to bathe, shower, or change clothes, all looked haggard and unkempt. Their only permitted amenity was sleeping at night in tents put up by the UNHCR just outside the terminal building. We were also surprised to learn that most of them also complained of constipation.

In effect, the Rwandans were somaticizing their ordeal. Having narrowly escaped death, the refugees now found themselves at the end of whatever affective, familial, and economic life they had led in Rwanda and at the beginning of a new life as yet undefined in terms of where they would live or what they would do. None at the time had much confidence that the situation in Rwanda would be quickly resolved. Most were resigned to the probability that they would never return to Rwanda and that all the other members of their family were dead. In virtually all ways that one can envision human existence, whether in social or psychological terms, the lives of these refugees had reached an impasse. Coupled with this state of suspended animation was the fact that the Rwandans were virtual captives at the Nairobi airport, anxiously awaiting the results of delicate negotiations between the UNHCR and the Kenyan government. It was thus appropriate that their bodies express these various modes of obstruction through symptoms that made sense in terms of Rwandan cultural experience.

The image of the body as conduit was not discernible only in modes of somaticizing psychological distress on the part of victims; it could also be seen in the techniques of cruelty used by the perpetrators of violence. Perhaps the most vivid example of this during the genocide was the practice of impalement. Recalling Liisa Malkki's observation concerning the 1972 violence against Hutu in Burundi, Rwandan Tutsi men in 1994 were also impaled from anus to mouth with wooden or bamboo poles and metal spears. Tutsi women were often impaled from vagina to mouth. Although none of the refugees that I interviewed in Nairobi spoke of having witnessed impalement, it was reported in Kenyan newspapers that I read during the summer of 1994. More recently it has been cited in an African Rights report entitled "Rwanda: Killing the Evidence" as a means by which perpetrators of the genocide still living on Rwandan soil terrorize surviving witnesses (Omaar and de Waal 1996). For example, the report cites the case of a certain Makasi, a resident of the Kicukiro suburb of Kigali, who, several months after the genocide, found a leaflet shoved under his door threatening his life and that of several others: "You, Makasi are going to die no matter what. And it will not only be you. It will be Bylingiro as well. Let your wife know that she will be killed with a pole which will run from her legs right up to her mouth. As for Charles' wife, her legs and arms will be cut off" (ibid.:15).

Even before the genocide, impalement was occasionally depicted in the popular Rwandan literature of Hutu extremism as one of the preferred means of torture used by the RPF and other Tutsi to dispatch their Hutu victims. Notice that in the cartoon depicting Melchior Ndadaye's death, in addition to impalement there are two other aspects that also require analysis: castration and crucifixion.[16] As explained above, one of the royal rituals involved adorning the royal drum, Karinga, with the genitals of slain enemies. That is what is depicted in this scene, as the captions show:

> *An onlooker:* "Kill this stupid Hutu and after you cut off his genitals, hang them on our drum."
>
> *Ndadaye:* "Kill me, but you won't exterminate all the Ndadayes in Burundi."
>
> *Kagame (prominent RPF general, now president and defense minister of Rwanda):*
> "Kill him quickly. Don't you know that in Byumba and Ruhengeri we did a lot of work. With women, we pulled the babies out of their wombs; with men, we dashed out their eyes."
>
> *The drum:* "Karinga of Burundi."

There is perhaps no other pictorial image in the annals of Rwandan Hutu extremism in which so much violent imagery is condensed. At one level we see a clear reference to the often repeated charge of Hutu extremists that the RPF were "feudo-monarchists" intent upon restoring the king and the royal rituals, including the monarchy's principal emblem—the drum named Karinga. Another ideological claim is advanced in depicting Hutu victims of the RPF as Christlike martyrs, for Ndadaye is not just impaled, he is also crucified. Yet at another level a complex synthesis has been forged. Specifically Rwandan symbols with deep historical and ontological roots have merged with those that are the more recent product of Christian evangelization.

In precolonial and early colonial times, Rwandans impaled cattle thieves. The executioners inserted a wooden stake into the thief's anus and then pushed it through the body, causing it to exit at the neck or the mouth. The pole with its agonizing charge was then erected, stuck into the earth, and left standing for several days. Dramatically gruesome and public, this punishment carried a clear and obvious normative message intended to deter cattle thievery. In a more subtle way, the message can be interpreted symbolically. Because cattle exchanges accompany, legitimize, and commemorate the most significant social transitions and relationships, most notably patron-client relations, blood brotherhood, and marriage, obviating the possibility of such exchanges or subverting those that have already occurred by stealing cattle removes all tangible mnemonic evidence of the attendant social relationships. Diverting socially appropriate flows of cattle by means of thievery is a way of gusiba inzira, or "blocking the path," between individuals and groups united through matrimonial alliance, blood brotherhood, or patron-client ties. It

Figure 6.1. L'assassinat de Ndadaye. (Cartoon from Chretien 1995:364–65.)

is symbolically appropriate, therefore, that people who obstruct the conduits of social exchange have the conduit that is the body obstructed with a pole or spear.

Quite obviously, between the precolonial and early colonial times, when Rwandan executioners impaled cattle thieves, and 1994, when genocidal murderers impaled Tutsi men and women, many things have changed. The more recent victims of the practice were clearly not cattle thieves. Were they in some sense like cattle thieves in the minds of those committing the atrocities? My feeling is that they were, although the more recent terms used in Hutu extremist discourse to describe Tutsi only occasionally make reference to the actual actions of which they might be guilty, such as theft. Instead, "Tutsi are invaders from Ethiopia," "cockroaches," "eaters of our sweat," or "weight upon our back." The Tutsi, much like the archetypal aga-keecuru discussed above, exert their malevolent influence on the social group not so much by what they do as by inherent qualities that they supposedly embody. In that sense they approach being "blocking beings," the mythical nemeses of Rwandan tradition—the agakeecuru, impenebere, or impa—and like those figures they possess fearful powers. In this case they were obstructors of the cosmic unity of the nation as that unity was imagined by the Hutu extremist elite: a purified nation with a purified, reified "Hutu culture" expunged of all elements of "Tutsi culture" and rid of all who would resist the encompassing powers of the state. The torturers not only killed their victims; they transformed their bodies into powerful signs that resonated with a Rwandan habitus even as they improvised upon it and enlarged the original semantic domain of associated meanings to depict an entire ethnic group as enemies of the Hutu state.

OTHER VIOLENCE

Among other violence reported during the Rwandan genocide, there were frequent instances of emasculation of Tutsi males, even those too young to reproduce. Attackers also slashed off the breasts of Tutsi women. These techniques of cruelty had also been employed during earlier periods of Rwandan history. Both emasculation and breast oblation manifest a preoccupation with the reproductive system, and specifically with parts of the body that produce fertility fluids. In both cases, the symbolic function interdigitates with and reinforces the pragmatic function, but the symbolic function cannot simply be reduced to the pragmatic one of destroying the future capacity of a group to reproduce. The torturers were assaulting specific and diverse human subjects as well as attacking a group's capacity to reproduce. In order to convince themselves that they were ridding the polity of a categorical enemy and not just assaulting specific individuals, they first had to transform their victims' bodies into the equivalent of "blocked beings." A logic, a posteriori, was operative: reclassify through violence bodies that do not, a priori, manifest the imagined inadequacy. Reconfigure specific bodies through torture so that they become the categorical abomination.

In other instances Tutsi women were taken captive and repeatedly raped by RGF soldiers or Interahamwe militia members before being killed.[17] Some Tutsi women were referred to as "wives" by their rapists, who kept them as sexual slaves and even brought them into the refugee camps in Zaire after the RGF was defeated. Among Tutsi women who escaped their captors, many became pregnant and then subsequently sought abortions in Catholic Rwanda, where abortion is illegal. Today in Rwanda there are many children who are the products of these rapes. In many cases these children have been rejected by their mothers and are now in orphanages run by international relief organizations (Boutros-Ghali 1996:67).

There were also cases of forcing adult Tutsi to commit incest with one of their children before killing them (ibid.). Here the image of misdirected flows is quite clear, for incest causes blood and semen to flow backward upon one another in a closed circuit within the family rather than in an open circuit between families. Not only were the victims brutalized and dehumanized by this treatment but, in addition, their bodies were transformed into icons of asociality, for incest constitutes the preemption of any possible alliance or exchange relation that might have resulted from the union of one's son or daughter with the son or daughter of another family.

OTHER METAPHORS OF VIOLENCE

Not all of the violence or the metaphors associated with it that occurred during the genocide followed the symbolic patterns that I have outlined above. Many of the explicit metaphors used by promoters of the violence actually show little overt relation to this symbolism. I do not see this as problematic; there were many levels to the genocide, some quite conscious, others less so.

For example, the killers' frequently made reference to the violence as *akazi kacu,* or "our work." In my opinion, this reference addressed more the killers' psychological discomfort with their unenviable social condition of un- and underemployment rather than any implicit aspect of Rwandan habitus. Just by becoming an Interahamwe and executing Tutsi, one could elevate oneself to the status of state employee. One could even expect eventual compensation from the state for one's services, and indeed that was sometimes given and much more frequently promised. In addition, the genocidiaires frequently employed horticultural imagery. Hutu citizens were instructed to cut the "tall trees" down to size, an indirect but easily understood reference to the physiognomic stereotype of Tutsi height. In other cases the nation-state became a garden, as Hutu extremists called upon their followers to clear away the "weeds." Following this metaphor, promoters exhorted their followers to remove both the "tall weeds" (adults) and the "shoots" (children).

The symbolization of Tutsi malevolence also drew upon other cultural sources. Some of the Hutu extremist theories, for example, show the probable influence of Nazi theories. Was this a coincidence, or was it a conscious appropriation of anti-Semitic imagery? For example, the differing physiognomies of Hutu and Tutsi were said to have moral implications, and particular attention was paid to the nose. (It should be recalled that in Nazi Germany posters depicted various forms of the so-called Jewish nose.) One extremist theory that I heard in Rwanda made the claim that the degree of human goodness that one possessed was directly proportional to the width of one's nose. Hutu stereotypically have wider noses than Tutsi.

In other instances the styles affected in the improvised uniforms of the Interhamwe militia, their gestures, and body language showed the influence of James Bond, Bruce Lee, Rambo, and Arnold Schwarzenegger films, all of which were readily available and popular in pregenocide Rwanda. Violence, it would appear, has its fashions and its styles, and these are partly transnational in origin.

THE RWANDAN GENOCIDE AND
HISTORICAL TRANSFORMATION

Although I believe that the imagery of flow and obstruction was pervasive during the genocide, it would be wrong to conclude from the above argument that Rwandan culture is simply a *machine a tropes* constantly replicating the same structures and hermetically sealed off from all influences arising from within or beyond its borders. As Bourdieu (1977, 1990) maintains, people tend to reproduce the "structured and structuring logic" of the habitus. Nevertheless, although older generations subtly inculcate this logic to their juniors, the socialization process is never perfect or complete. Transformed objective circumstances always influence socialization. The tendency to reproduce a structured logic thus should not be seen as simple and volitionless replication. There is always improvisation and innovation, even if many of the basic patterns retain their saliency.

In the Rwandan instance, colonialism and concomitant transformations in economic and political conditions influenced the perception and depiction of evil. Because of these changes, the symbolism of malevolent obstruction could be applied to an entire ethnic group. This was a radical departure from the past. During precolonial times, the image of the menacing "blocking being" was confined to a limited number of individuals. These included impa—women who had reached childbearing age and had never menstruated; impenebere—women who had reached childbearing age and had not developed breasts; individual enemies of the Rwandan king, and sorcerers. All these malevolent beings were mythically presaged in the legend about the agakeecuru and the origin of Death. Occasionally, in the rituals associated with sacred kingship, such individuals were publicly sacrificed to rid the polity of their potentially nefarious influence.

It was not until Tutsi and Hutu ethnic identities had become substantialized under colonialism, and then privileges were awarded by the colonial rulers on the basis of these identities, that an entire group of people could be thought of as a source of obstruction to the polity as a whole. Tutsi could be easily assimilated to the category of "invaders" because of their alliance with German, then Belgian, outsiders and the colonialists' reliance on Hamitic theories. When Belgians quickly shifted their allegiance to Hutu in the late 1950s, supporting the Hutu Revolution, Tutsi were left to fend for themselves while retaining their substantialized identity. Tutsi assimilation to the imagery of malevolent others, "blocked" or "blocking be-

ings," was facilitated by the fact that a minority among them had indeed been favored socially and economically under the colonial regime. Where once there had
been a sacred king whose actions were thought to ensure a religious and material
redistributive function—the downward flow of celestial beneficence, wealth, and
prosperity—under colonialism popular credence in the ritual and pragmatic functions of kingship was undermined. In its place a privileged class of Tutsi, Tutsi administrators in the colonial state apparatus, were perceived by other Rwandans to
have become rich by subverting the redistribution process, or, in a symbolic sense,
by impeding the flow of imaana.

The 1959–62 revolution in Rwanda was not anticolonial; Belgians were not endangered or forced to flee the country, Tutsi were. Nor were Belgian economic
and cultural interests seriously threatened. Belgians continued to enjoy privileged
status in Rwanda until some time after 1990, when Belgium withdrew its military
support of the Habyarimana regime. The symbolism of obstruction is indeed precolonial in origin, but its application to an entire group of people is a thoroughly
recent, modern application reflecting transformed consciousness of the polity and
of the people composing it.

Second, many of the actual and symbolic forms of violence became syncretized
to Euro-American or transnational forms. This is apparent in the cartoon depicting Melchior Ndadaye's death and in other juxtapositions of transnational images
and those of local vintage. Clearly, the violent imaginary looks for inspiration to
all possible sources. According to Jean-Pierre Chretien in *Les medias du genocide* (1995),
Nazi symbols were attributed to the RPF by Hutu extremists. The French government's habit of referring to the RPF as "Khmers noirs" followed in this pattern
and echoed their Hutu extremist allies. Nevertheless, it was Hutu extremists who
were more like Nazis and Khmers Rouges in actual practice.

CONCLUSION

Methodological individualists might very well object that atrocities occur in all violent conflicts, and that they are at their worst in fratricidal disputes and civil wars.
The Rwandan atrocities would then have followed an instrumental logic based on
maximizing the number of enemies killed, or maximizing the psychological effect
by the sheer horror of atrocity. Such an explanation might concur with what the
authors of the atrocities themselves claim was the reasoning behind their acts. Although such an explanation is not inexact, it is incomplete. It cannot explain the
depth of passion that clearly lay behind the Rwandan violence, nor the fact that it
assumed specific forms. But one type of logic to the cruelty does not preclude all
others; pragmatism and symbolism in a general way are not necessarily conflic-
tual (cf. Sperber 1975). Killing one's adversaries while communicating powerful
messages about them and oneself are not mutually exclusive. Pragmatic explanations alone, however, cannot account for the sheer number of roadblocks that
refugees reported to me that they had encountered. There was certainly a point of

diminishing returns where adding new barriers was concerned, and it would appear that this point had been more than surpassed. Nor is impalement the only way of making one's victims endure atrocious and exemplary suffering. Does it make sense to sever the Achilles tendons of those who have very little chance of running away? Does it make sense to castrate prepubescent boys? Does it make sense to cut the leg tendons of cattle rather than killing them outright?

This is where instrumental logic alone does not fully explain the Rwandan violence. The forms of the violence encountered here were enracinated in Rwandan ways of bodily experience and bodily predispositions lurking beneath the level of verbalization and calculation. Although these predispositions were political in the sense that they influenced thought and action where power was concerned, they were certainly not political in the ordinary sense of symbols consciously used by one group to advance its claims in opposition to another group and its symbols. This symbolism was logically prior to its instantiation in a political form and not the other way around.

Moreover, the use of the symbolism was ultimately contradictory. The power of the sacred king in precolonial and early colonial times emanated as much from his capacity to interdict flows as well as to catalyze them, but he was usually depicted as a "flowing being" rather than a "blocking" one, even to the point of being represented as a lactating male. Similarly, it made symbolic sense during the 1994 violence to make the claim of power—when power was no longer clearly defined, no longer in the hands of a single hierarchical authority, when power was diffuse and in the streets—by eliminating all who would subvert the encompassing order of the Rwandan state. This entailed obstructing the obstructors, sacrificing the malevolent "blocking beings" in the nation's midst, as these latter represented both potential pathology to individuals and a threat to collective order. Sacrifice took the form of interdicting the flight of Tutsi, obstructing the conduits of their bodies, impeding their bodies' capacity for movement, subverting the ability of Tutsi to reproduce socially or biologically, and in some instances turning their bodies into icons of their imagined moral flaw—obstruction. Yet it led the murderers into a paradox: in order to parry the imagined obstructor, they were forced to obstruct.

From a purely pragmatic viewpoint, one might object that the imagery of obstruction and its relation to power are quite general, even transcultural. A petty bureaucrat manifests his power over petitioning citizens by impeding the passage of papers and forms through the administrative conduits. But the same argument can be made for many, if not most, other symbols. Many symbolic forms are universal. Nevertheless, the universality of "image schemata" does not really detract from the assertion that the Rwandan violence should be understood in terms of its cultural specificity, for the question that really should be asked is not whether a certain symbolic image is transcultural or specific, but what degree of elaboration and use a specific group makes of the image. That Rwandans make extensive use of "flow/blockage" imagery in relation to the body seems clear from a study of popular medicine. That these images would reappear in the context of the genocide

makes sense in light of Kafka's *The Penal Colony* and the comments of Pierre Clastres, for it is the human body that serves as the ultimate tablet upon which the dic-
tates of the state are inscribed.

The Rwandan genocide was certainly about power, but not all aspects of power
are of the same nature. Although most of the events leading up to and during the
genocide involve power in their overt ideological manifestation, something that was
openly discussed and contested, there were other potencies at work, those that social
actors during the genocide possessed less conscious awareness of. These potencies were
not of the kind that competing factions could argue about or readily explicate. On
the contrary, it is likely that many people in this conflict, whether they were Interahamwe extremists or RPF soldiers, whether they were Hutu or Tutsi, shared a similar habitus and at least some of the same ontological predispositions. That is also why
many Burundian forms of violence perpetrated by Tutsi against Hutu in 1972 resemble Rwandan forms perpetrated by Hutu against Tutsi in 1994. It is also why Hutu
extremists depicted forms of violence that Hutu would presumably suffer at the hands
of Tutsi "feudo-monarchists," but yet actually represented what Hutu extremists en-
visioned doing to Tutsi. As for the representations themselves, these were not Hutu
symbols any more than they were Tutsi symbols. This was a system of representations that permitted Rwandans to cognize potencies of diverse sorts, potencies that include political power but yet are not confined to it. The symbols that lie at the core of
Rwandan culture cannot be reduced to simple surrogates for political action and struggle; they must be examined on their own right. Nor should these symbols be seen as
antagonistic to human agency, for in many ways they were constitutive of it.

NOTES

1. Before the genocide, Rwanda's population numbered in excess of seven million people. Approximately 80 to 85 percent of that population was Hutu, 15 to 20 percent Tutsi,
and less than 1 percent Twa. As many as 80 percent of the pregenocide Tutsi population
may have died in the violence.

2. "Kafka designe ici le corps comme surface d'ecriture, comme surface apte a recevoir
le texte lisible de la loi" (Clastres 1974:153).

3. "Le corps mediatise l'acquisition d'un savoir, ce savoir s'inscrit sur le corps" (ibid.:154).

4. "[La] societe imprime sa marque sur le corps des jeunes gens.... La marque est un
obstacle a l'oubli, le corps lui-meme porte imprimees sur soi les traces d'un souvenir, *le corps
est une memoire*" (ibid.:157).

5. Kapferer is cognizant of the criticism often leveled at Dumont's scheme as reminiscent of unilineal evolutionism with its accompanying dichotomization of tradition and
modernity. Kapferer responds by explaining that both egalitarian and hierarchical forms are
equally modern, but that the contrast is justified in that the two incorporate different notions of the state, nation, society, and the person. "In Foucault's sense the two ideologies ar-
ticulate rather different discursive 'technologies of power'" (Kapferer 1989:165).

6. Ubuhake is the name of the patron-client arrangement that emblematically characterized Tutsi/Hutu relations during the colonial era. In this arrangement a Tutsi patron

(*umushebuja*) would give a cow to a Hutu client (*umugaragu*) in exchange for the latter's occasional services in labor. All female offspring of the cow were to be returned to the Tutsi patron, but the Hutu client could keep all male calves. Perceived as exploitative by many Hutu, the arrangement was proscribed in the wake of the Hutu Revolution.

7. Interahamwe means "those who attack together." Most Rwandan political parties had youth wings, and for the MRND Party, theirs was the Interahamwe. Recruited largely from among un- or underemployed young males who had drifted into Rwandan cities, the Interahamwe received political and arms training from MRND party officials, Rwandan government soldiers, and possibly also from French military advisors. Virtually every urban neighborhood possessed at least one Interahamwe member, and in the rural areas, every hillside. They aided the pregenocidal apparatus in keeping regularly updated lists of all Rwandan opposition party members and all Tutsis. Before the outbreak of wholesale massacres, the Interahamwe intimidated people on their lists with actual or threatened violence and extorted "protection" money from them. Even before the genocide, Interahamwe were occasionally given the authorization to set up roadblocks and to rob, beat, and sometimes kill the people they trapped, or to steal or damage their vehicles. During the genocide Interahamwe weapons of choice were the machete, the nail-studded wooden club, and the grenade.

8. This opposition is certainly not the only one that characterizes Rwandan popular medicine; there are others, such as purity vs. pollution, hot vs. cold, and wet vs. dry. However, the flow/blockage opposition appears to be the dominant one in healing and may be dominant as well in other domains of Rwandan symbolic thought. Its analysis has nevertheless been neglected in the earlier ethnographic writing on Rwanda.

9. Francoise Heritier's work among the Ivory Coast Samo is quite germane here. Her work addresses some of the same concerns that I encountered in Rwanda: female sterility, amenorrhea, analogies between human bodily states and natural phenomena such as aridity and drought. While her work emphasizes the opposition between "hot" and "cold," that does not preclude other oppositions, such as "flow" vs. "blockage." Similar overall concerns are likely to be encountered elsewhere in sub-Saharan Africa but with varying symbolic expressions. While among the Samo the hot/cold opposition may be the dominant metaphor, among Rwandans and others in central Africa (cf. De Mahieu, Devisch) the flow/blockage opposition may be dominant.

10. The distinction between witchcraft and sorcery is not applicable in Rwanda. The Kinyarwanda verb *kuroga* refers to the introduction of poisons or other harmful substances into a victim's food or drink, or to the performance of ritual actions intended to harm another person.

11. Many rural Rwandans say that conception is most likely to occur after both partners have had orgasm. Moreover, the ideal, local form of making love, called *kunyaza*, which means "to make urinate," requires that the woman have profuse vaginal secretions during sex.

12. The Nyabarongo River eventually joins the Akagera River, which forms Rwanda's eastern boundary with Tanzania. The Akagera then empties into Lake Victoria, which is where the Nile River begins. In 1994 Rwanda's rivers served as disposal points for thousands of bodies that then began to collect on the shores of Lake Victoria, creating a health hazard. The importance of these rivers during the genocide in an ideological and symbolic sense will be discussed below.

13. Mystical harm in Rwanda is never an innate, congenital potentiality as it is among some African peoples (cf., E. E. Evans-Pritchard, *Witchcraft . . . among the Azande*); instead it is

always what Evans-Pritchard has termed "sorcery," involving the idea of the ingestion of harmful substances (even when no substances may have actually been ingested by the victim). "Les Rwandais sont obsédés par les effets néfastes de l'alimentation qui exige mille précautions, d'autant plus que la sorcellerie est toujours conçue comme un empoisonnement" (Smith 1975:133). (Rwandans are obsessed by the possible harmful effects of eating, which demands the observation of a thousand precautions, even more so because sorcery is always conceived of as poisoning.)

14. It is interesting to note that among the news and political magazines that came into existence in the 1990s, there was one called *Isibo*. Politically speaking, *Isibo* was an opposition magazine representing the viewpoint of southern and central Hutu allied to the Twagiramungu faction of the MDR and opposed to the MRND and the Habyarimana regime (Chretien 1995:383). Although I have been unable to determine the significance of the magazine's title to its promoters and readers, it does seem to indicate that the term *isibo* retains cultural and political significance in the modern context and possesses associations that go beyond that of sacred kingship.

15. During the several days that French troops controlled the center, this man had occasion to speak with the center's director twice on the phone. When he explained that he and other Rwandan employees marooned at the center had nothing to eat, she suggested that they take the plantains from trees growing on the center's grounds. (None of the plantain trees were bearing fruit at the time.) When he expressed his anxiety about the unwillingness of the French troops to evacuate him and others, she told him that maybe the RPF would rescue them. (The RPF did not take this section of Kigali until almost two months later.)

16. Melchior Ndadaye was Burundi's first democratically elected president and first Hutu president. Elected in June of 1993, Ndadaye was taken prisoner in late October and then murdered (though not by impalement) by Burundian Tutsi army officers in a coup attempt. Almost universally condemned by other nations, the coup eventually failed, but not before it had provoked reprisal killings in which thousands of Tutsi civilians died and counterreprisal violence in which thousands of Hutu were killed. The coup and Ndadaye's death served the cause of Hutu extremism in Rwanda quite well, and extremists lost no time in exploiting it. Unfortunately the extremists' point that the Tutsi could never be trusted as partners in a democracy gained enormous credibility in Rwanda in the wake of Ndadaye's tragic death.

17. Violence against women also characterized another recent fratricidal conflict where genocidal acts occurred—Bosnia. While the logic of violence against Tutsi women in Rwanda appears to have been motivated largely by Hutu extremist fear of interethnic marriages (cf. Taylor 1999), there was an additional logic in Bosnia, though it too was of a cultural nature. Among Mediterranean societies characterized by strong notions of "honor" (cf. Pitt-Rivers 1977), much is invested in the perceived sexual purity of a group's women. Rape, as long as it is unavenged, is not just an act that violates an individual; it is an act that subverts the honor of a family.

REFERENCES CITED

Assad, Talal. 1972. "Market Model, Class Structure and Consent: A Reconsideration of Swat Political Organisation." *Man* 7:74–94.

Barth, Fredrik. 1959. *Political Leadership among the Swat Pathans.* London: Athlone.

Beattie, John. 1960. *Bunyoro, an African Kingdom.* New York: Holt, Rinehart, and Winston.

Beidelman, Thomas. 1986. *Moral Imagination in Kaguru Modes of Thought.* Bloomington: Indiana University Press.

Bourdieu, Pierre. 1977. *Outline of a Theory of Practice.* Cambridge: Cambridge University Press.

———. 1990. *The Logic of Practice.* Stanford: Stanford University Press.

Bourgeois, Rene. 1956. *Banyarwanda et Barundi, religion et magie.* Brussels: Academie Royale des Sciences Coloniales.

Boutros-Ghali, Boutros. 1996. "Introduction." In *The United Nations and Rwanda, 1993–1996.* United Nations Blue Books Series, vol. 10. New York: United Nations Department of Public Information.

Braeckman, Colette. 1994. *Rwanda: Histoire d'un genocide.* Paris: Fayard.

Chretien, Jean-Pierre. 1991. "Burundi: Le Metier d'historien: Querelle d'ecole?" *Canadian Journal of African Studies.* 25(3):450–70.

———. 1995. *Rwanda: les medias du genocide.* Paris: Editions Karthala.

Clastres, Pierre. 1974. *La societe contre l'etat: recherches d'anthropologie politique.* Paris: Editions de Minuit.

Clifford, James, and George Marcus. 1986. *Writing Culture: The Poetics and Politics of Ethnography.* Berkeley: University of California Press.

Comaroff, John, and Jean Comaroff. 1992a. "Ethnography and the Historical Imagination." In *Ethnography and the Historical Imagination.* Pp. 3–48. Boulder: Westview Press.

———. 1992b. "Of Totemism and Ethnicity." In *Ethnography and the Historical Imagination.* Pp. 49–67. Boulder: Westview Press.

De Mahieu, Wauthier. 1985. *Qui a obstrué la cascade?* Cambridge: Cambridge University Press.

Devisch, René. 1984. *Se recréer femme.* Berlin: Dietrich Reimer Verlag.

Dumont, Louis. 1980. *Homo Hierarchicus: The Caste System and Its Implications.* Chicago: University of Chicago Press.

Ehret, Christopher. 1974. *Ethiopians and East Africans.* Nairobi: East African Publishing House.

Evans-Pritchard, Edward. 1937. *Witchcraft, Oracles and Magic among the Azande.* Oxford: Clarendon Press.

Farquhar, Judith. 1994. *Knowing Practice: The Clinical Encounter of Chinese Medicine.* Boulder: Westview Press.

Fenton, James. 1996. "A Short History of Anti-Hamitism." *New York Review of Books,* Feb. 15, 7–9.

Foucault, Michel. 1977. *Discipline and Punish: The Birth of the Prison.* New York: Pantheon.

Gledhill, John. 1994. *Power and Its Disguises: Anthropological Perspectives on Politics.* London: Pluto Press.

Goldhagen, Daniel. 1996. *Hitler's Willing Executioners: Ordinary Germans and the Holocaust.* New York: Knopf.

Harroy, Jean-Pierre. 1984. *Rwanda, du feodalism a la democratie (1955–1962).* Brussels: Hayez.

Heritier, Françoise. 1984. "Stabilité, aridité, sècheresse: Quelques invariants de la pensée symbolique." In *Le sens du mal.* Marc Augé and Claudine Herglich, eds. Pp. 123–54. Paris: Editions des Archives Contemporaines.

d'Hertefelt, Marcel. 1971. *Les clans du Rwanda ancien.* Serie in 8o, Sciences Humaines. Tervuren (Belgium): Musee Royal de l'Afrique Centrale.

d'Hertefelt, Marcel, and Andre Coupez. 1964. *La royautee sacree de l'ancien Rwanda.* Annales, Serie in 8o, no. 52, Sciences Humaines. Tervuren (Belgium): Musee Royal de l'Afrique Centrale.

de Heusch, Luc. 1966. *Le Rwanda et la civilisation interlacustre.* Brussels: Universite Libre de Bruxelles.

————. 1994. "Anthropologie d'un genocide: le Rwanda." *Les Temps Modernes* 579:1–19.

Hubert, Henri, and Marcel Mauss. 1981 [1964]. *Sacrifice: Its Nature and Functions.* Chicago: University of Chicago Press.

Jacob, Irenee. 1984, 1985, 1987. *Dictionnaire Rwandais-Francais: Extrait du dictionnaire de l'Institut National de Recherche Scientifique.* 3 vols. Kigali (Rwanda): L'Imprimerie Scolaire.

Johnson, Mark. 1987. *The Body in the Mind.* Chicago: University of Chicago Press.

Kagame, Alexis. 1956. *La philosophie bantu-rwandaise de l'être.* Memoire In 80, nouvelle serie, tome XII, fascicule 1, Classe des sciences morales et politiques. Brussels: Academie royale des sciences coloniales.

————. 1959. *Inganji Karinga.* Kabgayi (Rwanda).

Kakar, Sudar. 1982. *Shamans, Mystics and Doctors: A Psychological Inquiry into India and Its Healing Traditions.* Chicago: University of Chicago Press.

Kapferer, Bruce. 1988. *Legends of People, Myths of State.* Washington, D.C.: Smithsonian Institution Press.

————. 1989. "Nationalist Ideologies and a Comparative Anthropology." *Ethnos* 54(3–4):161–99.

Lacger, Louis de. 1930. *Ruanda I. Le Ruanda ancien.* Kabgayi (Rwanda).

Lemarchand, Rene. 1970. *Rwanda and Burundi.* New York: Praeger.

————. 1990. "L'ecole historiques burundo-francaise: Une ecole pas comme les autres." *Canadian Journal of African Studies* 24(2):235–48.

Linden, Ian. 1954. *Le systeme des relations sociales dans le Ruanda ancien.* Tervuren (Belgium): Musee Royal de l'Afrique Centrale.

————. 1977. *Church and Revolution in Rwanda.* Manchester: Manchester University Press.

Malkki, Liisa. 1995. *Purity and Exile.* Chicago: University of Chicago Press.

Nordstrom, Carolyn, and Jo-Anne Martin, eds. 1992. *The Paths to Domination, Terror, and Resistance.* Berkeley: University of California Press.

Omaar, Rakiya, and Andre de Waal, eds. 1996. "Rwanda: Killing the Evidence." London: African Rights.

Ortner, Sherry. 1995. "Resistance and the Problem of Ethnographic Refusal." *Comparative Studies in Society and History* 37(1):173–93.

Pages, Rene. 1933. *Un royaume Hamite au centre de l'Afrique.* Brussels: Institut Royal du Congo Belge.

Peters, Edward. 1996. *Torture.* Philadelphia: University of Pennsylvania Press.

Pitt-Rivers, Julien. 1977. *The Fate of Schechem: Or, the Politics of Sex: Essays in the Anthropology of the Mediterranean,* Cambridge: Cambridge University Press.

Prunier, Gerard. 1995. *The Rwanda Crisis.* New York: Columbia University Press.

Sahlins, Marshall. 1999. "Two or Three Things That I Know about Culture." *Journal of the Royal Anthropological Institute* 5(3):399–421.

Smith, Pierre. 1975. *Le recit populaire au Rwanda.* Paris: Armand Colin.

Sperber, Dan. 1975. *Le symbolisme en general.* Paris: Hermann.

Taussig, Michael. 1984. "Culture of Terror, Space of Death." *Comparative Studies in Society and History* 26(3):467–97.

————. 1987. *Shamanism, Colonialism and the Wild Man.* Chicago: University of Chicago Press.

Taylor, Christopher. 1988. "Milk, Honey and Money: Changing Concepts of Pathology in Rwandan Popular Medicine." Ph.D. dissertation, University of Virginia.

————. 1990. "Condoms and Cosmology: The Fractal Person and Sexual Risk in Rwanda." *Social Science and Medicine* 31(9):1023–28.

————. 1992. *Milk, Honey and Money.* Washington, D.C.: Smithsonian Institution Press.

————. 1999a. "A Gendered Genocide: Tutsi Women and Hutu Extremists in the 1994 Rwanda Genocide." *Political and Legal Anthropology Review* 22(1):42–54.

————. 1999b. *Sacrifice as Terror: The Rwandan Genocide of 1994.* Oxford: Berg Press.

Turner, Victor. 1977. *The Ritual Process.* Ithaca: Cornell University Press.

7

Dance, Music, and the Nature of Terror in Democratic Kampuchea

Toni Shapiro-Phim

INTRODUCTION

On a wooden platform in front of hundreds of weak, emaciated people, dancers dressed in loose tops and trousers, checkered scarves around their necks or waists, dark caps on their heads, and rubber tire sandals on their feet, stand in formation. Armed Khmer Rouge soldiers patrol around the silent audience. The dancers then proceed to march—walking in unison, arms swinging in rhythm with their legs— in choreographed linear and circular patterns. Wooden guns in hand, the performers dance to a song that makes explicit reference to *Angkar*, the Khmer Rouge revolutionary organization:

> We are young men and women
> protecting the coast.
> Children of the people of Kampuchea
> receiving new tasks of great importance
> to protect the integrity of our great country...
> However much the rain falls, the waves roll, the wind blows,
> Together we follow Angkar's tasks forever.
> We love our Angkar, homeland and people,
> along with the cooperative that makes our produce plentiful.[1]

Such would have constituted part of a typical performance of revolutionary song and dance in Democratic Kampuchea, the official name of the Khmer Rouge revolutionary regime (1975–79)[2] headed by Pol Pot.

In what follows I will discuss the conjunction of aesthetic practice with terror under the Khmer Rouge, viewing terror as both strategy and effect. Looking at dance and music as they were incorporated into the Khmer Rouge's exercise of power, I hope to shed light on one aspect of the nature of their evil. I am referring to what Michael Taussig has called, regarding the situation in Colombia, the "sinister quality [that] depends on the strategic use of uncertainty and mystery" (1992:16), which, at the receiving end, resembles the terror experienced by many Cambodians under Khmer Rouge rule.

Khmer Rouge leaders recognized the signifying power of songs and dances.[3] They created and organized public displays of revolutionary songs and dances through which they attempted to define reality and indoctrinate accordingly. Meanwhile, they forbade the practice of dance as Cambodians had known it (in all its variety) and allowed no performance of prerevolutionary popular, folk, or ritual songs.[4] Following a brief overview of Pol Pot's regime, I will talk about the new songs and dances, and then move on to stories that turn our understanding of officially sanctioned art during those years on its head. Viewing both corporeal and musical expression as loci of meaning-making, I aim to show how an examination of them as aesthetic practices may becloud the picture of state terror. Dance and music contributed to the fear-inspiring effects of Khmer Rouge rule, not only through the literal messages of hatred and violence in some revolutionary pieces but also through the inconsistency of responses to nonrevolutionary arts, evidence of a capriciousness that many informants reveal was unbearable.

THE REGIME

Scholars and survivors have documented the horrors experienced by the country and people of Cambodia in the 1970s.[5] As the decade dawned, civil war along with spillover from the conflict in neighboring Vietnam resulted in the deaths of hundreds of thousands of people, the uprooting of millions, and the destruction of vast amounts of arable land. When the war ended in 1975 with the Khmer Rouge defeat of the Khmer Republic headed by Lon Nol, many welcomed what they thought would be an era of peace and rebuilding. Instead, Democratic Kampuchea unleashed unfathomable suffering upon the populace as the upheaval and destruction continued, but on an unprecedented scale.

The revolution's leadership, known by the appellation of Angkar, or "organization," strove to be the sole focus of people's loyalties. Policies of mass relocation and family separation tore people from their communities. Religious worship, markets, and free association were banned. Constant surveillance was the norm for the masses in this "great leap"[6] toward a self-reliant, agrarian, socialist state. The populace was divided into two main categories: the "old" or "base" peasantry, which had been under Khmer Rouge rule in its liberated zones prior to 1975; and the "new" or "April 17th" people, who had lived in towns or villages under the control of the Khmer Republic.[7] Some "base" people held positions of local authority, while the "new" people were often subject to much more deprivation and harassment than the others. Forced hard labor, lack of access to modern medicine and adequate food, and brutal punishment led to the death of close to two million people (almost a quarter of the population).[8] The victims died from overwork, starvation, disease, torture, and execution, in just under four years of Angkar rule.[9]

THE REVOLUTIONARY IDIOM

Possessing the power to capture imaginations and emotions, and thus to "transport" people to other times and places, dance and music are sensually and socially impassioned. Dance and music are integral components of spiritual life and rites of passage, and popular forms of entertainment for people the world over. In Cambodia, that is true as well.[10] As symbols of identity, they are particularly compelling; social boundaries are often manipulated in the practice of performance.

In Democratic Kampuchea, dances and songs became instruments of battle, used to implicate enemies in the context of an ongoing struggle. A Khmer Rouge notebook from the 1970s, containing what appear to be notes from political education sessions, lists "Contemporary Principles of Cultural Politics." These include the notion that "every kind of art production among the masses is intended to wipe out the enemy's art(s) and to build new art(s) [and to] serve the people's war (*sangkriem praciecon*) to the extent possible."[11] Excerpts from an example of this new art, "The Red Flag" song, follow:

> Glittering red blood blankets the earth—blood given up to liberate the people...
> The blood swirls away, and flows upward, gently into the sky,
> turning into a red revolutionary flag.
> Red flag! red flag! flying now! flying now!
> O beloved friends, pursue, strike and hit the enemy.
> Red flag! red flag! flying now! flying now!
> Don't spare a single reactionary imperialist: drive them from Kampuchea.
> Strive and strike, strive and strike, and win the victory, win the victory.
> (CHANDLER, KIERNAN, AND LIM 1982:326)

An examination of songs must take into account limits placed on style and content (and transgressions of such), along with response by listeners. Understandings of ethnic, social, and political identities are enacted through music and song, and their reception (Radano and Bohlman 2000).

One person recalls that "[singing and listening to their songs] was the most effective tool of indoctrination. You started to believe in it" (interview cited in Um 1998:148). At the worksite, in the communal eating hall, even while packed in trucks during a relocation, people were force-fed songs extolling the virtues of Angkar and the new Cambodia. Played on transistor radios, blared over loudspeakers, and even sung by the workers, as expressed in a novel: "This was one of the Angkar's ways of killing us since it made our imaginations die by causing them to shrivel and run dry" (Oum 1997:28).

It was particularly important to Angkar that children started to believe what the faceless yet omnipresent Angkar was telling them. Ben Kiernan has noted that

"[Democratic Kampuchea] could not trust those outside of its creation or control" (1996:4). Children—"pure," clean slates in the eyes of the Khmer Rouge leadership—were perceived to be pivotal in building, enforcing, and continuing the revolution, as they could (potentially) be molded to fit the vision of a new society. There was an entire repertoire of songs composed for and taught specifically to children, songs that revealed not only the Khmer Rouge conceptions of their revolution but also the place of children in it.

During the Khmer Rouge regime, both attitudes toward and expectations of young people were upturned, factors that contributed greatly to the destabilizing of the general population. Whereas Cambodian children had always been trusted to be deferential to their elders, under the Khmer Rouge it was often they who gave orders and meted out punishment to people two and three times their age. And whereas (biological) family had been so key in people's lives in terms of identity and loyalty, Angkar strove to take the place of parents and siblings. What del Pino H. has said about Peruvian communities under Shining Path control holds true for Democratic Kampuchea: "[R]evolutionary values were to rule over affective ties, traditional family relations, and daily life" (1998:159).[12] Songs were instrumental in the process of creating and raising Angkar's (young) revolutionaries.

Lyrics from the song "Children of the New Kampuchea," found in a Democratic Kampuchea songbook, proclaim the battle-readiness of the boys and girls and their gratitude to be guided by the revolution. Here are excerpts:

> We the children have the good fortune
> to live the rest of our time in precious harmony
> under the affectionate care
> of the Kampuchean revolution, immense, most clear and shining.
> We the children of the revolution
> make the supreme resolution to strive
> to increase our ability to battle,
> and to make the stand of the revolution perfect.
> (MARSTON 1994:110–11)

Workers, young and old, often formed the audience for performances of revolutionary art troupes, as part of a celebration of the anniversary of the Khmer Rouge victory or in connection with other large meetings. There were, as well, separate performances explicitly for Khmer Rouge cadres, foreign visitors, or residents of Phnom Penh. Someth May (1986:177) recalls that after completion of a dam, a performing group entertained the workers. Of the performers, he writes:

> They sang of our love for the Angkar—it was as wide as the sea, it had no boundary. We were masters of our work. There was no more exploitation. We could do whatever we wanted. The canals were the veins of the Angkar.[13] We were no longer reliant upon rain. We could produce as much rice as we wanted.

They sang to the workers who had survived. Hundreds had died while laboring on the project. This is one example of how "the official voice can so strikingly contradict reality and by means of such contradiction create fear" (Taussig 1992:30).

After a twelve-hour day at a labor site, a work brigade might be marched, sometimes several kilometers, to a political gathering and required to listen to speeches and songs, and to watch the dances. Many were too exhausted—and too uninterested—to watch. But, said a woman who was a little girl at the time, "We would be punished if we didn't pay attention. Many of us learned to sleep with our eyes open" (personal interview, 1992).

In addition to being instruments of battle, dances, in their enactment, also modeled ideal revolutionary behavior and attitudes. The efficacy of their kinesthetic statements stemmed in part from the formulaic pattern harnessed as a means of educating and militarizing the populace in body and social space, thereby attempting to discipline both.

In dance, the cultural significance of "the training and deployment of bodies" is far reaching and includes "what it can tell us about the range of allowable representations of the body in motion and the policing of bodily form in a specific time and place" (Koritz 1996:91). The body, as the "tangible frame of selfhood in individual and collective experience" (Comaroff 1985:6), possesses both "materiality and . . . forces" (Foucault 1979:26), which can be manipulated by power relations that "invest [the body], mark it, train it, torture it, force it to carry out tasks, to perform ceremonies, to emit signs" (ibid.:25). But that very materiality and those very forces, through the bodily discourse of dance, can also actuate a creation of meanings independent of the intentions of the powers that be, as we shall see.

When the lyrics in dance songs referred to the glories of agricultural work, the dancers carried, for example, hoes and shovels; when the words praised industrial development, they wielded wrenches or other appropriate instruments. Lyrics aside, performers modeled ideal revolutionaries through their militaristic demeanor with backs held straight and faces devoid of emotion and, as was often the case, by carrying a real gun slung over one shoulder. They also modeled this through a lack of pronounced gender differentiation in gesture, although there were exceptions, and in dress, though women sometimes performed in a *sampot* (a long, straight skirt).

Staged "folk dances" meant to represent peasant lives and activities had been created by professional artists in Phnom Penh in the 1960s and 1970s, and they became very popular across Cambodia. Opposition of the sexes, including flirtation, is a central motif of many of these, a theme rarely invoked in the Democratic Kampuchea-era creations. The comic elements of some of these theatrical folk dances are also absent in revolutionary pieces.[14]

Yet there was some variation in the revolutionary formula. A woman tells of being brought to a field nightly for almost a week in 1976, along with all the other teenagers in her area of Battambang province (personal interview, 2000). There she and the other "new" youth stood and watched as the "base" children performed a song about the work of a blacksmith. The boys who were performing remained in place, moving their arms and hands in imitation of the pumping of a bellows and the hammering on an anvil. The girls, in a separate corner, enacted the fluid, circular motion of reaching for and cutting rice stalks with the scythes just fashioned by the blacksmiths. The girls and boys displayed distinct, yet complementary, spheres of work (and movement). All present, including those gathered to watch, were instructed to sing the lyrics that reproduced the swoosh of the bellows and the clanging of the anvil.

Many performers of revolutionary dances were of the "base" or "old" peasantry, those the Khmer Rouge most trusted. But some "new" youth were recruited as well. Recalls one, "I took the job because they didn't cut rations for dancers if we were sick. Regular workers starved if they couldn't complete their tasks" (personal interview, 1993). Many were also soldiers who spent their time, when not performing, transporting supplies and attending educational or political indoctrination sessions. They heard repeatedly that anyone who expressed distrust in or disloyalty to Angkar, even a member of one's own family, was a traitor, an enemy in need of elimination. Embodying the understanding of such teachings, the performers were being educated to hate, and, in that aim, to dance.

Official speeches, as well as performances of the songs and dances, inculcated the notion that the entire population was an army engaged in combat with the elements—rain, the earth—and with human foes. Indeed, much of the way the leadership administered the country "appeared [to be] a direct continuation of... methods... employed in war" (Um 1998:142; see also Marston 1994). Haing Ngor wrote in his autobiography that at the conclusion of one performance, dancers pounded their chests with clenched fists and repeatedly shouted at the top of their lungs: "Blood Avenges Blood." On the word *avenges* they

> stuck their arms out straight like a Nazi salute, except with a closed fist instead of an open hand.... They shouted other revolutionary slogans and gave the salutes and finally ended with "Long live the Cambodian revolution!" It was a dramatic performance, and it left us scared.... Blood avenges blood. You kill us, we kill you. We... had been on the other side of the Khmer Rouge in the civil war... they were going to take revenge. (1987:140–41)

The enmity toward perceived/accused traitors worked through the body by means of redundant brusque gestural and verbal pronouncements evocative of battle, and even of killing, reinforcing divisions between people and instilling fear. Such staging of Angkar's vision of the body politic at once separated "base" from "new," while creating an illusion of unity, just as Manning (1993:195) notes about some Nazi spectacles involving dance, by "seemingly includ[ing] all, performers and spectators alike," in the event.[15]

TRANSGRESSIVE ACTS

While state-sanctioned practices, examined above, offer one view of the Khmer Rouge relationship to dance and music, those re-created or enacted from "below" present a notably different dimension of that connection. The stories that follow bring to the forefront the effect of that relationship on the overall sense of terror engendered in Democratic Kampuchea. I will begin with the story of a young man named Dara.[16]

As part of a mobile youth work brigade in Battambang province in northwestern Cambodia in 1977, Dara lived in a hut in the middle of the forest. Nights were engulfed in silence, and in fear. Because at night people were taken away and never seen again, "I prayed," said Dara, "that nights would never come":

> At four A.M. they would wake us. The rice fields were a one and a half hour walk from our base. People were so hungry and weak when they were harvesting or building irrigation paths that they would collapse. If they didn't work, they received no food, or worse, they were killed. So many of us became sick, especially with night blindness. Mine lasted three months. We needed to be led out into the forest from our huts to find a place to go to the bathroom. But because everyone was exhausted and sick, nobody had the strength to help anyone else. We had to crawl through excrement and garbage to find a place to relieve ourselves. I had given up hopes of surviving and decided I needed to do something to soothe my soul until my time came. I found some bamboo and, using a small knife I had carried with me since I had been evacuated from Phnom Penh, I carved a *khloy* [bamboo flute]. When I had first left the city, I carried several flutes with me, of plastic, of metal, of bamboo, my favorite possessions. But I left them along the road as I became afraid they would mark me for punishment. Then, eventually, I felt the need to play once more. I had no instrument to measure the proportions, and the bamboo I used was the wrong kind, but I made a crude flute one night and sat down and played. The sound of the flute carried through the silence of the forest. The local *chlop* heard.[17] He came to find me and called me in for questioning.

Dara's dormitory mates and work partners had been disappearing nightly. Each evening he changed the position and place in which he would sleep so as to elude those who might come for him as they had come for the others. But once called in for questioning, he felt his time was up, and, even though he had heard that "they were killing artists in another area just because they were artists," he decided to tell the truth. He had been a student of the arts. Yet, counter to what Dara expected, after admonishing him for making and playing the flute, the chlop told him that if he agreed to serenade him with the khloy every night, his life would be spared. So he did.

> One night, months later, they held a big meeting at about 8:30. There must have been thousands of people there, from many villages. They talked to us about socialism and how we should give up all our possessions so as to benefit the whole society. After the meeting they asked me to play [my flute] for everyone. I played [an improvised medley of] lullabies. Everyone started to cry. The leaders were furious. "How dare you sabotage our meeting?!" they shouted. They had wanted to create an atmosphere of trust in the revolution, and I had made the people cry. But I hadn't really done anything. It's the power of the music and people's memories.

Indeed, these were the very memories that revolutionary music aimed to destroy. The man who had originally sanctioned Dara's performances rescued him from the grip of the enraged officials present. His fate is unknown.

Also in Battambang province, a young woman named Dani was likewise living in fear of the night, just as Dara was, and struggling to keep up with her workload during the day. She had been a member of the court (or classical) dance troupe of Cambodia in Phnom Penh.

The official history of Cambodian classical dance is linked with that of temples and monarchs. Inscriptions from as early as the seventh century tell us that dancers were important in temple life (Groslier 1965:283). And for centuries it was through the medium of the dancers that royal communication with the divinities was effected to guarantee the fertility of the land and the well-being of the people in the king's domain. In Cambodia today, such a ceremony involving sacred dance and music is still held under royal auspices at least once a year.

Girls and boys start training at a very young age, when they are supple enough to be molded into the seemingly unnatural poses (hyperextended elbows, flexed toes, arched backs, and so on), which require tireless discipline to master. When a certain virtuosity is attained, a classical dancer in the capital city becomes integral to particular royal rituals and national celebrations, as well as stage performances for dignitaries, tourists, and the local population.

It has been assumed that because of their intimate association with the state, and therefore, with previous regimes, classical dancers were a particular target of the Khmer Rouge. Indeed, the post–Democratic Kampuchea Cambodian government estimated that 80 to 90 percent of the country's professional artists perished. The high death toll resulted, perhaps, from a number of factors in addition to the artists' high-profile relationship with the state.[18] What we know more concretely is that this kind of dance *itself* was a target.

In Battambang in 1977, Dani would awaken daily at 4:00 A.M., missing her parents and feeling that it "would have been easier to be dead. We worked hard all day, then lived in fear all night." Indeed, the darkness and silence that might have provided shelter from the "panopticon" that ruled the days instead brought increased terror, as it did for Dara.

At one point Dani became seriously ill and couldn't work for several months. She was feverish and would shake uncontrollably every evening, then start singing and dancing. "It was as if I had gone crazy," she said.

Dani and her cousin, both from Phnom Penh, had been relocated to a village populated mainly by peasantry most trusted by the Khmer Rouge—as opposed to people from the cities or unliberated parts of the countryside before their national victory in 1975. Some local inhabitants took pity on her, leading a series of traditional healers to her one after the other.[19] "I don't know why they didn't just kill me or let me die, as, in my condition, I was worthless to them." Eight healers had not been able to cure her. The ninth, for reasons unknown, suspected that Dani might be in offense of the spirits of the dance. Those present asked her cousin whether Dani had been a dancer before. When her cousin answered that Dani had danced with the royal troupe, there was an audible sigh.

The residents of that region were familiar with court dance from the trips that then-Prince Sihanouk had made a decade earlier to a local temple to ask for blessings from the deities, during which dancers would perform as a means of communication with the heavens. Sacred dances connected heaven with earth, bringing, it was hoped, rain, prosperity, and well-being. Villagers had been involved in the preparation of offerings for those rites, and for Dani, they started the same sorts of preparations for a ceremony to appease the spirits that had been offended.

> After they had made the offerings they brought in an exorcism orchestra. The musicians played half the night, but their music didn't seem to help. Someone then said, "This woman needs a *pin peat* orchestra."[20] I don't know where they found the instruments and the people, but soon there was a full orchestra, just like we use today. And they started playing ... and even though I didn't "know" myself, I sat up and demanded a certain kind of dance shirt and pantaloons and a silver belt. When I was properly attired, the music started again, and I danced.

Dani danced and danced, her energy reaching to her extremities (fingers curved back and toes almost constantly flexed upward), in measured, controlled, yet lyrical movements devoid of hard edges and sharp displacements of weight. The music continued until dawn, with incense and candles continually lit. "In the morning I was able to go to work again" for the first time in months.

Before getting sick, Dani had entertained her cousin at night by dancing. One time she danced the role of the powerful and sacred character Moni Mekhala, a role passed down from teacher to pupil in a special ceremony (see Shapiro 1994). Dani had never received permission through the sacred ritual to practice or perform this role; she had only watched others in the palace from afar. But here in Battambang she had dared to perform. Traveling corporeally to a familiar and beloved locale from the new and torturous life she found herself leading, she believes the spirits of the dance had seen her and had registered their displeasure at her audacity to assume the role of Moni Mekhala by inflicting illness upon her.

The fact that any of this took place—the burning of incense and candles, a pin peat orchestra performance, a calling to the spirits, the execution of classical dance—might seem remarkable in itself, as each of these practices was forbidden. And in combination, with the participation of many, including the tacit consent of the local Khmer Rouge authorities (who neither protested nor stopped the proceedings), it might appear truly extraordinary. However, I contend that it is rather more prosaic than it seems. It is exactly the unexpected that kept everyone in suspense and maintained the ever-present possibility of arbitrary violence (and arbitrary benevolence). Even the positive surprises strengthened the overall sense of terror.

Across the country in Kompong Thom province, a man named Bun had also been sick for months. He was so weakened by malaria that he had to crawl to get water. "I could hardly even stand up." Then, one day, seemingly from out of nowhere, Khmer Rouge soldiers "captured me at gunpoint, and forced me into a boat.... I was crying." He was taken to a prison; he had no idea why. About sixty men were being held captive, chained and locked in by their feet. The first thing Bun noticed was the stench. Under each plank (used as a bed) was a box for excrement and urine.

At night, prisoners were taken for questioning. Some returned from the ordeal and fainted. Others were tortured (he heard their cries) and never came back. When Bun was interrogated, he told the truth, that he had been a classical dancer and dance teacher at the University of Fine Arts, and that he had traveled abroad to perform in Indonesia, Thailand, and the United States. "I told him that I did everything following the authorities at the university. Then he asked me what my specialty was. 'Hanuman,' I replied." (Hanuman is the monkey general in the *Reamker*, the Cambodian version of the Ramayana epic of Indian origin.)[21]

The interrogator grew silent. He eventually asked Bun to demonstrate a few dance moves. Skinny and bald (he had shaved his head when he was so sick, a customary form of prayer for the seriously ill), Bun struggled to lift his arms, to position his legs. The cadre was impressed with this wretched "monkey." He told Bun to perform that evening for all the guards and prisoners. So weak he could barely lift a foot to step over the sharp weeds on the ground, he danced in the prison courtyard. On his knees, he managed to push one leg back and turn the sole of that foot skyward, taking the position that represents flight in the classical dance.

From that day on, Bun was secretly supplied with food and called "*Ta* [Elder] Hanuman" by the Khmer Rouge. About a month later, the twenty men who were still alive were released. Why these particular prisoners had been taken, and why those surviving were set free remained destabilizing mysteries.

Given the Khmer Rouge's claim to have erased thousands of years of history and their excoriation of perceived feudal (including royalist) thought and action, as well as their need to orchestrate people's every move, one may wonder how it is that in the above examples the peasantry and the local cadres helped a sick or imprisoned person who would have been expected to be expendable simply because he or she danced—and in the royal tradition, no less. And one may wonder why someone who made and played a flute without permission wasn't punished. (It was quite often such seemingly small, individual actions that got people killed in Democratic Kampuchea.) Only 10 to 20 percent of the country's professional artists survived the regime. Yet here are some who are alive *because* of their art.

These stories, which muddle the public picture usually presented by and of the Khmer Rouge, in no way minimize the horrors and crimes they committed. The evil becomes even more inexplicable if they could save Hanuman and continue to kill those on either side of him in the prison. Such inhumane and disorienting capriciousness forms part of the very complicated canvas under study. It was the very nature of some Khmer Rouge violence to be completely arbitrary.

Being confronted with things that we now recognize to be symbols of prerevolutionary "Khmerness"—Hanuman, classical dance, a series of lullabies played on a khloy, and so on—peasants in the good stead of the Khmer Rouge or cadres themselves made choices about how to react. The choices they made in these cases were politically and "aesthetically oriented commentar[ies]" (Bull 1997:270) that contradicted expectations and that illustrate a key feature of Pol Pot's totalitarianism. Certain tales or characters, such as Hanuman, as well as physicality, spirituality, or music of a specific sort resonated with some members of the Khmer Rouge.

Lafreniere (2000:134) relates the experience of Daran Kravanh, a musician who, in Democratic Kampuchea, happened upon an accordion, the instrument of his expertise. The Khmer Rouge soldiers came to know him as the accordion player:

> A soldier came to me one day and said, "There is a girl I love and I want to find out if she loves me. I order you to play your accordion for us." This was an unusual request from a soldier, but of course I agreed. . . . I played my accordion while sitting on the floor between them. As I played, they looked at each other. After a time I suggested they dance and they did. . . . Then they began to sing a question and answer song back and forth.[22]

The accordion is not a particularly common instrument in Cambodia. Indeed, it is known to be a foreign import, something Khmer Rouge ideology might paint as anathema to the purity of the new society. But the music it held the possibility of creating kept it and Daran in demand, and gave Daran access to the personal, emotional world of his oppressors, a world, at least as far as romance was concerned, denounced by official rhetoric.

Prerevolutionary resonances coexisted with the Khmer Rouge contention that history had started anew with their rule. It is here that we can locate the production of the contradictions so essential for the maintenance of a state of terror.[23] Were we to try for an ethnography that brings to light more such contradictions, our understanding of the Khmer Rouge regime would be all the richer.

Terror haunts the constantly shifting ground upon which the inexplicable and the unspeakable dwell side by side.[24] The extreme confusion and intimidation experienced under the Khmer Rouge helped lay the groundwork for the emotional, physical, social, and spiritual scars lodged in Cambodia and her people.

NOTES

An earlier version of this essay appeared as *Anthropologies of the Khmer Rouge Part 1: Terror and Aesthetics,* Genocide Studies Program Working Paper GS 06 (New Haven: Yale Center for International and Area Studies, 1998). I would like to thank David Chandler, George Chigas, Alexander Hinton, Ben Kiernan, Edward Kissi, Sally Ness, Sally Nhomi, Niti Pawakapan, Thavro Phim, Puangthong Rungswadisab, Sek Sophea, Anne Sheeran, and Michael Vickery for their insightful comments and suggestions.

1. This dance was performed for me by a former Khmer Rouge dancer who also provided the lyrics.

2. Prince Norodom Sihanouk became king in 1941 and then, taking the title of prince, stepped down in the mid-1950s to become head of state until the 1970 coup d'état. He named

Cambodia's communist movement the "Khmer Rouge" in the 1960s. "Khmer Rouge" is commonly used both as a plural and a singular term.

3. Norodom Sihanouk had also recognized and manipulated the power of dance and music, as had Prime Minister Lon Nol in the early 1970s. See Shapiro 1994.

4. Some revolutionary songs retained traditional melodies while discarding old lyrics. See David Chandler's note in Chandler, Kiernan, and Lim (1982:326). Ry Kea (personal interview, 2000) has identified some songs she heard in Democratic Kampuchea as being of Chinese origin. In a private Chinese school in Phnom Penh a decade earlier, she had learned songs celebrating Mao Tse Tung's greatness. In revolutionary Cambodia, she heard the same songs—identical melodies with lyrics that were, according to her, direct translations from the Chinese—with one difference. Instead of honoring Mao—"When the sun rises a lotus appears with the face of Mao Tse Tung upon it, shining over the people. . . . Wherever there is Mao, there is freedom"—the songs revered Angkar. Henri Locard (1998) estimates that 10 percent of the Khmer Rouge revolutionary songs he has studied over the years employ melodies originating in the People's Republic of China.

5. Examples include Chandler 1991, 1999; Dith 1997; Him 2000; Hinton 1997; Kiernan 1993, 1996; Lafreniere 2000; May 1986; Ngor 1987; Oum 1997; Um 1998; Vann 1998.

6. See references to a "great leap" in the journal of the Ministry of Foreign Affairs 1997–98; and in Chandler, Kiernan, and Boua 1988.

7. The Khmer Rouge took control of the capital, Phnom Penh, on April 17, 1975.

8. Scholars' estimates range from 750,000 (Vickery 1984), to 1.7 million (Kiernan 1996), to 2 million (Heuveline 1998), out of a pre-1975 population of between 7 and 8 million.

9. For a cultural analysis of what he terms "genocidal practices," see Hinton 1997.

10. Along with Sally Ann Ness, who studies dance of the Philippines and Indonesia, I would like to "attempt to return bodily experience *as a form of consciousness and understanding* to a central place within the discipline of ethnographic inquiry, recognizing that to deny the interpretive potential of bodily/choreographic phenomena is to deprive ethnography of understanding an activity that may be as central to the human experience of another culture as it is marginal to that of mainstream U.S. society" (1992:239) [emphasis in original].

11. This is one of several hundred such handwritten notebooks in the collection of the Documentation Center of Cambodia, in Phnom Penh.

12. The same article presents a chilling account of Shining Path's attempt to incorporate children into its "war machine" (del Pino H. 1998:174), an attempt in many ways reminiscent of Khmer Rouge practice.

13. Ben Kiernan (personal communication 1998) has suggested that the concept of the embodiment of the country in Angkar could be extended to encompass the embodiment of Cambodia in the leader, Pol Pot, if we look at aspects of the use of the term *Angkar* by members of the Khmer Rouge. " '[T]he Organization' . . . has a home address, watches movies, is sometimes 'busy working,' but can be asked favors if one dares" (Chandler, Kiernan, and Boua 1988:232). See Shapiro 1994 for preliminary work on Khmer notions of carrying "Cambodia" within themselves.

14. For more on Cambodian folk dance, both ceremonial and theatrical, including the relationship of folk dance to Norodom Sihanouk's vision of modern nationhood, see Phim and Thompson 1999.

15. Such resonances with the role of spectacle in the Nazi propaganda machine are evident, but the analogy can be taken only so far. See Manning's examination of Nazi spec-

tacle in her study of dancer/choreographer Mary Wigman's life and work in Germany (1993).

16. The following narratives employ pseudonyms and are from personal interviews conducted by the author in Cambodia between 1990 and 1993, and in 1999.

17. A chlop had the power to arrest suspected transgressors on behalf of higher authorities.

18. A report from the People's Revolutionary Tribunal (convened in 1979 to try Khmer Rouge leaders in absentia for genocide) includes testimonies from survivors about the brutal killings of some individual performing artists. The report claims that it was Khmer Rouge policy "to massacre or at least to mistreat the artists" (Tribunal Populaire Revolutionnaire 1979:2). My own interviews suggest that status as a "new" person (from the city) or being a spouse or sibling of an official of the Lon Nol regime were among the various other reasons that people who happened to be dancers or musicians or actors were executed.

19. As with so many aspects of the regime, medical care varied by time (early or late in the regime) and by location. Most practitioners of modern (nontraditional) medicine were not allowed to administer to the sick. Some experienced traditional healers and midwives were able to continue practicing under the direction of the local Khmer Rouge. Teenage medics, newly trained as part of the revolution, were the norm.

20. The pin peat orchestra accompanies, among other things, classical dances, Buddhist temple ceremonies, and shadow puppet plays.

21. The interrogator knew that Cambodian dancers have "specialties." Perhaps he did not need an explanation of who Hanuman is, as he did not ask for one. There are some cultural cues that Khmer Rouge ideology did not override.

22. This is most likely a reference to repartee singing (ayai), in which a man and a woman improvise an often flirtatious, comic, and suggestive dialogue.

23. Similar contradictions in Nazi rule are described by Laks: "When an esman [SS man] listened to music ... he somehow became strangely similar to a human being. ... Could people who love music to this extent ... be at the same time capable of committing so many atrocities on the rest of humanity?" (1989:70). See also "The Rosner Family" chapter in Brecher (1994) on music, the Nazis, and concentration camp inmates.

24. Terror manages to take hold of those in power as well as the oppressed. Hanna Arendt points out that "the ultimate consequence of rule by terror [is] ... that nobody, not even the executioners, can ever be free of fear" (1979:6), which certainly held true in this case, as many members of the Khmer Rouge were eventually purged.

REFERENCES CITED

Arendt, Hanna. 1979[1951]. *The Origins of Totalitarianism.* New York: Harcourt Brace Jovanovich.

Brecher, Elinor J. 1994. *Schindler's Legacy.* New York: Plume/Penguin Books.

Bull, Cynthia Jean Cohen. 1997. "Sense, Meaning, and Perception in Three Dance Cultures." In *Meaning in Motion, New Cultural Studies of Dance.* Jane C. Desmond, ed. Pp. 269–87. Durham, N.C.: Duke University Press.

Chandler, David P. 1991. *The Tragedy of Cambodian History.* New Haven: Yale University Press.

———. 1999. *Voices from S-21: Terror and History in Pol Pot's Secret Prison.* Berkeley: University of California Press.

Chandler, David P., Ben Kiernan, and Chanthou Boua. 1988. *Pol Pot Plans the Future: Confidential Leadership Documents from Democratic Kampuchea 1976–1977.* Monograph Series 33. New Haven: Yale University Southeast Asia Studies.

Chandler, David P., Ben Kiernan, and Muy Hong Lim. 1982. "The Early Phases of Liberation: Conversations with Peang Sophi." In *Peasants and Politics in Kampuchea 1942–1981.* Ben Kiernan and Chanthou Boua, eds. Pp. 318–29. London: Zed Press.

Comaroff, Jean. 1985. *Body of Power, Spirit of Resistance.* Chicago: University of Chicago Press.

del Pino H., Ponciano. 1998. "Family, Culture, and 'Revolution': Everyday Life with Sendero Luminoso." In *Shining and Other Paths.* Steve J. Stern, ed. Pp. 158–92. Durham, N.C.: Duke University Press, 1998.

Dith Pran. 1997. *Children of Cambodia's Killing Fields.* New Haven: Yale University Press.

Foucault, Michel. 1979. *Discipline and Punish.* New York: Vintage Books.

Groslier, Bernard Philippe. 1965. "Danse et musique sous les rois d'Angkor." In *Felicitation Volumes of Southeast Asian Studies.* Pp. 283–92. Bangkok: Siam Society.

Heuveline, Patrick. 1998. "Between One and Three Million: Towards the Demographic Reconstruction of a Decade of Cambodian History (1970–79)." *Population Studies* 52:49–65.

Him, Chanrithy. 2000. *When Broken Glass Floats.* New York: W. W. Norton and Company.

Hinton, Alexander Laban. 1997. "Cambodian Shadow: An Examination of the Cultural Origins of Genocide." Ph.D. dissertation, Emory University.

Kiernan, Ben, ed. 1993. *Genocide and Democracy in Cambodia.* Monograph Series 41. New Haven: Yale University Southeast Asia Studies.

———. 1996. *The Pol Pot Regime: Race, Power and Genocide in Cambodia under the Khmer Rouge, 1975–1979.* New Haven: Yale University Press.

Koritz, Amy. 1996. "Re/Moving Boundaries: From Dance History to Cultural Studies." In *Moving Words, Re-writing Dance.* Gay Morris, ed. Pp. 88–103. New York: Routledge.

Lafreniere, Bree. 2000. *Music through the Dark.* Honolulu: University of Hawaii Press.

Laks, Szymon. 1989. *Music of Another World.* Evanston, Ill.: Northwestern University Press.

Locard, Henri. 1998. "Les chants revolutionnaires khmers et la tradition musicale cambodgienne ou La Revolution triomphante." In *Khmer Studies: Knowledge of the Past and Its Contributions to the Rehabilitation and Reconstruction of Cambodia.* Sorn Samnang, ed. Pp. 309–348. Proceedings of the August 1996 International Conference on Khmer Studies. Phnom Penh.

Manning, Susan A. 1993. *Ecstasy and the Demon: Feminism and Nationalism in the Dances of Mary Wigman.* Berkeley: University of California Press.

Marston, John. 1994. "Metaphors of the Khmer Rouge." In *Cambodian Culture since 1975.* May Ebihara et al., ed. Pp. 105–18. Ithaca, N.Y.: Cornell University Press.

May, Someth. 1986. *Cambodian Witness.* London: Faber and Faber.

Ministry of Foreign Affairs. 1997–98. "Ieng Sary's Regime: A Diary of the Khmer Rouge Foreign Ministry." Phat Kosal and Ben Kiernan, trans. Yale University Cambodian Genocide Program website (www.yale.edu/cgp).

Ness, Sally Ann. 1992. *Body, Movement, and Culture.* Philadelphia: University of Pennsylvania Press.

Ngor, Haing. 1987. *A Cambodian Odyssey.* New York: Macmillan.

Oum Suphany. 1997. *Under the Drops of Falling Rain.* Phnom Penh.

Phim, Toni Samantha [Shapiro], and Ashley Thompson. 1999. *Dance in Cambodia.* New York: Oxford University Press.

Radano, Ronald, and Philip Bohlman, eds. 2000. *Music and the Racial Imagination.* Chicago: University of Chicago Press.

Shapiro, Toni. 1994. "Dance and the Spirit of Cambodia." Ph.D. dissertation, Cornell University.

Taussig, Michael. 1992. *The Nervous System.* New York: Routledge.

Tribunal Populaire Revolutionnaire. 1979. "Rapport sur les crimes commis par la clique Pol Pot Ieng Sary a l'encontre de la culture, de l'information et de la presse au Kampuchea." Phnom Penh.

Um, Katharya. 1998. "The Broken Chain: Genocide in the Re-construction and Destruction of Cambodian Society." *Social Identities* 4(1):131–54.

Vann Nath. 1998. *A Cambodian Prison Portrait.* Bangkok: White Lotus Press.

Vickery, Michael. 1984. *Cambodia 1975–1982.* Boston: South End Press.

8

Averted Gaze

Genocide in Bosnia-Herzegovina, 1992–1995

Tone Bringa

This chapter examines some of the social and political structures that converged in the case of Bosnia-Herzegovina (B-H) and created a framework that enabled certain people to commit crimes against humanity at the end of the twentieth century in Europe. It argues that the particular kind of personalized violence directed toward individuals because they belonged to, or were identified with, a specific nationality or ethnic group was the expression of a politically organized attempt at radically redefining categories of belonging.[1] This implied the redrawing of boundaries of exclusion/inclusion (that is, excluding certain people with their knowledge and their skills from a certain territory having a certain history, resources, and social fabric, while including certain others). These were new boundaries both in a physical (political/territorial) and in a symbolic sense. The criteria for who was included and who was excluded were new, too. The violence was directed not only toward those who because of their nationality were redefined as "not belonging" but also toward anyone (irrespective of nationality) who resisted this redefinition.[2] I shall argue that this forced redrawing of boundaries of exclusion was the eventual resolution of authority—a delayed transition of authority—after modern Yugoslavia's founder and post–World War II leader, Tito, died in 1980. This delayed transition coincided with and was influenced by the end of communist regimes in Europe, while the criteria according to which the new boundaries were drawn were a legacy of the political and social structures of communist (Titoist) Yugoslavia.

Several strategies were used by the "new" power elites that came into power in Yugoslavia after the end of the Cold War in 1989/90 in order to redefine social categories of exclusion and inclusion (such as, for instance, "enemies" and "friends"). Some of these strategies were directed toward members of the group that the new boundaries were meant to include, in order to convince them of the need to redraw these boundaries. Measures included the use of a "rhetoric of exclusion" (such as the renaming of neighbors and compatriots as foreigners/intruders and enemies) and the manipulation of fear (on the "rhetorics of exclusion," see Stolcke 1995). Other strategies were directed toward those people who were to be excluded. Yet others were directed toward members of the included group who resisted the restructuring. (Measures were a combination of those applied to the first group—that is, "the included"—and the second group—that is, "the excluded.") The most ferocious and violent strategies were reserved for the second group. Measures included the rhetoric of exclusion and the actual exclusion from positions of power or influence; harassment, terror, and the redefinition of public space as the "private" ethnic space of the group in power; and, finally, the physical removal by violent means of most or all members of the "excluded" group from their homes in villages and towns. The violent removal or expulsion was done in such a way as to make it very difficult or even impossible for the expelled ever to return. This is the policy of "ethnic cleansing," and in some instances when it was pursued to its extreme logic—as in the case of Srebrenica—it turned into genocide.

THE MESSENGER OF GENOCIDE

On July 22, 1995, I sat on the grass next to the tarmac at Tuzla airbase in North Eastern Bosnia. I was listening to the story of a man from the Srebrenica region. I was there with an UNPROFOR human rights team.[3] About a week earlier thousands of women and children had started arriving in Tuzla from the Srebrenica region. These traumatized people had been accommodated in tents along the tarmac at the airbase where a Nordic U.N. battalion was stationed, and they were demanding to know where their men where.[4] Women were crying for their husbands, sons, brothers, and fathers, who had been forced to stay behind at the mercy of Serbian soldiers, while they themselves had walked to Tuzla and Bosnian government-controlled territory after the Bosnian Serb Army commander, Ratko Mladić, had organized for them to be bused to the front line. The camp was crowded and seething hot. This is where the U.N. human rights team turned up to take witness statements from refugees and survivors. (This was routinely done in the wake of any military offensive, or whenever there were reports or suspicion of human rights abuses in U.N.-controlled areas. However, access for the team was not always forthcoming. Thus there was no human rights team in Srebrenica itself.) An appeal was made over the loudspeakers for witnesses to come forward. Suddenly, I saw a man hurrying to the information desk by the tarmac. Both his body language and words expressed intense urgency: "I have to speak to them"; "I must tell them." He was agitated. He had come to look for his family but said he had to tell us his story first. While the human rights officer was asking, through an interpreter, the specific and detailed questions she is trained to ask, I was listening in to the man's account in Bosnian. For the officer, this was a routine statement; initially, perhaps, she thought she had listened to many similar stories during the wars in Bosnia-Herzegovina and Croatia—stories from people who were victims of what had become known as "ethnic cleansing." It was perhaps hard to see that this man's story was any different. And a human rights officer's concern is always with credibility. She had experienced people who made up stories about atrocities; perhaps this man's story was one of those? As the man's story unfolded, I had the terrible realization about the fate of the missing boys and men of Srebrenica. A mass killing of unimaginable proportions had taken place, and the man in front of me was one of only a few survivors. I was in no doubt whatsoever that his story was true, and that he was talking from personal experience. He was very concentrated as he spoke, and his language was factual and to the point. His descriptions were detailed and specific, citing place names, giving an exact chronology of events, and using personal pronouns.[5]

The Srebrenica survivor showed us the marks around his wrists left by the rope that had been used to tie his hands behind his back. He had been lined up with hundreds of other men, who all died of gunshot wounds to their head or other vital parts of their body. The bullet that was meant for him just missed and touched his chin. He survived because he was protected by the dead bodies on top of him. He escaped at night with one other survivor. More than seven thousand men of all ages where executed during a few hot July days in 1995 in the picturesque fields and forests around the town of Srebrenica, a town that had been designated a U.N. "safe area."[6]

The story of the massacres of Bosnian Muslim men and boys in the days following the Bosnian Serb Army takeover of the U.N. "safe area" of Srebrenica on July 11, 1995, is now accessible through some well-researched documentary books and films, as well as through the indictments for genocide and crimes against humanity issued by the International Criminal Tribunal for the former Yugoslavia in The Hague.[7] There are two main stories: on the one hand, what the Bosnian Serb Army planned and executed under the command of Ratko Mladić, and on the other the complacency, incompetence, and unwillingness to act to prevent genocide represented by the international community through its U.N. peacekeeping forces. The UNPROFOR human rights team filed a cautiously worded report which stated that grave human rights abuses had occurred in the aftermath of the Bosnian Serb takeover of Srebrenica. It cited testimonies from witnesses and suggested that assaults may have occurred that resulted in numerous deaths, but that those accounts were "as yet unconfirmed."[8] The report that failed to identify the enormity of the crimes that were taking place was transmitted to the United Nations Secretariat, but the head of UNPROFOR did not see any need to alert his superiors or an international public of the team's "unsubstantiated findings," and in the meantime the killings in the hills around Srebrenica continued.[9]

PRELUDES TO GENOCIDE

The organized massacre was the worst in Europe's history since World War II. But it was a crime that could have been prevented, inasmuch as it could have been predicted. For Srebrenica was the final push in a campaign of "ethnic cleansing" and genocide—an orgy in violence—that had started three years earlier in Northern and Eastern Bosnia in order to establish a Serbian state rid of all non-Serbs (that is, Bosnian Muslims and Croats). In its final report, the U.N. Commission of Experts for the International Criminal Tribunal researched the developments in the municipality (*Opština*) of Prijedor. Their findings formed the bases for the later indictments of individual Serbs for crimes against humanity and genocide. The report that was published on December 28, 1994, concludes: "It is unquestionable that the events in *Opština* Prijedor since 30 April 1992 qualify as crimes against humanity. Furthermore, it is likely to be confirmed in court under due process of law that these events constitute genocide."[10]

The campaign of "ethnic cleansing" had been preceded by a rhetorical campaign of exclusion (intolerance), fear, and hatred. For instance, in Sarajevo in 1992, on the eve of the war, the Bosnian Serb nationalist leader Radovan Karadžić uttered what was to become his personal mantra throughout the war waged to carve out an ethnically homogeneous Serbian state in ethnically diverse and complex Bosnia-Herzegovina: "We cannot live with the Muslims and the Croats, for there is too much hatred, centuries old hatred. Serbs fear the Muslims. They cannot live together. Because of genocide committed against them (the Serbs), they have to defend themselves." In a speech to the Bosnian parliament, he also threatened people with a war that might result in the disappearance of the "Muslim people" (*Muslimanski narod*) should they go ahead and vote for independence.[11] His words were echoed by General Ratko Mladić when he gave a casually chosen Muslim schoolteacher the responsibility for disarming Muslim men in Srebrenica in the wake of the Serbian takeover: "The Muslim people can disappear (*nestati*) or survive (*opstati*): it's up to you."[12]

The former Yugoslav republics of Slovenia and Croatia had declared their independence in June 1991. Within five months of Croatia's declaring its independence from Yugoslavia, the JNA (Yugoslav People's Army) and local Serb paramilitaries occupied more than one-third of Croatia. (These were areas with a Serbian and a Croatian population.) Fifteen thousand people were killed, and more than 250,000 were driven from their homes. While war raged in Croatia, the mainly Bosniac (ethnically Muslim) leadership of Bosnia-Herzegovina and many of its citizens hoped that war could be averted. However, with the majority of its population being non-Serb, Bosnia-Herzegovina would not want to stay in a Yugoslavia that would be no more than Greater Serbia. In a referendum held on February 29 and March 1, 1992, Bosnia-Herzegovina voted in favor of independence, although Serb-controlled areas did not participate. More than two months earlier, warlike martial law conditions had been reigning in numerous cities and townships in Northern and Eastern Bosnia, areas bordering on Serbia and/or with large Serbian settlements. Here the Serb Nationalist Party, the SDS, led by Radovan Karadžić, had not gained a majority in the 1990 elections but organized a parallel Serb administration consisting of so-called Crisis Committees. These committees were secretly arming local Serbs with guns coming from Belgrade and the JNA.[13] In November of 1991, the SDS organized a referendum in those areas they considered Serbian on whether the Serbs wanted to remain in Yugoslavia (with Montenegro, the Krajina, and Eastern Slavonija, the latter two areas in Croatia). This was in effect a vote for Greater Serbia, and an overwhelming majority of those who voted, voted "yes." (We have no reliable figure for how many Serbs actually voted.) On January 9, 1992, when the SDS declared the foundation of the Serbian Republic of Bosnia and Herzegovina, later renamed Republika Srpska, the harassment and violent terrorizing of non-Serbs in SDS areas of control was already under way.[14]

CAMPAIGNS OF "ETHNIC CLEANSING"

On April 5, 1992, the day before Bosnia-Herzegovina was recognized as an independent state by the EU, Serb snipers near the Hotel Holiday Inn and in the nearby neighborhood of Grbavica fired at a Sarajevo peace demonstration, killing two young women.[15] The Sarajevans had been chanting "We want to live together" and "Peace"; hours earlier barricades had been put up at various sites in the city. The next day, Sarajevans woke up to a partitioned city under siege. It was the day the war reached Sarajevo. From that date on, the Western media began to report almost daily about the shelling of civilians; about massacres; forced expulsions; the herding of civilians into camps; the burning of homes, mosques, and churches; and the everyday suffering of ordinary people in cities under siege and constant bombardment. While the attention of Western media was focused on the shelling and siege of Sarajevo, non-Serbs were being herded into detention centers that served as death camps outside of Sarajevo in Eastern and Northern Bosnia. It was part of the organized attempt at eliminating the non-Serb population from Serbian-controlled territory. The outside world became aware of what was going on only after some brave British and American journalists published pictures and stories from the Serbian-run death camps in the district of Prijedor in Northern Bosnia: Omarska, Keraterm, and Trnopolje (see Gutman 1993; Vulliamy 1994). The camps were part of a political and military strategy to rid Northern and Eastern Bosnia (territory that either borders with Serbia or had a sizable Bosnian Serb population) of all political opposition to a partition of Bosnia-Herzegovina and the creation of a separate Bosnian Serb state. According to the logic of ethnic politics in the former Yugoslavia, which I discuss below, a member of the opposite ethnic group or "nationality" translated into a political enemy.

The case of Prijedor shows the gradual increase in acts of intimidation, provocation, and terror directed toward the non-Serb population. "The Final Report of the UN Commission of Experts" documents how those (non-Serb) Muslims and Croats—the greatest numbers were Muslim—in positions of leadership or with higher education were systematically targeted: these included political leaders, teachers, physicians, lawyers, religious instructors, journalists, and intellectuals.[16] The obvious result of the organized targeting of the educated and powerful strata of a community or "ethnic group" is the weakening, marginalization, and possible destruction of the community's economic and political capability to prosper and to influence society. By killing or humiliating men and women through trespassing their most intimate sphere (that is, entering and destroying their homes, raping or mutilating them), the effect was not only to destroy the person physically and mentally but also to break their community by destroying persons who contributed to its social, moral, and economic strength. Furthermore, the community or targeted nationality's ability to reproduce members would be (at least in the short term) reduced. These effects were in addition to the immediate and obvious one of eliminating or pacifying (potential) enemy soldiers.

The Convention for the Prevention and Punishment of the Crime of Genocide, or, for short, the Genocide Convention, was adopted by the U.N. General Assembly in 1948. It states that genocide consists of killing, serious assault, starvation, and measures aimed at children "committed with the intent to destroy, in whole or in part, a national, ethnical, racial or religious group, as such." Raphael Lemkin, who first coined the term *genocide*, suggested a definition that is more elaborate and explanatory: "a coordinated plan of different actions aiming at the destruction of essential foundations of the life of national groups with the aim of annihilating the groups themselves." The objective of such a plan was "the disintegration of the political and social institutions of culture, language, national feelings, religion and the economic existence of national groups and the destruction of personal security, liberty, health, dignity, and even the lives of the individuals belonging to such groups" (quoted in Schabas 1999:2). With the rich documentation that exists about the crimes committed against the non-Serb population in Eastern and Northern Bosnia, the International Criminal Tribunal based in The Hague has already charged individual Serb commanders with genocide. The main challenge for the International Criminal Court will be to prove the perpetrators' intent to commit genocide.[17]

By the summer of 1992, Serbian forces had taken control over and "ethnically cleansed" 70 percent of Bosnia-Herzegovina. An alliance of ill-prepared Croat and mainly Bosnian Muslim Army units (but including Serbs and others who sided with the Sarajevo government and supported an integrated and undivided Bosnia-Herzegovina) held out against the militarily superior Serb forces until January of 1993, when it became obvious that the Bosnian Croat forces (HVO) were working hand in hand with the political forces that wanted an independent Croatian Republic of Bosnia and Herzegovina. Although a majority of the Bosnian Croat population voted for an independent and undivided Bosnia-Herzegovina at the referendum in February/March 1992, the Bosnian Croat sister party of the Croatian Nationalist Party—the HDZ, led by Franjo Tudjman—had already on November 18, 1991, declared "The Croat Republic of Herceg-Bosna" at their Herzegovinian headquarters in Grude. The Bosnian government forces were now fighting a two-front war against Serb and Croat separatists. There was more "ethnic cleansing": destroyed houses, prison camps, refugees, and deaths.

In April 1993, Muslim settlements in Kiseljak and other towns and villages in central Bosnia were attacked by the HVO (Croatian Defense Force) as part of what has become known as the "Lašva Valley Offensive." The offensive is described in several U.N. Criminal Tribunal documents in connection with indictments of HVO soldiers who are believed to have held command responsibilities during the offensive. In 1999, General Tihomir Blaškič was sentenced to forty-five years in prison by the court at the International Criminal Tribunal in The Hague for "having ordered the commission of a crime against humanity for persecution of the Muslim civilians of Bosnia in the municipalities of Vitez, Busovača and Kiseljak." Particularly aggravating was the massacre of 116 inhabitants, including women and children, in Ahmići, a small village in the municipality of Vitez, an area believed to be under the command of General Blaškić. (Five other Croat military and political leaders have been indicted on the same accounts.) Although the HVO initially had considerable military and political success in carving out a Croatian "statelet," by the summer of 1993 the HVO was losing ground to Bosnian government forces (ABiH—Armija Bosne i Hercegovine), who were also engaging in revenge attacks in central Bosnia and expelling Croats and burning and looting their homes. In Zagreb, politicians and intellectuals were becoming increasingly critical of President Tudjman's policies in Bosnia. At a point when domestic and international criticisms against Tudjman's war in Bosnia were running high, and the HVO continued to lose ground to the Bosnian government forces, the United States took the initiative to create a federation between the Croats and the Bosniacs in B-H.[18]

The Washington Agreement was signed in March 1994. The agreement set the framework for a future common administration and state structure, and provided for an immediate cessation of hostilities between the two parties. The war between the HVO and the ABiH (and by extension between the Croat and the Muslim communities) started almost a year later and ended a year and a half before the war ended between the Bosnian Serb Army (BSA) and the ABiH with the signing of the Dayton Agreement in November 1995. It had several of the characteristics of the war in Northern and Eastern Bosnia that the Bosnian Serb Army was waging against non-Serb civilians, but it was also different in many respects. It was preceded by a public rhetoric of exclusion portraying Muslims first in demeaning and dehumanizing ways, and then as attackers out to destroy the Croats. Muslim inhabitants were persecuted through campaigns of terror, expulsions, and the destruction of homes and mosques. The ferociousness of the campaign to force Muslims from territory controlled by the Croat separatists (HVO/HDZ) varied quite considerably from area to area, and particularly between Herzegovina and parts of central Bosnia. The HVO do not appear to have organized or committed mass killings on a scale comparable with that of the Bosnian Serb Army. This may be explained by several factors, though I will suggest only a few. First, the Bosnian Army was better equipped and better prepared for combat at the time when war broke out with the HVO (indeed, when the BSA attacked there was no Bosnian Army). Second, there was a vocal opposition among Croats within Bosnia, but more important within Croatia, against the war with the Sarajevo government and "the Muslims" in Bosnia. Furthermore, Croatian popular opinion as well as that of the government was susceptible to international pressure. Also, the absence of a history of violent conflict between Croats and Muslims, combined with the fact that both were victims of Serbian aggression at the beginning of the war, provided the Croat separatists with less fuel in their manipulation of fear and memory (although plenty has been produced in the recent war).

More than five years passed after the signing of the Washington Agreement before people expelled from their homes in the municipality of Kiseljak and other central Bosnian municipalities in 1993 could return home safely. (Both the Washington Agreement and the Dayton Agreement ensured the right for refugees and displaced people to return to their homes.) In central Bosnia, Bosniacs and Croats are again living together in towns and villages. This development in large parts of the Bosniac-Croat Federation (one of two entities in the state of Bosnia and Herzegovina constituted by the Dayton Agreement) is strikingly different from the one (or lack of one) in the Serbian-controlled part of Bosnia-Herzegovina (the Republika Srpska entity). Here a much smaller number of Bosniacs and Croats have moved back. The two developments reflect both the degree of ferociousness in the ethnic cleansing campaigns (the fact that genocide—including mass rape—was the defining crime against non-Serbs in the Serbian entity), and the different policies pursued in central Bosnia (the Bosniac-Croat Federation) and in Eastern and Northern Bosnia (Republika Srpska). Changes in policies in central Bosnia that facilitate refugee return are due to, first, the absence of certain key military and political leaders from positions of influence, and, second, continuous political pressure from the international community combined with aid for reconstruction. The nationalists did not, in other words, succeed in erasing the physical trait of "the other"; houses are being rebuilt and so are mosques.

The war in Bosnia probably cost about 250,000 lives.[19] Thousands remain unaccounted for. Out of a prewar population of more than 4 million, 1.8 million people were displaced or became refugees (1,259,000 were exiled outside B-H), and about 30 percent of all residential buildings were damaged or destroyed (65 percent of those are in the Bosniac-Croat Federation, 35 percent in the Republika Srpska entity).[20] In addition, public and civilian institutions were destroyed, such as schools, libraries, churches, mosques, and hospitals—in Sarajevo the hospital was frequently targeted by shelling, and the National Library was one of the first buildings to go up in flames. Cultural monuments such as mosques and libraries associated with the Ottoman Muslim heritage were also prime targets for shelling, both by the Bosnian Serb and the Bosnian Croat armies.

"ETHNIC CLEANSING" AND THE
RHETORIC OF "ANCIENT HATREDS"

The two phrases "centuries-old hatred" and "they cannot live together," and the term *genocide,* all referred to in the above-mentioned speech by the Serb nationalist leader Karadžić (a few weeks before the barricades were set up in Sarajevo and a Serb-controlled Sarajevo separated from the rest of the city), became a staple of Karadžić's public speech repertoire. Indeed, it frequently appeared in speeches made by the top brass of the Serbian leadership. The two phrases were quickly picked up by many representatives of the Western media and would shape policy makers' understanding of the conflict. With some honorable exceptions, international mediators would parrot this Serbian propaganda. They became simultaneously an explanation both for the war and one excuse for Western inaction in the face of atrocities (such as the death camps in Northern Bosnia and the siege and daily shelling of Sarajevo).

The implication behind the "centuries-old hatred" mantra was that the war could not be stopped but had to run its natural cause, or, as E.U. mediator Lord Owen suggested, that "the warring fractions would have to fight it out." (Other prominent believers of the "centuries-old hatred" explanatory model were Douglas Hurd, the British foreign minister at the time, and President Bill Clinton, although the latter later changed his views.) The war was, in other words, portrayed as a natural disaster at best, or as biologically determined at worst: driven by a peculiarly primordial or instinctive "Balkan" hatred. By implication, the international community could only try to alleviate some of the suffering by making sure that food and medicines were delivered to the survivors.[21] By the end of four years of atrocities and war committed in the name of one people against another (members of all three groups—Croats, Muslims, and Serbs—had been victimized), many Bosnians would finally agree that Karadžić was right: "[We] cannot live together."

GENOCIDE IS EVERYWHERE AND THEREFORE NOWHERE

Genocide was a favorite rhetorical device for the nationalist policy makers and hatred mongers. They made it sound more scientific and factual by prefixing it with specific adjectives. Such imaginative use of the term may be traced back to the 1986 "Memorandum" of the Serbian Academy of Science and Arts: "The physical, political, legal, and cultural genocide of the Serbian Population in Kosovo and Metohija is a worse defeat than any experiences in the liberation wars waged by Serbia from the First Serbian Uprising in 1804 to the uprising of 1941."[22] According to Roger Cohen, *genocide* was the most overused word in Serbian (and later Yugoslav) president Slobodan Milošević's vocabulary. He referred to the "demographic genocide against the Serbs" (in Kosovo the natality of the Albanians was much higher than that among any other people in the former Yugoslavia, including the Serbs). He talked about "the Croatian genocide against the Serbs" (a reminder to Serbs of what happened during World War II, when Serbs living under the Croatian Ustasha regime were victims of the regime's genocidal policies against Jews, Serbs, and Gypsies) and set up a direct association between the former Ustasha regime and the contemporary Republic of Croatia run by Franjo Tudjman and his nationalist party, the HDZ. He spoke of "the international embargo on Yugoslavia as the last genocidal attack against the Serbs" (the international embargo [sanctions] was imposed on Yugoslavia and the Milošević regime by the U.N. Security Council in 1992 for engaging in aggression against Bosnia-Herzegovina).[23]

The frequent use of the term *genocide* (not as an absolute term, but in combination with various adjectives) had at least three implications: First, the repetitive use in public propaganda instilled fear in Serbs about threats (from neighbors) to their own existence. Second, the Serbian leaders thus presented their own aggressive project toward non-Serb neighbors in defensive terms.[24] Third, by the time the non-Serb victims of genocide (or their spokespersons) in Bosnia were presenting their plight to the outside world, their claims were dismissed as propaganda.[25]

To many policy makers in Europe and the United States it was convenient to describe what was going on as "ethnic cleansing." Describing the crimes against non-Serb civilians as genocide would carry an obligation to intervene—although there may not exist a legal obligation to intervene, either to prevent genocide from happening or to stop it while in progress. It is not clear under the 1948 U.N. "Convention for the Prevention and Punishment of the Crime of Genocide" what prevention entails, and whether it implies an obligation to intervene (see Schabas 1999). However, I believe there would have been a moral obligation (pushed by public opinion) for the international community (and primarily the West) to intervene had "genocide" and not "ethnic cleansing" become the defining crime of the wars in Bosnia-Herzegovina. That is not to say, however, that "ethnic cleansing" in all cases became a euphemism for "genocide." The systematic murder of Muslim and Croat civilians that took place in Eastern and Northern Bosnia was not the pattern everywhere in Bosnia ("ethnic cleansing" does, however, entail crimes punishable as grave breaches of the Geneva Conventions and as crimes against humanity). But at least during the first half of the war the phenomenon of ethnic cleansing exoticized the war in Bosnia, and, I believe, made it more difficult for people to engage. The concept also contributed to blurring the lines in people's minds between perpetrator and victim, between attacker and attacked. The term is vague in that what constitutes "ethnic cleansing" is often vague, so it was easier to accuse all sides in the conflict of ethnic cleansing (and thus treat them as equally guilty).

Ethnic cleansing is not a legal term, and while genocide is defined as a crime of intent in legal terms, *ethnic cleansing* was originally used to describe the expulsions of unwanted populations (in order to create an ethnically pure territory) through terror tactics such as intimidation, discrimination, rape, torture, murder, looting and burning of homes, and the destruction of religious and cultural objects. However, through overuse and politically motivated misuse, the term was watered down. It was even used about the consequences of negotiated changes of political-military borders. (One example would be when Serb inhabitants, who in many cases set fire to their own houses first, fled areas of Sarajevo that were returned to the control of the Sarajevo government under the Dayton Peace Agreement.)

Genocide and *ethnic cleansing* have been used as powerful polemic terms by local political players in the war and by international observers and commentators. Yet while *genocide* was used mainly by the Serbian nationalists in a propaganda strategy, *ethnic cleansing* was used polemically and according to varying criteria (often dependent on the political point the speaker wanted to make) by foreign commentators as well.

THE POLICY OF ETHNIC CLEANSING

In the Final Report of the United Nations Commission of Experts, *ethnic cleansing* is defined as "rendering an area ethnically homogenous by using force or intimidation to remove from a given area persons from another ethnic or religious group." This is a very general definition that does not specify the violent means involved. However, the report is more specific in referring to actual campaigns of "ethnic cleansing"; it continues: " 'Ethnic Cleansing' has involved means, such as the mass killing of civilians, sexual assault, the bombardment of cities, the destruction of mosques and churches, the confiscation of property and similar measures to eliminate or dramatically reduce, Muslim and Croat populations that lie within Serb held territories." The report states that Croat forces, too, have engaged in ethnic cleansing against Serbs and Muslims, and that "while Bosnian Muslim forces have engaged in practices that constitute 'grave breaches' of the Geneva Conventions and other violations of international humanitarian law, they have not engaged in 'ethnic cleansing operations' " and that "the forceful population removal of Serbs by Bosnian Muslims has happened but not as part of a policy." Indeed, the organized and systematic character of the "ethnic cleansing" campaigns, and the fact that they were backed up with a propaganda led by a political leadership, should encourage us always to preface references to ethnic cleansing with "the policy of" or "campaign of."

It is not clear how the term *ethnic cleansing* originated. However, Bosnians have told me that *rasčistiti*, the word for "to clean up" or "to cleanse" (or *čišćenje*, the word for "cleaning") was used in the vernacular during World War II to describe a military action akin to "mopping up," as in the term *rasčistiti teren* ("mopping up the terrain"). I suggest that the term *ethnic* was added on by foreign journalists or human rights rapporteurs. To my knowledge, *ethnic (etnički)* was not a term widely known or used in Bosnia except by sociologists. But older people were familiar with the use of the term *čišćenje* (or *rasčistiti*) from armed attacks on villages during World War II (including by Tito's Partisan forces). Although the abhorrent practices associated with ethnic cleansing are not new, the term that has become a generalized expression of them is.

However, "ethnic purification," which is the English translation of *etnički čišćenje*, may better convey the Nazi era ideas behind the violent and bigoted practices the term is meant to stand for (see also Letica 1997). It could be argued that the wide use of *ethnic cleansing* (usually leaving out a clarifying "policy of") in the media coverage of the war in Bosnia during the first few years blurred the international public's conceptions of what was going on. "Ethnic cleansing" sounded like something peculiarly "Balkan," and indeed for some Balkan scholars who were applying their political views and academic analysis of the Greek experience with Turkey between the two World Wars, "ethnic cleansing" seemed familiar, and akin to, "population transfers/exchanges."[26] The suggestion is that "organized" or supervised "ethnic cleansing" would have reduced war casualties and even avoided the war and ensured a long-lasting peace. In this instance *ethnic cleansing* is given a positive connotation, in accordance with the "ethnic cleansers'" own evaluation. This view, however, is problematic for several reasons. First, it perceives multiethnicity itself as a problem. Second, the population transfers early in the last century raised significant moral, political, and social concerns and resulted in significant human suffering. Third, there is no reason to believe that social engineering elsewhere in the world at the start of the twentieth century is usefully applicable to Bosnia-Herzegovina in the 1990s. Last, it ignores the fact that the practices entailed in campaigns of ethnic cleansing are war crimes and in many cases will qualify under international law as crimes against humanity. Indeed, to start using *ethnic cleansing* to mean population transfers intended to protect people from war is to sanitize atrocities committed under the banner of "ethnic cleansing" (the same is true when *ethnic cleansing* is used to denote any kind of human rights abuses of ethnic minorities). Third, it assumes that the cause of the problem (the political and military drive for ethnically "pure" territories) is also the solution to the problem. This view, in other words, takes for granted that a majority of people (of their own free will) wanted to live not in Bosnia but in politically and militarily engineered "ethnically pure" statelets. I will argue that the very personalized violence that is the hallmark of ethnic cleansing and the wars in Bosnia-Herzegovina proves that a majority of people did not want the new social order that was being imposed on them.

The personalized violence, directed toward individuals because of their association with a certain ethnic community was poignantly conveyed by a Bosnian friend of mine. We were sitting in her home in a village and hearing shells falling a few kilometers away. I asked her whether she was afraid. She told me: "I do not fear shells for they do not ask me my name. I fear only the shock troops, they enter your house and do all sorts of things to you. Shells fall on you by chance and death is instant. They do not ask me my name." (It should be added by way of explanation that in Bosnia one can usually tell a person's ethnic identification by her or his first and last name or a combination of the two.) The level of terror and violence needed to force Bosnians to separate is a testimony, first, to the lack of fit between the ethnically homogenous political and geographical space desired by the "ethnic cleansers" and their engineers and the ethnically heterogeneous reality on the ground, and, second, and perhaps more important, to the lack of fit between the ideological and totalitarian view of ethnicity and the practical and flexible perception of ethnicity on the ground.[27] Indeed, the fact that a very high level of coercion was needed is a clear indication that most people wanted to continue to live together.

Yet what many people say and want at the end of ten years of hatred and fear propaganda, and almost four years of war with neighbors, is not necessarily what they said or wanted at the outset. To suggest otherwise would be to disregard social processes completely. For instance, many (if not most) Bosnian Serbs who live in the Republika Srpska entity of B-H "justify the 'homeland war' as righteous and necessary, as an ultimately defensive measure to rescue Serbs from an Islamic state reminiscent of Ottoman Turkish rule under which Serbs languished for centuries."[28] Surely, a crucial question to try to answer is: What where the frameworks, the social and political structures, that not only allowed and encouraged some people to commit crimes against their neighbors but also resulted in those people being seen as heroes by many of those who shared their ethnic affiliation?

YUGOSLAVIA AND BOSNIA'S DESCENT INTO WAR

For the Socialist Federative Republic of Yugoslavia, the end of communism meant that parts of the country suffered an almost five-year-long war that has completely devastated the country and its peoples. It was the bloodiest regime transition in central and eastern Europe at the end of the Cold War. This is ironic, as Yugoslavia was also the most open toward the West in terms of trade, foreign policy, less regulated markets, and the possibility for Yugoslavs to travel and work in Western Europe. Yugoslavia's transition from a one-party state socialist system should have been the least traumatic of all countries that rejoined democratic Europe after the fall of the Berlin Wall. Instead, the opposite was true.

Volumes have been written about the "fall," "destruction," "disintegration," "end," and so forth of Yugoslavia since 1991, and I am sure new titles will be added. Different authors stress different aspects of the developments that led to the wars: the economic crisis, the stifling of democratic movements, the rise to power of one man—Slobodan Milošević—and his brand of nationalism, old ethnic antagonisms dormant through communist times being reactivated, the role of the international community (primarily Europe) or lack of such a role, and even a "clash of civilizations."[29] Certainly, however, the breakup of Yugoslavia and the ensuing wars cannot be explained by one factor, but only as the result of a combination of factors—a series of circumstances whereby domestic and international structural changes and certain political players came together at the end of the century in Yugoslavia.

TRANSITION OF AUTHORITY AND THE TITOIST LEGACY

I would like to examine one element in this web of factors that I believe has received less attention than it should: namely, the problems entailed in the transition from one form of authority to another. The premise for my discussion is that issues of succession and political legitimacy following the death of Tito in 1980 were not properly addressed by the Yugoslavs, and that no mode of authority other than the one embodied by Tito was allowed to develop.[30] This was the "Tito we swear to you" (*Tito me te kunemo*) model of paternal authority that Tito passed on, not to one successor but to six in a rotating presidency. (Each successor represented the special interests of his or her republic and its people—with the exception of the representative from Bosnia-Herzegovina, who had to represent the interests of all three peoples living within it.) The issue of the successors to Tito deals with the macro level of the beginning of the end for Yugoslavia. The challenge is to connect events on the macro level to what eventually happened locally in villages, townships, and urban neighborhoods. This is an area where research is still needed. But I would like to propose some possible connections.

After the end of the Cold War, both the institutions at the base of the Yugoslav state structure and the ideological organizing principles were discredited (became illegitimate), made irrelevant, or were restructured. I will look at these in turn: The two main institutions were the league of Yugoslav communists (the party) and the Yugoslav People's Army (JNA). The ideological pillars were Self-Management, Nonalignment, and Brotherhood and Unity.

After Tito's death in 1980, the Yugoslav Communist Party was further propelled into a process of decentralization (which had begun with the 1974 constitution). Decisions were increasingly being made at the local/republican level, and the Croatian, Serb, Slovenian branches of the party were representing the interests of the republics and not those of a unified Yugoslavia (see Denitch 1994). With the fall of the Berlin Wall and the discrediting of communism, the era of the communist party in Yugoslavia, too, was coming to an end. In some areas communists reinvented themselves as nationalists (for example, Milošević in Serbia). This was not necessarily a radical ideological change, as communism and nationalism have some important traits in common. According to Zwick (1983), both communism and nationalism emerge in transitional societies and are as such an "expression of social collective grievances." Furthermore, he argues, they have both "quasi-religious characteristics," and they are "millenarian world views in that they promise secular deliverance and salvation in the form of a perfect world order and their followers are willing to justify virtually anything in the name of their millenarian goals" (ibid.:11–12). Both movements arise as a reaction to an (imagined) enemy or enemies. Although in the case of communism another class and the capitalist "foreign" Western world are depicted as the enemy, in the case of nationalism the primary enemy is the other nation (see ibid.:11). The dissolution of the Cold War polarization between the capitalist West and the communist East (and the disappearance of a so-called Soviet threat) not only removed traditional enemy categories from the repertoire of the Yugoslav state; it also deprived it of the rationale for its geopolitical status and identity—its "non-aligned" status. Backed up by nationalism as the new ideology of the Yugoslav republics, the successors to Tito redefined the enemy from being the outside foreign capitalist or Soviet powers to becoming the other competing "Yugoslav" nations within.

"Self-management" was the distinguishing feature of Tito's own brand of socialism, permeating all levels of official institutions and work places. The self-managing system "meant the installation of a multiple hierarchy of assemblies, from the communities to the republic and the federation." There was self-management in the workplace, on ownership to property (so-called social property), and in the area of military and defense, which meant "a network of civilian defense militias in every workplace and community" (Thompson 1992:32). Self-management as a system for managing the economy had already been discredited by the severe economic crisis and the ineffectiveness of the state apparatus in dealing with the crisis. Self-management as a principle in organizing and decentralizing Yugoslavia's military and defense forces, however, had critical importance for the military structure of the recent wars in Bosnia-Herzegovina and in Croatia. When the principles of self-management were applied to defense and military forces, it meant decentralized command structures and that citizens were involved on all levels in the defense of the country. It also meant that the access to arms was decentralized. A central element of this decentralized military structure was the Territorial Defense Units. Chairman Bassiouni of the U.N. Commission of Experts gives a clear analysis of the implications of this military defense system for the structure and dynamics of the wars in the former Yugoslavia:

> The governments of the various republics would participate with the federal government for regional defense. This strategy required universal military service and coordinated training in guerrilla warfare. This ensured that cadres of soldiers, trained in guerilla warfare, would be available nationwide and capable of operating in decentralized command fashion. Training facilities, weapon caches, and supply stores were placed throughout the country. The military also organized reserve units or so-called Territorial Defense Units around workplaces to ensure the wide distribution of weapons. Thus, with the breakup of the former Yugoslavia, trained soldiers were available for mobilization, and weapons and ammunition were also available for distribution to national and local political or military leaders and their followers. These leaders sometimes used these resources to further their own political, military, or personal goals.[31]

When the Yugoslav communist party disintegrated, only one state institution remained: the Yugoslav Peoples Army. When Slovenia declared independence, the JNA moved in; the same happened in Croatia a few months later. The JNA generals were loyal to Yugoslavia and saw their role as preventing it from disintegrating. But as non-Serbs started to realize that the JNA was used against Yugoslav compatriots and that it was a tool of Milošević and his new Serbian nationalist regime, they started to pull out of the JNA. It lost its last remnant of credibility (as became clear with JNA's siege of Vukovar) among non-Serbs when it shelled the old town and Adriatic port of Dubrovnik in 1991. In Bosnia the JNA pulled out when the republic declared independence, but it handed all its weaponry over to the Bosnian Serb insurgents and officers switched uniforms. The JNA did not even pretend to be protecting the Yugoslav state and all its peoples anymore; it had become the tool of Milošević and his project of creating a greater Serbia.

Subsequently, new armies were established that fought for one nation and one state (except in the Bosnian case, where the Bosnian Army in the first half of the war fought for one state but for all nations within it) and were the military arm of ethno-nationalist political parties. Tito, who had formed and headed both of the state-bearing institutions, the communist party and the JNA, had been dead for more than ten years when both of them disintegrated. It was the end of his state. His image, which had been religiously kept alive for ten years, was not only fading into the background but had also suffered from years of being debunked by the popular media and opposition forces. The allegiance to a dead Tito and the slogan "Tito we swear to you, we will not stray from your path" was no longer strong enough to withstand the forces of disintegration—forces that were very much helped by structures Tito himself had put in place. But what happened to the last of Tito's three ideological pillars—namely, Brotherhood and Unity?

BROTHERHOOD AND UNITY

This was the key transcendent of Titoist Yugoslavia: it was the idiom for solidarity and cooperation between the different nations and nationalities of Yugoslavia. The basis for this unity of the South Slav peoples was the common struggle (which cut across ethnic affiliation) against fascism (German, Italian, and Croatian) led by the partisans. It was the heartbeat of Tito's creation. This idea, however, both glossed over the animosities created by the communal fighting during World War II and, as far as Bosnia is concerned, was a Titoist appropriation of its long tradition of cooperation between the different ethno-religious communities. The new regimes had to establish legitimacy (and a popular base of support) through destroying the legitimacy of the previous regime, so multiethnicity was conveniently seen by the new nationalist and separatist leaders as a communist legacy. Multiethnicity would undermine their power base: the ethnically defined region or republic. Its most poignant expression—interethnic marriage—was portrayed as the ultimate communist invention. Indeed, it was considered (and probably rightly so) as a threat to the mobilizing effect of nationalism. It so happens that Bosnia was the region of the former Yugoslavia where so-called intermarriage was the most common. Not only was multiethnicity portrayed as another word for Brotherhood and Unity, but it was also an obstacle to creating homogenous nation states, both in terms of demography and geography—villages and towns all over B-H were ethnically heterogeneous—and from a political perspective. To better understand why multiethnicity (or ethnically heterogeneous communities) were perceived by the new ethno-nationalist leaders as a political obstacle to creating their desired new nation-states, it is helpful to examine the way in which the political and the ethnic were intertwined in Titoist policies.

In Tito's single-party state, the only opportunity to express diversity was through ethnicity. Indeed, in many instances political representation was based on ethnicity. That is, every governmental body had to be represented by a member from each of the ethnic groups in that republic (for example, in the rotating presidency that Tito had designed, all seats were allocated on the basis of ethnic or national identity). Tito regime's had an ambivalent attitude toward ethnic relations. On the one hand, it encouraged national identities through the political and administrative system, since political representation and allocation of resources were on the basis of ethnic identification (this system is still in force in Bosnia through the government structures laid down by the Dayton Agreement). On the other, it ethnicized political opposition: demands for more democracy were branded as outbursts of nationalism and an anathema, a threat to the very existence of Yugoslavia (based on the principle of Brotherhood and Unity), and therefore considered antistate and prosecuted. (Several crackdowns and court cases involved current leaders who were sentenced to prison terms for nationalist activities during Titoist rule.) Ten years after Tito's death, and a year after the fall of the Berlin Wall, all the Yugoslav republics decided to hold democratic multiparty elections.

The foundation for a political system based on ethnicity was already in place, and thus it should have come as no surprise that the 1990 elections in the Yugoslav republics swept to power nationalist parties and their leaders. During the elections, a critical theme was the relations between majority populations (or so-called constituent peoples) and ethnic minorities. People were worried about the outcome of the free elections and the new divisions of power it would create. Since there was no political tradition of democracy or pluralism, and resources and political office traditionally had been allocated on the basis of ethnic or national identity, people feared that to be a minority in a local community or political-administrative area could mean having no rights or having reduced access to resources. (Under one-party rule, only those who supported the party—that is, the majority—had political rights, so nobody wanted to be a minority.) The new nationalist leaders representing aggressive nationalist parties played on these fears. Thus on the eve of the elections there were the legacy of totalitarian one-party rule combined with the ethnification of political representation and allocation of resources, plus a worry about the change in status from a constituent people to a minority under the new democracies.

In a process that started with the 1974 Yugoslav constitution (resulting in the devolution of power to the republics), the "people-as-one" principle characteristic of totalitarian rule was moved from the Yugoslav (federal) to the ethnonational level (see Bringa, forthcoming). This element, together with the fact that there was a tradition of viewing political conflict or competition in ethnic terms, accounts for the branding of all people identifiable as belonging to a particular ethnic group as political opponents. In the case of Milošević's political project for a Greater Serbia (and later Tudjman's for a greater Croatia), all non-Serbs (or non-Croats, in Tudjman's HDZ-controlled areas) were considered enemies that had to be removed. That the war was primarily motivated by political ideology (of which nationalism was the main ingredient) is clear from the fact that Serbs who opposed the project (for example, who publicly expressed solidarity with non-Serb neighbors) were targeted too; anyone who was against the nationalist project was targeted. This meant that Bosnian Muslims (and other non-separatists, such as people of ethnically mixed backgrounds) became particularly vulnerable.

FEAR AND THE POLITICS OF MEMORY

There was yet another aspect of the Tito regime's ambivalent attitude toward ethnic relations and ethnic communities. It was its reluctance to deal with past injustices, such as atrocities toward civilians of a specific ethnic identification, for fear of stirring things up. The civil wars that ran parallel to and intertwined with World War II in Yugoslavia were never properly dealt with in the official history after 1945. It operated with two mutually exclusive categories: the fascists (the evil perpetrators) and the partisans (the heroic victors and the victims of the fascists).[32] The suffering and injustices experienced by anyone falling outside these categories were never publicly acknowledged. Civilians who had been caught in between, or those who had suffered at the hands of the partisans, did not have a place in the official account. No memorial was ever erected over the graves of those victims. In the late 1980s and early 1990s, "the nameless dead" were in many cases exhumed and given a religious burial, a burial that imbued these victims with an ethnic identity (see Verdery 1999). They became Serb victims of the Croat Ustasha or Croat victims of communists (Serbs).[33] Finally, there was public acknowledgment of the suffering and loss that had been silenced under Tito, but the public acknowledgment was only to those living members of the victims' ethnic/national groups. It was therefore not a ritual that could be part of a process of reconciliation; on the contrary, there was another, hidden message: a collapsing of time identifying the victims with all other members of the same ethnicity and the perpetrators with all other living members of the group they were seen to represent. As argued by Verdery (ibid.), the underlying message was, "They may do it to you again."

Cultivation of the death cults was a central element in the politics of memory and the manipulation of fear (see Borneman, forthcoming). (It should be noted, however, that the leaders of the Muslim community did not engage in exhumation and reburial rituals, as that would have run contrary to both Muslim tradition and Islamic belief: desecration of consecrated graves is believed to result in divine punishment. In addition, Alija Izetbegovic, the leader of the Bosnian Muslim Party [SDA], was reluctant to use inflammatory and divisive rhetoric. After all, at least in the first half of the war, Izetbegovic saw himself as the leader of a multiethnic Bosnia—when there was still a multiethnic B-H to consider.)

So there were atrocities and injustices at the hands of co-Yugoslavs that Tito had not wanted to deal with and therefore had buried under the slogan of Brotherhood and Unity. But the public process of remembering those events from 1989 onward did not form part of a process of reconciliation, since it was not owned by the local communities where the events had taken place; instead, it was hijacked by nationalist leaders as a tool to manipulate fear and create a social climate in which supporters would rally behind them for "protection."

The violent breakup of the Socialist Federal Republic of Yugoslavia into national(ist) republics was both a revolt against the Titoist regime and the result of conditions created by that regime, conditions that shaped developments and limited the number of possible outcomes. The most significant break with the old regime was the change in the transcendent from Brotherhood and Unity to its antithesis, ethnonationalist "purity." But structural and ideological traits of the old regime remained, among which the ethnification of political life was crucial. Indeed, the new ethnonationalist leaders relied on some of the previous regime's key political controlling mechanisms for their own hold on power.

FORGING NATIONS THROUGH TERROR AND WAR

As state structures crumble, institutions lose their legitimation, and there is no money left, people feel lost (a way of life is disappearing); they worry about the immediate future, which seems to hold only uncertainties. Insecurity and fear about the present and the future motivates people to withdraw into safe "we groups" in which you need not qualify to become a member—it is your birthright, and loyalty and protection are taken for granted. This may be your kin group or your ethnic group or your nation (the largest group of people using the idiom of kinship). As persecution, assaults, and violence become personal experience, the individual's fear turns into hatred for the enemy and all the members of his or her group. Fear and war help to coalesce populations into clearly defined nations. (I do believe that for most people when this kind of manipulated fear disappears, the hatred goes. The fear disappears when people feel safe again.)

The war experiences of individuals in turn serve to confirm the nationalist propaganda of the need for "ethnic unity" and the threat from the "ethnic other." War experiences change the way people and communities think and feel about their own identity and that of others. Indeed, the experience of violence and war seems crucial for the strong ethnic and national identification people in most of the former Yugoslavia developed (Povrzanović 1997). In Bosnia in 1993, you could no longer choose if you wanted to be a Bosnian rather than a Croat, or if you wanted to be a Yugoslav rather than a Muslim (or Bosniac). Any category other than Croat, Serb, or Muslim fell outside the dominant discourse (that is, the discourse of power). This development toward closed and rigid nationality-defined communities in Bosnia, should, as Gagnon has argued, be understood in the context of political elites pursuing a strategy for restructuring political circumstances so that the only way to obtain anything is by identifying oneself exclusively with one ethnic/national community (see Gagnon 1995, 1996).

Opposition and resistance became impossible. If you opposed the harassment or expulsion of your neighbor with, say, a Muslim name, you were a traitor; you risked being killed (or were killed), or, even worse, the "ethnic cleansers" threatened to kill (or killed) your son or another close relative. The brave persons who resisted and opposed were, in other words, given impossible choices. The method the Serbian paramilitaries in particular were applying were very efficient. Serbs who protected their Muslim friends and neighbors or voiced opposition to the mistreatment of non-Serbs in any other way were effectively dealt with: tortured and killed and left in view for others to contemplate. Individuals who refused to be separated from their friends or neighbors along ethnic lines were dealt with, too.

A Sarajevo journalist told me what happened in his neighborhood in Dobrinja (a residential area by the Sarajevo airport that had a high number of professionals and people who identified themselves as Bosnians or Yugoslavs among its residences). People were herded out of their apartments by Serbian paramilitaries, lined up in front of the building, and those with Serbian names were asked to step out of the line and join the paramilitaries. This had happened before elsewhere, and two of the Serbs knew that they might be asked to shoot and kill their non-Serb neighbors. They refused, and were killed on the spot. Potential witnesses to massacres were silenced by implicating them in the acts. David Rhode, the journalist who was captured by Serb forces while researching the Srebrenica massacre and then wrote the book *Endgame*, a comprehensive account of the political and military circumstances surrounding the Srebrenica massacre, told me that one of the bus drivers who had been ordered to bus Muslim men to the field where they were executed was himself forced to shoot and kill. In other words, a witness was turned into an accomplice. In this fashion, even if a person wanted to disassociate himself from acts of violence committed in the name of the ethnic or national group he identified with, it would be difficult, since every attempt was made to implicate everybody. Thus whatever opposition there was to divide Bosnians along so-called ethnic lines was effectively dealt with. Bosnians quickly learned the lesson: you do not argue with a gun. "Ethnic cleansing" then was not only, and perhaps not even primarily, about "ethnic purification." It was primarily, to borrow a term from Gordy (1999), about the "destruction of alternatives" and the elimination of people who represented those alternatives by virtue of identifying or being identified with another ethnic or political community.

BOSNIA'S MUSLIMS: THE VULNERABLE OPPOSITION

The fact remains that the main victims in the war (in terms of number of dead, destroyed homes, and cultural and religious monuments) were Bosnian Muslims. The Bosnian Muslims were the largest group in Bosnia-Herzegovina, but their losses were disproportionately large relative to the size of the their population. The destruction of cultural monuments, mosques, and so forth associated with Bosnian Muslim culture and tradition was also disproportionally large. I have argued above that "ethnic cleansing" was not just "ethnic" but also about the elimination of citizens who were believed to be hostile to the new political order that was being imposed on them. But why were the Muslims perceived as hostile by Serb and Croat nationalists and subsequently by their electorate?

It was clear that an overwhelming majority of Bosnian Muslims did not want to live in a Greater Serbia (or a Greater Croatia) but wanted to continue to live in

Bosnia-Herzegovina; that is what they voted for and that is what most Bosnian Army soldiers fought for. They opposed the partition of Bosnia-Herzegovina into a Serbian Belgrade-ruled half and a Croatian Zagreb-ruled half. There were also Serbs and Croats who opposed them, but they had few representatives in public and, most important, did not control any armies; consequently, international peace negotiators were not interested in talking to them. In addition, Bosnians of no clear Serb, Croat, or Muslim ethnic identification also opposed such a division. They had something in common with Bosnians who defined themselves as ethnically Muslim. They had no other homeland than Bosnia to aspire to, feel connected to, or identify with—multiethnic Bosnia was their homeland.

It is telling that after the Serb-Croat nationalist war for territory and political and economic control spread to Bosnia-Herzegovina, the overwhelming number of those who continued to declare themselves to be Bosnians and supportive of a multinational state of Bosnia-Herzegovina were Muslims and those of an ethnically mixed origin. Bosnia-Herzegovina was the only republic in the former Socialist Federal Republic of Yugoslavia that was not defined as the national home of one particular *narod*—that is, people or nation.[34] Instead it had three—Muslims, Serbs, and Croats—and none of them carried an ethnonym that identified them with the Republic of Bosnia-Herzegovina in the same way as Serbs were or could be identified with Serbia and Croats with Croatia (see Bringa 1995:25). The Bosnian Muslims as a people (narod) were blocking a simple two-way partition of Bosnia-Herzegovina, both politically and by their numerically strong presence in all parts of Bosnia-Herzegovina, both rural and urban, where they lived among Serbs and Croats. They were not geographically confined to any particular region.

The project of getting rid of the "opposition" had to be presented by the Serb and Croat nationalists to their electorate in defensive terms in order to be accepted. The wartime leader of Croatia, Franjo Tudjman, suggested to Western diplomats that he was fighting a war on behalf of the West to protect it from Muslim fundamentalism (that is, Islam). In making peace with the Bosniacs, he saw that, too, in terms of helping the West to reduce the influence of Islam and Muslims in Europe. To what extent nationalist leaders actually believed their own rhetoric is irrelevant to my present argument. It is clear, though, that this rhetoric had the desired effect of turning the Bosnian Muslims into the "other," "the intruder," "those who do not belong," "those who threaten our well-being, power, and prosperity"; in order to pacify them, they had to be dominated or eliminated.

The rhetoric of exclusion, which drew on demeaning, anti-Muslim imagery, was followed by physical exclusion by violent means. A great part of the imagery used by Serb separatist/nationalist leaders in public speeches and by the media that supported them was drawn from Serbian folklore (epics, folk songs, and traditional folk perceptions). A close examination of the imagery and vocabulary that was chosen by Serbian nationalists to justify exclusion of non-Serbs (and in particular Bosnian Muslims) and the violent redrawing of boundaries may help us better understand the process of dehumanization of the Muslims and the brutality they suffered at the hands of Serbs (see Sells 1996). A favorite theme of Serbian folktales and epics is the fight between good and evil, expressed in the fight between Serbs and (Ottoman) Turks—Christian and Muslim. Some of the most popular and well-known Serbian epics incite Serbs (and Montenegrins) to kill Muslims in the most bestial ways. The best-known example is "The Mountain Wreath" by the Montenegrin poet Njegos. (For a detailed analysis of this epic, the anti-Muslim iconography of Serbian epics more generally, and their reactivation at the end of the twentieth century in Serbia, see Sells 1996.) However, we can find prejudice and even dehumanizing images about "other" people in folklore, epics, songs, myths, and literature in many parts of the world. The presence of such images (and even of such attitudes) is not a sufficient explanation for the cruel treatment of Muslims in Bosnia-Herzegovina. The critical issue is the public appropriation of such images to serve political ends—that is, their use (primarily by elites) in public discourse.

Bosnian Muslims had an awkward position in both Serbian and Croatian nationalist historiography: both claimed that the Bosnian Muslims were ethnically really one or the other but had switched sides politically and religiously during Ottoman Turkish rule. There were times in the history of Yugoslavia when Croat or Serb leaders had found it opportune to stress the commonality of ethnicity between Muslims and Croats or Muslims and Serbs, respectively (as with the Ustasha during World War II). But during the recent conflict, nationalist leaders found it opportune to stress the "conversion" part of Bosnian Muslim history. Both Serbian and Croatian nationalist propaganda presented the "war against the Muslims" as a fight against the establishment of an Islamic state in B-H. The Bosnian Serb nationalist leader Radovan Karadžić and his then-patron in Belgrade (Slobodan Milošević) are only two examples of Bosnian Serb leaders who would use overt associations between present-day Bosnian Muslims and their rise to political office after the 1990 elections and the Turkish Ottomans and their rule in Bosnia and Serbia, which ended in the second part of the nineteenth century after having lasted for more than four hundred years. "Turk," the derogatory folk term for Bosnian Muslim, was elevated to a quasi-official term of reference.

In communist times dissidents and political opposition were branded "cominformists" or "nationalists" (that is, traitors) or as "fifth columnists" (foreign agents or spies). In a speech given in early 2000, Yugoslav President Milošević stressed that "[we] have no opposition, but rather contemporary janissaries. These latter-day turncoats (*poturice*) are at the service of foreign masters."[35] In other words, President Milošević branded his political opponents as janissaries and *poturice*. Both terms are associated with Muslims and refer to the Ottoman period. *Poturice* literally means "those who have become Turks." The term refers to those South Slavs who converted to Islam during Ottoman rule in the Balkans. But in some contexts it is used as a synonym for "traitors" or "turn-coats." The term is often used in that way in Serbian folklore. Janissaries were soldiers and members of the Sultan's guard and were often recruited from among young Christian boys in the Ottoman Empire. In Milošević's usage it is another term for fifth-columnists. The communist turned nationalist has changed his label and the targets for repression, but the rhetorical strategy remains the same: a twenty-first-century nationalist is using sixteenth-century terms to express his twentieth-century communist worldview.

A comparison between the iconography in Serbian and Croatian folklore in relation to the Muslims is called for. On the basis of such an analysis, can we speculate that the iconography in Croatian folklore is not sufficiently dehumanizing and violent toward Muslims to move Croats to commit genocide against the Muslims? I believe that ultimately the vocabulary of such epics and traditions of hatred do not motivate people's actions per se. It is the activation of the images that matters; the reconnection of those historic images and attitudes with the present and their translation into contemporary action. People have to be made to act upon them— but how?

THE MANIPULATION OF FEAR

In all societies at all times there exist both the potential for conflict and the potential for peaceful coexistence. At all times what becomes dominant is dependent on what the economically and politically powerful in a society choose to stress. Societies in radical transition, where state structures and the institutions regulating law and order disintegrate, as was the case in the former Yugoslavia, have a greater potential for conflict, and they are more vulnerable to individuals and organizations that seek to exploit the potential for conflict. The political leadership who instigated and drove the war in Bosnia (aided by the media they controlled) consciously exploited the potential for conflict as part of their divide-and-rule strategy. Manipulation of fear became the most important tool for the nationalists. The media (controlled by the various nationalist governments) would dwell on past atrocities committed by members of other nationalities and reinterpret them in the light of the present political development. Or they would simply fabricate incidents— such as massacres—perpetrated by "the other group." Such "incidents" were broadcast repeatedly in the nationalist-party-controlled media. Incidents were provoked in local communities by police or paramilitaries before the war broke out. It was hoped that incidents involving one or a few persons from the "enemy group" would lead to retribution, providing an excuse for a more massive attack on the local "enemy" population as a whole. Intimidation and provocations could consist of beating people up and bombing shops owned by members of the perceived enemy group. This happened in municipalities throughout Bosnia. Barricades were put up, people were stripped of their freedom of movement, war was raging elsewhere in the country, and citizens asked themselves: are we next? A siege mentality developed with fear of an imminent attack by members of the other group.

The media propaganda and individual incidents of intimidation did not bring immediate results, and ultimately violence and war proved to be the only means by which Bosnians could be separated and convinced of the truth of the doctrine that they could not live together. Many people resisted for quite some time and did not change their attitude toward their neighbors and friends. They refused to take part in a process whereby cocitizens were depersonalized and recategorized as the enemy and ethnic other. Indeed, in some local communities and neighborhoods the destruction of the social fabric and the partition of the population along ethnonational lines never succeeded. In others, separation turned out to be a phase, and people are returning to live in communities with their prewar neighbors and wartime enemies. In yet others, that has become almost impossible. First, because of the intransigence of the local political leadership to letting people they once expelled back into their area of control. Second, the area is still unsafe for those who do not belong to the same ethnic community as those who rule. And third, some people who had to flee cannot face the painful memories of the atrocities committed against them in their own homes and local communities.

KINSHIP, ETHNICITY, AND POLITICAL MOBILIZATION

Why did the Serbian (and later Croat) nationalist leaders in the former Yugoslavia rely on the appeal to ethnic solidarity to mobilize (or more accurately, to enlist people's cooperation, or at the least to ensure their lack of obstruction) for the project of restructuring relations of power by redrawing boundaries of exclusion and inclusion?[36] Before the war, Bosnia was neither a society of simmering ethnic hatreds, where members of different ethnic groups had "always been killing each other," nor the ideal model of a harmonious multiethnic society free of ethnic prejudices, as some Western intellectuals like to portray it. Rather, Bosnia contained within itself several different models for coexistence among people with different ethnoreligious backgrounds, and those models were not mutually exclusive. (In postwar Bosnian public discourse these models have been reduced to two: the multiethnic, pluralist model favored by the international community and nonnationalist Bosnians, and the ethnically pure, favored by Serb and Croat—and as a result of the war by some Bosniac—separatists. Unofficially, in terms of the everyday interaction of ordinary people, other models still exist.)

Instead, people existed along a continuum of degrees of intimacy: from people belonging to exclusive and parallel communities where members interacted only in publicly defined places (such as the school or workplace) to people who engaged in close and lifelong friendships and intermarriage. The kind of interethnic relationships people pursued varied from region to region, between town and country, sometimes from one village to the next, from neighborhood to neighborhood, from family to family, and from one person to the next. Elsewhere, I describe some of the ways in which people from different ethnic, religious, and socioeconomic backgrounds would live together: "Although in villages people from different ethnoreligious backgrounds would live side by side and sometimes have close friendships, they would rarely intermarry. In some neighborhoods or hamlets they would not even live side by side and would know little about each other. In towns, especially among the urban educated class, intermarriage would be quite common and would sometimes go back several generations in a single family. Here the socioeconomic strata a person belonged to was more important than was his or her nationality" (Bringa 1995:4).

In some villages relationships between members of different ethnoreligious groups were friendly and relaxed; in others there were tensions, mutual distrust, and separation. In many cases, tensions were due to injustices during or immediately after World War II that had not been addressed, or to neighborhood quarrels that had mobilized people along kinship lines. And this brings me to the point about the emotional appeal of nationalist rhetoric. In rural Bosnia (which is where the nationalist appeal is perhaps the strongest), kinship networks are important— kinship is the primary bond of loyalty. In rural areas, ethnic intermarriage is rare and therefore kinship overlaps with ethnicity. In other words, kin are also members of the same ethnic community. This fact may help explain a mobilizing potential in conflicts based on the rhetoric of nationalism, because nationalist ideologies use the idiom of kinship.[37] It is, in other words, kinship and not ethnicity that holds the primary emotional appeal and is the mobilizing factor. Nevertheless, it should be remembered that for most civilians on all sides mobilization was primarily based on fear (and therefore perceived in defensive terms) and the need to protect one's family and kin. Indeed, it could be argued that the level of fear and violence needed to engage people (or rather to disengage people—that is, to silence their opposition) is an indicator of the weak power of ethnic sentiment as a mobilizing factor (see Gagnon 1996). Furthermore, for the perpetrators of crimes the motivation was often economic gain (through extensive looting), power, and prestige. Prestige was forthcoming because acts that in a functioning state governed by the rule of law would be considered criminal were now considered heroic by those in whose name and on whose behalf the crimes were committed; they were portrayed as acts in defense of the nation.

As this nationalist rhetoric of "ethnic solidarity" takes hold, it becomes almost impossible to resist, because, as has already been argued, national identity becomes the only relevant identity, nationalism the only relevant discourse, and people who resist are exiled, treated as traitors, or forced to become accomplices to crimes committed in the name of the group.

A FINAL WORD

Each July 11 on the anniversary of the start of the Srebrenica massacre, survivors and relatives of those who were killed travel to Potocari (the site of the 1995 U.N. compound where men were separated from women) to mourn the dead. This is as close as these Bosnian Muslims come to "returning" to their prewar homes. In a tunnel near Tuzla north of Srebrenica, four thousand unidentified bodies are kept in body bags, and thousands more are dispersed in unmarked and undetected mass graves in the mountains and fields around Srebrenica. No memorial has been erected on any of the execution sites.[38] But more important, there is no public acknowledgment of the genocide in the Serbian-run entity of Bosnia-Herzegovina. Many Serbs do not believe that the genocide ever took place, and they have no incentive to believe otherwise ("if any Muslims were killed they were killed in combat or attacking Serbs"). Indeed, the only story that is being told is that of the Serbs as the victims, dying in defense of the Serbian homeland or in village raids by Muslim terrorists.[39]

The enormity of the crime in the face of an international presence brought the international community and particularly the fraught U.N. peacekeeping mission into deep crisis (which ended with NATO intervening). It has led to some soul-searching (see the U.N. Srebrenica report) and some suggestions for reform, among others the idea of a more specialized and permanent U.N. peacekeeping force. The Serbian takeover and subsequent execution of almost the entire male population of the Srebrenica U.N. "safe area" made a complete mockery of the "prevention" part of the "Convention for the Prevention and Punishment of the Crime of Genocide." This is particularly so inasmuch as the United Nations and the international community already had detailed knowledge of the Bosnian Serbs' political and military strategy and of the willingness of Serbian forces to kill civilians on a large scale. The international community through the United Nations has (almost in spite of itself) established a successful court to deal with perpetrators of genocide and crimes under the Geneva Conventions. The process is well under way to ensure that the Criminal Tribunal for the Former Yugoslavia and Rwanda will be turned into a permanent international court with a worldwide jurisdiction. There remains the very difficult task to decide and agree on strategies and mechanisms to prevent genocide.

If we want to take the part of the Genocide Convention that addresses prevention seriously in the case of Bosnia-Herzegovina, we (that is, scholars, international organizations, and institutions) must keep up our engagement with postwar Bosnia in order to prevent a replay of Srebrenica among those "who did not know" and their victims. As scholars, first, we can contribute by continuing to research, analyze, and write about social and cultural processes, institutions, and structures that are conducive to massive human right abuses against individuals. And second, we should work with our colleagues from the region and together look at ways in which the past can be dealt with locally—not through omission or denial but by ensuring that people are given a chance to acknowledge documented facts, and by allowing for the painful process of recognition that certain political, military, and emotional structures forced many of us into the role of silent bystanders, or even accomplices.

NOTES

This paper draws on information gathered and observations made on several trips to Bosnia during the war in 1993 and 1995, as well as field research conducted in 1987–88 and 1990. In 1995, I visited Bosnia several times while I was based in Zagreb as political and policy analyst for the special representative of the secretary general for the U.N. peacekeeping operations for the former Yugoslavia (UNPROFOR). In 1993 I visited Bosnia with a Granada film crew in connection with the filming of the documentary *We Are All Neighbours;* the film depicts the descent of one village into war. This article is based in part on a paper entitled "Power, Fear and Ethnicity in Bosnia-Herzegovina: Or Forging National Communities through War," which I presented at a seminar at the Weatherhead Center for International Studies at Harvard University in April 1999. While working on the article, I enjoyed the friendly hospitality and inspiring atmosphere of the U.S. Institute of Peace, where I was a guest scholar. I dedicate this article to Peter Galbraith, who acted to make the voices of the survivors of genocide heard when others failed, and who worked hard to prevent another Srebrenica.

1. The concept of nationality in the socialist multiethnic states such as Yugoslavia differed significantly in meaning from that used within Western European discourse. Although in Western Europe citizenship and nationality are synonyms and nationality refers to the relation of a person to a state, in the multiethnic former socialist states national identity was different from, and additional to, citizenship. Thus, for instance, everybody held Yugoslav citizenship, but no one held Yugoslav nationality. The term *nationality* is still used to refer to one of three collective identities—Bosniac, Croat, or Serb—and not to citizenship in Bosnia-Herzegovina after the breakup of Yugoslavia. This particular use of the concepts of nationality and nation is perhaps particularly confusing to native speakers of American English, since *nation* and *state* are often used interchangeably. (For a more lengthy discussion of the nationalities system in the former Yugoslavia, see Bringa 1995:22–26.)

2. Schabas points to the problem in defining the ethnic, religious, etc. group referred to in the Genocide Convention: "At the heart of the definition, it would seem, is the fact that it is the perpetrator who had defined or identified the group for destructions" (1999:3). And thus, I would add, who belongs to that group and who does not.

3. UNPROFOR is the acronym for the United Nations Protection Force in the former Yugoslavia.

4. At its peak, the airfield was dotted with tents that housed more than twenty thousand refugees from the Srebrenica area. About seventeen thousand were subsequently moved to collective centers outside the base. At the time I was there, approximately six thousand refugees remained at the airfield.

5. During the war in Bosnia, I learned that people who portray themselves as victims of atrocities that have not taken place, or that did not involve them, use language characterized by vagueness—particularly as far as time, place, and personal pronouns are concerned. They also will use a vocabulary and syntax that stylistically are not their own but are more reminiscent of a politician's language, or of a propaganda report in the nationalist media.

6. The number of Muslim men and boys who went missing after the Bosnian Serb Army takeover of Srebrenica on July 11, 1995, is believed to be 7500 or more. At the moment of writing, approximately four thousand bodies have been found in various mass graves by U.N. exhumation teams, but only seventy of those have been positively identified.

7. See in particular David Rhode's book *Endgame: The Betrayal and Fall of Srebrenica;* the 1999 BBC documentary "A Cry from the Grave" by Leslie Woodhead; and the U.N. Srebrenica Report (Report of the Secretary-General pursuant to General Assembly Resolution 53/35-1998).

8. The U.S. ambassador in Zagreb, Peter Galbraith, in the meantime had cabled a strongly worded report repeating the Srebrenica survivor's account of the mass executions and names of some of the places where they had taken place, to the U.S. secretary of state,

Warren Christopher, who immediately dispatched the assistant secretary of state for human rights to Tuzla to corroborate the account. With the names and descriptions of places where the massacres took place now available, the CIA reviewed spy photographs of the area and were able to identify execution sites and mass graves. The U.S. ambassador to the United Nations, Madeleine Albright, consequently presented U.S. government aerial photographs to the U.N. General Assembly and called for air strikes against Bosnian Serb Army positions in Bosnia.

9. The report of the UNPROFOR human rights team is quoted in the U.N. Srebrenica Report VIII:G (383–90). Tadeusz Mazowiecki, special rapporteur of the Commission of Human Rights for the United Nations, resigned in protest after the fall of the U.N. "safe havens" of Srebrenica and Zepa and the failure of the United Nations to protect the population in those "havens" from the onslaught of the Bosnian Serb Army.

10. Annex V Prijedor, IX Conclusions (prepared by Judge Hanne Sophie Greve), in Annex Summaries and Conclusions, Final Report of the United Nations Commission of Experts, December 28, 1994.

11. This is a paraphrase of Radovan Karadžić's utterance. He put forward his threat at a four-day session of the Bosnian Parliament (*Skupština BiH*) to consider a memorandum declaring B-H as a "democratic sovereign state of equal citizens—peoples of B-H—Muslims, Serbs, Croats and members of other nations and nationalities (*naroda* and *narodnosti*) living in it." Radovan Karadžić, who was not a deputy in the parliament, nor did he hold any positions in the government, regularly attended sessions there. "Don't you think that you are not going to lead Bosnia into hell, and probably the Muslim people into disappearance (*nestanak*) because the Muslim people cannot defend itself[?]—[It] is going to war." Alija Izetbegovic, the president of the collective presidency replied: "Muslim people will not raise its hand against anyone, but it will defend itself energetically and it won't as Karadžić said disappear. We really don't have an intention to live in a Yugoslavia that is being built on messages like this one that Mr. Karadžić just gave us" (Oslobodjenje, Sarajevo, October 15, 1991; see also Branka Magaš and Ivo Zanić, eds., *Rat u Hrvatskoj i Bosni i Hercegovini 1991–1995* [London: Bosnian Institute, 1999]).

12. This encounter between Ratko Mladić and the Srebrenica schoolteacher is shown in "A Cry from the Grave," the BBC documentary by Leslie Woodhead.

13. See Final Report of the United Nations Commission of Experts, Annex IV.

14. Ibid., Annex V.

15. The official history of the war in Sarajevo is that a young female student from Dubrovnik, Suada Delberović, was its first victim. The bridge where she was killed has been named after her, and a plaque commemorating her was fixed to the railings. However, in the spring of 2001, the plaque was taken down and reappeared with another name added— that of a young woman and mother, Olga Sučić, who also was killed on the bridge that day. She had been taking part in the same demonstration for peaceful coexistence, on April 5, 1992, as Suada. Suada and Olga were from different ethnic origins, one Bosniac (Muslim) and the other Serb (Orthodox). Moments before she was killed by a sniper, Olga had told a television journalist covering the peace demonstration: "I am the mother of two children, and I will defend this city" (*Oslobodjenje,* March 8, 2001).

16. Ibid. compares the 1991 population census figures for *opština* (municipality) Prijedor with the results of a population count in June 1993. It shows the number of Muslims reduced from 49,454 to 6,124; the number of Croats reduced from 6,300 to 3,169; and "Others" from 8,971 to 2,621 (the non-Serb population in the same period increased from 47,745 to 53,637).

17. Several Bosnian Serbs have been publicly indicted for genocide by the International Criminal Tribunal for the former Yugoslavia in The Hague. In addition to the indictments of the commanders of the death camps (at Luka, Keraterm, and Omarska), several of the Bosnian Serb military and political leaders have been indicted for genocide for their alleged role in directing the violent persecution and killing of non-Serbs in areas of Bosnia-Herzegovina under their control. Three men have, at the moment of this writing, been indicted for their alleged role in the genocide following the takeover of Srebrenica in Eastern Bosnia. Of the nine Serbs who have been indicted for genocide, six have been arrested and either stand or await trial in The Hague (and one accused has been acquitted). Radovan Karadžić (the leader of the Bosnian Serb Nationalist Party) and Ratko Mladić (the general of the Bosnian Serb Army) are among the three who are still at large. For further details on the indictments, see the U.N. International Criminal Tribunal's website at www.un.org/icty /index.html.

18. *Bosniac* is the official term for Bosnian Muslim; it is used in both the 1994 Washington Agreement and the 1995 Dayton Agreement. The Bosnian Muslim leadership favored the revived, historical term *Bosniac* in order to avoid the confusion and misconceptions that *Muslim* seems to have created abroad. Furthermore, it would establish both a conceptual and a historical link between Bosnian Muslims and Bosnia-Herzegovina as a territory and as a geopolitical unit. In Tito's Yugoslavia, *Muslim* referred to a nationality in the same way as Croat and Serb did. When *Muslim* was used to refer to a religious identity, it was written with a lower-case "m." (For a further discussion of ethnonyms and the collective Bosnian Muslim identity question, see Bringa 1995:30–36).

19. Numbers vary according to the source. The official number of the BiH authorities in Sarajevo is 328,000 people dead or disappeared. (This number is quoted in Murat Praso, "Demographic Consequences of the 1992–95 War," *Most (Mostar)* 93 (March–April 1996). More conservative sources quote about 200,000 dead or disappeared.

20. See *Bosnia and Herzegovina: War—Damaged Residential Buildings and Status on Repair/Reconstruction and Funding Requirements* (Sarajevo: International Management Group [IMG], Housing Sector Task Force, January 1999).

21. In early 1995, when Sarajevo had endured almost three years under siege, the Sarajevo daily *Oslobodjenje* printed a cartoon. It shows a citizen of Sarajevo dying on the pavement after being hit by a shell (or perhaps a sniper's bullet). Leaning over him is a person in a U.N. helmet holding out a package of "humanitarian aid." The caption reads: "Please let me feed him first." For the inhabitants of besieged Sarajevo, the U.N. peacekeeping mission was appearing increasingly absurd.

22. The "Memorandum" (drafted by the novelist and nationalist dissident under Tito, Dobrica Ćosić) is a fifty-page-long document "elaborating on two nationalist themes, the victimization of Serbia and Serbs and the conspiracy on non-Serb Communist leaders against Serbia" (Pavković 1997:89). The "Memorandum" was condemned by the Serbian party leadership as nationalistic, but it struck a chord among many disillusioned Serbs and caused a stir in the other republics where Serbian dominance and nationalism were feared. Among Yugoslavia scholars it is considered the road map to post-Tito Serbian nationalism and the ideological underpinnings for the idea of a Greater Serbia. The document can be found in *Former Yugoslavia through Documents: From Its Dissolution to Peace Settlements,* ed. Snezana Trifunovska (The Hague: University of Nijmegen, Martinus Nijhoff Publ., 1999).

23. Roger Cohen discussed Milošević's use of the word *genocide* in his 1999 lecture at the Holocaust Museum in Washington, D.C.

24. These two points were made by Roger Cohen in his lecture at the Holocaust Museum.

25. In many European countries, scholars, journalists, and others who used the word *genocide* when talking about the fate of the non-Serb population in Northern and Eastern Bosnia were dismissed as Muslim propagandists (or worse, accused of upsetting the "peace-process"). It was not until the findings and conclusions in the Final Report of the Commission of Experts (for the International Criminal Tribunal) were made public that it gradually became acceptable to talk about genocide in connection with the crimes that had taken place in Eastern and Northern Bosnia.

26. I have been confronted with these views in connection with lectures I have given at various academic institutions in Europe and the United States. But the population-transfers-to-forward-peace argument has also been put forward by academics in international political science and policy journals. For two examples, see John Mearsheimer and Robert Rape, "The Answer: A Partition Plan for Bosnia," *New Republic* (June 14, 1993):22–28; Chaim Kaufman, "Possible and Impossible Solutions to Ethnic Civil Wars," *International Security* 20(4):136–75.

27. For a similar argument and further discussion, see Gagnon, forthcoming. For examples of perceptions of ethnicity on the ground, see Bringa 1995.

28. Natasha Tesanović of Independent Alternative Television, quoted in "The Changing Face of Republika Srpska," Institute of War and Peace Research, May 2000.

29. "Clash of civilizations" refers to the title of Samuel Huntington's 1996 book, *The Clash of Civilizations and the Remaking of World Order.* His delineation of the world into different civilizational zones has been embraced by both politicians and academics seeking an explanatory framework for the wars in the former Yugoslavia.

30. I owe this formulation to John Borneman. The issue involved in the transition of power such as succession, legitimacy, and mode of authority just prior to and particularly after Tito's death is the subject of my article "The Peaceful Death of Tito and the Violent End of Titoism," in John Borneman, ed., *Death of the Father: An Anthropology of Closure in Political Authority,* forthcoming. Issues concerning transition of authority and political legitimacy in paternalistic and authoritarian states, including the former Yugoslavia are presented at a website accompanying the forthcoming book at http://cid.library.cornell.edu/DOF.

31. "Annex III-Military Structure, Strategy and Tactics of the Warring Factions," in Final Report of the United Nations Commission of Experts: Annex and Summaries, December 28, 1994.

32. This point is also made by Catherine Verdery in her 1999 book.

33. In 1990 a group of Serbs led by Christian Orthodox clergy went to the Surmanci ravine in Herzegovina where about five hundred Serb women, young girls, and children under the age of fifteen from the village of Prebilovici were hurled to their deaths down a four-hundred-foot pit by local Ustasha men in 1941. They wanted to excavate the bones and give them a Christian Orthodox burial in Serbian soil. "The bones lay in the depths until 1961, when the government . . . raised a memorial to the dead and sealed the pit with concrete" (Hall 1994:207). This pit was excavated along with twelve others in Herzegovina. "Afterwards, the hole was resealed and in the new cover was embedded a black marble Orthodox cross. Accompanied by Serbian television teams, a procession of pickup trucks transported the bones, in hundreds of small caskets draped with the Serbian coat of arms . . . to the old site of Prebilovici" (ibid.:208).

34. The former Yugoslavia was a multinational federation with a three-tier system of national group rights. The first category was the *Jugoslovenski narodi* (Yugoslav "peoples" or "nations"), among which were the Serbs, Croats, and Muslims. Each had a "national home" based in one of Yugoslavia's six republics (except Serbs and Croats, who had two: Serbia and Croatia, respectively, plus Bosnia-Herzegovina) and a constitutional right to equal political representation.

35. Slobodan Milošević gave this speech at the Congress of his Socialist Party of Serbia. See RFE/RL (Radio Free Europe/Radio Liberty) Balkan Report, vol. 4. no. 15, February 22, 2000.

36. For a discussion of ethnicity as a "demobilizer" in the conflict, see Gagnon 1995, 1996.

37. Michael Herzfeld inspired this point.

38. The marker stone for a memorial and cemetery in Potočari was uncovered during a ceremony on July 11, 2001, on the sixth anniversary of the Srebrenica genocide. Some thirteen hundred policemen, including antiriot units (from Republika Srpska and the U.N. international police force) were deployed at the ceremony. The three-ton marble stone was unveiled by five women from Srebrenica whose husbands, sons, and other male relatives were killed in the massacres. The ceremony was attended by more than three thousand people, including survivors, relatives of those massacred, and representatives of the international community and of the local authorities from the Federation half of B-H. Not a single official from the Republika Srpska was, however, present at the ceremony (see Office of the High Representative B-H Media Round-up 11/07 and 12/07/2001 at www.ohr.int).

39. See "The Changing Face of Republika Srpska," Institute of War and Peace Research Report, May 2000.

BIBLIOGRAPHY

Borneman, John. Forthcoming. "Introduction." In *Death of the Father: An Anthropology of Closure in Political Anthropology.* John Borneman, ed.

Bringa, Tone. 1995. *Being Muslim the Bosnian Way: Identity and Community in a Central Bosnian Village.* Princeton: Princeton University Press.

———. 1996. "The Bosniac-Croat Federation: The Achilles Heel of the Dayton Agreement." Nordisk Øst-Forum, 2, [published in Norwegian; original text in English available from the author on request].

———. Forthcoming. "The Peaceful Death of Tito and the Violent End of Titoism." In *Death of the Father: An Anthropology of Closure in Political Anthropology.* John Borneman, ed.

Denitch, Bette. 1994. "Dismembering Yugoslavia: Nationalist Ideologies and the Symbolic Revival of Genocide." *American Ethnologist* 21:367–90.

Gagnon, V. P., Jr. 1995. "Ethnic Nationalism and International Conflict: The Case of Serbia." *International Security* 19(3) (winter 1994/95):130–66.

———. 1996. "Ethnic Conflict as Demobilizer: The Case of Serbia." Cornell University, Institute for European Studies Working Paper, 96(1). http://www.ithaca.edu/gagnon/articles/demobil.

———. Forthcoming. *The Yugoslav Wars of the 1990s: A Critical Reexamination of "Ethnic Conflict."*

Glenny, Misha. 1993. *The Fall of Yugoslavia: The Third Balkan War.* London: Penguin.

Gordy, Eric. 1999. *The Culture of Power in Serbia: Nationalism and the Destruction of Alternatives.* University Park: Pennsylvania State University Press.

Gutman, Roy. 1993. *A Witness to Genocide.* New York: Macmillan.

Hall, Brian. 1994. *The Impossible Country: A Journey through the Last Days of Yugoslavia.* Boston: David R. Godine.

Letica, Bartoland Slaven. 1997. *Postmodernity and Genocide in Bosnia: "Ethnic Cleansing": The Great Fraud of our Time.* Zagreb: Naklada Jesenski i Turk.

Pavković, Aleksandar. 1997. *The Fragmentation of Yugoslavia: Nationalism in a Multinational State.* Basingstoke: Macmillan.

Povrzanović, Maja. 1997. "Identities in War: Embodiments of Violence and Places of Belonging." *Ethnologia Europaea, Journal of European Ethnology* 27(2).

Rhode, David. 1997. *Endgame: The Betrayal and Fall of Srebrenica: Europe's Worst Massacre since World War II.* New York: Farrar, Strauss and Giroux.

Schabas, William. 1999. "The Genocide Convention at Fifty." United States Institute of Peace Special Report. January 1999.

Sells, Michael. 1996. *The Bridge Betrayed: Religion and Genocide in Bosnia.* Berkeley: University of California Press.

Silber, Laura, and Allan Little. 1996. *Yugoslavia: Death of a Nation.* London: Penguin.

Stolcke, Verena. 1995. "Talking Culture—New Boundaries, New Rhetorics of Exclusion in Europe." *Current Anthropology* 36(1):1–24.

Thompson, Mark. 1992. *A Paper House: The Ending of Yugoslavia.* London: Vintage.

Verdery, Catherine. 1999. *The Political Lives of Dead Bodies: Reburial and Postsocialist Change.* New York: Columbia University Press.

Vulliamy, Ed. 1994. *Seasons in Hell: Understanding Bosnia's War.* London: Simon and Schuster.

Zwick, Peter. 1983. *National Communism.* Boulder, Colo.: Westview Press.

REPORTS

All these reports may be found at the Bridge Betrayed War Crimes Reports Page website by Professor Michael Sells at www.haverford.edu/relg/sells.

Final Report of the United Nations Commission of Experts, established pursuant to Security Council resolution 780 (1992) Annex Summaries and Conclusions. S/1994/674/Add. 2 (Vol. I), December 28, 1994. (www.ess.uwe.ac.uk/comexpert/ANX/summary.htm)

Final Report on the Situation of Human Rights in the Territory of the Former Yugoslavia, submitted by Tadeusz Mazowiecki, Special Rapporteur of the Commission on Human Rights, August 22, 1995.

Report of the Secretary-General pursuant to General Assembly Resolution 53/35 (1998). Srebrenica Report.

PART FOUR

Genocide's Wake

Trauma, Memory, Coping, and Renewal

9

Archives of Violence

The Holocaust and the German Politics of Memory

Uli Linke

This essay is an attempt to understand the transformative potential of public memory. My focus is on the modalities of symbolic violence in German culture after 1945 and their historical nexus with Nazism and genocide. My research suggests that German public memory is infused with visions of corporeal violence that have persisted in a more or less unbroken trajectory from the Third Reich until today. In postwar West Germany, Nazism and the murder of Jews are contested and highly charged domains of cultural reproduction. The horror of the past inspires an intense fascination that generates both desire and repulsion. In a diversity of public domains (everyday life, mass media, politics, and leftist protest), the past is brought into focus through violent iconotropic repertoires that are seized for the contemporary construction of identity and difference. My work suggests that the National Socialist phantasms of race, with their tropes of blood, body, and contagion, continue to organize German political thought to the present day. Contemporary Germans invest bodies and physicalities with meanings that derive significance from historical memory: of Nazi atrocities, the Holocaust, and the Judeocide. These events are implanted in public memory through a repertoire of images and symbols, which, by nature of the violence of representation, sustain and even reproduce the culture of the past. Such mimetic evocations, while often tangibly inscribed on bodies, remain below the level of conscious acknowledgment because they exist in disguised or highly aestheticized form.

My analysis of German memory practices proceeds by examination of a basic, organizing metaphor: the body. In post-Holocaust Germany, standing in the midst of the "ruins of culture" after Auschwitz, the body endures as a central icon of the past. Yet as Theodor W. Adorno suggests, this relation between body, history, and memory is skewed and pathological: "In all instances, where historical consciousness has been mutilated or maimed, it is hurled back onto the body and the sphere of bodiliness in rigid form [*Gestalt*], inclined to violence ... even through the terror of language, . . . as if the gestures of speech were those of a barely controlled bodily violence" (1969:91–92). Traumatized historical consciousness is housed in memory icons of the human body, and these images are in turn connected to cultural agency and political practice. In this chapter, in short, I examine how a specific form of "catastrophic nationalism" (Geyer 2001), which culminated in global war and genocide, reverberates in German body memory.

BODY MEMORY AND THE GERMAN NATION

German nation-building after 1945 was driven by the formative power of a public imaginary that sought to anesthetize the trauma of war and violence. Indeed, postwar nationhood was dramatically confronted with the aftermath of the Third Reich: with the reality of wounded bodies, ruined landscapes, and mountains of corpses (Barnouw 1996). But in the complex attempts at national reconstruction, the gaze of ordinary Germans turned away from the past: the "powerfully visible enormity of the atrocities *and* the burden of their responsibility for these acts" (ibid.:xiv). The postwar experience, marked by mass dislocation, urban devastation, and political uncertainty, produced an overwhelming sense of victimization: Germans came to see themselves as victims of 'war, not as perpetrators of Judeocide (Bartov 1998). Moreover, with the conclusion of the Nuremberg trials, which led to the execution of prominent Nazi officials, the West German parliament began to pursue a "politics of the past" that was to impose a further closure of history: former Nazi civil servants, including judges, bureaucrats, and teachers, were exonerated by an act of amnesty (Frei 1997). Such procedures of postwar state formation were synchronized with the recuperation of a retrograde archaism of national state culture: older sediments of a cultural aesthetic of state violence were transposed in the remetaphorization of the political landscape. The deforming effects of historical trauma were thus domesticated by implanting into the political vernacular of everyday life residual memories of national belonging: ethnic Germanness, organic (blood) unity, and a racial logic of citizenship.

Seeing nationalism as a generalized condition of the modern political world, Liisa Malkki suggests "that the widely held common sense assumptions linking people to place, and nation to territory, are not simply territorializing but deeply metaphysical" (1996:437). My analysis of the politics of German memory offers a schematic exploration of further aspects of this metaphysics. In postwar West Germany, national identity came to be dissociated from the very fixities of place that are normally associated with the spatial confines of the modern nation-state. The formation of German nationhood was complicated by a corporeal imaginary: blood, bodies, genealogies. German images of "the national order of things" (Malkki 1995b) seem to rest on metaphors of the human organism and the body. Among the potent metaphors is blood (Brubaker 1992; Borneman 1992b). Nationality is imagined as a "flow of blood," a unity of substance (Linke 1999a). Such metaphors are thought to "denote something to which one is naturally tied" (Anderson 1983:131). Thinking about the German nation takes the form of origins, ancestries, and racial lines, which are *naturalizing* images: a genealogical form of thought.

Much recent work in anthropology and related fields has focused on the processes whereby such mythographies of origin and ancestry are constructed and maintained by states or national elites (Anderson 1983; Hobsbawm and Ranger 1983; Linke 1997a). Here I focus on powerful metaphoric practices in German public life and examine how media discourse, body practice, and political language are deployed both to endure and act upon the volatile boundary conditions of nationhood in postwar Germany. My emphasis is on the location of violent history in German political memory, and I inquire how bodies, as racial constructs and potential sites of domination, are mobilized in the public discourse of commemoration and forgetting. My aim is to shed light on the evasions of collective memory in postwar West Germany, where the feminized body of the outsider (foreigner, refugee, other) has been reclaimed as a signifier of race and contagion; where violence defines a new corporal topography, linked to the murderous elimination of refugees and immigrants; and where notions of racial alterity and gendered difference are publicly constructed through iconographic images of blood and liquidation.

In earlier works (Linke 1995, 1997b, 1999a), I traced the (trans)formation of these conceptual models from the turn of the century through the postunification era, thus illuminating the persistence of German ideas about racial purity and contamination. I proposed that modern forms of violence are engendered through "regimes of representation" that are to some extent mimetic, a source of self-formation, both within the historical unconscious and the fabric of the social world (de Lauretis 1989; Feldman 1997). I began by drawing attention to the racist biomedical visions of blood that emerged under fascism. The representational violence of such blood imagery, which was firmly implanted in the popular imagination through political propaganda, emerged as a prelude to racial liquidation. Genealogies of blood were medicalized, conceived as sources of contamination that needed to be expunged through violent bloodletting. Documenting cultural continuities after 1945, I explored the implications of a racialist politics of blood for the German nation-building process in the postwar period. I analyzed more closely the linkages of blood to gendered forms of violence, focusing on the central role of masculinity and militarism for a German nationalist imaginary. Images of blood, women, and contagion became fused in fascist visions of a bio-organic unity of German nationhood. By exploring the metaphoric extensions of such a "symbolics of blood" in postwar German culture, I attempted to show how easily a misogynist militarism was reconfigured to (re)produce a violent body politic that legitimated the brutalization of immigrants and refugees (Linke 1997b, 1999a). Throughout my work, I emphasized the interplay of race and gender against the background of medical models, documenting how fears of "natural disasters" (women, Jews, refugees) and medical pathologies such as dirt and infection—bodily infestations—were continuously recycled to reinforce a racialist postmodern. Although in postwar West Germany, such corporeal landscapes are forged in the course of political battles over history and memory, the racial logic of exclusion is synchronized with a recuperation of the German body.

In this chapter, I attempt to show (through a critical analysis of German public memory) the highly ambivalent and stressed relation of the national order to the modern, and its eventual escape from modernity through the essentialisms of blood, race, and body. My ethnographic material derives from a diversity of historical sources, not only to illustrate the diachrony of events but also to highlight the fact that German history and memory overlap and appear as repetition—a frozen continuum—in which certain templates and motifs are re-encountered or return again and again, and where the new is mediated by a refurbished sameness via the essentializing metaphors of race: a tropology of corporeality. This mode of historicization, of tracing the anatomy of German nationhood, exposes past experience as a pathology, a traumatic syndrome.

BORDERS OF SHAME: MEMORY, HISTORY, AND OPPOSITION

What were the effects of Nazism on German public culture? How was the past, specifically the murder of Jews, configured in the imagination, language, and body practices of a postwar generation that was firmly committed to the restoration of a nonviolent democratic society? Or was the social world after 1945 in fact "the same world that produced (and keeps producing) genocide" (Bartov 1998:75), a claim perhaps supported by the overt manifestations of racial hatred and anti-Semitism that reappeared in the postwar period and the late twentieth century (Link 1983; Gerhard 1992, 1994; Linke 1997b; Kurthen et al. 1997)? Although the concentration camps, particularly Auschwitz, have become a dominant cultural symbol around which guilt, Germanness, and identity cohere in the national imagination of the postwar German state (Borneman 1992a; Maier 1989), post-Holocaust memory formations remain a critical issue. Germans tend to practice forgetting with regard to their past, particularly with regard to the murder of the Jews. The problem of collective memory and its evasions in postwar German politics has been extensively documented by cultural historians (Berenbaum and Peck 1998; Geyer 1996; Hartman 1994; Friedländer 1992; Grossmann 1995; Baldwin 1990).[1] Denial and concealment are clearly efforts to deal with a painful, guilt-producing subject. The excesses of inhumanity and brutal murder that occurred during the Third Reich were difficult to confront by a nation defeated in war. For many years after 1945, countless Germans pleaded ignorance of the death camps or claimed that the atrocities never happened at all (Vidal-Naquet 1992; Lipstadt 1993). The horror of the Judeocide was either repressed or silenced. And while the victimization of Jews was denied, as Omer Bartov points out, Nazi criminality was repeatedly associated with the *suffering of the Germans:*

> Germans experienced the last phases of World War II and its immediate aftermath as a period of mass victimization. Indeed, Germany's remarkable reconstruction was predicated both on repressing the memory of the Nazi regime's victims and on the

assumed existence of an array of new enemies, foreign and domestic, visible and elusive. Assertions of victimhood had the added benefit of suggesting parallels between the Germans and their own victims. Thus, if the Nazis strove to ensure the health and prosperity of the nation by eliminating the Jews, postwar Germany strove to neutralize the memory of the Jews' destruction so as to ensure its own physical and psychological restoration. (Bartov 1998:788)

Any attempt to tackle this denial of history on the part of the postwar generation (that is, the sons and daughters of those who had known or played a part in Nazism) was countered with silence (Moeller 1996, 1997; Naumann 1996; Markovits and Reich 1997).[2] Collective shame became a central issue for these younger Germans, who refused responsibility for the atrocities committed by their elders. The Holocaust was defined as an event carried out by others: the Nazis, members of another generation, one's parents or grandparents.[3] While refuting accountability for the horrors of the past, in particular for the murder of the Jews, these younger Germans experienced their own suffering and shame very keenly. As individuals, and as a group, they began to identify with the fate of the Jews insofar as both were victimized, although in different ways, by Nazism: "In this manner, the perpetrators of genocide were associated with the destroyers of Germany, while the Jewish victims were associated with German victims, without, however, creating the same kind of empathy" (Bartov 1998:790). Opposition to and rebellion against a murderous past were used by these young Germans as organizing tropes in their ongoing battles with identity and memory.

In postwar West Germany, intergenerational frictions over issues of morality, body, and sex were appropriated as "sites" where such battles could be waged, both in public and in private, and at which younger Germans "worked through their anxieties about their [specific] relationship to the mass murder in the nation's recent past" (Herzog 1998:442). Interestingly, in the experience of many young Germans, the entry into adulthood was somehow linked to their access to forbidden knowledge, their induction into the repressed memories of genocide. In the following example, Barbara Köster, a leftist 1968er activist, remembers "her own and her generation's coming-of-age" (ibid.:442) as a *rite of passage,* staged by detour to the past:

I was raised in the Adenauer years, a time dominated by a horrible moral conformism, against which we naturally rebelled. We wanted to flee from the white Sunday gloves, to run from the way one had to hide the fingernails behind the back if they weren't above reproach. Finally then we threw away our bras as well. . . . For a long time I had severe altercations with my parents and fought against the fascist heritage they forced on me. At first I rejected their authoritarian and puritanical conception of child-rearing, but soon we came into conflict over a more serious topic: the persecution of the Jews. I identified with the Jews, because I felt myself to be persecuted by my family. (Köster 1987:244)[4]

Köster's claim to adulthood, which provoked her rebellion against her parents, relied on "a disturbing and simplistic, even offensive, appropriation of the suffering of others. . . . [But] Köster (who eventually visited Israel, which caused the final break with her parents) was not alone" (Herzog 1998:442 n. 113). The "persecution of the Jews," she recalls, "was a permanent and painful topic, and it was only when I got to know other students that I understood that this was not just my problem, that the shame about the persecution of the Jews had brought many to rebel against parental authority!" (Köster 1987:244).[5] During the 1960s, student rebels, in their private and public battles, perpetually invoked the mass murder of Jews as a representational sign: the Judeocide became a signifier of German shame, of their own suffering, a tactic that according to Herzog (1998:444) ultimately "blocked" and subverted "direct engagement with the racial politics" of the Third Reich.

Leftists and conservatives alike deployed Holocaust images in their political battles, "bludgeoning each other with the country's past."[6] The invocation of Auschwitz and the Third Reich, according to Herzog (1998:440), "became a sort of *lingua franca* of postwar West German political culture, saturating ideological conflict over all manner of issues. Thus, for instance, antinuclear activists from the 1950s to the 1980s warned that nuclear war would mean 'a burning oven far more imposing than the most terrible burning ovens of the SS-camps,'[7] or a catastrophe compared to which 'Auschwitz and Treblinka were child's play.'[8] Or [another example from the 1970s describes] global economic injustice as 'a murderous conspiracy measured against which the consequences of Hitler's 'final solution' seem positively charming.'[9]" What do we make of such pronouncements that relate the magnitude of a nuclear disaster or the trauma of economic injustice to Judeocide? While this sort of rhetoric was clearly meant to break open the taboo of the past, to shock and startle a complacent German public with the provocative invocation of Nazi crimes, as Herzog argues, these verbal tactics also reveal that the murder of Jews became an auxiliary concern in a discourse dominated by identity politics and the crisis of political self-definition:

> In a peculiar but crucial way the Holocaust is at once absent *and* present in all that talk. . . . [T]he centrality of the Judeocide to the Third Reich is the very [subject] that is constantly being evaded when facile comparisons are put forward in the context of other political agendas, [but] it is also—however paradoxically—precisely the Holocaust's existence that allows self-definitions in opposition to fascism to serve as a sort of shorthand to anchor and assert the legitimacy and morality of one's own claims. (Herzog 1998:443)

But at the same time, this rhetorical preoccupation with Judeocide, often invoked "in an analogic or metaphorical way," was suggestive of a deeper pain—the immense historical burden—that many younger Germans experienced and longed to alleviate by "substitution or displacement" (ibid.:441).

THE NAKED BODY: COUNTERMEMORY AND
THE OPTICS OF SHAME

In postwar West Germany during the 1960s, the public remembrance of violent history was tied to the terrain of the body: memory practices were transported into body space. The disclosure of Nazi violence and the shifting borders of shame were structured by a new corporeal aesthetic. The naked body became an iconographic tool with which leftist activists could proclaim their opposition to Nazism. Public displays of nudity were contrasted with images of political order, bourgeois authority patterns, conformity, and consumption—that is, tropes of the Nazi state and the economic structures that had produced fascism. "Student radicals were among the most open and provocative defenders of the new publicity of sexual styles and practices and most explicitly made the case that sexual repressiveness was the bulwark of a politically and economically repressive society" (Herzog 1998:395). The practice of public nudity, understood as a sign of liberation, emerged as an attempt at social transformation, setting into motion a rebellious process of countermemory production.

The rejection of consumer capitalism, the commitment to democratic values, and an opening of bourgeois morality by "furthering the sexual revolution" were central themes of the political rebellion "of the sixties and seventies," a rebellion that "was closely intertwined with the New Left's effort to bring the subjects of fascism and the Third Reich . . . into public discussion" (ibid.:394–95).[10] Sexual liberation, and nudity, were closely linked to "political revolution":

> [The West German Left was] appalled by many forms of social and political injustice . . . and supported a broad array of resistance struggles, both in the Third World and at home. The damaging consequences of capitalism, racism, imperialism, and militarism worldwide were major preoccupations, and . . . the war in Vietnam [and] the struggles of the Palestinians . . . figured as prominently [in leftist activism] as did the legacy of Auschwitz. . . . It was ultimately no coincidence that members of the West German generation of 1968 repeatedly made reference to the Third Reich, and to the Holocaust, in their battles with each other and with members of their parents' generation. (ibid.:395)

Such battles often raged over the sexual mores and sexual politics of bourgeois culture, as Herzog (1998) documents, and the links between Nazi libidinal pathologies and genocide.

Whereas "church and political leaders" presented "sexual sobriety as the most effective cure for the nation's larger guilt and moral crisis,"[11] the New Left focused on Nazism's "sexual politics as inseparable from" the legacy of the Judeocide: "Throughout their programmatic writings on sex, members of this generation returned frequently to the problems of genocide and brutality within the concentration camps, suggesting that it was male sexual repression that engendered the Nazi capacity for cruelty and mass murder" (ibid.:397). The intense antifascism of the German New Left was centrally preoccupied with "assaults on male sexuality" because of the perceived connection between men's "release of libido" and "evil" (Herzog 1998:399; see also Theweleit 1987; Heider 1986; Preuss-Lausitz 1989; Siepmann 1984): "One noteworthy feature of so many of the debates within the left scene about sex and about sex and fascism [was] their focus on the male body and male desires and anxieties in particular. In postwar West German struggles over various sexual lessons of Nazism, male bodies were called to a kind of public visibility and accountability that most scholars of the history of sexuality generally assume to be reserved for women" (Herzog 1998:398). Remarkable is "the obsessiveness," says Herzog (ibid.:399), "with which [this postwar generation] tried to make public some of the most intimate ways in which men related to their own bodies and the bodies of others." The public exposure of the male body, including men's sexual desires, became a political agenda in leftists' attempts to reform gender relations and revolutionize the bourgeois/fascist individual (Bookhagen et al. 1969:92; Dürr 1994:418–20). By 1968, various socialist collectives, including the infamous *Kommune 2* in West Berlin, had integrated radical male nudity into both their domestic lifestyle and their public political program.

The West German Left had initiated such nudist body practices in part, as Herzog (1998:398) put it, "to strengthen their case for sexual liberation with the most shocking metaphors available" (see Figure 9.1):

> One group that did so—with spectacular flair—were the members of the *Kommune 1*, a small but endlessly publicized and debated experiment in communal living and anarcho-radicalism launched in Berlin in 1966. A classic example of the *Kommune 1*'s provocative style was provided by the photo of its members—including one of the two children living with them—distributed by the members themselves on a self-promotional brochure. . . . This photo has been reprinted many times—usually in a spirit of humor and/or nostalgia—and now counts as one of the icons of this era (ibid.:404–6, 405).[12]

What was the political subtext of this portrait of collective nudity? Some twenty years later, in 1988, as noted by Herzog, the former leader of the Socialist Student Union (Sozialistischer Deutscher Studentenbund—SDS), Reimut Reiche, interpreted the photo as follows:

> Consciously this photo-scene was meant to re-create and expose a police house-search of the Kommune 1. And yet these women and men stand there as if in an aesthetically staged, unconscious identification with the victims of their parents and at the same time mocking these victims by making the predetermined message of the picture one of sexual liberation. Thereby they simultaneously remain unconsciously identified with the consciously rejected perpetrator-parents. "Sexuality makes you free" fits with this picture as well as "Work makes you free" fits with Auschwitz. (Reiche 1988:65)[13]

Commenting on this persistent tactic by the German New Left to represent instances of their own political victimization in terms of Judeocide and Auschwitz, cultural historian Dagmar Herzog (1998) concludes:

Figure 9.1 "Naked Maoists before a Naked Wall": Members of the *Kommune 1*—A Socialist Collective of Young Maoists, West Berlin 1967. From a brochure by the *Kommune 1*. When reprinted in German newsmagazines, the nude bodies were retouched to erase visual signifiers of gender and sex (see Panorama 1967: 20; Spiegel 1999a:171; Stiftung Haus der Geschichte 1998: 49). Courtesy Spiegel-Verlag Rudolf Augstein GmbH, Hamburg, Germany. Photograph copyright Thomas Hesterberg.

> The apparent inability to leave the past behind—indeed, the apparently unquench-
> able urge to bring it up over and over again precisely in the context of sexual rela-
> tions—not only reveals how intense was the felt need to invert the sexual lessons of
> Nazism drawn by their parents' generation but also, and perhaps even more signifi-
> cantly, suggests something about the difficulty of theorizing a sexual revolution—of
> connecting pleasure and goodness, sex and societal justice [nudity and freedom]—in
> a country in which only a generation earlier pleasure had been so intimately tied in
> with evil. (p. 400)

The mnemotechniques of genocide, as practiced by the West German Left, re-
made the body into a public site of contestation. Retrieved from the dark under-
ground spaces, where the state had deposited its records of historical knowledge,
the pathogenic memories of violence were made visible on the topographic surface of the body. The body emerged as a *chronotope* of violence, the material and

temporal figuration on a landscape, "where time takes on flesh and becomes visible for human contemplation" (Bakthin 1981:7). And as traumatic history gradually came to visibility, the nude body was treated as revelationary: a repository of German historical consciousness. The exposure of past violence, with its allegories of fragmentation and ruin, placed the naked body on center stage in a monumental theater of public remembrance.

POPULAR NUDITY: CULTURAL PROTEST
AND OPPOSITIONAL MEMORY

The West German revival of body consciousness, and the privileging of nakedness, received its initial impetus from the student rebellion of the 1960s: nationhood was reconfigured through the icon of the naked body. During this era of leftist political protest, public nudity became a central emblem of popular opposition. The unclothed body signified liberation in several ways: it symbolized freedom from the "moral economy" of a consumer capitalism that relied on sexual sobriety as a technique of unremembering the past; it suggested disengagement from the materialist values of a society that equated Western democratization with commodity choice and conspicuous consumption (Boehling 1996; Carter 1997); and it facilitated deliverance from the burden of German history by political opposition to the anesthetizing effects of a booming postwar economy. While rallying against a seemingly repressive and inhumane society, and in defending a new openness of lifestyles, student radicals adopted public nudity as a crucial component of their political activism (Herzog 1998). Such a public showing of naked bodies gave rise to a corporeal aesthetic of Germanness that staged national privilege in relation to society's salient victims: the dead, the subjugated, and the betrayed. Public displays of nudity used the body in a novel dramaturgy of memory: nakedness was staged to expose a violent past and to render visible, on the canvas of the body, the legacies of the Third Reich.

The demand for sexual liberation and the promotion of nudity transported the subjects of Nazism and the Third Reich into public discourse by drawing on an iconography of shame: sexuality, gender relations, and nakedness belong to the affective structure of society, the moral economy of feelings. In their political battles with German history and memory, leftist activists deployed public body exposure to mobilize this residual archaeology of sentiments in several ways. Disillusioned (and angered) by their parents' inability to acknowledge the murder of millions, student protesters used public nakedness as a symbolic expression of their own victimhood and shame. Although this iconography of public nudity greatly facilitated the students' self-representation as casualties of Nazism, full-body exposure also provided a metaphor for the attempt to uncover the past by stripping Germany's murderous epoch of its protective and defensive armor. Public nudity was thus fiercely politicized and emotionally charged. Driven by a programmatic call for sexual liberation, the act of becoming naked in public signified a return to the authentic, the natural, and the unrepressed—that is, to a way of life untainted by the legacy of Auschwitz. Public displays of nudity were perceived as liberatory, both in a social and historical sense. By rejecting the cultural machinations of a murderous civility (clothing, commodities, memories), leftist political activists were rendered "free" of shame.

The program for such a body politic, which employed public nudity as a means of transforming German historical consciousness, was first launched by members of the radical New Left—the founders of various socialist communes in Berlin, Cologne, and Munich in the 1960s. Advocating a lifestyle opposite to that of the Nazi generation, these New Leftists, or "68ers," attempted to eradicate the private and "hidden" in favor of a public intimacy: "to be able to sleep with anyone; to be able to show oneself naked in front of everyone; to be honest without restraint and willing to speak one's mind without hesitation; to call a spade a spade, never to keep anything to oneself, and never to withhold or repress anything" (Guggenberg 1985:1, col. 2). Honesty, sexual freedom, and social equality were among the values that governed the new cult of nudity. The democratization of the German body politic was to be achieved by the public shedding of clothes: "bare skin" emerged as a new kind of uniform, an authentic body armor unmediated by the state or history.

In West Germany, political membership, like national identity, came to be visually encoded, physically grafted onto the skin (Gilman 1982). But this iconolatry of public nudity, which emphasized the "natural innocence" of unclothed bodies, was not devoid of historical meaning. The New Left's rejection of bourgeois culture took form through an ensemble of images that had their origin in the nationalist reform movements of the Weimar Republic. In Germany in the 1920s, the antimodernist revolt gave rise to a racialist vision that was articulated through the body. Corporality became a symbolic site in the nationalist rebellion against modernity: the unnatural, the impermanent, the decadent. Modern styles of life, with their materiality and pornographic sexuality, were "condemned as breeding grounds of immorality and moral sickness" (Mosse 1985:52). The terrain of the city, presumed to induce bodily ills, was set in opposition to the terrain of nature, which was extended to include the natural body: human nudity. German nationalism, with its antiurban focus and its rejection of the modern lifeworld, was marked by a rediscovery of the body. Societal reforms were tied to the reformation of the body. In other words, the German disenchantment with the modern was to be cured by purging the body of its materialist wrappings. Public nudity and the unclothed human body became important signifiers of this new nationalist consciousness.

In West Germany, during the 1960s, the leftist critique of society took form through nearly identical mythographies. The naked (white) body was imagined as a privileged, presocial site of truth. Public nakedness, deployed as a strategy for the promotion of societal reform, emerged as a new terrain of resistance against consumer capitalism. The public exposure of the body, a "marginalized pastime of anti-urbanists at the turn of the century" (Fehrenbach 1994:4), became a prevalent symbol of cultural protest and opposition in postwar German politics. The naked body, stripped of its materialist trappings, stood outside society: an emblem of nature, liberated from violent history. As in the 1920s, public nudity came to symbolize freedom from the deceptive armor of clothing: the naked body was purged of the artificial, the illicit, the erotic. But unlike the aestheticization of white nudity at the turn of the century, the West German critique of postfascist culture was not at first driven by an overtly nationalist agenda. That dimension was to be added later. Rather, the unclothed body (as an authentic truth-claim) was imagined in opposition to society and the state.

Encoded by these messages of opposition and rebellion, public nudity was soon employed by many young Germans as a personal gesture of cultural protest. Seemingly unconventional and provocative, the practice of disrobing in public was widely adopted as a pastime with countercultural significance. Offering a "language of commodity resistance" (Appadurai 1986:30), and inverting the logic of capitalist consumption, public nudity signified freedom from the constraints of modern German society. During the 1970s naked sunbathing established itself as a popular leisure activity, and as urban parks were increasingly thronged by those who preferred to bask in the sun without clothes, full-body exposure became commonplace (see Figure 9.2). By the late 1970s, nudity in public parks was so pervasive that local prohibitions against body exposure were no longer enforced unless "it caused offense": naked sunbathing was exempt from public indecency codes (Brügge 1985:149). The public display of naked bodies, in particular the public viewing of nude men, was rendered acceptable or normal by severing the links with historical memory. Confined to natural settings, the naked body seemed devoid of erotic or libidinal meanings. The topographic surface of the body, regarded as a natural figuration, was purged of its violent historiography.

NAKED MASCULINITY: ICONIC MEMORIES OF VIOLENCE

This perception of the "natural innocence" of naked bodies was contested in 1981, when public nudity moved beyond conventional urban spaces. Transgressing the designated boundaries of parks and park-related greens, nudists began to congregate along river shores, on beaches, in playgrounds, swimming pools, and cemeteries, even city centers. In downtown Munich, for instance, nudes were now often sighted in historic fountains, on streetcars, and in shopping centers (Brügge 1981, 1985). Such a migration of unclothed bodies into the metropolis, the apparent escape of nakedness from "nature," provoked among some segments of the German public deep anxieties about unfettered sexuality.

At issue was the naked male. Exposed masculinity was met with suspicion and unease. Uncovered male genitalia, the public sight of "dangling and swinging penises" (Brügge 1981:150), was experienced by many Germans as a threat. The open display of the phallus was traditionally prohibited, a thematic much belabored by the cultural critics of the 1960s. Among leftists, male nudity had been encour-

Figure 9.2. Nude Sunbathers in an Urban Public Park (Englischer Garten), Munich, 1981. From Brügge (1981:150). Courtesy Spiegel-Verlag Rudolf Augstein GmbH, Hamburg, Germany. Photograph copyright Marcel Fugere, Hamburg.

aged as a way of achieving sexual liberation, but "in order to experience corporal freedom, the unclothed [man] often long[s] to walk upright [thereby exposing himself and his sex], something which is still taboo" (ibid.:151). When voicing their discomfort, passersby conjured visions of rape and sexual violence. "I have to look at that," shouted a sixty-three-year-old housewife when encountering a naked man in public, "and I know what is to come after" (ibid.). As suggested here, public body exposure, specifically that of men, was read by mainstream Germans through images of sexual deviancy and unacceptable behavior (Guggenberg 1985:1, col. 3). In German popular consciousness, the shedding of clothes signified a release from civil restraint, an incitement to general rebellion and political unruliness: the naked male was judged capable of anything.

In order to preempt such anxieties, public displays of nudity had to be carefully packaged to seem natural or artistic: the inoffensive naked body stood outside of history, untainted by society and memory. Such a management of nakedness had several unintended consequences. Although awareness of the sexual side of nude bodies could be repressed by confinement to natural settings, this naturalness had to be rendered civilized and aesthetically pleasing.

"Today nobody cares if thousands take off their clothes in the English Garden [in Munich]. But those thousands, who unintentionally walk by, are forbidden to look. Shame works the other way around: nakedness must be veiled—by beauty" (Friedrich 1986:50). This emphasis on nature as an aesthetic construct worked by exclusion. The naked/natural body was idealized by juxtaposition to the biologically "ugly": "[German] public nudity always implies a privileging of the beautiful and youthful body. The display of nakedness in parks or cafes creates a situation of merciless scrutinization that intensifies the social marginalization of those who are physically disadvantaged: the fat and the overly thin, the misshapen or disfigured, and the handicapped" (Guggenberg 1985:1, col. 4). In West Germany, public nudity came to be governed by an ideology of difference that celebrated the unblemished body as a natural symbol. Naked "nature" was to be rendered free of the unsightly. Natural nakedness, as a quasi-mythical construct, could not be tainted by physiological markers of age, death, or history. Public nudity, like nature, was to present a facade of eternal beauty, unmarred by signs of physical weakness. Such iconographies of essentialized perfection (youth, beauty, and health) were integral to a postwar aesthetic that sought to rehabilitate the German body after Auschwitz.

MEMORY IMPLANTS: A MYTHOGRAPHY OF NATURAL NUDITY

The public display of naked German bodies was symptomatic of a return to a corporal aesthetic that celebrated the essential, natural, and authentic. Not surprisingly, the construction of national identity in postwar West Germany came to be governed by familiar visions of the racial body. The social geography of bare skin, with its symbolic emplacement of national identity and selfhood, made use of iconographic representations of undesirable difference. In an exemplary illustration, a photographic glimpse of a public park in West Berlin, two naked Germans—a man and a woman—are enjoying the tranquil outdoors: domesticated nature (see Figure 9.3). Positioned against a canvas of trees and bushes, the couple is sitting in the shady cover of the foliage. The display of nudity draws on existing social fantasies of "paradise," as indicated by the graffiti on the park's sign. This iconography of public nudity, the imagery of naked German bodies reposed on green grass, enveloped by shrubs and tall grass, hearkens back to early pictorial images of Adam and Eve in the Garden. Nakedness is staged in a mythic realm, in which the unclothed body signifies freedom from original sin. The scene evokes domesticated wilderness, a sense of the sublime world of nature, even as this carefully crafted landscape seeks to shroud the exposed body, repressing it, incarcerating it, and thereby protecting it from the gaze of a nation that does not invite all bodies to be sexual objects. In the photo, nakedness and body exposure are staged as a consumerist retreat. Leisure, experienced as an escape from the collective social world, is displaced to a domesticated natural interior: a mythic realm devoid of struggle or violence.

Figure 9.3. German Nudists and Clothed Third World Others in the "Garden of Eden" (Paradise), West Berlin, 1989. From Wahlprogramm (1989:24). Copyright Bündnis 90/Die Grünen, Berlin. Photograph by Ralph Rieth.

The German nudists (much like Adam and Eve) are positioned as overlords of nature. This is signified by their elevated station. The dark-skinned Mediterranean (Turkish) others, who are assembled in the foreground of the photo, are in tactile contact with the park's natural setting—a tactility that encodes physical labor as the primary relation of these others to nature. Sitting directly on the ground, their physicality is visually accentuated: by their clothing, their cooking of food on a grill, their tending to an open fire. The photographic gaze connects their bodies to images of work and consumption, signifying a dangerous preoccupation with corporal matters—that is, food, labor, and reproduction.

The immigrants, sitting in the middle of the grass, in the foreground of the picture, are rendered highly visible. This position places them on the nation's social periphery, on the margins, on the "outside," while the naked Germans, sitting in the background, partially hidden by the vegetation, are positioned within the nation's innermost center, the "inside," which is encoded as a "natural" domain. White naked bodies, equated with a civilized and privileged state of nature (paradise), can be imagined as sites of an authentic, national interior. The visual emphasis on natural and national privilege, which conceals the historic dimensions of nudity, was crucial in the symbolic reconstruction of the postwar German body politic. Such a reading in corporal aesthetics suggests that, as a terrain of signification, the naked body (like skin color) served as a political icon: not all bodies were equally invited to represent the German nation.

THE NAKED MALE: A MORPHOLOGY
OF FASCIST BODY MEMORY

During the early 1980s, when immigrants and refugees were depicted as an inundating biological threat (Linke 1997b), West German commercial culture began to display white bodies through images that idealized, and visually sculpted, the nude flesh. Often stripped of carnal sensuousness and raw sexuality, the visual desirability of white skin relied on image-constructions that made such bodies appear inaccessible, distant, and unattainable. Invigorating visions of white superiority, the naked, upright body—the Aryan male—stood firm against the feminine onslaught: the foreign flood.

This is suggested by a series of West German advertisements for men's cologne, in which complete male nudity took center stage (Jeske et al. 1987a, 1987b; Schirner 1987; Soltau 1987). Adopting the pose of classic statues, the male models were typically clad only with the scent of the commercial product (see Figure 9.4). The advertisement texts reiterate this point: "He wears Care" or "Care allures/attires" (*zieht an*). The classic beauty of the male nude, with his fortified and hardened body, seems impervious to seduction. Standing immobile, upright, and somewhat remote, the nude models resemble white statues: a perfected masculinity, reminiscent of the classic (Aryan) ideal.

These images of male nudity were introduced by German advertisers as a cultural provocation: The naked man had market value and effectively supplanted the standard fetish of the female nude (Köhler 1985). Working against the public perception that mass media was productive only in its creation of imaginary worlds and illusory needs, West German image-makers "began to produce a new materiality, a new essentialism; terminating all artificiality, . . . [there] stood suddenly the naked, unadulterated human body . . . the naked man . . . a signifier of . . . fundamental transformations. . . . In our *Care* campaign, we could finally unveil the monument for the postmodern man in its entirety . . . an entirely naked human being/man, but rendered particular through the unveiling of the most distinctive of male body parts—the penis" (Schirner 1987:39–41). But in West German advertising, such a novel exposure of naked masculinity, the denuding of the phallus, was immediately aestheticized through familiar iconographies and images:

> Whatever was unthinkable a few years ago, has today become a matter of course. . . .
> The borders of shame have shifted. A segment of the male population has been exposed. . . . These men show themselves as they are . . . naked, and bare . . . Sun-tanned
> and smooth . . . Beautiful, perfect, and immaculate . . . staged to perfection. . . . The
> male body has been cleverly positioned like an antique statue . . . the pose is unmistakable. . . . The image toys with our memories. (Soltau 1987:42–43, 44, 45, 46–47)

The aestheticization of male nudity, by a reliance on mimetic tools of classic iconography, and the corresponding emphasis on marble, rock, and art, liberated the naked male body from its sexual and political history. It became a "timeless" image, a

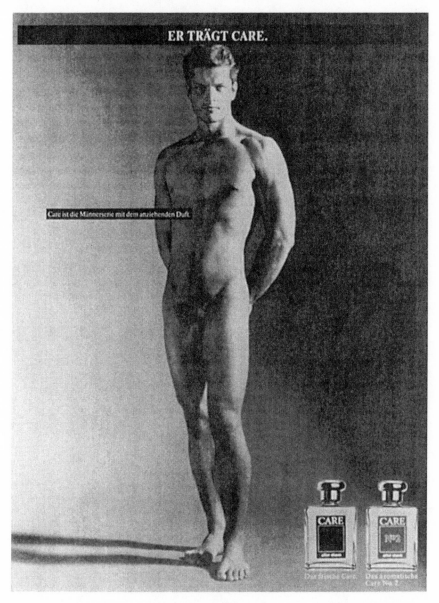

Figure 9.4. "He Wears Care": White Naked Male Bodies as Commodity Fetish, West Germany, 1985–87. From Jeske, Neumann, and Sprang (1987b:41). Copyright Jahrbuch der Werbung, ECON Verlag GmbH, Düsseldorf, Germany. Photography by Peter Knaup.

Figure 9.5. "Self-Empowerment through Nudity": Leftist Activists Protest Western Imperialism by Exposing White Masculinity, West Berlin, 1988. From Mayer, Schmolt, and Wolf (1988:138). Courtesy Steintor, Bremen Verlags und Buchhandelsgesellschaft. Photography copyright Ann-Christine Jansson.

"natural" artifact, which could be put on display without evoking traumatic memories of male libido and violence.

NUDE AUTHENTICITY: THE NAKED BODY
AS THE REBELLIOUS TERRAIN OF NATURE

These configurations of public memory were further enhanced by the sudden re-emergence of nudity in radical political discourse. In West Germany during the early 1980s, a time of heightened anti-immigrant sentiments, economic inequities, and the shaping of consumer consciousness by idealized images of white masculinity, leftist activists retrieved the naked body as an emblem of political struggle. Nudity became a performative icon of the West German environmental movement, where the public exposition of nakedness supported strategic forms of countercultural and anticapitalist protest. The naked body, a symbol of popular rebellion, was mobilized as a natural symbol, an authenticating sign, which was pitted against the facade of the German state. This is suggested by a series of political rallies in West Berlin, where public nudity took center stage. For instance, in 1988, unclothed male activists used their nude bodies in a dramaturgical battle against police brutality (Mayer et al. 1988:97). The protesters' performance framed the police officers' violent transgressions in terms of the terror of the Nazi regime. The naked male body, a visual assertion of an unmediated political self, was staged in opposition to the legacy of German state violence. In another mass demonstration, in 1988, leftist criticism of global capitalism featured male nudity as a form of ridicule, a message of debasement and negation of state power (see Figure 9.5). The unclothed male body was exhibited as an oppositional sign, a signifier of a rebellious subjectivity, which was displayed in protest against market-driven forms of inequality and violence (ibid.:138). Likewise in 1981, unclothed male activists used their bare bodies as subversive icons in protest against a presumed urban crisis: air pollution, lack of housing, unemployment, and inadequate public transportation (Volland 1987:20). The protesters' naked volatility stood in stark contrast to the defensive armor of state police (see Figure 9.6). The visual juxtaposition of male nudes and male officers in riot gear brought into focus the postulated distinction between political enemies (perpetrators) and victims. In 1988, student activists in Bonn, stripped to their undergarments, protested the shortfall in state funding for education (*Spiegel* 1988:62). The unclothed students argued their case while standing collectively before the minister of education, a man attired with the insignia of his office—dressed in a dark suit and tie: a political uniform. The visual emphasis marked the contrast between body armor and nudity—that is, between the political symbols of state authority and disempowerment. In such instances, public nudity served as a naturalizing truth claim: a signifier of the irrefutable reality of a victimized (albeit rebellious) national interior.

Throughout the 1980s, the West German Left employed public nudity to demonstrate its commitment to democracy, freedom, and equality. The bare/ex-

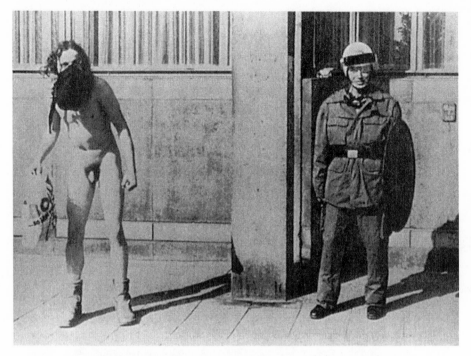

Figure 9.6. "Proclaiming Opposition through Male Nudity": Using Their Bodies as Performative Icons, Leftist Activists Rally against City Government (TUWAT Demo— Rathaus Kreuzberg), West Berlin, 1981. From Volland (1987:20). Copyright Voller-Ernst Agentur für komische und ungewöhnliche Fotos, Berlin. Photograph by Peter Hebler.

posed white body, a tangible icon of the physical world ("nature" and the "natural environment"), was equated with physical vulnerability and victimization. Environmental issues such as pollution, ozone depletion, and deforestation, as well as concerns about economic deprivation and male domination, were publicized through open displays of the unclothed human body. For instance, in Frankfurt in 1981, environmental activists opposed the destruction of urban woodlands, a designated site of airport construction, by protecting the endangered trees with their bare bodies—thereby heightening the public's awareness of the forest as a living organism (Pohrt 1991:27). During such demonstrations, the iconography of nudity was inseparably equated with the world of nature. Similarly, in West Berlin in 1989, several hundred men and women assembled in a protest against air pollution by displaying their nude bodies (*tageszeitung* 1989:16). Naked nature was exhibited as a terrain of potential destruction and suffering: German bodies endangered by the state's indifference to global ozone depletion. The nude body, unprotected and vulnerable, sought to reveal itself as a potential environmental casualty. Such a strategy, with its appeal to universal human values and its recuperation of German bodies as templates for a global ethics, unwittingly subverted recognition of existing racial inequality and ethnic difference. Leftist environmental activists invested naked bodies and white physicality with meanings that had a profound significance for the national body politic: German bodies were presented as perpetual victims of state violence.

NUDE NOSTALGIA: SUBLIME NATURE AGAINST STATE VIOLENCE

In contemporary Germany, during the late 1990s, when the governing apparatus was reconfigured by an uneasy alliance of leftists (the centrist Social Democrats and the radical Greens), and when German soldiers, as members of NATO, began to intervene in the war in Kosovo by dropping bombs on Serbia, the practice of public nudity was recovered as a medium of radical protest. At the national party convention of the AllianceGreens, in May 1999, the members of the New Left, now composed of old pacifists, 68ers, and government supporters, clashed with fervor over fundamental differences in ideological commitments. In this context, the naked body, as an icon of authenticity, nature, and nonviolence, was mobilized by the opponents of war. Among the utensils of protest, the whistles, posters, slogans, and blood-filled projectiles, which were hurled at Joschka Fischer (the foreign minister) and his supporters with accusations of "murder" and "war mongering," there also surfaced the conventional male nude: "proud, almost Jesus-like, wandering about, a stark-naked opponent of war" (*Spiegel* 1999b:303). The male nude, stepping out of the terrain of violent memory, stood as a reminder of past left-wing radicalism, when political opposition had a purging function, and when the battle against German state authority could erase the shame of "catastrophic nationalism" (Geyer 2001). But at this convention, the arsenal of unclothed indignation was mobilized against those members of the New Left, who, as part of the German governing body, had consented to acts of military violence abroad. The dramatic use of nude masculinity sought to expose the changeover of a party, whose radical pacifism took form some twenty years ago, emerging out of a political movement of antifascist protest: the opposition to state violence. But the naked war-opponent did not verbalize his discontent. In speechless rage, he provided his well-dressed party leaders with a signpost to the beginning. The male nude, according to critical media commentary, sought to convey the following:

> Undress yourselves, with naked buttocks wander back to nature, so that you become just as innocent as nature itself... or like Adam and Eve in their paradise phase. Others should bite into the bitter fruit from the tree of political knowledge. But after paradise—after the party convention. (*Spiegel* 1999b:303)

The nude body, as an icon of natural innocence and goodness, persists as a prominent symbol of leftist opposition to state militarism. Thus a few months later, in July 1999, in Berlin, groups of naked protesters disrupted an official military ceremony: the annual pledge of allegiance by newly drafted German recruits. The military ritual was symbolically charged. Staged in a public place, the soldiers' show of surrender to the German state was performed openly, in full view, before the nation. Scheduled on July 20, in commemoration of the assassination attempt against Hitler in 1944, the event was carried out at the very site on which the former conspirators were executed (Stadelmann 1999:2). The performative function of this military ritual was not unintentionally framed by a paradox. The soldiers' pledge of allegiance to a democratic state was simultaneously to commemorate German opposition to a totalitarian regime: the Nazi state. According to Rudolph Scharping, the minister of defense: "The men and women of the resistance gave their lives because of their respect for human dignity and human rights. . . . These values are also decisive markers of the independent tradition of the [postwar] German army (*Bundeswehr*)" (ibid.). Despite their initial criticism of the event, seen as a recuperation of martial nationalism, the AllianceGreens eventually consented to the symbolic mesh of military ceremonial and historical legacy. Angelika Beer, the party's political speaker, declared: "It is correct to confront the new recruits with this occurrence on the 55th anniversary of the day, on which Germans attempted to remove the dictator [Hitler]. . . . [T]he German army (*Bundeswehr*) is not the Nazi army (*Reichswehr*)" (ibid.). But other leftists, who had campaigned against mandatory military service, remained hostile. And despite the tight security measures, including sharpshooters, border patrols, and police, a group of nude protesters managed to break through the protective cordon. Just as Chancellor Schröder had familiarized the young recruits with the history of the German resistance, ten naked men and women burst into the center of the festivities. Shouting "soldiers are murderers," the nude demonstrators tried to take possession of the battalion pennant before they were thrown to the ground by military police.

The protesters' nude performance provoked severe measures of retribution by the German state (*Tagblatt* 1999:1): Two of the nudes were arrested; another twenty were charged with bodily injury, breach of the public peace, and resistance against the "supreme power of the state." The nudes' assault on the corporate military body, and on the symbolic armor of state power, was not devoid of national pathos. Nude opposition provoked retaliatory measures fraught with emotional charge. Once again, violent history and countermemory were pushed into the field of public vision through the emblematic meanings of the naked body.

INTERLUDE: VIOLENCE, MEMORY, REPRESENTATION

The problem with violence, as I have tried to show, is not merely one of behavior. It is also a matter linked to the production and consolidation of reference and meaning: the performance and discourse of memory. I argue, in short, that violence may be engendered by iconographic representations. In postwar Germany, public nudity was mobilized as a specific form of countermemory that could be transported through the iconography of bodies. Naked skin, equated with nature and natural signifiers, sought to expel the body from the terrain of social violence. Natural nakedness, as a symbolic construct, preempted presence, identity, and propriety: it produced a closure of history. Such a refusal of history, the very attempt to suppress or control fields of violent memory through a corporal aesthetic, seems to be a retreat, a departure, into a mythic realm: the innocent and wholesome world of nature. These mythographic phantasms of "natural nudity" enable Germans to exhibit their bodies publicly without shame: the theater of nakedness is staged against the traumatic memories of Nazi racial/sexual violence.

But such a reinvigoration of nudist body practices seems particularly significant in a global world order. Placed within the context of transnational economies, transnational commodity culture, and guestworker immigration, German nakedness is once again becoming "white." In turn, this form of racialization echoes tropes of an earlier era, a circumstance that may well be suggestive of the (re)emergence of a racial aesthetic that demands the erasure and suppression of difference.

Moreover, the public staging of the naked body, with its evocation of "nature"—an antithesis of "history"—is paradoxically tied to an oppositional language of violence and annihilation. Leftist activists, including supporters of the 1960s antifascist movement, promote the use of verbal violence as a medium for political contestation. In demonstrations, political rallies, and election campaigns, the mobilization of traumatic memory formations is accomplished through linguistic, visual, and performative practices that are staged in an effort to remake (and fortify) a democratic public sphere. Although the German New Left emphasizes its commitment to liberal democratic values (antimilitarism, minority rights, feminism), my research uncovered a perpetual reliance on metaphors and images that was (and is) historically problematic. The organic imagery, with its evocation of nature, that is prevalent in leftist body practices is synchronized with a verbal discourse of violence and annihilation. A range of highly charged image schema, focused on death, silencing, and physical brutality (typified by the swastika, SS sign, gallows, Nazi rhetoric, death camps) are appropriated as antisymbols, transformed into a language of resistance: the opposition to a violent past. Fantasies of violence, directed against the political "other," are thereby not merely historicized but reproduced as templates of action and identity. Holocaust images, deployed as oppositional signs, seem to facilitate a profound dissociation from shame.

In the following section, I attempt to scrutinize how social memories of genocide, Nazi terror, and race-based violence are verbally invoked by postwar German antifascists. With a focus on Germany's New Left activists, who belong to a broad-based democratic social movement (headed by the party of the Greens), I explore how the historical experience of Nazism and the Holocaust emerged as a formative discourse in leftist political protest. The body, as in the public theater of nudity, figures as a central memory icon in the New Left's verbal battles.

TRANSPOSED MEMORY: RACIAL PHANTASMS
AS OPPOSITIONAL SIGNS

The production of death and the erasure of Jewish bodies were central to the Nazi politics of race. The aim of genocide was to maintain the "health" of the German body by enforcing a strict regimen of racial hygiene (Proctor 1988; Müller-Hill 1988; Aly et al. 1994). German political fantasy employed a model of race that relied on images of disease, dirt, and infection. Blood became a marker of pathological difference, a signifier of filth and contagion: Jews and outsiders were equated with excrement that had to be eliminated or expunged (Dundes 1984). After 1945, these same images reappeared in right-wing protest against immigrants: foreigners, seen as pollutants, a dangerous racial threat, became victims of street violence (Linke 1995, 1997b). The political Right called for the expulsion of all ethnic others. One example, graffiti that appeared on the radio tower in Frankfurt, expressed the desire to purge the German nation of foreign (and polluting) matter (Müller 1985):

> Foreigners out of Germany!
> Excrement/shit out of the body!
> *(Ausländer raus aus Deutschland!*
> *Scheisse aus dem Körper!)*

These same motifs surface in the political language of the German Left. In their public protests against the street terror against immigrants, leftist activists, like the supporters of the Anti-Fascist League in West Berlin, made use of the following formulaic slogans.[14] The verbal repertoire of Leftist speech acts articulates a desire to eradicate the "enemy" by tapping into a paradigm of elimination:

> Turks in! Nazis get out!
> *(Türken rein. Nazis raus!)*
> Garbage out! Human beings in!
> *(Müll raus! Menschen rein!)*
> Nazi dirt must be purged!
> *(Nazi Dreck muss weg!)*
> Keep your environment clean! Get rid of the brown filth!
> *(Halte Deine Umwelt sauber! Schmeiss weg den braunen Dreck!)*
> Nazis out! Cut away (exterminate) the excrement!
> *(Nazis raus! Hau weg den Scheiss!)*

The German language of expulsion, as exemplified by the oppositional terms *rein* and *raus*, transcends historical and ideological boundaries. Unlike the corresponding *into* and *out of* in English, the German terms *rein* and *raus* are not merely spatial referents. Their use is grounded in a paradigm in which the nation, the imagined political community, is a human body. The denial of membership, and the expulsion of people, is linguistically conceptualized as a process of bodily discharge: a form of excretion or elimination. German *raus* belongs to a semantic field that defines expulsion as a physiological process, a process of termination and death (*aussen, ausmachen, heraus, Garaus, austilgen, ausmerzen*, etc.). The German *raus* is a historical cognate of terms denoting belly, stomach, uterus, intestines (Pokorny 1959:1103–5). *Raus*, whether in language use or semantic practice, retains a metaphoric connection to body parts that expel or excrete waste matter.

The converse of this discorporative symbolism, designated by the German term *rein*, is likewise based on a physiological model. The affirmation of membership, and the inclusion of people, is linguistically conceptualized as a process of incorporation and simultaneously as a process of homogenization and cleansing (ibid.:945–46). Indeed, *rein* belongs to a semantic field that comprises both meanings (*herein, reinlich, einig*). This duality is reflected in contemporary German usage. *Rein* signifies inclusion, as in *Türken rein*, literally "Turks in," a slogan coined in the 1980s by the New Left, advocating a national agenda of ethnic integration. The term also denotes purification or cleanliness, as in *Judenrein*, meaning "cleansed of Jews," an expression coined in the 1930s, articulating the Third Reich's programmatic concern with racial purity. One of the announced Nazi goals was to make Germany *Judenrein*—that is, "free of Jews," an imperative for racial purging (Bauman 1989:104; Dundes 1984:126). The metaphoric equation of bodily purity with membership is further attested by evidence from semantic reconstructions: German *rein* is a historic cognate of terms denoting cut, separate, rip, slice, tear, sever (Pokorny 1959:945–46). As suggested by this language of violence, the claim to German membership always requires some form of purging: the excretion of presumed filth or the excision and amputation of contaminants.

Images of ethnic integration or German solidarity are often expressed in terms of this corporal language of expulsion, a language through which killing is redefined as therapeutic. Interestingly, physicians who participated in genocide under Nazism often used the same rationalization to legitimate their participation in mass killing. Frequently, they drew analogies to surgery: just as a physician, in order to heal, will cut off a gangrenous leg, so the "social" physician must amputate the sick part of society (Lifton 1986). Racial differences were presented, and treated, as matters of medical pathology.

German Leftists have appropriated the motif of expulsion as an oppositional symbol: through a transposition of memory and meaning, their speech acts convey a message of protest. But, paradoxically, the antifascist discourse perpetuates racist axioms:

Nazis get out!
(*Nazis raus!*)

This text, which appeared on a house wall in Berlin's city center, demands the expulsion of Nazis (see Figure 9.7). Spray-painted in red capital letters, the implied urgency of the postulate is supported by visual means. The typographic message fades into the image of a grotesque, masklike face, a template of the despised "Nazi." Drawn with exaggerated oriental features, the image signifies the alien or

Figure 9.7. "Nazis Out!": Antifascist Graffiti, Berlin, 1994. Photograph copyright Uli Linke.

foreign. This leftist graffiti is an attempt at demonization, accomplished by a disturbing reliance on race-based iconographic markers. Such a depiction of evil, which envisions "Nazis" as an Asiatic threat that must be stopped, expunged, or driven out, entails an unsettling confusion between the perpetrators of genocide and their victims. As Omer Bartov (1998) observed:

> West German representations of the past have often included the figure of "the Nazi." This elusive type, rarely presented with any degree of sympathy, retains a complex relationship with its predecessor, "the Jew." Serving as a metaphor for "the Nazi in us," it inverts the discredited notion of "the Jew in us" [a racist axiom propagated by National Socialists]. . . . Simultaneously, it presents "the Nazi" as the paradigmatic other, just as "the Jew" had been in the past. . . . The new enemy of postwar Germany, "the Nazi," is thus both everywhere and nowhere. On the one hand, "he" lurks in everyone and, in this sense, can never be ferreted out. On the other hand, "he" is essentially so different from "us" that he can be said never to have existed in the first place in any sense that would be historically meaningful or significant for . . . contemporary Germany [or] the vast majority of individual Germans. . . . Hence "we" cannot be held responsible for "his" misdeeds. Just like the Devil, "the Nazi" penetrates the world from another sphere and must be exorcized. (pp. 792–94)

For the New Left, "the Nazi" is a metaphor of the satanic element in postwar German society: a legacy of the Holocaust. The spray-painted portrait of "the Nazi" reveals deep-seated anxieties about the ubiquity of evil—an elusive threat that is rendered tangible through images of racial difference. Such a representation of Nazis as Asian (Jewish) other serves two purposes. It distances leftist Germans from the past and acquits them of their sense of guilt by placing Nazis into a separate, race-marked category. Moreover, their conflation of the Nazi threat with "the Asian/Jewish menace" (a postulate of the Third Reich that is rehabilitated by unthinking anti-Semitism) also greatly facilitates the New Left's sense of martyrdom and victimhood.

Another text, painted across the facade of a university building in West Berlin (see Figure 9.8), demands the expulsion of Nazis, while opposing the extradition of non-Germans:

> Nazis get out!
> Drive the Nazis away! Foreigners stay!
> (*Nazis raus!*
> *Nazis vertreiben! Ausländerinnen bleiben!*)

Written as a political protest, these antifascist slogans advocate tolerance of ethnic diversity. But the chosen language of expulsion (*raus*, "get out"; *vertreiben*, "drive away") and emplacement (*bleiben*, "stay") operates from assumptions of a "pure" nation, and taps into postwar memory formations of blood, history, and homeland. The German term *vertreiben* ("expulsion") refers to the forced removal or extradition of people from a national domain: it conjures images of territorial dislocation or displacement. Un-

Figure 9.8. "Drive the Nazis Away! Foreigners Stay!": Antifascist Graffiti, West Berlin, 1989. Photograph copyright Uli Linke.

der Hitler, before 1945, this meaning of expulsion was employed by National Socialists to describe their policy of Judeocide: to kill and "drive out the Jews" (*Juden vertreiben*). After 1945, with the collapse of the Third Reich, the language of expulsion became a signifier for victimization, referring to those Germans displaced by Hitler's war in Eastern Europe (*die Vertriebenen*). In such contexts, and as used by these slogans, expulsion means "termination," an uprooting, which kills, renders homeless, and exiles. The German discourse of expulsion works from assumptions of a political community, a "homeland," that is defined by contrast to all that is foreign or distant: as a quasi-mythical realm—fixed, unitary, and bounded—it privileges "racial purity" and "homogeneity" (Peck 1996:482–83). In the German historical imagination, this concept of homeland (*Heimat*) is invoked as "a synonym for race (blood) and territory (soil)—a deadly combination that led to exile or annihilation of anyone who did not 'belong.' . . . Under the National Socialists [it] meant the murderous exclusion of anything 'un-German'" (Morley and Robins 1996:466). As an act of rhetorical violence, the slogan's demand to banish or to expel "Nazis" (that is, right-wing extremists) taps into this nationalist discourse of "murder" and "homeland."

These acts of narrative violence tend to follow a predictable pattern: intended as a political response to the brutalization of refugees and immigrants, these critical utterances by leftist protesters transpose racial violence into a medium of opposition. For instance, in West Berlin, in January 1989, immediately after the senate elections, antifascist activists and members of the Green/Alternative Party assembled in protest. Their anger was directed against the militant right-wing party of Republicans, which had unexpectedly gained eleven seats in the Berlin Senate. The protesters organized nightly demonstrations, where they displayed banners expressing their political sentiments. One banner showed a clenched human fist smashing a swastika, fragmenting it. Another banner, a white cardboard poster fastened to a stick, showed a tightly closed fist squashing (with a top-down movement) a black swastika, crushing it beneath. One banner, made to resemble a national flag, fashioned from red and green cloth (the emblems of the urban environmentalists and the Old Left), showed a large fist smashing a black swastika (hitting it dead center, fragmenting it). Other banners demanded the annihilation of political opponents—that is Nazis, fascists, or right-wing supporters—by reducing them to muck or dirt: *brown filth* (see Figure 9.9):

Hack/smash away the brown filth!
(*Hau weg den braunen Dreck!*)

The enemy's reduction to filth, specifically excrement, taps into race-based fantasies of "elimination"—a legacy of the Holocaust. Until 1945, under Hitler, German anti-Semitism was promulgated by an obsessive concern with scatology: Jews were equated with feces and dirt, a symbolic preoccupation that encoded Germany's drive for "racial purity" (Dundes 1984). The protesters' banner, which demands the violent erasure of "brown filth"—a circumlocution for Nazis (for example, Brown Shirts, or SA, Hitler's militia) as fecal waste—is accompanied by a large skeletal figure. The skeleton (made of cardboard and paper) reiterates this connection between filth and fascism: the emblematic "death's-head" (*Totenkopf*), this iconography of skull and bones, was the insignia and symbol of Hitler's terror-inspiring elite troops (*SS*, or *Schutzstaffel*). The "skeleton" conjures images of the persistent existence of Nazi perpetrators: life-takers, death-givers. Extermination or the removal of "filth" (neo-Nazis) is rendered by leftists as the legitimate disposal of an enduring threat.

In an another instance, leftist opposition to right-wing extremism, accentuated by the smashing of a swastika, is made verbally explicit (see Figure 9.10). One banner, carried by several protesters, reads:

University rage against the Nazi brood!
(*Uni-Wut gegen Nazi-Brut!*)

The sign's red-lettered text appeared on a white cloth, which, as its centerpiece, displayed a black swastika smashed (broken) by a clenched fist. The slogan names the protesters' target of wrath: "the Nazi brood!" (*Nazi-Brut*). In this instance, violent opposition is directed not against fascism but its postwar legacy: Hitler's

Figure 9.9. "Annihilate the Brown Filth!": Antifascist Iconography (Image and Banner), West Berlin, 1989. Photograph copyright Uli Linke.

Figure 9.10. "Eradicate the Nazi Brood!": Antifascist Protest Banner, West Berlin, 1989.
Photograph copyright Uli Linke.

progeny. The reference to Nazi "brood" (*Brut*) conjures frightful images of evil:
beastly offspring, a litter of nonhuman fiends, which—hatched and cared for—
populate the world. By drawing on genealogical metaphors of "progeny" and
"breeding," the protesters speak of their right-wing opponents as a colonizing
threat. But this language of propagation also entails an act of racialization: the political enemy is typified by reference to dehumanizing and biologizing symbols.
Such a choice of signs compels the use of violence. Brutality and uncontrolled anger
are turned into a weapon of defense. Painted in red (a leftist symbol for sacrifice
and revolution), the word *rage* alludes to a berserker state (German *Wut*, "fury"),
an irresistible drive that relies on bloodshed as a violent or cathartic release (Jones
1951:262). The slogan's accompanying visual image recommends annihilation: a
fist smashes a swastika. The fist extends from the figure of a bear, the traditional
emblem of the city of Berlin. This identification of leftist activists with a geopolitical site expresses the overt desire to eradicate or banish "Nazis" from a concrete
social terrain.

What are the implications of these racist iconographies, produced by German
leftists, for the formation of postwar civil society? How does the mimetic reproduction of fascist signifiers (blood, race, contagion) in leftist political discourse

effect the reconstruction of a democratic public sphere in postwar/postunification Germany? And why are such images of contagion, annihilation, and death continuously recycled in the New Left's effort to fortify a nonviolent liberal democracy, a political project that is imagined through the utopic iconicity of naked/natural bodies?

DECENTERING VIOLENCE:
THE LANDSCAPES OF POST-HOLOCAUST MEMORY

The public culture of violence in Germany, which follows a pattern of invocation and dissociation, has found anchorage in a variety of social settings. It is reproduced, albeit in sanitized form, by academic responses to my research on memory and violence. Often delivered in scathing polemics and personalized attacks, scholarly criticisms tend to dismiss the validity of such research. For instance, at a conference in 1994, a well-known German historian angrily responded:

> I live there and I don't recognize the Germany you describe. That's not the Germany I know. I suggest you go back and check your sources. Nobody would say such things. I've never heard anybody say anything like that. It's taboo. You cannot say these things in public without an inevitable scandal. Political parties would never endorse such statements. Who are these people you cite? They are irrelevant, insignificant people. They are not representative. I am sure that this person you quote does exist, but she would have never said anything like that. So my suggestion to you is: go back and check your sources!

Such objections to my work, which I consistently encountered, were based on the rejection of my ethnographic sources. German academics contested the existence of discursive violence by denying the validity of my evidence: local-level politics, graffiti, slogans, everyday sociolinguistics, street violence, normal ways of speaking, and the language and vocabulary of popular media were rejected as legitimate data. After presenting my work at an international symposium in 1994 in Berlin, a meeting focused on violence and racism, I was told that my research had missed the mark entirely by examining political language. As one historian instructed me:

> In politics, the rhetorical aim is to annihilate the opponent. But the selection of metaphors, with which one can accomplish this, is limited. There are only few methods, few possibilities: stabbing, hanging, shooting. And these methods should not be taken literally. To put it bluntly: language is different from action; rhetoric is a matter of theater—political drama—and cannot be taken too seriously.

According to my German critics, language and violence were antithetical discourses. Verbalization was privileged as a cognitive tool, while violence was interpreted as an unmediated practice, an expression of primordial hatred. Based on these conceptions, my descriptive exposure of narrative violence was dismissed as insignificant and even meaningless.

Puzzled by my treatment of language as cultural practice, some German scholars were even more incensed by my investigation of violence across political boundaries. How could I suggest that rightist militants and antifascists produced a common cultural discourse? Did I not realize that leftists were engaged in an ideological struggle against fascism? According to my German critics, violent fantasy was engendered by a specifically right-wing agenda. While the Left *spoke* violence, which was dismissed as a rhetorical tactic, the right *enacted* violence. This attempt to attribute the practice of violence exclusively to right-wing agency was perceived as unproblematic. According to several German commentators, violence was a characteristic expression of a conservative or rightist mentality. In contradiction to the empirical evidence offered by several sociological studies (Heitmeyer 1992; Held and Horn 1992; Hoffmeister and Sill 1993), rightist perpetrators were imagined as uneducated members of the lower classes, who were unemployed and dispossessed of stable social relationships; they were typified as social marginals, who used violence to compensate for their inability to verbalize (*die Unfähigkeit zu Versprachlichen*). Here the use of language was defined as a transformative medium, which converted primordial desires into rational social precepts. Since verbal articulation was perceived to be a leftist prerogative, rightists were constructed as "primitive others" whose rational faculties were impaired without this mediating capacity of language. In any case, such presuppositions (in fact, conjured stereotypes) might account for the fact that my descriptions of right-wing violence were never once contested.

Of course, some German academics conceded that my disclosure of leftist discourses of violence was basically correct. But even during those moments of covert agreement, the perpetration of violence was quickly dissociated from the moderate left and projected onto a more militant, antisocial periphery. At a symposium on identity in March 1993, a young German scholar thus angrily explained:

> I was really disturbed by your presentation about the Green/Alternatives. As you should know, most supporters of this party are committed pacifists. The Greens, even in Berlin, never use violence in their public protests. So when you are describing the violent discourse of the German left, you are really referring to political alliances other than the Greens. Violence is used systematically by members of the autonomous and anarchist factions. They still believe in armed struggle. In Berlin, they live in Kreuzberg. That's a completely different scene. They don't work within the system. You can't just lump them all together like that.

The displacement of annihilatory discourses to the fringes of German society was a common ploy of critique and denial. Contesting the pervasiveness of discursive violence, some German scholars tended to dismiss my ethnographic evidence by these strategies of displacement. Such attempts at invalidation were sometimes coupled with other forms of dismissal: included were demands for greater relativization; accusations of a totalization and exaggerated cultural criticism;

charges of implementing a program of language purism; and an advocacy for American-style political correctness. How dare I tell Germans how to speak?

These angry objections to my findings sometimes took the form of outright denial. A young woman at an international conference in 1994 responded as follows to my presentation:

> I worked with the Greens for several years, and among them were some of the kindest and gentlest people I have ever met. How can you say these things about them? I think you are wrong to say that the Greens have a problem with violence or pollution. If that was true they would advocate the use of pesticides against insects or promote the dumping of toxic wastes into the oceans. These are things which they oppose.

Such attitudes of denial and dissociation by German academics were on occasion coupled with their plea for my silence. For example, at a meeting for area specialists in April 1994, I was angrily reproached by a German legal scholar: "You just can't say these things about the left. The left has made headway, changed many things with their initiatives, and if you say such things it leads to setbacks."

My ethnographic documentation of exterminatory violence and its perpetual contestation by members of my German audiences engender a paradox: genocide, both as a practice and a discourse, is clearly linked to modernity, yet some German scholars prefer to deny this. Their attitude toward violence is embedded in a theoretical approach that promotes a basic assumption of progress. Modernity is equated with the development of a civil society, in which outbursts of violence are suppressed by the state's pacification of daily life. From such a perspective Nazism, genocide, and annihilatory racism are interpreted as anomalies, as regressive aberrations, resulting from temporary social breakdown.

GENOCIDE, MODERNITY, AND CULTURAL MEMORY

What are we to make of these collective imaginings? Zygmunt Bauman, in *Modernity and the Holocaust* (1989), argued that genocide in Germany must be understood as a central event of modern history and not as an exceptional episode. The production of mass death was facilitated by modern processes of rationalization. Exterminatory racism was tied to conceptions of social engineering, to the idea of creating an artificial order by changing the present one and by eliminating those elements that could not be altered as desired. Genocide was based on the technological and organizational achievements of an advanced industrial society. A political program of complete extermination became possible under modernity because of the collaboration of science, technology, and bureaucracy.

Such an interpretation of mass violence requires a critical reconsideration of modernity as a civilizing process, as a progressive rationalization of social life (see, for example, Elias 1939; Weber 1947). It requires rethinking genocide, not as an exceptional episode, a state of anomie and a breakdown of the social, a suspension of the normal order of things, a historical regression, or a return to primitive instincts and mythic origins (for example, Sorel 1941; Girard 1979), but as an integral principle of modernity. Comprehensive programs of extermination are neither primitive nor instinctual (Fein 1979; Melson 1992). They are the result of sustained conscious effort and the substitution of moral responsibility with organizational discipline (Hilberg 1985; Friedlander 1988; Bartov 1996).

This concept of modernity emphasizes the "normalcy" of the perpetrators. In the 1930s and 1940s, ordinary German citizens participated in the killings: "As is well known by now, the SS officers responsible for the smooth unfolding of operations were not particularly bestial or, for that matter, sadistic. (This is true of the overwhelming number of them, according to survivors.) They were normal human beings who, the rest of the time, played with their children, gardened, listened to music. They were, in short, civilized" (Todorov 1990:31). The genesis of the Holocaust offers an example of the ways in which ordinary Germans—"otherwise normal individuals"—could become perpetrators by their passive acceptance of the "political and bureaucratic mechanisms that permitted the idea of mass extermination to be realized" (Mommsen 1991:252–53). The technocratic nature of Nazi genocide attests to the "banality of evil"—that is, the sight of a highly mechanized and bureaucratized world where the extermination of entire groups of people who were regarded as "contagion" could become a normal occurrence (Arendt 1964). From this perspective, race-based violence and public machinations of mass death cannot be understood as regressive historical processes (Feldman 1997; Kuper 1981; Malkki 1995a; Tilly 1970): they are manifestations of new forms of political violence and the centralizing tendencies of modern state power.

But such a modernist conception of genocide, while it seeks to comprehend the industrial efficiency with which Jews were killed, is also deeply disturbing. As Omer Bartov (1998:799) suggested: "Recent works on the links between genocide and modernity have both the potential of distancing us from the horror (by sanitizing it) and of making us all complicit in it (since we belong to an age that perpetrates horror)." The perpetration of mass murder, even in a modern age, must be understood in its relation to the existence of a powerful political imaginary through which everyday understandings of national belonging, race, and body are defined. How do we analyze a cultural history of genocide? Modernity, as Yehuda Bauer (1998:13) points out, whatever the definition of the concept, did not affect only Germany, and in any case, it does not explain why the Jews were the victims. As I have tried to show, the study of the social consensus formed by ideologies, attitudes, and symbolic practices transmitted over historic time produces the possibility of answering why it occurred.

MODERNITY AND BODY MEMORY:
THE ARCHAEOLOGICAL RUINS OF STATE CULTURE

In my analysis of post-Holocaust memory practices, our understanding of German historicity was mediated by the concept of the unconscious, of dream work,

and of fantasy formation. Recognizing the material force of the historical unconscious, I emphasized the formation, inheritance, and devolution of essentialist symbolic systems or grids of perception. What are the building blocks of such essentialist constructs? My analysis contributes to an archaeology of essentialist
metaphysics in the public sphere of modern Germany. Throughout I inquired how
essentialism is made. How does it achieve such a deterministic and habitual hold
on the experience, perception, and processing of reality?

My treatment of essentialism as a formative construct and my orientation toward the notion of a historical unconscious mean that the point of emergence of
ethnographic data in this type of study does not conform to the highly local-
ized/bounded profiling or extraction of data typical of conventional anthropological analysis. A major historical condition for the replication of essentialism, as
I document in this chapter, is the continuous oscillation between free-floating fantasy formations and their frightening instantiations in precise locales and in specific
performances: public nudity and eliminationist speech acts. From what discreet sites
of social experience, class affiliation, or gender identity does essentialist fantasy
originate? We are no longer within the circumscribed space of childhood socialization, the nuclear family, the residential community. Popular culture and mass
media have deterritorialized fantasy, although instantiations of fantasy can be given
a discrete coordinate or topography. In many cases, the fantasy formations, particularly those embedded in linguistic and visual icons, as I demonstrate, crisscross
divergent class and political positions: thus the common symbolic grammar of
blood between the fascists and the New Left, or the disturbing evidence for a common logic of elimination between the antifascist Left and the Nazis. Such essentialist fantasy formations gather force and momentum precisely because of their
indistinct parameters in cultural repertoires. This fuzziness evades simplistic
cause/effect analysis. Rather, as my research suggests, it requires ethnographic exploration on a heterogeneity or montage of discursive and image-making sites: political demonstrations, the mass media, popular memory, linguistic substrata, body
practices, and symbolic geographies, which all share a translocal, national scope.

The German instrumental imagination of current ideologies of violence works
with mystified bits and pieces of materiality, rehabilitating old positivities in the
search for social anchorage. We are in the material culture of the body (blood, race,
nudity), and the linked somatic and medicalized nationalism that has specific German (but also trans-European) coordinates. A root metaphor of the German state
defines citizenship by blood (as opposed to soil—that is, place of birth—as in the
case of France). Blood and soil, body and space, constitute the materialist theory
of national interiority and foreign exteriority. There exists a fundamental contradiction between the liberal state's promotion of tolerance and the founding charter of familial blood membership, which underwrites stigmatizing imageries of oth-
erhood. For the pathos of the nation state, that is, the political community as an
object of patriotic feeling, derives from the liberal revolution, with its infantiliza-
tion and gendering of the subjects of the "fatherland."

In the twentieth century, however, the familial model of the organic nation was medicalized. By the early 1930s, fascist sociologists began to envision nations as "units of blood." A good deal of German social theory during the first part of this century was in effect a medical anthropology, a diagnostic science of the racial body. Accordingly, the nation was imagined as a "unity filled with blood," an "organic river basin," which functioned as a genealogical reservoir for a *healthy* German body politic: "Thus 'nationhood' drives time, indeed history out of history: it is space and organic fate, nothing else" (Bloch 1990:90). Nationality came to be accepted as a medical fact by the fascist state and its supporting racial ideologies. Such a medicalized vision of nationhood resulted in the transposition of earlier forms of state culture into the political vernacular of everyday life, as is evident in contemporary Germany. My ethnographic material shows that a retrograde archaism of national state culture is continuously repositioned in the present. Crucial to this reappearance is the fact that the current manifestations of the civil state remain both neutral and even opposed to those ideologies of organic unity and spatial purification, but nevertheless abet them. This is dialectical necessity, since it is precisely such residual archaeological strata, older sediments, earlier ideological manifestations, and cultural memories of a violent state that are thrown up and expropriated to organize the political perceptions of the present. Thus blood imagery, nude nature, and organicism, as a devolved language of the nation-state, also inflect the discourse of the German Left. There exists, as I have tried to show, a cultural complicity of the Left with the organistic iconography of the Right. The German New Left unwittingly accepts the fascist polarity between defilement and sealed armament: the national body. The historical project of this masculinist enclosure is focused on the containment, indeed, the eradication, of "filthy" bodies, foreign and other. When thus attempting to decipher this logic of German national fantasy, as Allen Feldman (1996) suggests:

> We cannot escape the image of the archeological ruins of Nazi state culture emerging from a forest of public memory as a substructure of everyday life.... It is as if a flea market of former bureaucracies and ideologies opens up for ideological traffic, with its used dusted-off contents of gas chambers, military campaigns, racial hygiene, racist economic rationalities, war imagery, and formulaic linguistic codes. These antiques are excavated by the anxieties of everyday life, and are superimposed on contemporary German social space, endowing it with the aura of authenticated ruins: a ruined modernity... [with] an attic full of authenticating artifacts.[15]

The ideological ruins of the Third Reich, of race and soil and body and space, are thus required by Left and Right for a massive remetaphorization of the postwar political landscape, a performance that indicts the poverty of available "nonviolent" political depiction and of the failure of existing institutional optics, which can no longer visualize contemporary experience with any public satisfaction.

NOTES

This chapter builds on some of my earlier works, notably *Blood and Nation: The European Aesthetics of Race* (Philadelphia: University of Pennsylavnia Press, 1999) and *German Bodies: Race and Representation after Hitler* (New York: Routledge, 1999), however with substantial revisions. Short segments of this chapter also appeared in *Transforming Anthropology* 8, nos. 1–2 (1999): 129–61; *City and Society: Annual Review 1997* (1998): 135–58; and *American Anthropologist* 99, no. 2 (1997): 559–73, all © American Anthropological Association.

 1. The literature on the politics of post-Holocaust memory is enormous. Here I have made reference to only some of the outstanding recent examples.

 2. This list of publications is not meant to be exhaustive; it merely samples some of the excellent recent works on this issue.

 3. As Omer Bartov (1998:793) has pointed out, the enthusiastic reception by third-generation Germans of Goldhagen's book, which argued that in the Third Reich Nazis and Germans were synonymous, was related to this desired sense of the past being "another country," or rather the grandparents' fatherland. See, for example, Roll (1996); Ullrich (1996); and Joffe (1996).

 4. English translation from Herzog (1998:442).

 5. English translation from ibid. (p. 442, n. 113).

 6. From ibid. (p. 440).

 7. From Sauer (1955:426).

 8. A prevalent 1980s peace movement slogan cited by Claussen (1986:61).

 9. From Piwitt (1978:39).

 10. For a discussion about the comparative importance of the German student movement, consult Bude (1995:17–22, 41–42).

 11. From Herzog (1998:397), who provides an in-depth analysis of the recurrent coupling of politics and sex in the debates of the German New Left movement during the late sixties. For a contemporary rendering, see Haug (1965:30–31).

 12. The photo caption text was translated by Herzog (1998:405).

 13. English translation from Herzog (1998:405).

 14. I recorded these slogans and texts during different stages of fieldwork in Germany: 1988–89, 1994 (Berlin), 1995 (Coblenz). For similar versions documented elsewhere, see, for example, *Spiegel* (1989:26–50); *Interim* (1989:cover jacket); Jäger (1993); and Link (1983).

 15. Personal communication (July 16, 1996).

BIBLIOGRAPHY

Adorno, Theodor W. 1969. *Stichworte. Kritische Modelle 2*. Frankfurt: Suhrkamp Verlag.

Aly, Goetz, Peter Chroust, and Christian Pross. 1994. *Cleansing the Fatherland: Nazi Medicine and Racial Hygiene*. Belinda Cooper, trans. Baltimore: Johns Hopkins University Press.

Anderson, Benedict. 1983. *Imagined Communities: Reflections on the Origin and Spread of Nationalism*. London: Verso.

Appadurai, Arjun, ed. 1986. "Introduction." In *The Social Life of Things*. Pp. 3–63. New York: Cambridge University Press.

Arendt, Hannah. 1964. *Eichmann in Jerusalem*. Munich: R. Pieper.

Bakthin, Mikhail. 1981. *The Dialogic Imagination*. M. Holquist, ed. Austin: University of Texas Press.

Baldwin, Peter, ed. 1990. *Reworking the Past: Hitler, the Holocaust, and the Historians' Debate.* Boston: Beacon Press.

Barnouw, Dagmar. 1996. *Germany 1945: Views of War and Violence.* Bloomington: Indiana University Press.

Bartov, Omer. 1996. *Murder in Our Midst: The Holocaust, Industrial Killing, and Representation.* New York: Oxford University Press.

———. 1998. "Defining Enemies, Making Victims: Germans, Jews, and the Holocaust." *American Historical Review* 103(3):771–816.

Bauer, Yehuda. 1998. "The Past That Will Not Go Away." In *The Holocaust and History.* M. Berenbaum and A. J. Peck, eds. Pp. 12–22. Bloomington: Indiana University Press.

Bauman, Zygmunt. 1989. *Modernity and the Holocaust.* Ithaca: Cornell University Press.

Berenbaum, Michael, and Abraham J. Peck, eds. 1998. *The Holocaust and History.* Bloomington: Indiana University Press.

Bloch, Ernst. 1990. *Heritage of Our Times.* Cambridge: MIT Press.

Boehling, Rebecca. 1996. *A Question of Priorities: Democratic Reform and Economic Recovery in Postwar Germany.* Providence: Berghahn Books.

Bookhagen, C., E. Hemmer, J. Raspe, E. Schulz, and M. Stergar. 1969. *Kommune 2. Versuch der Revolutionierung des bürgerlichen Individuums.* Berlin: Oberbaumverlag (reprint: Cologne: Kiepenheuer and Witsch, 1971).

Borneman, John. 1992a. *Belonging in the Two Berlins: Kin, State, Nation.* Cambridge: Cambridge University Press.

———. 1992b. "State, Territory, and Identity Formation in the Postwar Berlins, 1945–1989." *Cultural Anthropology* 7(1):45–62.

Brubaker, Rogers. 1992. *Citizenship and Nationhood in France and Germany.* Cambridge: Harvard University Press.

Brügge, Peter. 1981. " 'Nächstes Jahr nackert in d'Oper': über den Münchner Streit zwischen Katholiken und den Nackten." *Der Spiegel* 34 (August 17):150–51.

———. 1985. " 'Braun wennst bist, hast überall Kredit.' über die Münchner Kulturrevolution der Nacktbader." *Der Spiegel* (August 5):148–49.

Bude, Heinz. 1995. *Das Altern einer Generation: Die Jahrgänge 1938 bis 1948.* Frankfurt/Main: Suhrkamp.

Carter, Erica. 1997. *How German Is She? Postwar West German Reconstruction and the Consuming Woman.* Ann Arbor: University of Michigan Press.

Claussen, Detlev. 1986. "In the House of the Hangman." In *Germans and Jews since the Holocaust.* Anson Rabinbach and Jack Zipes, eds. New York: Holmes and Meier.

de Lauretis, Teresa. 1989. "The Violence of Rhetoric: Considerations on Representation and Gender." In *The Violence of Representation.* N. Armstrong and L. Tennenhouse, eds. Pp. 239–58. London: Routledge.

Dirke, Sabine von. 1997. *"All Power to the Imagination!": The West German Counterculture from the Student Movement to the Greens.* Lincoln: University of Nebraska Press.

Dundes, Alan. 1984. *Life Is Like a Chicken Coop Ladder: A Portrait of German Culture through Folklore.* New York: Columbia University Press.

Dürr, Hans Peter. 1994. *Nacktheit und Scham: Der Mythos vom Zivilisationsprozeß.* Frankfurt/Main: Suhrkamp Verlag.

Elias, Norbert. 1939. *Über den Prozess der Zivilisation.* 2 vols. Basel: Haus zum Falken.

Fehrenbach, Heide. 1994. *German Body Politics.* Postdoctoral fellow's project, Rutgers Center for Historical Analysis, Rutgers University.

Fein, Helen. 1979. *Accounting for Genocide*. New York: Free Press.

Feldman, Allen. 1997. *Formations of Violence: The Narration of the Body and Political Terror in Northern Ireland*. 3d ed. Chicago: University of Chicago Press.

Frei, Norbert. 1997. *Vergangenheitspolitik. Die Anfänge der Bundesrepublik und die NS-Vergangenheit*. Munich: Beck.

Friedlander, Henry. 1988. *The Origins of Nazi Genocide: From Euthanasia to the Final Solution*. Chapel Hill: University of North Carolina Press.

Friedländer, Saul, ed. 1992. *Probing the Limits of Representation: Nazism and the "Final Solution."* Cambridge: Harvard University Press.

Friedrich, Dorothea. 1986. "Not der Augen. Die Nacktheit oder der nackte Körper nackt." *Frankfurter Allgemeine Zeitung* 211 (September 9), Beilage—Frankfurter Magazin, Heft 341, pp. 46–50.

Gerhard, Ute. 1992. "Wenn Flüchtlinge und Einwanderer zu 'Asylantenfluten' werden. Zum Anteil des Mediendiskurses an rassistischen Progromen." In *Der Diskurs des Rassismus*. Siegfried Jäger and Franz Januschek, eds. Pp. 163–78. Oldenburg: Red. Osnabrücker Beiträge zur Sprachtheorie.

———. 1994. "Diskurstheoretische überlegungen zu Strategien des Rassismus in Medien und Politik. Flüchtlinge und Zuwanderer in Deutschland als wiederkehrendes Thema im 20. Jahrhundert." In *"Überall in den Köpfen und den Fäusten." Auf der Suche nach Ursachen und Konsequenzen von Gewalt*. Hans Tiersch et al., eds. Pp. 138–52. Darmstadt: Wissenschaftliche Buchgesellschaft.

Geyer, Michael. 1996. "The Politics of Memory in Contemporary Germany." In *Radical Evil*. Joan Copjec, ed. Pp. 169–200. London: Verso.

———. 2001. " 'There Is a Land Where Everything Is Pure: Its Name Is Land of Death.' Some Observations on Catastrophic Nationalism." In *Sacrifice and National Belonging*. Greg Eghigian, ed. Arlington: Texas University Press.

Gilman, Sander L. 1982. *On Blackness without Blacks: Essays on the Image of the Black in Germany*. Boston: G. H. Hall.

Girard, René. 1979. *Violence and the Sacred*. Patrick Gregory, trans. Baltimore: Johns Hopkins University Press.

Grossmann, Atina. 1995. "Unfortunate Germans: Victims, Victors, and Survivors at War's End, Germany 1945–1950." Working paper, Center for German and European Studies, University of California, Berkeley.

Guggenberg, Bernd. 1985. "Die nackte Wahrheit ist nicht immer das Wahre. Über die Grenzen zwischen Intimität und Öffentlichkeit." *Frankfurter Allgemeine Zeitung* 177 (August 3), Beilage: Bild und Zeit, pp. 1–2.

Hartman, Geoffrey, ed. 1994. *Holocaust Remembrance: The Shapes of Memory*. Oxford: Oxford University Press.

Haug, Fritz Wolfgang. 1965. "Vorbemerkung." *Das Argument* 32:30–31.

Heider, Ulrike. 1986. "Freie Liebe und Liebesreligion: Zum Sexualitätsbegriff der 6oer und 8oer Jahre." In *Sadomasochisten, Keusche, und Romantiker: Vom Mythos neuer Sinnlichkeit*. U. Heider, ed. Pp. 92–109. Hamburg: Rowohlt.

Heitmeyer, Wilhelm. 1992. *Die Bielefelder Rechtsextremismusstudie*. 2d ed. Weinheim: Juventa.

Held, Josef, and H. W. Horn. 1992. *Du musst so handeln, daß Du Gewinn machst...* Text No. 18. Duisburg: Duisburger Institut für Sprach- und Sozialforschung.

Herzog, Dagmar. 1998. "Pleasure, Sex, and Politics Belong Together: Post-Holocaust Memory and the Sexual Revolution in West Germany." *Critical Inquiry* 24 (Winter):393–444.

Hilberg, Raul. 1985. *The Destruction of the European Jews.* 3d rev. ed. New York: Holmes and Meier.

Hobsbawm, Eric, and Terence Ranger, eds. 1983. *The Invention of Tradition.* Cambridge: Cambridge University Press.

Hoffmeister, D., and O. Sill. 1993. *Zwischen Aufstieg und Ausstieg: Autoritäre Einstellungsmuster bei Jugendlichen und jungen Erwachsenen.* Opladen: Leske und Budrich.

Interim. 1989. "Müll raus, Menschen rein." *Interim: Wöchentliches Berlin-Info.* 59 (June 29):cover page.

Jäger, Margret. 1993. "Sprache der Angst." *die tageszeitung* (March 24).

Jeggle, Utz. 1997. "Phasen der Erinnerungsarbeit." In *Erinnern gegen den Schlußstrich: zum Umgang mit dem Nationalsozialismus.* K. Schönberger and M. Ulmer, eds. Pp. 70–82. Freiburg: Joachim Haug Verlag.

Jeske, J. Jürgen, Eckhard Neumann, and Wolfgang Sprang, eds. 1987a. "Körperpflege und Pharmazie." *Jahrbuch der Werbung* 24:418–23.

———. 1987b. "Diskussion: Das Nackte in der Werbung." *Jahrbuch der Werbung in Deutschland, Österreich und der Schweiz* 24:39–55.

Joffe, Josef. 1996. "Goldhagen in Deutschland." *New York Review of Books* (November 28):18–21.

Jones, Ernest. 1951. *On the Nightmare.* New York: Liveright.

Köhler, Michael. 1985. "Stimmen zu Nacktheit und Sex in der Werbung. Eine Dokumentation." In *Das Aktfoto.* M. Köhler and G. Barche, eds. Pp. 274–81. Munich: Verlag C. J. Bucher.

Köster, Barbara. 1987. "Rüsselsheim Juli 1985." In *Wir haben sie so geliebt, die Revolution.* Daniel Cohn-Bendit, ed. P. 244. Frankfurt/Main: Athenäum.

Kuper, Leo. 1981. *Genocide.* New Haven: Yale University Press.

Kurthen, Hermann, Wener Bergmann, and Rainer Erb, eds. 1997. *Antisemitism and Xenophobia in Germany after Unification.* New York/Oxford: Oxford University Press.

Lifton, Robert Jay. 1986. *Nazi Doctos: Medical Killing and the Psychology of Genocide.* New York: Basic Books.

Link, Jürgen. 1983. "Asylanten, ein Killwort." Auszüge aus einer Bochumer Vorlesung vom 15. Dezember 1982. *kultuRRevolution* 2 (February):36–38.

Linke, Uli. 1995. "Murderous Fantasies: Violence, Memory, and Selfhood in Germany." *New German Critique* 64 (winter):37–59.

———. 1997a. "Colonizing the National Imaginary: Folklore, Anthropology, and the Making of the Modern State." In *Cultures of Scholarship.* Sally Humphreys, ed. Pp. 97–138. Ann Arbor: Michigan University Press.

———. 1997b. "Gendered Difference, Violent Imagination: Blood, Race, Nation." *American Anthropologist* 99:559–73.

———. 1999a. *Blood and Nation: The European Aesthetics of Race.* Philadelphia: University of Pennsylvania Press.

———. 1999b. *German Bodies: Race and Representation after Hitler.* New York/London: Routledge.

Lipstadt, Deborah. 1993. *Denying the Holocaust: The Growing Assault on Truth and Memory.* New York: Free Press.

Maier, Charles S. 1989. *The Unmasterable Past: History, Holocaust, and German National Identity.* Boston: Harvard University Press.

Malkki, Liisa H. 1995a. *Purity and Exile.* Chicago: University of Chicago Press.

————. 1995b. "Refugees and Exile: From 'Refugee Studies' to the National Order of Things." *Annual Review of Anthropology* 24:495–523.

————. 1996. "National Geographic." In *Becoming National.* Geoff Eley and Ronald Grigor Suny, eds. Pp. 434–53. New York: Oxford University Press.

Markovits, Andrei S., and Simon Reich. 1997. *The German Predicament: Memory and Power in the New Europe.* Ithaca: Cornell University Press.

Mayer, Elkebarbara, Martina Schmolt, and Harald Wolf, eds. 1988. *Zehn Jahre Alternative Liste.* Bremen: Steintor.

Melson, Robert. 1992. *Revolution and Genocide.* Chicago: University of Chicago Press.

Moeller, Robert G. 1996. "War Stories: The Search for a Usable Past in the Federal Republic of Germany." *American Historical Review* 101 (October):1008–48.

Moeller, Robert G., ed. 1997. *West Germany under Construction: Politics, Society, and Culture in the Adenauer Era.* Ann Arbor: University of Michigan Press.

Mommsen, Hans. 1991. *From Weimar to Auschwitz.* Princeton: Princeton University Press.

Morley, David, and Kevin Robins. 1996. "No Place Like *Heimat:* Images of Home(land) in European Culture." In *Becoming National.* Geoff Eley and Ronald G. Suny, eds. Pp. 456–78. New York: Oxford University Press.

Mosler, Peter. 1977. *Was wir wollten, was wir wurden: Studentenrevolte—zehn Jahre danach.* Hamburg: Rowohlt.

Mosse, George L. 1985. *Nationalism and Sexuality: Middle-Class Morality and Sexual Norms in Modern Europe.* Madison: University of Wisconsin Press.

Müller, Siegfried. 1985. *Graffiti: Tätowierte Wände.* Bielefeld: AYZ.

Müller-Hill, Benno. 1988. *Murderous Science.* George R. Fraser, trans. Oxford: Oxford University Press.

Naumann, Klaus. 1996. "Die Mutter, das Pferd und die Juden: Flucht und Vertreibung als Themen deutscher Erinnerungspolitik." *Mittelweg* 36 (August–September):70–83.

Panorama. 1967. "Kahle Maoisten vor einer kahlen Wand." *Spiegel* 27 (June 26):20.

Peck, Jeffrey M. 1996. "Rac(e)ing the Nation: Is There a German 'Home'?" In *Becoming National.* Geoff Eley and Ronald G. Suny, eds. Pp. 481–92. New York: Oxford University Press.

Piwitt, Hermann Peter. 1978. "Niemand muß hungern: Das Gerede von der 'Überbevölkerung' ist ein verbrecherischer Mythos. Zwei Amerikaner haben ihn zerstört." *Konkret* 8 (August):39.

Pohrt, Wolfgang. 1991. "Stop den Mob." *Konkret* (May) 5:34–35.

Pokorny, Julius. 1959. *Indogermanisches Wörterbuch.* 2 vols. Bern: Francke Verlag.

Preuss-Lausitz, Ulf. 1989. "Vom gepanzerten zum sinnstiftenden Körper." In *Kriegskinder, Konsumkinder, Krisenkinder: Zur Sozialisationsgeschichte seit dem zweiten Weltkrieg.* U. Preuss-Lausitz, ed. 2d ed. Weinheim: Beltz.

Proctor, Robert. 1988. *Racial Hygiene: Medicine under the Nazis.* Cambridge: Harvard University Press.

Reiche, Reimut. 1988. "Sexuelle Revolution—Erinnerung an einen Mythos." In *Die Früchte der Revolte. Über die Veränderung der politischen Kultur durch die Studentenbewegung.* Lothar Baier, ed. Pp. 55–67. Berlin: Wagenbach.

Roll, Evelyn. 1996. "Goldhagens Diskussionsreise: Der schwierige Streit um die Deutschen und den Holocaust; Eine These und drei gebrochene Tabus." *Süddeutsche Zeitung* (September 9).

Sauer, Hermann. 1955. "Zwischen Gewissen und Dämon: Der 20. Juli gestern und heute." *Junge Kirche* (1955):426.

Schirner, Michael. 1987. "Hatten Sie schon mal den Weltgeist als Kunden?: Das Nackte in der Werbung." *Jahrbuch der Werbung* 24:39–41.

Siepmann, Eckhard, ed. 1984. *CheSchaShit: Die Sechziger Jahre zwischen Cocktail und Molotov.* 2d ed. Berlin: Elefanten Press.

Soltau, Heide. 1987. "Erotische Irritationen und heimliche Spiele mit der Lust: Das Nackte in der Werbung." *Jahrbuch der Werbung* 24:42–50.

Sorel, Georges. 1941. *Reflections on Violence.* T. E. Hulme, trans. New York: P. Smith.

Spiegel, Der. 1988. "Hochschulen bis aufs Hemd." *Der Spiegel* 52:62–63.

———. 1989. "Die neuen Deutschen. Einwanderungsland Bundesrepublik, I: Fremdenfurcht verändert die politische Landschaft." *Der Spiegel* 43(7):26–50.

———. 1999a. "Das Jahrhundert der Befreiung: 1968, das Jahr der Rebellion." *Der Spiegel* 13 (March 29):171–88.

———. 1999b. "Wieso nackt?" *Der Spiegel* 20 (May 17):303.

Stadelmann, Bernd. 1999. "Bundeswehr/Rekrutengelöbnis am Jahrestag des Hitler-Attentats." *Schwäbisches Tagblatt* 165 (July 21):2.

Stiftung Haus der Geschichte. 1998. *Bilder die lügen: Begleitbuch zur Austellung im Haus der Geschichte der Bundesrepublik Deutschland, Bonn.* Bonn: Bouvier.

Tagblatt. 1999. "Störern drohen harte Strafen." *Schwäbisches Tagblatt* 167 (July 23):1.

tageszeitung [taz]. 1989. "Volks-frei-tag vor der Wahl." *die tageszeitung* (January 27): 15–16.

Theweleit, Klaus. 1987. *Male Fantasies.* Vol. 1, *Women, Floods, Bodies, History.* Minneapolis: University of Minnesota Press.

Tilly, Charles. 1970. "The Changing Place of Collective Violence." In *Essays in Theory and History.* Melvin Richter, ed. Cambridge: Harvard University Press.

Todorov, Tzvetan. 1990. "Measuring Evil." *New Republic* (March 19):30–33.

Ullrich, Volker. 1996. "Daniel J. Goldhagen in Deutschland: Die Buchtournee wurde zum Triumphzug." *Die Zeit* 38 (September 13).

Vidal-Naquet, Pierre. 1992. *Assassins of Memory: Essays on the Denial of the Holocaust.* Jeffrey Mehlman, trans. New York: Columbia University Press.

Volland, Ernst. 1987. *Gefühl und Schärfe.* Bremen: Rixdorfer Verlagsanstalt.

Wahlprogramm. 1989. *Wahlprogramm der Alternativen Liste.* Berlin: Alternative Liste.

Weber, Max. 1947. *The Theory of Social and Economic Organization.* A. M. Henderson and T. Parson, trans. New York: Oxford University Press.

Aftermaths of Genocide

Cambodian Villagers

May Ebihara and Judy Ledgerwood

This paper explores some effects of the massive mortality rate that Cambodia sustained in the 1970s, especially during the regime of Democratic Kampuchea (DK) under Pol Pot. It focuses in particular on a Khmer peasant village of rice cultivators, Svay, that Ebihara originally studied in 1959–60 and that she and Ledgerwood revisited several times through the 1990s.[1] Genocide, coupled with the Khmer Rouge regime's attempt to create a revolutionary new society though simultaneous destruction of customary social institutions, had dramatic repercussions on village life even after Pol Pot was routed in 1979. Under subsequent regimes over the past two decades, villagers have undergone various processes of recovery and rebuilding under changing demographic, sociocultural, economic, and political circumstances. The discussion here will focus on several dimensions of the manifold repercussions of the "Pol Pot time" (*samay a-Pot*):[2] (1) the reconstitution of families/households, kinship bonds, and social networks in the face of numerous deaths, as well as coping with an initial gender imbalance created by high mortality among males during DK; (2) the revitalization of Buddhism after years of suppression; and (3) the creation of a climate of fear and continued social and political violence. We cannot deal with the profound question of why the Cambodian genocide occurred, an issue that has been discussed and debated by a number of scholars (for example, Chandler 1992; Kiernan 1996; Thion 1993; Hinton 1997; Jackson 1989). Rather, we look at the circumstances and effects of genocide at the local level of a specific community.

BACKGROUND

It would be useful to recap recent Cambodian history as context for this discussion. In 1970 a coup overthrowing Prince Norodom Sihanouk precipitated a brutal civil war between the Lon Nol government and the insurgent Khmer Rouge, as well as intensive covert bombing of the countryside by the United States in a spillover from the conflict in Vietnam. During the early 1970s the communist rebels expanded rapidly throughout the county until they captured Phnom Penh on April 17, 1975, ushering in Pol Pot's infamous Democratic Kampuchea. The regime was short-lived, lasting only through the end of 1978, when the Vietnamese, goaded by DK incursions into Vietnam, invaded Cambodia and routed the Khmer Rouge, who retreated to bases on the border with Thailand and certain other regions. At that time, many people were forced by or escaped from the Khmer Rouge to the Thai border area, where enormous refugee camps with hundreds of thousands of people were created under the auspices of the United Nations High Commissioner for Refugees (on camp life, see French 1994a). Over a period of years following 1979, some 250,000 refugees were eventually relocated to such countries as the United States, France, Canada, and Australia, creating an extensive Cambodian diaspora (Ebihara 1985).[3]

In Cambodia after 1979, the government (initially called the People's Republic of Kampuchea, or PRK, renamed the State of Cambodia, or SOC, in 1989) moved gradually from an initially semisocialist system to restoration of various features of prerevolutionary Cambodian society, including private property, a market economy, and the revival of Buddhism. Peace, however, was elusive, as the country experienced renewed civil conflict between the incumbent PRK/SOC government and several resistance forces: the militant Khmer Rouge, a royalist group loyal to Sihanouk, and a pro-Western faction. Following negotiations and a peace agreement among the contesting political groups, the United Nations sponsored a nationwide general election in 1993. The country was yet again renamed, this time as the Kingdom of Cambodia, with Sihanouk as figurehead leader over an ostensibly coalition government of officials from several political parties or factions. In fact, however, the Cambodian People's Party (under Prime Minister Hun Sen) holds primary political power.

MORTALITY

Even prior to the genocide of the DK regime, the civil war period caused some 275,000 "excess deaths" (Banister and Johnson 1993:87). The village of Svay was located in a region of intense fighting between Lon Nol government soldiers and rebel Khmer Rouge; several villagers were killed by random gunfire in the early 1970s, and people began to flee the countryside as it became too dangerous to tend the rice fields. Villagers escaped to what they hoped would be safe havens in and around Phnom Penh, and their abandoned houses and fields fell into ruin. Immediately after the Khmer Rouge victory in 1975, when people were forcibly ejected from Phnom Penh, many villagers tried to return to Svay but found only what they characterized as an overgrown "wilderness" (*prey*) where their homes had once stood.[4] DK cadres sent the wanderers to a barren area nearby, where the evacuees were forced to live for several months in makeshift shelters with little food or water. Eleven West Hamlet villagers died there from starvation and illness before the surviving evacuees were dispersed to Svay and other sites that were rebuilt as communes in the region.

During DK, Svay was controlled by Khmer Rouge cadres and so-called Old People—that is, ordinary people who had either joined or been "liberated" by the Khmer Rouge before their victory in 1975. Urbanites and rural peasants who had not been part of the revolutionary movement prior to 1975—including Svay villagers who had fled to Phnom Penh during the civil war—were pejoratively labeled "New People," "April 17 People," "Lon Nol People," and, more ominously, "the enemy." Although Svay villagers were actually from the politically correct stratum of poor peasantry, the Khmer Rouge suspected everyone of concealing former lives as prosperous urbanites, government soldiers, educated people, or even CIA agents. One villager reported an exchange with a DK cadre when he was ill:

> [The cadre] said, "The reason you're sick is that you're used to living well." I replied, "How can you say that? I've been a farmer all my life." They said, "You're used to living in comfort and never worked hard. *We* fought all the battles and liberated you. You just came here with your two empty hands and your empty stomach. So *we* have the right to tell you what to do. What *we* say, goes."

Defined as "the other" (compare Hinton's introduction to this volume), New People were subject to extremely harsh conditions. With the abolition of private property, markets, and money, production and consumption became communal. As part of DK's determination to maximize agricultural output, people were organized into work teams that were segregated on the basis of age and gender; they were forced to endure unrelenting hard labor on the communes growing rice and other crops, constructing dams and enormous irrigation systems, reshaping rice paddies, tending animals, making fertilizer, and pursuing an endless array of other tasks. Ironically, however, New People were given grossly inadequate food rations, consisting largely of thin rice gruel and whatever wild foods might be foraged. They also suffered endemic illnesses (such as fevers, dysentery, malaria, and infections) with little or no medical aid, and stringent discipline that included severe physical punishments, imprisonment, and execution for breaking rules or upon suspicion of being "enemies" of the regime.[5] Villagers described DK in such terms as these:

> People's worth was measured in terms of how many cubic meters of dirt they moved. We had to dig canals: measure and dig; measure and dig. I'd fall carrying heavy loads . . . so you'd walk and fall, walk and fall. Even when you got sick you didn't dare stop working because they'd kill you, so you kept working until you collapsed. They used people without a thought as to whether we lived or died.

> We worked so hard planting and harvesting; there were piles of rice as big as this house, but they took it away in trucks. . . . You'd be killed if you tried to take anything for yourself. You could *see* food, but you weren't allowed to eat it. We had no freedom to do anything: to eat, to sleep, to speak. We hid our crying, weeping into our pillows at night.

From 1977 on, people were taken away to be killed (*vay chaol*). [One day in 1977, seven men in Svay] were taken away. [The Khmer Rouge cadre] said, "Come on, load up everything, you're being taken to build houses." They lied. They didn't tell you they were going to kill you; they said you're going to work. But I knew. C [one of the men being called up] also knew. He cried and embraced his father. I went up to C and he said, "We're about to be separated now. I'm going." When people were taken away, I knew in my heart that they were going to die. I knew when they were taken away with their hands tied behind their backs, but also when they were called away to work. I kept thinking, when will *I* be taken away? But you couldn't ask, and you couldn't run away—or even kill yourself—because then they'd get your wife and children.

All of the preceding made for massive mortality, estimated at some 1.7 million (possibly as many as 2 million) deaths out of a total population of about 7.9 million Cambodians in 1975 (compare Kiernan 1996:458; Cambodian Genocide Program 1999:1).[6] Further, the death rate for males was higher than for females because men were more likely to die from starvation or execution (as well as combat deaths during the civil war). Looking more specifically at Svay, the following mortality figures were calculated for a delimited population of 159 persons whom Ebihara had known during her original fieldwork in 1959–60 in one particular section, West Hamlet, of Svay.[7] Taking into account the inhabitants who died natural deaths and four who were killed during the civil war preceding DK, 139 persons were still alive in 1975 at the outset of the Pol Pot regime. During DK some of these people remained in the Svay region, while others were dispersed to communes elsewhere, including some northern provinces with especially harsh conditions. Of these 139, 70 died of starvation, overwork, illness, or execution during DK, a mortality rate of 50 percent among West Svay villagers Ebihara had previously known (see also Ebihara 1993b).[8] During DK every adult villager suffered the deaths of close family members, whether parents, grandparents, siblings, or children, not to mention deaths of other relatives and close friends—and they also lived with the constant threat of their own possible death.

AFTERMATHS: FAMILY/HOUSEHOLD, KIN, AND SOCIAL NETWORKS

Part of Democratic Kampuchea's attempt to create a radical new society involved undermining a crucial social group in prerevolutionary life: the family/household, which had been the basic unit of economic production and consumption, as well as the locus of the strongest emotional bonds. Beyond the family, individuals also felt attachments and moral obligations toward members of a broadly defined bilateral kindred of relatives by both blood and marriage (*bang-b'aun*). During DK, a number of measures aimed to undercut sentiments and cohesion among family and kinfolk. Huge numbers of people were moved around the country in the deployment of the labor force, thus fracturing family and kin relationships. Forced separation occurred also at the local level. Even when family or kin were based in the same commune, they were placed in work teams segregated by age and gender such that husbands and wives saw one another only at night, and parents and offspring could meet only occasionally.[9] Household commensality was replaced by communal dining halls (which allowed the state to control food distribution down to the grass roots level). Children were encouraged to spy upon and turn against their "reactionary" elders. Marriages, formerly decided upon by individuals and parents, were now arranged between strangers or had to be approved by Khmer Rouge cadres. Expressions of love for family members—such as weeping over the death of a spouse or child—were denigrated, scorned, and even punished. One woman managed to remain impassively silent when her husband was summoned to a work project—that is, almost certain execution—but she could not contain herself when her newborn infant died shortly thereafter. In response to her uncontrollable wails, the KR cadre responded disdainfully: "You're crying over that little thing? We lost all those people in our struggle, and you don't see us crying."

After the Khmer Rouge were ousted and tight controls over the population were lifted, people moved about the country searching for family and kin from whom they had been separated, and many returned to their home communities. Svay was transformed once more, reorganized as an ordinary village again, as many of its original inhabitants returned from other regions to which they had been relocated during DK. "It was then," one villager said, "that we found out who was alive and who was dead." Families reconstituted themselves with whatever members survived. As in prerevolutionary times, present-day Svay households are either nuclear or extended families. Some of the latter are three-generational stem families (a couple or widow[er] with a married child plus the latter's spouse and children), such as was common in the past. Other extended family households, however, have more varied composition, as people followed the prerevolutionary practice of sheltering needy kin, and some took in relatives left orphaned or widowed after DK. (One household, for example, has a wife and husband, the wife's widowed sister and a widowed aunt, plus the couple's married daughter and her husband and children.) Ties with kinfolk in the village and nearby communities were also reactivated, with mutual aid of various kinds that include labor exchange for rice cultivation, financial help in times of need, assistance for one another's life cycle and other rituals, and a sense of mutual concern and moral obligation for one another's welfare (see also Uimonen 1996:45).[10]

Contemporary patterns of reciprocal aid and cooperation among kinsmen—and also among close friends—are perceived by villagers as revivals of customary (that is, prerevolutionary) patterns of behavior. In discussing aspects of present-day life (such as cooperative labor during rice cultivation), villagers often say that a certain practice occurs "as in times before" (*douc pi daoem*). In fact changes have occurred, but the villagers' reference to earlier times seems to invoke a belief or hope that life has returned to what they knew in a peaceful prewar Cambodia.[11]

On the issue of mutual assistance in the context of this particular village, it is important to recall that most of Svay's present population are former residents who returned home after the upheavals of DK.[12] Thus many villagers have known one another since birth. Their families have been acquainted for generations, and most are related to each other by blood or marriage. The former residents of West Hamlet Svay belong to overlapping kindreds such that everyone is kin, friends of kin, or kin of friends. They demonstrate a kind of tolerance for one another's personalities and habits that is found only among people who know each other very well. There are also reports of other villages on the central plains of Cambodia that have returned to patterns of mutual assistance, including labor exchange (see, for example, Uimonen 1996; McAndrew 1997).

There are, however, assertions in some development (and other) literature that Cambodian society was so fragmented and atomized by the horrific conditions of DK that people, even kinsmen, no longer help one another.[13] Frings (1994:61) argues that Khmer no longer care about each other, have no sense of moral obligation or genuine desire to help, are motivated only by self-interest, and will provide assistance only if they get something in return. Ovesen et al. (1996:68) take this argument a step further to assert that a Cambodian village is nothing more than a cluster of houses that does not constitute a significant social entity, let alone a moral community. Indeed, they question whether a village ever had "normal" traditional social cohesion (ibid.:66).

Although Ledgerwood has critiqued this literature elsewhere (1998b), we would note several points regarding the issue of whether mutual aid and cooperation do or do not exist among Cambodian villagers. Part of the problem in this debate is a romanticized notion that mutual aid in Khmer social networks before DK was based on purely altruistic generosity and kindness, but that survivors of the DK firestorm have become greedy and (following Frings) expect something in return. Taking a more general perspective, however, anthropologists have long noted systems of reciprocity in which gift giving and forms of assistance create a system of obligations that bind people together as a social unit.[14] Thus while Western development researchers may perceive a system in which people help one another to get something in return, Marston argues that being enmeshed in a network of social obligations is the only relatively safe haven in a dangerous world (1997:59). Indeed, he suggests that in the aftermath of genocide, personal and kin networks become all the more important because other kinds of institutions have proven to be unreliable (ibid.:81). In addition, people who have suffered the deaths of so many family members would cleave all that much more closely to those who survived.

Emphasizing resentments and conflicts within a community can create a false picture of a collection of houses with no sense of social cohesion. On the other hand, overemphasizing the social bonds of kinsmen and friends could present another mistaken view of a community in perfect harmony. In fact, any community will be characterized by its own particular set of social relations that falls along a continuum between these extremes, although the notion of a cluster of houses with no social ties would seem the more improbable situation.

If Cambodian villagers sometimes appear to outsiders to be more selfish and self-serving than in the past, even as (following Marston's argument) their dependency on one another has increased, what are the possible reasons for that perception? For one thing, the social circles within which assistance is provided may be smaller than in the past. Vijghen has discussed this shrinking circle of relatives and asserts that needy kin are often given only enough food so they will not starve, but they are not provided with equipment, land to farm, or investment capital (Vijghen, cited in Frings 1994; Vijghen and Ly 1996). We would interpret such a situation as indicating not lack of concern for one's fellows but rather the poverty of most villagers, who have little or no spare money or land to give to others.[15] It is true that the extreme deprivation and violence of the Pol Pot period made people watch out for themselves more than ever before. But there are numerous instances in Svay of people helping each other in a variety of ways, including sharing food, providing cash donations or loans, giving emergency financial and other assistance, and offering psychological support (see Ebihara 1994; Ledgerwood 1998b). Such aid is most often proffered to relatives and close friends, but we have also seen Svay villagers give whatever help was possible to mere acquaintances whose dire straits evoked compassionate responses.

GENDER IMBALANCE

In the years immediately following the ouster of Pol Pot, a major issue for the People's Republic of Kampuchea during the early 1980s was the large number of widows left by high male mortality during DK. Banister and Johnson estimated that about "ten percent of men and almost three percent of women in young adult and middle age years were killed above and beyond those who died due to the general mortality situation" (1993:90). In some parts of the country during the 1980s, widows were said to constitute anywhere from 65 to 80 percent of the adult population (Ledgerwood 1992; Boua 1982). Of the specific West Hamlet population who died during DK, some 56 percent were male, which is lower than the Banister and Johnson estimates. However, looking at the newly created administrative unit of West Svay village, local census figures for 1990 noted that the total village population (including all ages) was 80.5 percent female (although those figures are open to question; see below).

Such shortage of male labor, as well as of draft animals and agricultural implements, led the early PRK government to institute a semisocialist system with communal production and distribution of rice and certain other foodstuffs by so-called solidarity groups (*krom samaki*), although other subsistence activities were left to private household production and consumption as in prerevolutionary times (see also Boua 1982; Vickery 1986; Curtis 1990). Although this system was intended to benefit widows and other needy folk, Svay villagers were averse to such communal effort—perhaps because it reminded them all too vividly of the hated Pol Pot years, when they had been forced into labor teams—and de facto household production and consumption for all subsistence activities re-emerged by around 1986. Although some Western analysts (for example, Frings 1994) have bemoaned the failure of collectivization during the PRK, Svay villagers express no such regrets.

Earlier studies of women and development in Cambodia (including Ledgerwood 1992) reported that widow-headed households were much poorer than their neighbors, because they needed to hire male labor for cultivation and pay with return labor exchange or money.[16] However, further analysis of Svay's widow-headed households (as well as similar households in two other communities studied by Ledgerwood) indicates that widowing per se is not a predictor of poverty. Rather, the critical factors affecting the relative economic position of a widow are whether or not she has able-bodied male labor power (especially sons and sons-in-law) within her own household or in other closely related households, moderate landholdings, and (in the best of all possible worlds) some cattle (see also Taylor, quoted in Boyden and Gibbs 1997:96). Manpower and oxen are critical for plowing rice fields, and obviously a household's relative prosperity is tied in large measure to the amount of rice paddy land it owns.[17]

Some works have asserted that widows are falling into debt and being forced to sell their lands and move to the city (for example, Frings 1994; Secretariat of State for Women's Affairs 1994). This pattern is not yet evident in Svay, possibly because Phnom Penh is not far away and villagers can easily travel to the city to seek additional income rather than giving up precious land. Only one widow reported selling a bit of land.

According to Boua (1982), the highly skewed sex ratio also created another sort of problem for women in the early 1980s: men, knowing that adult males were in short supply, often took advantage of the situation by consorting with many women, abandoning wives and taking "second wives," concubines, or lovers, although polygyny is no longer legal.[18] Wife abandonment or multiple liaisons may also occur in situations when soldiers are moved around to different parts of the countryside; or, possibly, men leave wives that they were forced to marry during DK. In one case near Svay, a young man had not totally abandoned his wife but would disappear for periods of time, and it was quite certain that he had a "second wife" in Phnom Penh.[19] While divorces (which were relatively easy to obtain) and remarriages were not uncommon in prerevolutionary Svay (see Ebihara 1974), divorce nowadays involves a lengthy, cumbersome, and sometimes expensive procedure (that often works to the detriment of the woman). Thus many couples may simply separate (whether by mutual consent or not) without obtaining formal divorces, and former mates may enter new relationships. Although villagers certainly knew or had heard of examples of wife abandonment in nearby communities, the great majority of marriages in Svay appear to be relatively stable, with responsible and faithful spouses.

Throughout the 1990s the formerly highly skewed gender ratio evened out dramatically, with 1996 population figures for West Svay (encompassing all age groups) having an almost equal number of males and females (recall that the 1990 West Svay census indicated 80.5 percent females). Nationwide the 1995 statistics showed that the population over twenty years of age was 48 percent male and 56 percent female, and the 1998 census showed a national population (including all age groups) that was 51.8 percent female (United Nations Population Fund 1995:5–7; National Institute of Statistics 1999). We believe that it is difficult to explain this rapid balancing out of the sex ratio simply in terms of a high birth rate producing more male babies. Rather we suspect that adult males were undercounted everywhere in earlier censuses because they were away from home for a variety of reasons: they were in the government army, or had joined antigovernment resistance groups in northwestern Cambodia, or were in refugee camps in Thailand, or had been sent abroad by the government to get various kinds of technical training, or had been hiding somewhere to avoid conscription. (Examples of virtually all of these can be found in Svay.) The return of the men, as well as a healthy birth rate of 2.5 to 3 percent over the past fifteen or so years (such that 47 percent of the current population is under fifteen years of age), has thus made the sex ratio and household composition more normal in the country as a whole (United Nations Population Fund 1995:5–7; National Institute of Statistics 1999).

AFTERMATHS: THE REVIVAL OF BUDDHISM

Another aspect of DK's attempt to turn people's loyalties exclusively to the state was the effort to destroy Buddhism. Buddhist monks were forced to disrobe and even were executed, while Buddhist temples were either demolished or desecrated by being put to menial uses as, for example, pigsties or storehouses. Thus in 1979, at the beginning of the PRK period, there was a grave shortage of both religious sites and personnel. Although the government allowed Buddhism to be revived, it was limited both by state policy and by lack of material resources. The PRK initially stipulated that only men over fifty could become monks because young males were needed for agricultural labor and for the military. Communities had to apply for permission to reconstruct temple compounds, and funds for construction (raised through ceremonies and through soliciting donations) had to be used first and foremost to rebuild temple schools and only secondarily to restore the temples themselves. As Keyes has written: "Buddhism was still viewed in Marxist terms as having a potential for offering people 'unhealthy beliefs' " (1994:62). Given such circumstances, there is a question as to whether an entire generation of Cambodians who were children during DK and adolescents during PRK lacked exposure to, and hence became estranged from, Buddhism.

In 1989 the State of Cambodia formally designated Therevada Buddhism as being once again the state religion, as it had been prior to DK, and broadcasts of daily prayers were immediately revived on the national radio. Buddhism blossomed throughout the 1990s. The hierarchy of Buddhist monks was reinstated; young men and boys were again allowed to become monks and novices; Pali schools for monks reopened around the country; and Buddhist texts are being reprinted and distributed with the help of Japanese and German funding. The number of monks, estimated at 6,500 to 8,000 in 1985–89 during the PRK, jumped to 16,400 in 1990, about 20,000 in 1991 (ibid.:62–63), and 50,081 in 1998–99, affiliated with 3,685 temples (Ministry of Cults and Religion 1999).[20]

Fearing that events of the recent past disrupted people's relationship to the spiritual realm (see also Mortland 1994), rural communities have expended considerable effort toward rebuilding local temples that were destroyed, damaged, or neglected during the Khmer Rouge and PRK periods. Families across the country used whatever small amounts of surplus they may have accrued to make donations for restoring temples, building or repairing *chedey* (repositories for ashes of the dead), and performing ceremonies for the spirits of relatives who died during DK. Many overseas Khmer returning to their homeland or sending money from abroad have also contributed large sums to this process, as have wealthy Phnom Penh residents who sometimes support a specific temple in the region where they or their forebears were born. Furthermore, contributions to temples (whether in the form of money, material goods, labor, or attendance at ceremonies) are considered highly virtuous deeds, and donors earn much religious merit.

Svay's temple compound suffered considerable destruction and deterioration during the civil war and DK periods. The central temple (*vihear*), which was a beautiful structure with the graceful curving roof characteristic of Khmer temples, was completely destroyed with explosives by the Khmer Rouge.[21] In 1990 the building that had been used as a dormitory for the monks was still standing, but its walls were pockmarked with holes from bullets and artillery; the *salaa*, or open-sided meeting hall, was in shabby condition after having been used as a hospital by the Khmer Rouge. After DK, villagers continued to worship in the salaa, but there was deep desire to construct a new vihear. Beginning in 1990 with the erection of a gate and wall that defined the sacred space of the temple compound, work on the vihear proceeded slowly in gradual steps over many years, because there were few funds for rebuilding and construction depended largely on the voluntary labor of local villagers. By 1997 the vihear was largely completed (and looked in many ways more resplendent than it had in the past), and several chedey had also been newly erected. Work was still progressing on some smaller structures in the compound.

Each rebuilt temple has a group of resident monks who are critical for celebrations of the full round of annual Buddhist rituals, as well as essential participants in familial ceremonies such as weddings and funerals. Buddhism is especially important in offering people a means to renew the social and moral order of society. Through ritual, villagers can formally reconstruct the proper order of relationships between the world of the living and the spiritual realm. At the same time they may make peace with their own feelings of guilt and remorse over the suffering of their fellows during the past twenty years. As Meas Nee has written:

> Looked at from the outside, religion, the teaching of the monks, music, traditional games, and traditional skills are a way to strengthen the culture. But I see them as not just that. They are the way to build unity and to heal hearts and spirits. They help

to create a community where everything can be talked about, even past suffering. They help create a community where the poorest are cared about. They help to restore dignity. (1995:70)

Impressions from contemporary village life suggest that children born after 1979 are once again being socialized into religious practices, and contingents of monks at local Buddhist temples include novices who are young adolescents.[22]

AFTERMATHS: UNCERTAINTY, FEAR, AND VIOLENCE

Survivors of DK live with an undercurrent of fear and uncertainty. One of the legacies of genocide is that people's confidence in personal safety is stripped away. As Myerhoff has written about the experience of Jewish holocaust survivors, the self-assurance that

> it can never happen to me, comforts on-lookers, but not survivors. They know by what slender threads their lives are distinguished from those who died; they do not see in themselves soothing virtues or special merits that make their survival inevitable or right; to these people complacency is forever lost. (1978:24)

For many years after 1979, the fear most commonly and fervently expressed by rural villagers was that the Khmer Rouge would return to power. Memories of DK were indelibly etched in the minds of survivors, and Democratic Kampuchean resistance forces remained active in certain regions. In the early 1990s, although there were no Khmer Rouge in the immediate vicinity,[23] villagers (and Ledgerwood and Ebihara) sometimes heard explosions, whether muffled thumps coming from mountains to the southwest where DK camps were located, or frighteningly loud blasts from unexploded ordnance left buried in nearby fields that was accidentally detonated. Some families had dug trenches alongside their houses to serve as foxholes in case of sudden attack. Svay residents declared emphatically that they could not survive a second DK regime and would fight to the death before succumbing again to Khmer Rouge rule. Such sentiments were strongly encouraged by the PRK government, whose legitimacy was based in large part on its having liberated Cambodia from Pol Pot. Vivid reminders of the DK's horrors contained in photographs of victims, paintings of killings, and implements used for torture are on display at the Tuol Sleng Museum of Genocidal Crimes, a former school that had become a deadly interrogation center during DK (see Ledgerwood 1997; Chandler 1999), as well as in a monumental display of skulls and bones at Chhoeung Ek, a former killing field where one can still see bits of bone and cloth in the soil of what had been mass graves. The PRK also instituted an annual observance called The Day of Hate, in which people were gathered at various locales to hear invectives heaped on the Khmer Rouge.[24] State propaganda played on this theme with such slogans as: "We must absolutely prevent the return of this former black darkness," and "We must struggle ceaselessly to protect against the return of the Pol Pot, Ieng Sary,

Khieu Samphan genocidal clique." These formulaic and state-sanctioned expressions were genuine and often expressed in conversations among ordinary folk.

Cambodians today have a second generalized fear about violence within their midst. Although violent outbursts occurred periodically in pre-1970 Cambodia (for example, a street crowd in Phnom Penh battering a thief), acts of violence have become much more commonplace. After nearly thirty years of war, there are now many more armed men than in prewar times. Fear focuses in particular on soldiers and former soldiers who still move through the countryside, and there is also apprehension about police or even ordinary people with weapons who may engage in robbery, extortion, or hostile confrontations that result in injury or death (see also Ovesen et al. 1995:28; Boyden and Gibbs 1997:93–94, 127). Military units expropriate land from peasants and sell it for themselves; forest areas are also taken over by force and logged for the personal profit of officials. Abuse of military power incurs no consequences in contemporary Cambodian society, and police often violate laws with impunity.[25]

Another kind of weapon, land mines, creates an extremely serious and frightening problem in various regions of Cambodia that experienced fighting after DK. With several contending forces laying down scores of land mines over more than a decade of civil conflict, large portions of land remain uninhabitable or dangerous even to cross. Despite demining efforts, great numbers of people are still wounded by mines and suffer not only physical and psychological traumas but oftentimes problems of economic survival and social marginalization as well (see also French 1994b).[26]

Finally, domestic violence, especially wife abuse, is said to be a serious problem in contemporary Cambodia (see Zimmerman, Men, and Sar 1994; Nelson and Zimmerman 1996) that has developed because of the brutality to which people were exposed in DK.[27] The precise extent of abuse, however, is uncertain, because it is virtually impossible to know exactly how widespread domestic violence may be at present or was in the past. So far as Svay is concerned, Ebihara saw no evidence of wife or child abuse in her original fieldwork, and present-day villagers state that domestic violence is not a problem within the community.

Our impression is that there was a general decline in fearfulness across the central plains of Cambodia from the late 1980s through the U.N.-sponsored elections of 1993. Aid workers report that in the early 1980s villagers hesitated to plant sugar palm trees (*daom tnaot*) because they take so long to mature, and there was no way to know whether one might have to flee the area again, or even if one would live long enough to benefit from the effort. But when we visited Svay in the early 1990s, we found that sugar palms as well as coconut, mango, and many other trees had indeed been planted and were bearing fruit, and that living conditions gradually improved for most (if not all) villagers. Around the time of the 1993 elections, people had high hopes that there would finally be peace and with it increased prosperity.

This hopefulness, however, was muted by periodic political instability after 1993; Prime Minister Hun Sen's coup in 1997, which ousted a co–prime minister with whom he was supposed to share power; and brutal attacks on antigovernment protesters in 1998–99. Although with the death of Pol Pot and the defections of Ieng Sary, Khieu Samphan, and other leaders in 1998–99 the Khmer Rouge themselves ceased to constitute a serious threat, continued political infighting among top officials of the ostensibly coalition government perpetuates a climate of general political uncertainty and recurring violence. Cambodians feel that there is always the possibility that society could collapse again into warfare and destruction.[28] Some people regularly consult a work called the *Buddh Damneay*, which is believed to contain prophecies by the Buddha about events that will occur at the midpoint of the next *kalpa*, or cycle of time before the coming of the next Buddha. The text speaks of multiple wars and devastation, and many Cambodians believe that the horrors of the DK period fulfilled those prophecies (see also Smith 1989). However, they cannot be certain that the time of destruction is over and that the reign of the new and righteous ruler is at hand. Thus they consult the text and wait, still fearful.

CONCLUDING REMARKS

The Cambodian genocide under Pol Pot drew international attention for its massive death toll, which occurred in a small population within a short period. In addition, the DK regime was infamous for its attempt to destroy cultural institutions as well as people in its headlong plunge to "leap" into a revolutionary new society more quickly than any other society in history (Chandler, Kiernan, and Boua 1988:36). DK obviously had a number of profound and disruptive effects on Cambodian life, only some of which have been discussed here. What has particularly struck us, however, is the remarkable strength of the Cambodian survivors we know, who, after experiencing devastating social upheavals and personal traumas, nonetheless got on with their lives. Also, possibly because the DK regime was so short-lived, its effort to crush certain fundamental aspects of Cambodian society and culture did not take hold. Thus after 1979 various elements of prerevolutionary life—for example, families, Buddhism, private property, a market economy—were revived, albeit with modifications caused by changing socio-political-economic circumstances (see Ebihara 1993a).

Svay villagers remain peasant rice cultivators who lead a rather precarious existence, with their harvests often diminished by droughts or floods and their small savings suddenly drained by illness. As one man remarked with a sigh: "It's still a struggle to live; you still have to work hard to grow rice." Some villagers may get added income from other sources, such as nonagricultural jobs (for example, as schoolteachers), financial assistance from offspring or relatives working in Phnom Penh, or remittances from relatives who became refugees abroad. According to villagers, relatively few households are "rich," but most families have adequate resources, and impoverished households are few (see ibid.). Over the course of periodic visits to Svay between 1989 and 1997 we have seen many visible improvements in people's daily lives. We were struck in particular by the increasing number of families building wooden houses raised on piles above the ground in the traditional Khmer style, after having lived since Pol Pot times in rather shabby thatch houses built directly on the ground with dirt floors. No one looks malnourished; people have nicer clothes; virtually every household has a bicycle, and increasingly over time, some have acquired motorcycles; most families have radios, and nowadays some even have tiny black-and-white television sets that run (in the absence of electricity) on car batteries.[29] (On some other aspects of contemporary village life, see Ebihara 1993a and 1993b; Meas Nee 1995; Uimonen 1996.)

Despite some material improvements to their lives, present-day villagers obviously bear scars, both physical and emotional, from the horrors of the Pol Pot regime. People believe that the harsh conditions of DK caused the deaths of several villagers in the years following 1979; and many survivors are plagued by profound fatigue, lack of strength, weak limbs, faulty memories, and other problems that are thought to be the consequence of overly arduous work, severe deprivations, and beatings during DK. Villagers report such difficulties as: "My legs are still weak from all the work; sometimes they collapse and I fall down." "They beat me on my head and shoulders and back . . . and now I can't lift heavy things." "I've forgotten how to read and write Khmer since Pol Pot." Only one person admits that she had a mental breakdown during DK; now, she says, "Sometimes I laugh or cry for no reason." But she has managed to hold down a job and functions quite capably in daily life. We found no other evidence of serious psychological problems, although it is quite possible that some of the villagers' physical ailments could be somaticizations of emotional reactions to past horrors. Although it is certainly true that numerous Cambodians endured intense psychological traumas during DK and that some continue to suffer emotional distress, we do not agree with periodic statements (largely in journalistic media) that Cambodia has become a nation of the mentally unbalanced.[30] (See Ledgerwood 1998c for fuller discussion of this issue.)

The present-day life of Svay villagers remains difficult in many respects. But in listening to people speak of their horrendous experiences and profound losses during the "Pol Pot time," and in watching transformations in their lives throughout the 1990s, we are deeply moved above all by their astonishing fortitude, resilience, courage, and endurance. As is probably true of humankind almost everywhere, the villagers are ordinary people with *extra*ordinary strength and spirit. They are survivors.

NOTES

1. Ebihara's original fieldwork was sponsored by a Ford Foundation Foreign Area Training Fellowship; subsequent research during the 1990s was supported by the Social Science Research Council, the Wenner-Gren Foundation for Anthropological Research, and the PSC/CUNY Faculty Research Awards Program. Ledgerwood's work has been funded by the Social Science

Research Council, the Wenner-Gren Foundation, UNICEF, and the East-West Center. We are grateful to all these sources. We conducted research in Svay in the 1990s both individually and collaboratively. (Note: In earlier publications, Svay was given the pseudonym Sobay.)

2. The prefix a- appended to a name or term is pejorative, in this case connoting a meaning such as the "loathsome Pol Pot."

3. Some refugees were relocated earlier, in the late 1970s (see Ebihara 1985). About 360,000 people, however, remained in Thai refugee camps until 1992, when they began to be repatriated back to Cambodia, creating resettlement problems and internal dislocation (Boyden and Gibbs 1997:138–40).

4. In the summer of 1973, the region around Svay was also one of the areas subject to intense "strategic bombing" by the United States, which was attempting to destroy Khmer Rouge bases. Fortunately, Svay's residents had already fled, but some houses were destroyed and there are still outlines of bomb craters in the rice fields. On Cambodian conceptions of *prey*, see Chandler 1996 [1978] and Ebihara 1993a:150.

5. Vickery 1984 points out that conditions varied in different parts of Cambodia and over time, with some places being less harsh than others. Svay, however, was located in a region where conditions and discipline were stringent from the outset. On conditions during DK, see also Toni Shapiro-Phim's chapter in this volume and Ebihara 1987, 1993a, 1993b.

6. There has been debate over the number of deaths, with estimates ranging from less than a million to three or more million. Kiernan 1996:458 (Table 4) notes 1,671,000 deaths; the 1.7 million figure comes from the most recent report of the Cambodian Genocide Project at Yale, which has been conducting detailed studies of the mortality toll.

7. At that time Svay was divided into three hamlets, and Ebihara's most intensive research focused on so-called West Hamlet of Svay, which was somewhat separate from the other hamlets and in some ways like a small community in itself. Ebihara's research in the 1990s concentrated specifically on survivors from West Hamlet and some of their descendants.

8. This death toll does not include spouses and offspring from marriages that occurred after Ebihara left Svay in 1960.

9. Children were taken from their parents at about the age of six or seven and placed in their own work teams. Adolescents and other young unmarried adults were put in mobile labor teams sent to various parts of the country; they sometimes saw their parents only once or twice a year.

10. Similar forms of household composition and mutual aid occur also among refugees (see Ebihara 1985). In addition, refugees often feel a strong sense of obligation to send remittances to close kin in Cambodia, even though refugees in the United States are themselves often very poor; contacts between kin are maintained through exchange of letters, tape cassettes, and videos. In recent years, some refugees have made visits to or returned to work in Cambodia. See also Boyden and Gibbs 1997; Breckon 1998; Smith-Hefner 1999; Ledgerwood 1998c.

11. For patterns of mutual aid in prerevolutionary Cambodia, see Ebihara 1968. On contemporary social relationships, see Ebihara 1993a and 1994; on economic organization, see Ledgerwood 1992. The latter notes that in a 1992 survey, Svay villagers voiced a preference for hiring field labor rather than practicing labor exchange (ibid.:57–60), but actual observation of cultivation in 1994 indicated that few villagers can afford hired help.

12. During the PRK period following DK there was a territorial administrative change in Svay, such that the former Middle and West Hamlets were joined together and named West Svay, while East Hamlet became a separate (if contiguous) community. After DK, many former residents of West Hamlet established new homes on sites different from their prewar locations, but social relationships with one another were maintained.

13. Such claims often go along with arguments that the DK period irrevocably shattered the entire society and that Khmer culture is dead or dying; for discussion of such assertions, see the introduction to Ebihara, Mortland, and Ledgerwood 1994; and Ledgerwood 1998a.

14. The most famous work on reciprocity is, of course, Marcel Mauss's *The Gift*. For discussion of these issues as applied to exchange in the Khmer context, see Marston 1997:chap. 4; Kim 2001.

15. Similar conclusions are reached by Uimonen 1996:45; Boyden and Gibbs 1997; and Davenport, Healy, and Malone 1995:48–49. The latter, writing about families limiting assistance to relatives returning from refugee camps on the Thai border, write: "[It] seems that most families, unless they are wealthy, can ill afford to do more [than provide emergency assistance]."

16. The term *widow* is a direct translation of the Khmer term *memai*, which denotes women whose husbands are known to be dead. *Memai* is also used to refer to divorced women, as well as those who are separated from or have been abandoned by their husbands and may not know if the latter are alive.

17. In the land redistribution of 1986 (formalized by constitutional restoration of private property in 1989), each villager received approximately 0.16 to 0.18 hectare of rice paddy lands. While there is individual ownership of land, members of a household generally pool all the paddies and cooperate in their cultivation. Holdings in Svay now range from a low of about 0.3 hectare for an elderly couple to almost 2 hectares for a large extended family. Ledgerwood conducted a survey of Svay in 1992 that indicated that 70 percent of families had less than 1 hectare of land, which was somewhat below the national average of 1.2 cited by Curtis 1989.

18. Polygyny was legal in prerevolutionary Cambodia, although it was practiced mainly by men in higher socioeconomic strata. See Ebihara 1974, however, for a situation in which a Svay villager's attempt to take a second wife was quashed by his irate (first) wife.

19. There is a case in Svay in which a man had left a wife of more than twenty years standing to live with another woman (the widow of a friend who had died during DK). The first wife certainly *felt* abandoned because she got no economic help from her former mate and was quite poor (she managed with help from married daughters). Ebihara feels, however, that this man was not a heedless philanderer but someone who had developed a strong attachment to another woman with whom he has continued to live for the past two decades.

20. These statistics indicate that the number of monks and temples has rebounded almost to prewar figures for 1969, which noted 3,369 temples and 65,062 monks (Cambodia Report 1996).

21. Another temple compound several kilometers distant was also blown up with explosives, and any sections of wall or foundation that remained intact were broken up by hand and taken to provide steel rods and filler for a huge dam that was constructed on a nearby river during DK. While the DK had ideological reasons for destroying temples as symbols of Buddhism, in this case the remnants of a religious building were incorporated and transformed into a secular structure (a dam) that had enormous practical importance

for a major concern of DK: building irrigation systems to maximize agriculture. Remains of the Svay temple were used to fill in a bathing pond so that the space could be used for growing food plants.

22. It is important to note that Khmer religion also includes a variety of animistic beliefs, practices, rituals, and religious specialists (such as healers, spirit mediums, and other practitioners), all of which survived DK and continue to be active.

23. In the early 1970s, when the Khmer Rouge began to make forays into the area and the civil war began to rage, a few Svay families evidently decided to go to Khmer Rouge base camps rather than move to Phnom Penh. Some years after the fall of DK, a few families of these former Old People eventually moved back to Svay. Villagers say that it would be against Buddhist morality and civil law to take revenge on those people, but the latter are held in scorn and largely ostracized.

24. At one such gathering of local officials, schoolteachers, and students near Svay, the children burned an effigy of Pol Pot. There is also a huge pile of skulls and bones heaped up in a ruined school several kilometers from Svay that had been used as a prison and killing ground during DK (see Ebihara 1993b). Similar local displays are scattered throughout the country. Craig Etcheson (personal communication) recently told Ledgerwood that the skeletal remains at a former prison in this region were removed in 1999–2000, but we are not certain if he is referring to the same place that we visited.

25. See the United Nations Report of the Special Representative of the Secretary General on the Situation of Human Rights in Cambodia, 1998.

26. The Svay region was not mined during the post-DK civil conflict as were some regions of Cambodia, but one Svay resident lost a leg to a land mine when he was sent to northwestern Cambodia to labor on a PRK government work project. There have been periodic problems, however, with unexploded shells and the like from the civil war of the early 1970s left in the fields around Svay.

27. For a discussion of this issue, see Zimmerman, Men, and Sar 1994; Boyden and Gibbs 1997:93–95. The problem is shared with other countries emerging from extended periods of warfare (compare Enloe 1993:chap. 4).

28. Some women told Ledgerwood that prior to the 1993 general election they had their IUDs removed because if society collapsed again, medical services would not be available to remove the devices, and they wanted to be able to bear children again after the turmoil.

29. Ledgerwood, who has traveled widely throughout Cambodia, believes that although Svay is not a prosperous village, it is nonetheless better off than many communities elsewhere, especially those that are distant from Phnom Penh. Cambodia as a whole still suffers from a relatively low standard of living with respect to such criteria as infant mortality and child malnutrition (see, for example, Boyden and Gibbs 1997).

30. There is considerable literature on psychological problems among Cambodians in refugee camps and resettlement communities (to give but a few examples, see Eisenbruch 1991; Mollica 1986; Kinzie 1987). While we have not conducted psychological research, we believe that many Cambodian refugees have generally suffered more severe disruptions in their lives after DK—including harsh conditions in refugee camps followed by difficult adjustments to alien environments abroad—than did Cambodians who remained at home. Svay villagers, despite their relative poverty and the insecurities of an agricultural life, stayed in a familiar cultural setting with kin and other support systems. (See also Boyden and Gibbs 1997; Meas Nee 1995; Ebihara 1985; Smith-Hefner 1999.)

REFERENCES CITED

Banister, Judith, and Paige Johnson. 1993. "After the Nightmare: The Population of Cambodia." In *Genocide and Democracy in Cambodia.* Ben Kiernan, ed. Pp. 65–139. Yale University Southeast Asia Studies, Monograph Series 41. New Haven: Yale Center for International and Area Studies.

Boua, Chanthou. 1982. "Women in Today's Cambodia." *New Left Review* 131:45–61.

Boyden, Jo, and Sara Gibbs. 1997. *Children of War: Responses to Pycho-Social Distress in Cambodia.* Geneva: United Nations Research Institute for Social Development.

Breckon, Lydia. 1998. "To Rebuild Our Cambodia: An Examination of Khmer-American Sojourns in Cambodia." In *Diasporic Identities.* Selected Papers on Refugee and Immigrant Issues 6, Cambodia Report. Carol Mortland, ed. Pp. 113–32. Arlington, Va.: American Anthropological Association.

Cambodian Genocide Program. 1999. Cambodian Genocide Program, 1997–1999. Ben Kiernan, director. New Haven: Yale Center for International and Area Studies.

Cambodia Report. 1996. Newsletter of the Center for Advanced Study, Phnom Penh. Special issue on Buddhism in Cambodia, 2(2) (March/April).

Chandler, David. 1992. *A History of Cambodia.* 2d ed. Boulder, Colo.: Westview Press.

———. 1996 [1978]. "Songs at the Edge of the Forest." In *Facing the Cambodian Past, Selected Essays 1971–1994.* Pp. 76–99. Chiang Mai, Thailand: Silkworm Books.

———. 1999. *Voices from S-21: Terror and History in Pol Pot's Secret Prison.* Berkeley: University of California Press.

Chandler, David P., Ben Kiernan, and Chanthou Boua. 1988. *Pol Pot Plans the Future, Confidential Leadership Documents from Democratic Kampuchea, 1976–79.* Yale University Southeast Asia Studies, Monograph Series 33. New Haven: Yale Center for International and Area Studies.

Curtis, Grant. 1990. *Cambodia: A Country Profile.* Stockholm: Swedish International Development Authority.

Davenport, Paul, Sr., Joan Healy, and Kevin Malone. 1995. *Vulnerable in the Village: A Study of Returnees in Battambang Province, Cambodia, with a Focus on Strategies for the Landless.* Phnom Penh: UNHCR.

Ebihara, May. 1968. "A Khmer Village in Cambodia." Ph.D. dissertation, Department of Anthropology, Columbia University.

———. 1974. "Khmer Village Women in Cambodia." In *Many Sisters: Women in Cross-Cultural Perspective.* Carolyn Matthiasson, ed. Pp. 305–47. New York: Free Press.

———. 1985. "Khmer." In *Refugees in the United States: A Reference Handbook.* David Haines, ed. Pp. 127–47. Westport, Conn.: Greenwood.

———. 1987. "Revolution and Reformulation in Kampuchean Village Culture." In *The Cambodian Agony.* David Ablin and Marlowe Hood, eds. Pp. 16–61. Armonk, N.Y.: M. E. Sharpe.

———. 1993a. " 'Beyond Suffering': The Recent History of a Cambodian Village." In *The Challenge of Reform in Indochina.* Börje Ljunggren, ed. Pp. 149–66. Cambridge: Harvard Institute for International Development, Harvard University Press.

———. 1993b. "A Cambodian Village under the Khmer Rouge, 1975–1979." In *Genocide and Democracy in Cambodia.* Ben Kiernan, ed. Pp. 51–64. Yale University Southeast Asia Studies, Monograph Series 41. New Haven: Yale Center for International and Area Studies.

————. 1994. "Plus Ça Change? Social Relations in a Khmer Village." Paper presented at the annual meetings of the Association for Asian Studies, Honolulu.

Ebihara, May, Carol A. Mortland, and Judy Ledgerwood, eds. 1994. *Cambodian Culture since 1975: Homeland and Exile.* Ithaca: Cornell University Press.

Eisenbruch, Maurice. 1991. "From Post-Traumatic Stress Disorder to Cultural Bereavement: Diagnosis of Southeast Asian Refugees." *Social Science and Medicine* 33(6):673–80.

Enloe, Cynthia. 1993. *The Morning After: Sexual Politics at the End of the Cold War.* Berkeley: University of California Press.

French, Lindsay. 1994a. "Enduring Holocaust, Surviving History: Displaced Cambodians on the Thai-Cambodian Border, 1989–1991." Ph.D. dissertation, Department of Anthropology, Harvard University.

————. 1994b. "The Political Economy of Injury and Compassion: Amputees on the Thai-Cambodia Border." In *Embodiment and Experience: The Existential Ground of Culture and Self.* Thomas Csordas, ed. Pp. 69–99. Cambridge: Cambridge University Press.

Frings, Viviane. 1994. "Cambodia after Decollectivization (1989–92)." *Journal of Contemporary Asia* 24:50–66.

Hinton, Alexander. 1997. "Cambodia's Shadow: An Examination of the Cultural Origins of Genocide." Ph.D. dissertation, Department of Anthropology, Emory University.

Jackson, Karl, ed. 1989. *Cambodia 1975–1978, Rendezvous with Death.* Princeton: Princeton University Press.

Keyes, Charles. 1994. "Communist Revolution and the Buddhist Past in Cambodia." In *Asian Visions of Authority: Religion and the Modern States of East and Southeast Asia.* Charles F. Keyes, Laurel Kendall, and Helen Hardacre, eds. Pp. 43–73. Honolulu: University of Hawaii Press.

Kiernan, Ben. 1996. *The Pol Pot Regime: Race, Power, and Genocide in Cambodia under the Khmer Rouge, 1975–79.* New Haven: Yale University Press.

Kim, Sedara. 2001. "Reciprocity: Informal Patterns of Social Interactions in a Cambodian Village near *Angkor* Park." M.A. thesis. Department of Anthropology, Northern Illinois University.

Kinzie, David. 1987. "The Concentration Camp Syndrome among Cambodian Refugees." In *The Cambodian Agony.* David Ablin and Marlowe Hood, eds. Pp. 332–53. Armonk, N.Y.: M. E. Sharpe.

Ledgerwood, Judy. 1992. *Analysis of the Situation of Women in Cambodia.* Bangkok: UNICEF.

————. 1997. "The Cambodian Tuol Sleng Museum of Genocidal Crimes: National Narratives." *Museum Anthropology* 21:1:82–98.

————. 1998a. "Does Cambodia Exist? Nationalism and Diasporic Constructions of a Homeland." In *Diasporic Identities.* Selected Papers on Refugee and Immigrant Issues 6. Carol Mortland, ed. Arlington, Va.: American Anthropological Association.

————. 1998b. "Rural Development in Cambodia: The View from the Village." In *Cambodia and the International Community: The Quest for Peace, Development and Democracy.* Frederick Z. Brown and David G. Timberman, eds. Pp. 127–48. New York: Asia Society.

————. 1998c. "The Social Legacies of Genocide: Fear, Uncertainly, But Not Madness." Paper presented in a series on Legacies of Genocide in Cambodia, Program in Southeast Asian Studies, University of Wisconsin, Madison.

Marston, John. 1997. "Cambodia 1991–94: Hierarchy, Neutrality and Etiquettes of Discourse." Ph.D. dissertation, Department of Anthropology, University of Washington.

Mauss, Marcel. 1954 [1924]. *The Gift.* I. Cunnison, trans. New York: Free Press.

McAndrews, John P. 1997. *Interdependence in Household Livelihood: Strategies in Two Cambodian Villages.* Phnom Penh: Cambodia Development Resource Institute.

Meas Nee. 1995. *Towards Restoring Life: Cambodian Villages.* Phnom Penh: NGO Forum on Cambodia.

Ministry of Cults and Religion. 1999. "Statistics." Mimeo. Phnom Penh: Ministry of Cults and Religion.

Mollica, Richard. 1986. "The Trauma Story: Psychiatric Care of Refugee Survivors of Violence and Torture." In *Post Traumatic Therapy and Victims of Violence.* Frank Ochberg, ed. Pp. 295–314. New York: Brunner and Mead.

Mortland, Carol. 1994. "Khmer Buddhism in the United States: Ultimate Questions." In *Cambodian Culture since 1975: Homeland and Exile.* May Ebihara, Carol Mortland, and Judy Ledgerwood, eds. Pp. 74–90. Ithaca: Cornell University Press.

Myerhoff, Barbara. 1978. *Number Our Days.* New York: Simon and Schuster.

National Institute of Statistics. 1998. *General Population Census of Cambodia.* Phnom Penh: National Institute of Statistics, Ministry of Planning.

Nelson, Erin, and Cathy Zimmerman. 1996. *Household Survey of Domestic Violence in Cambodia.* Phnom Penh: Ministry of Women's Affairs and Project against Domestic Violence.

Ovesen, Jan, Ing-Britt Trankell, and Joakim Ojendal. 1996. *When Every Household Is an Island.* Uppsala, Sweden: Uppsala University.

Secretariat of State for Women's Affairs. 1994. "Report Submitted by the Secretariat of State for Women's Affairs, Kingdom of Cambodia." Mimeo. Second Asia and Pacific Ministerial Conference in Jakarta, June 7–14, 1994; Fourth World Conference on Women in Beijing, September 1995.

Smith, Frank. 1989. *Interpretive Accounts of the Khmer Rouge Years: Personal Experience in Cambodian Peasant World View.* Center for Southeast Asian Studies, University of Wisconsin, Wisconsin Papers on Southeast Asia, Occasional paper no. 18. Madison: University of Wisconsin.

Smith-Hefner, Nancy. 1999. *Khmer American: Identity and Moral Education in a Diasporic Community.* Berkeley: University of California Press.

Thion, Serge. 1993. *Watching Cambodia.* Bangkok: White Lotus.

Uimonen, Paula. 1996. "Responses to Revolutionary Change: A Study of Social Memory in a Khmer Village." *Folk, Journal of the Danish Ethnographic Society* 38:31–51.

United Nations. 1998. "Report of the Special Representative of the Secretary General on the Situation of Human Rights in Cambodia." Posted to camnews@lists.best.com, April 24, 1998.

United Nations Population Fund (UNFPA). 1995. *Cambodia: Demographic Profile.* Phnom Penh: National Institute of Statistics of Cambodia, Ministry of Planning.

Vickery, Michael. 1984. *Cambodia: 1975–1982.* Boston: South End.

———. 1986. *Kampuchea: Politics, Economics, and Society.* Boulder, Colo.: Lynne Riener.

Vijghen, John, and Sareoun Ly. 1996. *Customs of Patronage and Community Development in a Cambodian Village.* Phnom Penh: Cambodian Researchers for Development.

Zimmerman, Cathy, Men Savorn, and Sar Samen. 1994. *Plates in a Basket Will Rattle.* Phnom Penh: Asia Foundation.

11

Terror, Grief, and Recovery

Genocidal Trauma in a Mayan Village in Guatemala

Beatriz Manz

In the hot, humid afternoon of Saturday, February 13, 1982, a long column of soldiers moved with an angry, deliberate gait down a muddy path toward Santa Maria Tzejá, a small, isolated village in the rain forest of northern Guatemala. As the troops approached, the terrified inhabitants scattered in every direction into the surrounding forest, having heard that the military had massacred the people of a nearby village two days before. When the military unit arrived, it found an eerily quiet, deserted community. Only one woman inexplicably remained. The soldiers beat, repeatedly raped, and murdered her. They then dumped her battered body near the building housing the village's cooperative. This heinous act was only the prelude to the horrors to come.

Over the next two days, the soldiers looted and torched every structure in the village. Then, as the flames consumed more than a decade's worth of hard work and dreams, a long line of troops hiked down a path that skirted an area where two terrified groups, a total of fourteen women and children, were quietly hiding. Crouching in fear in the dense foliage, mothers had stuffed rags into the mouths of their infants so they would not cry. As the last soldier passed, a little dog suddenly began to bark. The unit halted and then returned to scan the area more closely. They soon discovered the first group, a pregnant woman, her infant, and two boys left in her care. A young boy, who was running to warn his siblings of the approaching army, heard the soldiers say something to the terrified woman, and then the troops opened fire upon them, after which a soldier threw a grenade to finalize the carnage. The unit then moved on, locating the second group of eight children, their pregnant mother, and a grandmother. As they did with the first group, the troops methodically and mercilessly slaughtered everyone. Some were shot, others hacked to death, some decapitated. Soldiers slit open the stomach of the pregnant woman, killing mother and child. Others, laughing, threw babies into the air.

The only survivor was a six-year-old boy who ran and hid behind a tree, a silent witness to the bloodletting that destroyed the only world he knew.

When news of the massacre reached the hiding places of those who had escaped, the stunned villagers took further precautions to save their lives—among them the gruesome task of killing their own dogs, about fifty in all. There is no doubt that the army would have slaughtered every villager had they found those who had eluded them—as they did in nearby villages days before and days after this massacre. After several months in hiding, more than half the families made the arduous and emotionally devastating journey to find refuge in Mexico, where they stayed for more than a decade. The army eventually placed those who remained behind—about fifty families—under military control, literally on the ashes of the original village, and brought in new peasants to occupy the lands of those in refuge.

Santa Maria Tzejá was part of the much larger tragedy endured in Guatemala. Governments, at various times and in various places, have unleashed state-sponsored terrorism across a wide swath of territory, at times engulfing a region or even drenching an entire nation in blood. On occasion the intensity, extent, and purpose of the violence is so extreme that it becomes genocide. In Guatemala, the Commission for Historical Clarification (CEH)—as the Truth Commission is officially called—was created in June 1994 as part of the Oslo Accords between the Guatemalan government and the umbrella group of insurgent forces, the Guatemalan National Revolutionary Unity (URNG). "Truth commissions are born of compromise between two extremes: institutional justice vs. silence and sanctified impunity," Amy Ross (1999b:39) observes. There was little equivocation, however, in the commission's conclusions. In a stunning judgment, the CEH charged the Guatemalan military with genocide: "[T]he CEH concludes that agents of the State of Guatemala, within the framework of counterinsurgency operations carried out between 1981 and 1983, committed acts of genocide against groups of Mayan people" (CEH 1999b:41). According to its findings, 83 percent of the victims were Maya. "After studying four selected geographical regions," the commission concluded "that between 1981 and 1983 the Army identified groups of the Mayan population as the internal enemy, considering them to be an actual or potential support base for the guerrillas, with respect to material sustenance, a source of recruits and a place to hide their members." Based on that assessment, "the Army, inspired by the National Security Doctrine, defined a concept of internal enemy that went beyond guerrilla sympathizers, combatants or militants to include civilians from specific ethnic groups" (ibid.:39).

As if to confirm the charge, a spokesman for the regime of de facto president General Rios Montt confided the military's thinking to an American journalist in the summer of 1982. "The guerrillas won over many Indian collaborators, therefore, the Indians were subversives, right? And how do you fight subversion? Clearly, you had to kill Indians because they were collaborating with subversion. And then they would say, 'You're massacring innocent people.' But they weren't innocent.

They had sold out to subversion" (Nairn 1982). Echoing these views, Colonel By-ron Disrael Lima, who graduated at the top of his military academy class of 1962, told the *Wall Street Journal* (Krauss 1985:1) that his heroes in history are Napoleon and Hitler because "I respect conquerors." He evidenced little respect for civilians or democracy. "The civilians don't work until we tell them to work. They need our protection, control and direction." As the front page *Wall Street Journal* article points out, the Reagan administration in 1980 resumed $300 million in military aid. Col. Lima confidently showed disdain for elected civilian leaders: "There's a civilian wave in Latin America now," he observed in 1985 as Guatemala was in the midst of a presidential campaign, "but that doesn't mean military men will lose their ul-timate power." Concluding, he smugly boasted, "Latins take commands from men in uniform" (Krauss 1991:45).

In a place hammered into silence and accustomed to impunity, the CEH re-port—particularly the charge of genocide—stunned the country by its straight-forward language and the thoroughness of its documentation. It was as if the whole country had burst into tears, tears repressed for decades and tears of vindication. The public understandably had been skeptical about what the CEH would docu-ment and conclude. Thus when the report was released on February 25, 1999, "the public was shocked at its strength," Ross observes (1999b:42). "In addition to more than 3,500 pages of information on atrocities, including more than 600 massacres, the commission found the state responsible for more than 93 percent of the viola-tions" (ibid.; see also Ross 1999a). "And they called it genocide," Ross reminds us, a charge that inspired long, wrenching discussions within the CEH itself. The pur-pose of the terror in this and countless other villages, the commission forcefully charged, "was to intimidate and silence society as a whole, in order to destroy the will for transformation, both in the short and long term" (CEH 1999b:27). With-out question, the army's horrific actions ripped deep psychological wounds into the consciousness of the inhabitants of Santa Maria Tzejá—a village involved in a much larger trauma. The army's brutal and targeted repression, especially in the province of El Quiché, where Santa Maria Tzejá is located, went far beyond the threat posed by the armed insurgency. In El Quiché, 344 massacres took place, rep-resenting more than half of the total deaths and over 45 percent of the human rights violations in the country. The commission documented that 200,000 people were killed or disappeared throughout Guatemala over more than three decades of war (ibid.:18, 20; see also Oficina de Derechos Humanos del Arzobispado de Guatemala 1998a, 1998b, 1998c). During the most intense period of the military onslaught, from 1981 to 1983, as many as 1.5 million people were internally dis-placed or had to flee the country, including about 150,000 who sought refuge in Mexico (CEH 1999b:30; Manz 1988a, 1988b).

The roots of the genocide against Mayan communities are anchored in the tor-tured history of Guatemala, according to the CEH report. "The proclamation of independence in 1821, an event prompted by the country's elite, saw the creation of an authoritarian State which excluded the majority of the population, was racist in its precepts and practices, and served to protect the economic interests of the privileged minority" (CEH 1999b:17). The contemporary context led from repression to slaughter through a path of sharply escalating bloodletting and brutality, according to *Guatemala: Never Again!*, the official report of the Human Rights Office of the Archdiocese of Guatemala (1999). "During the sixties, in addition to combat between the guerrillas and the army, government violence targeted peasants in the eastern part of the country," the report asserts. "In the seventies, state violence was particularly virulent in the cities. It was trained on leaders of social movements and sectors opposing the successive military regimes, in addition to the guerrillas' infrastructure." The violence of those two decades escalated to genocidal forms during 1981–83. "In the early eighties, counterinsurgency policy took the form of state-sponsored terrorism featuring systematic mass destruction, particularly of indigenous communities and organized peasant groups" (ibid.:xxxii). The CEH report adds that "the massacres, scorched earth operations, forced disappearances and executions of Mayan authorities, leaders and spiritual guides, were not only an attempt to destroy the social base of the guerrillas, but above all, to destroy the cultural values that ensured cohesion and collective action in Mayan communities" (CEH 1999b:23).

The scale of this nightmare defies comprehension. The terror and the lasting wounds, however, are endured on a far more immediate though no less horrific scale by individuals, families, and communities. This chapter explores the process of grieving by focusing on Santa Maria Tzejá, a unique community whose devastating experience was all too common. Let me summarize a key point in my argument: communities face a fundamental challenge in how to reconcile deep, inescapable mourning over the traumas of the past with hope for a better future. Grieving, then, goes beyond even the heavy burden of grief itself and encompasses interpreting and reinterpreting the past as a guide to engaging the future. This community has chosen the most difficult of paths: an unflinching look at what took place as a foundation for shaping the future. This approach raises a number of questions. How do communities cope with this level of atrocity coupled with impunity? What are the long-term effects of people's sense of deep sorrow, distress, regret, and melancholy? Years after the savagery, how does remembrance take place when forgetting seems an act of salvation? How is the past retrieved when powerful social institutions, individual actors, and the fallibility of memory itself all conspire to redefine what took place?

The village's short, turbulent, thirty-year history encompasses a profound hope along with a legacy of desperation. Founded in 1970, Santa Maria Tzejá was the ambitious attempt of land-starved peasants from the highlands and Catholic clergy—particularly an energetic and deeply committed priest, Luis Gurriarán— to settle the nearly inaccessible rain forest near the Mexican border. I first visited this remote outpost in the summer of 1973, perhaps walking down the same muddy path that the murderous troops would soak in blood less than a decade later. Little did I know at the time that my involvement would span the next three decades and continue today—let alone what those years would hold. I knew immediately that I had entered an unusual community, but I didn't realize right away the ways in which that community would become part of my life.

On that first trip, the dense green canopy of the virgin rain forest still surrounded the village. Conditions were harsh and resources meager when I arrived, but the spirit was remarkable and the enthusiasm infectious. It had taken a grueling hike on a jungle path over the rough terrain to get there, but it turned out to be far harder emotionally to leave. During the 1970s, I was amazed at the village's success and spirit and all too aware of the encroaching military. I remembered those dreams in the mid-1980s as I walked over the ashes of what the army had incinerated and then watched the slow, demanding process of rebuilding. I traveled back and forth between the village and the refugee camps in Mexico, often providing the only source of news between families torn asunder by events, carrying photos I took, carefully folded letters, cassette tapes, and treasured keepsakes. In the 1990s, the return of the refugees from Mexico once again offered a moment of hope in a context of continued apprehension.

Prior to the January 1970 morning on which the first pioneers set off to establish the village, generations of highland peasants had been losing ground as cornfields were divided and divided again and as land became exhausted and eroded. Economic desperation in their highland ancestral homes made peasants ever more dependent on wage labor in the sprawling southern-coast plantations. There, mostly Mayan laborers cut sugar cane, picked coffee, and harvested cotton, toiling for low pay in slavelike, disease-ridden conditions. For many, the lack of land and the dreaded plantation labor conspired to create a spiral of desperation where the harder one worked, the further one sank. Following the overthrow of the democratically elected Arbenz government in 1954, a succession of generals, either in the presidential office or controlling it, made reform impossible and land reform, in particular, a dangerous subject. Under those circumstances, the forgotten, dense, isolated rain forest in the north offered the tantalizing hope of land at the same time that it posed seemingly insurmountable challenges.

The social and political problems of the village, and Guatemala more generally, were framed by the Cold War (Immerman 1982; Schlesinger and Kinzer 1982; McClintock 1985; Gleijeses 1991). A rich ethnographic literature has explored issues of cultural identity and transformation in the context of village life in Guatemala (Brintnall 1979; Warren 1978, 1992; Nash 1967; Melville and Melville 1971; Falla 1978; Annis 1987; Smith 1984, 1990; Adams 1970; Berryman 1984; Watanabe 1992). Less explored has been the experience of the Mayans during the past two decades, which has been so shaped by conflict and traumatized by atrocity (Stoll 1993; Falla 1994; Manz 1988a, 1988b, 1988c, 1995; Wilson 1995; Nelson 1999; Green 1999). Without question, the Cold War has provided the dominant context of contemporary Guatemala, but it is important not to overstate its role. The Cold War exacerbated, rather than created, the social, class, and ethnic tensions that have racked the country. The army and the economic oligarchy seized the opportunity of the Cold War to legitimate their continued domination. In the name of anticommunism, elites and the military sought to reinforce their position by tapping into the vast economic, military, and political support eagerly supplied by the U.S. government.

The 1960s and 1970s were a prologue to the period of mass terror that ravaged Guatemala in the early 1980s. What was happening in the Mayan communities during this prologue? The Catholic Church was vigorously involved in religious organizations such as Catholic Action and secular organizations such as cooperatives. Religious traditions and generational positions were challenged and at times displaced. The Christian Democratic Party made inroads as a party with popular support. External institutions such as the Peace Corps and the Agency for International Development were involved in rural development. The transistor radio revolutionized information in remote villages, as did fluency in Spanish. New agricultural techniques and the resettlement of thousands of highland peasants in the Ixcán jungle were reshaping rural Guatemala. These activities underscore the fact that Mayan communities—the youth in particular—were far from quiescent observers. In fact, some were undergoing profound ideological changes. Instead of a more resigned acceptance of their fate—never willing or complete by any means—they were active interrogators of their current situation and seeking to be architects of their future.

These activities, especially new movements in the Catholic Church throughout Latin America (theology of liberation, preferential option for the poor), produced some of the most far reaching changes in the Mayan communities in the twentieth century. Foreign priests, nuns, and a vibrant network of lay church workers involved communities in wide-ranging forms of social promotion. They encouraged community participation—including previously marginal women and youth—in education, health, and communication. These activists did not shy from the conflictive issues surrounding land. Since agrarian reform programs were politically out of the question, the colonization of undesirable and impenetrable rain forests seemed the only viable option. Although these lands were ill suited for the type of agriculture practiced by modern-day peasants—and moreover would become even further damaged by burgeoning population density—these untouched areas nonetheless fulfilled the dreams of landless peasants. Surprisingly, the initial economic results confounded the justifiably dismal expectations of many observers. In the early 1970s, peasant cooperatives were established and flourished throughout the Ixcán. Success bred a new spirited confidence, and this confidence, in turn, fueled social transformations.

Two years after the formation of the village, a little-noticed but momentous event occurred: a small group of armed insurgents entered the Ixcán from Mexico in 1972. This ragtag band of fifteen combatants would eventually become the Guerilla Army of the Poor (EGP), the strongest of the insurgent groups (see Payeras 1982; Black, Jamail, and Chinchilla 1984). The guerrillas slowly built support in the isolated villages of the Ixcán and in the populated highlands throughout the 1970s. The army lashed out with unexpected ferocity, seeking to permanently terrorize or, if need be, annihilate Mayan communities. And it was the Mayan population, as the CEH report documents, not simply the guerrillas, who became the target. The early 1980s became the vortex of a genocidal storm. In the aftermath of this maelstrom, the military sought to suture the wounds by establishing a new version of the past by portraying the army as the savior from the guerrillas rather than the perpetrator of unspeakable criminal acts. The language of the Cold War remained after the fighting stopped—after the peace accords were signed in 1996, after the Cold War itself slid into history. What Guatemalans are saying, however, is that they have a right to know—a right to the truth.

Today, the community is seeking to come to terms with the past, not simply to remain a victim of it. The collective memory of the village is in transition, burdened by the legacy of military action but also shaped by the return of the refugees from Mexico and informed by a more open national dialogue. Refugees returned with a deeper awareness of their rights, developed in a more open atmosphere in years of exile. The fuller national dialogue was enhanced by the negotiations leading to the December 1996 peace accords, an amnesty, and a resultant national desire, at times hesitant and still fearful, to come to terms with a bitter history.

One cannot look forward in Guatemala, however, without confronting the grief of the past, and here the role of memory is crucial. Many scholars have written extensively and eloquently about the need to recover the memory and interpret the Mayans' situation in the war (Hale 1997a, 1997b; Wilson 1991, 1995, 1997; Warren 1993; Green 1999; Nelson 1999). "In discrete and relatively brief moments, societies in different parts of the world have developed an intense collective need to remember their past as a precondition for facing the future," Hale writes (1997a:817). These scholars also recognize the complexity and difficulty of the task. As anthropologist Kay Warren (1998:86) states, "*La violencia* gives a shape to memories and to later experiences of repression." Memory is tangled in trauma, and unraveling the tangle is itself traumatic.

On one level, memory is individual, reflecting the struggle of individuals to deal with what has taken place. "Human memory is a marvelous but fallacious instrument," Primo Levi (1988:23) tells us, expanding, contracting, filling in, obliterating, and rearranging its silhouette. Following social and political turmoil, let alone the unimaginable ravages of genocide, events are rethought and reorganized even more rapidly. Those who fell under military control may not consciously be rewriting the past, in their minds, but history is a remarkably heavy millstone to come to terms with. Some "lie consciously, coldly falsifying reality itself," Levi observed, "but more numerous are those who weigh anchor, move off, momentarily or forever, from genuine memories, and fabricate for themselves a convenient reality. The past is a burden to them; they feel repugnance for things done or suffered and tend to replace them with others" (ibid.:27). Over time, if not challenged, the distinction between the early and the later remembrance "progressively loses its contours" (ibid.). It does not take much to reshape a suggested image: an omission here and some embellishing there until a new picture emerges that mirrors the current context and, over time, barely resembles the original. As one witness told the CEH, "[People] don't just remember the event as it was, under what circumstances, the time and all that, but all the subjective interpretation," a subjectivity infused with fear (CEH 1999a:tomo IV:29).

On another level, memory has a collective dimension, transcending the individual and reflecting the social. This broader dimension of memory provides its own dynamic. "Collective memory is biased towards forgetting that which is negative," Halbwachs suggests (Marques, Paez, and Serra 1997:258), and painful or shameful events are even more difficult to handle. The social dimension of memory also shapes individual recollection. In formulating an account of what took place that is shared with others, individuals tap their own recollections, based on their observation of major events as well as exchanges with each other. These perceptions of the past filter not only through their own experiences but also through the social arena—the public and private discussion of these events and the ways in which they are interpreted and understood by society as a whole.

In the case of Santa Maria Tzejá, what is this social context? It is a context that those in power seek to define. "Everything that exists, no matter what its origin," Nietzsche writes, "is periodically reinterpreted by those in power in terms of fresh intentions" (Nietzsche 1956:209). A Guatemalan military officer echoes Nietzsche in a contemporary context: "[T]here is a historic truth in Guatemala, which is a truth from the perspective of power and that is the one that we know and accept" (Cifuentes 1998:89). One way of legitimizing the present is by denying the past or, if faced with undeniable truths, by providing an interpretation capable of rationalizing the terror that took place. Nonetheless, as Arendt (1968:259) puts it, facts possess "a strength of [their] own: whatever those in power may contrive, they are unable to discover or invent a viable substitute for [them]." This tension between interpretation and reality is the terrain on which memory is constituted.

Social scientists face a particular challenge in doing research among populations subjected to terror and fear. How is one to understand and interpret the recollections people provide? More than usual, it is important, even decisive, to decipher or decode the meanings in people's stories, to sort out the public voice and the concealed, unspoken thoughts. It is not as straightforward as simply counterposing truth versus falsehood, but rather seeking to understand what is said and what is not said. That which remains purposefully unspoken can indicate agency, defiance, resistance, control, autonomy, contestation, and resilience. Silence, at times, is remarkably eloquent. A social science researcher needs to locate the hidden voice, the codes or the double meanings, the thoughts that reside "between the lines."

Guatemala provides an unusually difficult, troubling challenge. The act of remembering, let alone the act of retelling, is a highly charged, politicized event, fraught with danger (see Manz 1999). Not surprisingly, fear leads people to provide partial information, and often misinformation, until trust is established and it becomes clear what, if any, consequences might befall the respondent. "It is as if denial and a low profile would bring protection from a world that merited greater distrust than ever," Warren (1998:93) found in the village of San Andrés. Confidence becomes the medium that encourages a fuller picture to emerge, that allows the shards of shattered lives to be pieced back together.

How, then, does one conduct research on grief? If terror continues to pierce the grief, how does one enter that desperate place and then interpret what respondents are saying? What methodology does one employ? Often, and in the case of Guatemala with certainty, a respondent's perception of the researcher influences, at times determines, what is said. Given the apprehension peasants feel, the challenge is to discover what people thought when the events were unfolding, and to understand the factors that have molded current memory. In many Guatemalan villages, diverse, often contradictory, memories coexist concerning relations with the insurgent forces. What dynamics shape and reshape these multiple narratives? Over time, memories of the same events sometimes evolve into mirror images of each other when viewed from the recollections of those inside and outside the country.

Communities that have traversed the unimaginable and grieve in the aftermath of the unspeakable, confront the past in varying ways. A central challenge is the recovery of trust and, in particular, rebuilding it within the community. The absence of trust cripples the present and hobbles the future. How does a society subjected to butchery and forced to cower in the face of impunity change course? How do people have confidence in legal institutions when they have seen these institutions as either complicit with the agents of destruction or as decimated by them? How do people participate in society and social institutions when the terror has instilled a numbing silence? How do survivors deal with the weight of their guilt—guilt for having survived, guilt for not having spoken out, guilt for having become accomplices in the repression suffered by others, guilt for having carved for themselves *Una Vida Tranquila.*

Resignation and passivity as a strategy for survival is a heavy albatross that chokes the possibility of recovery. Everyone in this village experienced a tremendous sense of guilt, fear, depression, loss, abandonment, despair, humiliation, anger, and solitude. For some, deep religious faith was able to carry them through. For others, even for some of the most religious, the blow was so devastating that it shattered their faith in God. And, as the CEH observed, "the terror does not disappear automatically when the levels of violence lessen, instead it has cumulative and perdurable effects which require time, effort and experience of a new type in order to overcome it" (CEH 1999a:tomo IV:15).

In some Guatemalan villages, the burden of the past has paralyzed the present. They have retreated into passivity, conformity, and mistrust. A phantomlike omnipotent impunity for those who perpetrated the massive terror grinds glass into open wounds. No crime, no matter how excessive, no matter how cruel and degrading, no matter how many times repeated, was ever punished. There were no limits, there was no recourse, and the result is a profound sense of continued vulnerability. If a society does not render a judgment and the truth is not declared, communities understandably feel that the terror of the past could reoccur. There is no closure and no sense of justice. The past lurks in the present and threatens to overwhelm the future.

But even in a culture of silence, quiet voices challenge themselves and others to speak out. Villagers in Santa Maria Tzejá began to view their silence as making them accomplices. Silence affirms—as the terrorist state expects—that nothing indeed has happened and binds the murderers and the survivors into a depraved covenant. The unspeakable horrors this village suffered should logically throttle any progress, optimism, energy, confidence, enthusiasm, ambition, or collective action (political or social). Yet this extraordinary community has become a model of success, an engaged population that is looking onward with confidence—not by avoiding the nightmare that took place but, on the contrary, by facing it head on. Through human rights workshops, speaking about the past, and engaging with it, they have moved forward and are determined—despite all the continued threats and attacks—not to move one step back. Key to this process is the public nature of their grieving: sharing the grief, hearing each other, receiving responses and reactions to their deep pain. This open grief allows for reciprocity and that, in turn, links the individual to the collective process of coping with fear, stress, and recovery. Also important has been a past of participatory experience and a venue to participate publicly—a strong community experience infused with democratic practices. The result is a process of private suffering, public grieving. The public space unveils pathways not always available in other villages that enable individuals to better cope with private wounds.

Nonetheless, the process of healing will take time. Ramon, a former combatant with the guerrilla forces, emphasizes the psychological scars of the war: "We were left psychologically wounded as a result of the war. It will take a long time to achieve an emotional stability." A Maya-K'iche' man, so poor he lacked land of his own in the village, recalls the decision he made when captured at the age of thirty-two and taken to be tortured at the military base. He had made up his mind not to collaborate with the army, not to provide any information. "I thought, no, I would rather just die by myself, why should I kill my brothers? I didn't even think of my family, I forgot, so let them kill me, I thought." I ask him how he felt when he left the army base after four months. "One leg was totally swollen, I couldn't walk. My feet were totally swollen," he recalls with a pained look twisting his features. "I only wanted water. My family and I were thrown in a thick forest, without food, nothing." Leandro was told he could not go back to his destroyed village because that was "a red zone, we could not cultivate there." He says he was devastated and demoralized. The physical pain and damage bled into the psychological wounds. In the beginning, it was not simply the terrible, debilitating physical pain that was immobilizing, he recalled, but rather the desire to live had seeped out of him. He says his wife began to cut wood and work so they could survive in the wasteland in which they had been dumped. He just sat there cowering: devastated, humiliated, and without energy or will. Hope for recovery was derailed because the military ordered him to appear at the army base—the same place where he had been tortured—every week, as if on a perverse parole that caused him to revisit the scene of the crimes of his tormentors.

When I conducted the first lengthy interview at his home in 1987, he nearly lost control as he began to describe the tortures. His wife and children looked on stunned by the physical representations of the torture techniques the army applied; then he threw himself exhausted onto a hammock, sobbing uncontrollably and covering his face with a towel. He said, "[T]his is the first time I have told anyone about what happened at the military base—I had not even told my wife about it." In my most recent interview in the mid-1990s, he told me that he still suffers pain in his stomach, and he becomes inexplicably irritable at times, unable to control his nerves or patience. He does not participate much in community activities because, he says, the smallest comment provokes unconscious outbursts. Today, fifty years old, he looks far older than his age, the deep wrinkles in his face betraying a permanent pain.

Claudio, a former combatant, also spoke of the psychological problems, saying, "[We] feel sad and desperate. [Before], when we were in the mountains [fighting with the guerrilla forces], we were free, happy, we sang, but then you leave the organization, you give up your weapon, you no longer have security, you never know when someone may threaten you, or kill you. That is why some *compañeros* cried when they surrendered their weapons."

Many villagers confide a deeply felt sorrow and talk of being haunted by the memories of those violent days. Leonardo tells of unexpectedly suffering near nervous breakdowns "because of the enormous fright of the past." He somberly reflects that "sometimes I remember and I cannot sleep. I feel very frightened." In those first days when he returned to the village after twelve years in refuge, he felt convulsed with anger at the sight of the army. "I felt such anger I almost could not stand it. I could not look at them." He says it was very difficult to adjust. "When I would see the army I would remember the bullets they would fire, the bombs, the screams and I would say to myself, 'Ay, they are looking at me, maybe they will fire at me.'"

Adelina recollects the time the family spent hiding in the jungle when she was a child: "I don't remember much but that we were hiding in the jungle. They would cover my mouth so I would not cry. I remember thorns tearing our knees and we would bleed. That is when I began to experience suffering and I learned that something very grave was happening and I felt that we were all going to suffer."

Manuel Canil, who lost his wife and all but two of his children in the massacre, said that, in the days following the butchery, while he was escaping the army in the jungle, he "had no feelings. It was like a dream I had. What hurt me the most is the manner by which they died, that hurt me a lot. I didn't feel any more. I only felt as if I was dreaming. I thought I will go crazy." His son, Edwin, six years old at the time, remembers the emotional state of his father during those days. "My father was feeling tremendous sadness, and I remember that in church they had said that to forget something very heavy, the best thing is to leave the place and go to another far-off place so that one would begin to abandon the pain." It was at that point that a broken-hearted, dispirited Manuel and his two surviving sons began the long and frightening walk to the border of Mexico to seek refuge.

This small village seems to have experienced all the horrors suffered in Guatemala in the early 1980s: massacres, torture, rape, disappearance, persecution, displacement. In some cases, the closest relationships were irretrievably altered. The army captured two children during an offensive although the family had hidden successfully for years in the jungle. Interviewed some twenty years later, the mother and father cry as they provide details about that tragic day, even though they did locate the children a decade later. At the time, they frantically looked everywhere for days, hoping that the children had only gotten lost during the army incursion. They went to the place where the children knew that food was hidden, "but, nothing, there was nothing"—no signs that the children had been there. "We couldn't do anything. That is how it was, that is how this history happened, so sad. It was a great sadness," the mother painfully remembers. "Truthfully we could not eat anymore. We began to fight among ourselves. He would say, '[It] was your fault, why didn't you take care of them?' And I also blamed him. We just didn't know what to do. We were already crazy, truly. Oh God! It was an immense sadness, truly." Although hope was crushed during the day, it would creep in at night. "I spent a year dreaming about them. I would dream that they were arriving. What hope! What wish! When I would wake up, there was nothing." She stops. Contemplatively, she looks out of her house and continues to sob and sigh as she and her husband traverse back to memories of those heartbreaking days. The schism that separated them from their children, physically as well as emotionally and ideologically, tangled the normal bonds between parents and children.

The residents of Santa Maria Tzejá have sought to confront the past publicly, through an especially innovative strategy: theater. A group of teenagers and Randall Shea, a North American teacher and director of the community's school, wrote a play documenting what Santa Maria Tzejá has experienced. They call the play *There Is Nothing Concealed That Will Not Be Discovered (Matthew 10:26)*, and the villagers themselves perform it. The play not only recalls what happened in the village in a stark, unflinching manner but also didactically lays out the laws and rights that the military violated. The play pointedly and precisely cites articles of the Guatemalan constitution that were trampled on, not normally the text of great drama. But in Guatemala, publicly reading the constitution can be a profoundly dramatic act. Performances inevitably lead to moving, at times heated, discussions. At first some were upset that a play was written at all, fearing that the theater group would provoke retaliation from the army. Some of the play's critics were fearful about what might happen, but others simply did not want to revisit the past. Nonetheless the production went ahead, and it had a cathartic impact on the village. Nicanor, who was taken to the military base in 1982 and apparently cooperated with the army and thus avoided lengthy torture, was quite disturbed about the play, arguing, "We don't want to recall again; to disturb again those situations that perhaps we are already leaving behind." He questioned whether the promoters and the performers of the play may have done it for money. He was disturbed, warning that all that scratching (*escarbar*, as chickens do) and provoking will bring a response.

When asked if he can forget what happened, he replied: "*Como no*, of course, after a long while yes, it can be forgotten, so long as there is no one reminding you, but with a reminder . . ." He left the sentence unfinished, as if to say that this play forced him to deal with the past. Should what happened in Santa Maria Tzejá be told? He remained silent for a very long time, and then said, "If it were told as it was, then magnificent. But there are a lot of things in the play that are missing." He was obviously uncomfortable with the portrayal of events and by the fact that his two boys are asking him questions about the past. His complaint was that the army takes all the hits and the guerrillas get off too easily.

Villagers who remained in the militarized community were afraid that a military attack might result, given the portrayal of the army, according to Leonardo, a young man who spent years in refugee camps in Mexico. Leonardo joined the guerrilla forces for a few years, along with half a dozen outraged teenagers, after the army's massacre and destruction of the village. Given his experiences, Leonardo should have been fearful of military retaliation, but he was more alarmed at leaving the past unexplained. Overall, however, even its critics have come to terms with the play. To the surprise of everyone involved, the play achieved national and international recognition. The theater group has gone on national tours, and the BBC both filmed the play and included extensive excerpts in a documentary about Guatemala.

Adelina Chom, a young Mayan woman who fled to the jungle, survived, and spent twelve years as a refugee in Mexico, is the lead actress. The play opens with Adelina addressing the audience directly, and then the following exchange takes place:

> *Santa Ortiz:* Ladies and Gentlemen, in 1982, my village of Santa Maria Tzejá, along with almost all the communities of the Ixcán, was attacked and destroyed by the army. Army soldiers massacred 17 people in Santa Maria Tzejá; in addition in the months after the attack, at least 8 more people died, from the illnesses and malnutrition they suffered living in the jungle. The army was carrying out its scorched earth campaign. . . .
>
> *Drunk*
> *(Santiago Boton-Simai):* Hey, I don't agree with what you're saying. You don't have the right to say things that stain the reputation of our sacred army. God in the heavens, and the army on the earth.
>
> *Santa:* Excuse me, sir, but it's our understanding that the army exists to defend the sovereignty of the Guatemalan people. The highest authority in Guatemala is the people. You have it backwards; the people do not exist to serve and honor the army.

Antonio: She's right. Article 35 of the Guatemalan constitution guarantees freedom of speech. The constitution is the most important law in Guatemala; it is above all other laws. All of the state institutions: the police, the army, even the firemen, have to function in accordance with the constitution. Neither the army, nor you, sir, have the right to take away any of our constitutional rights.

Midway into the play, in scene 6.3, Adelina returns to deal specifically with the tragedy of Santa Maria Tzejá:

Adelina: In the February 15th massacre, the following people were killed: [Adelina kneels, her head down. Church bell rings once, then twice; six of the performers walk on stage with wooden crosses in their hands. At the end Aurelio comes to stage dressed in army clothes.]

Santa: Second article of the Guatemalan constitution. Duties of the state: it is the duty of the state to guarantee for all of the inhabitants of the republic life, liberty, justice, security, peace, and the integral development of each person. Christian Canil Suar, 7 years old. Eufrasia Canil Suar, 14 years old. [Aurelio, as the soldier, with a knife in each hand, moves behind Santa, lets out a yell, and gives the impression of slitting her throat. Santa slumps to the ground, and Aurelio freezes.]

The play goes over somberly, yet forcefully, several articles of the constitution relevant to the abuses committed in the village, and then the scene concludes with a reference to international law:

Article 5 of the Universal Declaration of Human Rights. "No one shall be subjected to torture or any treatment which is cruel, inhuman or degrading."

This is followed by details of torture at the military base.

Scene 7 begins with the first "disappeared" person from the village:

Nazario: My name is Santos Vicente Sarat. I was one of the first people killed by the army. Soldiers kept watch on my house for three weeks, but I wasn't afraid. I had done nothing wrong. But finally one night, they kidnapped me. My corpse was never found. I died in 1975; I was 22 years old. My life was only just beginning. [A wooden block is struck against a desk to create a powerful, abrupt sound. Nazario strikes a pose and freezes.]

The play recites the names and ages of those murdered. Finally, it concludes:

All: Our lives were only just beginning. [Final ring of the bell, and candles are blown out.]

The play is a powerful vehicle for confronting the past, but it is able to succeed only because of the broader context that supports its performance. This village is fortunate to have neutral, concerned, and constructive mediators, respected by all, that are helping in the process. Most significant has been the steady, uncompromising involvement over the past thirty years of Father Luis Gurriarán, bringing a measure of comfort and stability to a grueling journey. While the community is determined to move on, the country as a whole, and the international community, still need to do their part. Signing a peace agreement may end the conflict between the army and insurgents, but it falls far short as the main means for the ideal of reconciliation. As a South African astutely observed, there is an inherent contradiction in a call for "re-conciliation" when the parties were never "conciliated" to begin with (Simpson 1998:491). For conciliation to be taken seriously, the efforts have to be deeprooted, requiring a serious look at the very core of social relations and not simply to concentrate on the period of most recent conflict.

The village has received national attention not only because of the play but also because of the bold charges leveled at the military. As a front-page headline in Guatemala's leading newspaper, *Prensa Libre*, announced on Tuesday, May 2, 2000: "Acusan Hermanos Lucas (Lucas Brothers accused)." The story mentioned Santa Maria Tzejá. The following day, Edwin Canil, now a law student at San Carlos University, testified about what he had seen.

The village has made remarkable strides both economically and socially. The cooperative has been a vital force in their material success, and an intense belief in education has resulted in a vibrant school and close to a hundred students pursuing professional degrees. Nonetheless, the attacks against Santa Maria Tzejá continue. On May 14, 2000, at 2:10 A.M., the cooperative store was set on fire. Everything was destroyed: merchandise, accounting books, records, and office equipment. Villagers estimated the loss at $52,000. The various attacks are "not mere chance," according to the board of the cooperative, but rather "follow a premeditated plan to destabilize the regular operations of our cooperative." In fact, the fire was set ten days after members of the community filed charges of genocide against military generals in power in 1982, and on the very day the community was celebrating the sixth anniversary of the return of the refugees. The villagers call May 13 the Holiday of Reconciliation and Initiation of the Reconstruction of the Community, a feat no other community has been able to achieve thus far. To the surprise of neighboring villages, there was a unified, determined response to rebuild. They secured new funds, rebuilt once again, and now have a more effective security system. This initiative is yet another sign that the village can cope with fear and adversity.

I will conclude by returning to the beginning—to the little boy that survived the massacre by hiding behind a tree and to the woman's body that was dumped by the cooperative building.

I received the following message from Edwin Canil at the end of August 2000:

Hola Beatriz,
I am writing to tell you that on Sunday August 20th the remains of my aunt Vicenta Mendoza were located. Finally, after 18 years, we were able to see her again, though

now only in bones. Nonetheless we feel a little bit more tranquil. But, only when justice is done, then, our souls and their souls will rest in peace. When I heard the news I cried a lot, everything came back to me, and I felt as if all had happened yesterday. Then, after all the crying, I began to feel calm again, but I do feel a thirst for justice. I think that only with justice will we feel more secure that it would not be so easy for it all to happen again. . . .

My family has not been found. The exhumations continue and I hope they will be found. . . .

I want to tell you that at the University I am involved in a research project and I chose the theme of Genocide and Crimes Against Humanity. I am very interested in this and pushing along. . . . All of this gives me more courage to get involved. I am becoming more conscious of the situation in Guatemala. Next month I will give my testimony before a prosecutor and then the public debate will begin.

I want to tell you also that a few days ago the video of the Santa Maria Tzejá play, "There is nothing hidden that will not be discovered" was presented here in Guatemala City. A lot of people came, the place was packed for two nights.

This message is an example of villagers bridging the painful and unjust past—with a hope for justice and a better future. The charge of genocide against army generals, the planners of appalling savagery, is one step families have taken toward justice. The words of Edwin Canil tell us that moral strength can defeat intimidation; that courage, understanding, and hope can undermine silence.

I would like to acknowledge and thank the John D. and Catherine T. MacArthur Foundation for their Research and Writing grant, which supported the writing phase of this research. I am grateful to two University of California, Berkeley, students, Monica Pons and Carina Carriedo, for their dedicated and first-rate assistance. Both took part in Berkeley's Undergraduate Research Apprentice Program. Pseudonyms were used for some villagers to protect their identities.

BIBLIOGRAPHY

Adams, Richard N. 1970. *Crucifixion by Power: Essays on Guatemalan National Social Structure, 1944–1966*. Austin: University of Texas Press.

Annis, Sheldon. 1987. *God and Production in a Guatemalan Town*. Austin: University of Texas Press.

Archdiocese of Guatemala. 1999. "Guatemala: Never Again!" The Official Report of the Human Rights Office, Guatemala. Maryknoll, N.Y.: Orbis Books.

Arendt, Hannah. 1968. *Between Past and Future*. New York: Viking Press.

Berryman, Phillip. 1984. *The Religious Roots of Rebellion: Christians in Central American Revolutions*. Maryknoll, N.Y.: Orbis Books.

Black, George, with Milton Jamail and Norma Stoltz Chinchilla. 1984. *Garrison Guatemala*. New York: Monthly Review.

Brintnall, Douglas E. 1979. *Revolt against the Dead: The Modernization of a Mayan Community in the Highlands of Guatemala*. New York: Gordon and Breach.

Cifuentes H., Juan Fernando. 1998. *Historia moderna de la etnicidad en Guatemala. La visión hegemónica: rebeliones y otros incidentes indígenas en el siglo XX*. Guatemala: Universidad Rafael Landivar, Instituto de Investigaciones Económicas y Sociales.

Comisión para el Esclarecimiento Histórico (CEH). 1999a. Tomo IV. *Consecuencias y efectos de la violencia. Guatemala: Oficina de Servicios para Proyectos de las Naciones Unidas.*

———. 1999b. *Guatemala: Memory of Silence.* Report of the Commission for Historical Clarification. Conclusions and Recommendations. Guatemala.

Falla, Ricardo. 1978. *Quiche rebelde: estudio de un movimiento de conversión religiosa, rebelde a las creencias tradicionales, en San Antonio Ilotenango, Quiché (1948–1970).* Ciudad Universitaria, Guatemala: Editorial Universitaria de Guatemala.

———. 1994. *Massacres in the Jungle: Ixcán, Guatemala, 1975–1982.* Boulder, Colo.: Westview Press.

Gleijeses, Piero. 1991. *Shattered Hope: The Guatemalan Revolution and the United States, 1944–1954.* Princeton: Princeton University Press.

Green, Linda. 1999. *Fear as a Way of Life: Mayan Widows in Rural Guatemala.* New York: Columbia University Press.

Hale, Charles R. 1997a. "Consciousness, Violence, and the Politics of Memory in Guatemala." *Current Anthropology* 38(5):817–38.

———. 1997b. "Cultural Politics of Identity in Latin America." *Annual Review of Anthropology.* 26:567–90.

Immerman, Richard. 1982. *The CIA in Guatemala: The Foreign Policy of Intervention.* Austin: University of Texas Press.

Krauss, Clifford. 1985. "Guatemela Will Elect a Civilian, but Will He Control the Military?" *Wall Street Journal,* October 30.

———. 1991. *Inside Central America: Its People, Politics and History.* New York: Summit Books.

Levi, Primo. 1988. *The Drowned and the Saved.* New York: Vintage International.

Manz, Beatriz. 1988a. *Refugees of a Hidden War: The Aftermath of Counterinsurgency in Guatemala.* Anthropological Studies of Contemporary Issues Series. Albany: State University of New York Press.

———. 1988b. *Repatriation and Reintegration: An Arduous Process in Guatemala.* Washington, D.C.: Georgetown University (HMP/CIPRA).

———. 1988c. "The Transformation of La Esperanza: An Ixcán village." In *Harvest of Violence.* Robert Carmack, ed. Norman: University of Oklahoma Press.

———. 1995. "Fostering Trust in a Climate of Fear." In *Mistrusting Refugees.* E. V. Daniel and J. Knudsen, eds. Berkeley: University of California Press.

———. 1999. "La importancia del contexto en la memoria." In *De la Memoria a la Reconstrucción Histórica.* Beatriz Manz, Elizabeth Oglesby, and José García Noval, eds. Guatemala: Asociación para el Avance de las Ciencias Sociales en Guatemala—AVANCSO.

Marques, Jose, Dario Paez, and Alexandra F. Serra. 1997. "Social Sharing, Emotional Climate, and the Transgenerational Transmission of Memories: The Portuguese Colonial War." In *Collective Memory of Political Events: Social Psychological Perspectives.* J. W. Pennebaker, D. Paez, and B. Rimé, ed. Mahway, N.J.: Lawrence Erlbaum Associates.

McClintock, Michael. 1985. *State Terror and Popular Resistance in Guatemala.* Vol. 2. *The American Connection.* London: Zed Books.

Melville, Thomas, and Marjorie Melville. 1971. *Guatemala: The Politics of Land Ownership.* New York: Free Press.

Nairn, Allan. 1982. "Guatemala Can't Take Two Roads," Op-Ed page, *New York Times,* July 20:23.

Nash, Manning. 1967. *Machine Age Maya: The Industrialization of a Guatemalan Community.* Chicago: University of Chicago Press.

Nelson, Diane M. 1999. *A Finger in the Wound: Body Politics in Quincentennial Guatemala*. Berkeley: University of California Press.

Nietzsche, Fredrich. 1956. *The Birth of Tragedy and the Genealogy of Morals*. Francis Golffing, trans. New York: Doubleday and Company.

Oficina de Derechos Humanos del Arzobispado de Guatemala. 1998a. *Nunca Más*. Tomo I. *Impactos de la Violencia*. Guatemala: Oficina de Derechos Humanos del Arzobispado de Guatemala.

——. 1998b. Tomo II. *Los Mecanismos del Horror*. Guatemala.

——. 1998c. Tomo III. *El Entorno Histórico*. Guatemala.

Payeras, Mario. 1982. *Los Días de la Selva. Relato sobre la implantación de las guerrillas populares en el norte del Quiché, 1972–1076*. Mexico: Nuestro Tiempo.

Ross, Amy. 1999a. "The Body of the Truth: Truth Commissions in Guatemala and South Africa." Ph.D. dissertation, Department of Geography, University of California, Berkeley.

——. 1999b. "Truth Commissions as Sites of Struggle." In *Guatemala, Thinking about the Unthinkable*. Ruth M. Gidley, Cynthia Klee, and Reggie Norton, eds. Association of Artists for Guatemala. England: Farringdon.

Schlesinger, Stephen, and Stephen Kinzer. 1982. *Bitter Fruit: The Untold Story of the American Coup in Guatemala*. New York: Doubleday.

Simpson, 1998. "The Second Bullet: Transgenerational Impacts of the Trauma of Conflict within a South African and World Context." In *International Handbook of Multigenerational Legacies of Trauma*. Yael Danieli, ed. New York: Plenum Press.

Smith, Carol A. 1984. *Indian Class and Class Consciousness in Prerevolutionary Guatemala*. Washington, D.C.: Latin American Program, Wilson Center.

——. ed. 1990. *Guatemalan Indians and the State, 1540 to 1988*. Austin: University of Texas Press.

Stoll, David. 1993. *Between Two Armies in the Ixil Towns of Guatemala*. New York: Columbia University Press.

Warren, Kay B, 1978. *The Symbolism of Subordination: Indian Identity in a Guatemalan Town*. Austin: University of Texas Press.

——. 1992. "Transforming Memories and Histories: The Meanings of Ethnic Resurgence for Mayan Indians." In *Americas: New Interpretive Essays*. Alfred Stepan, ed. New York: Oxford University Press.

——. 1998. *Indigenous Movements and Their Critics: Pan-Maya Activism in Guatemala*. Princeton: Princeton University Press.

Warren, Kay B, ed. 1993. *The Violence Within: Cultural and Political Opposition in Divided Nations*. Boulder, Colorado: Westview Press.

Watanabe, John M. 1992. *Maya Saints and Souls in a Changing World*. Austin, Texas: University of Texas Press.

Wilson, Richard. 1991. "Machine Guns and Mountain Spirits: The Cultural Effects of State Repression among the Q'eqchi' of Guatemala." *Critical Anthropology* 11:33–61.

——. 1995. *Maya Resurgence in Guatemala: Q'eqchi' Experiences*. Norman, Oklahoma: University of Oklahoma Press.

——, ed. 1997. *Human Rights, Culture and Context: Anthropological Perspectives*. London: Pluto Press.

12

Recent Developments in the International Law of Genocide

An Anthropological Perspective on the International Criminal Tribunal for Rwanda

Paul J. Magnarella

Anthropologists have always been concerned with the well-being of politically weak peoples around the world. Consequently they find the genocidal attacks on defenseless populations in Rwanda, Burundi, Bosnia, Kosovo, East Timur, and other lands especially distressing. As part of their humanistic and scientific enterprise, anthropologists endeavor to understand the root causes and nature of these most aberrant of human acts. This chapter contributes to this endeavor by focusing on the evolving conceptualization of genocide in international law and its application to the recent genocide in Rwanda.

Since the 1940s, when Raphael Lemkin coined the term *genocide*, scholars have offered a wide variety of concepts to carry that label (see Andreopoulos 1994). Although scholarly conceptualization is useful for research purposes, it is important for anthropologists and others to know the legal definition of genocide as presented in the United Nations' 1948 Convention on the Prevention and Punishment of Genocide, as well as the recent judicial expansion of this definition in the 1998 case of *Akayesu* in the International Criminal Tribunal for Rwanda (discussed below).[1] The convention's definition of genocide has been adopted into the legal systems of at least 127 countries. It is in the statutes of the U.N. International Criminal Tribunals for the former Yugoslavia and Rwanda, and the proposed permanent International Criminal Court. Consequently, this definition has legal power.

THE INTERNATIONAL LEGAL DEFINITION OF GENOCIDE

Article II of the Genocide Convention defines the crime of genocide as:

any of the following acts committed with intent to destroy, in whole or in part, a national, ethnical, racial or religious group, as such:

(a) Killing members of the group;

(b) Causing serious bodily or mental harm to members of the group;

(c) Deliberately inflicting on the group conditions of life calculated to bring about its physical destruction in whole or in part;

(d) Imposing measures intended to prevent births within the group;

(e) Forcibly transferring children of the group to another group.

Article V of the Genocide Convention requires ratifying states to enact the legislation necessary to give effect to the convention and to provide effective penalties for persons found guilty of genocide or any of the acts enumerated in Article II (above). Although only 127 of the almost 200 countries sharing our earth have ratified the Genocide Convention, legal authorities maintain that the prevention and punishment of the crime of genocide are part of customary international law, and, therefore, all states are legally obligated to take the measures necessary to prevent genocide in their territories and to punish those who perpetrate it. As early as 1951, the International Court of Justice (ICJ) characterized the prohibition of genocide as a peremptory norm of international law (*jus cogens*) from which no derogation is permitted.[2]

Article VI of the Genocide Convention requires that persons charged with genocide be tried either by a state court of the country in which the genocide was allegedly committed or by a recognized and competent international penal tribunal. To date, the anticipated international penal tribunal has not been created. In July of 1998, however, state delegates at a U.N.-sponsored conference in Rome overwhelmingly approved a statute for a permanent International Criminal Court (ICC) by a vote of 120 to 7 with 21 abstentions (Baron 1998). The ICC will become a reality after sixty countries ratify its statute—a process that may take four to five years.

With respect to the prevention or stoppage of genocide, Article VIII of the Genocide Convention provides that any state party may call on the United Nations to take appropriate action, and Article IX provides for recourse to the interstate jurisdiction of the International Court of Justice:

> Disputes between the Contracting Parties relating to the interpretation, application, or fulfillment of the present Convention, including those relating to the responsibility of a State for genocide . . . shall be submitted to the International Court of Justice at the request of any of the parties to the dispute.

Consequently the convention, by means of Articles V, VIII, and IX, contemplates prevention of genocide by national legislation, state governments, and competent U.N. organs, which may include (but are not limited to) the General Assembly, the High Commission for Human Rights, the General Secretariat, and the Security Council. Clearly, the most powerful of these is the Security Council, which has the authority and obligation under Chapter VII of the U.N. Charter to maintain and restore international peace by taking diplomatic, economic, or military measures. Once the Security Council determines which of these measures it will employ to deal with threats to peace in any part of the world, all U.N. member states are obligated to lend their support as needed (U.N. Charter, Art. 43).

The Genocide Convention calls for judicial enforcement by means of national courts, an international penal tribunal (that may not be established until the year 2003), and the ICJ. To date, none of these mechanisms has been effective in the prevention of genocide. In the 1990s, for example, ethnic cleansing in the former Yugoslavia and mass murder of Tutsi in Rwanda continued while national courts, state governments, and the ICJ looked on in despair.

Since the perpetrators of genocide are often persons who control a government or a national army, national courts are unlikely venues for their prosecution. Countries where genocide occurs usually do not have independent judiciaries. As for the ICJ, it is not a criminal court. It deals with disputes between states that voluntarily recognize its jurisdiction. The ICJ can determine whether a state party has breached the Genocide Convention and can decide the amount of reparations for such a breach, but it cannot convict the individuals responsible for the breach (see ICJ Statute Art. 36). Only rarely has the ICJ been called upon to address the issue of genocide.

Significantly, recent action by the U.N. Security Council has led to the punishment of individual genocide perpetrators in the former Yugoslavia and Rwanda. Acting under Chapter VII of the U.N. Charter, the Security Council took unprecedented steps by establishing the International Tribunal for the Former Yugoslavia (ICTY) in 1993 and the International Tribunal for Rwanda (ICTR) in 1994 as measures to restore international peace and security.[3]

Of those two tribunals, the ICTR was the first to deal head-on with the crime of genocide. During 1998 the ICTR made significant progress in the prosecution of persons responsible for the 1994 mass murder of Tutsi. In its first completed trial, the case against former Taba *bourgmestre* (mayor) Jean-Paul Akayesu, the ICTR created a number of important jurisprudential concepts and reasoning paths that it and other tribunals will likely apply in future genocide cases (*Pros. v. Akayesu* 1998).

In addition, this trial reached several milestones on the evolving road of international humanitarian law. Just fifty years after the United Nations had adopted the Genocide Convention, Jean-Paul Akayesu became the first person in history to be found guilty of genocide after a trial by an international tribunal. His trial also represents the first time in history that an international tribunal conceptualized sexual violence (including rape) as an act of genocide.

The details of these developments are discussed below against the backdrop of recent Rwandan history.

MASS MURDER IN RWANDA

Following the assassination of Rwanda's Hutu president, Juvenal Habyarimana, when the plane carrying him was shot down near Kigali's airport (probably by hardline Hutu) on April 6, 1994, Rwanda burst into horrifying violence resulting in the murder of about 800,000 people (mostly Tutsi), the uprooting of about two million within Rwanda's borders, and the exodus of more than two million (mostly Hutu) to the neighboring countries of Zaire, Burundi, Tanzania, Kenya, and Uganda (Prunier 1995). Immediately after Habyarimana's death, the Presidential Guard, the Hutu-dominated national army, and the *Interahamwe* (Hutu death squads) unleashed a systematic campaign of murder against hundreds of moderate Hutu and all Tutsi.

Rwanda was Africa's most densely populated country, with rural peasants constituting the bulk of its inhabitants. It had a pregenocide population of approximately eight million, all speaking Ikinyarwanda, a Bantu language. About 85 percent of the people were officially classified as Hutu, 14 percent as Tutsi, and 1 percent as Twa or Pygmies. Intermarriage among these people, many of whom are Christian, was not uncommon (Newbury 1988).

Precolonial rule by the minority but aristocratic Tutsi, as well as indirect rule later by Belgian colonialists through Tutsi royalty, had created resentment among the majority Hutu. Rwanda became independent of Belgium in 1962, and various Hutu factions controlled the government and military until July of 1994. Periodically throughout the years of independence there were outbreaks of violence, resulting in the flight of Tutsi to surrounding countries, especially to Uganda where they formed the Rwandan Patriotic Front (RPF) and Army. In the 1960s, some exiled Tutsi invaded Rwanda in unsuccessful attempts to regain power.

Major-General Juvenal Habyarimana came to power in 1973, as the result of a military coup. During his twenty-one years of rule (1973–1994), there were no Tutsi mayors or governors, only one Tutsi military officer, just two Tutsi members of parliament, and only one Tutsi cabinet minister (Prunier 1995:75). In addition, Hutu in the military were prohibited from marrying Tutsi, and all citizens were required to carry ethnic identity cards. For purposes of these identity cards, ethnicity was determined by patrilineal descent. Hence even the children of mixed marriages were classified as Hutu, Tutsi, or Twa, depending on the identity cards of their fathers.

Habyarimana promoted a policy of internal repression against Tutsi. In the 1990s, especially, his government indiscriminately interred and persecuted Tutsi, claiming that they were actual or potential accomplices of the RPF (Jefremovas 1995; Newbury 1995). From 1990 to 1993, Hutu ultranationalists killed an estimated two thousand Tutsi; they also targeted human rights advocates, regardless of ethnicity (Newbury 1995:14).

The genocide campaign following Habyarimana's death ended in July 1994, when the RPF Army routed the Hutu militias and army. The RPF and moderate Hutu political parties formed a new government on July 18, 1994, but the country was in chaos. The government pledged to implement the Arusha peace agreement on power sharing previously reached by Habyarimana's regime and the RPF on August 3, 1993. On August 10, 1995, in a presidential statement, the U.N. Security Council called upon the new Rwandan government to ensure that there would be no reprisals against Hutu wishing to return to their homes and resume their work, reminded the government of its responsibility for a national reconciliation, and emphasized that the Arusha peace agreement constituted an appropriate framework for reconciliation.[4]

The new Rwandan government was a coalition of twenty-two ministers drawn from the RPF (with nine ministers) and four other political parties (U.S. Department of State 1994). Both Tutsi and Hutu were among the top government officials. The government committed itself to building a multiparty democracy and to discontinuing the ethnic classification system utilized by the previous regime (Bonner 1994).

On July 1, 1994, the U.N. Security Council adopted resolution 935, in which it requested the secretary general to establish a commission of experts to determine whether serious breaches of humanitarian law (including genocide) had been committed in Rwanda. In the fall of 1994, the commission reported to the Security Council that genocide and systematic, widespread, and flagrant violations of international humanitarian law had been committed in Rwanda, resulting in massive loss of life. On November 8, 1994, the secretary general submitted to the Security Council a statute for the International Criminal Tribunal for Rwanda, stating that he was "convinced" that "the prosecution of persons responsible for serious violations of international humanitarian law [in Rwanda] ... would contribute to the process of national reconciliation and to the restoration and maintenance of peace."[5] He recommended that this tribunal, like the one created by the Security Council in 1993 for the former Yugoslavia, be established under Chapter VII of the U.N. Charter. The Security Council adopted the secretary general's report and the ICTR statute without change.

Article 1 of the tribunal's statute limits the ICTR's temporal jurisdiction to the year 1994. That article also states that the ICTR "shall have the power to prosecute persons responsible for serious violations of international humanitarian law committed in the territory of Rwanda and Rwandan citizens responsible for such violations committed in the territory of neighboring states." Consequently, the statute gives the tribunal both personal and territorial jurisdiction in Rwanda, as well as limited personal and territorial jurisdiction in surrounding states.

Because the Security Council is not a legislative body, it lacked authority to enact substantive law for the tribunal. Instead, it authorized the tribunal to apply existing international humanitarian law applicable to noninternational armed conflict. The humanitarian law included in the tribunal's statute consists of the Genocide Convention (ratified by Rwanda), crimes against humanity (as defined by the Nuremberg Charter), Article 3 Common to the Geneva Conventions, and Additional Protocol II (also ratified by Rwanda).[6] Both the prohibition and punishment of acts of genocide and crimes against humanity are part of customary international law imposing legal obligations on all states.

THE CASE AGAINST JEAN-PAUL AKAYESU

As stated above, the case against Jean-Paul Akayesu is significant for a series of reasons: it was the first trial before an international tribunal of someone charged with genocide, and it was the first trial in which an international tribunal conceptualized sexual violence (including rape) as an act of genocide. Also, because this was the ICTR's first judgment based on a contested trial, the justices had to face many jurisprudential issues for the first time. The trial chamber's lengthy judgment of September 2, 1998, carefully explicates the facts, reasoning, and rules it relied upon to reach its conclusions. By so doing, this judgment will stand as a historic precedent for future tribunals dealing with similar issues.

Akayesu's Background

Jean-Paul Akayesu, a Rwandan national, was born in 1953.[7] He is married, with five children. Prior to becoming bourgmestre of Taba commune in the Gitarama prefecture of Rwanda, he was a teacher, then an inspector of schools. Akayesu entered politics in 1991, becoming a founding member of the Mouvement Démocratique Républicain (MDR). He served as chairman of the local wing of the MDR in Taba commune. In April 1993, Akayesu, with the support of several key figures and influential groups in the commune, was elected bourgmestre of Taba. He held that position until June 1994, when he fled to Zambia.

Arrest and Indictment

Jean-Paul Akayesu was arrested in Zambia on October 10, 1995. On November 22, 1995, the ICTR prosecutor requested the Zambian authorities keep Akayesu in detention for a period of ninety days while awaiting the completion of the investigation into potential charges against him. The prosecutor's indictment contained a total of fifteen counts individually charging Akayesu with genocide, complicity in genocide, direct and public incitement to commit genocide, extermination, murder, torture, cruel treatment, rape, other inhumane acts and outrages upon personal dignity, crimes against humanity, and violations of Article 3 Common to the 1949 Geneva Conventions and Additional Protocol II.[8] Judge William H. Sekule confirmed the indictment and issued an arrest warrant. Akayesu was transferred to the ICTR detention facilities in Arusha, Tanzania, on May 26, 1996. His case was assigned to Trial Chamber I, consisting of Judges Laïty Kama (Senegal), Lennart Aspegren (Sweden), and Navanethem Pillay (South Africa)—the only female judge at the ICTR.

Trial and Testimony

During the seventeen-month-long trial, punctuated by defense-requested adjournments, the justices heard forty-two witnesses, many being eyewitnesses and victims who told gruesome stories of their ordeals.[9] The first person to testify for the prosecution was a thirty-five-year-old Tutsi woman, known as Witness JJ to protect her identity. She explained how within days after President Habyarimana's plane crashed, Hutu killed her husband, tore down her family's home, then slaughtered and ate her cows. She fled, with her twenty-month-old son on her back, to the farm of a Hutu neighbor, but he was too scared to hide her, so she and the baby spent the night in a field of coffee plants. The next morning her Hutu neighbor brought her food and advised her to go to the Taba municipal office of Mayor Jean-Paul Akayesu, where Tutsi were seeking refuge.

When she arrived at the municipal compound, about sixty Tutsi, mostly women and children, were already there. She saw Akayesu standing next to two policemen armed with pistols. Soon, she said, Hutu thugs began beating her, her child, and many of the other Tutsi refugees. Witness JJ fled to a nearby banana plantation, but a policeman found her there and beat her with the butt of his pistol. The next morning Witness JJ and about ten other Tutsi women went to Mayor Akayesu and asked him to shoot them, because they could no longer endure the brutal beatings. He told them there were no more bullets, and even if there were, he would not waste them on Tutsi women.

Witness JJ and the others went back to the banana plantation. Shortly thereafter soldiers came and began raping the women. The next day some soldiers took Witness JJ and some other women to the communal office, known as the "cultural center," where drunken soldiers were raping screaming girls. Three of them also raped Witness JJ. The next day she was raped twice more. The rapes were especially humiliating because many took place in public, before children. She testified that Akayesu told the rapist, "Don't tell me that you won't have tasted a Tutsi woman. Take advantage of it, because they'll be killed tomorrow." "He spoke as though he were encouraging players," she said.

Desperate and weak, she took her child and limped off to a cornfield. Later she accepted the offer of a Hutu couple who said that they would care for her baby while she was on the run. They had a cow and said they would give the child milk. Instead, Witness JJ testified, they killed the baby and let their dogs eat his body. Somehow, she escaped with her life. She met with ICTR prosecutors in June 1997.

According to Witness JJ, "Akayesu did not kill with his own hands, but with his orders." She said that Akayesu had declared all Tutsis as enemy and had asked the Hutu to get rid of them. He made the call at a public meeting in Taba on April 19, 1994, following a security meeting of mayors and members of the interim government in Murambi the day before. Witness JJ claimed that Akayesu specifically told people, "[If] you knew what the Tutsis were doing. I have just found out at the security meeting. I have no more pity for them, especially the intellectuals. I will give them to you."

In cross-examination, the defense asked Witness JJ how Akayesu was to blame for her ordeal. "Did he have the means to prevent the rapes?" She responded that Akayesu was an authority. He could have protected the women and children, but he did nothing for them. "When I went to see him for help, he had the police get me away." Other witnesses also testified to Akayesu's change in attitude following the security meeting held twelve days after the start of the genocide.

Akayesu testified in his own defense on March 12, 1998. He portrayed himself as a helpless, low-level official who had no control over events in Taba commune. He told the court that the Interahamwe was responsible for the killings. Akayesu claimed he had asked the *préfét* of Gitarama Province for gendarmes to maintain law and order but received no support. He said that when he tried to save some Tutsi, he was accused of supporting the RPF and his life was threatened.

Are the Tutsi a Protected Group?

Before determining whether Akayesu was guilty of acts of genocide, the trial chamber had to determine whether genocide as defined in Article 2 of the ICTR statute, which replicates the Genocide Convention, had occurred in Rwanda. The chamber reasoned that since the special intent to commit genocide lies in the intent to destroy, in whole or in part, a national, ethnic, racial, or social group, it was necessary to determine the meaning of those four social categories. Because neither the Genocide Convention nor the ICTR statute had defined them, the task fell upon the chamber itself. Based on its reading of the *travaux préparatoires* (preparatory work) of the Genocide Convention, the chamber concluded that the drafters perceived the crime of genocide as targeting only stable, permanent groups, whose membership is determined by birth. The drafters excluded more mobile groups, such as political and economic groups, that one joins voluntarily.[10] The chamber then proceeded to define each of the social categories listed in the ICTR statute.

It maintained that a national group is "a collection of people who are perceived to share a legal bond based on common citizenship, coupled with reciprocity of rights and duties." An ethnic group is "a group whose members share a common language or culture." A racial group is "based on the hereditary physical traits often identified with a geographical region, irrespective of linguistic, cultural, national or religious factors." A religious group "is one whose members share the same religion, denomination or mode of worship" (*Pros. v Akayesu* 1998:§6.3).

Significantly, the Tutsi-Hutu distinction in Rwanda does not fit into any of the above categories. The Tutsi belong to the same religious groups and national group as do the Hutu. Tutsi and Hutu share a common language and culture. And any hereditary physical traits formerly distinguishing Hutu from Tutsi have become largely obliterated through generations of intermarriage and a Belgian classification scheme based on cattle ownership.[11] Consequently, had the ICTR justices stopped there, they would have been forced to conclude that genocide, as legally defined in the convention and statute, had not occurred in Rwanda.

Fortunately the justices did not stop there. They next asked "whether it would be impossible to punish the physical destruction of a group as such under the Genocide Convention, if the said group, although stable and membership is by birth, does not meet the definition of any one of the four groups expressly protected by the Genocide Convention [and Article 2 of the ICTR Statute]" (ibid.). They concluded that the answer is "no," because it is "important to respect the intention of the drafters of the Genocide Convention, which according to the *travaux préparatoires*, was patently to ensure the protection of any stable and permanent group" (ibid.:§7.8).

Next the chamber asked whether the Tutsi constituted a stable and permanent group for purposes of the Genocide Convention. To answer this question, the chamber considered evidence provided by eyewitness and expert testimony during the trial. The chamber noted that the Tutsi constituted a group referred to as "ethnic" in official Rwandan classifications. Identity cards prior to 1994 included a reference to *ubwoko* in Kinyarwanda or *ethnie* (ethnic group) in French, which referred to the designations Hutu, Tutsi, and Twa. The chamber noted that all the Rwandan witnesses who appeared before it invariably answered without hesitation the prosecutor's questions regarding their ethnic identity.

Earlier in its judgment, the chamber noted that witnesses testified that "[e]ven pregnant women, including those of Hutu origin, were killed on the grounds that the foetuses in their wombs were fathered by Tutsi men, for in a patrilineal society like Rwanda, the child belongs to the father's group of origin" (ibid.:§3). Witness PP testified that Akayesu had made a public statement to the effect that "if a Hutu woman were impregnated by a Tutsi man, the Hutu woman had to be found in order 'for the pregnancy to be aborted'"(ibid.). Given these and related facts, the chamber found that at the time of the alleged events, "the Tutsi did indeed constitute a stable and permanent group and were identified as such by all" (ibid.:§7.8). Consequently they were protected by the Genocide Convention and Article 2 of the ICTR statute.

Here, the chamber made two critical determinations that will greatly influence the international law of genocide and should interest anthropologists. By adding "stable and permanent group, whose membership is largely determined by birth," to the four existing social categories (that is, national, ethnical, racial, and religious) of the Genocide Convention, the chamber significantly expanded the kinds of populations that will be protected by the convention. Anthropologists might wonder whether unisexual groups, homosexuals, or persons mentally or physically impaired permanently at birth might constitute protected groups under the tribunal's expanded definition.

The chamber also expanded upon the categories of protected peoples by refusing to confine itself to an objective (etic), universalistic definition of ethnic group. Instead it relied on the subjective (emic) perceptions of the Rwandan people. Consequently it established as a precedent the idea that a court may regard any stable and permanent group, whose membership is largely determined by birth, as an ethnic group for purposes of the Genocide Convention as long as the people of the society in question perceive that group to be different from others according to local, emic criteria. With that approach, the chamber has linked the international law of genocide with the rich tradition of ethnoscientific inquiry.

DETERMINING INTENT

Because genocide involves the intent to destroy a protected group, in whole or in part, intentionality is a constitutive element of the crime. Intent is a mental factor that is difficult to determine with precision in the absence of a sincere confession or public admission by the accused. The chamber provided another jurisprudential roadway by maintaining that in the absence of a confession, the accused's intent can be inferred from a number of presumptions of fact. The chamber reasoned that "it is possible to deduce the genocidal intent inherent in a particular act charged from the general context of the perpetration of other culpable acts systematically directed against that same group, whether these acts were committed by the same offender or by others" (ibid.:§6.3.1). Specific factors that the chamber believed could enable it to infer the genocidal intent of a particular act included the scale of atrocities committed, their general nature, and the deliberate and systematic targeting of people because of their membership in a particular group, while excluding members of other groups.

Here the chamber offers a method for judicially constructing an individual's genocidal intent. This method involves placing an accused's particular act(s) against a victim within the broad context of prevalent and culpable acts directed at other persons because they are members of the victim's group, even if those acts were perpetrated by persons other than the accused. The method turns an emic category—intent—into an etic one—constructive intent. Hence an individual who attacks only one person and never explains why can be convicted of genocide (a special intent crime) as long as his one attack fits into an overall pattern of genocidal acts by others against members of the same protected group.

SEXUAL VIOLENCE AS A CRIME OF GENOCIDE

Those counts in the indictment charging Akayesu with the crime of genocide made no specific reference to sexual violence or rape. However, noting that the Genocide Convention and Article 2(2) of the ICTR statute offer as one of the definitions of genocide the "causing [of] serious bodily or mental harm to members of a group," the trial chamber chose to consider sexual violence in connection with the charge of genocide. The three justices reasoned that acts of sexual violence constituted genocide provided they were committed with the specific intent to destroy, in whole or in part, a particular group—in this case, the Tutsi. Rape and sexual violence certainly constitute inflictions of "serious bodily and mental harm" on victims.

In light of all the evidence before it, the chamber was satisfied that the acts of sexual violence (including rape) described by witnesses were committed solely against Tutsi women, many of whom were subjected to the worst public humiliation, mutilation, and multiple sexual violations on the municipal premises or in other public places. These sexual attacks, the chamber concluded, resulted in physical and psychological destruction of Tutsi women, their families, and their communities. Sexual violence was an integral part of the process of destruction, specifically targeting Tutsi women and specifically contributing to the destruction of the Tutsi group as a whole.

The tribunal found that Akayesu had aided and abetted the acts of sexual violence by allowing them to take place in his presence in or near the municipal building and by verbally encouraging the commission of those acts. By virtue of his authority, his overt encouragement sent a clear signal of official tolerance for sexual violence, without which these acts would not have taken place. Consequently the chamber concluded that the acts of sexual violence alleged in the indictment and subsequently proven at trial constitute the crime of genocide for which it found Akayesu individually criminally responsible.

CONCLUSION

The *Akayesu* case has immense factual and jurisprudential importance for Rwanda, international humanitarian law, and the anthropological study of genocide. During the trial, the chamber heard forty-two witnesses (including five expert witnesses). Many of those testifying were eyewitnesses and victims who told gruesome stories of their ordeals. The proceedings generated more than four thousand pages of transcripts and 125 evidentiary documents. The final judgment runs over two hundred pages.

This chapter has addressed only a limited number of the case's many important issues. With its *Akayesu* decision, the ICTR added to the four groups specified in the Genocide Convention and Tribunal Statute. It also introduced an emic standard for determining what groups in a particular society are protected by the Genocide Convention. Arguably, by definition there would have been no genocide in Rwanda had the trial chamber not done so. In addition, the chamber explicated a method for determining an individual's constructive genocidal intent, thereby making it easier for prosecutors to win convictions in the absence of a confession or admission of intent. The ICTR also became the first international tribunal in history to conceptualize sexual violence as a crime of genocide.

This case has generated some major contributions to the legal analysis and conceptualization of genocide. It also contributed to a better understanding of the events that constituted the horrors of Rwanda.

NOTES

1. Convention on the Prevention and Punishment of the Crime of Genocide, approved December 9, 1948, S. TREATY DOC. NO. 1, 81st Cong., 2d Sess., 78 U.N.T.S. 277 (registered January 12, 1951) [Hereinafter Genocide Convention]. As of January 1, 1999, 127 states were party to the Genocide Convention (Henkin et al. 1999:332).

2. The court made this pronouncement in the case entitled: "Reservations to the Convention on Genocide," 1951 I.C.J. p. 23 (May 28).

3. The full name of the Yugoslavian Tribunal is International Tribunal for the Prosecution of Persons Responsible for Serious Violations of International Humanitarian Law Committed in the Territories of the Former Yugoslavia since 1991 [Hereinafter the Yugoslavian Tribunal, or the ICTY]. For a discussion of the establishment of the ICTY, see Bassiouni (1995). For a description and analysis of its legal structure, see Magnarella (1995) and Meron (1994).

The full name of the U.N. Rwandan Tribunal is International Criminal Tribunal for the Prosecution of Persons Responsible for Genocide and Other Serious Violations of International Humanitarian Law Committed in the Territory of Rwanda and Rwandan Citizens Responsible for Genocide and Other Such Violations Committed in the Territory of Neighboring States between 1 January and 31 December 1994 [Hereinafter Rwandan Tribunal or ICTR]. For a discussion of the ICTR's history, statute, and organization, see Akhavan (1996) and Magnarella (1994, 2000).

4. U.N. SCOR, *Statement by the President of the Security Council,* 3414th mtg. at 1, U.N. Doc. S/PRST/1994/42 (1994).

5. S.C. Res. 955, U.N. SCOR, 3453 mtg. at 1, U.N. Doc. S/RES/955 (1994) [Hereinafter ICTR Statute].

6. For the text of the ICTR Statute defining each of these laws, see Magnarella (2000: Appendix A).

7. Information in this chapter concerning Akayesu's background, arrest, indictment, and trial comes from *Prosecutor v. Akayesu* 1988.

8. For the full indictment, see Magnarella (2000:Appendix C).

9. For a detailed presentation of witness testimonies and sources, see Magnarella (ibid.:103–8).

10. Crimes Against Humanity include widespread attacks against civilian populations on political grounds.

11. A number of modern scholars and early explorers have commented on the physical differences between Tutsi, Hutu, and Twa. For example, American anthropologist Helen Codere (1962:48) writes that "although there has been sufficient intermixture to blur racial lines, the majority of each caste is racially distinct. In stature, for example, the differences are striking: the average stature of the Tutsi is 1 m. 75; the Hutu 1 m. 66; and the Twa 1 m. 55." Unfortunately, Codere does not reveal the source, time, or sample size of her data.

Of the Tutsi, historian Lemarchand (1970:18) writes that "physical features [of the Tutsi] suggest obvious ethnic affinities with the Galla tribes of southern Ethiopia."

Duke Frederick of Mecklenburg, who traveled through Central Africa in 1907–8, writes:

> The Watussi [that is, Tutsi] are a tall, well-made people with an almost ideal physique. Heights of 1.80, 2.00, and even 2.20 meters (from 5 ft. 11 1/2 in. to 7 ft. 2 1/2 in.) are of quite common occurrence, ... their bronze-brown skin reminds one of the inhabitants of the more hilly parts of northern Africa.... Unmistakable evidences of a foreign strain are betrayed in their high foreheads, the curve of their nostrils, and the fine oval shape of their faces. (1910:47–48)

During 1933–34 the Belgians conducted a census and introduced an identity card system that indicated the Tutsi, Hutu, or Twa "ethnicity" (*ubwoko* in Kinyarwanda, and *ethnie* in French) of each person. However, the Belgians "decided to classify any individual [that is, male farmer] with fewer than ten cows as a Hutu" (Vassall-Adams 1994:8). According to African Rights (1995:9), the Belgians used "ownership of cows as the key criterion for determining which group an individual belonged to. Those with ten or more cows were Tutsi— along with all their descendants in the male line—and those with less were Hutu. Those 'recognized as Twa' at the time of the census were given the status of Twa." This basis for classification contributed to the physical mix found in each of the various "ethnic" categories.

REFERENCES CITED

African Rights. 1995. *Rwanda: Death, Despair, and Defiance.* London: African Rights.

Akhavan, Payam. 1996. "The International Criminal Tribunal for Rwanda: The Politics and Pragmatics of Punishment." *American Journal of International Law* 90:501–10.

Andreopoulos, George J. 1994. *Genocide: Conceptual and Historical Dimensions.* Philadelphia: University of Pennsylvania Press.

Baron, Xavier. 1998. "Statute for a War Crimes Court Adopted." *Agence France Presse,* July 18, 1998, Lexis News File.

Bassiouni, M. Cherif. 1995. "Former Yugoslavia: Investigating Violations of International Humanitarian Law and Establishing an International Criminal Tribunal." *Fordham International Law Review* 18:1191–1211.

Bonner, Raymond. 1994. "Rwanda's Leaders Vow to Build a Multiparty State for Both Hutu and Tutsi." *New York Times,* Sept. 7, p. A10.

Codere, Helen. 1962. "Power in Rwanda." *Anthropologica* 4:45–85.

Henkin, Louis, et al. 1999. *Human Rights.* New York: Foundation Press.

Jefremovas, Villia. 1995. "Acts of Human Kindness: Tutsi, Hutu and the Genocide." *Issue* 23:28–31.

Lemarchand, René. 1970. *Rwanda and Burundi.* London: Pall Mall.

Magnarella, Paul J. 1994. "Expanding the Frontiers of Humanitarian Law: The UN Criminal Tribunal for Rwanda." *Florida Journal of International Law* 9:421–41.

————. 1995. "Trying for Peace through Law: The UN Tribunal for the Former Yugoslavia." *Human Peace* 10:3–8.

————. 2000. *Justice in Africa: Rwanda's Genocide, Its National Courts and the UN Criminal Tribunal.* Aldershot, England: Ashgate.

Mecklenburg, Frederick, Duke of. 1910. *In the Heart of Africa.* London: Cassel.

Meron, Theodor. 1994. "War Crimes in Yugoslavia and Development of International Law." *American Journal of International Law* 88:76–87.

Newbury, Catharine. 1988. *The Cohesion of Oppression: Clientship and Ethnicity in Rwanda: 1860–1960.* New York: Columbia University Press.

————. 1995. "Background to Genocide in Rwanda." *Issue* 23:12–17.

Prosecutor v. Jean-Paul Akayesu. 1998. Case No. ICTR 96–4-T (September 2).

Prunier, Gerard. 1995. *The Rwanda Crisis: History of a Genocide.* New York: Columbia University Press.

U.S. Department of State. 1994. "Rwanda Human Rights Practices." Washington, D.C. (Available in Lexis, News Library).

Vassall-Adams, Guy. 1994. *Rwanda.* Oxford: Oxfam.

PART FIVE

Critical Reflections

Anthropology and the Study of Genocide

13

Inoculations of Evil in the U.S.-Mexican Border Region

Reflections on the Genocidal Potential of Symbolic Violence

Carole Nagengast

Simply describing genocide or denouncing it after it occurs has certain uses but is a far cry from "doing good."

GOUREVITCH (1998)

INTRODUCTION

The shortcomings of the present world order have never been so glaringly apparent as when we consider the failure of the international system either to predict or forestall genocide. Political philosopher Richard Falk argues that international intervention in genocide and, presumably, measures taken to prevent it will always be interest-based rather than driven by moral values. In view of what Falk calls the prevailing "politically conditioned moral advocacy" and the absence of clear geopolitical rationales for prevention/intervention, liberal democracies and intergovernmental agencies need to be pushed from below by transnational social forces (Falk 2000:169–70). Few NGOs or other international actors are equipped to deal with genocide or other extreme forms of political violence in a preemptive way, however willing they might be, partially because it is not always possible for them to recognize and evaluate genocidal processes until they are already well under way and difficult or impossible to combat.

Alexander Hinton suggests in the introduction to this volume and in a forthcoming publication that there are certain "priming mechanisms" that encourage genocidal processes, or, to use another metaphor, processes or circumstances that *heat up* and are capable of setting off a chain reaction. These ought to be apparent at an early stage. Genocide, in this view, is the culmination of a number of apparently far lesser occurrences of symbolic and physical violence performed against groups that the dominant society has defined in one way or another as lesser human beings. Indeed, genocide can only be committed against people who are perceived as outsiders, never against equals (Chalk and Jonassohn 1990:28). The critical word is *perceived*. The differences capable of triggering first ethnic violence and then genocide are not primordial but rather are constructed along linguistic, "racial," or ethnic lines with class often disguised as "race" or ethnicity (Bowen 1996; Appadurai 1998). In this formulation, difference equals inequality.

One of the most frightening aspects of genocide is the dual recognition that first, those who commit atrocities against categorical others (however constructed) are not very different from ourselves, and second, that all of us through a range of societal circumstances including "disaster fatigue"—the failure to be moved by human suffering if it is sufficiently removed from our own lives—are indirectly responsible for its continuation (Lifton and Markusen 1990; Falk 2000:163). Robert Jay Lifton suggests that the roots of genocide can be found in a combination of the human personality and the economic-social hierarchy of society. Therefore a "moralistic denunciation on its own is an empty gesture that obscures the pervasive and continuing potential for genocide to erupt almost anywhere in the social landscape of humanity" (Falk 2000:165).[1] Genocide is always a possibility, and none of us can be complacent.

If prediction is the first step in preventing ethnic violence and genocide, we need to ascertain what the first steps in an escalation of violence that culminates in genocide might look like. Drawing on my fieldwork in the U.S.-Mexican border region, I will examine the informal and formal, the institutional and cultural constructions of difference through which Latinos in the United States are separated and labeled and made victims of mostly symbolic but sometimes physical violence. These processes constitute potential first steps toward what might, in other times and places and in the absence of political controls, become widespread ethnic violence that could culminate in genocide. Although there is always the possibility of "devaluing an important concept by allowing it to become a catch phrase for the dispossessed" (Harff 1992:28), I think the heuristic of using domestic examples to illustrate what is to most Americans inconceivable justifies the risk.

SYMBOLIC VIOLENCE LEADS TO PHYSICAL VIOLENCE

I suggested above that Latinos along the border are subjected to symbolic violence. By symbolic violence I mean what Bourdieu (1977:191) calls the "censored but euphemized" violence that is part of daily hegemonic practice, but in "disguised and transfigured" form. These are the multitude of everyday violences that can be found in the workplace, in schoolyards, in jails, and in the media (see Scheper-Hughes, this volume) and that often precede and always accompany physical violence. Bowen's (1996) discussion of colonial Rwanda and Burundi illustrates both the process through which various forms of violence succeed each other and the ways in which economic inequality can be recast as ethnicity. He argues that ethnic violence is likely to occur in postcolonial situations in which the colonial powers and later independent states promoted and elaborated differences among groups as a way of amassing and consolidating power (ibid.:6). German and Belgian colonial powers admired the minority Tutsis, who were tall and handsome. They therefore gave them privileged access to jobs and higher education and even instituted a minimum height requirement for college entrance. So that they could tell who were Tutsi, they required everyone to carry an identity card with a tribal label. Complex social differences were reduced to simple physiological variations, which were then inscribed on people's bodies such that people believed they could distinguish one group from the other (see also Malkki 1995). Privilege accrued to one group and symbolic violence was levied against the other. Bowen continues:

> Many Tutsis are tall and many Hutus short, but Hutus and Tutsis had intermarried to such an extent that they were not easily distinguishable (nor are they today). They spoke the same language and carried out the same religious practices. In most regions of the colonies the categories became economic labels: poor Tutsis became Hutus, and economically successful Hutus became Tutsis. Where the labels "Hutu" and "Tutsi" had not been much used, lineages with lots of cattle were simply labeled Tutsi; poorer lineages, Hutu. Colonial discrimination against Hutus created what had not existed before: a sense of collective Hutu identity, a Hutu cause. (1996:6)

Tutsi identity was created as well. A long-term result of the emergence of collective identities and symbolic violences was the series of genocides in Rwanda in which vast numbers were killed in often gruesome circumstances (Malkki 1995). Although the state instigated the violence that led to genocide to begin with, it was ordinary people who committed most of the atrocities, thus removing any uncertainly about who was a *real* Hutu or Tutsi.[2] Death at the hand of the other irrevocably established one's identity (Appadurai 1998). Each putative Tutsi and Hutu had to believe that the other group was truly the enemy. Bowen cautions us to remember, however, "that it is fear and hate generated from the top, and not ethnic differences, that finally push people to commit acts of violence" (1996:6). I now turn to top-down violence and the issue of the state.

THE STATE AND HUMAN RIGHTS ABUSES[3]

Although NGOs are increasingly turning the spotlight on nongovernmental entities, corporations, and individual actors, the state is still held responsible as the major perpetrator/facilitator of human rights abuses (Steiner and Alton 1996; Amnesty International 1998; Andreopoulos 1994). This creates a fundamental contradiction in the international human rights system constituted in and by the United Nations. Although member states have a clear interest in not challenging the sovereignty of the state or undermining the stability of the nation-state as the world's core political entity, the organization's own declarations, treaties, and covenants, endorsed by member states, charge states themselves with preventing human rights abuses, ameliorating the conditions that give rise to them, and punishing transgressors. It should not surprise us that nongovernmental organizations are better monitors of human rights abuses than the United Nations.

Few states, especially liberal democracies, typically or openly exercise their power over their constituency through unmediated violence, though it is always held in reserve. Rather, they try to ensure conformity to a set of images that create the illusion of unity, the illusion of an indivisible, homogenous nation-state, the illusion of consensus about what is and what is not legitimate, what should and should not be suppressed. "The refusal of multiplicity, the dread of difference . . . is the very essence of the state" (Clastres 1974:110). For example, the unmarked category in the United Sates, the category from which all else requires an adjectival form, is a white, employed, middle-class, heterosexual, male, monolingual English-speaker who is married with children. It is not that everyone does not know that huge numbers of people do not fit that profile, but that the more dimensions on which one deviates from it, the greater the possible application of symbolic violence intended to "punish" deviance and to coax one into apparent homogeneity.

In order to understand how people who share the characteristics of political majorities implicitly agree to the repression of certain segments of society, we need to examine the role of "the state" in promoting conformity to the ideal. Typically, the state is defined as a Weberian set of institutions staffed by bureaucrats who serve the public interest and exercise power and authority over a bounded territory. Philip Abrams examines the epistemological basis for the state, referring to it as "an ideological artifact attributing unity, morality, and independence to the disunited, a-moral and dependent workings of the practices of government" (1988:81). The state also incorporates cultural and political forms, representations, discourse, practices, and activities, and specific technologies and organizations of power that together define "public interest" and establish agreed-upon meaning. The contemporary state as ideological artifact is naturalized (Barthes 1988:190) and rendered the inevitable container of a "people," control over whom is the mark of international legitimacy. The state legitimates what would, if seen directly, be understood as illegitimate, "an unacceptable domination" (Abrams 1988:2). Thus as we saw in the Rwandan case, the state also defines and naturalizes available identities (cf. Comaroff and Comaroff 1991; Alonso 1994; Joseph and Nugent 1994; Abrams 1988).

There is nothing "natural" about identities of this sort; they often arise in opposition to other more or less powerful social positions. It is meaningless, for example, to say that my identity is constituted by the fact that I am a brown-eyed blonde unless such an appearance gives me greater or lesser power vis-à-vis blue-eyed blondes or some other hair-eye combination. The opposition between so-called white skin and brown skin, however, does provide a social and often a class identity in a racialized state in which hierarchy is informally legitimated (even though formally outlawed). I am arguing, in other words, that a specious distinction between public institutions of the state and so-called private or civil society renders opaque the state's intrusion into what people think is their private life. Let us illustrate this by considering some aspects of daily life in the U.S.-Mexican border region.

THE U.S.-MEXICO BORDER REGION

The United States arguably was a colonial power in the American Southwest in the nineteenth century, a circumstance that created ethnic tension between Americans and Mexicans and in due course rendered Mexicans and Mexican-Americans second-class citizens (McWilliams 1948; Anazaldua 1987; de la Garza 1985; Montejano 1977, 1987). Although there has been significant progress in recent decades, Mexican Americans and newly immigrant Mexicans (and others from Latin America) who live in the border area still suffer discrimination, racism, and both symbolic and physical violence directed toward them by individuals and the state (Montejano 1999; Zavalla 1987).

Throughout the 1990s, U.S. opinion makers, the media, politicians, and Congress portrayed the U.S.-Mexican border area and the communities within it as places "infested" with hordes of drug runners, welfare cheats, and foreigners looking for a free ride.[4] The Border Patrol, as an arm of the state, has been charged with keeping the country safe from these "scourges." Consequently, the Border Patrol often treats working-class Latino border communities as hostile territory that gives refuge to undesirables. It also often racializes Latinos and Chicanos and treats them as lesser citizens. Roberto Martinez, a Chicano, an American citizen, and the director of the Immigration Project of the American Friends Service Committee (AFSC) in San Diego, notes: "[Politicians] keep saying this is a country of laws. Where were the laws when people like me were being arrested and they tried to deport me? When U.S. citizens are coming across the border and their documents are being confiscated. We [the AFSC] have three lawsuits going where police and the Border Patrol are breaking into people's homes without search warrants. This is under the pretext of looking for drugs or illegals. Then they beat up the people, mace them, put bogus charges on them. Then they have to go to court. Why aren't *they* playing by the rules? They lump us all together. We're all suspects. We're all illegal immigrants, criminals or drug traffickers."[5]

Martinez's colleague, Maria Jimenez, director of the Immigration Project of the American Friends Service Committee in South Texas, agrees: "Part of our work is increasing public awareness that we [Chicanos, Latinos] are an abused community. I have coined that phrase—the abused community syndrome. It has gone on so long that we no longer see the abuse. This doesn't happen to other communities. [Mexican Americans] are the only ones saying, Oh, I'm a 4th generation, 5th generation, 8th generation American. We are continually reinforcing our right to be here because we are constantly being *asked* about our right to be here. We are the only ethnic group in the whole country who can claim to have a national police force we can call our very own."[6]

Immigrant rights organizations such as the AFSC have established hot lines for citizens and noncitizens who are caught in INS nets and need legal advice or want to voice a complaint about agents. In the Nogales, Arizona, INS office, a poster advertising such services had the telephone number blacked out and the words 1–800 EAT-SHIT substituted. Although an America's Watch investigator complained to the head of the station, the defaced poster was still there four months later (Human Rights Watch 1995).

As outspoken defenders of the marked category of Latino in the United States, Martinez, Jimenez, the American Friends Service Committee, America's Watch, and Amnesty International use the legal system and the media to defend the rights of Latinos and thereby forestall violence against them. Nonetheless, neither their activities nor Latino inclusion in the United States through citizenship has resolved the inequalities of a racialized exploitation in a political and economic system that has been constituted historically by the simultaneous exclusion and demand for the labor of racialized migrants (Lowe 1996). While the Immigration and Naturalization Service is charged with upholding the law, Andreas (2000) charges that it also enforces class and racial hierarchies by targeting more susceptible underclasses. In the process, people learn what is acceptable from within a narrow range of social identities and behaviors. Further, when some categories of people are reduced to a less than human status, it becomes easier for those higher in the hierarchy to imagine that those lower somehow deserve to be brutalized (Scarry 1985; Nagengast 1994). Thus *all* are controlled, and hierarchy based on skin color and language, and less obviously but even more centrally on class, is rendered natural.

THE MILITARIZATION OF THE BORDER

The gradual militarization of the Border Patrol since the 1980s has played an integral role in the escalation of violence directed toward Latinos and Latino communities, legal and illegal alike (Heyman 1995; Dunn 1996; Andreas 2000). In 1984, elite Border Patrol units known as Border Patrol Tactical Teams (BORTAC) began receiving special paramilitary training similar to that of SWAT teams. The 1986 Immigration Reform Control Act (IRCA) was intended to reduce illegal immigration, and the federal government was prepared to back it up with force. By 1989 Congress had authorized five thousand federal troops for border duty. According to a former army officer, "It is . . . absurd that the most powerful nation on earth cannot prevent a swarming land invasion by unarmed Mexican peasants. The U.S. Army is entirely capable of plugging the holes permanently and border patrol [is] excellent military training" (Bassford 1991 quoted in Andreas 1994). Furthermore, between 1989 and 1999 the budget and number of Border Patrol agents increased dramatically. By 1998, for example, 2,350 agents were patrolling a sixty-six-mile strip of border in San Diego County, California, where there had been only 890 in 1993.

The presence of army troops and marines and many more Border Patrol agents has made border crossings more dangerous for migrants than ever before. A 1997 University of Houston study provides the particulars on twelve hundred people, presumably all or mostly Mexicans, who died between 1993 and 1996 trying to cross the border and whose bodies were found. The researchers believe the actual number who died to be much higher, but their bodies have not been located. Many of the twelve hundred died of the extreme heat of the desert, where daytime temperatures routinely reach 120 to 125 degrees. Others drowned in the Rio Bravo/Rio Grande, or were hit by cars, in some instances while being chased by the Border Patrol or the military.

Between January and early September of 1998, at least one hundred corpses turned up in southeastern California alone. This is the most remote, hottest, and driest part of the border region. The discovery of five desiccated bodies in a single location in August 1998 unleashed a flood of apparent concern, and numerous new signs telling of the dangers of summer crossings were posted in isolated areas. Further, warnings about the heat and lack of water in the desert were broadcast on Spanish-language radio stations that service the border region. These official gestures, however, obscure the official U.S. policy that forces migrants away from the more populated and therefore safer areas. Bodies continue to be found, especially in the summer. Drowning or dying of heat exhaustion and dehydration in the desert to escape the Border Patrol is no less violent than being shot.

INS officials contend that prompt apprehension and immediate return to the country of origin is still the best deterrent to illegal immigration. In spite of the hazards and repeated "voluntary" deportations, most migrants who are apprehended simply try again later. "How many times have you crossed?" anthropologist Michael Kearney asked a migrant from Oaxaca during a 1988 NBC special on the "New Immigrants." "Oh, at least one hundred times," replied the man. "And why do you come back?" "Because there is work." He and others have told us of many traumatic experiences having to do with hunger, thirst, heat and cold, harrowing chases through the underbrush, injuries suffered as a result of captures, and verbal and physical abuse by citizens (Nagengast et al. 1992; Zabin et al. 1993; Nagengast and Kearney 1990). As Estevan Torres, Democratic member of Congress from California, remarked, "We will catch a few [illegal migrants], round them up, and send them back, but not too many, because then who will do the work?" (quoted in Andreas 1994:233). Indeed, increased surveillance seems not to have seriously affected the number of undocumented workers. All reports suggest that as of mid-2000 there were between five and six million undocumented workers in the United States. That is at least as many as there were in 1986. One might reasonably conclude that many of the controls implemented on the U.S.-Mexico border, violent though they may be, are not really intended to prevent all workers from crossing; their purpose is to control and regulate the flow of labor power to agriculture and business in North America (Cockcroft 1986; Dunn 1996; Andreas 2000).

The Border Patrol and, more broadly speaking, the Immigration and Naturalization Service (INS)—both arms of the U.S. government—have been charged with responsibility for numerous instances of violence against Latinos in the border region. The stated mission of the Border Patrol is to, among other things, prevent drug runners, terrorists, and illegal migrants from penetrating the borders of the United States.

In recent years, Border Patrol forces have been augmented with National Guard and military units to protect what all agree are still permeable barriers along the two-thousand-mile-long border with Mexico. Amnesty International, Americas Watch, and other human rights organizations charge that Border Patrol agents and federal troops assigned to border duty have fired on and sometimes killed unarmed Latinos, mostly Mexican men. They also charge that agents have beaten men and boys, sexually abused and raped women and girls, and deprived many men, women, and children of food, water, and medical treatment (Amnesty International 1998b; Human Rights Watch 1992, 1995; Nagengast, Stavenhagen, and Kearney 1992; Chavez 1992). Hardly any of the alleged incidents have been explained to the satisfaction of these internationally renowned human rights organizations, and few of the victims appear to have been drug runners; none were terrorists. Although large quantities of illegal drugs *do* come across the U.S.-Mexico border, a former Drug Enforcement Agency agent notes that 70 to 85 percent of the total comes through legal ports of entry in large transport trucks that are exempt from inspection as part of the North American Free Trade Agreement (NAFTA), an exemption that is currently under review.[7] Drug smugglers who cross the U.S.-Mexican border on foot are reprehensible and not to be tolerated, but they are probably responsible for a small proportion of the drugs that enter the United States.

Several cases of Border Patrol shootings during the late 1990s have been especially notorious. In May 1997, a U.S. Marine on border duty with the Immigration and Naturalization Service (INS) shot and killed Ezequiel Hernandez near Redford, Texas, his home along the U.S.-Mexican border. Hernandez was an American citizen, an eighteen-year-old high school sophomore who was simultaneously tending his family's goat herd and hunting rabbits with a .22 rifle, as he did early every morning before going to school. Although the court eventually instructed the U.S. government to pay damages to Hernandez's family, it allowed the government to do so "without prejudice"—that is, without admitting wrongdoing. The Marines eventually were officially exonerated of any blame in the shooting because the boy "fit the profile of a Mexican drug runner," meaning that he had brown skin, was young, carried a rifle, and was out and about near the border before dawn.

On September 27, 1998, Border Patrol agents shot and killed a man who had crossed from Mexico with two others near San Ysidro, California. According to agents, the three men raced back toward the Mexican side when they realized that they had been spotted. The Border Patrol caught one man on the U.S. side, while a second managed to get safely back to the Mexican side. The third man allegedly turned and charged the agents with a rock in his hand. The agents shot and killed him, they said, when he refused their order to stop. Eyewitnesses who claim that the victim only picked up the rock and turned to throw it, presumably in self-defense, after agents opened fire on the backs of the running men, however, contradict the Border Patrol version. On the following day, Border Patrol agents shot and killed another man under similar circumstances on almost the same spot. In this fourth fatal shooting in San Diego County, California, in three days, witnesses also contradicted the Border Patrol version of events.

Finally, in September 1999, agents shot and killed a mentally unbalanced man, a long-time legal resident of the United States who was originally from Mexico. The man allegedly had thrown rocks at a water company employee in a remote area ten miles north of the border, through which undocumented Mexicans sometimes cross. The water employee sought help from passing Border Patrol agents, who hunted the man down and opened fire on him after he threw additional rocks at them. According to the *Los Angeles Times*, "U.S. officials speculated at the time that he *might* have been an illegal border crosser or a drug smuggler" (September 3, 1999:A3, A26, emphasis added).

Each of these incidents is open to multiple interpretations. The Border Patrol agents might have feared for their lives; some or all of the shootings might have been the result of errors of judgment or honest mistakes. Nonetheless, "racial" and ethnic profiling by police and other agents of the state is increasingly recognized in the United States as a serious problem (Cole 1999), and these incidents and others may also be part of what critics regard as a larger and disturbing pattern of subconscious politically motivated violence against Latinos.

In addition to the physical dangers to migrants entailed by the militarization of the border, there is mounting evidence of other contradictions. Because the border has become so difficult and dangerous to cross, unauthorized migrants now tend to stay longer in the United States. Children are born into citizenship and go to school here. More and more families are bootstrapping themselves out of abject poverty and, in some cases, becoming vocal critics of a system that deprives them of rights guaranteed by both the U.S. Constitution and the Universal Declaration of Human Rights (Nagengast, Stavenhagen, and Kearney 1992). Those who are forced to move back and forth across the border depend more on *coyotes* (professional smugglers) than they did in the past. As both the physical danger and the danger of apprehension increase, the price charged by smugglers also increases. The rate in 1994 was about seven hundred dollars per person for transport from Tijuana to Los Angeles, payable whether or not the migrant reached his or her destination (Andreas 1994:232). According to some informants, smuggler fees had increased to more than a thousand dollars by early 1999. Not only has the border become a "balloon" (squeeze it in one place and it bulges in another) but official border policies have helped to create and augment a profitable business in human trafficking, another area of human rights concern.

Until mid-2000 there had been little public outcry in the United States about migrant and Latino rights outside the Latino and human rights communities themselves, in part because the stripping away of peoples' basic human rights has been naturalized and rendered acceptable to the greater public. The 1996 changes in national legislation curtailed the economic rights of migrants/immigrants, and voter referenda in California have tried to bar the children of migrants from access to schools, colleges, and universities. Although not all referenda have been successfully implemented, they have in some cases drastically limited social services to children, including their access to food.[8] The 1998 California proposition to ban bilingual education for documented and undocumented alike was at least in part a reflection of anti-immigrant and anti-Latino sentiment. "If they want to live here, they should become more like 'real' Americans" is the general tenor of any number of letters to the editor that appeared in the *Los Angeles Times,* the *San Diego Union,* and other Southern California newspapers during the months preceding that election. Thus the media can both promote and undercut basic fairness. These events and processes have been augmented by further limitations on immigrants' and migrants' civil rights. On February 24, 1999, the Supreme Court limited the First Amendment rights of illegal immigrants by ruling that people who are in the United States without papers cannot avoid deportation by claiming that they are targeted for their political views. This ruling, which was the result of a case against several Palestinians and a Kenyan, is unlikely to affect most of the undocumented people in the United States since few actually claim that they have been deported or marked in some way because of their politics. Nonetheless, it is a chilling exception to what was once a general rule in the United States that "aliens" enjoy civil rights more or less equal to those of citizens (Nagengast et al. 1992). Further, it effectively discourages the undocumented from speaking out publicly about any matter that might be interpreted as political. Finally, it may endanger the rights of those who are awaiting either asylum hearings or are in the United States legally (Biskupic and Branigin 1999:A1). It certainly flies in the face of Kuper's stipulation that nongenocidal societies guarantee the legal rights of minorities.

Latino citizen activism following Ezequiel Hernandez's killing in Redford, Texas, did contribute to the defeat of a 1998 congressional bill to put an additional ten thousand soldiers on the border and to remove those already there, an encouraging outcome that suggests the power of oppositional politics. Further, the 2000 AFL-CIO call for a new amnesty for illegal immigrants and an end to employer sanctions, which it has supported since the mid-1980s, surprised many. The *Los Angeles Times* attributed the large turnout at a Los Angeles rally in support of the AFL-CIO to the end of the recession in California.[9] Indeed, the extremely low unemployment rate in California in 2000 meant that the lowest-paying jobs were going begging. Labor shortages rather than a concern with immigrant rights per se may motivate the AFL-CIO, an illustration of Falk's point about interest-based rather than morality-based advocacy.

In mid-2001, President George W. Bush indicated that he favors a new amnesty policy to possibly legalize millions of Mexicans already in the United States, but he immediately retreated from his position in the face of scathing criticism from Congress and much of the public. Nonetheless, a new immigration policy of some kind is in the air. In spite of mildly hopeful signs of a shift in public opinion, the military continues to provide assistance to the INS in a variety of areas along or close to the border, including the building and upgrading of helicopter pads and roads so that they are suitable for "enhanced operations." Federal troops are also involved in the construction of miles of steel and concrete walls that may one day extend from San Diego to Brownsville, Texas.[10] Most important, when it withdrew, the army left behind a highly militarized Border Patrol trained in low-intensity conflict (LIC) military tactics. This makes large numbers of troops unnecessary.

Low-intensity conflict methods were first developed as Cold War tactics and used extensively by the U.S. military in Southeast Asia in the 1960s.[11] The military objective was to establish and maintain social control over targeted civilian groups in order to further foreign policy aims—namely, to counter communism and secure the global expansion of Western capitalism and liberal democracy. Low-intensity conflict strategies, which include counterinsurgency, antiterrorism, and peacekeeping, are based on the premise that it is the "enemy within" that poses the greatest threat to the national security of any country. Although communism (other than that emanating from Cuba) is no longer perceived as a threat to the United States, the orderly reproduction and expansion of neoliberal capitalist hegemony is a major concern of policy makers. Thus LIC tactics developed during the Cold War have been updated, reterritorialized, and redeployed in the United States in order to ensure that American markets and the American "way of life" are protected. Illegal aliens, immigrant-rights groups, welfare recipients, and any persons or organizations perceived as subversive to the neoliberal order have been cast as the enemy within, internal foes of the United States, threats to "our" way of life, "our" social institutions, and even to the viability of "our" language. If the enemy is everywhere, the system needs a military that is capable in the name of national security of intervening in all aspects of domestic politics and social policy.

A classic low-intensity conflict counterinsurgency technique, one taught by the U.S. Army to generations of military officers from Latin America at special institutions like the School of the Americas at Fort Benning, Georgia, is to enlist the domestic police force into military and paramilitary operations. The widely televised images of Riverside County, California, sheriff's deputies chasing down a truckload of suspected undocumented workers in 1996 and beating unarmed men and women across the back and head with truncheons poignantly revealed counterinsurgency strategies in action.

So-called peace-keeping operations are also part of low-intensity conflict measures. The way this mission has been adopted by the Border Patrol is illustrated by the role it played in the Los Angeles riots in 1992. Four hundred members of BORTAC, the elite and specially trained Border Patrol squads, were brought in to assist local police in controlling the looting and burning. BORTAC agents, who were deployed only in Latino neighborhoods throughout the Los Angeles area, arrested more than a thousand people whom they suspected were illegal immigrants, whether or not they had committed or were suspected or accused of committing any criminal offense. Interestingly, these arrests accounted for 10 percent of all arrests made during the disturbances. More than seven hundred of the thousand were immediately subjected to voluntary deportation without any charges whatsoever being brought against them (Dunn 1996:81–82). These events were widely publicized by the press and presumably were approved of by the general public, which was apparently and erroneously led to believe that "illegals" were heavily implicated in looting and burning.

Another low-intensity conflict tactic is to enlist civilians in the fight against internal enemies. California's well-known Proposition 187, for example, attempted to enlist health care workers, teachers, and social service agencies in reporting the presence of undocumented workers and their children. Although teachers and medical personnel have largely refused to cooperate, other public sector workers risk their jobs if they do not work together with the Immigration and Naturalization Service. In an interview, a Chicano intake officer at a correctional institution in California told me that he and his fellow employees are expected to notify the INS immediately if they suspect that an inmate they are processing is undocumented. He says that most inmates who come under suspicion are Spanish-speaking, and less often Asian. He also says that undocumented inmates report that Irish, Polish, Italian, and other European construction workers who are illegally in the country look on while Border Patrol agents take away all the Spanish-speakers.[12] In fact, 90 percent of the people that the Border Patrol detains as "illegals" are Mexican, even though people from all Latin American countries combined compose only 40 percent of the undocumented workers in the United States. By demanding and receiving the cooperation of civilians and local law enforcement agencies in their campaigns, the Border Patrol teaches them first to be participants in the categorizing of people into the desirable and the undesirable, and second how to deploy symbolic violence against the subordinate. It also trains them to participate in the hierarchical categorization of individuals and communities.

The Border Patrol has taken to sponsoring Explorer Scout groups in Texas. Youth are given uniforms complete with Border Patrol badges and sometimes are allowed to accompany agents on patrol. The idea is to teach the Scouts to be "good" Americans, to build the prestige of the INS, and to undermine the work of grassroots, largely Latino community organizations that oppose the militarization of the Border Patrol, support immigrant rights, or have other agendas that are officially defined as anti-American, "leftist," or antifamily (ibid.:82).[13] The Border Patrol also sponsors a soccer league in the Laredo area (ibid.) and conducts public education seminars and elementary and high school forums in counties in southeastern California that focus on "how to identify illegals" and "why they are bad for the economy." In October 1998 I spent a night in a town in eastern Riverside County, not far from the U.S.-Mexican border. The local television station aired several spots featuring Border Patrol agents advertising these seminars. Further, the community access station televised agents talking about how they do their jobs and which attributes and aspects of a person—skin color, language, quality of clothing—arouse their suspicion of illegal status and cause them to search that person and ask for official documentation. This is, of course, another permutation of widespread and substantiated charges that many police forces routinely use racial profiling to target Latinos and African Americans (Cole 1999).[14] All of these activities give the Border Patrol a benign visibility that is explicitly intended to draw in civilians, including children, as participants in the state's fight against the enemy within.

Consensus about hierarchies and "enemies" also is expressed in television, films, theater, music, newspaper editorials, letters to the editor, and more, as Lowe (1996) has demonstrated. These depict the degree to which "minorities" can deviate from the "norm" and are class specific. For example, Spanish-speakers cannot with impunity paint their house bright colors in middle-class neighborhoods. I have some Latino colleagues in California who live in a predominately Anglo neighborhood close to the university where they both work. When they painted their formerly beige house pink and started to lay out their gardens in a fashion found throughout Mexico and the Caribbean, their neighbors marched on them, demanding that their house be returned to "neighborhood standards."[15]

The hegemony of "our" cultural practices and the denigration of what is represented as the less valuable parts of the social body are so strong that, according to an ABC poll several years ago, 66 percent of those surveyed favored random searches of houses, cars, and personal belongings, even if the police had *no* suspicion of any wrongdoing. These searches would presumably not be in middle-class neighborhoods, but in barrios and poor working-class areas. Virtually all Americans seem willing to submit to the many Border Patrol checkpoints on north-south highways throughout the Southwest, many miles from the border itself. People have been so inoculated with the fear of "the enemy within" and with the myth about the relationship of repression to the cure of society, that they are willing to give up their own rights for what they have become convinced is the good of "their" society.

Although Border Patrol agents have never been renowned for their gentleness, as the Immigration and Naturalization Service adopts and successfully implements low-intensity conflict tactics throughout the Southwest, there are new opportunities for human rights violations. These may be directed toward suspected drug smugglers and terrorists, as well as toward illegal migrants whose labor power contributes so much to the success of neoliberal capitalism, but it could also be more often turned upon legal residents or citizens who "look like" migrants or who object to the treatment of migrants, or who are simply poor, brown skinned, and Spanish-speaking, or who live in a Latino neighborhood.

POLITICAL AND SYMBOLIC VIOLENCE AGAIN

Political violence, a subset of violence in general, is state-sponsored or tolerated "action taken or not taken by the state or its agents with the express intent of realizing certain social, ethnic, economic, and political goals in the realm of public affairs, especially affairs of the state or social life in general" (Nagengast 1994:114). Political violence subsumes war, terrorism, torture, and genocide. Genocide as a subset of political violence is "the criminal intent to destroy or permanently cripple a human group, whether that group is political, religious, social, or ethnic" (Andreopoulos 1994:1).[16] As is the case in other forms of political violence, the state is the major perpetrator. If the police or military are not the major actors, they may stand by while civilians act with impunity, unrestrained by the institutions of the state. Civilian paramilitaries may even act with the implicit collusion of the state, as they did in El Salvador, Guatemala, and Cambodia, among other places (see contributors to this volume; Totten, Parsons and Charney 1997). State officials also may find reasons to not enforce the law, or perpetrators of genocide might be civilians who learn who and what to despise and go on rampages when the state is weakened or collapses.[17]

It cannot be emphasized too strongly that official institutions of the state, such as the military and the police, are directly or indirectly responsible for genocide against *groups* of people. Scholars and politicians who insist on analyzing the accounts of ethnic violence or the shootings described above as inexplicable tribal violence, primordial evil, or individual happenings with individual and unconnected actors fatally obscure the overall historical, economic, social, and cultural processes and the semantic space in which the events are embedded. Just as in Rwanda, unfolding social relations in the U.S.-Mexican border region and the cultural practices with which its inhabitants "construct and represent themselves and others, and hence their societies and histories" (Comaroff and Comaroff 1992:27) illuminate the processes of domination, representation, and, to some degree, resistance that underpin political violence.

Part of peoples' everyday construction of their world—whether they are politicians, news reporters, or others—entails the process through which popular consensus is built around the idea that the state ought to control certain others, usually minorities,[18] by jailing them, depriving them of basic services and civil rights, deporting them, or even killing them. The result of these processes are analogous to Hinton's primers, in the sense that political violence is activated by injecting just a little bit of ethnic conflict into daily fare in order to "get it going," just as a water pump is primed by pouring a little fluid into it. It is, of course, largely underclass status that makes certain people susceptible to violence, whether it is manifest symbolically or physically. It is their ambiguity as both sub- and superhuman that allows dominant groups to crystallize the myths about the evils that subordinates represent, whether they are citizens, residents and holders of green cards, or undocumented. This justifies first symbolic and then all too often physical violence against them. And that requires the implicit agreement and cooperation of ordinary nice people who have been inoculated with evil, who learn to take myths at face value, and who do not question the projects of the state in defense of a social order that requires hierarchy. Only when general consensus has been created can "ordinary people" (read the dominant group) actively participate in human rights abuses, explicitly support them, or turn their faces and pretend not to know even when confronted with incontrovertible evidence of them. My hypothesis is that similar processes of pump priming by means of consensus-building around the domination of despised minorities (ethnic, religious, or political) preceded the actual violence that led to genocide in states such as Nazi Germany, Cambodia, East Timor, Bosnia, Rwanda, and Kosovo, where genocide has or is taking place or is threatened.

Central to this hypothesis is the notion that state-perpetrated or -tolerated physical violence toward an identifiable group could not occur unless it is preceded by symbolic violence. Scholars of subaltern peoples argue that symbolic violence is important in the structuring and ordering of the social relations of domination and subordination that assign subalterns a lower place in a hierarchy (see, for example, Chatterjee 1986). Indeed, symbolic violence is displayed in the myths that depict certain groups of people as both somewhat less than human beings, and who therefore deserve their subordinate position, and at the same time as superhumans who are capable of subverting the given social order. The Nazis depicted Jews (and others) as rats or insects, but also as perpetrators of a worldwide conspiracy (see, for example, Keen 1986; Müller-Hill 1988). Ordinary Russians call Chechens "shit people," a phrase and concept they no doubt learned during the earlier Chechen genocide of 1943 to 1957 (Harff 1992:32). Psychologist Sam Keen demonstrates that demonizing others creates the possibility, even the probability, of war atrocities against enemy civilians. Democratic societies are by no means immune to this process, as recent revelations about atrocities committed by U.S. soldiers against Koreans during the Korean conflict amply demonstrate.

Essential to myth is the process through which the collective imagination is immunized by means of a small inoculation of acknowledged evil in order to protect it against the risk of generalized subversion (Barthes 1988; Taussig 1991). A handful of Mexican drug runners or illegal migrants who take the jobs of citizens, or a few foreign-born terrorists are sufficient to inoculate a shaky social order with evil. This justifies raids on Latino neighborhoods, discrimination and mistreatment of Spanish-speakers, even the killing of suspected drug runners—and then anyone who knows a drug runner, or anyone who looks like or speaks the same language as a drug runner, or anyone who is found at a time and in a place—such as along the border at dawn or in a remote area ten miles from the border—that drug runners might frequent.

Such inoculations of evil are crucial to human rights violations because they become part of socially accepted notions of common sense, a kind of social knowledge of the "everyone knows" variety that enters public discourse and helps build popular consensus around who and what is suspect, who and what ought to be repressed, what constitutes difference and how the state ought to control it. Thus even when accused of brutality, excessive use of force, murder, or other human rights abuses and brought to trial, neither Border Patrol agents nor police officers are usually convicted. Human Rights Watch suggests that juries are more inclined to believe Border Patrol versions of events than those of "Mexicans" or "aliens" or those who defend them by providing alternative versions of events. Indeed many citizens applaud the "strong measures" taken by the Border Patrol, and some encourage even stronger ones. What is more, Border Patrol agents who accuse their fellow agents of abusing suspects or other wrongdoing up to and including murder, or who testify against them in court, often suffer retaliation and are sometimes fired (Human Rights Watch, 1992, 1995).

Most of the people that the Border Patrol apprehends are not drug runners or terrorists, but migrant workers who cross or attempt to cross without papers. Migrants have long come to the United States both seeking a better life and responding to demands for their labor power (Hoffman 1976; Cockcroft 1986), but the most recent of them have done so within the context of the global economic restructuring that, in this hemisphere, is epitomized by the North American Free Trade Agreement (NAFTA). Although NAFTA, combined with Mexican government measures that have removed price supports for food staples and "liberalized" agriculture, have meant increased prosperity for some, it has also translated into increased poverty for many others, the reduction of social services, privatization of once communal land, and ever larger numbers of foreign-owned corporations moving into the border zone looking for cheap labor and relaxed environmental standards (Barry 1995; Ross 1995; Collier 1994; Kearney and Nagengast 1990). When labor is regulated but capital is not, workers from countries to which globally mobile assembly plants have relocated are discouraged from immigrating. However, the number of export assembly factories (*maquiladoras*) along the Mexican side of the border has quadrupled since the mid-1980s, drawing far more displaced small farmers and urban poor to the area than can be employed (see, for example, Tiano 1994). If potential workers still manage, or are allowed, to cross the border illegally, their illegality renders them economically and politically vulnerable. They can be better channeled into U.S. secondary and tertiary labor markets as agricultural workers, gardeners, or day laborers. In those markets they are often underpaid and exploited (Zabin et al. 1993; Sassen 1991, 1996). Historically, vast numbers of Mexicans went into the agricultural labor market in the United States, but the expansion of the service sector and the restructuring of urban manufacturing since the 1980s has meant the growth of manufacturing: "sweat shop" jobs that are filled by illegal workers. For example, undocumented workers fill some 90 percent of Los Angeles garment factory positions (Andreas 1994; Sassen 1996; cf. Tiano 1994). When they no longer need them, agricultural, service sector, and manufacturing employers often dispose of their labor force by calling the Border Patrol (Zabin et al. 1993).

The employer sanctions that were mandated by the much-heralded Immigration and Reform Act (IRCA) of 1986 and that are supposed to punish employers who knowingly hire undocumented workers are sporadically enforced at best. "There are 7.2 million employers out there," said an immigration official. "In their lifetime, they're never going to see an immigration officer unless they stand up and scream that they've got a factory full of illegal immigrants" (quoted in Andreas 1994:232; see also Andreas 2000). The 1996 immigration legislation is more draconian than IRCA; not only does it target illegal migrants, but it also deprives some legal immigrants or residents of the United States of social security entitlements, limits their rights to education, and so forth. In effect, "a special category of residents [has been created] with significantly fewer rights than the population as a whole and which cannot legally work or receive social benefits, and can be apprehended, incarcerated, and deported at any time" (Bacon 1996:137). The INS in effect enforces labor management, now better than ever, and more and more migrants suffer trying to better their lives.

Many studies indicate that migrant workers are responding to the ongoing demands for their labor power in the United States by entering legally if they can and illegally if they must (Cockcroft 1986; Sassen 1996). Other studies indicate that migrants and Latino immigrants contribute as much as they take from the economy, if not more; do jobs that native-born workers are unwilling to take; and in the first generation are far less likely to be involved in crime than citizens (Zabin et al. 1993). Nonetheless, public sentiment against migrants, especially in the Southwestern states, and citizen violence, including beatings and robberies, is as commonplace as the official violence of the Border Patrol (Chavez 1992; Dwyer 1994; Human Rights Watch 1992, 1995; Nagengast et al. 1992). Understandably, illegal workers rarely call the police when they are attacked, but members of the legal Latino community are also reluctant to do so, believing that they will not be treated justly. Although the Immigration and Naturalization Service portrays official violence by Border Patrol agents and federal troops as a series of individual and isolated incidents—accidents or mistakes—I contend that both official and civilian violence against migrants in general, but Latinos in the border region in particular, is an expectable result of U.S. policy. As such, it is the raw material of which human rights violations are made. That these violations fall far short of genocide should not blind us to their importance.

CONCLUSION

I have offered an illustration of some cultural and political forms, representations, and practices through which dominant sectors of the population deploy symbolic violence against others—symbolic violence, which I think always precedes political violence and human rights violations. I note, however, that even general symbolic violence against a named minority does not always signal that genocide is imminent (indeed symbolic and physical violence are part of a more generalized inequality manifest in the various *isms*). An examination of the factors that prime the genocide pump must also account for situations in which symbolic violence is present but genocide does not result. Political scientist Donald Horowitz (cited in Bowen 1996:12) asserts that a crucial difference between genocidal and nongenocidal society when all other things are equal is whether states have constructed multiethnic coalitions that force politicians to seek political support across ethnic groups. Leo Kuper (1981:188–89) suggests that genocide does not occur in societies in which: (a) differences among racial, ethnic, or religious groups are either insignificant or not a source of deadly conflict; (b) there is willingness on the part of the dominant sectors to accept strangers and offer them access to the resources of society; (c) the rights of minorities are legally guaranteed; (d) there are complex webs of social relations or voluntary groups that crosscut perceived racial, religious, or ethnic differences; or (e) there is balanced accommodation between recognized groups such that there is at least an attempt to share power, as for example among blacks, whites, and colored in South Africa, or Catholics and Protestants in Northern Ireland. Other social constraints against genocide might include a high level of development, a vocal and more or less unfettered media, and citizen groups that are able to publicize injustices and oppose violence against minorities (Andreopoulos 1994).[19]

In the global south the overt and subtexual rationales for the repression of minorities is often to ensure "development" that ostensibly benefits the majority, to seize political control from a rival ethnic group, to preserve cultural or religious traditions, or to eliminate class enemies. Although "development" does not appear on the surface to be an issue in the United States, it may need to be taken into account when discussing the human rights of Latino migrants and immigrants. The disparity in the economic situations of Mexico and the United States that motivates many migrants to cross the border, as well as the ongoing demand for Mexican labor power in the United States, is a development issue. On the other hand, the media in the United States is as free as anywhere in the world. Further, there are numerous Latino organizations and voluntary groups, civic associations, and political parties that include Latinos (and other minorities), and Latinos play a growing role in national politics. Although there is an apparent declining readiness to accept strangers in the United States and to offer them access to all the resources of society, differences among "racial" and ethnic groups have not resulted in sustained deadly conflict. Even though the legal guarantees of the rights of minorities have come under increasing threat in the United States, they have not been eliminated. Finally, some portion of the general public, at least in California, favors a new amnesty for migrants.

We can easily conclude that the United States is not on the verge of committing or tolerating the widespread and systematic abuse of minorities, a first step in the direction of genocide. The presence of symbolic violence toward migrants in general and Latinos in particular in the border region suggests a *potential*, not yet and, it is hoped, never to be realized. Nonetheless the treatment of immigrants/migrants should alert us to the potential for escalations of human rights abuses, especially if international development issues are not addressed and if political processes are perceived as fundamentally flawed. Acknowledging the importance of symbolic violence and taking steps to alleviate it may help human rights monitors prevent genocidal behavior before its actual advent (Dugger 1996; Kuper 1981, 1985; Kapferer 1988). However, it is only a first step.

NOTES

A shorter version of this paper appeared in November 1998 as "Militarizing the Border Patrol," in *NACLA: Report on the Americas* XXXII (3):37–41.

1. Accounts of atrocities in distant places often appear on the front pages of national newspapers but usually focus on their inhumanity, rather than their politics. See, for example, the article by Dean Murphy entitled "W. African Rebels on Mutilation Rampage," which appeared in the *Los Angeles Times* on March 14, 1999, pp. A1, A29.

2. Stanley Milgram, whatever one may think about the ethics of his experiments, was among the first to examine the psychology of the torturer. Subjects were asked to administer ever larger electrical shocks to volunteers who were instructed not to comply with experimenter requests. (The volunteers were in fact not hooked up to the electrical current.) Surprisingly large numbers of subjects were willing to shock volunteers even when the voltage was clearly marked as dangerous, even potentially fatal. Further, Amnesty International produced a docudrama entitled *Your Neighbor's Son: The Making of a Torturer* in the 1970s. Set in Greece in the early 1970s and using interviews with actual torturers, the film depicts the steps taken by the Greek military that turned ordinary young men into brutal torturers.

3. This section draws on Nagengast (1994).

4. The language of contagion and infestation is commonplace when people are dehumanized (see, for example, Sontag 1978; Keen 1986).

5. Interview with Roberto Martinez, "Immigration and Human Rights on the U.S. Mexico Border," *Motion Magazine* (on the Internet, July 1997).

6. Interview with Maria Jimenez, *Motion Magazine* (as it appears on the Internet; n.d. [between June and December 1997]).

7. According to an article in the *Dallas Morning Star* on May 11, 1998, an independent task force led by the U.S. Customs Service reported that NAFTA is directly linked to the increase in illegal drug traffic across the U. S.-Mexico border. Peter Andreas doubts that the INS will take meaningful steps to examine all traffic from Mexico into the United States in order to stem the narcotics trade. He asserts in a recent volume (2000) that if Customs examined every truck arriving along the U.S.-Mexican border, the line of traffic would extend 1200 miles from the border to Mexico City.

8. An article in the *Los Angeles Times* (May 27, 1998, A1) stated that the children of migrant workers are suffering malnutrition in unprecedented numbers.

9. *Los Angeles Times,* June 11, 2000, B1–3.

10. *Dallas Morning Star,* November 20, 1997.

11. This section draws on Timothy Dunn, *The Militarization of the U.S. Mexico Border: 1978–1992* (Austin: University of Texas Press, 1996).

12. Author's personal interview with R. P. Flores, August 3, 1998.

13. Recall the antigay stance taken by the Boy Scouts in mid-1998 and upheld by the Supreme Court in 2000.

14. See, for example, the Amnesty International 1999 report, *United States: Rights for All,* especially chapter 3 on police brutality and "prejudiced policing."

15. The *Los Angeles Times* ran an article in November 1998 about other Latinos who found themselves ostracized by Anglo neighbors who objected to their lavender, pink, and blue houses.

16. Andreopoulos's definition finesses the one contained in the United Nations Convention on Genocide, which many scholars have found limiting because it does not include social, political, or economic groups. This issue has been taken up by Helen Fein (1992), Kurt

Jonassohn (1992), and Barbara Harff (1992), among others. They have either agreed to expand the U. N. definition or to coin additional terms such as *politicide*, to describe the state violence against groups that are not ethnically, "racially," or religiously based.

17. There are a number of other issues having to do with, for example, intentionality and other preconditions for genocide, all of which are ably raised and discussed in a volume edited by George Andreopoulos entitled *Genocide* (Philadelphia: University of Pennsylvania Press, 1994).

18. I use the term *minority* reluctantly and only because it is in general usage. People described as "minorities" often object to the terminology because of its connotations of minor, less than, with fewer rights than.

19. Harff (1992) argues that genocide is far less likely in a democracy than in an authoritarian or totalitarian state. While this may be so, we should not to be too sanguine about democracy in and of itself as a deterrent to political violence. While it may prevent it in the metropoles or at least restrict it to "tolerable" numbers there, democratic states have been direct or indirect participants or supporters of political violence in client states around the world (see, for example, Ebihara and Ledgerwood, this volume). Like economics and politics in general, political violence, including genocide is or has become an aspect of the contemporary transnational world (Falk 2000).

BIBLIOGRAPHY

Abrams, Philip. 1988. "Notes of the Difficulty of Studying the State." *Journal of Historical Sociology* 1:58–89.

Alonso, Ana. 1994. "The Politics of Space, Time and Substance: State Formation, Nationalism, and Ethnicity." *Annual Review of Anthropology* 23:379–504.

Amnesty International. 1998a. *Annual Report.* London: Amnesty International Publishers.

———. 1998b. "From San Diego to Brownsville: Human Rights Violations on the USA Mexico Border." Amnesty International Report, May 20, 1998.

———. 1999. *United States of America: Rights for All.* London: Amnesty International Publishers.

Anazaldua, Gloria. 1987. *Borderlands/La Frontera.* San Francisco: Aunt Lute Press.

Andreas, Peter. 1994. "Border Troubles: Free Trade, Immigration, and Cheap Labour." *Ecologist* 24(6):230–34.

———. 2000. *Border Games: Policing the U.S.-Mexico Divide.* Ithaca: Cornell University Press.

Andreopoulos, George, ed. 1994. *Genocide: Conceptual and Historical Dimensions.* Philadelphia: University of Pennsylvania Press.

Appadurai, Arjun. 1998. "Dead Certainty: Ethnic Violence in the Era of Globalization." *Public Culture* 10(2):225–47.

Bacon, David. 1996. "Immigration Policy and Human Rights." *Social Justice* 23:137–53.

Barry, Tom. 1995. *Zapata's Revenge: Free Trade and the Farm Crisis in Mexico.* Boston: South End Press.

Barthes, Roland. 1988. *The Semiotic Challenge.* New York: Hill and Wang.

Bassford, C. 1991. "What Wars Can We Find for the Military Now?" *Newsday*, September 17.

Biskupic, Joan, and William Branigin. 1999. "Court Curbs Free Speech of Illegal Immigrants." *Washington Post*, February 25, 1999, p. A01.

Bourdieu, Pierre. 1977. *Outline of a Theory of Practice.* Cambridge: Cambridge University Press.

Bowen, John. 1996. "The Myth of Global Ethnic Conflict." *Journal of Democracy* 7(4):3–14.

Chalk, Frank, and Kurt Jonassohn. 1990. *The History and Sociology of Genocide: Analyses and Case Studies.* New Haven: Yale University Press.

Chatterjee, Partha. 1986. *Nationalist Thought and the Colonial World—A Derivative Discourse.* London: Zed.

Chavez, Leo. 1992. *Shadowed Lives: Undocumented Immigrants in American Society.* Fort Worth, Tex.: Harcourt, Brace, Jovanovich.

Clastres, P. 1974. "De l'ethnocide." *L'Homme* 14(3–4):101–10.

Cockcroft, James. 1986. *Outlaws in the Promised Land: Mexican Immigrant Workers and America's Future.* New York: Grove Press.

Cole, David. 1999. *No Equal Justice: Race and Class in the American Criminal Justice System.* New York: New Press.

Collier, George (with Elizabeth Lowery Quaratiello). 1994. *Basta! Land and the Zapatista Rebellion in Chiapas.* Oakland: Institute for Food and Development Policy.

Comaroff, John, and Jean Comaroff. 1991. *Of Revelation and Revolution: Christianity, Colonialism, and Consciousness in South Africa.* Chicago: University of Chicago Press.

De la Garza, Ernesto, et al., eds. 1985. *The Mexican-American Experience.* Austin: University of Texas Press.

Dugger, Ronnie. 1996. "To Prevent or To Stop Mass Murder." In *Genocide, War, and Human Survival.* Charles Strozier and Michael Flynn, eds. Pp. 59–74. Lanham, Md.: Rowman and Littlefield.

Dunn, Timothy. 1996. *The Militarization of the U.S. Mexico Border: 1978–1992.* Austin: University of Texas Press.

Dwyer, Augusta. 1994. *On the Line: Life on the US-Mexican Border.* New York: Monthly Review Press.

Falk, Richard A. 2000. *Human Rights Horizons: The Pursuit of Justice in a Globalizing World.* New York: Routledge.

Fein, Helen, ed. 1992. *Genocide Watch.* New Haven: Yale University Press.

Gourevitch, Philip. 1998. *We Wish to Inform You That Tomorrow We Will Be Killed with Our Families.* New York: Farrar, Strauss and Giroux.

Harff, Barbara. 1992. "Recognizing Genocides and Politicides." In *Genocide Watch.* Helen Fein, ed. Pp. 27–41. New Haven: Yale University Press.

Heyman, Josiah McC. 1995. "Putting Power in the Anthropology of Bureaucracy: The Immigration and Naturalization Service at the Mexico-United States Border." *Current Anthropology* 36(2):261–87.

Hoffman, Abraham. 1976. *Unwanted Mexican Americans in the Great Depression.* Tucson: University of Arizona Press.

Horowitz, Donald. 1985. *Ethnic Groups in Conflict.* Berkeley: University of California Press.

Human Rights Watch. 1992. *Brutality Unchecked: Human Rights Abuses along the U.S. Border with Mexico.* New York: Human Rights Watch.

———. 1995. *Human Rights Abuses along the U.S. Border with Mexico Persist amid a Climate of Immunity.* New York: Human Rights Watch.

Jonassohn, Kurt. 1992. "What Is Genocide?" In *Genocide Watch.* Helen Feim, ed. Pp. 17–26. New Haven: Yale University Press.

Joseph, Gilbert, and Daniel Nugent, eds. 1994. *Everyday Forms of State Formation: Revolution and the Negotiation of Rule in Modern Mexico.* Durham: Duke University Press.

Kapferer, Bruce. 1988. *Legends of People, Myths of State: Violence, Intolerance, and Political Culture in Sri Lanka and Australia.* Washington, D.C.: Smithsonian Institution Press.

Kearney, Michael, and Carole Nagengast. 1990. *Anthropological Perspectives on Transnational Communities in Rural California.* Davis: California Institute on Rural Studies.

Keen, Sam. 1986. *Faces of the Enemy: Reflections of the Hostile Imagination.* New York: Harper and Row.

Kuper, Leo. 1981. *Genocide.* New Haven: Yale University Press.

————. 1985. *The Prevention of Genocide.* New Haven: Yale University Press.

Lifton, Robert Jay, and Eric Markusen. 1990. *The Genocidal Mentality: Nazi Holocaust and Nuclear Threat.* New York: Basic Books.

Lowe, Lisa. 1996. *Immigrant Acts: On Asian American Cultural Politics.* Durham: Duke University Press.

Malkki, Liisa. 1995. *Purity and Exile: Violence, Memory, and National Cosmology among Hutu Refugees in Tanzania.* Chicago: University of Chicago Press.

McWilliams, Carey. 1948. *North from Mexico: The Spanish-Speaking People of the United States.* New York: Praeger.

Montejano, David, ed. 1977. *Race, Labor Repression and Capitalist Agriculture: Notes from South Texas, 1920–1930.* Berkeley: University of California Press.

————. 1987. *Anglos and Mexicans in the Making of Texas, 1936–1986.* Austin: University of Texas Press.

————. 1999. *Chicano Politics and Society in the Late Twentieth Century.* Austin: University of Texas Press.

Müller-Hill, B. 1988. *Murderous Science: The Elimination by Scientific Selection of Jews, Gypsies, and Others, Germany 1933–1945.* Oxford: Oxford University Press.

Nagengast, Carole. 1994. "Violence, Terror, and the Crisis of the State." *Annual Review of Anthropology* 23:109–36.

Nagengast, Carole, and Michael Kearney. 1990. "Mixtec Ethnicity: Social Identity, Political Consciousness, and Political Activism." *Latin American Research Review* 25(1):61–91.

Nagengast, Carole, Rodolfo Stavenhagen, and Michael Kearney. 1992. *Human Rights and Indigenous Workers: The Mixtecs in Mexico and the United States.* San Diego: Center for U.S.-Mexican Studies, University of California.

Ross, John. 1995. *Rebellion from the Roots.* Monroe, Maine: Common Courage Press.

Sassen, Saskia. 1991. *The Global City.* Princeton: Princeton University Press.

————. 1996. "Beyond Sovereignty: Immigration Policy Making Today." *Social Justice: A Journal of Crime, Conflict, and World Order* 9:20.

Scarry, Elaine. 1985. *The Body in Pain.* Oxford: Oxford University Press.

Sontag, Susan. 1978. "Disease as Political Metaphor." *New York Review of Books* 23 (February): 29–33.

Steiner, Henry J., and Philip Alston. 1996. *International Human Rights in Context.* Oxford: Clarendon Press.

Taussig, Michael. 1984. "Culture of Terror, Space of Death: Roger Casement and the Explanation of Torture." *Comparative Studies in Society and History* 26:467–97.

————. 1991. *Shamanism, Colonialism, and the Wild Man: A Study in Terror and Healing.* Chicago: University of Chicago Press.

Tiano, Susan. 1994. *Patriarchy on the Line: Labor, Gender, and Ideology in the Mexican Maquila Industry.* Philadelphia: Temple University Press.

Totten, Samuel, William S. Parsons, and Israel W. Charny. 1997. *Century of Genocide: Eyewitness Accounts and Critical Views.* New York: Garland Publishing.

Zabin, Carol, Michael Kearney, Anna Garcia, David Runsten, and Carole Nagengast. 1993. *Mixtec Migrants in California Agriculture.* Davis: California Institute for Rural Studies.

Zavalla, Patricia. 1987. *Women's Work and Chicano Families: Cannery Workers of the Santa Clara Valley.* Ithaca: Cornell University Press.

14

Coming to Our Senses

Anthropology and Genocide

Nancy Scheper-Hughes

Modern anthropology was built up in the face of colonial genocides, ethnocides, mass killings, population die-outs, and other forms of mass destruction visited on the marginalized peoples whose lives, suffering, and deaths have provided us with a livelihood. Yet, despite this history—and the privileged position of the anthropologist-ethnographer as eyewitness to some of these events—anthropology has been, until quite recently, relatively mute on the subject. To this day most "early warning signals" concerning genocidal sentiments, gestures, and acts still come from political journalists rather than from ethnographers in the field. And most theories concerning the causes, meanings, and consequences of genocide come from other disciplinary quarters—history, psychology and psychiatry, theology, comparative law, human rights, and political science. In all, anthropology is a late arrival to the field, and this volume, published in 2001, represents, as it were, anthropology's opening gambit. Why is this so?

As Alex Hinton and several contributors to this volume have noted, violence is hardly a natural subject for anthropologists. Everything in our disciplinary training predisposes us *not* to see the blatant and manifest forms of violence that so often ravage the lives of our subjects. Although the term *genocide* and its modern conception were first coined by Raphael Lemkin (1944) following and in response to the Holocaust, genocides and other forms of mass killing clearly existed prior to late modernity and in societies relatively untouched by Western "civilization." Indeed, the avoidance of this topic by anthropologists was surely dictated by a desire to avoid further stigmatizing indigenous societies and cultures that were so often judged negatively and in terms of Eurocentric values and aims.

A basic premise guiding twentieth-century ethnographic research was, quite simply, to see, hear, and report no evil (and very little violence) in reporting back from the field. Classical cultural anthropology and its particular moral sensibility orients us like so many inverse bloodhounds on the trail and on the scent of the good and the righteous in the societies that we study. Some have even suggested that evil is not a proper subject for the anthropologist.[1] Consequently, as Elliot Leyton (1998a) has pointed out, the contributions of anthropology to understanding *all* levels of violence—from sexual abuse and homicide to state-sponsored political terrorism and "dirty wars" to genocide—is extremely modest. Those who deviated from the golden rule of moral relativism were forever saddled with accusations of victim-blaming. But the moral blinders that we wore in the one instance spilled over into a kind of hermeneutic generosity in other instances—toward Western colonizers, modern police states, and other political and military institutions of mass destruction. Although genocides predate the spread of Western "civilization," the savage colonization of Africa, Asia, and the New World incited some of the worst genocides of the eighteenth to early twentieth centuries. The failure of anthropologists to deal directly with these primal scenes of mass destruction as they were being played out in various "ethnographic niches" is the subject of this epilogue or postscript to the story of anthropology and genocide.

Although averting their gaze from the scenes of genocide and other forms of graphic and brutal physical violence, anthropologists have always been astute observers of violence-once-removed. We are quite good at analyzing the *symbolic* (see Bourdieu and Waquant 1992), the *psychological* (see Devereux 1961; Goffman 1961; Edgerton 1992; Scheper-Hughes 2000b), and the *structural* (see Farmer 1996; Bourgois 1995) forms of everyday violence that underlie so many social institutions and interactions—a contribution that may provide a missing link in contemporary genocide studies.

In my own case, it took me more than two decades to confront the question of overt political violence, which, given my choice of early field sites—Ireland in the mid-1970s and Brazil during the military dictatorship years—must have required a massive dose of denial. While studying the madness of everyday life in the mid-1970s in a small, quiet peasant community in western Ireland, I was largely concerned with *interior* spaces, with the small, dark psychodramas of scapegoating and labeling within traditional farm households that were driving so many young bachelors to drink and bouts of depression and schizophrenia. I paid scant attention then to the mundane political activities of Matty Dowd, from whom we rented our cottage in the mountain hamlet of Ballynalacken, and who used our attic to store a small arsenal of guns and explosives that he and a few of his Sinn Fein buddies were running to Northern Ireland. Consequently, I left unexamined until very recently (Scheper-Hughes 2000b) the possible links between the political violence in Northern Ireland and the tortured family dramas in West Kerry that I so carefully documented, and which certainly had a violence of their own.

Since then I have continued to study other forms of "everyday" violence: the abuses of medicine practiced in bad faith against the weak, the mad, and the hungry, including the bodies of socially disadvantaged and largely invisible organ donors in transplant transactions (see Scheper-Hughes 2000a); and the social indifference to child death in Northeast Brazil that allowed political leaders, priests, coffin makers, *and* shantytown mothers to dispatch a multitude of hungry "angel-babies" to the afterlife. In Brazil I did not begin to study state and political violence until, in the late 1980s, the half-grown sons of some of my friends and neighbors in the shantytown of Alto do Cruzeiro began to "disappear"—their mutilated bodies turning up later, the handiwork of police-infiltrated local death squads.

TRISTES ANTROPOLOGIQUES

In his professional memoir, *After the Fact*, Clifford Geertz (1995) notes somewhat wryly that he always had the uncomfortable feeling of arriving too early or too late to observe the really large and significant political events and the violent upheavals that descended on his respective field sites in Morocco and Java. But, in fact, he writes that he (understandably) consciously *avoided* the conflicts, moving back and forth between his respective field sites during periods of relative calm, always managing to "miss the revolution" (Starn 1992), as it were.

Consequently there was nothing in Geertz's ethnographic writings hinting at the "killing fields" that were beginning to engulf Indonesia soon after he had departed from the field, a massacre of suspected communists by Islamic fundamentalists in 1965 that rivaled more recent events in Rwanda. It was an extraordinary bloodbath—a political massacre of some sixty thousand Balinese following an unsuccessful Marxist-inspired coup in 1965. Perhaps one could interpret Geertz's celebrated analysis of the Balinese cock fight as a coded expression of the fierce aggression lying just beneath the surface of a people whom the anthropologist otherwise described as among the most poised, controlled, and decorous in the world.

Today, the world, the objects of our study, and the uses of anthropology have changed considerably. Those privileged to observe human events close up and over time and who are thereby privy to local, community, and even state secrets that are generally hidden from view until much later—after the collective graves have been discovered and the body counts made—are beginning to recognize another ethical position: to name and to identify the sources, structures, and institutions of mass violence. This new mood of political and ethical engagement (see Scheper-Hughes 1995a) has resulted in considerable soul-searching, even if long "after the fact."

Claude Levi-Strauss (1995), for example, fast approaching the end of his long and distinguished career, opened his recently published photographic memoir, *Saudades do Brasil [Homesickness for Brazil]*, with a sobering caveat. He warned the reader that the lyrically beautiful images of "pristine" rain forest Brazilian Indians about to be presented—photos taken by him between 1935 and 1939 in the interior of Brazil—should *not* be trusted. The images were illusory, he cautioned. The world they portray no longer exists. The starkly beautiful, seemingly timeless Nambikwara, Caduveo, and Bororo Indians captured in his photos bear no resemblance to the reduced populations one might find today camped out by the sides of busy truck routes or loitering in urban villages looking like slums carved out of a gutted wilderness. The Nambiquara and their Amerindian neighbors have been decimated by wage labor, gold prospecting, prostitution, and the diseases of cultural contact: smallpox, TB, AIDS, and syphilis.

But the old master's confession goes further. These early photos capturing simple, naked Indians sleeping on the ground under romantic shelters of palm leaves have nothing to do with a state of pristine humanity that has since been lost. The photos taken in the 1930s already show the effects of a savage European colonization on the once-populous civilizations of Central Brazil and the Amazon. Following contact, these indigenous civilizations were destroyed, leaving behind only sad remnants of themselves—a people not so much "primitive," he cautions, as "stranded," stripped of their material and symbolic wealth. Levi-Strauss's camera had captured images of a particularly virulent kind of human strip mining, an invisible genocide, the magnitude of which the anthropologist was at the time perhaps naively unaware.

Earlier, Levi-Strauss had recognized that a good deal more was required of the anthropologist than dedication to a purely scholarly pursuit (see also Sontag 1964 on anthropology as a spiritual vocation). He wrote (1966:126): "Anthropology is not a dispassionate science like astronomy, which springs from the contemplation of things at a distance. It is the outcome of a historical process which has made the larger part of mankind subservient to the other, and during which millions of innocent human beings have had their resources plundered and their institutions and beliefs destroyed whilst they themselves were ruthlessly killed, thrown into bondage, and contaminated by diseases they were unable to resist. Anthropology is the daughter to this era of violence: its capacity to assess more objectively the facts pertaining to the human condition reflects, on the epistemological level, a state of affairs in which one part of mankind treated the other as an object." Sadly, however, more often than not, anthropologists have served as passive bystanders, as silent rather than engaged witnesses to the genocides, ethnocides, and die-outs they have so often encountered in the course of pursuing their "vocation."

Late-in-life professional examinations of conscience by anthropologists with regard to their "recovered memories" of the scenes of violence and ethnocide go back to the days of Bronislaw Malinowski (1884–1942). Malinowski began his anthropological career under considerable duress as an "enemy-alien," a Polish-born Austrian citizen detained in Australia while en route to his first fieldwork expedition during the outbreak of World War 1. Granted *libera custodia* by the Australian government, Malinowski was permitted to conduct his ethnographic research in New Guinea as long as the war continued, which artificially expanded his intended term of fieldwork.

Malinowski's field diary, covering the period from 1914 to 1918 and published posthumously by his widow in 1967, records the anthropologist's conflicting emotions and identities as a European gentleman, a child of Western imperialism, and a natural scientist trying to reinvent himself and carve out a new science and method for recording and understanding human and cultural difference. His sympathies were initially aligned with the values of his own European civilization. In a wry and, one hopes, ironic entry to his diary, Malinowski repeats the words of the savage colonizer, Kurtz, from Joseph Conrad's *Heart of Darkness:* "My feelings toward the natives are [on the whole] decidedly tending to 'exterminate the brutes' " (1967:69). Here the anthropologist and racist imperialist seem one in spirit. But Malinowski was profoundly homesick and morbidly depressed while "captive" in the field, and his fevered diary musings might best be understood as just that: the nightmarish daydreams of a diseased, hyperactive, and hypochondriacal imagination. Surely the true measure of Malinowski's anthropological genius lay not in his private musings but in his public writings and in his method of "participant observation," which required an empathic identification with "the native."

After the traumas of fieldwork, when Malinowski sat down to reflect on the moral underpinnings of his discipline, he concluded: "The duty of the anthropologist is to be a fair and true interpreter of the Native and . . . to register that Europeans in the past sometimes exterminated whole island peoples; that they expropriated most of the patrimony of savage races; that they introduced slavery in a specially cruel and pernicious form" (1945:3–4, cited by James 1973:66). Malinowski noted that while Europeans were generous in distributing their spiritual gifts to the colonized, they were stingy in circulating the cultural and material instruments of power and self-mastery. Europeans did not, he wrote (1945:57), give African peoples "firearms, bombing planes, poison gas, and all that makes effective self-defense or aggression possible." In the end Malinowski argued passionately against the anthropologist as a neutral and objective "by-stander" to the contemporary history of colonial and postcolonial genocides and ethnocides. But these later writings were largely discredited by his profession as the irresponsible babbling of an old man past his intellectual prime.

KROEBER AND ISHI: LAST OF THEIR TRIBES

Alfred Kroeber died before he could imagine a radically different role for the anthropologist as an engaged witness rather than disinterested spectator to the scenes of human suffering, cultural destruction, and genocide even then being visited on the native peoples of Northern California. When Kroeber arrived in San Francisco in 1901 to take up the post of museum anthropologist at the University of California, it was at the tail end of a terrible, wanton, and officially sanctioned extermination of northern California Indians that had begun during the Gold Rush and continued through the turn of the twentieth century.

In the coldly objective words of a historian of the period (Cook 1978:91): "Like all native people in the Western Hemisphere, the Indians of California underwent a very severe decline in numbers following the entrance of White civilization. From the beginning to the end of the process the native population experienced a fall from 310,000 to approximately 20,000, a decline of over 90% of the original number. This collapse was due to the operation of factors inherent in the physical and social conflict between the White and the Red races." Cook identified disease epidemics as the primary factor in "depressing the local population" (p. 92). But the historical record belies this more neutral explanation. In fact, military campaigns, massacres, bounty hunts, debt peonage, land grabbing, and enclosures by Anglo settlers and ranchers produced the far greater toll of suffering and death on the native populations.[2]

From first contact to 1860, American military attacks took the lives of 4,267 native Californians. But the worst was yet to come: with the California Gold Rush, Indians in California began to experience a total assault on their communities. For example, in May 1852 a mob of whites led by the sheriff of Weatherville, California, attacked, without warning, a peaceful Indian rancheria, killing men, women, and children: "Of the [original] 150 Indians that constituted the rancheria, only 2 or 3 escaped, and those were supposed to be dangerously wounded; so probably not one . . . remains alive" (*Daily Alta California*, May 4, 1852, cited by Churchill 1997:220). The devastation suffered by the greater Maiduan community is captured by the following numbers. In 1846 there were eight thousand Maiduan people; in 1850 there were between thirty-five hundred and forty-five hundred; by 1910 only nine hundred Maidu people remained (Riddell 1978:386).

In 1850 the California legislature passed a law that marked the transition of the California Indian from peonage to virtual slavery. The law decreed that any Indian, on the word of a single white, could be declared a vagrant, thrown into jail, and his labor sold at auction for up to four months without pay. Moreover, it permitted the kidnapping of Indian children, a practice that lasted through the end of the nineteenth century. An editorial published on December 6, 1861, in the local newspaper of Marysville, California, reported: "It is from these [local] mountain tribes that white settlers draw their supplies of kidnapped children, educated as servants, and women for the purpose of labor and lust. . . . It is notorious that there are parties in the northern countries of this state, whose sole occupation has been to steal young children and squaws . . . and to dispose of them at handsome prices to the settlers, who being [largely] unmarried willingly pay 50 or 60 dollars for a likely young girl" (cited in Castillo 1978:109).

Like many anthropologists of his day, including Margaret Mead, whose sense of urgency ("We must study them before they disappear!") was dictated by the accelerating die-outs of indigenous peoples and their languages and cultures, Kroeber spent his first two decades in California conducting what was then called salvage ethnography. That was the attempt to document the cultures of disappearing peoples by relying on the memories of the oldest living members of the group. It was a work of intense concentration that culminated in Kroeber's monumental 925-page *Handbook of the Indians of California*, which he completed and delivered to the Smithsonian Institution, although the volume was not published until 1925.

In the *Handbook* and elsewhere, Kroeber (see, for example, 1917; 1952) operated from the premise that Native Americans were destined to disappear through an inevitable social evolutionary trajectory determined by the inevitable and progressive march of civilization. It was an anthropological version of the American doctrine of Manifest Destiny. The remaining "scattered bands" of hunting and gathering tribes in northern California would, Kroeber argued, inevitably give way to Anglo farming, ranching, and mining ventures. Some indigenous groups fell quickly. Others fought bravely, and others went into hiding. Their survival was, as Kroeber (1972a:9) commented, "remarkable." He referred, for example, to the "elusive Mill Creek Indians" (1911a; 1972a) as the "last free survivors of the American red man, who by a fortitude and stubbornness of character, succeeded in holding out against the overwhelming tide of civilization twenty-five years longer even than Geronimo's famous band of Apaches." But Kroeber warned that the "final chapter" of the Mill Creek survivors was fast approaching. And he was right.

By the time he completed the *Handbook*, Kroeber had come to view "salvage ethnography"—gathering the remembered remnants of dying aboriginal societies from survivors in blue-jeans living in ruined and "bastardized" cultures (Kroeber 1948a:427)—as less than satisfying work. And he returned to an earlier interest in the peoples and cultures of the American Southwest, where a more vibrant (and viable) Native American experience persisted, even flourished, among Pueblo Indians. More significantly, after the traumatic death of Ishi, his singular Yahi informant, Kroeber turned away from "particularistic" ethnography to take up more broadly theoretical writings, which, following the German idealist tradition, focused on the collective "genius" of a given cultural tradition to which the individual and his personal history were largely irrelevant.

Kroeber treated the disappearance of entire populations of native Californians in massacres and bounty hunts by Anglo ranchers and gold miners as a small, inconsequential sidebar in the *long duree* of social evolutionary time. "After some hesitation," Kroeber wrote in 1925, "I have omitted all directly historical treatment . . . of the relations of the natives with the whites and of the events befalling them after such contact was established. It is not that this subject is unimportant or uninteresting, but that I am not in a position to treat it adequately. It is also a matter that has comparatively slight relation to aboriginal civilization" (cited by Buckley 1996:274). The vanquished peoples and cultures were already "ruined," anthropologically speaking, and could cast little light on the "authentic" aboriginal civilizations that preceded their decline, which Kroeber viewed as the true subject of his scientific research.

Perhaps the suffering, premature deaths, and cultural devastation of his native California informants was just too difficult for Kroeber to face, and he retreated into the safety zone of a theory that put their losses into a broader, cultural historical perspective. Kroeber once confided to a colleague (A. R. Pilling, cited by ibid.:277) that he did not delve into his Yurok informants' experiences of the contact era because he "could not stand all the tears." And so Kroeber began to write the individual out of his works to the extent that even as stalwart an objectivist and empiricist as Eric Wolf (1981:57–58) later referred to Kroeber's disembodied and impersonal approach to culture (the "superorganic") as "very abstract, very Olympian, even frightening, ultimately." Kroeber's belief in the power of the highly abstract "superorganic" was the expression of a kind of scientific faith (see Kroeber 1948:22–24). But in turning away from the tragic personal and collective histories of his informants, Kroeber's anthropology failed to grapple with the destructive animus of his adopted state toward its indigenous peoples. And he described the genocide that reduced the indigenous population of California from 300,000 in the mid-1840s to less than 20,000 at the close of the century as a relatively minor affair, as "a little history . . . of pitiful events" (cited by Buckley 1996).

It is difficult to know whether the tangled, intense, but ultimately tragic relationship between Kroeber and his key native Californian informant, Ishi (that spanned the years 1911–16) was a cause or consequence of the anthropologist's sentiments regarding the inevitability of the decline and death of California's indigenous cultures. But this much is known. The arrival of Ishi into Kroeber's life—and therefore into our anthropological and historical consciousness—was uncannily overdetermined.

In the first of two journalistic articles that Kroeber wrote about the Yahi Indians first published in the summer of 1911, Kroeber described the "discovery" by California surveyors of a ragtag band of Mill Creek Indian Yahi survivors. "The Elusive Mill Creeks" (republished in 1972 by the Lowie/Hearst Museum of Anthropology) describes how a team of local surveyors for a power company came upon a cleverly concealed camp site in the tangled woods near Deer Creek in 1908. This site was in all likelihood one of the last hiding places of Ishi and his few remaining family members. Inside the camp the surveyors found a middle-aged woman and two aged Indians, a man and a woman. The old woman, resting under a pile of rabbit skins, was very ill, and she begged for water, which one of the surveyors brought to her after the other members of the group ran off to hide. Then the whites cruelly and inexplicably carried away all the blankets, bows and arrows, and other supplies left behind in the encampment.

In this piece written for popular consumption, Kroeber used words and phrases that he normally avoided in his scientific writings. He refers, for example, to "a totally wild and independent tribe of Indians, without firearms, fleeing at the approach of the white man" (1972a:1) who managed for forty years to elude detection. Elsewhere in the article Kroeber described the Mill Creek Indians as "a handful of savages" while describing their Anglo bounty hunters as "the enterprising pioneer and miner."

The best outcome Kroeber could imagine for this "remnant" band of Indians was for them to be captured by a posse of American soldiers sent by the Office of Indian Affairs: "How they can be captured and brought in is, however, another and more difficult problem. It is the unanimous opinion of those acquainted with them that a troop of cavalry might scour the region of Deer Creek and Mill Creek for months without laying hands on them. Possibly a gradually narrowing circle of men might enclose them and finally drive them to the center" (p. 9). Then the goal would be to integrate them with other "survivors of landless tribes that have lived for many years as scattered outcasts on the fringes of civilization." Alternatively, Kroeber argued, they could be granted "a few square miles in the inaccessible and worthless canyon of Deer Creek where they now live." Otherwise, their future was extremely dire: "If they continue their present mode of life, the settlers in the vicinity are likely to suffer further loss of property and livestock. If the Indians are ever caught in the act of marauding it may go hard with them, for the rancher in these districts rarely has his rifle far from his hand *and can scarcely be blamed for resorting to violence* [emphasis mine] when his belongings have been repeatedly seized" (p. 8).

Then, as if on cue, in July 1911, the last member of that renegade band, the man the anthropologists would later call "Ishi" and whom Kroeber would describe (in a letter to Sapir) as the "last California aborigine" appeared in downtown Oroville, Butte County, California, a historical gold mining town on the Feather River. Driven by hunger or desperation the Indian came out of the foothills of Mt. Lassen and was found cowering in the corner of an animal slaughterhouse. Scarcely had the ink dried on Kroeber's article on the Last Mill Creek Indians when he received a call from the Oroville jailhouse asking for his help in communicating with the "wild man." The Indian was cold and frightened, and although he was obviously very hungry he refused to accept the food and water that was offered to him. His only clothing was a ragged canvas cloak.

In the first photo taken of Ishi just hours after his capture (see figure 14.1), the man's startled expression and his state of advanced emaciation are frighteningly familiar. It is reminiscent of photos taken of Holocaust survivors immediately after their liberation from concentration camps at the end of World War II. The camps at Kosovo also come to mind. Ishi's hair was clipped or singed close to his head in a traditional sign of Yahi mourning. Had the old woman left behind in the camp at Mill Creek died? Ishi's cheeks cling fast to the bones and accentuate his deep-set eyes. The photo reveals a man of intelligence and of deep sorrow.

Indeed, Ishi has been described as northern California's Anne Frank. Cruelly hunted, his family reduced until, the last of his group, Ishi was flushed out of his wooded hideout. There is speculation among some northern California Indians that Ishi may have been in search of refuge at the nearby Feather River (Maidu Indian) rancheria. The Maidu, like the Pit River rancheria Indians to the north of Mt. Lassen, were known to sometimes offer sanctuary to their escaping Yahi neighbors. "Ishi wasn't crazy," Art Angle, chair of the Butte County American Indian Cultural Committee in Oroville, told me in the spring of 2000. "He *knew* where he was headed." But betrayed by barking guard dogs, Ishi fell into the hands of whites instead.

Other native Californians in the area suspect that Ishi was "a loner," trained by his mother and other close adult relatives to avoid *all* humans. One Pit River man said that Ishi, in his view, had "lost his bearing" as well as his bonds to other Indians. "Too many years alone," is what others said. "He didn't really trust anyone anymore—white or Indian, it was all the same to him." "He suffered too much,"

Figure 14.1. Portrait of Ishi, August 29, 1911. From Theodora Kroeber, *Ishi in Two Worlds* (Berkeley: University of California Press, 1961).

another native person said. White people who live and work today near Ishi's family's Mill Creek camp also still talk about Ishi. It seems as though he is never very far from their consciousness. "You know," one young white man, a deer hunter, told me angrily in a general store overlooking Mill Creek where he had stopped for supplies: "They hunted Ishi just like a fox—I don't know how *they* could have done that to a man like him."

After his "rescue" by Kroeber and his associates, Ishi lived out his final years (1911–16) as an assistant janitor (paid twenty-five dollars week), a key informant to A. L. Kroeber, and a "living specimen" at the museum of anthropology at the University of California, then located in San Francisco. Ishi was given his own private quarters in the museum, but his room was located next to a hall housing a large collection of human skulls and bones that appalled and depressed the Indian. During the period that Ishi lived among whites (mostly UCSF doctors and anthropologists), he served as a key anthropological informant to Kroeber, to Tom Waterman, and to other local and visiting anthropologists, including Edward Sapir of Yale University, whom Waterman accused of overworking Ishi, already weak from illness. Like thousands of other "first contact" peoples, Ishi contracted tuberculosis, an urban, white man's disease, although his condition was not properly diagnosed until the final weeks of his life. Kroeber had anticipated and feared this outcome, as his first wife, Henriette, was carried away by this dreaded disease, then endemic in many cities of the United States, soon after Ishi arrived at the museum. Ishi finally succumbed to what was described as "galloping consumption" in March 1916 while Kroeber was away on sabbatical leave in New York City.

Illiterate and unlettered, Ishi (unlike Anne Frank) did not write his own diary, but he told parts of his life story to Alfred Kroeber, who recorded those fragments by hand. Kroeber also captured on primitive wax cylinders Ishi's rendition of Yahi myths, origin stories, and folktales. There were many things, however, that Ishi would *not* talk about: the death of his close relatives and his last, horrible years around Deer Creek before his decision to travel south, far beyond the normal boundaries of Yahi country. Ishi's silence on some topics was dictated by a Yahi taboo against naming the dead.

In the end, Kroeber did not write the definitive history of Ishi and his people. After the Indian's death, Kroeber avoided talking about his friend, and he put aside for many years his materials and field notes on Ishi and Yahi culture. In her biography of A. L. Kroeber, Theodora Kroeber (1970) writes that the subject of Ishi caused her husband considerable discomfort and so was generally avoided in the Kroeber household. Perhaps Kroeber was observing the Yahi custom that forbade naming and speaking of the dead. I like to think so. But many years after these sad events, Kroeber did allow his second wife, Theodora, to use her husband as a key informant on Ishi's last years. And so, it was Theodora Kroeber who told the story that the anthropologist could not bring himself to write, and she produced two memorable and highly literary accounts: *Ishi in Two Worlds* (1961) and *Ishi: Last of*

His Tribe (1964). Consequently, what we know and remember about Ishi today is based mostly on what Theodora wrote.

Ishi in Two Worlds directly confronted what Kroeber had studiously avoided: the history of the California Indian genocide at the hands of white settlers and ranchers. Chapters 3 through 5 of her book stand as one of the most unflinching renditions of the brutality and savagery of California's white settler history. And because of Theodora Kroeber's compelling rendition of Ishi's life and times, Ishi lent a face, a name, and a personalized narrative to the hidden genocide of his people. Ishi came to represent more than the life of a single man but to symbolize, instead, the broader experience of Native Americans.

By contrast to the permanency of Theodora's simple text, the fragile plastic cylinders on which Kroeber (and later Sapir) recorded Ishi's songs and folktales were stored too close to the heaters in the anthropology museum archives, and a great many melted. One of the early recordings that remains, however, is Ishi's telling of the Yahi myth "Coyote Sleeps with His Sister," which has been carefully transcribed by Leanne Hinton and her students at U.C. Berkeley and compared with similar and related tales collected from nearby tribes. At the conference entitled "Legacies of Ishi," held in Oroville on May 12, 2000, Professor Hinton remarked on Ishi's intense enjoyment in telling this long tale, with its many complicated subtexts filled with intimate details of Yahi practices of acorn gathering, cooking, and home-keeping. Why Ishi, a man who was by all accounts excessively modest (even prudish), chose to recount this particular tale with its explicitly sexual content dealing with a profound Yahi taboo—brother-sister incest—remained a bit of a mystery to Hinton. But the theme must have been a powerful one for Ishi, an adult male, who was forced to live, travel, and hide out with blood relations, all of them sexually restricted to him. Among the many forms of violence suffered by Ishi at the hands of the white miners and ranchers who hunted his people were the restrictions on his sexuality and of his right to reproduce. This was genocide in another form. Even after his capture or rescue by whites, Ishi's sexuality was often the butt of public jokes. The local press had, for example, invented Ishi's supposed sexual infatuation for Lily Lena, a lowbrow music hall entertainer from London who appeared at the Orpheum Theater in San Francisco in the fall of 1911. But Kroeber pointed out (1911b) that Ishi was far more impressed with the architecture of the building and with the crowds below the balcony where he was sitting than he was with Miss Lena, to whom he paid scant attention.

In this same short, journalistic piece Kroeber recounts the arrival of Ishi to San Francisco on Labor Day, 1911. When the man called Ishi stepped off the ferry boat and into the glare of electric lights, hotel runners, and clanging trolley cars on Market Street, he was frightened and distraught. Ishi, Kroeber writes, was "a curious and pathetic figure in those [first] days. Timid, gentle, an almost ever-pervading fear held down and concealed to the best of his ability, he nevertheless startled and leaped at the slightest sudden sound. A new sight, or the crowding around of half a dozen people, made his limbs rigid. If his hand had been held and was released, his arm remained frozen in the air for several minutes. The first boom from a canon fired in the artillery practice at the Presidio several miles away, raised him a foot from his chair.... His one great dread, which he overcame but slowly, was of crowds. It is not hard to understand this in light of his lonely life in a tribe of five [later reduced to three and then, finally, to one]."

In this jarring passage Kroeber describes the symptoms of what would today be considered a classic description of PTSD, posttraumatic stress disorder. Ishi's startle reflex, his phobias, and his mobilization for flight are similar to those of many "recovering" victims of so-called shell shock following wars, mass killings, kidnap, torture, rape, and physical assault (see Herman 1992). Yet despite his physical vulnerability to urban diseases and his psychological fragility as a survivor of extreme trauma, Ishi was exhibited at the anthropology museum where families came on Sunday excursions to watch the "wild man of California" make arrows and fishing spears. Given Ishi's acute phobia of crowds, one wonders why Kroeber allowed him to be exhibited before the masses at the Panama Pacific Trade Exhibition.

In 1915 Ishi began his inevitable decline after contracting tuberculosis. Initially he was misdiagnosed by his great friend and personal doctor Saxton Pope (1920:192), who also failed to notice (until days before Ishi's death) how thin and ravaged his friend's body had become. In February 1916, a month before Ishi died, Pope (p. 205) recorded the following: "All this time he had a moderate cough; but repeated examination failed to show any tubercle bacilli.... [A]fter taking food he apparently experienced great pain. Even water caused him misery and I have seen him writhe in agony, with tears running down his cheeks, yet utter no sound of complaint. At this period, when he seemed to be failing so rapidly that the end must be near, I coaxed him to get out of bed and to let me take his picture once more. He was always happy to be photographed and he accommodated me. *It was only after the picture was developed that I recognized to what a pitiful condition he had been reduced*" [emphasis mine]. Ishi's last medical record at UCSF hospital admission (ibid.) reads: "Ishi.—No. 11032. March 19, 1916. Well developed but extremely emaciated, dark skinned Indian lying in bed ... vomiting and retching occasionally, evidently in great distress ... broad and prominently arched nose; high malar bones and sunken cheeks; orbital depressions deep, apparently from wasting."

Kroeber knew when he decided to leave the University of California to take up a sabbatical year abroad and in New York City in 1916 that his good-byes might constitute his final leave-taking from Ishi. But Ishi reportedly reversed the situation in the larger metaphorical sense when he said to Alfred: "*I* go, *you* stay." In the final days of Ishi's life, Kroeber communicated frequently from New York City by telegrams in which he demanded timely postings on his friend's deteriorating condition. Ishi had entrusted Kroeber to ensure the proper care and treatment of his remains after his death, but in the end Kroeber, hampered by distance, was unable to prevent an autopsy on Ishi's body during which the Indian's brain was removed "for science."

When Kroeber returned to Berkeley he inexplicably arranged for Ishi's brain to be shipped to the Smithsonian Institution for curation. The man to whom the brain was directed, Ales Hrdlička, was a prominent physical anthropologist of the old school, a man obsessively dedicated to collecting and measuring brain "specimens" from various orders of primates, human "exotics" (like Ishi), and from Western "geniuses" (like John Wesley Powell, the first chief of the Bureau of American Ethnology). Kroeber knew that Ishi reviled the white man's science of collecting skulls and body parts. But perhaps he thought that it was too late for such "sentimental" reservations. Ishi was dead, and the damage to his remains had been done and was irreversible. Perhaps he believed that the science to which he had unreservedly dedicated his life might be able to benefit from the tragedy of his friend and informant's death. If so, it was a triumph of science over sentiment. In any event, Kroeber wrote to Hrdlička on October 27, 1916: "I find that with Ishi's death last spring, his brain was removed and preserved. There is no one here who can put it to scientific use. If you wish it, I would be pleased to deposit it in the National Museum collection." Hrdlička replied on December 12, 1916, that he would be "very glad" to receive the brain, and he would have it "properly worked up." There is no evidence, however, that Ishi's brain was ever included in any physical anthropological or scientific study. It was simply forgotten and abandoned in a Smithsonian warehouse, kept in a vat of formaldehyde with several other brain "specimens."

Alternatively, Kroeber's behavior was an act of disordered mourning. Grief can be expressed in a myriad of ways, ranging from denial and avoidance to the rage of the Illongot headhunter (Rosaldo 1989). According to Theodora Kroeber (1970), her husband suffered greatly at the news of his friend's death and at the violence done to his body. He fell into a long depression, and he went into a flight pattern that lasted seven years. Kroeber characterized this unsettling period in his life (from 1915 to 1922) as his *hegira*—a dark period of journey, soul-searching, and melancholia. It was marked by seemingly bizarre symptoms: physical disequilibrium, nausea, vertigo, strain, and exhaustion. His condition was similar to what used to be called neurasthenia. Freud's essay on mourning and melancholia comes to mind with respect to Kroeber's "swallowed grief" concerning the deaths in close succession of his first wife and his friend and key informant, both from the same disease.

Immediately after Ishi's death, Kroeber again left California in order to take up a temporary position at the Museum of Natural History in New York. But he also went to New York in order to enter a classic psychoanalysis with Dr. Jelliffe, a former student of Anna Freud. Kroeber recognized that the signs were of his own disequilibrium. With the death of Henriette, Kroeber's personal life was shattered. With the death of Ishi his professional life seemed meaningless. And so, at the age of forty, Kroeber was for the first time questioning his choice of career and his long-term professional goals. And when Kroeber returned to Berkeley he began a practice in psychoanalytic therapy at the Stanford Clinic. Later he opened a private office in San Francisco.

When he resumed his anthropological career full time in 1922, Kroeber threw himself into new fields and approaches. He took up archeology and experimented with more objective, statistical methods, which gave him some distance from the more personal, intimate, and psychological aspects of human life. The individual and the small group were now interpreted as part of a much larger design that Kroeber called the "superorganic." Similarly, his new interest in "culture areas" allowed Kroeber to compile masses of statistically comparable data for the whole of native California (T. Kroeber 1970:163). In all, it was a flight into objectivism driven by a desire to map the inevitable ebb and flow of cultures, which Kroeber came to believe were as inevitable as cycles of night and day, birth and death.

It is easy today with the advantage of hindsight to identify the blind spots of our anthropological predecessors—in this instance, Kroeber's intellectual denial of the genocide of Northern California Indians and his seemingly callous behavior toward Ishi's remains. Kroeber was not indifferent toward his *living* native Californian informants, and the Kroeber compound on Arch Street in North Berkeley was frequently host to Kroeber's key informants and friends, some of whom lived with the family for weeks at a time (ibid.:158–59). And in the 1950s, at the end of Kroeber's long and distinguished career, he emerged from his normal reticence toward "applied anthropology" to argue the side of California Indians in a major land claims case, *Indians v. the United States of America* (ibid.:221). Although he found the case dispiriting, the Indians did eventually win the suit, and six years after Kroeber's death the Indians were awarded a token sum for their collective losses (Shea 2000:50). Theodora Kroeber (1970) described the land claims case as conceived in white guilt and in bad faith. Eighteen years after the case was first opened, President Johnson authorized a bill that awarded eight hundred dollars to each "properly identified" and "qualified" Indian man, woman, and child alive in the United States in September 1968. It was just the "sort of expensive but meaningless denouement that Kroeber had most feared" (ibid.:223).

Still, it is reasonable to ask what might have been done differently. What options did Kroeber have? Before Ishi became ill might Kroeber have considered broaching the delicate topic of just where and to whom Ishi had been headed when he was caught on the run in Oroville? If it was (as some present-day Maidu Indians believe) to find sanctuary among related native peoples, might not that have been a possible solution? And after Ishi's health began to fail, were the museum and hospital the best places for the man to have been confined? To this day there is a strong investment in the idea that Ishi was a happy man (see Gerald Vizenor's satire [2000:esp. pp. 137–59]) who enjoyed his new life among his white friends, who was charmed by matches, window shades, and other manifestations of the white man's ingenuity, and who was content in his roles of museum janitor and Sunday exhibit. Perhaps he was. But the evidence (see esp. Heizer and T. Kroeber 1979) leans toward another interpretation—that Ishi was simply bone tired of life on the run. The Museum of Anthropology was his end of the line. Although it was not of his choosing, Ishi accepted his final destiny with great patience, good humor, and grace. He was exceptionally learned in the art of waiting.

ISHI'S ASHES

The final chapter in the sad history of Ishi and Berkeley anthropology opened in the spring of 1999 with the "rediscovery" of Ishi's brain, which had languished for three-quarters of a century in a vat of formaldehyde at a Smithsonian warehouse, and the demands of native Californians for its immediate repatriation. Members of the Department of Anthropology at Berkeley differed in their opinions of what, if anything, should be said or done with respect to these developments. A special departmental meeting was held and a compromise statement was ultimately voted and agreed upon. Although falling short of the apology to Northern California Indians that a large number of the faculty had signed after an earlier draft, the final statement concluded:[3]

> We acknowledge our department's role in what happened to Ishi, a man who had already lost all that was dear to him. We strongly urge that the process of returning Ishi's brain to appropriate Native American representatives be speedily accomplished.... We invite the peoples of Native California to instruct us in how we may better serve the needs of their communities through our research related activities. Perhaps, working together, we can ensure that the next millennium will represent a new era in the relationship between indigenous peoples, anthropologists and the public. (March 29, 1999, Department of Anthropology, University of California, Berkeley)

The following words and phrases were deleted from the earlier draft: "What happened to Ishi's body, in the name of science, was a perversion of our core anthropological values. Science proceeds by correcting past error and through a gradual process of critical self-reflection.... We are sorry for our department's role, however unintentional, in the final betrayal of Ishi, a man who had already lost all that was dear to him at the hands of Western colonizers. We recognize that the exploitation and betrayal of Native Americans is still commonplace in American society. The anthropology that emerged in the early 20th century—so-called 'salvage anthropology'—was a human science devoted to 'salvaging' what was left of indigenous peoples and cultures following a national genocide." This longer statement was, however, read by me into the record at a state legislature hearing on the repatriazation of Ishi's remains in Sacramento in April 1999.

Some representatives of the Native Californian communities, such as Art Angle of the Butte County American Indian Cultural Committee, appreciated and accepted the apology, which he recognized as a "big step" for anthropology and for the University of California. Other Indian spokespeople, such as Gerald Vizenor, professor of Native American studies at Berkeley, dismissed the "pained rhetoric" and the apology, which he characterized as "too little and too late." Obviously, the century of mistrust between Indians and anthropologists (see Deloria

364 CRITICAL REFLECTIONS

1988 [1969]; Thomas 2000) rooted in a history of genocide requires, as Vizanor noted, a great deal more than an apology or a scholarly conference. But the return of Ishi's brain from the Smithsonian Institution to representatives of the Pit River tribe on August 8, 2000, closed one sad chapter in the history of anthropology-Indian relations. Perhaps it has also opened the way for more constructive and meaningful engagements between anthropologists and the survivors of U.S. genocides and ethnocides.

Compared with the role that anthropology played in providing a "scientific" rationale and conceptual "tool kit" for the Jewish Holocaust (as described in the unflinching chapters by Arnold and Schafft, this volume), the "little history" of anthropology's complicity in the erasure of the history of the genocides in California or in the reification of Ishi as an object of anthropological analysis might seem minor. But within the conceptual framework that I am proposing here—the genocidal continuum—it is essential not to lose sight of the ease with which the abnormal is normalized and the deaths of our "anthropological subjects" rendered inevitable or routine.

ANTHROPOLOGY AND APARTHEID

Another, and more extreme, instance of the application of anthropological ideas, methods, and concepts to an officially genocidal public policy—one not treated in this volume—is the ideological and applied role that the German-Dutch tradition of cultural anthropology (known in South Africa as *volkekunde*) played in the rationale and design of grand apartheid in South Africa. The idea that people were naturally divided into discrete cultural groups and "populations" based on recognizable differences in physical type, in social organization, in language, and in cultural institutions, along with the key concepts of race, tribe, ethnic group, community, and ethos, were readily drafted into the service of implementing the South African Bantu "homelands," the Group Areas Act (1950), and various other institutions of cultural and racial segregation. These policies were defended by the architects of apartheid as fostering the unique cultural heritage of different "peoples" (see Boonzaier and Sharp 1988). This perverse application of anthropological discourses was a fairly transparent ploy for a ruthless form of white domination and suppression of the black majority, a system that was supported in some Afrikaner universities and departments of anthropology.

Volkekunde provided the blueprint and scientific rationale for apartheid. It was a tradition of anthropology that was inspired both by late-nineteenth-century German ethnology and folklore, *and* by twentieth-century American anthropology, especially that of the Boasian/Kroeberian "school," which integrated biological, linguistic, and cultural anthropology, as well as by the romantic cultural configurationalist "school" of Ruth Benedict. Indeed, Benedict's *Patterns of Culture* was read in some South African circles during the 1970s and 1980s as a romantic Magna Carta for grand apartheid— an argument for the need to preserve highly reified notions of cultural patterns and social distinctions. Afrikaner cultural anthropology, drawing on the tradition of American "culture and personality" studies of the 1950s and early 1960s, provided the National Party government with reductionist theories of culture, community, and basic personality structure that were used to justify the apartheid policy of "parallel" cultural development. American Indian reservations were often cited by apartheid planners as a model for the creation of the hated Bantustands.

Still, it was something of a shock during a visit to the Afrikaner University of the Orange Free State in 1994 to see large photographs of the founding fathers and mothers of American anthropology gracing the walls of the Department of Anthropology there. I wondered what the great antiracist Franz Boas, and the Berkeley ethnographer of the Plains Indians, Robert Lowie, and Alfred Kroeber, the founder of the Berkeley department, and even that irascible mother of us all, Margaret Mead, would have thought about their images being displayed at an institution that had more or less faithfully served the apartheid state in South Africa. The explanation given for their presence was genealogical: both American cultural anthropology and Afrikaner anthropology emerged from the same nineteenth-century tradition of German idealism dedicated to discovering the specific "genius" of each cultural group, a genius that needed to be carefully cultivated and developed according to its own intrinsic values and in its own cultural (and geographical) space. This ideal was the original goal of apartheid as imagined by "the great South African anthropologist" H. F. Verwoerd. In the context of this vexed history I wondered (Scheper-Hughes 1996:344–46) what, if any, role a reinvented and deracinated cultural anthropology might play in the building of a new South Africa.

While one could supply other instances of the misuse of anthropological ideas and practices in fostering structural and political violence, one can also cite far more numerous examples of anthropological ideas and methods used as a tool of human liberation and as a defiant wedge in opposition to state projects of mass killing and genocide. The oppositional and Marxist tradition of social anthropology as it was practiced by some anthropologists at Witswatersrand, the University of Cape Town, and at the University of the Western Cape in South Africa during the apartheid years is one case in point.

The courageous political work of forensic anthropologist Clyde Snow, in collaboration with Mary Clare King, is another example of politically committed anthropology in the face of genocide. Snow helped to organize and train the vital *Equipo Argentino de Antropologia Forense* of Buenos Aires, one of the first groups to use the technology of DNA to identify the remains of the politically disappeared exhumed from mass graves. More recently, these methods have been used to locate and identify the adult children and grandchildren of some of those politically "disappeared" who were adopted by military families during the Argentine "dirty war" (1975–83). Similar work is going on today in Salvador, Guatemala, and Bosnia with the help of applied forensic anthropologists. This new field of politically engaged forensic anthropology has emerged in the past two decades as a potent political and scientific practice in defense of human rights during and after genocides and other mass killings.

If some key anthropological concepts—from Lowie's notion of culture, to Boas's notion of race, to Ruth Benedict's "configurationalism," to Mead's notions of national character—have been perversely applied to advance "scientific racism" and mass killings, these same concepts have been used at other times and places to foster the social and human rights of individuals and of disadvantaged cultural groups. Finally, as this volume illustrates, there are a growing number of anthropologists who have not "missed the revolution" or turned their gaze away from genocides and who have positioned themselves squarely on the side of the victims and survivors of political and ethnic violence in bold attempts to write and act subversively (see Aretxaga 1995; Binford 1996; Borneman 1997; Bourgois 1999; Daniel 1996; Das 1996; Feitlowitz 1998; Feldman 1991; Green 1999; Leyton 1998b; Nelson 1999; Malkki 1995; Pedelty 1995; Quesada, 1998, 1999; Robben 2000; Suarez-Orozco 1987; Swendenburg 1995; Taussig 1987, 1991; Zulaika 1988).

THE MODERNITY OF GENOCIDE

Bauman's (1991) controversial thesis linking genocide to a specific level of state formation, technological efficiency, rationality, and subjectivity is belied in many of the ethnographic examples provided by contributors to this volume. Although the legal concept of genocide is new, the "eliminationist" impulse can be found under premodern as well as modern and late-modern conditions. A spiritual charter for genocide can be found in Genesis when God the Creator turns into God the destroyer of humankind in an expression of genocidal fury. The God of the desert Hebrews willed a flood to destroy all evidence of human life (save Noah and his family). The destruction of Sodom and Gomorra is another biblical prototype of mass killing, as is King Herod's decree ordering the destruction of all first-born infant sons in Judea. In these scriptural accounts God is constructed in the problematic image and likeness of man.

Genocides and mass killings have been attributed to "weak states" (Bayart 1993; Reno 1998) and to statelessness, for example, in Robert Kaplan's (1994) controversial and contested "coming of anarchy" thesis with reference to the chaos and violence that has marked postcolonial equatorial Africa (especially, Angola and Sierra Leone), and which Totten, Parsons, and Hichcock (this volume) have rather surprisingly and uncritically embraced. Conversely, genocides have also been linked to strong, authoritarian, and bureaucratically efficient states, such as Germany at mid-twentieth century (Goldhagen 1997; Arendt 1963). And genocides have been linked to anomic individualism and, at other times and places, to communalism and its demands for obedience and human sacrifice (Gourvitch 1998:33–34; Zulaika 1988).

Witch-hunts and witch burnings in parts of Africa and highland New Guinea have led in some small-scale and premodern societies to forms of demographic collapse that could be viewed as alternative examples of political genocide. The impulse to identify and eliminate all witches, seen as disease objects in given societies, is motivated by the same kind of "social hygiene" thinking characteristic of genocide in modern states. Massacres and mass killings that have sometimes resulted in the die-outs of entire populations of indigenous peoples living in isolated bands by small groups of bounty hunters, gold prospectors, and white or mixed-race settlers seem far removed from the kinds of "modernity" referred to in Bauman's thesis. Indeed, mass killing, genocides, and provoked die-outs of scapegoated populations have occurred in prestate societies, and in ancient as well as modern states.

Uli Linke (this volume), writing in the Weberian tradition, sees the Holocaust, as do Hannah Arendt (1963) and Daniel Goldhagen (1997), as a kind of mad triumph of rational efficiency, a distorted end product of the increasing rationalization of social life. Recently, Agamben (1999) identified the modern concentration camp as the prototype of late-modern biopolitics in its creation of a population of "living dead" people, those whose bodies and lives can be taken by the state at will or at whim, neither for (religious) sacrifice nor for crimes committed (capital punishment), but merely because of their "availability" for execution.

Hence the Holocaust is something of a misnomer. It is not about religion or about bodies that have been "sacrificed" as burnt offerings to placate the gods. Rather, if Agambem is correct, modern forms of genocide are about actualizing the capacity and availability of certain vulnerable populations for mass killings, a dangerous theory that is reminiscent of Arendt's condemnation of the collaboration of Jewish leaders with the Nazis. Despite this, as Agamben and Foucault recognize, the body is at the heart of modern biopolitics, as it is, of course, to the racist rationales for genocide, as it was in Germany (see Linke, this volume) and in Rwanda (see Taylor, this volume).

With the shocking reappearance of genocides and other mass killings in the late twentieth century—in Africa (Malkki 1995), South Asia (Das 1996; Daniel 1997), and Eastern Europe (Olujic 1998), in Central and South America (Green 1999; Suarez-Oroxco 1987; Robben 2000)—anthropologists have been witness to the recurrence of what moderns once thought, following the Holocaust, could not happen again. In Central and South America during "dirty wars" and military-sponsored "social hygiene," the eliminations of despised populations were enacted through techniques and practices of torture that could hardly be described as "modern."

The apartheid government's security forces reinvented "primitive" witch burnings, and they discarded their political enemies by slowly burning them—sometimes while still alive—over barbecue pits (see Scheper-Hughes 1998). And the Brazilian and Argentinean military's "parrot's perch" torture resembled nothing so much as a technique of the Inquisition. True, the Argentine military did use modern planes to dispose of, by air drops into the sea, the dead bodies produced by their medieval tortures, and Rwandan "genocidaires" relied heavily on the mass media, radio in particular, to mobilize the Hutu killers in "barbarous" acts of cruelty (see Gourvitch 1998). Meanwhile, the presumably modern invention of political "disappearances" is spoken about by the terrorized populations subject to these roundups for mass slaying in the premodern idiom of "body snatching," "blood and organ stealing," and ritual killings.

What kinds of modernity do the genocides in Cambodia, Rwanda, and Burundi represent? Characteristic of all of them is the "corporeal imaginary" that Linke and Taylor (this volume) address—the obsessive focus on the body—on blood and genealogy to be sure, but also on defining phenotypes and body types—the particular shape and length of heads, arms, legs, buttocks, hair, and lips, the race-mad "corporeal imaginary" of the late-modern world.

In light of these recent atrocities we are forced to revisit the question that so vexed a generation of post-Holocaust social theorists: *What makes genocide possible?* What, after all, can we say about anthropos? What are its limits and its capacities? And how do we explain the complicity of ordinary people, the proverbial and necessary bystanders, to new outbreaks of genocidal violence? Adorno and the post–World War II Frankfurt School suggested that participation in genocidal acts requires a strong childhood conditioning that produces almost mindless obedience to authority figures. More recently Goldhagen (1997) argued, to the contrary, that thousands of ordinary Germans participated willingly, even eagerly, in the Holocaust, not for fear of punishment or retribution by authority figures but because they *chose*, sometimes eagerly, to do so, guided by race hatred alone.

Nonetheless, modern theorists of genocide have proposed certain prerequisites necessary to mass participation in genocides. Indeed, mass killings rarely appear on the scene unbidden. They evolve. There are identifiable starting points or instigating circumstances. Genocides are often preceded, for example, by social upheavals, a radical decline in economic conditions, political disorganization, or sociocultural changes leading to a loss in traditional values and anomie. Conflict between competing groups over concrete and material resources—land and water—can escalate into desperate mass killings when combined with social sentiments that question or denigrate the humanity of the opposing group. Extreme forms of us-vs.-them can result in a social self-identity predicated on a stigmatized, devalued notion of the other as a-less-than-human enemy. The German example has alerted a generation of post–World War II scholars to the danger of social conformity and the absence of dissent. More recently, the conflict in the Middle East, in the former Yugoslavia, and in many postcolonial societies of sub-Saharan Africa suggests that a history of social suffering and woundedness, especially a history of racial victimization, leads to a vulnerability to mass violence. A kind of collective posttraumatic stress disorder may predispose certain "wounded" populations to a hypervigilance that can lead to another cycle of "self-defensive" mass killings and genocide.

Ritual sacrifice and the search to identify a generative scapegoat—a social class or ethnic or racial group on which to pin the blame for the social and economic problems that arise—are also common preconditions in the evolution of genocide. Finally, there must be a shared ideology, a blueprint for living, a vision of the world and how to live that defines certain obstacles to the good or holy life in the form of certain kinds of people who must be removed, eliminated, wiped out. There is the belief that everyone will benefit from this social cleansing, even the dead themselves.

Finally, there must be a broad constituency of *bystanders* who either (as in the case of white South Africa) simply "allow" adverse and hostile policies to continue affecting the targeted victims without massive forms of civil disobedience or (as in Nazi Germany and in Rwanda) can be recruited to participate in acts of genocidal violence. But less well analyzed is the role of external or global "bystanders," including strong nation-states and international and nongovernmental agencies such as the United Nations, whose delays or refusals to intervene can aid and abet genocides at a time when the tide could still be reversed. In the case of Rwanda, for example, U.N. peace-keepers were explicitly instructed to do nothing. Similarly, during the Holocaust and during the worst phases of apartheid's program of political terror, a great many U.S. corporations continued to do business with the perpetrators of mass violence. The origins and evolution of genocide are complex and multifaceted, but they are not inscrutable or unpredictable.

PEACETIME CRIMES—THE GENOCIDE CONTINUUM

I have suggested a genocide continuum (see Scheper-Hughes 1997, 2001) made up of a multitude of "small wars and invisible genocides" conducted in the normative social spaces of public schools, clinics, emergency rooms, hospital wards, nursing homes, court rooms, prisons, detention centers, and public morgues. The continuum refers to the human capacity to reduce others to nonpersons, to monsters, or to things that gives structure, meaning, and rationale to everyday practices of violence. It is essential that we recognize in our species (and in ourselves) *a genocidal capacity* and that we exercise a defensive hypervigilance, a hypersensitivity to the less dramatic, *permitted,* everyday acts of violence that make participation (under other conditions) in genocidal acts possible, perhaps more easy than we would like to know. I would include all expressions of social exclusion, dehumanization, depersonalization, pseudo-speciation, and reification that normalize atrocious behavior and violence toward others. A constant self-mobilization for alarm, a state of constant hyperarousal is a reasonable response to Benjamin's view of late-modern history as a chronic "state of emergency."

I realize that in referring to a genocide continuum I am walking on thin ice. The concept flies directly in the face of a tradition of genocide studies that argues for the absolute uniqueness of the Jewish Holocaust, for example, and for vigilance with respect to a careful and restricted use of the term *genocide* itself (see Kuper 1885; Chaulk 1999; Fein 1990; Chorbajian 1999). But I share with Carole Nagengast (this volume) the alternative view that we *must* make just such existential leaps in drawing comparisons between violent acts in normal and in abnormal times. If there is a moral risk in overextending the concept of "genocide" into spaces and corners of everyday life where we might not ordinarily think to find it (and there is), an even greater risk lies in failing to sensitize ourselves, in misrecognizing protogenocidal practices and sentiments daily enacted as normative behavior by "ordinary" good enough people.

Here Pierre Bourdieu's partial and unfinished theory of violence is useful. By including the normative, everyday forms of violence hidden in the minutia of "normal" social practices—in the architecture of homes, in gender relations, in communal work, in the exchange of gifts, and so forth—Bourdieu forces us to reconsider the broader meanings and status of violence, especially the links between the violence of everyday life and explicit political terror.

Similarly, Franco Basaglia's notion of "peace-time crimes"—*crimini di pace*—imagines a direct relationship between wartime and peacetime, between war crimes and peace crimes. Here, war crimes might be seen as the ordinary violence, crimes of public consent, when they are applied systematically and dramatically in times of war and overt genocide. Peacetime crimes force us to consider the parallel uses and meanings of rape during peacetime and wartime as well as the family resemblances between border raids and physical assaults by official INS agents on Mexican and Central American refugees, as described by Carole Nagengast (this volume), and earlier state-sponsored genocides such as the Cherokee Indians' forced exile, their "Trail of Tears."

Everyday forms of state violence—peacetime crimes—make a certain kind of domestic "peace" possible. In the United States (and especially in California), the phenomenal growth of a new military, postindustrial prison complex has taken place in the absence of broad-based opposition. How many public executions of mentally deficient murderers are needed to make life feel more secure for the affluent? How many new maximum-security prisons are needed to contain an expanding population of young black and Latino men cast as "public enemies"? Ordinary peacetime crimes such as the steady evolution of American prisons into alternative black concentration camps constitute the "small wars and invisible genocides" to which I refer. So do the youth mortality rates in Oakland, California, and in New York City. These are invisible genocides not because they are secreted away or hidden from view but quite the opposite. As Wittgenstein observed, the things that are hardest to perceive are those that are right before our eyes and taken for granted.

In light of these phenomena we would do well to recover the classic anagogic thinking that enabled Erving Goffman and Jules Henry (as well as Franco Basaglia) to perceive the logical relations between concentration camps and mental hospitals, nursing homes, and other "total" institutions, and between prisoners and mental patients. This allows us to see the capacity and the willingness of ordinary people—society's "practical technicians"—to enforce, at other times, "genocidal"-like crimes against classes and types of people thought of as waste, as rubbish, as "deficient" in humanity, as "better off dead" or even as better off never having been born. The mad, the disabled, the mentally deficient have often fallen into this category, as have the very old and infirm, the sick-poor, and despised racial, religious, and ethnic groups. Erik Erikson referred to "pseudo-speciation" as the human tendency to classify some individuals or social groups as less than fully human—a necessary prerequisite to genocide and one that is carefully honed during the unremarkable peacetimes that can precede the sudden, and only seemingly unintelligible, outbreaks of genocide.

Denial is a prerequisite of mass violence and genocide. In *Death without Weeping* (1993), I explored the social indifference to staggering infant and child mortality in shantytown *favelas* of Northeast Brazil. Local political leaders, Catholic priests and nuns, coffin makers, and shantytown mothers themselves casually dispatched a multitude of hungry "angel-babies" to the afterlife each year, saying: "Well, they *themselves* wanted to die." The babies were described as having no "taste," no "knack," and no "talent" for life.

Medical practices such as prescribing powerful tranquilizers to fretful and frightfully hungry babies, Catholic ritual celebrations of the death of "angel-babies," and the bureaucratic indifference in political leaders' dispensing free baby coffins but no food to hungry families and children interacted with maternal practices such as radically reducing food and liquids to severely malnourished and dehydrated babies so as to help them, their mothers said, to die quickly and well. Perceived as already "doomed," sickly infants were described as less than human creatures, as ghostly angel-babies, inhabiting a terrain midway between life and death. "Really and truly," mothers said, "it is better that these spirit-children return to where they came."

The ability of desperately poor women to help those infants who (they said) "needed to die" required an existential "letting go" (contrasted to the maternal work of holding on, holding close, and holding dear). Letting go required a leap of faith that was not easy to achieve. And these largely Catholic women often said that their infants died just as Jesus died so that others—especially themselves—could live. The question that lingered, unresolved, in my mind was whether this Kierkegaardian "leap of faith" entailed a certain Marxist "bad faith" as well.

I did not want to blame shantytown mothers for putting their own survival over and above that of their infants and small babies, for these were moral choices that no person should be forced to make. But they resulted in "bad faith" whenever the women refused authorship of their acts and blamed the deaths of their "angel-babies" on the desire and willingness of the doomed infants themselves. I gradually came to think of the shantytown angel-babies in terms of Rene Girard's (1987) idea of sacrificial violence. The given-up, given-up-on babies had been sacrificed in the face of terrible conflicts about scarcity and survival. And it was here, for example, that peacetime and wartime, maternal thinking and military thinking, converged. When angels (or martyrs) are fashioned from the dead bodies of those who die young, "maternal thinking" most resembles military, especially wartime, thinking. On the battlefield as in the shantytown, triage, thinking in sets, and a belief in the magical replaceability of the dead predominate.

Above all, ideas of "acceptable death" and of "meaningful" (rather than useless) suffering extinguish rage and grief for those whose lives are taken and allow for the recruitment of new lives and new bodies into the struggle. Just as shantytown mothers in Brazil consoled each other that their hungry babies died because they were "meant" to die or because they "had" to die, Northern Irish mothers and South African township mothers have consoled each other at political wakes and funerals during wartime and in times of political struggle with the belief that their sacrificed and "martyred" children died purposefully and died well. This kind of thinking is not exclusive to any particular class of people. Whenever humans attribute some meaning—whether political or spiritual—to the useless suffering of others we all behave, I have argued, a bit like public executioners.

Similarly, the existence of two childhoods in Brazil—"my" child (middle class, beloved, a child of family and home) versus the hated "street child" (the child of the other, unwanted and unwashed) has given rise in the late twentieth century to police and death squad attacks that are genocidal in their social and political sentiments. "Street children" are often described as "dirty vermin" so that unofficial policies of "street cleaning," "trash removal," "fly swatting," and "pest removal" are invoked in garnering broad-based public support for their extermination.

The term *street child* reflects the preoccupations of one class and segment of Brazilian society with the proper place of another. The term represents a kind of symbolic apartheid as urban space has become increasingly "privatized." As long as poor, "dirty" street children are contained to the slum or the favela, where they "belong," they are not viewed as an urgent social problem about which something must be done. The real issue is the preoccupation of one social class with the "proper place" of another social class. Like dirt, which is "clean" when it is in the yard and "dirty" when it is under the nails, "dirty" street children are simply children out of place. In Brazil the street is an unbounded and dangerous realm, the space of the "masses" (*o povo*), where one can be treated anonymously. Rights belong to the realm of the "home." Street children, barefoot, shirtless, and unattached to a home, represent the extreme of social marginality. They occupy a particularly degraded social position within the Brazilian hierarchy of place and power. As denizens of the street, these semiautonomous kids are separated from all that can confer relationship and propriety, without which rights and citizenship are impossible.

In the cohort of forty semiautonomous, mostly homeless street children in the interior market town of Bom Jesus in Pernambuco that I have been studying since 1982, twenty-two of the original group are dead. Some were killed by police in acts designated as "legitimate homicides"; others were killed by death squads and hired guns, some of them by former street children themselves. Others are "disappeared" and suspected dead. Among the survivors a third are in jail, or released from jail, and some of these have already become killers, recruited by off-duty police and by corrupt judges to help clear the streets of their own social class. And so the cycle of violence turns, with children killing children, urged on by the so-called forces of state law and order.

But we need go no further than our own medical clinics, emergency rooms, public hospitals, and old age homes to encounter other classes of "rubbish people" treated with as much indifference and malevolence as "street kids" in some parts of South America. As ever increasing numbers of the aged are both sick and poor because of the astronomical cost of late-life medical care, they are at risk of spending their remaining time in public or less expensive private institutions for the aged, where the care of residents is delegated to grossly underpaid and undertrained workers. Economic pressures are strong and bear down on staff to minimize the personal care and attention given to the residents, especially those whose limited savings have already been used up by the institution and who are now supported by Medicare. And so, nursing home staff often protect themselves by turning the persons and bodies under their protection into things, into bulky objects that can be dealt with in shorter and shorter intervals.

When the body is rolled from one side or the other for cleaning or to clean the sheets [body and sheets are equated]; or when the resident is wheeled conveniently into a corner so that the floor can be more easily mopped; when cleaning staff do little to suppress expressions of disgust at urine, feces, or phlegm out of place—on clothing, under the nails, on wheelchairs, or in waste paper baskets—the person trapped inside the failing body may also come to see themselves as "dirty," "vile," "disgusting"—as an object or nonperson. An essay by Jules Henry (1966) on "Hospitals for the Aged Poor," documenting the attack on the elderly individual's dwindling stock of personal and psychological "capital" by unconscious hospital and nursing home staff, is as true today as when it was first written.

The institutional destruction of personhood is aided by the material circumstances of the nursing home. When all personal objects—toothbrush, comb, glasses, towels, pens and pencils—continue to disappear no matter how many times they have been replaced, the resident (if he or she knows what is good for him or her) finally accepts the situation and adapts in other ways. Eventually, residents are compelled to use other objects, which are more available, for purposes for which they were never intended. The plastic wastepaper basket becomes the urinal, the urinal the wash basin, the water glass turns into a spittoon, the hated adult diaper is used defiantly for a table napkin, and so forth. Meanwhile, the institutional violence and indifference are masked as the resident's own state of mental confusion and incompetence. And everything in the nature of the institution invites the resident to further regression, to give up, to lose, to accept his or her inevitable and less than human, depersonalized status. But where are the forces of liberation or a "human rights watch" responding to invisible genocides in such normative institutions (of caring) as these?

The point of my bringing into the discourses on genocide such everyday, normative experiences of reification, depersonalization, and acceptable death is to help answer the question: What makes genocide possible? I am suggesting here that genocide is part of a continuum, and that it is socially incremental and often experienced by perpetrators, collaborators, bystanders—and even by victims themselves—as expected, routine, even justified.

In all, the preparation for mass killing can be found in social sentiments and institutions from the family, to schools, churches, hospitals, and the military. The early "warning signs" (see also Charney 1991), the "priming" (as Hinton, this volume, calls it), or the "genocidal continuum" (as I call it) refers to an evolving social consensus toward *devaluing certain forms of human life* and lifeways (via pseudo-speciation, dehumanization, reification, and depersonalization); *the refusal of social support and humane care* to vulnerable and stigmatized social groups seen as social parasites ("nursing home elderly," "welfare queens," "illegal aliens," "Gomers," etc.); *the militarization of everyday life* (for example, the growth of prisons, the acceptance of capital punishment, heightened technologies of personal security, such as the house gun and gated communities); *social polarization and fear* (that is, the perceptions of the poor, outcast, underclass, or certain racial or ethnic groups as dangerous public enemies); *reversed feelings of victimization* as dominant social groups and classes demand violent policing to put offending groups in their place.

GETTING OVER

Remorse, reconciliation, and reparation have emerged as master narratives of the late twentieth century/early twenty-first century as individuals and entire nations struggle to overcome the legacies of suffering ranging from rape and domestic violence to collective atrocities of state-sponsored dirty wars, genocides, and ethnic cleansings. Several chapters in this volume (but especially those by Linke, Ebihara and Ledgerwood, Manz, and Magnarella) discuss individual and collective attempts at reconciliation and healing, the repair of fractured bodies, broken lives, and destroyed societies after the facts of genocide.

Linke presents us with a terrifying proposition—the irreversibility, the impossibility of undoing so massive a wound as the Jewish Holocaust for new generations of German youth, the children and grandchildren of perpetrators, bystanders, and, one can hope, a few just men and women. There seems to be no exit, no escape, from that spoiled history that continues to return, like the repressed, to haunt German youth trying to reinvent themselves and to free themselves from inherited, generational guilt and complicity. They seem altogether trapped by that history, when youth culture embraces nudity as transparency and as innocence but which also bears striking resemblances to the Nazi youth cults of the forest, the natural, the German heroic. And the childlike display of unfettered nudity is seen by Linke as a cruel, though surely unintended, parody of "naked life" in the concentration camps.

In marked contrast, Ebihara and Ledgerwood present an almost uncomplicated picture of community recovery in rural Cambodia in the mere two decades following the Pol Pot regime. That which was destroyed—from Buddhism to subsistence-based peasant farming—appears to have returned relatively unscathed, while extreme demographic imbalances—the virtual absence of men in rural villages—is being corrected. Perhaps it is too soon in the history of the Khmer Rouge to assess the real damages that may, as in the German instance, return to haunt subsequent generations. It is for this reason that many recovering nations and wounded populations—from post–military dictatorship Chile to postapartheid South Africa to postgenocide Rwanda (see Magnarella, this volume)—have put their faith in international tribunals or in independent truth commissions to deal with burying the ghosts of the past. At times this has meant uncovering mass graves and re-

burying the unquiet dead. At other times—as in the South African Truth and Reconciliation Commission (based on the experience of Chile)—this has meant a complicated political gamble in which justice is traded for truth telling.

Finally, what special contributions can anthropology make to the interdisciplinary discourses on mass violence and genocide? The postcolonial critiques of
anthropological ways of seeing and knowing have resulted in a relentless form of
institutional and professional self-analysis. It is one thing to rethink one's basic epis-
temology, as many social sciences have done under the spell of deconstructionism.
It is quite another to rethink one's way of being and acting in and on the world.
Anthropologists have been asked to transform their central and defining practice
of fieldwork and to decolonize themselves and reimagine new relations to their anthropological subjects, some the victims and others the perpetrators of genocide
and mass killings.

The irony is that cultural anthropology is all about meaning, about making sense
in a world that is so often absurd. Can one "make sense" of mass violence and genocide? In recent years an anthropology of suffering has emerged as a new kind of
theodicy, a cultural inquiry into the ways that people attempt to explain, account
for, and justify the presence of pain, death, affliction, evil in the world (see Kleinman and Kleinman 1997; Farmer 1996). But the quest to make sense of suffering
and chaotic violence is as old as Job, and as fraught with moral ambiguity for the
anthropologist-as-witness as it was for the companions of Job who demanded an
explanation compatible with their own views of a just God (for secularists, a just
world). As Geertz pointed out many years ago, the one thing humans seem unable
to accept is the idea that the world may be ultimately deficient in meaning.

The gift of the ethnographer remains some combination of thick description,
eyewitnessing, and radical juxtaposition based on cross-cultural insight. But the
rules of our living-in and living-with peoples on the verge of extermination remain
as yet unwritten, perhaps even unspoken. What, during periods of genocide or ethnocide, is an appropriate distance to take from our subjects? What kinds of "par-
ticipant-observation," what sorts of eyewitnessing are adequate to the scenes of
genocide and its aftermath? When the anthropologist is witness to crimes against
humanity, is mere scientific empathy sufficient? At what point does the anthropologist as eyewitness become a bystander or even a coconspirator?

Although these remain vexing and unresolved issues, the original mandate of
anthropology and ethnography remains clear: to put ourselves and our discipline
squarely on the side of humanity, world-saving, and world-repair, even when we
are not always certain exactly what that means or what is being asked of us at a
particular moment in the fraught lives of our friends, research subjects, and informants. In the final analysis we can only hope that our time-honored methods
of empathic and engaged witnessing—a "being with" and "being there"—as tired
as those old concepts may seem—will provide us with the tools necessary for anthropology to grow and develop as a "little practice" of human liberation.

NOTES

1. During a lively debate at the American Anthropological Association meetings several years ago, the late Paul Riesman concluded that when anthropologists try to intervene in critical situations (of life and death) in the field they betray their discipline, and they/we: "leave anthropology behind... because we abandon what I [Paul Riesman] believe to be a fundamental axiom of the creed we [anthropologists] all share, namely that all humans are equal in the sight of anthropology.... Once we identify an evil, I think we give up trying to understand the situation as a human reality. Instead we see it as in some sense inhuman, and all we try to understand is how best to combat it. At this point we leave anthropology behind and enter the political process." This point of view is contested. One contrary example is provided by the several anthropologists who contributed to the volume *Sanctions for Evil* (Nevitt Sanford and Craig Comstack, eds., 1971), a project sponsored by the Wright Institute at Berkeley, largely in response to the My Lai massacre during the American-Vietnam War.

2. In a letter to the commissioner of Indian Affairs, a government agent, Adam Johnson (cited by Castillo 1978:107) reported the following with respect to the "Indian wars" in California: "The majority of the tribes are kept in constant fear on account of the indiscriminate and inhuman massacre of their people for real or supposed injuries. They have become alarmed about the increased flood of [settlers].... [It] was just incomprehensible to them.... I have seldom heard of a single difficulty between the whites and the Indians in which the original cause could not be traced to some rash or reckless act of the former."

3. At a regular faculty meeting on March 29, 1999, the Department of Anthropology voted to issue the following statement on Ishi's brain:

> The recent recovery of a famous California Indian's brain from a Smithsonian warehouse has led the Department of Anthropology at the University of California Berkeley to revisit and reflect on a troubling chapter of our history. Ishi, whose family and cultural group, the Yahi Indians, were murdered as part of the genocide that characterized the influx of western settlers to California, lived out his last years at the original museum of anthropology at the University of California. He served as an informant to one of our department's founding members, Alfred Kroeber, as well as to other local and visiting anthropologists. The nature of the relationships between Ishi and the anthropologists and linguists who worked with him for some five years at the museum were complex and contradictory. Despite Kroeber's lifelong devotion to California Indians and his friendship with Ishi, he failed in his efforts to honor Ishi's wishes not to be autopsied and he inexplicably arranged for Ishi's brain to be shipped to and to be curated at the Smithsonian. We acknowledge our department's role in what happened to Ishi, a man who had already lost all that was dear to him. We strongly urge that the process of returning Ishi's brain to appropriate Native American representatives be speedily accomplished. We are considering various ways to pay honor and respect to Ishi's memory. We regard public participation as a necessary component of these discussions and in particular we invite the peoples of Native California to instruct us in how we may better serve the needs of their communities through our research related activities. Perhaps, working together, we can ensure that the next millennium will represent a new era in the relationship between indigenous peoples, anthropologists, and the public.

REFERENCES CITED

Agamben, Giorgio. 1999. *Remnants of Auschwitz.* New York: Zone Books.
Arendt, Hannah. 1963. *Eichmann in Jerusalem: A Report on the Banality of Evil.* New York: Viking Press.

————. 1969. *On Violence.* New York: Harcourt, Brace and World.

Aretxaga, Begona. 1995. "Dirty Protest: Symbolic Overdetermination and Gender in Northern Ireland Ethnic Violence." *Ethos* 23(2):123–48.

Basaglia, Franco. 1987, "Institutions of Violence." *Psychiatry Inside Out: Selected Writings of Franco Basaglia.* Nancy Scheper-Hughes, ed. Pp. 59–85. New York: Columbia University Press.

Bauman, Zygmunt. 1989. *Modernity and the Holocaust.* Ithaca: Cornell University Press.

Bayart, Jean-Francois. 1993. "The Politics of the Belly." In *The State in Africa: The Politics of the Belly.* Pp. 228–59. London: Longman.

Binford, Leigh. 1996. *The El Mozote Massacre.* Tucson: University of Arizona Press.

Blanchor, Maurice. *The Writing of the Disaster.* Lincoln: University of Nebraska Press.

Boonzaier, Emile, and John Sharp. 1988. *South African Key Words.* Cape Town, South Africa: Phillips.

Borneman, John. 1997. *Settling Accounts: Violence, Justice, and Accountability in Postsocialist Europe.* Princeton: Princeton University Press.

Bourdieu, Pierre, and Loic Waquant. 1992. *Invitation to Reflexive Sociology.* Chicago: University of Chicago Press.

Bourgois, Philippe. 1995. *In Search of Respect: Selling Crack in El Barrio.* New York: Cambridge University Press.

————. 1999. "Reconfronting Violence in El Salvador and the U.S. Inner City with a Cold War Hangover." Paper presented to the Society for Cultural Anthropology. San Francisco, May 1999.

Buckley, Thomas. 1989a. "Kroeber's Theory of Culture Areas and the Ethnology of Northwestern California." *Anthropological Quarterly* 62(1):15–26.

————. 1989b. "Suffering in the Cultural Construction of Others: Robert Spott and A. L. Kroeber." *American Indian Quarterly* 13(4):437–45.

————. 1996. " 'The Little History of Pitiful Events': The Epistemological and Moral Contexts of Kroeber's Californian Ethnology." In *Volkgeist as Method and Ethic: Essays on Boasian Ethnography and the German Anthropological Tradition.* History of Anthropology Series, vol. 8. George Stocking, ed. Madison: University of Wisconsin Press.

Camus, Albert. 1960. "The Artist and His Time." In *Resistance, Rebellion and Death.* Pp. 181–89. New York: Alfred A. Knopf.

Charny, Israel. 1999. "Toward a Generic Definition of Genocide." In *Studies in Comparative Genocide.* L. Chorbajian and G. Shirinian, eds. Pp. 64–93. New York: St. Martin's Press.

Chaulk, Frank. 1999. "Redefining Genocide." In *Studies in Comparative Genocide.* L. Chorbajain and G. Shirinian, eds. Pp. 47–63. New York: St. Martin's Press.

Chorbajian, Levon. 1999. "Introduction." In *Studies in Comparative Genocide.* L. Chorbajain and G. Shirinian, eds. New York: St. Martin's Press.

Churchill, Ward. 1997. *A Little Matter of Genocide: Holocaust and Denial in the Americas: 1492 to the Present.* San Francisco: City Lights Books.

Cohn, Carol. 1987. "Sex and Death in the Rational World of Defense Intellectuals." In *Signs* 12(4):687–718.

Cook, Sherburne F. 1978. "Historical Demography." In Heizer, ed. Pp. 91–98.

Daniel, Valentine. 1996. *Charred Lullabies.* Princeton: Princeton University Press.

Darnell, R. 1969. "The Development of American Anthropology 1879–1920." Doctoral dissertation, University of Pennsylvania.

Das, Veena. 1996. "Language and Body: Transactions in the Construction of Pain." *Daedalus* 125(1):67–92.

Deloria, Vine. 1988 [1969]. *Custer Died for Your Sins*. Norman: University of Oklahoma Press.

Devereux, George. 1961. "Mohave Ethnopsychiatry and Suicide." Smithsonian Institution, Bureau of American Ethnology, Bulletin No. 175, Washington, D.C.

Eargle, Dolan. 2000. *Native California Guide: Weaving the Past and Present*. San Francisco: Trees Company Press.

Edgerton, Robert B. 1992. *Sick Societies: Challenging the Myth of Primitive Harmony*. New York: Free Press.

Fanon, Frantz. 1963. "Colonial Wars and Mental Disorders." In *Wretched of the Earth*. Pp. 254–316. New York: Grove Press.

Farmer, Paul. 1996. "On Suffering and Structural Violence: A View from Below." *Daedalus* 125(1):245–60.

Fein, Helen. 1990. "Genocide—A Sociological Perspective." *Current Sociology* 38:23–35.

Feitlowitz, Marguerite. 1998. *A Lexicon of Terror: Argentina and the Legacies of Torture*. New York: Oxford University Press.

Feldman, Alan. 1991. *Formations of Violence: The Narrative of the Body and Political Terror in Northern Ireland*. Chicago: University of Chicago Press.

Finnagan, William. 1992. *A Complicated War: The Harrowing of Mozambique*. Berkeley: University of California Press.

Foucault, Michel. 1979. *Discipline and Punish: The Birth of the Prison*. New York: Vintage Books.

Freud, Sigmund. 1957. "Mourning and Melancholia." In *The Standard Edition of the Complete Psychological Works of Sigmund Freud*. Vol. 14, pp. 243–58. London: Hogarth.

Geertz, Clifford. 1995. *After the Fact*. Cambridge: Harvard University Press.

Girard, René. 1987. "Generative Scapegoating." In *Violent Origins*. R. Hameram-Kelly, ed. Pp. 73–105. Stanford: Stanford University Press.

Gladwell, Malcom. 1996. "The Tipping Point." *New Yorker*, June 3, 1996.

Goffman, Erving. 1961. *Asylums*. New York: Doubleday.

Goldhagen, Daniel Jonah. 1997. *Hitler's Willing Executioners: Ordinary Germans and the Holocaust*. New York: Vintage Books.

Gourvitch, Philip. 1998. *We Wish to Inform You That Tomorrow We Will Be Killed with Our Families*. New York: Farrar, Strauss and Giroux.

Green, Linda. 1999. *Fear as a Way of Life*. New York: Columbia University Press.

Heizer, Robert F. 1978. *California*. Vol. 8. Washington: Smithsonian Institution.

Heizer, Robert F., and Theodora Kroeber. 1979. *Ishi the Last Yahi: A Documentary History*. Berkeley: University of California Press.

Henry, Jules. 1966. "Hospitals for the Aged Poor." In *Sham, Vulnerability and Other Forms of Self-Destruction*. New York: Vintage.

Herman, Judith. 1992. *Trauma and Recovery*. New York: Basic Books.

Hinton, Leanne. 1999. "Ishi's Brain." *News from Native California* 13(1): 4–9.

Hrdlicka, A. 1931. "The Most Ancient Skeletal Remains of Man." In *Source Book in Anthropology*. Kroeber and Waterman, eds. Pp. 43–66. New York: Harcourt, Brace and Company.

Jacknis, Ira. 2000. "From Performance to Record: Ishi's Music and Speech." Paper presented at the international conference "Who Owns the Body," University of California, Berkeley, September 20–23.

James, Wendy. 1973. "The Anthropologist as Reluctant Imperialist." In *Anthropology and the Colonial Encounter*. T. Asad, ed. Pp. 41–69. New York: Humanities Press.

Jaspers, Karl. 1961. *The Question of German Guilt.* New York: Capricorn Books.

Kaplan, Robert. 1994. "The Coming of Anarchy." *Atlantic Monthly* (February):44–76.

Kleinman, Arthur, and Joan Kleinman. 1997. "The Appeal of Experience; the Dismay of Images: Cultural Appropriations of Suffering in Our Times." In *Social Suffering.* A. Kleinman, V. Das, and M. Lock, eds. Berkeley: University of California Press.

Klinenberg, Eric. 1999. "Denaturalizing Disaster: A Social Autopsy of the 1995 Chicago Heat Wave." *Theory and Society* 28:239–95.

Kroeber, Alfred L. 1911a. "The Elusive Mill Creeks: A Band of Wild Indians Roaming in Northern California Today." *Travel* 17(4):510–13, 548, 550. New York.

———. 1911b. "Ishi, the Last Aborigine." *World's Work Magazine* 24(3):304–8. New York.

———. 1917. "The Superorganic." *American Anthropologist* 19:163–213.

———. 1925. "Handbook of the Indians of California." Smithsonian Institution. Bureau of American Ethnology. Bulletin 78. Government Printing Office. Washington, D.C.

———. 1939. *Cultural and Natural Areas of Native North America.* Berkeley: University of California Press.

———. 1948a. *Anthropology: Race, Language, Culture, Psychology and Prehistory.* New York: Harcourt, Brace and World.

———. 1948b. "My Faith." In *The Faith of Great Scientists: A Collection from the American Weekly.* Pp. 22–24. New York: Hearst Pub. Co.

———. 1952. *The Nature of Culture.* Chicago: University of Chicago Press.

———. 1972a. *The Mill Creek Indians and Ishi—Early Reports by A. L. Kroeber.* Berkeley: University of California Printing Department. [Reprint of 1911 articles.]

———. 1972b. *More Mohave Myths.* Anthropological Records. Vol. 27. Berkeley: University of California Press.

———. 1976. *Yurok Myths.* Berkeley: University of California Press.

Kroeber, A. L., and T. R. Waterman. 1931. *Source Book in Anthropology.* Rev. ed. New York: Harcourt, Brace and Company.

Kroeber, Theodora. 1961. *Ishi in Two Worlds.* Berkeley: University of California Press.

———. 1964. *Ishi, Last of His Tribe.* Berkeley: Parnassus Press.

———. 1970. *Alfred Kroeber: A Personal Configuration.* Berkeley: University of California Press.

Krog, Antjie. 1998. *Country of My Skull.* South Africa: Random House.

Kuper, Leo. 1982. *Genocide: Its Political Use in the Twentieth Century.* New Haven: Yale University Press.

———. 1985. *The Prevention of Genocide.* New Haven: Yale University Press.

Lévi-Strauss, Claude. 1995. *Saudades do Brasil.* Seattle: University of Washington Press.

Leyton, Elliot. 1998a. "Discussant Comments, Following Plenary Panel on the Anthropology of Violence." Canadian Anthropological Society Meetings, St. John's, Newfoundland.

———. 1998b. *Touched by Fire: Doctors without Borders in a Third World Crisis.* Photographs by Greg Locke. Toronto: McClelland and Stewart.

Malinowski, Bronislaw. 1945. *The Dynamics of Culture Change.* New Haven: Yale University Press.

———. 1967. *A Diary in the Strict Sense of the Term.* New York: Harcourt, Brace and World.

Malkki, Lisa H. 1995. *Purity and Exile: Violence, Memory, and National Cosmology among Huti Refugees in Tanzania.* Chicago: Chicago University Press.

Nelson, Diane. 1999. *A Finger in the Wound: Body Politics in Quincentennial Guatemala.* Berkeley: University of California Press.

Olujic, Maria. 1988. "Children in Extremely Difficult Circumstances: War and Its Aftermath in Croatia." In *Small Wars*. N. Schefer-Hylon and C. Sargent, eds. Pp. 318–30. Berkeley: University of California Press.

Pedelty, Mark. 1995. *War Stories: The Culture of Foreign Correspondents*. New York: Routledge.

Pope, Saxton. 1920. "The Medical History of Ishi." *University of California Publications in American Archaeology and Ethnology* 13(5):175–213.

Quesada, James. 1998. "Suffering Child: An Embodiment of War and Its Aftermath in Post-Sandinista Nicaragua." *Medical Anthropology Quarterly* 12(1):51–73.

Reno, William. 1998. "The Distinctive Political Logic of Weak States." In *Warlord Politics and African States*. Boulder, Colo.: Lynn Rienner.

Riddell, Francis A. 1978. "Maidu and Konkow." In Heizer, ed. Pp. 370–86.

Rieff, David. 1996. "An Age of Genocide." *New Republic* (January 29):27–36.

Robben, Antonius. 2000. "State Terror in the Nether World: Disappearance and Reburial in Argentina." In *Death Squad: The Anthropology of State Terror*. J. Sluka, ed. Philadelphia: University of Pennsylvania Press.

Rosaldo, Renato. 1989. "Grief and a Headhunter's Rage." In *Culture and Truth*. Pp. 1–21. Boston: Beacon.

Sanday, Peggy. 1990. *Fraternity Gang Rape: Sex, Brotherhood and Privilege on Campus*. New York: New York University Press.

Sanford, N., and C. Comstack, eds. 1971. *Sanctions for Evil*. Boston: Beacon Press.

Sartre, Jean Paul. 1952. "Reply to Camus." In *Situations*. Pp. 88–105. New York: Braziller Pubs.

———. 1963. "Preface." In *Wretched of the Earth*, by Frantz Fanon. Pp. 7–31. New York: Grove Press.

Scheper-Hughes, Nancy. 1993. *Death without Weeping: The Violence of Everyday Life in Brazil*. Berkeley: University of California Press.

———. 1994. "The Last White Christmas: The Heidelberg Pub Massacre." *American Anthropologist* 96(4):805–32.

———. 1995a. "The Primacy of the Ethical: Propositions for a Militant Anthropology." *Current Anthropology* 36(3):409–40.

———. 1995b. "Who's the Killer? Popular Justice and Human Rights in a South African Squatter Camp." *Social Justice* 22(3):143–64.

———. 1996. "Reply—White Writing." *Current Anthropology* 37(2):344–46.

———. 1997. "Peace-Time Crimes." *Social Identities* 3(3):471–97.

———. 1998. "Undoing—Social Suffering and the Politics of Remorse in the New South Africa." *Social Justice* 25(4):114–42.

———. 1999. "The Body and Violence." *Theater Symposium* 7(1):7–30.

———. 2000a. "The Global Traffic in Organs." *Current Anthropology* 41(2):191–224.

———. 2000b. Preface and Epilogue to the new, expanded edition of *Saints, Scholars and Schizophrenics: Mental Illness in Rural Ireland*. Berkeley: University of California Press.

———. 2000c. "Sacred Wounds: Writing with the Body." Introduction to *The Soft Vengeance of a Freedom Fighter*, by Albie Sachs. Pp. xi–xxiv. Berkeley: University of California Press.

———. 2001. "The Genocidal Continuum." In *Power and Self*. J. Mageo, ed. Cambridge: Cambridge University Press.

Schulrz, Paul E. 1988. *Indians of Lassen*. Mineral, Calif.: Loomis Museum Association.

Sennett, Richard, and Jonathan Cobbs. 1975. *The Hidden Injuries of Class*. New York: Vintage.

Shea, Christopher. 2000. "The Return of Ishi's Brain." *Lingua Franca* (February): 26–55.

Smith, Carol, ed. 1990. "Conclusion: History and Revolution in Guatemala." In *Guatemalan Indians and the State: 1540 to 1988*. Austin: University of Texas Press.

Sontag, Susan. 1964. "The Anthropologist as Hero." In *Against Interpretation*. Pp. 68–81. New York: Dell.

Starn, Orin. 1992. "Missing the Revolution: Anthropologists and the War in Peru." In *Rereading Cultural Anthropology*. George Marcus, ed. Pp. 152–79. Durham: Duke University Press.

———. n.d. "Ishi's Brain." Unpublished manuscript.

Steward, Julian. 1961. "Alfred Louis Kroeber: Obituary." *American Anthropologist* 63:1038–87.

Stoll, David. 1993. *Between Two Armies in the Ixil Towns of Guatemala*. New York: Columbia University Press.

Suarez-Orozco, Marcelo. 1987. "The Treatment of Children in the Dirty War: Ideology, State Terrorism, and the Abuse of Children in Argentina." In *Child Survival*. Nancy Scheper-Hughes, ed. Pp. 227–46. Dordrecht: D. Reidel.

Swendenburg, Ted. 1995. "Prisoners of Love: With Genet in the Palestinian Field." In *Fieldwork under Fire: Contemporary Studies of Violence and Survival*. Pp. 25–40. Carolyn Nordstrom and Antonius C. Robben, eds. Berkeley: University of California.

Taussig, Michael. 1987. *Shamanism, Colonialism and the Wildman*. Chicago: University of Chicago Press.

———. 1991. "Terror as Usual: Walter Benjamin's Theory of History as State of Siege." In *The Nervous System*. Pp. 11–35. New York: Routledge.

Thomas, David Hurst. 2000. *Skull Wars: Kennewick Man, Archaeology, and the Battle for Native American Identity*. New York: Basic Books.

Vizenor, Gerald. 2000. *Chancers: A Novel*. Norman: University of Oklahoma Press.

Wallace, Grant. 1911. "Ishi, the Last Aboriginal Savage in America, Finds Enchantment in a Vaudeville Show." *San Francisco Call*, October 8, 1911.

Williams, Ray. 1976. "Violence." In *Keywords*. Pp. 329–31. New York: Oxford University Press.

Wolf, Eric. 1981. "Alfred L. Kroeber." In *Totems and Teachers: Perspectives on the History of Anthropology*. Sydel Silverman, ed. New York: Columbia University Press.

———. 1982. *Europe and the People without History*. Berkeley: University of California Press.

Wooden, Wayne, and Jay Parker. 1982. "The Punks in Prison." In *Men behind Bars: Sexual Exploitation in Prison*. New York: Da Capo Press.

Zulaika, Joseba. 1988. *Basque Violence: Metaphor and Sacrament*. Reno: University of Nevada Press.

15

Culture, Genocide, and a Public Anthropology

John R. Bowen

What is, or should be, the distinctive anthropological contribution to the study of genocide? The essays in this book point toward what we might call the cultural analysis of group violence, a mode of analysis that focuses on both individual acts of violence and public representations of group differences, and that searches for connections between the two.[1] Ultimately we wish to know whether some ways of representing differences contribute to tolerance, intolerance, or violence.[2] Such causal links might be direct, as when hate speech leads to hate crimes, or indirect, as when social scientific representations of difference lead to policies that in turn either exacerbate or lessen conflict. We need to include as an object of study the public policy consequences of our own anthropological ways of speaking. After years of self-criticism over past uses of "race," we ought to consider the policy implications of other ways of representing human variation and human conflict. To the extent that anthropologists wish to play a more prominent public role in shaping international political affairs, the variable resonances of our own professional categories will need to be given greater scrutiny than ever before.

FRAMING CONFLICT

It is surely one of anthropology's key contributions to the study of social life to point out that categories—labels, names, ways of classifying things—shape our perceptions and actions. This insight can be brought to bear on the task of analyzing how public discourse shapes political policies toward violent conflicts. The labels used to characterize groups involved in conflict index specific theories about group cohesion, the genesis of conflict, and the motivations of those involved, and these theory-saturated labels in turn shape subsequent policy decisions.

Take, for example, two sets of labels that might be used to build alternative descriptions of the same set of events. The first set includes the phrase "ethnic conflict," along with other phrases such as "primordial tensions," "religious wars," and "communal strife." All these terms attribute local, endogenous origins and deep historical roots to conflicts. The second set of labels includes the key word in this volume, "genocide," but also other phrases such as "political killings" and "ethnic cleansing" that attribute exogenous origins and more proximate causes for the events in question. Each set of labels identifies a problem, provides a set of narratives about that problem, and suggests a feasible set of solutions.

"Ethnic conflict" highlights group differences as the causes of violence and ascribes a degree of primordialness to those differences.[3] Politics and the state lie in the background in the narratives implied by this phrase, as do types of identity other than ethnic, religious, or national identities—for example, cosmopolitan, or class-based, ways of self-identification. The label implies ground-up, nearly inevitable historical processes, sometimes alluded to as "seething cauldrons" (usually applied to Europeans or near-Europeans) or "tribal hatreds" (usually reserved for Africa). These phrases ascribe a set of basic, underlying, and relatively stable motives to killers, motives that turn on historical resentments or visceral dislikes of other groups, and that have psychological salience prior to other more superficial and fleeting motives, such as fear, or anger over the loss of resources, or incitement by politicians.

Now consider the implications of choosing from the second set of labels. "Genocide" brings into the mind a very different narrative from that just described: one in which leaders seek to wipe out a group of people and engage in cunning efforts to mobilize their supporters against their target. The leaders' motives are not specified by the phrase, but the events are marked as having required planning. "Genocide" and related terms leave relatively open the motives of those who carry out the killings, making analytical room for complex motives of fear, desires for retribution, and highly scripted images of the "pure" community that would exist after the elimination of the enemy. Such terms also direct research toward the processes of fanning fear and hatred, selectively commemorating events of the past, creating a climate receptive to authoritarianism.[4] Totten, Parsons, and Hitchcock's paper in this volume is an excellent example of such research: in their case research into the environmental sources of the fear, increasing resource scarcity, and competition that increase the likelihood of intense conflict among local groups. They correctly point out that this line of study is an effective way of disarming those who view such conflict as merely the nature of things among "those" people.

In the analytical discourses surrounding the murder of Yugoslavia, the label of "ethnic conflict" lent to Milosevic's and Tudjman's actions a certain legitimacy: "Yes, they acted terribly, but after all, there was a point to the idea of separating peoples who are so strongly driven by ancient hatreds." The label diffuses responsibility across a people, rather than isolating it in the initial actions that increased levels of fear and hatred. It lends support to some policy moves by other powers: letting the conflict run its course because of its inevitability, for example, rather than refusing to allow wholesale bombardment of cities.

This way of thinking has different cultural resonances in each country. In France, for example, it reinforces the idea that a unitary republic (such as guess where?) is a much better way to arrange things than is the oxymoronic idea of a "multicultural society."⁵ In the United States the resonances of "ethnic conflict" were different. President Clinton was reportedly strongly influenced by Robert Kaplan's (1993) writings on the Balkans, which portrayed the violence as a popular replay of the fifteenth century and made military intervention appear inappropriate. What if Mr. Clinton had happened to read a different account, such as that by Misha Glenny (1992), which stressed the proximate, political causes of the conflict? Perhaps the early Serb bombardments of Croatian cities would have met with a stronger U.S. response.

Of course, alternative labels, such as "genocide," may also be inappropriate in many of these cases, such as the events attending the death of Yugoslavia.⁶ What anthropologists really should question is the tendency in U.S. public discourse to try to assimilate conflicts elsewhere in the world to one of these two categories. All too often, political killings are quickly termed "genocide," and local-level conflicts are tagged as "ethnic" or "religious." Each of these last two relabelings gives an inappropriate culturalist spin to the bloodshed, and in fact can converge on a supposition that the conflict is rooted in unresolvable hatreds between peoples. "Genocide" also can imply motives of racial or religious hatred toward a particular group, and thus ultimately primordial causes for the violence, not unlike the effects on readers of the use of the label "ethnic conflict."

For example, the conflicts occurring in Indonesia after the 1998 fall of Suharto have been frequently described either as religious/ethnic conflict (in the case of killings in Ambon, Kalimantan, and Aceh) or as genocide (in the case of East Timor—the latter description is found in some of the essays in this volume). Both labels mislead. East Timor was the site of a running battle between an invading state and a resisting collection of peoples and movements, some of which had been battling each other just prior to the invasion (giving Jakarta a pretext for the initial invasion). The massacres during and after the late 1999 referendum on autonomy for the region were carried out by the Indonesian army and by local pro-Jakarta militias in order to destabilize the referendum, and then to punish those who had supported independence. They were not genocidal but political; they were intended not to wipe out a people but to discourage voting, silence dissidence, and punish those who favored autonomy, of whatever ethnicity they might be.

Other conflicts, in Ambon, Kalimantan, and Aceh, arose for combinations of motives, all of which included struggles for the control of local resources. In Ambon, rival gangs had grown up in Muslim and Christian parts of the city, and indeed were based in mosques or churches. Conflict between them activated long-simmering conflicts between immigrants and locals, and led to rather ineffectual calls for support from coreligionists elsewhere. Something of the same sort arose in Kalimantan, this time pitting (among others) two Islamic groups against each other, one of which resented the other's monopoly of resources and what was perceived of as "coarse" behavioral differences. (Immigrant Sulawesi people were so perceived by local Dayaks and by Malay immigrants, who joined to fight those from Sulawesi.) Conflicts in Aceh have involved resentment against Jakarta's siphoning off of oil and gas resources, and its slaughter of people accused of ties to the Acehnese liberation movement. Conflicts are over autonomy, control, and survival.

Crossing from one of the available discursive frames to the other can create scandals. One could view Daniel Goldhagen's (1996) argument, that anti-Semitic political culture was internalized by most Germans and explains the success of the Holocaust, as an effort to reframe the very prototype of genocide as if it were a kind of "ethnic conflict." Such reframing has indeed caused a scandal, and it is worth reflecting on why it has done so. As many have pointed out, it spreads responsibility for the massacres to all Germans, which is quite inconvenient. But it also violates an assumption of post-Enlightenment, social evolutionary self-understanding that shapes the norms about "proper" identification of different events of violence, to wit: "We, the good, civilized people of Western Europe and their descendants, do not have 'ethnic conflict.' We are more purposeful than that. In our nastier moments we might wipe out a people, but down deep we are rational, in control of ourselves. Even the Nazis had their Werner von Brauns. 'They,' however, the primitive peoples of the world, unfortunately have not yet reached that stage of social development; their primordial urges still well up and lead to irrational slaughter." (Hayden's [1996] argument that mass expulsions of peoples—called "ethnic cleansing" in Yugoslavia—are more common to modern European history than "we" would like to think caused a similar scandal within the smaller world of Slavic studies.)

It might appear that the more culturalist the account of mass or political violence, the more it underscores the way culture shapes killing, the more likely it is to relegate political agency to the background. This possibility poses a challenge to anthropologists: can we use our tools of cultural analysis to explain the genesis of violent conflicts without reinforcing public perceptions that such societal self-immolations are inevitable among "them"? (Were we to reinforce such perceptions we would not only be stumbling rhetorically but also erring analytically.)

In his analysis of the Rwandan genocide of 1994 (this volume), Christopher Taylor shows one way to walk this thin line. He shows the political killings for what they were, ordered from the top and fueled by fears of retribution by the "ordinary" Rwandan killers. Yet he also shows that they followed a cultural logic. Taylor carefully distinguishes between the motives for killing and torturing, and the internalized "generative cultural schemes" that shaped how people killed and tortured. On the one hand, he shows, quite effectively, how the state set out to enforce "ethnicist politics" (a phrase I appreciate), and did so murderously, against efforts by some citizens to build cross-ethnic political parties. On the other hand, he points to the ways older ideologies of Rwandan sacred kingship and about the health-related importance of the flow of bodily fluids shaped the ways Rwandans killed. He highlights systematic actions that did not make rational sense in terms of the objectives of the killers, but that followed a cultural logic of blockage—putting up too many road-blocks, impaling victims, cutting leg tendons rather than killing outright.

Taylor also highlights the rhetorical and psychological processes by which the state reframed its own violence as "the anger of the people," processes that included incorporating "the people" into the cruelty, by forcing those who passed a road-block to hit a captured Tutsi with a hammer. "Prove that you're one of us" is a logic used by state agents in many similar situations—in Indonesia in 1965–66, for example, when the army made as many people as possible tools of murder, in order to more plausibly frame the events as a mass uprising, and thereafter to more effectively silence the incorporated killers.

Taylor argues persuasively for attention to the cultural logics surrounding power and hierarchy that shape violent actions, without attributing to those logics a causal force in producing violence. Taylor's argument does not take ethnicity as an explanatory primitive, but acknowledges that it is a salient, and historically constructed, set of representations. In similar fashion, Linke's and Phim's essays add to our understanding of the ways in which a particular aesthetics of the body can evoke or contribute to violence. Linke's shocking article points to the continuity of imagery of the naked male body and of pristine nature from the Nazi era to current antifascist politics. Nazis, neo-Nazis, antifascists, Greens—all want to purge Germany of pollution, participating in a "logic of expulsion." Linke recounts how many German academics have dismissed her study, by saying that political discourse is "just words." She also reminds us that images and discourse are the very substance of the mechanisms by which "ordinary Germans" or anyone else can be turned into a mass murderer. Representations can provide a cultural logic to killing, even though that killing then requires an additional push—a panic, fear of retaliation, incitement by leaders.

The study of national corporeality is also at the center of Phim's account of how Khmer Rouge soldiers harnessed dance and music to revolutionary ends. Khmer Rouge theorists saw creating a new aesthetics as part of the process of instilling terror and enforcing compliance. And yet, as she tells it, a nostalgia that lingered among the guards and officials caused some of them to spare and even to favor those artists who performed the old music and dance. Images, sounds, movements leap across even the sharpest shifts in political ideology.

Here we begin to see the way that anthropological analyses of violence can draw out the cultural logics that lead ordinary people to accept that others in their country ought to be harassed or eliminated. Such violence may well not become genocidal; indeed, as Nagengast suggests (this volume), we should take into account the continuum of oppressive measures that are supported by popular opinion, which can stretch from everyday harassment (such as that experienced by middle-class blacks in many U.S. suburbs) to efforts at annihilation, or genocide in the strict sense.

The challenge, then, to an anthropology of violence is to keep in play both the analysis of a cultural logic of action and the analysis of individuals' motives, without reducing the one to the other. Rwandans killing other Rwandans acted from motives of fear and hatred, churned up by state agents and local militias; the manner in which the terror was thought out drew on specifically Rwandan ideas about power, the body, and properties accruing to different categories of people.

Group violence, then, is doubly "framed" by specific representations: first, in a local structure of representations that incites violence and guides its execution; second (and third . . .), and in the many second-order representations by public officials and observers (including anthropologists) whose manner of speaking may shape subsequent international responses.

THE PROBLEM OF HUMAN TYPES

Anthropology's (and not only anthropology's) direct place in this structure of representations and violence lies both in how we portray the nature of general human social, cultural, and biological variation, and in how we speak out on public issues. Ours is the science entrusted to discern the mechanisms underlying human variation, and we have the opportunity to provide news commentators, politicians, and "public intellectuals" with a well-considered set of categories and examples. How well have we carried out this task?

We could start with the discipline's darkest hour—that is, with the direct involvement of anthropologists in the Third Reich. Schafft (this volume) describes in illuminating detail how anthropologists of the Kaiser Wilhelm Institut steered their research in the direction pointed out by the leaders of the Third Reich. Their "applied anthropology" included "salvage" studies of Jews about to be annihilated, with the goals of understanding how to prevent a re-emergence of their "domination tendencies." But most important for our own current reflections on power and knowledge is her account of how the goal of finding the racial types underlying the confusing surface variation in human bodies shaped the research. In other words, the problem was, and is, not that research was perverted to bad ends, but that the very way that human variation was framed pushed the studies in a particular direction, one that was consistent with Nazi policies.

This close relationship between the idea of racial types and direct involvement in Nazi "fieldwork" ought to lead us to ask, in a more general fashion, about the advisability of searching for "human types" at all. It is clear that constructing typologies of people can be, although it is not necessarily, dangerous to human health. The difficulty lies of course in identifying which ways of conceiving of human variation add substantially to the risks of serving the causes of human annihilation. Surely the study of human variation is an important part of the human sciences; surely also, eugenics studies are not, and, as Schafft shows, the questions asked by those studies made it much easier for researchers to rationalize as "good science" their complicity in Nazi atrocities, if not their direct hand in carrying them out.

The very idea of a type comes into question here, linked as it is to notions of normality and goodness of fit. The use of types can be oppressive, even in the relatively innocuous manner with which images of an "average Frenchman" or "average American" have inevitably been of white, middle-class persons of median height and build, and have immediately marginalized all other bodily types. Once harnessed to policy ends, the use of a metric together with the notion of "normal" can be shifted to accommodate any existing hierarchies, just as the original Binet test was renormed on white Americans after its original French version showed them to tend toward idiocy, but was not renormed after it showed immigrants to the United States to be subnormal (Gould 1981).

The problem with constructing human types goes well beyond the use of a category of "race." In her essay in this volume, Bettina Arnold questions archaeology's assumption that material culture assemblages map onto peoples, ethnic groups, or protonations. She shows how this assumption can be put to the service of political projects, as occurred in the Germany of the 1930s and 1940s. Nazi-era narratives about German historical identity depended on claims of ethnic-racial continuity and autochthonousness. Of course, claims of long lineage are found in many times and places, but their specific content changed when harnessed to the project of legitimating exclusive nationalism. In Germany, ethnicity meant "race" (as it does elsewhere in Europe), and Nazi ideological requirement of racial purity did not allow a finding that Germans had migrated from somewhere else. Germans had to be indigenous people, or as nearly so as archaeology could make them by identifying a continuity of material assemblages over the territory then inhabited by Germans. No longer did the ruler descend from Greece or Rome, but the people arose from the forest itself—an idea of the nation-state that was particularly dependent on anthropology for its scientific validation.

The ideology of the nation-state, regnant in international political discourse during the interwar period, has been so frequently held responsible for atrocities that the arguments need not be rehearsed here. And yet, plans to redraw boundaries in, say, Bosnia, to conform to the distribution of "peoples" or "nations" follows that same logic—"Once we get the borders right, we will have peace."[7] Moreover, the general way of thinking that tries to map "peoples" onto political units transcends the nation-state. The possibility of thinking in terms of "Europe" makes possible new ways of projecting an indigenous peoplehood. Bruno Mégret, leader of the breakaway faction of the French National Front, now claims that "his" France is that of the Gauls; Breton regionalists claim a Celtic identity that links them to the British Isles (and perhaps even to the Basques!); Afro-Celt musicians find a way to marry immigrant heritage to European antiquity.

The same cultural logic that equates peoples with material cultures can also be used to deny historical continuity, when racialist politics require. It was just not thinkable, for example, that the Mound Builders could have been native Americans. To have acknowledged historical continuity between the builders of the giant mounds and current natives would have required whites to recognize them as culturally advanced and as thus in a position to make certain claims. The same logic is at work: continuity on a territory grants certain rights.

These examples attest to an insecurity surrounding the political-cultural idea of the nation-state, and more generally to the problematic character of claims that a political unit maps onto a long-term cultural unit. This insecurity helps explain nervousness over linguistic and cultural pluralism, why even in the avowedly pluralistic United States some residents feel threatened by the public use of Spanish. Carol Nagengast (this volume) examines this sense of threat, but also the ways in which public constructions of Mexicans as a cultural type leads many U.S. residents to tolerate harassment of Mexican immigrants. Symbolic violence is required in order to generate sufficient public support for state action against this minority. The violence involves treating this group of people as essentially the same in some negative respect, usually on the "evidence" of acts taken by some individual members of that group. She links U.S. Border Patrol violence against Mexicans entering the country to a more general public opinion about assimilation and difference in Southern California, to opposition to bilingual education on the grounds that "they" should become more like "us," and to a general erosion of rights for resident noncitizens. Civilian employers are taught to report undocumented aliens, but they soon learn that it is Spanish-speaking workers who are the sole target, a minority among the total population of undocumented workers in the United States.

The U.S. and German cases both involve ideas of "natives" (in the former case, nicely ignoring the irony in a land of immigrants) versus "foreigners." But any discourse about "peoples" can have negative effects when it reinforces tendencies to attribute characteristics to groups rather than to individuals. The legal scholar Martha Minow (1990) terms this consequence one horn of the "dilemma of difference," whereby recognizing the legitimate claim of a social category (women, Jews, Spanish speakers) may also raise the probability that others will attribute stereotypes to individuals as members of that category. The problem of human types is not that we fail to "get the types right" but that we characterize the motives, actions, or qualities of individuals in terms of group characteristics, whether "ethnic," "national," "racial," or gendered.

PROTOTYPES AND INTERNATIONAL LAW

The problem of constructing categories to capture human variation is of course central to the project of extending the rule of law more effectively in the international sphere. International law must be constructed in Janus-like fashion. Definitions and procedures need to be crafted with the histories of crimes and prosecutions in mind—indeed, legal categories often have been developed with a specific past event in mind. These categories also need to be given sufficient generality to be useful in the future as well, and may require continual reinterpretation. Such reinterpretations move the definitions away from the original "prototypes"—by which I mean both the model for the category and the psychologically immediate image or example—and toward new cases that stretch the categories.

For most of us today, the term *genocide* prototypically refers to the Nazi efforts to annihilate the Jews. It also has an unquestionably appropriate and unproblematic (psychologically, morally, and legally) application to the efforts by European conquerors to wipe out certain peoples of the New World—and elsewhere, as David Maybury-Lewis reminds us in his discussion of the sad history of Tasmania.

The legal definition of genocide comes from the 1948 U.N. convention, which stipulates that those accused have intended to destroy a "national, ethnical, racial, or religious group" (Article 2). As Paul Magnarella points out (this volume), the convention has been interpreted to refer to "stable and permanent groups" that are in some sense objective—that is, which exist prior to the efforts to wipe them out. This interpretation makes sense in terms of the prototypical referents of the concept.

However, this idea of ethnic (or racial, or national) identity is one that anthropologists increasingly understand to be problematic, for reasons that soon were perceived by the international tribunals. Ethnic identification is itself a social process, subject to both gradual social changes and abrupt political manipulation, in Europe and North America as much as elsewhere. Much of modern European history has consisted of attempts to regiment self-identifications along nation-state lines, with some success, especially in the mid-twentieth century (fewer Bretons, more French). The violent dismembering of Yugoslavia in the 1990s was accompanied by the withdrawal from "Yugoslavs" of the right to claim that identity, and the substitution of ethnically specific alternatives.

As Magnarella points out, this point was not lost on the judges serving on the U.N. International Criminal Tribunal for Rwanda who sought to apply the 1948 genocide convention to Rwanda. What many had assumed to be a physically obvious distinction between Hutus and Tutsis in fact was the artifact of (a) initial distinctions that were relatively fluid, and (b) a subsequent hardening of those categories by colonial and postcolonial regimes. The judges realized that these ethnic labels did not designate what an outside observer would see as objective groups, making the designation of the massacres as "genocidal" legally, if not politically, problematic. And yet the actions of Rwandans presupposed the existence of such categories. The justices concluded that self-identifications as "Hutu" or "Tutsi," classifications by the Rwandan government of people into these two categories, and the fact that slaughtering mothers and infants was intended to prevent the birth of new "Tutsi," defined in terms of patrilineal descent, made the Tutsi a "stable and permanent group" for purposes of finding that genocide had occurred. In other words, sufficient violent behavior was organized around the psychologically real categories of "Hutu" and "Tutsi" that they could be taken to designate socially real groups. Ethnic groups come into existence legally, then, when someone is trying to wipe them out.

Here we see an instance where international categories have responded to a gathering of new evidence and perspectives about social and cultural processes. International law will doubtless continue to refine its categories as the International Criminal Court takes form and begins to set out its codes and procedures. Alongside of genocide, as defined by the United Nations, such tribunals may likely recognize a broader category of state violence used to intimidate or oppress political as well as ethnic groups, and also government efforts, violent or nonviolent, to compel or induce members of a group to move from one region to another, whether as "ethnic cleansing" or as policies intended to keep certain types of individuals out of certain areas—such as targeting by police or immigration officials of certain "profiles," or Israeli settlement policies. Such state policies are hardly "genocide" but are similarly aimed at categories of individuals. Different again are efforts to wipe out a language, or religion, or various culturally specific patterns of behavior, including forced assimilation, such as of U.S. Native Americans in reservation schools, or of Bretons in French schools.

A concern for "cultural survival" against these types of violence has supported anthropological attention to the plight of "indigenous peoples"—who often also are targets of genocide. David Maybury-Lewis (this volume) reminds us that in the New World, and in some other places colonized by Europeans, true genocide did take place, as colonists, either initially or in the process of establishing their domination, sought to wipe out the peoples who pre-existed them. In these situations the contrast between inhabitants of long standing and genocidal European colonizers is clear. Indeed, precisely because the New World cases are so clear, they have come to be the prototypes for how we think about indigenous peoples, who have come to be associated as a category with tribal knowledge and medicine, a special relationship to the earth, and prior claims on land. This particular conceptual package has been very effective in allowing a public anthropology to work for tribal rights over property, for example, including intellectual property.

But can we easily export the concept of "indigenous peoples" around the world? The question may seem anachronistic, because we clearly have done so. The 1994 U.N. Draft Declaration on the Rights of Indigenous Peoples enunciates the rights of "indigenous peoples" everywhere, guaranteeing them rights of self-determination, remaining on their territory, and even the right (Article 32) "to determine their citizenship in accordance with their customs and traditions." The declaration does not define what is meant by "indigenous peoples," but an influential definition was proposed by J. R. Martinez-Cobo, the author of a study that preceded and in some sense led to the declaration. Indigenous peoples, "having a historical continuity with pre-invasion and pre-colonial societies that developed on their territories, consider themselves distinct from other sectors of the societies now prevailing in those territories. . . . They form at present non-dominant sectors of society and are determined to preserve, develop and transmit to future generations their ancestral territories, and their ethnic identity, as the basis of their continued existence as peoples, in accordance with their own cultural patterns, social institutions, and legal systems."[8] To be an indigenous people, then, presupposes a demonstrable continuous relationship to ancestral territories and a sense of ethnic distinctiveness vis-à-vis other "peoples" in the state who are not indigenous.

Although New World tribal groups easily fit this definition, extending it across the world, as international law requires, encounters difficulties. Samuel Totten,

William Parsons, and Robert Hitchcock (this volume) discuss several problems in the efforts to identify "indigenous" peoples in Africa; these problems arise in other world areas as well. First, population movements may void the concept of "original residents" of any sense. Of course, some groups may claim indigenous status in order to make specific political claims, but there may be little evident relationship between the group's ways of self-identification and the idea of "ancestral territory." Ironically, the relationship between being indigenous and having an ancestral territory is particularly problematic for nomadic groups, which are often the prototypes of an "indigenous" people. In some societies, the categories used to distinguish among citizens may not be those of "peoples" at all, but distinctions of origin place, or clans, or religious affiliation—all of which can be less socially divisive than the concept of "peoples," which is all too easily assimilable into Western notions of race-and-ethnicity.

Let me consider the region where I do most of my own fieldwork, the province of Aceh in Indonesia, where the Acehnese Liberation Front claims to have been colonized by the Javanese after having been colonized by the Dutch. The Acehnese appear on lists of "indigenous peoples," probably because of that claim. And yet Acehnese have never thought of themselves as "indigenous." To the contrary, the folk etymology of Aceh is "Arab, Cina, Eropa, Hindi," to indicate that the area has been a land of immigration of people from many corners of the world, whose common element is Islam.

Second, there may be very good reasons for a state to emphasize the characteristics, interests, and rights shared by all citizens, rather than a division into indigenous and nonindigenous peoples. Distinguishing between natives and others is redolent of the very logic of internal minorities that was foundational to the apartheid policies of South Africa, for example. Alternatives exist: states may use categories such as economic marginality in order to target certain groups for assistance without stigmatizing them as different in kind—Botswana so categories the San, in part in order to avoid the "primitive museum" approach to the San favored by South Africa. A similar insistence on equal citizenship status, but for all Africans, is part of the justification for humanitarian interventions across state borders, such as those undertaken by the Organization of African Unity.

Third, in some countries the political resonance of the concept of "indigenous peoples" is to support attacks on minorities that can be defined as "foreigners." I realize that the definitions provided by international agencies (and underscored here by Maybury-Lewis) require a group to be "nondominant" to be "indigenous" (although it is unclear why one cannot have dominant indigenous groups).[9] However, the rather complex bureaucratic definitions—usually followed by statements of the type "we know them when we see them"—do not prevent other interest groups from expanding on their own definitions of "indigenous peoples." The concept can be appropriated by groups who dominate in one way or another but can claim not to dominate, however improbably, as did the Nazis by claiming that "international Jewry" was the real dominant group. As Taylor points out, some Hutus, in justifying their violence against Tutsi people, drew on narratives that depicted the Hutus as Rwanda's "indigenous people" who had been conquered by Tutsis. In similar fashion, narratives that portray Muslims as "conquerors" of the "indigenous" Hindus are available to villagers in northern India, alongside alternative narratives, genealogical in form, that, in depicting shared kinship between present-day Muslims and Hindus, describe processes of conversion to Islam. The former narratives are, of course, those picked up and disseminated by Hindu nationalist activists, and they fit into an available international discourse of "indigenous peoples." Some Malays and Javanese can draw on terms meaning "children of the soil" in claiming their rights as indigenous people vis-à-vis the Chinese, who dominate the economic sphere. From their perspective, then, the situation can be portrayed as one of "foreign domination" of a set of "indigenous peoples."

Finally, much as anthropologists have remarked on the unsuitability of an idea of distinct races for understanding human genotypical and phenotypical variation, so we might also remark on the unsuitability of a simple dichotomy of indigenous/foreign for understanding the various histories of immigration, agreements, population movements, ideas about territory and ownership, that characterize diverse societies in Asia, Africa, and the Americas.

Are there alternatives to "indigenous" that could serve the same or similar legal and public policy functions? Note that to condemn crimes of genocide and political violence we do not need to invoke a distinction between "indigenous" and "nonindigenous" peoples. Such crimes are equally condemnable, from a moral as well as from a legal basis, when carried out against any population.

However, for purposes other than recognizing these sorts of crimes, one might wish to distinguish as worthy of legal recognition claims for autonomy made by certain communities living within states. Will Kymlicka (1995:107–20) has proposed two major criteria for evaluating claims for special legal or political rights that are made by what he calls "national minorities": groups of people living in a distinct territory, who exercised sovereignty prior to being incorporated in a state. The first is that of equality. Special "group-differentiated" rights may be necessary to provide political equality in cases where members of minorities are disadvantaged with respect to a particular resource—whether land, language, or political representation—and where a group-differentiated right, such as protection for languages, reservation of hunting or fishing lands, or mechanisms to ensure electoral representation, would rectify the inequality.[10] Second, historical agreements may have been entered into either between pre-existing groups and encompassing states, or between groups that agreed to federate, such as Québec and the rest of Canada, or the provinces of Indonesia. These agreements can then be cited as justifications for contemporary political demands.[11]

Kymlicka's formulation provides a political-theoretic foundation for national minorities to advance claims as to their rights to autonomy with respect to particular resources. These arguments do not require distinguishing the "indigenous" from the "nonindigenous" people in a state. They may actually be more successful than "indigenous peoples" arguments in states that have already recognized general cultural rights, such as the right to preserve one's own language.

Our anthropological descriptive categories—"ethnic conflict," "genocide," "indigenous peoples"—have implications not only for how we set up research questions and attempt to answer them. These categories also send messages to broader publics about what science can tell them concerning the underlying reality, basic causes, and historical roots of group violence. These publics include not only "our own" governments and citizens but also the people involved in conflicts and the international agencies trying to resolve them.

The challenge to the anthropology of group violence, then, will be to study simultaneously the double framing of violence by culturally specific representations of social life. Our ethnographies of violence, and of the fears, resentments, and political manipulations leading to violence, will underscore the powerful role of rhetorics and images about social groups, those "mere discourses" scorned by Linke's critics. But we must then look outward, and afterward, to the categories through which others in the world apprehend and "explain" this violence. As we have done with race and racism, our public role may increasingly lead us to instruct ourselves about the political implications of "our own" (anthropological, scientific, public) cultural categories.

NOTES

1. Of course, a number of sophisticated accounts by journalists already pose such questions, such as Philip Gourevitch's writings (for example, 1998) on Rwanda, and Misha Glenny's (for example, 1992) on the Balkans, as do the ethnographies of many of our colleagues, for example Liisa Malkki (1995) and Christopher Taylor (this volume).

2. In doing so we also need to become more conversant with work by social psychologists, political scientists, and sociologists on group conflict, for example Horowitz (1985) and Hardin (1995).

3. Elsewhere (Bowen 1996) I have written at greater length about the problems associated with the use of this particular phrase. In this volume, Totten, Parsons, and Hitchcock point to the historical origins of ethnicity in Africa; they mention the process of ethnogenesis, as when two clans in Congo (former Zaire) began to label themselves and each other as groups, the "Luba" and the "Luluwa," as a result of conflicts over land and other resources. It is probably an overstatement to say that colonial rule gave birth to the idea of totally distinct, well-bounded "ethnic groups," but certainly the propensity to think in terms of distinct groups, along the model of racial groups, is a hallmark of European thinking. (It continues to haunt efforts to rethink plural societies throughout Europe, most notably in France.) The (by now) classic anthropological source for studying these processes of ethnic reformulation is Barth (1969).

4. As an example one might cite the birth of the subfield of social psychology as an attempt to explain the success of Hitler: a birth that was prompted by the shock to Europeans of fellow Europeans having done things that contradicted the assumption of post-Enlightenment rational grace.

5. During the Balkan conflicts, the association of the war against Serbia with a doomed policy of multiculturalism was most clearly evident in the reporting by the weekly news mag-

azine *Marianne,* the house organ for the new "nationalist-republican" coalition, but it was also visible in *Le Monde.*

6. For a heated debate about the use of the terms *genocide* and *ethnic cleansing* to describe events in former Yugoslavia, see Hayden (1996) and the comments thereafter.

7. For an extensive critique of this way of thinking, see Brubaker (1996). I suspect that Jim Scott (1998) might be willing to include such logic in that category of "high modernist thinking" that he has recently and effectively demolished.

8. From the report of the Sub-Commission on Prevention of Discrimination and Protection of Minorities of the U.N. Economic and Social Council, quoted in Pritchard (1998:43).

9. In an autonomous Inuit territory would the Inuit, who would become the dominant group, no longer be "indigenous"? Do political waxings and wanings shift groups in and out of "indigenous" status? What meaning would the term then retain?

10. For a similar argument regarding the specific issue of political representation, see Phillips (1995).

11. Anaya (1996) argues that, from the standpoint of international law, claims for sovereignty are stronger if they are based on inequalities, or basic human rights, than if they are based on historical agreements, because of the international law doctrine that current law applies to cases, not laws existing at the time of the relevant events.

REFERENCES

Anaya, S. James. 1996. *Indigenous Peoples in International Law.* New York: Oxford University Press.

Barth, Fredrik, ed. 1969. *Ethnic Groups and Boundaries.* Boston: Little, Brown.

Bowen, John R. 1996. "The Myth of Global Ethnic Conflict." *Journal of Democracy* 7(4):3–14.

Brubaker, Rogers. 1996. *Nationalism Reframed: Nationhood and the National Question in the New Europe.* Cambridge: Cambridge University Press.

Glenny, Misha. 1992. *The Fall of Yugoslavia.* New York: Penguin.

Goldhagen, Daniel. 1996. *Hitler's Willing Executioners.* New York: Knopf.

Gould, Stephen Jay. 1981. *The Mismeasure of Man.* New York: W. W. Norton.

Gourevitch, Philip. 1998. *We Wish to Inform You That Tomorrow We Will Be Killed with Our Families: Stories from Rwanda.* New York: Farrar, Strauss and Giroux.

Hardin, Russell. 1995. *One for All: The Logic of Group Conflict.* Princeton: Princeton University Press.

Hayden, Robert M. 1996. "Schindler's Fate: Genocide, Ethnic Cleansing, and Population Transfers." *Slavic Review* 55:727–78.

Horowitz, Donald L. 1985. *Ethnic Groups in Conflict.* Berkeley: University of California Press.

Kaplan, Robert. 1993. *Balkan Ghosts.* New York: St. Martin's Press.

Kymlicka, Will. 1995. *Multicultural Citizenship.* Oxford: Oxford University Press.

Malkki, Liisa. 1995. *Purity and Exile.* Chicago: University of Chicago Press.

Minow, Martha. 1990. *Making All the Difference: Inclusion, Exclusion, and American Law.* Ithaca: Cornell University Press.

Phillips, Anne. 1995. *The Politics of Presence.* Oxford: Oxford University Press.

Pritchard, Sarah, ed. 1998. *Indigenous Peoples, the United Nations and Human Rights.* London: Zed Books.

Scott, James C. 1998. *Seeing Like a State.* New Haven: Yale University Press.

Bettina Arnold is an associate professor in the Department of Anthropology at the University of Wisconsin-Milwaukee. She conducts field research in southwest Germany, with a particular emphasis on the pre-Roman Iron Age (see http://www.uwm.edu/~barnold/). She has been investigating the symbiotic relationship between archaeology and politics, especially in the context of National Socialist Germany, since 1985.

John R. Bowen is Dunbar-Van Cleve Professor of Arts and Sciences at Washington University in St. Louis, where he directs the Program in Social Thought and Analysis. He is the author of *Muslims through Discourse* (1993), *Religions in Practice* (2002), and the coeditor of *Critical Comparisons in Politics and Culture* (1999). He is completing *Entangled Commands: Islam, Law, and Equality in Indonesian Public Reasoning*, and working on Muslim public discourse in France.

Tone Bringa is associate professor of social anthropology at the University of Bergen in Norway. She is author of *Being Muslim the Bosnian Way* (1995), which describes life in an ethnically mixed village in central Bosnia just prior to the war. She served as the anthropologist to the 1993 award-winning Granada Television documentary "We Are All Neighbours," about the war in Bosnia, and in 1995 she worked as a political and policy analyst for the United Nations mission to the former Yugoslavia.

May Ebihara is professor emerita of anthropology, Lehman College and the Graduate Center, City University of New York. She is the only American anthropologist to have conducted ethnographic research in a Khmer peasant village before civil war and revolution tore Cambodia apart in the 1970s. She revisited the community during the 1990s to gather narratives of villagers' experiences during the past several decades and to explore continuities and transformations in their lives. She has written about many aspects of Cambodian village life and was a coeditor of *Cambodian Culture since 1975: Homeland and Exile* (Cornell 1994). She is currently working on an ethnographic social history of the village and its vicissitudes over some forty years.

Alexander Laban Hinton is an assistant professor in the Department of Sociology and Anthropology at Rutgers University, Newark (ahinton@andromeda.rutgers.edu). In addition to publishing a number of journal articles on genocide, Hinton's edited volume, *Biocultural Approaches to the Emotions*, was published with Cambridge University Press in 1999. He recently published an anthology, *Genocide: An Anthropological Reader* (Blackwell 2002) and is currently completing an ethnography of the Cambodian genocide entitled *Cambodia's Shadow: Cultural Dimensions of Genocide*.

Robert K. Hitchcock is a professor in the Department of Anthropology and Geography and the coordinator of African studies at the University of Nebraska-Lincoln. He is the coeditor of *Endangered Peoples of Africa and the Middle East: Struggles to Survive and Thrive* (Greenwood 2001). He has worked on human rights, development, and environmental issues among rural populations in eastern and southern Africa since 1975.

Judy Ledgerwood is associate professor of anthropology and Southeast Asian studies, Northern Illinois University. Her broad experience in Cambodia includes teaching at the Royal University of Fine Arts, work for the United Nations, and ethnographic research on a variety of topics. She coedited *Cambodian Culture since 1975: Homeland and Exile* (Cornell 1994) and *Propaganda, Politics, and Violence in Cambodia, Democratic Transition under United Nations Peace-keeping* (M. E. Sharpe 1996), and edited a forthcoming volume, *Cambodia Emerges from the Past* (Northern Illinois University Center for Southeast Asian Studies).

Uli Linke is an associate professor in the Department of Anthropology at Rutgers University. She is the author of *Blood and Nation: The European Aesthetics of Race* (1999) and *German Bodies: Race and Representation after Hitler* (1999), and coeditor of *Denying Biology*.

Paul J. Magnarella is professor of anthropology and affiliate professor of law at the University of Florida, where he directs the joint degree programs in anthropology and law. He has served as Expert on Mission with the International Criminal Tribunal for the Former Yugoslavia and pro bono legal researcher for the International Criminal Tribunal for Rwanda. He presently serves as legal counsel to the American Anthropological Association's Committee for Human Rights and as special counsel to the Association of Third World Studies. His most recent book—*Justice for Africa: Rwanda's Genocide, Its National Courts and the UN Criminal Tribunal* (2000)—won the Association of Third World Studies' book of the year award and was nominated for the Raphael Lemkin book award.

Beatriz Manz, an anthropologist and native of Chile, has conducted extensive research in Guatemala and Mexico. She has received several grants, including a Peace Fellowship from the Bunting Institute at Radcliffe for her research among Guatemalan refugees in Mexico. Most recently, she was the recipient of a John D. and Catherine T. MacArthur Foundation research and writing grant. She is currently associate professor of geography and ethnic studies at the University of California, Berkeley.

David Maybury-Lewis is Edward C. Henderson Professor of Anthropology at Harvard University and the founder and president of Cultural Survival, an organization that defends the rights of indigenous peoples.

Carole Nagengast is professor of anthropology at the University of New Mexico, where she teaches classes on human rights, class, gender, ethnicity, and transnationalism. She does research with Mixtecs from southern Mexico, the U.S.-Mexico border region, and in Poland. Major publications include articles in the *Annual Reviews of Anthropology* (1994), the *Journal of Anthropological Research* (1997), *Latin American Research Review* (1990), and the volume *Reluctant Socialists: Class, Culture and the Polish State* (1991). She has a forthcoming edited volume entitled *The Anthropologist as Activist* and is writing an ethnography of Mixtec migrants to the United States. Nagengast served on the board of directors at Amnesty International and was a member of the American Anthropology Association Committee for Human Rights. She currently chairs the American Anthropological Association Committee on Public Policy, the Association for the Advancement of Science Committee on Social Responsibility, and the AAAS Subcommittee on Human Rights.

William S. Parsons is the former director of education and now chief of staff for the United States Holocaust Memorial Museum in Washington, D.C. He is the author of the study guide *Everyone's Not Here: Families of the Armenian Genocide* (Armenian Assembly of America 1989), coauthor of *Facing History and Ourselves: Holocaust and Human Behavior* (Intentional Publications 1982), and coeditor of *Century of Genocide: Eyewitness Accounts and Critical Views* (Garland 1997).

Kenneth Roth is the executive director of Human Rights Watch, the largest U.S.-based international human rights organization. He has conducted human rights investigations around the globe, devoting special attention to issues of justice and accountability for gross abuses of human rights, standards governing military conduct in time of war, the human rights policies of the United States and the United Nations, and the human rights responsibilities of multinational businesses. He has written extensively on a range of human rights topics in such publications as the *New York Times,* the *Washington Post, Foreign Affairs,* the *Nation,* and the *New York Review of Books.* He appears often in the major media, including NPR, the BBC, CNN, PBS, and the principal U.S. networks. He has testified repeatedly before the U.S. Congress.

Gretchen E. Schafft is an applied anthropologist in residence at American University in Washington, D.C., where she teaches perhaps the first Holocaust class in an anthropology department. She has been a leader in the development of practicing anthropology, founding member and second president of the Washington Association of Professional Anthropologists. Schafft is active in contract research for government agencies, evaluating programs in the areas of health, education, and social welfare.

Nancy Scheper-Hughes is professor of anthropology at the University of California, Berkeley, where she also directs the doctoral program in critical studies of medicine, science, and the body. Her many publications include *Saints, Scholars and Schizophrenics: Mental Illness in Rural Ireland*, which received the Margaret Mead Award, and *Death without Weeping: The Violence of Everyday Life in Brazil*, which received several awards including the international Pitre Prize and the Welcome Medal of the Royal Anthropological Institute. She is currently writing two books, one entitled *Who's the Killer? Violence and Democracy in the New South Africa*, and the other entitled *The Ends of the Body: The Global Traffic in Organs*.

Toni Shapiro-Phim is a research associate with the Electronic Cultural Atlas Initiative at the University of California, Berkeley. She is completing a manuscript on the relationship between war and dance in late-twentieth-century Cambodia and has been working with artists at Cambodia's Royal University of Fine Arts on documentation of their dance technique. Coauthor of *Dance in Cambodia* (Oxford 1999), Shapiro-Phim has written numerous articles on the cultural context of Cambodian performing arts.

Christopher C. Taylor is associate professor of anthropology at the University of Alabama at Birmingham. He is primarily a specialist in symbolic and medical anthropology and has done fieldwork in Rwanda, Kenya, and the Ivory Coast. He also worked in applied medical anthropology on the sociocultural and behavioral aspects of HIV transmission. At the beginning of the genocide in Rwanda, he was employed by Family Health International under the auspices of the United States Agency for International Development.

Samuel Totten is professor of curriculum and instruction at the University of Arkansas at Fayetteville. He is the compiler/editor of *First Person Accounts of Genocidal Acts Committed in the Twentieth Century* (Greenwood 1991), coeditor of *Century of Genocide: Eyewitness Accounts and Critical Views* (Garland 1997), associate editor of *Encyclopedia of Genocide* (ABC-CLIO 1999). He is currently completing two books: *Pioneers of Genocide Studies* (Transaction Publishers, forthcoming) and *The Intervention and Prevention of Genocide: An Annotated Bibliography* (Greenwood, forthcoming).

INDEX

Abrams, Philip, 328
Aceh, 385, 392
Ache, 62–63
Adorno, Theodor W., 229–30
AFL-CIO, 334
Agamben, Giorgio, 367
Akayesu, Jean-Paul, 312, 314–17, 318, 319–20
AllianceGreens, 249, 250
Ambon, 384
American Anthropological Association, 2
American Friends Service Committee, 329
Amnesty International, 79
Andreopoulos, George, 106, 109
Angkor Wat, 109
anthropology/anthropologists: advocacy for social justice by, 74; apartheid and, 364–65; contribution to understanding genocide by, 375; genocide and, 28–29, 55–56; in Nazi Germany, 16–18, 123–31; silence on genocide of, 1–2, 348
apartheid, 364–65
archaeology: as contributing factor to genocide, 95–96; as cultural capital, 95–96; in Germany under National Socialists, 97–102; as handmaiden of nationalism, 106–10
Arendt, Hannah, 299
Arnold, Bettina, 15–16
Assyrians, 7
Atlantis, 105
Australia: genocide in, 46; nationalism in, 142

Bartov, Omer, 255, 263
Basaglia, Franco, 370

Bauman, Zygmunt, 12
Beer, Angelika, 250
Benedict, Ruth, 364
blood: German nationhood and, 14, 230, 231, 264–65
body: genocide and focus on, 367–68; German nationhood and, 230, 231; as icon of past, 229–30; and nudity as tool in West Germany, 235–42, 244–50; Rwandan practices relating to, 146–52, 153–57, 164–68, 172–73; and the state, 141–42
Border Patrol, 329, 331–32; militarization of, 330; use of low-intensity conflict methods by, 335–37; violence by, 332–33, 339–40, 341
Bosniac-Croat Federation, 201
Bosnia-Herzegovina: ethnic cleansing in, 22–23, 196–200, 205–6, 212–13; ethnic relations in, 217–18; federation of Bosnians and Croats in, 200, 201; independence of, 197, 198; manipulation of fear in, 198, 211, 216–17; Muslims in, 213–16; Serbian take over of, 199
Bosnian Muslims, 196, 213–16, 222n18
Bosnian Serb Army, 200
Boua, Chanthou, 279
Bourdieu, Pierre, 369–70
Bowen, John, 28–29, 326–27
Brazil, 57, 74, 350–51, 371, 372
Bringa, Tone, 22–23
Brügge, Peter, 240–41
Buddhism, 24, 280
Burma, 50, 76
Burundi, 140–41, 240–41